Criminal Procedure

Christopher E. Smith
Michigan State University

THOMSON
™
WADSWORTH

Australia • Canada • Mexico • Singapore • Spain • United Kingdom • United States

THOMSON

WADSWORTH

Senior Executive Editor, Criminal Justice: Sabra Horne

Senior Acquisitions Editor, Criminal Justice: Jay Whitney

Acquisitions Editor: Shelley Murphy

Assistant Editor: Dawn Mesa

Editorial Assistant: Paul Massicotte

Technology Project Manager: Susan DeVanna

Marketing Manager: Dory Schaeffer

Marketing Assistant: Neena Chandra

Advertising Project Manager: Stacey Purviance

Project Manager, Editorial Production: Jennie Redwitz

Print/Media Buyer: Becky Cross

Permissions Editor: Beth Zuber

Production Service: Vicki Moran, Publishing Support Services

Text Designer: Carolyn Deacy

Copy Editor: Margaret Moore

Cover Designer: Bill Stanton

Cover Images: Constitution: Corbis; Engraving of U.S. seal: © Bettmann/Corbis.

Compositor: Thompson Type

Text and Cover Printer: Phoenix Color Corp. (BTP)

For more information about our products, contact us at:

Thomson Learning Academic Resource Center

1-800-423-0563

For permission to use material from this text, contact us by:

Phone: 1-800-730-2214   **Fax:** 1-800-730-2215

Web: http://www.thomsonrights.com

Library of Congress Control Number: 2002112129

ISBN 0-534-61209-1

Wadsworth/Thomson Learning
10 Davis Drive
Belmont, CA 94002-3098
USA

Asia
Thomson Learning
5 Shenton Way #01-01
UIC Building
Singapore 068808

Australia
Nelson Thomson Learning
102 Dodds Street
South Melbourne, Victoria 3205
Australia

Canada
Nelson Thomson Learning
1120 Birchmount Road
Toronto, Ontario M1K 5G4
Canada

Europe/Middle East/Africa
Thomson Learning
High Holborn House
50/51 Bedford Row
London WC1R 4LR
United Kingdom

Latin America
Thomson Learning
Seneca, 53
Colonia Polanco
11560 Mexico D.F.
Mexico

Spain
Paraninfo Thomson Learning
Calle/Magallanes, 25
28015 Madrid, Spain

DEDICATION

With gratitude to the people who facilitated my opportunities to learn about constitutional law and civil rights in contexts outside the classroom: the Hon. Richard A. Enslen; Pamela S. Horowitz; Kathy Miller; Wayne M. Conner; Charles Morgan; Julia Hale-Harbaugh; Thao Tiedt; and the Black Prisoners' Caucus-WSR.

Trained as a lawyer and social scientist, Christopher E. Smith, J.D., Ph.D., is Professor of Criminal Justice at Michigan State University where he teaches courses on constitutional criminal procedure, corrections law, judicial process, and criminal justice policy. Dr. Smith holds degrees in political science, sociology, and law. He is a graduate of Harvard University, the University of Bristol (England), the University of Tennessee College of Law, and the University of Connecticut. In addition to writing more than 75 scholarly articles in legal studies journals and law reviews, he is the author of 20 books, including several titles with Wadsworth: *Criminal Justice in America,* Third Edition (2002) with George F. Cole; *The American System of Criminal Justice,* Ninth Edition (2001) with George F. Cole; *Law and Contemporary Corrections* (2000); *Courts, Politics, and the Judicial Process,* Second Edition (1997); *The Changing Supreme Court: Constitutional Rights and Liberties* (1997) with Thomas R. Hensley and Joyce A. Baugh; *Courts and Public Policy* (1993); *Politics in Constitutional Law* (1992); and *Courts and the Poor* (1991).

BRIEF CONTENTS

CONTENTS

Preface xvii

Contemporary textbooks on criminal procedure typically do a fine job of describing the procedural steps of criminal investigations, prosecutions, and trials. In addition, they inform students about U.S. Supreme Court decisions that define constitutional rights and provide guidelines for the appropriate exercise of authority by criminal justice officials. These topics are necessary elements in criminal procedure courses, but they represent a limited focus that does not provide students with a comprehensive understanding of criminal procedure, its importance, and its effects on the lives of human beings. *Criminal Procedure* seeks to remedy these deficiencies by broadening students' understanding of underlying contextual elements and consequences of constitutional criminal procedure.

UNIQUE THEMES

Students of criminal justice are both future justice system professionals as well as individuals bound for alternative careers who see criminal justice as providing an interesting social science subject that will supply analytical skills and a deeper understanding of human behavior, governmental organizations, and decision-making processes. When criminal procedure textbooks limit their attention to descriptions of processes and existing rule-defining judicial decisions, they do a disservice to both segments of our student audience. It is imperative for future justice system personnel as well as other citizens who will affect the justice system as voters and community leaders to understand that legal decisions can define rules but they cannot ensure that human behavior complies with those rules. There are often gaps between courts' announced definitions of rights and the actual decisions and processes that determine the fates of people drawn into the justice system. Thus, a major theme interwoven in chapters throughout this textbook is the need for professionals and citizens alike to recognize that court decisions cannot guarantee the protection of constitutional rights in the criminal justice process. Instead, the effectuation of rights requires that justice system professionals be educated, conscientious, and ethical, because the fulfillment of constitutional principles rests in their hands as they make discretionary decisions in the tens of thousands of daily interactions between criminal justice officials and citizens.

Textbooks that focus on procedures and rules may lull students into viewing constitutional criminal procedure as concerning only the rights of "criminals." Such a viewpoint creates risks: Justice system professionals may subconsciously regard constitutional rights as impediments to justice that can legitimately be manipulated and avoided in order to achieve crime control goals. Moreover, such a viewpoint may make future voters and community leaders insufficiently vigilant in monitoring the complete range of activities of justice system professionals whose actions may be guided, in part, by significant public pressure to achieve crime control goals. In light of rising public fears and aggressive law enforcement activity in the aftermath of the horrifying September 11th attacks on the World Trade Center and the Pentagon, both justice system officials and the American public face increasingly difficult questions about the appropriate priority to place on constitutional rights in criminal justice. Thus, a second important theme in *Criminal Procedure* concerns the need to recognize that anyone can be drawn into the criminal justice process and therefore constitutional rights in criminal procedure are important because they provide protections for the innocent as well as the guilty.

Contemporary textbooks with a limited focus on existing procedures, rules, and rights typically neglect to address adequately the nature of and prospects for change. Some books discuss past changes in rights definitions and rules as developmental steps toward the existing rule. However, they typically fail to convey the extent to which rights and rules are subject to change and the underlying social and political forces that may produce change. Changes may be produced by notable societal developments, such as the rapid expansion of technological innovations affecting criminal justice, and by political changes, such as the new appointments that change the composition of appellate courts. Thus, a third unique theme in *Criminal Procedure* concerns the prospects for change in criminal procedure based on societal developments that introduce new challenges, problems, and influences into the justice process.

IMPORTANT FEATURES

Criminal Procedure provides essential descriptions and analyses of stages in the criminal justice process and judicial decisions that define rights and provide guidelines for justice system decision makers. These important topics provide the core of any criminal procedure course but, in this textbook, they are not the sole focal points. In addition to textual discussion and case excerpts that cover these important topics, the foregoing themes that provide a comprehensive understanding of criminal procedure and its importance are integrated into textual discussion and highlighted in the book's special features.

Foundational Material

The initial chapters provide essential building blocks for understanding judicial opinions and the importance of constitutional criminal procedure in the justice process. Rather than begin by immersing students in a substantive topic, the initial chapters provide materials to help them understand the underlying interaction between discretionary decision making and rights, the structure of the court system and its processes, and even how to brief a case.

Instructors with students from a variety of majors or whose students would benefit from attention to foundational issues can use these chapters to ensure that their students have appropriate backgrounds for comprehending the later substantive topics. Instructors whose students have advanced knowledge of law and criminal justice may move more quickly through these chapters, but they will still find the boxed features (discussed below) that raise provocative questions to be valuable pedagogical tools for enhancing the analytical orientation of advanced students.

Case Excerpts

Criminal Procedure contains carefully edited excerpts of sixty-nine cases integrated within each chapter for easy pedagogical connection with related textual discussions. Most of the cases are important U.S. Supreme Court decisions interpreting the 4th, 5th, 6th, 8th, and 14th Amendments. These excerpts include recent opinions issued in 2000, 2001, and 2002. In addition, there are cases included from other courts to help students recognize that the U.S. Supreme Court is not solely responsible for defining rights in criminal procedure. Thus the case excerpts include *People v. Oliver* (Michigan Supreme Court, 2001) concerning the nature of reasonable suspicion that justifies stopping a motor vehicle to investigate a crime and *Burdine v. Johnson* (5th Circuit, U.S. Court of Appeals, 2001) concerning whether a defense attorney who sleeps during a murder trial has provided ineffective assistance of counsel. The cases in the book are supplemented by additional cases on the book's Web site so that instructors have options for assigning judicial opinions for their students to read.

Chapter-Opening Hypotheticals

Each substantive chapter begins with a plausible hypothetical scenario that illustrates how contemporary college students may be drawn into the criminal justice system and find specific criminal procedure rights relevant to their lives. In highlighting the theme of criminal procedure's importance and relevance for all Americans, these hypothetical scenarios raise such issues as the risks of witness misidentification, the authority of law enforcement officers to use their discretion in deciding to search people and homes, and the importance of bail and right to counsel for people who have been taken into custody.

Highlighted Discussion of Symbolic Aspects of Constitutional Rights

Each chapter contains a featured box entitled "Constitutional Rights: Symbol or Substance?" These boxes give examples and pose questions about apparent gaps between courts' declarations about the definitions of rights and the actual operations of the justice process. For example, these boxes raise such issues as: questions about Americans' commitment to the Bill of Rights in light of the federal government's detention of terror suspects in Guantanamo Bay, Cuba in order to avoid the application of constitutional criminal procedure; the manner in which law enforcement officers' discretionary decisions and adaptive behavior may undercut the rules established in 4th and 5th Amendment cases;

the actual substance of the constitutional right to a speedy trial in light of the vague standard established in *Barker v. Wingo*; and the nature of the right to counsel in light of the difficult standards of proof for demonstrating ineffective assistance of counsel. These features as well as other boxes about ethical issues help to reinforce the theme about the fulfillment of constitutional rights relying on the professionalism and ethics of justice system personnel.

Highlighted Discussion of the Impact of Technological Innovation

Throughout the book special boxes feature questions and discussions of the impact of technological innovation on constitutional rights. New developments in surveillance technologies, such as thermal imaging and Internet monitoring, will raise new issues about the government's permissible authority to conduct searches. In addition, scientific research is posing new questions about the potential development of "lie detection" devices that detect brainwave reactions to images and questions without requiring self-incriminating testimonial evidence from suspects.

Closer Examination of Special Issues

In order to facilitate analysis and discussion of important issues, special boxes throughout the book provide closer examination of such issues as police ethics, the rules of evidence, sample jury instructions, an actual transcript of the entry of a guilty plea, and the forms used by convicted offenders to file habeas corpus petitions. These features provide opportunities for instructors to give extra attention to subjects that are often treated only in a descriptive or cursory manner in criminal procedure textbooks.

Instructional Aids

Each chapter contains a glossary of keys terms highlighted in the text. There are also chapter summaries to aid students in reviewing and understanding the material.

SUPPLEMENTS

Available to qualified adopters. Please consult your local sales representative for details.

Web-Based Instructor's Manual

The *Instructor's Manual* has been prepared by the text author, Christopher E. Smith, a lawyer and social scientist who has taught criminal procedure for nearly two decades. The *Instructor's Manual* contains chapter outlines, hypothetical scenarios for class discussion, and exam questions, including multiple choice, true/false, and essay formats. It can be accessed from the Instructor Resources section of Wadsworth's Criminal Justice Resource Center at http://cj.wadsworth.com.

Web-Based Study Guide

The student study guide includes chapter outlines, practice matching questions on important concepts and cases, and advice for succeeding in the study of criminal procedure. The *Study Guide* can be easily accessed under the Student Resources section of Wadsworth's Criminal Justice Resource Center at http://cj.wadsworth.com.

Web-Based Supplemental Case Excerpts

In order to provide instructors with additional options for student reading and discussion, additional case excerpts of important U.S. Supreme Court cases are available on the Instructor Resources section of the Criminal Justice Resource Center at http://cj.wadsworth.com.

ACKNOWLEDGMENTS

I wrote this textbook because I found myself dissatisfied with the limitations of other books on criminal procedure. As indicated earlier in the Preface by my discussion of additional themes and topics, my training as a lawyer and a social scientist as well as my many years of teaching law classes for undergraduate students led me to conclude that there was a need for a textbook that provided greater attention to the human dimensions of criminal procedure. Students need to understand the steps in the justice process and the important court decisions that define rights, but they also need to understand these topics in the context of their human consequences and the pervasiveness of discretionary decision-making authority in the system. Hopefully, the materials in this book will be helpful in enabling instructors to provide their students with a comprehensive understanding of criminal procedure and its consequences.

My understanding of criminal procedure and its consequences has been greatly enhanced by my work with and questions posed to a number of individuals over a period of twenty years. They have had a particularly significant influence on my understanding of the subject, although they bear no responsibility for the interpretations and choices that shaped this book: George F. Cole, University of Connecticut; Thomas R. Hensley, Kent State University; Joyce A. Baugh, Central Michigan University; David A. Schultz, Hamline University; Steven B. Dow, Michigan State University; Abraham V. Hutt, Esq.; the late Hon. Doyle Rowland, U.S. Magistrate Judge for the Western District of Michigan; the Hon. Virginia Morgan, U.S. Magistrate Judge for the Eastern District of Michigan; and the Hon. James Carr, U.S. District Judge for the Northern District of Ohio. In addition, I learned many valuable lessons through feedback from my former students, especially those who are now practicing attorneys.

This book would not have been possible without the encouragement and support of Wadsworth's Senior Executive Editor for Criminal Justice, Sabra Horne, and the book's editor, Shelley Murphy. Dawn Mesa provided her usual invaluable assistance with the supplements. Equally important for the book's final form were the careful evaluations and constructive suggestions from a number of reviewers:

Jack Call
Radford University

Phyllis Gerstenfeld
CSU, Stanislaus

Milo Miller
Southeast Missouri State

Victoria Time
Old Dominion University

Although I did not adopt all of their suggestions, they deserve significant credit for improving the organization and content of the book. I give the reviewers full credit for the improvements that they initiated, but I remain fully responsible for the choices that determined the book's contents as well as any errors that may appear within its pages.

Christopher E. Smith
Michigan State University

smithc28@msu.edu

CHAPTER ONE

Law and the Legal System

Crime is a serious problem in the United States. Many Americans are fearful of being victimized by robbers and burglars, and they want the government to take action to prevent crime and punish lawbreakers. Imagine all the possible actions a government might take to combat crime. Police officers could be given orders to shoot suspected criminals on sight. Citizens could be required to have government-issued permits in order to leave their homes and drive to work. Government officials could systematically search every person, vehicle, and home to look for evidence of criminal activity. Criminals caught in the act could be tortured to death on live television. In sum, governments could take strong actions against crime and, indeed, in various countries and at different moments in history, governments carried out harsh actions similar to some of those just mentioned.

Why do we not see such strong actions employed in the United States if we truly believe that crime is a threatening problem? In considering this question, also ask yourself whether you would be comfortable with such actions being taken by your government. Should police officers be allowed to shoot "suspected" criminals? Should such officers be free from punishment if they are mistaken about a person's guilt? Should you be required to seek government permission to leave your home? Should you be subjected to searches at any time and for no good reason? Should the government use torture against someone who commits a crime? Most Americans would have trouble answering "yes" to these questions. Such anticrime actions would collide with American values about personal liberty and limited governmental authority. In countries with democratic governing systems, such as the United States, society's dominant values help to define governmental priorities and values. People select government officials with the expectation that those officials will produce rules and policies that reflect societal values. These rules and policies produced by government officials, especially legislators and judges, are called **law.** Law defines and limits the authority of government, and it establishes the protections that individuals enjoy against interference by government. Law also provides the rules for settling disputes when citizens have conflicts with each other. Thus, the answer to the original question about why we do not see such harsh anticrime actions in the United States is that law, which is defined by societal values, limits the authority of government.

The governing system of the United States, including the criminal justice process and the governmental actors in that process (i.e., police officers, prosecutors, judges, and corrections officers), is guided and limited by law. In this chapter we will examine the nature of law as it affects the criminal justice process as well as the institutions of the legal system that determine how law is applied in American society.

LAW AND CRIMINAL JUSTICE

What is law? In essence, law is the body of authoritative rules for society. These are the rules that are backed by the power of the American people and their government. In other words, these rules tell everyone, including government officials, what they can and cannot do and what will happen if someone violates these rules. In criminal justice, there are two primary categories of laws. Laws that define which behaviors will be subject to punishment by government constitute the body of **substantive criminal law.** Examples of criminal laws include the prohibitions on murder, rape, assault, and burglary. Violations of these laws cause people to be subjected to the government's power to punish. Punishment in criminal justice can, depending on the seriousness of the offense and the offender's prior record, range from relatively mild fines to significant restrictions on liberty through lengthy prison terms and even the death penalty.

Substantive criminal laws are spelled out in state and federal penal codes that are drafted and enacted as statutes by the citizens' elected representatives in legislatures. Congress enacts federal criminal laws, and state legislatures establish state crimes. Local city councils and county commissions can define low-level crimes by enacting ordinances. When there are disputes about the meaning of these statutes and ordinances, judges may be called on to interpret and clarify these laws. Because legislative bodies possess the ultimate authority over the meaning of their own enactments, they can revise and reenact their statute and ordinances if they disagree with the interpretations pronounced by judges.

The second category of law affecting criminal justice, called **procedural criminal law,** mandates the steps in the criminal justice process and provides legal protections for criminal suspects, defendants, and convicted offenders. Legal protections possessed by individuals against governmental actions are called **constitutional rights.** People in the United States possess rights against governmental actions within the criminal justice process and outside of criminal justice. Within the criminal justice process, individuals possess such familiar rights as the right to trial by jury and the protection against cruel and unusual punishments. Outside of criminal justice, such familiar rights as the right to freedom of speech and the right to free exercise of religion provide protections against governmental actions that would interfere with these liberties.

Although Americans are aware that they possess rights and they can list many of those rights (e.g., freedom of speech, trial by jury), two important aspects of rights are not clearly understood. First, the scope and meaning of rights is determined by judges' interpretations. Judges are not obligated to produce interpretations that are clear and consistent. Indeed, judges are not even obligated to define rights in a manner that follows the literal words of the federal and state constitutions. For example, although the Sixth Amendment to the U.S. Constitution says that "*[i]n all criminal prosecutions,* the accused shall enjoy the right to a speedy and public trial, by an impartial jury" (emphasis added), judges have interpreted the Sixth Amendment to provide a jury trial in only *some* criminal cases.[1] Moreover, the fact that the definition of rights is determined by judges' interpretations means that the nature of rights can change as new judges are appointed or elected to office and these new judges produce new interpretations.

Second, the rights described by constitutions and interpreted by judicial decisions may not be carried out properly. In other words, the judges may declare that people possess certain rights, yet the rights are not implemented. The rights exist on paper but do not provide the protections that people expect them to provide. For example, police may search automobiles only when there is a basis for a search, which may be provided by the driver's consent, the arrest of the driver, or the observation of a weapon or drugs lying on the floor of the car. Sometimes, however, officers may search a car without a proper basis. Judges say, in the words of the Fourth Amendment, that people are protected against "unreasonable searches," yet such declarations cannot guarantee that these searches will never take place. Thus the law must also be concerned with what, if anything, happens when someone violates a right. The box on p. 4 takes a closer look at rights, authority, and power.

Criminal justice is also affected by **civil law.** Unlike criminal law, which is based on government-imposed punishments for specifically defined misbehavior, civil law governs the relationships among individuals, corporations, and government agencies. Disputes about contracts, property, and personal injuries all fall under civil law. Typically, civil law is used to clarify people's obligations to each other or to institutional entities. For example, a court may determine whether or not you are obligated to pay for a piano that you purchased but later decided that you did not want. Civil law can also provide compensation to people who suffered injuries through the actions of others. These injuries may be physical injuries or financial injuries. Thus a court may order you to pay for someone's medical bills if you hit the person with your car. A court may also order payment of money for damage to property.

In criminal justice, civil law is very important because it provides the basis for lawsuits filed against government officials by individuals who claim that their rights were violated. If police officers mistakenly search the wrong house, they may be sued for damaging property during the search and for violating

A CLOSER LOOK   Terminology: Rights, Authority, and Power

People who study and discuss law must take care to use legal terms with precision. Words used in everyday conversations often have special, precise meanings when used in discussing law. Thus students of criminal procedure should think carefully about the words they use. For example, it is not uncommon to hear a college student make the following statement: "I was driving my car and I didn't break any laws, but this police officer stopped me and searched my car. Did the officer have a right to do that?" This statement helps to illustrate the care we must take in distinguishing three different but equally important concepts: rights, authority, and power. Look again at the definition of "rights" mentioned earlier. Rights are protections that individuals possess against actions by government. Thus, in the car scenario the officer does not have "rights." The officer is the representative of the government, so it is the driver's rights that are at issue. Instead, the question more precisely concerns whether the officer had the *authority*—not the "right"—to conduct the search. Someone possesses authority when an official source, such as a law or an agency regulation, gives him or her permission to legitimately undertake a certain action. Police officers possess the authority—granted to them by law—to arrest people whom they observe committing crimes. They do not possess the authority to demand that everyone who walks past a certain street corner give them twenty dollars. The law does not permit officers to take money away from people in this way. Thus we need to be careful to apply the words "rights" and "authority" to proper situations and not mix them together in an unthinking fashion.

Suppose that we change the student's statement to the following: "I was driving my car and I didn't break any laws, but this police officer stopped me and searched my car. Can the officer do that?" An accurate response to that question might be "Well, she did it, didn't she? So I guess that shows that she can." Here the question and response focus on what actually happened, not on what *should have* happened. When someone has a badge and a gun, how can you stop her or him from conducting a search? A gun gives the person *power,* which can be defined as the ability to make others do what they otherwise might not wish to do. Questions about authority concern what police officers (and other government officials) are supposed to be able to do legitimately under the law. Questions about power concern what police officers (and other government officials) can do because they have the ability to do it, even if they are not supposed to. Sometimes power and authority coincide. Do police officers possess both the authority and power to place handcuffs on people who are observed committing crimes? Yes. By contrast, do police officers possess both the authority and the power to force every pedestrian on a street to pay them twenty dollars? They clearly do not possess this authority, but they may possess power if they threaten people with arrest or physical harm. If police officers (or other government officials) choose to use power in a manner that exceeds their authority, especially when that exercise of power violates individuals' rights, then the police officers run the risk of being sanctioned. They may be arrested, fired, or sued for misusing their power.

For the sake of clarity, try to use appropriate terms when discussing criminal procedure issues. Reserve the word "rights" for situations in which an individual claims that a legal protection was violated by government officials. When discussing the actions of government officials, distinguish legitimate actions (authority) from actions taken without permission simply because the official chooses to do it (power).

the homeowner's right against unreasonable searches and seizures. If police officers or corrections officers are responsible for the personal injury or death of someone in custody, they may be liable for large sums of money to the injured person or the person's surviving family members. Because some police departments and correctional institutions have been ordered to pay thousands and even millions of dollars for actions that injured people and violated constitutional rights, law enforcement and corrections agencies make great efforts to develop policies and training programs that will prevent such unfortunate events from occurring. Thus the threat of civil lawsuits affects criminal justice by shaping the development of policies, practices, and training.

Rule violations in civil law may result in orders that individuals or corporations pay money to compensate people injured by improper actions or dangerous products. This would arise, for example, when someone is injured in an automobile accident caused by poor driving or a defective car. Other kinds of laws define the rights of individuals, describe the processes the government must follow before taking certain actions, or design governmental programs affecting criminal justice, health, education, and other policy issues.

We can look to several sources to find the law. These sources produce different forms of law, each with its own lawmaking processes.

Constitutions

Constitutions contain the fundamental laws for the United States and each state. They describe the design and powers of government and list the rights possessed by individuals. As previously discussed, constitutional rights are basic protections possessed by individuals to guard them against improper governmental interference with their liberty. For example, the United States Constitution, which was ratified in 1789, describes the design and authority of Congress, the President, and the Supreme Court. Similarly, each state has its own constitution describing the design and powers of its legislature, governor, and courts. Because people were initially worried that the U.S. Constitution granted too much power to the federal government, they added amendments to the Constitution which would, among other things, list the rights possessed by individuals to protect them against abusive actions by government. State constitutions also contain lists of rights applicable to people within their state boundaries. These rights were often included at the time each state constitution was written rather than added later as was the case with the U.S. Constitution.

Because constitutions provide the fundamental law of the nation or a state, we do not want constitutions changed without strong reasons. Therefore the processes for amending constitutions usually require that an amendment enjoy significant popular support before it is added to change a constitution. In most states, the people of the state must vote on constitutional amendments. For the U.S. Constitution, amendments can be initiated either by a two-thirds vote in Congress or by two-thirds of the states' legislatures. However, in order to be added to the U.S. Constitution, the amendment must subsequently be approved by the state legislatures or state constitutional conventions in three-fourths of the states. It can be extremely difficult to gain such levels of support for constitutional provisions. Thus relatively few amendments are added to constitutions.

The first ten amendments to the U.S. Constitution, known as the Bill of Rights, were ratified in 1791. These amendments contain the most famous and important rights, such as freedom of speech and religion, that Americans learn about as schoolchildren. These amendments also serve as a central focus of legal issues in criminal justice because of questions about the extent to which criminal suspects and defendants possess protections. An additional amendment ratified in 1868, the Fourteenth Amendment, provides other rights that affect criminal justice institutions and processes. As you read the Bill of Rights and the Fourteenth Amendment in the box on p. 6, try to identify which

The Bill of Rights and Fourteenth Amendment to the United States Constitution

First Amendment (ratified in 1791): Congress shall make no law respecting an establishment of religion, or prohibiting the free exercise thereof; or abridging the freedom of speech, or of the press; or the right of the people peaceably to assemble, and to petition the Government for redress of grievances.

Second Amendment (ratified in 1791): A well-regulated Militia, being necessary for the security of a free State, the right of the people to keep and bear Arms, shall not be infringed.

Third Amendment (ratified in 1791): No Soldier shall, in time of peace be quartered in any house, without the consent of the Owner, nor in time of war, but in a manner to be prescribed by law.

Fourth Amendment (ratified in 1791): The right of the people to be secure in their persons, houses, papers, and effects, against unreasonable searches and seizures, shall not be violated, and no Warrants shall issue, but upon probable cause, supported by Oath or affirmation, and particularly describing the place to be searched, and the persons or things to be seized.

Fifth Amendment (ratified in 1791): No person shall be held to answer for a capital or otherwise infamous crime, unless on a presentment or indictment of a Grand Jury, except in cases arising in the land or naval forces, or in the Militia, when in actual service in time of War or public danger; nor shall any person be subject for the same offence to be twice put in jeopardy of life or limb; nor shall be compelled in any criminal case to be a witness against himself, nor be deprived of life, liberty, or property, without due process of law; nor shall private property be taken for public use, without just compensation.

Sixth Amendment (ratified in 1791): In all criminal prosecutions, the accused shall enjoy the right to a speedy and public trial, by an impartial jury of the State and district wherein the crime shall have been committed, which district shall have been previously ascertained by law, and to be informed of the nature and cause of the accusation; to be confronted with the witnesses against him; to have compulsory process for obtaining witnesses in his favor, and to have the Assistance of Counsel for his defence.

Seventh Amendment (ratified in 1791): In Suits at common law, where the value in controversy shall exceed twenty dollars, the right of trial by jury shall be preserved, and no fact tried by a jury, shall be otherwise re-examined in any Court of the United States, than according to the rules of the common law.

Eighth Amendment (ratified in 1791): Excessive bail shall not be required, nor excessive fines imposed, nor cruel and unusual punishments inflicted.

Ninth Amendment (ratified in 1791): The enumeration in the Constitution, of certain rights, shall not be construed to deny or disparage others retained by the people.

Tenth Amendment (ratified in 1791): The powers not delegated to the United States by the Constitution, nor prohibited by it to the States, are reserved to the States respectively, or to the people.

Fourteenth Amendment (ratified in 1868)
Section 1: All persons born or naturalized in the United States, and subject to the jurisdiction thereof, are citizens of the United States and of the State wherein they reside. No State shall make or enforce any law which shall abridge the privileges or immunities of citizens of the United States; nor shall any State deprive any person of life, liberty, or property, without due process of law; nor deny to any person within its jurisdiction the equal protection of the laws.
Section 5: The Congress shall have the power to enforce, by appropriate legislation, the provisions of this article.

rights are most likely to affect the decisions and behavior of police officers, prosecutors, and judges.

States also have their own constitutions. These constitutions provide the basis for state courts' decisions overseeing corrections policies and practices. Many rights in state constitutions are based on the wording of the federal Bill of Rights. Note how closely Section 16 of the Michigan Constitution follows the Eighth Amendment of the U.S. Constitution:

> *Section 16: Bail; fines; punishments; detention of witnesses. Excessive bail shall not be required; excessive fines shall not be imposed; cruel or unusual punishment shall not be inflicted; nor shall witnesses be unreasonably detained.*

Although the parallels between Section 16 and the Eighth Amendment are evident with respect to the coverage of bail, fines, and punishments, there are important differences. Michigan's Section 16 contains an additional constitutional protection not provided by the Eighth Amendment: prohibition on the unreasonable detaining of witnesses. In addition, Section 16 is different from the Eighth Amendment in its coverage of improper punishments. The Eighth Amendment bans "cruel *and* unusual punishments" while Section 16 prohibits "cruel *or* unusual punishment." By its words, the Michigan Constitution appears to provide greater protection to criminal offenders. It prevents punishments that are either cruel or unusual while the Eighth Amendment protection seems to stop only those that are both cruel and unusual. In practice, the two phrases could be interpreted in a similar fashion, but the wording differences create the opportunity for Michigan's courts to make different, broader interpretations.

Statutes

Statutes are laws enacted by elected representatives in legislatures. These laws are passed in the legislatures at all levels of government. Congress bears responsibility for statutes governing the entire country. Each state has a legislature to enact statutes. Examples of lower-level legislatures would be county commissions and city councils whose enactments are generally called ordinances. At any given moment, a person in the United States is simultaneously subject to the legal rules enacted by the legislative bodies of multiple levels of government: city, county, state, and nation. The legislature for each level of government may possess the authority to enact laws governing various matters. However, the most significant statutes affecting criminal justice and corrections come from state legislatures and Congress.

State legislatures use statutes to define crimes and punishments within their borders. They enact statutes to determine how citizens will be taxed and how tax money will be spent. Laws passed by Congress define federal crimes and punishments and provide money for federal law enforcement agencies, courts, and prisons.

Whereas many provisions in constitutions are written in general terms, statutes are often very detailed and specific. In addition, statutes may change frequently. Legislatures regularly write and enact new statutes or modify existing statutes. It normally takes only a majority vote by the people's elected representatives within a legislature to change a statutory law or enact a new statute. Congress enacts statutes covering the entire country, but states have their own statutes to handle most matters related to criminal justice. As you read the portions of these statutes in the box "Sample Statutes" on p. 8, take note of the detailed language. Both the federal and state statutes appear to be more detailed than the constitutional provisions we previously examined. Is it easy to read and understand both statutes? What are these statutes about?

Sample Statutes: Federal and State

FEDERAL STATUTE

Preliminary Examination: **Title 18, United States Code, Section 3060**

[excerpt]

(a) Except as otherwise provided by this section, a preliminary examination shall be held within the time set by the judge or magistrate pursuant to subsection (b) of this section, to determine whether there is probable cause to believe that an offense has been committed and that the arrested person has committed it.

(b) The date for the preliminary examination shall be fixed by the judge or magistrate at the initial appearance of the arrested person. Except as provided by subsection (c) of this section, or unless the arrested person waives the preliminary examination, such examination shall be held within a reasonable time following initial appearance, but in any event not later than—

   (1) the tenth day following the date of the initial appearance of the arrested person before such officer if the arrested person is held in custody without any provision for release, or is held in custody for failure to meet the conditions of release imposed, or is released from custody only during specified hours of the day; or

   (2) the twentieth day following the date of the initial appearance if the arrested person is released from custody under any condition other than a condition described in paragraph (1) of this subsection.

(c) With the consent of the arrested person, the date fixed by the judge or magistrate for the preliminary examination may be a date later than that prescribed by subsection (b). . . .

(d) Except as provided by subsection (e) of this section, an arrested person who has not been accorded the preliminary examination required by subsection (a) within the period of time fixed by the judge or magistrate in compliance with subsections (b) and (c), shall be discharged from custody or from the requirement of bail or any other condition of release, without prejudice, however, to the institution of further criminal proceedings against him upon the charge upon which he was arrested.

(e) No preliminary examination in compliance with subsection (a) of this section shall be required to be accorded an arrested person, nor shall such arrested person be discharged from custody or from the requirement of bail or any other condition of release pursuant to subsection (d), if at any time subsequent to the initial appearance of such person before a judge or magistrate and prior to the date fixed for the preliminary examination pursuant to subsections (b) and (c) an indictment is returned, or, in appropriate cases, an information is filed against such person in a court of the United States.

STATE STATUTE

Waiver of Trial by Jury in Criminal Cases: **Michigan Compiled Laws 763.3**

Sec. 3. (1) In all criminal cases arising in the courts of this state the defendant may, with the consent of the prosecutor and approval by the court, waive a determination of the facts by a jury and elect to be tried before the court without a jury. Except in cases of minor offenses, the waiver and election by a defendant shall be in writing signed by the defendant and filed in the case and made a part of the record. The waiver and election shall be entitled in the court and case, and in substance as follows: "I, defendant in the above case, hereby voluntarily waive and relinquish my right to a trial by jury and elect to be tried by a judge of the court in which the case may be pending. I fully understand that under the laws of this state I have a constitutional right to a trial by jury."

Signature of defendant

(2) Except in cases of minor offenses, the waiver of trial by jury shall be made in open court after the defendant has been arraigned and has had opportunity to consult with legal counsel.

Legal cases are often filed concerning statutes. Some cases ask judges to interpret the statutes and provide clearer definitions of the statutory law's meaning. Other cases claim that the statute should be invalidated because it violates some provision of a state or federal constitution. Constitutional provisions are more important than statutes, and judges possess the power of **judicial review,** which permits them to determine if a law passed by a legislature and signed by a president or governor violates a constitution. Still other cases seek to have statutes enforced if someone believes that criminal justice officials are not properly obeying the rules created by the legislature.

Case Law

Case law is produced through judges' decisions. In deciding the cases presented to them, judges frequently interpret constitutional provisions, statutes, and other judges' decisions in prior cases. By interpreting law and applying it in deciding cases, judges create new law or modify existing legal rules through their judicial decisions. For example, suppose police officers approach a young person who is walking down the street carrying a paper bag. If the officers order this person to show them the contents of the bag and the person obeys the order, does the examination of the bag violate the Fourth Amendment's prohibition on "unreasonable searches and seizures"? In reaching a conclusion, the judge would be creating case law in the form of a legal rule concerning whether the ban on unreasonable searches applies to searches of containers carried by pedestrians who have not engaged in any behaviors that reasonably arouse police officers' suspicions. The judge's decision will be guided by prior judicial decisions, if any, concerning similar situations.

The United States inherited the **common law** process developed in England. Under the common law process, judges use judicial decisions in prior cases to help them decide new cases that arise. In the previous example of the search of the pedestrian's bag, a judge would not start from scratch in simply deciding if he or she believes that such searches violate the prohibition on unreasonable searches. The judge would first examine prior case decisions about search situations affecting pedestrians and containers they carry as well as case decisions about the meaning of "unreasonable searches and seizures." If there were prior decisions concerning such situations, the judge would likely follow the rule established by the judges in the prior cases. This would be especially true if the prior decisions came from the U.S. Supreme Court or a federal court of appeals (or a state supreme court for an issue of state constitutional law). If there were no prior decisions on such an issue, then the judge would use prior interpretations of the phrase "unreasonable searches and seizures" and prior decisions on searching containers to see if the rules from those cases ought to apply in some form to the case at hand. The judge can use his or her judgment about whether and how a prior decision should apply, but the prior cases provide important guidance. If this is a completely new situation that has never arisen in a prior case, then the judge has an opportunity to create a completely new rule that will help to provide guidance for any similar cases that arise later.

In relying on prior judicial decisions, judges use **case precedent.** In the common law, this is known as following *stare decisis*—adhering to decisions that have come before. The common law process of relying on case precedent, or *stare decisis,* provides several advantages for the legal system. The use of case precedent in judicial decisions provides consistency and stability in law. The same legal principles are applied to similar cases. People in one situation are treated in the same manner as other people who find themselves in a similar situation. Case precedent also increases efficiency in the administration of justice.

Judges do not have to start from scratch in deciding each case. They simply look to prior case decisions for guidance. Consistency in judges' decisions helps to maintain the image of justice that people want to see in the law. It helps to keep judges from appearing to make up legal rules on their own—even if they sometimes do just that.

Cases presented in court call on judges to interpret constitutions and statutes. Constitutions often have general phrases that lack clear, definite meanings. The Eighth Amendment's phrase "cruel and unusual punishments" is one such phrase. Its meaning is not obvious so judges must use their judgment, in light of case precedent, in determining the meaning of this and other constitutional phrases. Judges are the ultimate authorities over the meaning of constitutional language. Lower-court judges must obey the constitutional decisions of higher courts, but the **courts of last resort**—namely, state supreme courts and the U.S. Supreme Court—enjoy significant freedom to create new interpretations of constitutional phrases. If new justices are appointed to the U.S. Supreme Court or elected to a state supreme court, they can help make new law by reinterpreting constitutional provisions. For example, for most of American history the phrase "right to counsel" in the Sixth Amendment merely meant that a defendant could not be prevented from obtaining an attorney if he or she could afford to pay for legal representation. As the Supreme Court composition changed and the new justices' interpretations reflected different societal values than those of their predecessors, the Court eventually reinterpreted the "right to counsel" to mean an entitlement to have a defense attorney provided for defendants facing serious charges who could not otherwise afford to hire an attorney for themselves.

If legislators do not like constitutional interpretation decisions produced by judges, they cannot directly change those decisions. They can seek to initiate constitutional amendments to undo the judges' decisions, but such amendments usually require complicated processes in which legislative approval by a super majority of legislators (e.g., two-thirds) must be followed by a vote of the people (state constitutions) or by ratification in a super majority (i.e., three-fourths) of states (U.S. Constitution). Because of the multistep decision-making process and the need for the support of more than a mere majority of legislators, voters, and states, it is very difficult to succeed in amending a constitution.

By contrast, legislatures are supposed to be the ultimate authorities over the meaning of statutes. Despite legislatures' control over statutes' meaning, judges, in fact, have significant power to determine the meaning of statutory law. Cases raising questions about the meaning of statutes are presented in court. Judges must decide what the words of a statute mean and how those words apply to a specific situation. In theory, judges are supposed to interpret the statute in accordance with the meaning intended by the legislature that created the statute. Again, the judges look to prior judicial decisions for guidance. With statutes, however, they also look to discussions in legislative hearings and published statements by legislators to help them decide what the words of a statute mean.

Judges determine the meaning of statutory law in the cases presented to them, but legislators are the ultimate authorities because they can rewrite the statute's wording if they do not like judges' interpretations. A vote supported by a simple majority of legislators and endorsed by a governor (states) or the U.S. president (federal) can create new legislation that will undo a judge's statutory interpretation decision. In most instances, however, legislators do not enact new statutes to clarify the meaning of statutes or override a judge's decisions. Legislators are too busy with a variety of pressing issues to closely monitor and control judges' statutory interpretation decisions. When a majority of legislators strongly object to a judge's decision, they will take the time to enact corrective legislation. However, judges' interpretations usually control the meaning of statutes because legislatures have moved on to other issues and do not take the time to go back to correct judicial statutory interpretation decisions with which they disagree.

Judges' decisions, which are written in the form of **judicial opinions,** are not easy to read. They are typically elaborate and seemingly lengthy documents written in the language of lawyers. They are not written for the general public. Instead, they are written to give guidance to lawyers and judges who will look to the case as a precedent in preparing arguments or deciding future cases. Judicial opinions provide detailed reasons for the rule of law developed or endorsed by the court to decide the case at hand. They do not necessarily get right to the point. Nor do they always announce the rule of law in a clear, straightforward manner. Often, the rule of law established by a judicial opinion is itself subject to interpretation by judges and lawyers in subsequent cases.

Read the portion of the U.S. Supreme Court's judicial opinion in *Rummel v. Estelle* (1980) that is presented in the box on pp. 12–13. Try to pick out the important elements of a judicial opinion. First, look for the **facts,** which are a summary of the events and circumstances that produced a court case. Who did what to whom? Why is someone so unhappy with the situation that he brought the case to court? The facts in court cases may not include all actual events. Only matters that can be established through admissible evidence will count as legal facts to be included in making decisions. Second, try to identify the **issue** in the case. The issue is the question being addressed by the appellate court. Unlike trial courts, which in criminal cases hear testimony and examine other evidence before a jury or judge determines whether the defendant is guilty, appellate courts focus on narrow questions of law. Generally, appellate courts decide whether the trial court made an error in interpreting some aspect of law or court procedure. In most of the cases presented in this book, the issue will involve someone's claim that a constitutional provision or statute was violated. In *Rummel v. Estelle,* which part of the U.S. Constitution is being examined by the Supreme Court? Third, find the **holding,** which is the answer to the question posed by the issue. The holding is the rule of law established or endorsed in the judicial opinion. Technically, it is the only aspect of the judicial opinion that other courts are required to apply in subsequent cases concerning the same kind of issue. Fourth, look for the **reasoning,** which is essentially the list of reasons given by the court for deciding the case in the manner that it did. Why does the judicial opinion apply the rule of law as it did? Fifth, identify the reasoning in any concurring or dissenting opinions. **Concurring** opinions are written by judges (called "justices" on the U.S. Supreme Court and state supreme courts) who agree with the result of the case, but who believe that the result should be supported by one or more different reasons than those put forward by the majority of judges. **Dissenting** opinions are written by judges who disagree with the decision and believe that the losing side should really have won the case.

The box "Briefing a Case" on p. 14 contains a sample case brief based on *Rummel v. Estelle.*

Rummel v. Estelle, 445 U.S. 263 (1980)

JUSTICE REHNQUIST delivered the opinion of the Court [joined by CHIEF JUSTICE BURGER, JUSTICE BLACKMUN, JUSTICE STEWART, and JUSTICE WHITE].

Petitioner William James Rummel is presently serving a life sentence imposed by the State of Texas in 1973 under its [repeat offender or] "recidivist statute" . . . which provided that "[w]hoever shall have been three times convicted of a felony less than capital shall on such third conviction be imprisoned for life in the penitentiary."

. . . [Rummel is] arguing that life imprisonment is "grossly disproportionate" to the three felonies that formed the predicate for his sentence and that therefore the sentence violated the ban on cruel and unusual punishments of the Eighth and Fourteenth Amendments. . . .

In 1964 the State of Texas charged Rummel with fraudulent use of a credit card to obtain $80 worth of goods or services. Because the amount in question was greater than $50, the charged offense was a felony. . . . Rummel eventually pleaded guilty to the charge and was sentenced to three years' confinement in a state penitentiary.

In 1969 the State of Texas charged Rummel with passing a forged check in the amount of $28.36. . . . Rummel pleaded guilty to this offense and was sentenced to four years' imprisonment.

In 1973 Rummel was charged with obtaining $120.75 by false pretenses. . . . The prosecution chose, however, to proceed against Rummel under Texas recidivist statute, and cited in the indictment his 1964 and 1969 convictions as requiring the imposition of a life sentence if Rummel were convicted of the charge. A jury convicted Rummel of felony theft and also found true the allegation that he had been convicted of two prior felonies. As a result, on April 26, 1973, the trial court imposed upon Rummel the life sentence mandated by [the recidivist statute].

This Court has on occasion stated that the Eighth Amendment prohibits the imposition of a sentence that is grossly disproportionate to the severity of the crime. . . . In recent years this proposition has appeared most frequently in opinions dealing with the death penalty. . . . Rummel cites these . . . opinions dealing with capital punishment as compelling the conclusion that his sentence is disproportionate to his offenses. . . .

. . . [However,] [b]ecause a sentence of death differs in kind from any sentence of imprisonment, no matter how long, our decisions applying the prohibition on cruel and unusual punishments to capital cases are of limited assistance in deciding the constitutionality of the punishment meted out to Rummel.

Outside the context of capital punishment, successful challenges to the proportionality of particular sentences have been exceedingly rare. . . .

Undaunted by earlier cases [in which the Supreme Court rejected Eighth Amendment claims for severe prison sentences], Rummel attempts to ground his proportionality attack on an alleged "nationwide" trend away from mandatory life sentences and toward "lighter, discretionary sentences." . . . According to Rummel, "[n]o jurisdiction in the United States or the Free World punishes habitual offenders as harshly as Texas." . . . In support of this proposition, Rummel offers detailed charts and tables documenting the history of recidivist statutes in the United States since 1776. . . .

Rummel's charts and tables do appear to indicate that he might have received more lenient treatment in almost any State other than Texas, West Virginia, or Washington. The distinctions, however, are subtle rather than gross. A number of States impose a mandatory life sentence upon conviction of four felonies rather than three. Other States require one or more of the felonies to be "violent" to support a life sentence. Still other States leave the imposition of a life sentence after three felonies within the discretion of a judge or jury. It is one thing for a court to compare those States that impose capital punishment for a specific offense with those States that do not. . . . It is quite another thing for a court to attempt to evaluate the position of any particular recidivist scheme within Rummel's complex matrix.

Nor do Rummel's extensive charts even begin to reflect the complexity of the comparison he asks this Court to make. Texas, we are told, has a relatively liberal policy of granting "good time" credits to its prisoners, a policy that historically has allowed a prisoner serving a life sentence to become eligible for parole in as little as 12 years. . . . We agree with Rummel that his inability to enforce any "right" to parole precludes us from treating his life sentence as if it were equivalent to a sentence of 12 years. Nevertheless, because parole is "an established variation on imprisonment of convicted criminals," _Morrissey v. Brewer,_ 408 U.S. 471 . . . (1972), a proper assessment of Texas' treatment of Rummel could hardly ignore the possibility that he will not actually be imprisoned for the rest of his life. If nothing else, the possibility of parole, however slim, serves to distinguish Rummel from a person sentenced under a recidivist statute like Mississippi's, which provides for a sentence of life without parole upon conviction of three felonies including at least one violent felony. . . .

. . . Like the line dividing felony theft from petty larceny, the point at which a recidivist will be deemed to have demonstrated the necessary propensities and the amount of time that the recidivist will be isolated from society are matters largely within the discretion of the punishing jurisdiction.

We therefore hold that the mandatory life sentence imposed upon this petitioner does not constitute cruel and unusual punishment under the Eighth and Fourteenth Amendments. The judgment of the Court of Appeals is *Affirmed*.

JUSTICE STEWART, concurring.

I am moved to repeat the substance of what I had to say on another occasion about the recidivist legislation of Texas:

> *"If the Constitution gave me a roving commission to impose upon the criminal courts of Texas my own notions of enlightened policy, I would not join the Court's opinion. For it is clear to me that the recidivist procedures adopted in recent years by many other States . . . are far superior to those utilized [here]. But the question for decision is not whether we applaud or even whether we personally approve the procedures followed in [this case]. The question is whether those procedures fall below the minimum level the [Constitution] will tolerate. Upon that question I am constrained to join the opinion and judgment of the Court."* Spencer v. Texas, 385 U.S. 554. . . .

JUSTICE POWELL, with whom JUSTICE BRENNAN, JUSTICE MARSHALL, and JUSTICE STEVENS join, dissenting.

This Court today affirms the Fifth Circuit's decision. I dissent because I believe that (i) the penalty for a noncapital offense may be unconstitutionally disproportionate, (ii) the possibility of parole should not be considered in assessing the nature of the punishment, (iii) a mandatory life sentence is grossly disproportionate as applied to petitioner, and (iv) the conclusion that this petitioner has suffered a violation of his Eighth Amendment rights is compatible with principles of judicial restraint and federalism. . . .

The scope of the Cruel and Unusual Punishments Clause extends not only to barbarous methods of punishment, but also to punishments that are grossly disproportionate. Disproportionality analysis measures the relationship between the nature and number of offenses committed and the severity of the punishment inflicted upon the offender. The inquiry focuses on whether a person deserves such punishment, not simply whether the punishment would serve a utilitarian goal. A statute that levied a mandatory life sentence for overtime parking might well deter vehicular lawlessness, but it would offend our felt sense of justice. The Court concedes today that the principle of disproportionality plays a role in the review of sentences imposing the death penalty, but suggests that the principle may be less applicable when a noncapital sentence is challenged. Such a limitation finds no support in the history of Eighth Amendment jurisprudence. . . .

Examination of the objective factors traditionally employed by the Court to assess the proportionality of a sentence demonstrates that petitioner suffers a cruel and unusual punishment. . . . A comparison of petitioner to other criminal[s] sentenced in Texas shows that he has been punished for three property-related offenses with a harsher sentence than that given to first-time or two-time offenders convicted of far more serious offenses. The Texas system assumes that all three-time offenders deserve the same punishment whether they commit three murders or cash three fraudulent checks.

The petitioner has committed criminal acts for which he may be punished. He has been given a sentence that is not inherently barbarous. But the relationship between the criminal acts and the sentence is grossly disproportionate. For having defrauded others of about $230 [the total amount illegally taken in the three separate crimes], the State of Texas has deprived petitioner of his freedom for the rest of his life. The State has not attempted to justify the sentence as necessary either to deter other persons or to isolate a potentially violent individual. Nor has petitioner's status as a habitual offender been shown to justify a mandatory life sentence. . . .

We are construing a living Constitution. The sentence imposed upon the petitioner would be viewed as grossly unjust by virtually every layman and lawyer. In my view, objective criteria clearly establish that a mandatory life sentence for defrauding persons of about $230 crosses any rationally drawn line separating punishment that lawfully may be imposed from that which is proscribed by the Eighth Amendment. I would reverse the decision of the Court of Appeals.

When law students and lawyers read judicial opinions, they prepare a one-page "brief," which is a set of notes that helps them to boil down the case into understandable terms. For all of the cases presented in each chapter of this book, you may wish to create a case brief to assist you in understanding what the judges are saying in their judicial opinions. The following is a sample case brief based on *Rummel v. Estelle* (1980). Note how a series of numbers follows the case name in the case excerpt in the previous box and on the case brief. This is called the **citation** to the case. Every case has one or more citations. These numbers tell you where to find the case in a law library. The first number indicates the specific volume of the case reporter that contains the judicial opinion for the case. Usually, each kind of court has its own set of books called case reporters in which opinions are published. For example, there are three case reporters for U.S. Supreme Court opinions: U.S.

Supreme Court Reports, Supreme Court Reporter, and Lawyers' Edition Supreme Court Reporter. Opinions for the U.S. courts of appeals are published in volumes called Federal Reporter, and U.S. district court opinions are in Federal Supplement. Opinions from states' supreme courts and courts of appeals are published in separate reporters. Each case law reporter in a law library has a volume number on the spine of the book so that you can easily see the desired book on the library shelf. The set of letters in the middle indicates which case law reporter contains the case. In essence you can regard these letters as abbreviations for the name of the set of books in which the book can be found. The letters "U.S." in the *Rummel v. Estelle* citation stand for "U.S. Supreme Court Reports." The third number in the citation is the page number where the case begins within the appropriate volume. Finally, the citation contains the year in which the decision was issued.

Regulations

Government agencies create legal rules called regulations. Legislatures enact statutes to create and direct policies and programs. However, legislatures cannot always write all of the detailed rules that will be needed in every situations. Thus they frequently give government agencies the power to develop detailed regulations. For example, a county sheriff's department may create detailed rules for its officers about what steps to take when searching prisoners and processing them for entry into jail after arrest. Regulations are a form of law that guides that creates rules for society and guides the behavior of government officials, including criminal justice officials. In the context of corrections, they are often the subject of legal actions filed by prisoners or corrections employees. These legal actions may claim that the regulations violate constitutional provisions or statutes. Such legal actions may also claim that corrections officials are not properly adhering to the regulations they are obligated to follow. In the first instance, the legal action is filed to have particular regulations changed or abolished. In the second example, the legal action seeks to have the regulations enforced and obeyed by corrections officials.

Examine the sample regulations in the box on p. 16. Note that regulations can be as or more detailed than statutes. In addition, regulations can cover a wide range of subjects, including rules for people's behavior in specific contexts, processes used within administrative agencies, and the authority of government officials. Do these illustrative regulations raise any risks that administrative agencies might exceed their authority in creating rules or create rules that give themselves too much power?

Rummel v. Estelle, **445 U.S. 263 (1980)**

Vote: 5 (majority) v. 4 (dissenters)

Author of Majority Opinion: Justice Rehnquist

Facts: Rummel was convicted of fraudulent use of a credit card for $80 in 1964, passing a forged check for $28.36 in 1969, and obtaining $120.75 by false pretenses in 1973. Under Texas law, conviction of three felonies can lead to an automatic life sentence under the repeat offender statute. Rummel was sentenced to life in prison upon conviction of the third felony in 1973.

Issue: Was the life sentence imposed on Rummel for fraudulently obtaining a total of $230 in three separate felonies over a nine-year period so disproportionate to his crimes as to violate the Eighth Amendment's ban on cruel and unusual punishments?

Holding: The life sentence imposed on Rummel for fraudulently obtaining a total of $230 in three separate felonies over a nine-year period was not so disproportionate to his crimes as to violate the Eighth Amendment's ban on cruel and unusual punishments.

Reasoning: Very few claims of disproportionate punishment under the Eighth Amendment have been recognized except for death penalty cases. Imprisonment cases are very different from death penalty cases. Rummel's comparisons of the harshness of the Texas repeat offender statute with laws in other states is unpersuasive. Rummel's comparison does not include adequate consideration of the fact that he could be eligible for parole in as little as twelve years and therefore will not necessarily actually spend his life in prison as punishment for these crimes. States have significant authority to define for themselves the proper punishments for crimes committed within their borders.

Concurring Opinion: Justice Stewart: I personally disagree with the Texas law, but I am not authorized to decide cases on that basis. I can only see if the Texas law falls below the Constitution's standards. It does not.

Dissenting Opinion: Justice Powell: Noncapital sentences can be disproportionate. It was improper for the majority opinion to consider the possibility of parole as a reason to approve this sentence. The life sentence is too severe for the crimes committed by Rummel. Any person can see that Rummel's sentence is grossly unjust.

LEGAL ACTIONS AND THE COURTS

The United States has a "dual court" system, meaning that there are both state courts and federal courts. Both kinds of courts exist in each state. Indeed, there are separate state and federal courthouses next door to each other in many large cities. State and federal courts have separate **jurisdictions.** A court's jurisdiction is composed of the kinds of cases that the court is authorized to hear and the geographic area under the court's authority. The state courts can generally hear only cases that arise from events and situations within their borders.

Federal courts can handle three kinds of cases. First, they can handle cases concerning federal law, whether from the U.S. Constitution, federal statutes, or federal agency regulations. For example, cases involving the Eighth Amendment's ban on cruel and unusual punishments can be heard by federal courts because they concern a provision of the U.S. Constitution. Second, they can handle cases in which the United States government is involved. If someone files a lawsuit against the Federal Bureau of Investigation (FBI), which is a component of the U.S. Department of Justice, the case will be heard in federal

Code of Federal Regulations: Title 33, Navigation and Navigable Waters; Chapter I, Coast Guard, Department of Transportation; Part 6, Protection and Security of Vessels, Harbors, and Waterways; Section 6.04-7, Visitation, search, and removal

The Captain of the Port may cause to be inspected and searched at any time any vessel, waterfront facility, or security zone, person, article, or thing thereon or therein, within the jurisdiction of the United States, may place guards upon any such vessel, waterfront, facility, or security zone and may remove therefrom any and all persons, articles, or things not specifically authorized by him to go or remain thereon or therein.

Michigan Department of Corrections, Policy Directive, 04.05.110: Use of Force

[excerpt]

(I) If gunfire is used, except for warning shots, it shall be directed with the intent to stop the person or persons at whom the gunfire is directed. A verbal warning and a warning shot shall precede gunfire directed at a person, if time and circumstances permit such warnings. A warning shot must be directed in a manner which avoids risk to the prisoner(s) being warned. For example, a warning shot may be aimed into the ground or in another direction where there is clearly no one present. However, at times it may be appropriate to aim warning shots into the ground directly in front of a person or persons who are advancing on a target, or above their heads, if this is the only effective means of stopping them short of shooting to stop.

(J) Warning shots shall only be used in a situation which occurs inside the security perimeter of an institution or to prevent an escape or storming of the security perimeter from the outside if the institution is located in an area where a warning shot can be fired safely.

(K) Deadly force shall be used only in the following situations:

1. To prevent death or serious physical injury to self, other staff, offenders, or other persons who are threatened;

2. To prevent the taking of hostages;

3. To prevent escape of any prisoner assigned to an institution which is Level II or higher; however, Level II prisoners detailed to Level I assignments shall be treated as Level I prisoners;

4. To prevent major damage to State property during a disturbance within an institution if it is reasonably believed that the damage may cause death or serious injury to any person. For example, if prisoners are attempting to burn down a building. . . .

5. To prevent prisoners from unlocking other prisoners without authorization if it is reasonably believed that the unlocking may result in death or serious physical injury to others. . . .

court. For example, in June 2000 a federal court conducted the trial for a multi-million-dollar lawsuit against the U.S. government concerning the actions of FBI agents and Bureau of Alcohol, Tobacco, and Firearms (BATF) agents in the 1993 standoff at the Branch Davidian complex that ultimately led to the deaths of seventy-five people inside the complex when it burned down.[2] Many cases concerning criminal justice involve federal law or the U.S. government and are thereby heard in federal courts. The third category of cases in federal courts, "diversity of citizenship" cases in which a resident from one state sues the resident of another state for an amount exceeding $75,000, is much less likely to involve criminal justice.

| A CLOSER LOOK | **Implementation of Judicial Opinions** |

When judges make decisions concerning criminal procedure, they simultaneously affect the rights of criminal defendants and the range of criminal justice officials' authority. For example, a rule concerning a defendant's rights during the course of an interrogation obviously also tells police officers what they can and cannot do in questioning suspects. Judges' opinions do not always determine exactly what will happen in encounters between officials and citizens. Sometimes judicial opinions are not clear and law enforcement officials have difficulty interpreting them. Law enforcement officials may also be able to adapt their behavior to permit them to achieve their objectives without any interference from legal rules concerning constitutional rights. As we will discuss in Chapter 7, police officers have developed ways to question suspects without violating the requirements of court-mandated *Miranda* warnings. In other situations, law enforcement officials may disobey the judicial decisions. If there are no witnesses, a citizen who believes that his or her rights have been violated by police officers may have no way of proving that officers acted in a manner contrary to the rules established by the courts. Thus we cannot assume that rules about constitutional rights announced by courts are implemented properly or even implemented at all. An understanding of criminal procedure requires knowledge of the rules announced by the Courts as well as an understanding of how officials respond to those rules. The rules as well as the responses to those rules determine the extent to which citizens do—or do not—enjoy the constitutional rights discussed in legal cases.

Trial Courts

Federal trial courts are called **U.S. district courts.** There are ninety-four districts throughout the United States with at least one district in each state. For example, small states such as Connecticut are each covered by one district court. Connecticut's is called the U.S. District Court for the District of Connecticut, and the district's cases are handled by judges housed in federal courthouses in Hartford, New Haven, and Bridgeport. Larger states are often broken into multiple districts. Ohio, for example, has two districts, the Northern District of Ohio, with courthouses in Toledo, Cleveland, Akron, and Youngstown, and the Southern District of Ohio, with courthouses in Columbus, Dayton, and Cincinnati. Larger states, such as California and New York, are broken into even more districts.

State trial courts are often divided according to a state's counties, although rural counties may be combined into a single court. States have given their trial courts various names. Most commonly, such courts are called superior courts (e.g., in California), circuit courts (e.g., in Michigan), courts of common pleas (e.g., in Ohio), and district courts (e.g., in Texas).

Cases begin in trial courts. In criminal cases, charges are filed, plea bargaining occurs, and trials are conducted in trial courts. Trial judges impose sentences on convicted criminals. In civil cases, lawsuits are filed in trial courts. These lawsuits are ultimately dismissed for failing to provide sufficient evidence, or settled through negotiation between the opposing parties, or decided after a trial. Television shows and movies about lawyers usually take place in trial courts. A single judge presides over the courtroom as lawyers battle each other, sometimes before a jury and sometimes with the judge as the lone decision maker. It is in trial courts that witnesses testify, lawyers present evidence, and jurors issue verdicts. In many states, there are

FIGURE 1.1 **Court System and Path of Criminal Cases**

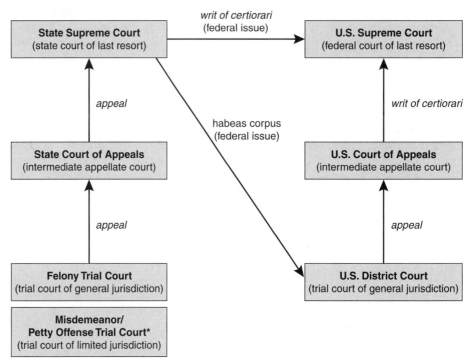

*Appeals from decisions in state trial courts of limited jurisdiction may go to state intermediate appellate courts or contested cases may be retried in trial courts of general jurisdiction, depending on the laws of each individual state.

two or more levels of trial courts. While the top-level trial courts have general jurisdiction and handle trials for felony cases, lower-level trial courts have limited jurisdiction. In criminal cases, these limited jurisdiction courts typically issue search and arrest warrants, set bail for arrested suspects, hold preliminary hearings, and process misdemeanor cases. Figure 1.1 shows a chart organization of court systems and path of cases through the system to courts of last resort.

Appellate Courts

After a case has passed through a trial court, some convicted offenders or losing parties in civil cases will file appeals. Appeals are legal actions filed in a higher court that claim an error was made by the police, prosecutor, trial judge, or jury. There are no juries in appellate courts. Lawyers do not present evidence to appellate courts. The lawyers' arguments and the judges' decisions focus on narrow issues concerning alleged mistakes in law and procedure that occurred in or were uncorrected by the trial court. In appellate courts, judges make decisions as a group. In most appellate courts, groups of three judges listen to lawyers' arguments and issue judicial opinions to decide the cases. In courts of last resort, however, the decisions are made by larger groups of judges. There are nine justices on the U.S. Supreme Court. On most state supreme courts, there are either five or seven justices.

The federal court system and all but a dozen states have intermediate appellate courts. The federal appellate courts are called **U.S. circuit courts of appeals.** Each circuit covers a specific geographic region. For example, the U.S. Court of Appeals for the Sixth Circuit handles appeals from federal cases arising in Michigan, Ohio, Kentucky, and Tennessee. When a losing party claims that an error occurred in a U.S. district court, an appeal may be filed in the U.S. circuit court of appeals which handles appeals from that district. Federal circuit judges sit in panels of three judges to hear cases. Because a circuit court may have as many as twenty-eight judges, these appellate courts can hear several cases simultaneously by breaking into groups of three. In important cases that generate significant disagreement among the judges of a circuit, the case may be heard for a second time with all the judges hearing the case together. When all the judges of an appellate court hear a case together, it is called an *en banc* **hearing.**

States also have intermediate appellate courts in which judges typically hear cases as three-judge panels. Some states have a single intermediate appellate court, typically called a court of appeals. Other states are divided into regions with an appeals court for each region.

The U.S. Supreme Court and state supreme courts nearly always hear cases *en banc*. Because they sit as an entire group, they must hear cases one at a time. Courts of last resort typically have significant **discretionary jurisdiction.** In other words, they have the power to pick and choose the cases they want to hear. They can turn down nearly all other cases. People generally have no automatic right to have their appeals heard by the U.S. Supreme Court or a state supreme court if they are unhappy with the decision of an intermediate appellate court. Individual states have created an entitlement to review by their state supreme courts in death penalty cases, and they could create similar entitlements for other kinds of cases if they chose to do so.

Most cases arrive at the U.S. Supreme Court in the form of a petition for a **writ of certiorari.** This is a special legal action that asks the high court to call up a case from a lower court. In the mid-1990s, the U.S. Supreme Court received nearly 7,000 certiorari petitions each year. Despite this large number of requests, the Court granted full hearings and decisions to fewer than ninety cases each year.

Although it is regarded as "the highest court in the land," the U.S. Supreme Court does not have the power to handle all cases. Like other federal courts, it, too, is limited to hearing cases that raise federal law issues, involve the United States government, or present lawsuits between residents of different states seeking more than $75,000. Cases can come to the U.S. Supreme Court from either the U.S. circuit courts of appeals or state supreme courts, provided a federal law issue is presented for the high court to decide. If a case concerns only the interpretation of a state statute or a provision of a state constitution, then the supreme court of that state is the final authority on that issue. Many criminal cases come to the U.S. Supreme Court from state supreme courts rather than from U.S. circuit courts of appeals. This is because state criminal cases frequently raise issues concerning federal constitutional rights. These cases may concern such matters as the defendant's Sixth Amendment right to counsel or Fourth Amendment protection against unreasonable searches and seizures. If, however, the state supreme court's decision about searches or arrests clearly states that the decision is based on its own state constitution, then the U.S. Supreme Court will not hear the case, unless the state supreme court interprets the state constitution as providing fewer or narrower rights than the U.S. Constitution. The U.S. Constitution provides the minimum, baseline of rights to which everyone in the United States is entitled. State supreme courts can interpret their constitutions to provide more or broader rights than those contained in the U.S. Constitution, but they cannot interpret their state's document as permitting fewer rights than those mandated by the U.S. Supreme Court's interpretations of the U.S. Constitution.

For example, in 1991 the U.S. Supreme Court examined the constitutionality of a Michigan statute that imposed a mandatory sentence of life without parole for possession of more than 650 grams of cocaine (*Harmelin v. Michigan*). In the case, a first-time offender who received the severe punishment claimed that the sentence was disproportionate to the crime and therefore violated the Eighth Amendment prohibition on cruel and unusual punishments. A slim majority of justices found that the statute did not violate the Eighth Amendment. One year later, however, the Michigan Supreme Court ruled that a life sentence without possibility of parole for possession of cocaine violated the Michigan Constitution (*People v. Bullock,* 1992). The Michigan court left open the possibility of life without parole for people who sold or transported cocaine, but the justices said that it was unconstitutional to deny parole eligibility for mere possession of cocaine. In effect, the Michigan Supreme Court interpreted its state's constitution to provide greater protection against severe mandatory sentences than that provided by the U.S. Supreme Court's interpretation of the Eighth Amendment.

HISTORY OF RIGHTS IN CRIMINAL PROCEDURE

For most of American history, federal judges interpreted the Bill of Rights narrowly. In the case of *Barron v. Baltimore* (1833), the Supreme Court declared that the Bill of Rights applies only against the federal government. Indeed, the very first words of the First Amendment, "Congress shall make no law . . . ," indicate that the amendments comprising the Bill of Rights were meant to keep the national government from infringing on citizens' liberties. Thus the rights described in the Bill of Rights did not protect people against actions by state and local governments. People did not think that states were free to do anything to interfere with people's rights and liberties. Instead, they believed that state constitutions provided protections for people against actions by state and local officials. For example, the Fourth Amendment's prohibition on unreasonable searches and seizures was not applied to searches and arrests undertaken by state and local governments. This meant that the Fourth Amendment had very little influence over criminal justice since the vast majority of criminal cases are handled by state and local law enforcement officers and then processed in state courts. Relatively few criminal offenders violate the limited number of federal crimes, such as counterfeiting and smuggling (although this has changed in recent years with the expansion of federal drug crimes). Similarly, the other parts of the Bill of Rights had little impact on criminal justice. As another example, until the 1960s, the Sixth Amendment's right to counsel meant that only defendants in federal cases could claim a right to be represented by a defense attorney—unless a state's statutes or constitution provided a comparable right in that state's criminal cases.

In addition to the limited applicability of the Bill of Rights, judges tended to take a narrow view of the definition of "rights." Judicial decisions interpreting the meanings of the U.S. Constitution and the state constitutions treated rights as being more limited than implied by the words of specific provisions. For example, although the First Amendment protects freedom of speech by forbidding Congress from enacting any law that abridges that freedom, judges did not regard free speech rights as permitting people to criticize the American system of government and advocate alternative systems, such as socialism or communism. It was not until the 1960s that very unpopular people, such as communists, were granted freedom of speech protections in decisions by federal judges.

The ratification of the Fourteenth Amendment (1868) after the Civil War provided a basis for extending some of the Bill of Rights' protections against actions by state and local officials. The Fourteenth Amendment is aimed to prevent states from violating rights. The amendment's very words say that "[n]o State shall . . ." violate certain rights. The amendment was created, in part, out of a fear that the former Confederate states would establish laws to limit the freedom of the African Americans who had been newly freed from slavery. Although the Fourteenth Amendment provided a specific basis for recognizing rights that applied against states, the rights listed in the amendment were much more vague than those listed in the original Bill of Rights. The Fourteenth Amendment provides rights to "due process" of law, "equal protection of the laws," and "privileges and immunities" of citizenship. Because the meaning of these rights was so unclear, courts were asked to define the specific rights that people enjoy against actions by state and local officials.

Initially, the Supreme Court declined to declare that the Fourteenth Amendment applied any specific rights against the states. Eventually, however, lawyers began to argue that the right to due process in the Fourteenth Amendment actually contained specific rights listed in the Bill of Rights. In *Hurtado v. California* (1884), for example, Hurtado's lawyer argued that the Fifth Amendment right to a grand jury should be considered as part of the right to due process provided by the Fourteenth Amendment. Hurtado had been charged with murder based on information filed by a prosecutor rather than through indictment by a grand jury. Hurtado lost the case, but his lawyer's argument began to receive more serious consideration among lawyers and judges. In the *Hurtado* case, one justice, John Marshall Harlan, dissented by advancing the argument that the Fourteenth Amendment's Due Process Clause had the effect of applying the entire Bill of Rights against state and local governments. Thus he argued that people should have the same rights against actions by state and local officials that they had against actions by federal officials. However, Harlan was the only justice making that argument prior to the mid-twentieth century. Over the course of several decades, the Court's composition changed and more justices arrived who were inclined to use the Due Process Clause as the basis for applying portions of the Bill of Rights against the states.

Beginning with the application of freedom of speech to protect people against state and local governments in 1925,[3] the high court gradually made state and local officials subject to specific provisions of the Bill of Rights over the next four decades. The justices took the vague right to due process and gave it meaning by saying that this right contains many of the specific rights in the Bill of Rights, such as the rights to free speech, free press, and free exercise of religion. This process of recognizing specific individual rights within the Fourteenth Amendment is referred to as **incorporation.** The Court incorporated rights from the Bill of Rights into the Due Process Clause of the Fourteenth Amendment.[4] The Court initially had incorporated rights from the First Amendment. Many of the rights related to criminal justice were not incorporated until the 1960s.

Incorporation occurred gradually as the Supreme Court's composition changed and new justices brought with them ideas about the applicability of the Bill of Rights to the states. Some justices believed that only "fundamental" rights should be incorporated into the Due Process Clause of the Fourteenth Amendment and applied to the states. As you read the excerpt from *Palko v. Connecticut* (1937) in the accompanying box, see if you agree with Justice Benjamin Cardozo's classification of those rights that protect people in state criminal justice systems and those that apply only against the federal government.

The *Palko* case is famous for establishing a "test" through which to determine which rights from the Bill of Rights are included in the Fourteenth Amendment's Due Process Clause and applied against state and local governments. According to Justice Cardozo, only those rights that are fundamental and essential to liberty are applicable to the states through the Fourteenth Amendment. Thus he recognizes freedom of speech as fundamental, but not the criminal justice right to jury trials and the protections against double jeopardy and compelled self-incrimination. However, later justices altered this test so that more rights could be incorporated, including some that Justice Cardozo did not believe were fundamental to liberty.

In *Adamson v. California* (1947), the defendant claimed that the Fifth Amendment privilege against compelled self-incrimination should be included in the Fourteenth Amendment right to due process. At Adamson's trial, the

---

CASE   *Palko v. Connecticut,* **302 U.S. 319 (1937)**

[*Frank Palko faced the death penalty during his trial for the murders of two police officers. The jury found him guilty of second-degree murder and sentenced him to life in prison. The state's Supreme Court of Errors granted the prosecution's request for a new trial based on errors in the trial judge's ruling on the admissibility of evidence and on instructions to the jury. After the second trial, Palko* was convicted of first-degree murder and sentenced to death. Palko unsuccessfully pursued an appeal through the state's Supreme Court of Errors before bringing to the U.S. Supreme Court his argument that double jeopardy rights ought to apply against the states through the process of incorporating components of the Bill of Rights into the Fourteenth Amendment.]

JUSTICE CARDOZO delivered the opinion of the Court.

. . .

The argument for appellant is that whatever is forbidden by the Fifth Amendment is forbidden by the Fourteenth also. The Fifth Amendment, which is not directed to the States, but solely to the federal government, creates immunity from double jeopardy. No person shall be "subject for the same offense to be twice put in jeopardy of life or limb." The Fourteenth Amendment ordains, "nor shall any State deprive any person of life, liberty, or property, without due process of law." To retry a defendant, though under one indictment and only one, subjects him, it is said, to double jeopardy in violation of the Fifth Amendment, if the prosecution is one on behalf of the United States. From this the consequence is said to follow that there is a denial of life or liberty without due process of law, if the prosecution is one on behalf of the people of a state. . . .

We have said that in appellant's view the Fourteenth Amendment is to be taken as embodying the prohibitions of the Fifth. His thesis is even broader. Whatever would be a violation of the original bill of rights (Amendments 1 to 8) if done by the federal government is now equally unlawful by force of the Fourteenth Amendment if done by a state. There is no such general rule.

The Fifth Amendment provides, among other things, that no person shall be held to answer for a capital or otherwise infamous crime unless on presentment or indictment of a grand jury. This court has held that, in prosecutions by a state, presentment or indictment by a grand jury may give way to informations at the instance of a public officer. *Hurtado v. California* [1884]. . . . The Fifth Amendment provides also that no person shall be compelled in any criminal case to be a witness against himself. This court has said that, in prosecutions by a state, the exemption will fail if the state elects to end it. *Twining v. New Jersey* [1908]. . . .

On the other hand, the due process clause of the Fourteenth Amendment may make it unlawful for a state to abridge by its statutes the freedom of speech which the First Amendment safeguards against encroachment by the Congress (*DeJonge v. Oregon* [1937]) . . . , or the like freedom of the press (*Near v. Minnesota* [1932]) . . . , or free exercise of religion (*Hamilton v. Regents of University* [1934]) . . . , or the right of peaceable assembly, without which speech would be unduly trampled (*DeJonge v. Oregon* [1937]) . . . , or the right of one accused of crime to the benefit of counsel (*Powell v. Alabama* [1932]). . . . In these and other situations immunities that are valid as against the federal government by force of the specific pledges in particular amendments have been found to be implicit in the concept of ordered liberty, and thus, through the Fourteenth Amendment, become valid as against the states.

The line of division may seem to be wavering or broken if there is a hasty catalogue of the cases on the one side and the other. Reflection and analysis will induce a different view. There emerges a perception of a rationalizing principle which gives to discrete instances a proper order and coherence. The right to trial by jury and immunity from prosecution except as the result of an indictment have value and importance. Even so, they are not of the very essence of a scheme of ordered liberty. To abolish them is not to violate a "principle of justice so rooted in the traditions and conscience of our people as to be ranked as fundamental." . . . Few would be so narrow or provincial as to maintain that a fair and enlightened system of justice would be impossible without them. What is true of jury trials and indictments is true also, as the cases show, of the immunity from compulsory self-incrimination. . . . This too might be lost, and justice still be done. . . . No doubt there would remain the need to give protection against torture, physical and mental. . . . Justice, however, would not perish if the accused were subject to a duty to respond to orderly inquiry. The exclusion of these immunities and privileges from the privileges and immunities protected against the action of the States has not been arbitrary or casual. It has been dictated by a study and appreciation of the meaning, the essential implications, of liberty itself.

We reach a different plane of social and moral values when we pass to the privileges and immunities that have been taken over from the earlier articles of the Federal Bill of Rights and brought within the Fourteenth Amendment by the process of absorption. These in their origin were effective against the federal government alone. If the Fourteenth Amendment has absorbed them, the process of absorption has had its source in the belief that neither liberty nor justice would exist if they were sacrificed. . . . This is true, for illustration, of freedom of thought and speech. Of that freedom one may say that it is the matrix, the indispensable condition, of nearly every other form of freedom. With rare aberrations a pervasive recognition of that truth can be traced in our history, political and legal. So it has

(continued)

come about that the domain of liberty, withdrawn by the Fourteenth Amendment from encroachment by the states, has been enlarged by latter-day judgments to include liberty of the mind as well as liberty of action. . . . Fundamental too in the concept of due process, and so in that of liberty, is the thought that condemnation shall be rendered only after trial. . . . The hearing, moreover, must be a real one, not a sham or pretense. . . . For that reason, ignorant defendants in a capital case were held to have uncondemned unlawfully when in truth, though not in form, they were refused the aid of counsel. . . . The decision did not turn upon the fact that the benefit of counsel would have been guaranteed to the defendants by the provisions of the Sixth Amendment if they had been prosecuted in a federal court. The decision turned upon the fact that in the particular situation laid before us in the evidence the benefit of counsel was essential to the substance of a hearing.

Our survey of the cases serves, we think, to justify the statement that the dividing line between them, if not unfaltering throughout its course, has been true for the most part to a unifying principle. On which side of the line the case made out by the appellant has appropriate location must be the next inquiry and the final one. Is that kind of double jeopardy to which the statute has subjected him to a hardship so acute and shocking that our polity will not endure it? Does it violate those "fundamental principles of liberty and justice which lie at the base of all our civil and political institutions?" . . . The answer surely must be "no." . . . The state is not attempting to wear the accused out by a multitude of cases with accumulated trials. It asks no more than this, that the case against him shall go on until there shall be a trial free from the corrosion of substantial legal error. . . . This is not cruelty at all, nor even vexation in any immoderate degree. If the trial had been infected with error adverse to the accused, there might have been review at his instance, and as often as necessary to purge the vicious taint. A reciprocal privilege, subject at all times to the discretion of the presiding judge . . . has now been granted to the state. There is here no seismic innovation. The edifice of justice stands, its symmetry, to many, greater than before.

The conviction of the appellant is not in derogation of any privileges and immunities that belong to him as a citizen of the United States. There is an argument in his behalf that the privileges and immunities clause of the Fourteenth Amendment as well as the due process clause has been flouted by the judgment. *Maxwell v. Dow* [1900] . . . gives all the answer that is necessary.

The judgment is affirmed.

prosecutor had made comments to the jury about the defendant's failure to testify in his own defense. Such comments may make defendants feel compelled to testify in order to avoid having their silence used against them. The Fifth Amendment is intended to prevent such pressure to testify, but it had not been incorporated into the Fourteenth Amendment for application to state criminal cases. A majority of justices failed to incorporate the Fifth Amendment's privilege against compelled self-incrimination in Adamson's case. The privilege was, however, incorporated in a later case so that it protects defendants in state cases today. The *Adamson* case was notable because it demonstrated how the Court's composition changes had affected views on incorporation. Unlike in the *Hurtado* case, in which one justice had supported incorporation, four justices in the *Adamson* case endorsed broad incorporation of the Bill of Rights.

The incorporation of most rights affecting criminal justice occurred during the **Warren Court era,** which lasted from 1953 to 1969. This era is defined by the time period in which Earl Warren, a former governor of California, served as chief justice and led the Supreme Court in making many decisions expanding rights for individuals throughout society. The Warren Court's most famous decision, *Brown v. Board of Education* (1954), stunned the nation by declaring that racial segregation in the public schools, which had long been regarded as an accepted component of American life, violated the Equal Protection

| A CLOSER LOOK | Incorporation of Rights in Criminal Justice |

Fourth Amendment

    Unreasonable searches and seizures   *Wolf v. Colorado* (1949)

    Exclusionary rule   *Mapp v. Ohio* (1961)

Fifth Amendment

    Compelled self-incrimination   *Malloy v. Hogan* (1964)

    Double jeopardy   *Benton v. Maryland* (1969)

Sixth Amendment

    Right to counsel: capital cases   *Powell v. Alabama* (1932)

    Right to counsel: serious charges   *Gideon v. Wainwright* (1963)

    Confrontation   *Pointer v. Texas* (1965)

    Trial by jury   *Duncan v. Louisiana* (1968)

Eighth Amendment

    Cruel and unusual punishments   *Robinson v. California* (1962)

Clause of the Fourteenth Amendment. In its other decisions, the Warren Court's interpretations of the Constitution expanded the definitions of freedom of speech, free exercise of religion, and other rights, including such criminal justice rights as the right to counsel, the right against unreasonable searches and seizures, and the privilege against compelled self-incrimination. The box "Incorporation of Rights in Criminal Justice" shows when the Supreme Court incorporated various criminal procedure rights and applied them against the states. Many people may believe that the rights enjoyed by Americans have been available since the new nation became independent of Great Britain in the eighteenth century. In reality, most rights relevant to criminal justice have protected citizens throughout the nation for less than fifty years.

The Supreme Court's decision in *Duncan v. Louisiana* (1968) presented in the box on pp. 26–27 helps to illustrate how many rights had been incorporated since freedom of speech was applied to the states in 1925. Look for Justice White's list of rights that had been incorporated and applied to the states by 1968. Remember that in *Palko v. Connecticut* (1937), Justice Cardozo had said that the right to trial by jury was *not* fundamental. How does Justice White take a different approach in order to reach the opposite conclusion about the importance of the jury trial right?

The incorporation process undertaken by the Supreme Court transformed the criminal justice system. Individual states no longer had control over how cases would be processed within their own courts. Instead, courts throughout the country came under a common set of rules about the rights of suspects and defendants that must be respected. In addition, the incorporation process placed the U.S. Supreme Court firmly in charge of identifying and defining rights applicable to courts at all levels, including state and local. State supreme courts still apply additional rights to their own states when they identify those rights as being required by their states' constitutions. However, state supreme courts cannot remove their

Duncan v. Louisiana, 391 U.S. 145 (1968)

[*On October 18, 1966, as Duncan, an African American towboat worker, drove down Highway 23, he saw two of his cousins, Bert Grant and Bernard St. Ann, confronted by four white boys. Grant and St. Ann were new students at the parish's previously all-white public high school, and they had complained that they were harassed by white students. Duncan stopped his car and asked his cousins about their dispute with the white boys. After hearing that his cousins believed the white boys wanted to start a fight, Duncan told his cousins to get into the car. Duncan then exchanged words with the whites. He claimed that he told one of the boys, Herman M. Landry, Jr., to go home and that he touched Landry on the elbow. Landry, however, claimed that Duncan had slapped him forcefully on the arm. The incident was observed by P. E. Lathum, the principal of an all-white private school established to maintain racial separation. Lathum reported the incident to a deputy sheriff, who intercepted Duncan's car and returned Duncan to the scene of the incident. The deputy released Duncan shortly thereafter upon concluding from questioning the white boys that Duncan had not assaulted Landry. Three days later, however, Duncan was arrested by parish authorities and charged with cruelty to juveniles.[5]*]

JUSTICE WHITE delivered the opinion of the Court.

Appellant, Gary Duncan, was convicted of simple battery[,] . . . a misdemeanor, punishable by a maximum of two years' imprisonment and a $300 fine. Appellant sought trial by jury, but because the Louisiana Constitution grants jury trials only in cases in which capital punishment or imprisonment at hard labor may be imposed, the trial judge denied the request. Appellant was convicted and sentenced to serve 60 days in the parish prison and pay a fine of $150. . . . [A]ppellant sought review in this Court, alleging that the Sixth and Fourteenth Amendments to the United States Constitution secure the right to jury trial in state criminal prosecutions. . . .

I

The Fourteenth Amendment denies the States the power to "deprive any person of life, liberty, or property, without due process of law." In resolving conflicting claims concerning the meaning of this spacious language, the Court has looked increasingly to the Bill of Rights for guidance; many of the rights guaranteed by the first eight Amendments to the Constitution have been held to be protected against state action by the Due Process Clause of the Fourteenth Amendment. That clause now protects the right to compensation for property taken by the State; the rights to speech, press, and religion covered by the First Amendment; the Fourth Amendment rights to be free from unreasonable searches and seizures and to have excluded from criminal trials any evidence illegally seized; the right guaranteed by the Fifth Amendment to be free of compelled self-incrimination; and the Sixth Amendment rights to counsel, to a speedy and public trial, to confrontation of opposing witnesses, and to compulsory process for obtaining witnesses.

. . . Because we believe that trial by jury in criminal cases is fundamental to the American scheme of justice, we hold that the Fourteenth Amendment guarantees a right of jury trial in all criminal cases which—were they to be tried in federal court—would come within the Sixth Amendment's guarantee.[14] . . .

We are aware of prior cases in this Court in which the prevailing opinion contains statements to the contrary to our holding today that the right to jury trial in serious criminal cases is a fundamental right and hence must be recognized by the States as part of their obligation to extend due process of law to all

---

[14]In one sense recent cases applying provisions of the first eight Amendments to the States represent a new approach to the "incorporation" debate. Earlier the Court can be seen as having asked, when inquiring whether some particular procedural safeguard was required of a State, if a civilized system could be imagined that would not accord the particular protection. For example, *Palko v. State of Connecticut* [1937] . . . stated: "The right to trial by jury . . . may have value and importance. Even so, they are not of the very essence of a scheme of ordered liberty. . . . Few would be so narrow or provincial as to maintain that a fair and enlightened system of justice would be impossible without them." The recent cases, on the other hand, have proceeded upon the valid assumption that state criminal processes are not imaginary and theoretical schemes but actual systems bearing virtually every characteristic of the common-law system that has been developing contemporaneously in England and in this country. The question thus is whether given this kind of system a particular procedure is fundamental—whether, that is, a procedure is necessary to an Anglo-American regime of ordered liberty. . . . [T]he question is not necessarily fundamental to fairness in every criminal system that might be imagined but is fundamental in the context of the criminal processes maintained by the American States.

. . . A criminal process which was fair and equitable but used no juries is easy to imagine. It would make use of alternative guarantees and protections. . . . Yet no American system has undertaken to construct such a system. . . .

persons within their jurisdiction. . . . [However,] [i]n neither *Palko* nor *Snyder* [*v. Massachusetts* (1934)] was jury trial actually at issue, although both cases contain important dicta asserting that the right to jury trial is not essential to ordered liberty. . . . These observations, though weighty and respectable, are nevertheless dicta, unsupported by holdings in this Court that a State may refuse a defendant's demand for a jury trial when he is charged with a serious crime. . . . Respectfully, we reject the prior dicta regarding jury trial in criminal cases. . . .

The State of Louisiana urges that holding the Fourteenth Amendment assures a right to jury trial will cast doubt on the integrity of every trial conducted without a jury. Plainly, this is not the import of our holding. Our conclusion is that in the American States, as in the federal judicial system, a general grant of jury trial for serious offenses is a fundamental right, essential for preventing miscarriages of justice and for assuring that fair trials are provided for all defendants. We would not assert, however, that every criminal trial—or any particular trial—held before a judge alone is unfair or that a defendant may never be as fairly treated by a judge as he would be by a jury. Thus we hold no constitutional doubts about the practices, common in both federal and state courts, of accepting waivers of jury trial and prosecuting petty crimes without extending a right to jury trial. However, the fact is that in most places more trials for serious crimes are to juries than to a court alone; a great many defendants prefer the judgment of a jury to that of a court. Even where defendants are satisfied with bench trials, the right to a jury trial very likely serves its intended purpose of making judicial or prosecutorial unfairness less likely.

. . . Crimes carrying possible penalties up to six months do not require a jury trial if they otherwise qualify as petty offenses. . . . But the penalty authorized for a particular crime is of major relevance in determining whether it is serious or not and may in itself, if severe enough, subject the trial to mandates of the Sixth Amendment. . . . In the case before us the Legislature of Louisiana has made simple battery a criminal offense punishable by imprisonment for up to two years and a fine. The question, then, is whether a crime carrying such a penalty is an offense which Louisiana may insist on trying without a jury.

We think not. . . .

. . . In 49 of the 50 States crimes subject to trial without a jury, which occasionally include simple battery, are punishable by no more than one year in jail. Moreover, in the late 18th century in America crimes triable without a jury were for the most part punishable by no more than a six-month prison term, although there appear to have been exceptions to this rule. We need not, however, settle in this case the exact location of the line between petty offenses and serious crimes. It is sufficient to hold that a crime punishable by two years in prison is, based on past and contemporary standards in this country, a serious crime and not a petty offense. Consequently, appellant was entitled to a jury trial and it was error to deny it.

The judgment below is reversed and the case is remanded for proceedings not inconsistent with this opinion.

Reversed and remanded.

JUSTICE HARLAN, dissenting [joined by JUSTICE STEWART].

. . .

. . . The Due Process Clause of the Fourteenth Amendment requires that those procedures be fundamentally fair in all respects. It does not, in my view, impose or encourage nationwide uniformity for its own sake; it does not command adherence to forms that happen to be old; and it does not impose on the States the rules that may be in force in the federal courts except where such rules are also found to be essential to basic fairness. . . .

Today's Court still remains unwilling to accept the total incorporationists' view of the history of the Fourteenth Amendment. This, if accepted, would afford a cogent reason for applying the Sixth Amendment to the States. The Court is also, apparently, unwilling to face the task of determining whether denial of trial by jury in the situation before us, or in other situations, is fundamentally unfair. Consequently, the Court has compromised on the ease of the incorporationist position, without its internal logic. It has simply assumed that the question before us is whether the Jury Trial Clause of the Sixth Amendment should be incorporated into the Fourteenth, jot-for-jot, and case-for-case, or ignored. Then the Court merely declares that the Clause is "in" rather than "out." . . .

II

. . .

The argument that jury trial is not a requisite of due process is quite simple. The central proposition of *Palko*, a proposition to which I would adhere, is that "due process of law" requires only that criminal trials be fundamentally fair. As stated above,

(continued)

apart from the theory that it was historically intended as a mere shorthand for the Bill of Rights, I do not see what else "due process of law" can intelligibly be thought to mean. If due process of law requires only fundamental fairness, then the inquiry in each case must be whether a state trial process is a fair one. The Court has held, properly I think, that in an adversary process it is a requisite of fairness, for which there is no adequate substitute, that a criminal defendant be afforded a right to counsel and to cross-examine opposing witnesses. But it simply has not been demonstrated, that trial by jury is the only fair means of resolving issues of fact. . . .

That trial by jury is not the only fair way of adjudicating criminal guilt is well attested by the fact that it is not the prevailing way, either in England or in this country. . . . Over all [in England], "the ratio of defendants actually tried by jury becomes in some years little more than 1 per cent."

In the United States, where it has not been as generally assumed that jury waiver is permissible, the statistics are only slightly less revealing. Two experts have estimated that, of all prosecutions for crimes triable to a jury, 75% are settled by guilty plea and 40% of the remainder are tried in court. . . . I therefore see no reason why this Court should reverse the conviction of appellant, absent any suggestion that his particular trial was in fact unfair, or compel the State of Louisiana to afford jury trial in an as yet unbounded category of cases that can, without unfairness, be tried to a court. . . .

. . . [T]he Court has chosen to impose upon every State one means of trying criminal cases; it is a good means, but it is not the only fair means, and it is not demonstrably better than the alternatives States might devise. . . .

states' criminal justice systems from the requirements of the Bill of Rights and the Fourteenth Amendment that have been imposed by the U.S. Supreme Court. The box "Continuity and Change in Criminal Procedure" discusses incorporation as an example of this process of change.

The Supreme Court's incorporation decisions applied most, but not all, rights in the Bill of Rights against state and local officials. Among criminal justice rights, the Supreme Court has never imposed on the states the Fifth Amendment's right to indictment by a grand jury. In the federal court system, which clearly comes under the entire Fifth Amendment, a grand jury of citizens must hear evidence in a preliminary proceeding before determining whether or not there is enough evidence for the prosecutor to pursue serious charges against a defendant. By contrast, because the grand jury right has never been incorporated, prosecutors in state courts can decide on their own whether or not to pursue charges against defendants, unless the constitution or laws of their own state require them to present evidence to a grand jury first. Likewise, the Eighth Amendment's prohibition on excessive bail has never been incorporated. The other provisions that have never been applied to the states are the Second Amendment's declaration concerning a well-regulated Militia and the "right" to bear arms, the Seventh Amendment's right to a jury trial in civil cases, and the Third Amendment's prohibition on quartering troops in private citizens' homes.[6]

CONCLUSION

Criminal procedure consists of the rules and constitutional rights that guide the sequential steps of the criminal justice process from the investigation of crimes through appeals filed by offenders convicted of violating criminal laws.

| **A CLOSER LOOK** | **Continuity and Change in Criminal Procedure** |

Criminal procedure does not consist of a set of fixed and enduring rules. The rules that define constitutional rights and guide police actions will change over time. The history of incorporation provides a good example of this process of change. One day the Sixth Amendment's right to trial by jury did not apply to the states. On another day, after the U.S. Supreme Court decided *Duncan v. Louisiana* (1968), the right to trial by jury did apply to the states. The fact that a single decision of the Supreme Court defines a change does not mean that the change occurred overnight. In the case of *Duncan,* the incorporation of the right to trial by jury can be understood as a long, gradual process that began with the Court's first interpretation of the Fourteenth Amendment in the *Slaughterhouse Cases* (1873) and continued step by step through *Hurtado* (1884), *Palko* (1937), *Adamson* (1947), and the other cases that provided the "building blocks" for incorporation as the Court considered when and how to apply rights to the states. These changes reflect the development

and gradual acceptance of specific legal arguments put forward by lawyers and judges over the course of many decades. The changes also reflect changes in the composition of the Supreme Court. As new justices arrive on the Court, they may bring values and interpretive philosophies that differ from those of their predecessors. In applying these values and philosophies to legal issues affecting criminal procedure, the justices can—if they gather at least a five-vote majority on the Court—alter the definitions of rights and rules for police actions in conducting investigations.

Does the concept of "law" mean what you thought it was supposed to mean when you recognize that the law can change? How is your view of law affected by the knowledge that judges who are selected through political processes are the ones who determine how law develops and changes? Because law is not necessarily permanent and enduring, why should people rely on it to determine what happens in society?

In order to understand criminal procedure, one must understand the different sources of law, including constitutions, statutes, and case law. Moreover, it is important to recognize that law is shaped by human beings whose decisions determine the content and interpretation of law. In addition, the ultimate impact of law is determined by whether and how officials in the criminal justice system implement (or fail to implement) the authoritative decisions by judges and other lawmakers. Police officers and other officials possess authority and power which, if they use their discretion inappropriately, can negate the principles articulated by judges as comprising the law that guides the criminal justice process and protects constitutional rights.

The American justice system is complex because it is comprised of agencies and organizations at the federal, state, and local levels. In addition, the multilevel court systems within each jurisdiction add complexity to criminal justice, in part because slightly different rules of criminal procedure may apply in each different court and jurisdiction.

The Bill of Rights provides the source of many constitutional rights that affect criminal procedure by providing legal protections for suspects and defendants and by limiting the authority of criminal justice system officials. The rights contained in the Bill of Rights originally applied only against federal officials, but through the gradual incorporation process carried out by the U.S. Supreme Court, most criminal justice rights were applied against state and local officials during the 1950s and 60s.

The Rights of Non-Citizens

The United States government's response to the terrorist attacks on New York City and Washington, D.C., in September 2001 raises questions about the nature of constitutional rights and whether the principles of the U.S. Constitution actually govern all the prosecutions undertaken by the American government.

In the aftermath of the devastating suicide attacks on the World Trade Center and the Pentagon by airplane hijackers on September 11, 2001, President George W. Bush issued an executive order titled "Detention, Treatment, and Trial of Certain Non-Citizens in the War Against Terrorism" (November 13, 2001). The order declared that when the president determines that there is reason to believe a non-citizen is a member of the al Qaeda organization blamed for the September 11th attacks or otherwise aided acts of international terrorism against the United States, such individuals, when captured, will be tried by "military commissions" rather than in the usual criminal proceedings of American courts. These proceedings would not follow the usual rules of evidence, and defendants could be convicted by a vote of two-thirds of commission members. By contrast, most states require criminal juries to find a defendant guilty only upon a unanimous vote. In addition, there would be no right to appeal a military commission's decision.

During the course of military action against al Qaeda and Taliban forces in Afghanistan in 2001 and 2002, hundreds of suspected enemies were captured. The United States sent dozens of these captives to its Navy base at Guantánamo Bay, Cuba, in order to interrogate them, consider whether to put them on trial, or send them to other countries for trial. They were sent to an American base in Cuba rather than to the United States in order to avoid legal questions about whether they would be entitled to constitutional rights for criminal defendants and whether they could be tried by military commissions rather than courts. A majority of U.S. Supreme Court justices had previously indicated that non-citizens of the United States are not entitled to the protections of the Fourth Amendment when their property located in foreign countries is searched by American law enforcement officers (*United States v. Verdugo-Urquidez,* 1990). This decision had led many legal analysts to conclude that the rights under the U.S. Constitution do not apply to protect people located in foreign countries, even when those people are arrested or searched by American officials. By sending the prisoners to Cuba, the government could assert that these non-citizens were not entitled to constitutional rights and that they were eligible for trial by military commissions under the executive order.

The American Bar Association (ABA), the national organization representing 400,000 lawyers, passed a resolution calling on the U.S. government to guarantee that defendants will receive traditional legal protections when tried before military commissions. The ABA argued that defendants should be presumed innocent, have their guilt proven beyond a reasonable doubt, and be convicted by a unanimous verdict before the death penalty could be imposed.

The American response to the prospect of prosecuting non-citizens for terrorist activities raises many interesting questions. If Americans are committed to the principles of the U.S. Constitution, should those principles not apply when the U.S. government is prosecuting non-citizens? In light of the fact that the United States criticizes China and other countries for failing to provide the kinds of constitutional rights that Americans receive under the Bill of Rights, is it hypocritical of the United States to hold prosecutorial proceedings without providing those rights to terrorism suspects? Is there a risk that people who are actually innocent of terrorism charges might be erroneously convicted by a military commission because they did not receive the benefits of the right to counsel, rules of evidence, strict standards of proof, and the opportunity to appeal?

Although Guantánamo Bay is located on the island of Cuba, it has been under the complete control of the United States for more than forty years. Thus American law could be easily applied without actually interfering with the sovereignty of a foreign government, especially since the United States does not recognize the legitimacy of Cuba's socialist government. Is the United States using the "technicality" of an overseas location merely to justify the denial of constitutional rights in a place that is actually completely controlled by Americans and their rules? If non-citizens suspected of terrorism can be denied protections under the U.S. Constitution in the aftermath of September 11th, are there any situations in which the Bill of Rights could be suspended or ignored for American suspects because the government has proclaimed the existence of an emergency?

Sources: Anne Gearan, "ABA Urges Military Tribunal Rights," Associated Press Wire Service, 4 February 2002; "Justice Kept in the Dark," *Newsweek,* 10 December 2001, 37–43.

SUMMARY

- Law guides and controls the actions of criminal justice officials.
- Substantive criminal law defines the behaviors subject to punishment by government, and procedural criminal law defines the steps in the criminal justice process and rights of individuals.
- The law of criminal justice is in several forms: constitutions, statutes enacted by legislatures, case law from judges' opinions, and regulations produced by government agencies.
- Judicial opinions present judges' reasoning for an audience of lawyers and judges.

- The American dual court system is composed of state and federal courts, both of which have trial and appellate courts.
- During the twentieth century, the Supreme Court gradually expanded its interpretations of the Bill of Rights and incorporated most of those rights into the Due Process Clause of the Fourteenth Amendment to protect people against actions by state and local governments.
- The incorporation of most criminal justice rights occurred during the Warren Court era (1953–1969).

Key Terms

case law   Legal rules produced by judges' decisions.

case precedent   Legal rules created in judges' decisions that serve to guide the decisions of other judges in subsequent similar cases.

citation   Formal abbreviated notation that identifies the case reporter, volume, and page where a complete printed version of a judicial opinion can be found.

civil law   Rules governing the relationships among individuals, corporations, and government agencies, including disputes about contracts, property, and personal injuries.

common law   Legal system that the United States inherited from England in which judges create law by deciding cases while relying on judges' opinions in prior similar cases.

concurring opinion   Opinion by an appellate judge who agrees with the outcome of a case but disagrees with some aspect of the reasoning in the majority opinion.

constitution   Fundamental law contained in a state or federal document that provides the design of government and basic rights for individuals.

constitutional rights   Legal guarantees, which are specified in the fundamental legal document of a state or nation, to protect individuals against improper actions by government.

court of last resort   Highest court in a judicial system, either a state supreme court or the U.S. Supreme Court.

discretionary jurisdiction   Power of courts of last resort to pick and choose which cases will be heard and thereby decline to hear other cases brought forward from lower courts.

dissenting opinion   Judicial opinion by an appellate judge who disagrees with the court majority's decision on the outcome of a case.

***en banc* hearing**   Hearing in which all the judges of an appellate court hear and decide a case together as a group rather than in three-member panels.

facts   The events and circumstances that produced a legal case. In a court case, the decision is based on legal facts developed through the presentation of admissible evidence.

holding   The statement of the legal rule in a judicial opinion that will serve as precedent for later cases.

incorporation   Process through which the U.S. Supreme Court applied provisions of the Bill of Rights against state and local governments by including them in the Due Process Clause of the Fourteenth Amendment.

issue   The question of law or procedure being addressed by an appellate court in a legal case.

judicial opinion   A written document issued by a judge that announces and explains a legal decision.

judicial review   The power of American judges to review actions by other branches of government to determine if those actions should be invalidated for violating constitutional law.

jurisdiction   The legal issues and territory under the authority of a court.

law   Rules and policies produced by government officials, especially legislators and judges, that define and limit the authority of government, including protections for individuals and rules for settling disputes.

procedural criminal law Statutes and judicial decisions that mandate the steps in the criminal justice process and provide legal protections for criminal suspects, defendants, and convicted offenders.

reasoning The portion of a judicial opinion that provides justifications for a judge's decision.

statutes Law created by the people's elected representatives in legislatures.

substantive criminal law Laws that define which behaviors will be subject to punishment by government.

U.S. circuit courts of appeals The intermediate appellate courts in the federal court system that each handle initial appeals from cases within a specific geographic region.

U.S. district courts The trial courts in the federal court system.

Warren Court era Time period from 1953 to 1969 in which the U.S. Supreme Court, under the leadership of Chief Justice Earl Warren, incorporated the Bill of Rights and expanded interpretations of constitutional protections for individuals.

writ of certiorari Legal petition used to ask the U.S. Supreme Court to accept a case for hearing by calling up the case from a lower court.

Additional Readings

Abraham, Henry J. 1988. *Freedom and the Court.* 5th ed. New York: Oxford University Press. A thorough history of the U.S. Supreme Court's decisions developing constitutional rights.

Baum, Lawrence. 1997. *The Puzzle of Judicial Behavior.* Ann Arbor: University of Michigan Press. A review and analysis of research on how judges make decisions.

Curtis, Michael Kent. 1986. *No State Shall Abridge: The Fourteenth Amendment and the Bill of Rights.* Durham, N.C.: Duke University Press. A historical analysis of the purpose of the Fourteenth Amendment and its relationship to the Bill of Rights with respect to the issue of incorporation.

Hensley, Thomas R., Christopher E. Smith, and Joyce A. Baugh. 1997. *The Changing Supreme Court: Constitutional Rights and Liberties.* St. Paul, Minn.: West. Detailed discussion of constitutional law, rights, the U.S. Supreme Court, and incorporation.

O'Brien, David M. 1990. *Storm Center: The Supreme Court in American Politics.* 2nd. New York: W.W. Norton. A detailed description of the U.S. Supreme Court and its decision-making processes.

Smith, Christopher E. 1997. *Courts, Politics, and the Judicial Process.* 2nd ed. Chicago: Nelson-Hall. A description and analysis of courts, law, and the legal process.

Notes

1. *Lewis v. United States,* 518 U.S. 322 (1996).
2. Bauer, Esther. "Lawyer Blames U.S. for Deaths in Texas Sect," *Washington Post,* 21 June 2000, A3.
3. *Gitlow v. New York,* 268 U.S. 652 (1925).
4. In *Duncan v. Louisiana,* 391 U.S. 145 (1968), the Court noted the rights that had been incorporated and applied to the states through the Due Process Clause of the Fourteenth Amendment. In the Court's words, by 1968, "That clause now protects the right to compensation for property taken by the State; the rights to speech, press, and religion covered by the First Amendment; the Fourth Amendment rights to be free from unreasonable searches and seizures and to have excluded from criminal trials any evidence illegally seized; the right guaranteed by the Fifth Amendment to be free of compelled self-incrimination; and the Sixth Amendment rights to counsel, to speedy and public trial, to confrontation of opposing witnesses, and to compulsory process for obtaining witnesses."
5. Richard C. Cortner, *The Supreme Court and Civil Liberties* (Palo Alto, Calif.: Mayfield, 1975), 10.
6. Henry J. Abraham, *Freedom and the Court,* 5th ed. (New York: Oxford University Press, 1988), 113–117.

CHAPTER TWO

The Criminal Justice Process

Imagine that you have spent a long day studying at the college library. As you arrive at your apartment's parking lot, you are surprised to see a police car parked in front of your building. When you enter the hallway, you see two police officers speaking with a neighbor whose apartment is three doors down from yours. You pull your keys from your pocket and prepare to enter your apartment. Then you notice that both officers are staring at you as the neighbor points his finger at you and jabs the air angrily as he speaks to the officers in an animated fashion. You hurry to turn the door handle as you get an uneasy feeling in your stomach. You had had a loud argument with this particular neighbor several days ago because he had thrown your clean clothes on the floor after removing them from the dryer in the laundry room. Once inside the apartment, you rush to the telephone and call a friend who lives on the same hallway.

"What's going on with the police? Why are they here?" you ask your friend.

Your friend hesitates before answering. "Well, this guy says that somebody broke the window on his car and stole a bunch of CDs that were sitting on the front seat." He hesitates again. "Even worse, he's been telling the police that he's sure you did it to get revenge for the big argument in the laundry room."

"What! That's crazy."

"I know it is. But that's what he says."

"That's really, really crazy! I would never . . ."

You are interrupted by a knock on the door.

"HEY, OPEN UP IN THERE. THIS IS THE POLICE AND WE WANT TO TALK TO YOU."

Your rapidly beating heart is making you almost dizzy as you drop the phone on the receiver and stand up to walk toward the door. With each footstep, your mind is racing as you ask yourself, "What should I say? What should I do?"

Step back from the scene. Could such events happen to you? Of course they could. A crime has been reported to the police, and they are doing their jobs by investigating the crime. They have the authority to make arrests and bring suspects into the criminal justice system for possible prosecution. In such circumstances, how much authority do police officers possess? Can they question you? Can they search your apartment? Can they hit you with a nightstick to force you to talk? As a practical matter, they have the *power* to do all of these things. Because they have guns and badges, there is little you can do at that moment to stop them. However, the fact that they possess the power to act does not mean they possess the proper *authority* to take such actions. Their authority is guided, in part, by the rights contained in the Bill of Rights. If they assert power without proper authority, there may be negative consequences for them. A judge may order you released from custody. Any evidence found during an improper search or questioning may be excluded from use in court. You may sue them for violating your rights and causing physical or psychological injuries.

In this chapter, we will undertake an overview of the steps in the criminal process in order to examine how constitutional rights define and limit the authority of officials in the criminal justice system. As we consider how individual amendments in the Bill of Rights apply to various steps in the criminal process, we must remember, however, that people may not always possess the rights that they believe they possess. Popular beliefs about rights do not always match reality. Moreover, even when the U.S. Supreme Court says that people possess rights, it is possible that police and prosecutors will exercise power that exceeds their proper authority anyway. Sometimes police officers and other officials misunderstand or ignore constitutional rights. In some of these situations, criminal justice officials will face few sanctions because there is little risk that certain rights violations will lead to successful lawsuits or other punitive actions against them.

INVESTIGATION

Searching for Evidence

Police officers may undertake investigatory activities either after a crime has been reported or as a part of their routine patrol duties. Sometimes an investigation is an elaborate, time-consuming process of piecing together bits of evidence from a crime scene and from witnesses. An investigation can also be quite brief if the police receive a complaint from a victim who can identify the perpetrator at the scene of the crime. Officers employ broad **discretion** in conducting investigations. Officers' own observations of suspicious behavior constitute a form of "investigation" that can lead to arrests. The investigation phase includes important discretionary decisions concerning which cases to pursue, which evidence to examine, which witnesses to believe, and which suspects to question. These seemingly small decisions have enormous consequences for the individuals eventually identified for further processing in the criminal justice system. As illustrated by the examples in the box "Discre-

A CLOSER LOOK	**Discretionary Decisions of Criminal Justice Officials**
Police	choosing which people to stop, question, search, arrest
	selecting which suspects should be subject to surveillance
	selecting investigation techniques for each case
	developing strategies for interrogation
Prosecutors	dismissing charges
	selecting which charges to pursue
	recommending bail amounts
	offering plea negotiations
	recommending sentences
Judges	issuing search and arrest warrants
	setting bail
	making probable cause determinations in hearings
	ruling on motions concerning evidence
	determining guilt in bench trials
	determining sentences (if not governed by mandatory sentences)
Corrections officials	classifying prisoners for security purposes
	making program assignments, including prison jobs
	issuing citations for infractions of rules
	recommending parole eligibility

tionary Decisions of Criminal Justice Officials," discretion is applied by decision makers throughout the criminal law process that shapes the outcomes of cases. This widespread use of discretion poses risks. For example, because discretionary decisions are central to criminal investigations, there are risks that officers' personal biases will determine which people are drawn into the criminal justice process. For example, there is evidence that some police officers target African Americans for unjustified traffic stops in order to question and search to seek evidence about other crimes.[1]

Are police officers authorized to conduct their investigations in any manner that they deem to be most appropriate? No. The U.S. Constitution's primary limitation on police officers' discretion in initiating investigations is the Fourth Amendment. The Fourth Amendment requires that officers have sufficient information to constitute "probable cause" in order to seek a search warrant or an arrest warrant from a judge. As we shall see in a later discussion, "probable cause" is a vague concept that judges must interpret and apply when deciding whether or not to issue warrants. From the perspective of police officers, the probable cause requirement means that they cannot simply ask for a warrant and they cannot justify their request for a warrant based on a hunch.

Officers on the street do not need warrants to conduct immediate investigations. Indeed, as we will see in later chapters, the Supreme Court has defined several situations in which police officers can conduct searches without warrants. The Fourth Amendment limitation most relevant to officers' discretionary decisions about whom to stop, question, or search is the prohibition on "unreasonable searches and seizures." Police officers can direct questions to passing pedestrians, because such actions are not "unreasonable." Such actions by police officers produce only a minor interference with people's privacy and liberty as long as they are not forced to stop and answer questions. More difficult Fourth Amendment issues arise when officers decide to command someone to stop and, especially, when officers want to conduct searches. The Supreme Court has made many decisions interpreting the Fourth Amendment in an effort to define the kinds of situations in which officers can use their discretion to make stops and conduct searches without violating the Fourth Amendment.

In *Delaware v. Prouse* (1979), the Court said that officers may not stop cars just because they want to check the driver's license and vehicle registration. In order to make a stop, the officers must be able to articulate a basis for reasonable suspicion that a violation of the law has occurred. Similarly, the Court said that officers cannot stop a pedestrian and arrest him for refusing to provide identification when they merely observed him walking in a high crime area (*Brown v. Texas,* 1979). Although these decisions warn officers away from making groundless stops, police officers still enjoy broad discretion, especially when they can provide a reason for the stop. Their authority applies even when their stated reason for the stop may not reflect their true motives. In *Whren v. United States* (1996), defendants questioned whether plainclothes narcotics officers in an unmarked car should be making traffic stops. There were fears expressed that police officers would make pretextual traffic stops when they really want to search for drugs. A pretextual stop would be one made by pretending that it was for one reason, such as a purported traffic violation, when the stop was actually made for a different purpose, such as a search for drugs. The issue is important because officers are supposed to have a legal basis for stopping a car. They cannot stop a car just because they wonder whether it contains drugs. Unjustified traffic stops can be regarded as a violation of the Fourth Amendment's prohibition on unreasonable seizures, since the term "seizure" applies to stopping people as well as to seizing property.

For example, if police officers stop someone by claiming, for example, that she failed to use her turn signal, how can she prove otherwise? This example shows the broad extent of police discretionary authority and the way society relies on police officers to be honest and professional. As you read the *Whren* case in the accompanying box, ask yourself whether or not courts should place any specific limits on police officers' discretion to make traffic stops and use those stops to investigate other crimes.

CASE   ### *Whren v. United States,* 517 U.S. 806 (1996)

[*Plainclothes narcotics officers in Washington, D.C., noticed a car with temporary license plates and youthful occupants that sat for an unusually long time at a stop sign. When the officers made a U-turn* *in their unmarked car to follow the vehicle, the vehicle made a quick turn—without signaling—and took off at an excessive speed. When the suspicious vehicle stopped behind traffic at a stoplight, the po-*

lice car pulled alongside and an officer approached the driver's side window. He identified himself as a police officer and instructed the driver to shift the vehicle into "park." He noticed two plastic bags that appeared to be crack cocaine in the hands of the car's passenger, and both the driver and the passenger were arrested. Both men were convicted of narcotics offenses. They challenged their convictions by claiming that the police had stopped their vehicle improperly.]

JUSTICE SCALIA delivered the opinion of the Court.

In this case we decide whether the temporary detention of a motorist who the police have probable cause to believe has committed a civil traffic violation is inconsistent with the Fourth Amendment's prohibition against unreasonable seizures unless a reasonable officer would have been motivated to stop the car by a desire to enforce traffic laws. . . .

. . . At a pretrial suppression hearing, [Whren] challenged the legality of the stop and the resulting seizure of the drugs. They argued that the stop had not been justified by probable cause to believe or even reasonable suspicion, that petitioners were engaged in illegal drug-dealing activity; and that Officer Soto's asserted ground for approaching the vehicle to give the driver a warning concerning traffic violations was pretextual. The District Court denied the suppression motion, concluding that the facts of the stop were not controverted, and "[t]here was nothing to really demonstrate that the actions of the officers were contrary to a normal traffic stop." . . .

Petitioners were convicted of the [four illegal narcotics] counts at issue here. The Court of Appeals affirmed the convictions, holding with respect to the suppression issue that, "regardless of whether a police officer subjectively believes that the occupants of an automobile may be engaging in some other illegal behavior, a traffic stop is permissible as long as a reasonable officer in the same circumstances could have stopped the car for the suspected traffic violation." . . .

. . . Temporary detention of individuals during the stop of an automobile by the police, even if only for a brief period and for a limited purpose, constitutes a "seizure" of "persons" within the meaning of this provision. . . . An automobile stop is thus subject to the constitutional imperative that it not be "unreasonable" under the circumstances. As a general matter, the decision to stop an automobile is reasonable where the police have probable cause to believe that a traffic violation has occurred. . . .

Petitioners accept that Officer Soto had probable cause to believe that various provisions of the District of Columbia traffic code had been violated. . . . They argue, however, that—in the context of civil traffic regulations—probable cause is not enough. Since, they contend, the use of automobiles is so heavily and minutely regulated that total compliance with traffic and safety rules is nearly impossible, a police officer will almost invariably be able to catch any given motorist in a technical violation. This creates the temptation to use traffic stops as a means of investigating other law violations, as to which no probable cause or even articulable suspicion exists. Petitioners, who are both black, further contend that police officers might decide which motorists to stop based on decidedly impermissble factors, such as the race of the car's occupants. To avoid this danger, they say, the Fourth Amendment test for traffic stops should be, not the normal one (applied by the Court of Appeals) of whether probable cause existed to justify the stop; but rather, whether a police officer, acting reasonably, would have made the stop for the reason given. . . .

. . . Petitioners' difficulty is not simply a lack of affirmative support for their position. Not only have we never held, outside the context of inventory search or administrative inspection . . . , that an officer's motive invalidates objectively justifiable behavior under the Fourth Amendment; but we have repeatedly held and asserted the contrary. . . . In *United States v. Robinson* [1973] . . . , we held that a traffic-violation arrest (of the sort here) would not be rendered invalid by the fact that it was not motivated by the officer-safety concern that justifies such searches. . . . We described *Robinson* as having established that "the fact that the officer does not have the state of mind which is hypothecated by the reasons which provide the legal justification for the officer's action does not invalidate the action taken as long as the circumstances, viewed objectively, justify the action." . . .

We think these cases foreclose any argument that the constitutional reasonableness of traffic stops depends on the actual motivations of the individual officers involved. We of course agree with petitioners that the Constitution prohibits selective enforcement of the law based on considerations such as race. But the constitutional basis for objecting to intentionally discriminatory application of laws is the Equal Protection Clause, not the Fourth Amendment. Subjective intentions play no role in ordinary, probable-cause Fourth Amendment analysis. . . .

(continued)

Moreover, police enforcement practices, even if they could practically be assessed by a judge, vary from place to place and from time to time. We cannot accept that the search and seizure protections of the Fourth Amendment are so variable, . . . and can be made to turn upon such trivialities. The difficulty is illustrated by petitioners' arguments in this case. Their claim that a reasonable officer would not have made this stop is based largely on District of Columbia police regulations which permit plainclothes officers in unmarked vehicles to enforce traffic laws "only in the case of a violation that is so grave as to to pose an immediate threat to the safety of others." . . . This basis of invalidation would not apply in jurisdictions that had a different practice. And it would not have applied even in the District of Columbia, if Officer Soto had been wearing a uniform or patrolling in a marked police cruiser. . . .

As indicated by *Whren,* the Court declined to prevent officers from making traffic stops, even if those stops were pretextual and based on officers' motives to look for drugs, as long as there was probable cause to believe that a traffic violation had occurred. The Court left police officers with the same broad discretion that they have always had, yet how could the Court have decided otherwise? In other words, would it be possible for the Court to formulate a rule that would satisfy concerns about pretextual or discriminatory discretionary stops while also giving the police the flexibility that they need to enforce the laws? It is not clear what kind of rule the Supreme Court might have created even if it was inclined to limit police discretion.

When a crime is reported to the police, they generally examine the crime scene to search for evidence and question the victim and witnesses. If the crime occurs in a public place or the victim invites the police into his or her home, there is no constitutional right that limits the ability of the police to visit the scene of the crime. If the police wish to search for evidence on private property where the property owner denies permission to enter, then the Constitution becomes relevant. The individual can look to the Fourth Amendment right against "unreasonable searches and seizures" as the basis for limiting police officers' authority to go wherever they wish to seek evidence.

One of the central elements of the Fourth Amendment is the warrant requirement. If prosecutors or police chiefs want officers to undertake a search of private property, they must typically seek a **search warrant** from a judge. Subsequent chapters will discuss situations in which searches may be conducted without a warrant. A warrant is a judicial order granting authority for officers to search a specific place. Judges also issue **arrest warrants** to authorize that specific individuals be taken into custody.

The purpose of the warrant requirement is to ensure that a neutral, detached decision maker determines that there is an adequate justification before criminal justice officials invade a person's private property or deprive that person of liberty by making an arrest. If police officers were always permitted to make their own determinations about when searches and arrests are justified, there are grave risks that such discretionary authority would violate the Fourth Amendment's stated intention to protect "[t]he right of the people to be secure in their persons, houses, papers, and effects, against unreasonable searches and seizures." Judges are presumed to be separate from prosecutors and police and, therefore, positioned to prevent excessive exercises of power by law enforcement officials. It should be noted that warrants are often issued by part-time judges, frequently called "magistrates," who have authority over a limited range of judicial tasks. In the federal system, warrants are issued by U.S. magistrate judges, full-time judicial officers who assist U.S. district judges with a wide array of responsibilities.[2]

In *Coolidge v. New Hampshire* (1971), the Supreme Court examined the issue of whether law enforcement officials can also be considered neutral magistrates for the purpose of issuing warrants. Under New Hampshire law, warrants could be issued by justices of the peace. Because police officers served as justices of the peace, police officers could ask fellow officers to issue warrants. In the *Coolidge* case, the state attorney general, who was to serve as chief prosecutor in a highly publicized murder case, issued search and arrest warrants in the case while acting in his role as justice of the peace. The Supreme Court invalidated these warrants because a prosecutor cannot be the "neutral and detached magistrate required by the Constitution."

Judges do not have unlimited authority to issue warrants whenever they want, and the warrants that they issue cannot grant unlimited authority to police officers. The Fourth Amendment limits officials' authority with respect to warrants in two ways. First, the amendment requires "no Warrants shall issue, but upon probable cause, supported by Oath or affirmation." This is a limitation on judges' authority to approve warrants. **Probable cause** is an ambiguous concept that attempts to define the amount of evidence that must be shown to the judge to justify the issuance of the warrant. Probable cause is usually defined as reliable information tending to show that additional evidence of a specific crime will be found at a certain location. For an arrest warrant, the information must convince the judicial officer that it tends to show a sufficient likelihood that a specific person is guilty of a crime. Police officers must swear or affirm the truthfulness of the evidence that they present to the judge when seeking approval for a warrant. Second, the Fourth Amendment limits the potential authority of police officers in undertaking the search by requiring that the search warrant "particularly describ[e] the place to be searched, and the persons or things to be seized."

It is difficult for police officers, prosecutors, and judges to know how much evidence is needed to constitute "probable cause" and thereby justify the issuance of a warrant. As we will see in later chapters, the Supreme Court has attempted to provide guidance on this issue, but the term has not been defined precisely. There is still room for significant discretion. Indeed, prosecutors and police may know that some judges will recognize "probable cause" and approve warrants based on less evidence than that required by other judges.

Interviewing and Questioning

In addition to examining crime scenes and conducting searches for evidence, the investigation phase of the criminal justice process involves interviewing witnesses and questioning suspects. The Fifth Amendment privilege against compelled self-incrimination and the Sixth Amendment right to counsel both limit police activities in questioning suspects. The Fifth Amendment says, in part, "No person . . . shall be compelled in any criminal case to be a witness against himself." Although this language may appear to refer to courtroom testimony, it has also been interpreted to limit the use of statements obtained in pretrial questioning of suspects. Police officers are not barred from using self-incriminating statements made by suspects. As subsequent chapters will discuss in greater detail, the police must simply follow rules to ensure that certain suspects, especially those in custody, are informed of their right to remain silent before they are questioned. In addition, the Supreme Court has developed rules for when and how the Sixth Amendment right to counsel enables suspects to be represented by attorneys during questioning and other stages in the criminal justice process.

Historically, the Supreme Court has also applied the Fourteenth Amendment right to due process of law as a limitation on police investigatory activities. As you read the excerpt from *Brown v. Mississippi* (1936) in the accompanying box, ask yourself several questions: What process was "due" to the suspects that was not provided to them by the police? What does this case tell us about the risks of abusive police actions if there are no courts or laws to limit discretionary exercises of power by law enforcement officers?

The *Brown* case occurred at a time in American history when the legal system was used as a tool of oppression against African Americans. Law does not automatically advance justice. Law is shaped and applied in the hands of decision makers who use their authority and discretion to determine people's fates. Racial biases in society can easily be reflected in the rules and decisions that guide the criminal justice process. Moreover, if those officials who are responsible for enforcing rules, such as judges, share the same biases, then the rules of law will not be applied in a fair and equal fashion. Fortunately, the Supreme Court's interpretations of constitutional rights in the twentieth century created limitations on officials' opportunities to use their power and authority in abusive and discriminatory ways. In addition, contemporary law enforcement officers are better educated, better trained, and more professional than police officers were early in the twentieth century. Thus there are well-established legal and ethical rules against the overt discrimination and violence that were common elements of law enforcement practices in prior decades. However, in a country with more than 700,000 law enforcement officers, it is not surprising that individual examples of misbehavior and abuse catch the public's attention periodically. The existence of constitutional rights cannot prevent discrimination and abusive behavior by criminal justice officials. These officials possess broad discretion, and often there are no witnesses to observe and verify claims of mistreatment that are raised by criminal suspects. Thus the precise extent of improper activities occurring during criminal investigations can never be measured. However, the availability of courts and legal actions based on rights can help to stop and correct many abuses when there is proof that such improper practices occurred. As you read the box "Legal Rules and the Risk of Police Misbehavior," on p. 42 consider your own views about the necessity and desirability of imposing extensive legal rules to limit the authority of police officers.

ARREST

After officers obtain information about a possible crime through a lengthy investigation or through a quick observation, they must decide whether or not to make an **arrest**. Officers enter people into the criminal justice system by formally taking the arrestees into custody when there is sufficient evidence for the officer to reasonably believe that probable cause exists to justify the deprivation of liberty. Police officers may, however, utilize their power to arrest even in cases in which they know that insufficient evidence exists concerning

CASE   *Brown v. Mississippi*, 297 U.S. 278 (1936)

[*The defendants were convicted of murder based solely on confessions that they gave to the police. There was no other evidence presented to the jury concerning their guilt. They sought to have the confessions excluded from evidence because they claimed the confessions were obtained through improper means.*]

CHIEF JUSTICE HUGHES delivered the opinion of the Court.

. . .

The crime with which these defendants, all ignorant negroes, are charged, was discovered about one o'clock p.m. on Friday, March 30, 1934. On that night one Dial, a deputy sheriff, accompanied by others, came to the home of Ellington, one of the defendants, and requested him to accompany them to the house of the deceased, and there a number of white men were gathered, who began to accuse the defendant of the crime. Upon his denial they seized him, and with the participation of the deputy they hanged him by a rope to the limb of a tree, and having let him down, they hung him again, and when he was let down a second time, and he still protested his innocence, he was tied to a tree and whipped, and still declining to accede to the demands that he confess, he was finally released and he returned with some difficulty to his home, suffering intense pain and agony. The record of the testimony shows that the signs of the rope on his neck were plainly visible during the so-called trial. A day or two thereafter the said deputy, accompanied by another, returned to the home of the said defendant and arrested him, and departed with the prisoner towards the jail in an adjoining county, but went by a route which led into the State of Alabama; and while on the way, in that State, the deputy stopped and again severely whipped the defendant, declaring that he would continue the whipping until he confessed, and the defendant then agreed to confess to such a statement as the deputy would dictate, and he did so, after which he was delivered to jail.

The other two defendants, Ed Brown and Henry Shields, were also arrested and taken to the same jail. On Sunday night, April 1, 1934, the same deputy, accompanied by a number of white men, one of whom was also an officer, and by the jailer, came to the jail, and the two last named defendants were made to strip and they were laid over chairs and their backs were cut to pieces with a leather strap with buckles on it, and they were likewise made by the said deputy definitely to understand that the whipping would be continued unless and until they confessed, and not only confessed, but confessed in every matter of detail as demanded by those present; and in this manner the defendants confessed the crime, and as the whippings progressed and were repeated, they changed or adjusted their confession in all particulars of detail so as to conform to the demands of their torturers. When the confessions had been obtained in the exact form and contents as desired by the mob, they left with the parting admonition and warning that, if the defendants changed their story at any time in any respect from that last stated, the perpetrators of the outrage would administer the same or equally effective treatment.

. . . It is sufficient to say that in pertinent respects the transcript reads more like pages torn from some medieval account, than a record made within the confines of a modern civilization which aspires to an enlightened constitutional government. . . .

. . . This deputy was put on the stand by the state in rebuttal and admitted the whippings. It is interesting to note that in his testimony with reference to the whippings of the defendant Ellington, and in response to the inquiry as to how severely he was whipped, the deputy stated, "Not too much for a negro; not as much as I would have done if it were left to me." Two others who had participated in these whippings were introduced and admitted it—not a single witness was introduced who denied it. The facts are not only undisputed, they are admitted, and admitted to have been done by officers of the state, in conjunction with other participants, and all this was definitely well known to everybody connected with the trial, and during the trial, including the state's prosecuting attorney and the trial judge presiding. . . .

The State is free to regulate the procedure in its own courts in accordance with its own conceptions of policy, unless in so doing it "offends some principle of justice so rooted in the traditions and conscience of our people as to be ranked as fundamental." . . . It would be difficult to conceive of methods more revolting to the sense of justice than those taken to procure the confessions of these petitioners, and the use of the confessions thus obtained as the basis for conviction and sentence was a clear denial of due process. . . .

Legal Rules and the Risk of Police Misbehavior

When most American children are told about police officers, they are given an idealized vision of uniformed "friends" who can be trusted to provide assistance when problems occur. This image of the police officer as a trustworthy public servant is useful in a society that relies on law enforcement officers to fulfill so many emergency, crime control, order maintenance, and service functions. Moreover, this positive image is reinforced in many beneficial encounters between police officers and citizens when there are calls for help in emergency situations.

However, there are other contexts in which police-citizen encounters are less universally positive. For example, many Americans are irritated by what they consider overzealous enforcement of certain laws, especially traffic laws (e.g., stopping a driver for not wearing a seat belt or for going only a few miles per hour over the speed limit). The irritation is compounded by evidence in some jurisdictions that traffic stops are made in a racially discriminatory manner. Studies and police records demonstrating that police officers disproportionately stop and search African American and Hispanic drivers in many states, including Maryland, New Jersey, Kentucky, and Washington, produced public outcry and civil rights lawsuits. In Washington, for example, African American, Hispanic, and Native American drivers were two and one-half times as likely as whites to be forced to submit to a search when stopped by the State Patrol.[3] A study conducted by the U.S. General Accounting Office found that African American women returning from abroad were nine times as likely as white American women to be subjected to an x-ray search, but only half as likely to be concealing illegal drugs.[4] Even worse are the situations in which police officers, not unlike the officers in *Brown v. Mississippi* (1936), abuse their authority in order to convict innocent people. For example, in the late 1990s, criminal convictions were overturned, including those of

prisoners on death row, because of evidence that Chicago police officers tortured and framed suspects. Similarly, a scandal hit the Los Angeles Police Department when one officer revealed that several officers had beaten and planted evidence on individuals whom they wished to see imprisoned.

Many of the public debates about criminal procedure concern whether police officers should be given greater flexibility in exercising their authority to combat crime or whether judges should impose stricter rules to control police conduct in criminal investigations. As you read the following excerpt from an opinion issued in 2000 by U.S. Supreme Court Justice John Paul Stevens, consider whether Stevens is correct in describing the reasonableness of Americans running away in order to avoid contact with the police. Do you think judges should adopt a skeptical view of police and use that view to broaden rights and limit police authority, even if it benefits criminal suspects? Bear in mind that Stevens's opinion was joined by three other justices (Ruth Bader Ginsburg, David Souter, and Stephen Breyer), so his views cannot be dismissed as simply reflecting his own peculiar perspective.

Justice John Paul Stevens:

> *Among some citizens, particularly minorities and those residing in high crime areas, there is also the possibility that the fleeing person is entirely innocent, but, with or without justification, believes that contact with the police can itself be dangerous, apart from any criminal activity associated with the officer's sudden presence. For such a person, unprovoked flight is neither "aberrant" nor "abnormal." Moreover, these concerns and fears are known to the police officers themselves, and are validated by law enforcement investigations into their own practices.* Illinois v. Wardlow, 528 U.S. 119, 132–133 (2000) (Stevens, J., concurring in part and dissenting in part).

the commission of a crime. They may wish to punish someone informally through a brief period of detention. An arrest may also provide a brief period of supervised control in which an individual can "sober up" or be referred to a social service agency. In circumstances in which an arrest is not supported by probable cause, there is a risk that the arrestee might sue the police officer for depriving him or her of Fourth Amendment protection against unreasonable seizures.

Under traditional common law rules that came from England to America with the early colonists, police can make arrests without warrants in two situations. First, they can use their discretion to make arrests when they have probable cause to believe that a person is committing or has committed a felony. Crimes classified as felonies are defined under each state's laws and typically involve crimes for which the punishment is more than one year of incarceration. Second, officers may make arrests without warrants for misdemeanors committed in their presence that involve a breach of the peace. Misdemeanors are usually defined as lesser offenses for which the prescribed punishment is a fine or less than one year in jail. The authority to make warrantless arrests for felonies is intended to protect public safety while the arrest authority for immediate breach-of-the-peace misdemeanors is intended to promptly restore public order.[5] The U.S. Supreme Court endorsed the common law tradition by authorizing officers to make warrantless felony arrests in public in *United States v. Watson* (1976).[6] In 2001 the Supreme Court endorsed an expanded definition of arrest authority by permitting police officers to make arrests for traffic violations for which the punishment upon conviction is merely a small fine (*Atwater v. City of Lago Vista*). In the case, a woman was arrested and taken to the police station when an officer saw that her children were not wearing seat belts in her motor vehicle. Although the punishment for the seat-belt offense was only a $50 fine, the officer was permitted to take her into custody. A five-member majority on the Court relied on its interpretation of the common law arrest authority in making the decision.

The Fourth Amendment's explicit language protecting the "right of the people to be secure in their persons, houses, papers and effects" has always been regarded as creating an expectation that people and their property would receive more protection inside homes than in public places. Thus officers are normally expected to obtain a warrant in order to arrest someone inside a home. However, the Supreme Court has established the "hot pursuit" doctrine to permit officers to make warrantless entries into buildings in order to make arrests (*Warden v. Hayden*, 1967). Judges have recognized that there may be circumstances in which it is not feasible to take the time to seek a warrant. When police are chasing a suspected felon from the scene of a crime, for example, there is a risk that the public will be endangered if the police must let the suspect escape in order to go to court to seek a warrant.

The example of the "hot pursuit" exception to the warrant requirement demonstrates that the Supreme Court attempts to strike an appropriate balance between the interests of the public and the rights of criminal suspects when it interprets the Fourth Amendment. The Court's use of a **balancing test** is evident in many search and seizure cases. There is no clear formula for determining the appropriate balance between individuals' rights and society's crime control interests. Instead, the justices make their own subjective evaluations. In effect, they seem to use their "gut reactions" to tell them in each situation whether an individual's rights are more important than the need for police officers to combat crime. Obviously, the use of this test leads to many disagreements among the justices about the scope of Fourth Amendment rights in specific situations.

The Court does not define the Fourth Amendment according to the broadest or clearest possible reading of its words. It would be possible, for example, to interpret the Fourth Amendment as requiring a warrant for all searches and seizures, including those seizures of persons that constitute arrests. The amendment is a single sentence in which warrants are emphasized. However, the Court treats the clause about warrants as separate from the clause forbidding unreasonable searches and seizures. Thus the Court leaves open the possibility of warrantless searches and arrests. As we will see in subsequent chapters, the Court's efforts to define which searches are "unreasonable" have led to the identification of several situations in which warrantless searches may be undertaken.

One purpose of the probable cause requirement for seizures under the Fourth Amendment is to protect people against unjustified arrests. An arrest is a form of seizure under the Fourth Amendment. In order for an arrest to be proper, it must be supported by sufficient information to indicate that the person arrested is likely to have perpetrated a specific crime. The Fourth Amendment and its probable cause, warrant, and reasonableness requirements do not, however, prevent innocent people from being arrested and prosecuted. As described in the box "Who Can Be Prosecuted for a Crime?" everyone must be aware that the U.S. Constitution cannot guarantee that no mistakes or improper actions will happen within the criminal justice system.

PRETRIAL PROCESSES

Soon after the arrest, the defendant goes through **booking**, the process of searching, photographing, fingerprinting, and creating a record of the arrest and jailing. Initially, arrestees are likely to be placed in a holding cell until they can be interviewed and their records can be checked to determine their security classification. The security classification determines where the individual will be housed within the jail depending on her or his need for close supervision because of a record of violent behavior, mental illness, medical problems, and other issues. If they have sufficient space, jails often attempt to keep people with records of violence separate from those being held for lesser offenses.

After suspects are in custody, there are several processing stages in which the application of discretionary decisions may either filter suspects out of the system through dismissals or increase the likelihood of conviction and punishment. It is important to remember that not-yet-convicted people are presumed to be innocent under the law. However, they still lose their liberty (at least temporarily), their rights are limited by the jail's security interests, and their fates are affected by discretionary decisions that may treat them differently than suspects accused of precisely the same crimes.

Initial Appearance

Soon after arrest, suspects are brought to court for their **initial appearance.** This first hearing serves several important purposes. If the suspect was arrested without a warrant, the judge must determine whether there is probable cause to support the arrest and the continued detention of the suspect. Thus the police and prosecutor must supply information to the judge about the evidence implicating the suspect in the crime. The judge also uses the first hearing to inform the suspect of her rights, including the right to counsel. The judge will ask the suspect whether she can afford to hire her own attorney. If

| A CLOSER LOOK | **Who Can Be Prosecuted for a Crime?** |

Many casual observers of the criminal justice system may feel a sense of detachment from its operation. News media reports highlight violent crimes, especially rapes and murders. These reports may make people feel fearful that crime is all around. This fear can lead people to view the police as the "thin blue line" that stands between them and harm at the hands of "bad" people. Under this detached view, the criminal justice system arrests, prosecutes, and punishes bad people who cause harm to society.

In reality, however, police possess the discretionary authority to make arrests and issue citations based on their own observations, their own investigations, and reports from witnesses. Because police officers are imperfect human beings, they will make mistakes. They may misinterpret someone's behavior. They may rely on reports from witnesses who mistakenly identify the wrong people as lawbreakers. If they lack proper professionalism and ethics, they may also intentionally arrest innocent people whom they wish to arrest. So, who can be prosecuted for a crime? Anyone. No one is free from the risk of arrest, no matter how innocent they may be.

Innocent people who are wrongly drawn into the criminal justice process may endure different levels of inconvenience and suffering when mistakes are made. One woman, who had always had complete faith in police officers, found that her views changed when officers cited her as a hit-and-run driver based on an erroneous report from a witness. She was shocked that the police did not care about her alibi (she was at a restaurant with two other people and had a credit card receipt to prove it at the time of the alleged accident). They also did not seem to care about the inconsistencies between the witness's description of the accident and vehicle and the color

and condition of her own vehicle. She was forced to hire a lawyer and go to court several times before a judge dropped the charges.

Although the innocent driver experienced the stress and financial cost of being drawn into the system, she did not lose her liberty. By contrast, a middle-class suburbanite arrested for trying to sell at face value his extra major league baseball tickets outside of the stadium had to spend time in jail. Although the maximum penalty for scalping tickets was a $50 fine, the police locked him in jail for twenty hours with a mix of arrestees, including someone charged with murder.

At the far end of the scale are people who experience years of imprisonment due to mistakes or misconduct by criminal justice officials. James Richardson, an illiterate farmworker, was sentenced to death in 1967. Prosecutors told the jury that he murdered his own children to collect insurance money, even though the prosecutors knew that there was no insurance policy. Richardson was released twenty-one years later when his supporters discovered that evidence in the case pointed to the children's baby-sitter as the murderer and that prosecutorial misconduct had led to Richardson's conviction.

The criminal justice system is operated by imperfect human beings who can make mistakes or engage in misconduct. In light of this reality, how important are constitutional rights? Which provisions of the Bill of Rights are most important for innocent citizens who may be drawn into the criminal justice system?

Drawn from James N. Baker, "From Tragedy to Travesty," *Newsweek*, 24 April 1989, 68; Chris Kridler, "Sergeant Friday, Where Are You?" *Newsweek*, 17 May 1999, 14; DeWayne Wickham, "Jailhouse View Alters Man's Views," *Lansing State Journal*, 20 July 2000, 10A.

she claims to be too poor to hire an attorney, the court may require evidence of her financial circumstances before appointing a defense attorney at the court's expense. In some jurisdictions with many poor defendants, the appointment of a public defender or defense attorney whose fee will be paid by the state may be virtually automatic when a suspect claims to be too poor to hire an attorney. If the suspect is charged with a misdemeanor, the judge may accept a guilty plea and resolve the case at the initial appearance. For example, such a guilty plea may produce a quick punishment of a fine or probation. If the judge will sentence a misdemeanant to a short jail sentence, then the judge must be especially careful to ensure that the individual understands he has a right to counsel. If he understands that he has a right to representation but wishes to waive his right to counsel in order to plead guilty immediately, the judge may impose a jail sentence. For people charged with felonies or those charged with misdemeanors who do not plead guilty immediately, the judge may also set bail at the initial appearance.

Bail

Bail is typically set by a judge after a hearing. **Bail** involves the suspect putting forward money or property to be forfeited if he or she does not return for scheduled hearings. Depending on the jurisdiction's practices and the seriousness of the offense, bail may be set at the initial appearance or at a separate bail hearing held later. The judge's decision on the appropriate amount for bail is based on an evaluation of the conditions necessary to ensure that the defendant returns to court and consideration of whether the defendant poses a threat to community safety. For minor charges, the police may set bail and impose conditions of release based on a standard schedule of bail amounts required for specific offenses. Some suspects may be released on their own recognizance, meaning that they are released in exchange for a promise to return for scheduled court dates. Others must pay bail money to gain pretrial release. In theory, bail should be set no higher than the amount necessary to ensure that the defendant will return for court hearings. Some defendants may make bail by paying a fee to a bail bondsman who puts up the money. Other defendants simply cannot afford to pay the required amount necessary to gain release. The decision concerning whether or not a criminal defendant will be released prior to trial ultimately affects the defendant's ability to assist in preparing a defense. Defendants who are held in jail have less ability to help their defense attorneys by locating witnesses and other evidence-gathering tasks. Defendants who are held in jail also suffer adverse personal consequences such as losing jobs or being unable to support their families or make their rent payments.

The Constitution purports to protect against inappropriately high bail amounts through the Eighth Amendment's Excessive Bail Clause. As discussed in the accompanying box on this constitutional right, it is not clear exactly what protection the Eighth Amendment provides for people who face the loss of liberty because they cannot afford to pay the required amount for bail.

Preliminary Hearing

In a **preliminary hearing,** the prosecutor and police must present enough evidence to persuade a judge that there is sufficient evidence to pursue criminal charges against the defendant. Many cases are dismissed prior to this stage by the prosecutor either because there is insufficient evidence to win the case or because the prosecutor feels the person was adequately punished in the process of being arrested and jailed. If a person has already spent several days in jail waiting for the preliminary hearings on a minor charge, the prosecutor may not wish to spend additional time and money pursuing a formal conviction, especially when the likely punishment is merely probation or a short jail sentence. The decisions about whether to pursue a case and which strategy to employ in seeking a conviction show how prosecutors' discretionary choices

CONSTITUTIONAL RIGHTS: SYMBOL OR SUBSTANCE?

The Eighth Amendment Prohibition on Excessive Bail

The Eighth Amendment says that "excessive bail shall not be required." There is no guidance in the Constitution, however, about what amount should be considered as "excessive." Such assessments must be made by courts if jailed suspects claim that their Eighth Amendment right against excessive bail has been violated. In general, judges rarely find that a bail amount was excessive. Thus the vague right expressed by the Eighth Amendment may seem largely symbolic. The right has no specific meaning or definition, and thus it is unclear whether it provides any actual protection to suspects. Is the right merely a slogan rather than a substantive protection?

In one case, the Supreme Court found a bail amount to be excessive in violation of the Eighth Amendment. *Stack v. Boyle* (1951) presented the case of several individuals charged with conspiring against the federal government during the era in which Americans' fear of communism around the world led to the prosecution of Americans who advocated communist ideas. Bail for each defendant was set at $50,000. The Supreme Court found this amount to be excessive because it was far more than the bail normally set for similar charges and the government had not demonstrated any special need to impose a higher bail in this case.

Chief Justice Fred Vinson wrote:

Upon final judgment of convictions, the petitioners face imprisonment of not more than five years and a fine of not more than $10,000. It is not denied that bail for each petitioner is fixed in a sum much higher than that usually imposed for offenses with like penalties and yet there has been no factual showing to justify such action in this case. The Government asks the courts to depart from the norm by assuming without the introduction of evidence that each petitioner is a pawn in a conspiracy and will, in obedience to a superior, flee the jurisdiction. To infer from the fact of indictment alone a need for bail in an unusually high amount is an arbitrary act. Such conduct would inject into our own system of government the very principles of totalitarianism which Congress was seeking to guard against in passing the statute under which petitioners have been indicted. (342 U.S. 1, 5–6)

The decision implies that a bail amount which exceeds the ultimate potential punishment for the crime or which exceeds the amount usually applied for similar offenses may violate the Constitution. The case also indicates, however, that a higher bail may be justified if the government presents evidence to support the amount. In light of the uncertainty about when a bail amount violates the Eighth Amendment, think of hypothetical examples of bail amounts that would violate the constitutional protection against excessive bail. Ask yourself how you know that each example would violate the Eighth Amendment. Is it possible to articulate a rule or guiding principle that judges could follow in order to make sure that no bail amounts are unconstitutional? Alternatively, if there is no workable rule or guideline, does that mean that this right is doomed to be largely symbolic and enforced only occasionally (and inconsistently) at the discretion of individual judges? If a right is not clear and applied consistently, can we really say that it is a "right" at all?

have a significant impact on the fates of individuals drawn into the criminal justice process. Judges dismiss other cases for lack of evidence or for misconduct by the police and prosecutors in obtaining evidence.

Defense attorneys can often use bail hearings and preliminary hearings as an opportunity to get a peek at the prosecutor's evidence in order to begin preparing an appropriate plea bargain offer or a trial defense strategy. In order to maximize the strength of their plea bargaining posture, prosecutors attempt to present enough evidence to justify continued prosecution without revealing all of their evidence. Thus they hope to bluff the defendants and defense attorneys into believing that more incriminating evidence is in the possession of the police. If defendants and their attorneys are fearful about the existence of additional damning evidence, they may be more inclined to offer a quick guilty plea in exchange for a reduced charge or sentence.

Grand Jury

In some jurisdictions, including federal courts, serious charges must be considered by a grand jury before formal charges are filed. A **grand jury** is a body of citizens drawn from the community to hear evidence from witnesses and prosecutors in order to determine if specific individuals should be charged with crimes. The grand jury's job is to ensure that prosecutions are justified and the government is not attempting to impose criminal punishments on people without proper reasons. Depending on the laws of a particular jurisdiction, the size of a grand jury can range from six to twenty-three members. Grand jury proceedings are not adversarial, and the usual rules of evidence and courtroom procedure do not apply. Evidence can be presented concerning suspects who do not even know that they are under investigation. Suspects who are asked to testify before a grand jury can decline to answer questions, but they are not entitled to have their attorneys in the courtroom providing arguments on their behalf. Witnesses who refuse to testify for reasons other than concerns about self-incrimination, which are protected by the Fifth Amendment, may be found in contempt of court and held in jail until they agree to testify. When a grand jury decides that the available evidence justifies prosecution, they issue an **indictment** against the suspect. The indictment serves as the formal charging mechanism. Critics of grand jury proceedings argue that they are one-sided proceedings controlled by the prosecutor rather than realistic restraints on inappropriate prosecutions.

At the **arraignment,** the defendant is formally informed of the charges lodged by the prosecutor or the grand jury. The defendant enters a plea, usually by saying "not guilty," and the attorneys for each side can then begin the plea negotiations in earnest. Although most defendants whose cases were not dismissed by the prosecutor or judge prior to arraignment will eventually plead guilty, very few enter a guilty plea immediately because their lawyers need time to seek a favorable deal from the prosecutor.

When cases are carried forward, there are frequently weeks or months in which both prosecutors and defense attorneys simultaneously continue their investigations, prepare their arguments and evidence, and negotiate possible plea bargain arrangements. Studies indicate that nearly half of all arrestees have their cases dismissed by prosecutors and judges. Of the remaining cases pushed forward, approximately 90 percent will result in negotiated guilty pleas and only 10 percent (or less) will lead to a trial.

As indicated by the foregoing description, prosecutors have significant discretion to determine which defendants will be charged. These decisions may be influenced by the prosecutor's priorities. Which crimes does the prosecutor think are most threatening to the community? The question can be posed differently by some prosecutors because local prosecutors in most communities are elected officials and many of them later hope to seek higher office. Thus their decisions may be influenced by asking themselves which prosecutions will gain the most publicity and support from the public. Prosecutors may also make decisions based on resource limitations. They may simply lack a sufficient number of assistants to prosecute all the cases that they believe are deserving of attention. If prosecutors pursue someone against whom there is no credible evidence, a judge may dismiss the case during a preliminary hearing. However, prosecutors have complete discretion about choosing to dismiss charges, no matter how much evidence exists. Prosecutors can also decide to pursue some suspects against whom evidence exists and ignore law violations by other suspects. Judges do not interfere with these decisions by prosecutors. Theoretically, the voters can turn the prosecutor out of office if they disagree with these decisions, but in reality voters have little knowledge about the many discretionary decisions that prosecutors make every day. These decisions are not visible to the public.

The exercise of discretion inevitably leads to unequal treatment. Some criminal suspects are pursued. Others are considered not worth prosecuting. Some defendants receive favorable plea agreements. Others are pushed all the way to trial. Because of the extent of prosecutors' discretion, many people worry that prosecutorial decisions may be infected by improper biases. Yet courts are reluctant to permit anyone to question prosecutors' decisions because our system places great emphasis on the need for prosecutors to use discretion. As you read *United States v. Armstrong* (1996) in the box on pp. 50–51, ask yourself whether courts should make it easier to question prosecutors' discretionary decisions.

In an 8-to-1 decision, the Court declined to permit the defendants in *Armstrong* to have access to the prosecutor's records in order to determine whether systematic racial discrimination was occurring. What evidence would a defendant need to show in order to move forward with a challenge to a prosecutor's discretionary decision making? How difficult is it to make such a showing? The *Armstrong* case reinforced the idea that judges are extremely reluctant to examine discretionary decision making by prosecutors, even when there are suspicious indications that the decision making may be improperly biased. Thus prosecutors continue to enjoy broad discretion in deciding whom to prosecute. The exercise of this discretion means that prosecutors bear a significant responsibility for ensuring the prosecutions are appropriate and fair. As with police officers, if prosecutors are self-interested, biased, unethical, or unprofessional, they can make unfair or discriminatory decisions that effectively defeat both the protection of constitutional rights and the aspirational goal of equal justice under law.

PLEA BARGAINING

The language of the Constitution indicates that all criminal cases will be determined by jury trials. With respect to the federal courts, Article III of the Constitution says that "[t]he Trial of all Crimes, except in Cases of Impeachment, shall be by Jury." The Sixth Amendment, which was incorporated and applied to all state cases through the Fourteenth Amendment Due Process Clause, says that "[i]n all criminal prosecutions, the accused shall enjoy the right to a speedy and public trial, by an impartial jury. . . ." In light of this seemingly clear language about the importance of jury trials, how is it permissible for any case, let alone a significant majority of cases, to be determined by plea bargaining?

One justification for plea bargaining is the accepted premise that defendants can voluntarily surrender their constitutional rights. In other words,

United States v. Armstrong, 517 U.S. 456 (1996)

[*A defendant claimed that the federal prosecutor in Los Angeles violated the Fourteenth Amendment's Equal Protection Clause by engaging in racial discrimination. According to the complaint, the prosecutor singled out African Americans for prosecution on charges related to the sale and possession of crack cocaine. Under federal law, prosecutions for crack cocaine can result in especially long prison terms—sentences much longer than those for smaller amounts of powder cocaine. The defendant attempted to present evidence indicating that many white people in Los Angeles used and sold crack cocaine, yet nearly all the defendants in cocaine cases were African American.*]

CHIEF JUSTICE REHNQUIST delivered the opinion of the Court.

In this case, we consider the showing necessary for a defendant to be entitled to discovery on a claim that the prosecuting attorney singled him out for prosecution on the basis of his race. We conclude that respondents failed to satisfy the threshold showing: They failed to show that the Government declined to prosecute similarly situated suspects of other races. . . .

In response to the[ir] indictment [for selling crack cocaine to undercover officers], respondents filed a motion for discovery or for dismissal of the indictment, alleging that they were selected for federal prosecution because they are black. In support of their motion, they offered only an affidavit by a "Paralegal Specialist," employed by the Office of the Federal Public Defender representing one of the respondents. The allegation in the affidavit was that, in every one of the [crack cocaine prosecution] cases closed by the office in 1991, the defendant was black. Accompanying the affidavit was a "study" listing the 24 defendants, their race, whether they were prosecuted for dealing cocaine as well as crack, and the status of each case.

The Government opposed the discovery motion, arguing, among other things, that there was no evidence or allegation "that the Government had acted unfairly or has prosecuted non-black defendants or failed to prosecute them." . . .

. . . The Government also submitted sections of a published 1989 Drug Enforcement Administration report which concluded "[l]arge-scale, interstate trafficking networks controlled by Jamaicans, Haitians, and Black street gangs dominate the manufacture and distribution of crack." . . .

In response, one of the respondents' attorneys submitted an affidavit alleging that an intake coordinator at a drug treatment center had told her that there are "an equal number of caucasian users and dealers to minority users and dealers.". . . Respondents also submitted an affidavit from a criminal defense attorney alleging that in his experience many nonblacks are prosecuted in state court for crack offenses, . . . and a newspaper article reporting that Federal "crack criminals . . . are being punished far more severely than if they had been caught with powder cocaine, and almost every single one of them is black." . . .

Respondents argue that documents "within the possession . . . of the government" that discuss the government's prosecution strategy for cocaine cases are "material" to respondents' selective-prosecution claim. . . .

We reject this argument [and decline to use a Federal Rule of Criminal Procedure to require the prosecution to open its files for the defense on this issue. . .].

In order to dispel the presumption that a prosecutor has not violated equal protection, a criminal defendant must present "clear evidence to the contrary." . . . We explained [in a prior case] why courts are "properly hesitant to examine the decision whether to prosecute." . . . Judicial deference to the decisions of these executive officers rests in part on an assessment of the relative competence of prosecutors and courts. "Such factors as the strength of the case, the prosecution's general deterrence value, the Government's enforcement priorities, and the case's relationship to the Government's overall enforcement plan are not readily susceptible to the kind of analysis the courts are competent to undertake." . . . It also stems from a concern not to unnecessarily impair the performance of a core executive constitutional function. "Examining the basis of a prosecution delays the criminal proceeding, threatens to chill law enforcement by subjecting the prosecutor's motives and decisionmaking to outside inquiry, and may undermine prosecutorial effectiveness by revealing the Government's enforcement policy. . . .

The requirements for a selective-prosecution claim draw on "ordinary equal protection standards." . . . The claimant must demonstrate that the federal prosecutorial policy "had a discriminatory effect and that it was motivated by a discriminatory purpose." . . . To establish a discriminatory effect in a race case, the claimant must show that similarly situated individuals of a different race were not prosecuted. . . .

Having reviewed the requirements to prove a selective-prosecution claim, we turn to the showing necessary to obtain discovery in support of such a claim. If discovery is ordered, the Government must assemble from its own files documents which might corroborate or refute the defendant's claim. Discovery thus imposes many of the costs present when the Government must respond to a prima facie case of selective prosecution. It will divert prosecutors' resources and may disclose the Government's prosecutorial strategy. The justifications for a rigorous standard for the elements of a selective-prosecution claim thus require a correspondingly rigorous standard for discovery in aid of such a claim. . . .

In the case before us, respondents' "study" did not constitute "some evidence tending to show the existence of the essential elements of" a selective-prosecution claim. . . . The study failed to identify individuals who were not black, could have been prosecuted for the offenses for which respondents were charged, but were not so prosecuted. This omission was not remedied by respondents' evidence in opposition to the Government's motion for reconsideration. The newspaper article, which discussed the discriminatory effect of federal drug sentencing laws, was not relevant to an allegation of discrimination in decisions to prosecute. Respondents' affidavits, which recounted one attorney's conversation with a drug treatment center employee and the experience of another attorney defending drug prosecutions in state court, recounted hearsay and reported personal conclusions based on anecdotal evidence. The judgment of the Court of Appeals is therefore reversed, and the case is remanded for proceedings consistent with this opinion.

[The concurring opinions of Justices Breyer, Ginsburg, and Souter are omitted.]

JUSTICE STEVENS, dissenting.

. . .

The District Judge's order should be evaluated in light of three circumstances that underscore the need for judicial vigilance over certain types of drug prosecutions. First, the Anti-Drug Abuse Act of 1986 and subsequent legislation established a regime of extremely high penalties for the possession and distribution of so-called "crack" cocaine. Those provisions treat one gram of crack as the equivalent of 100 grams of powder cocaine. The distribution of 50 grams of crack is thus punishable by the same mandatory minimum sentence of 10 years in prison that applies to the distribution of 5,000 grams of powder cocaine. . . . These penalties result in sentences for crack offenders that average three to eight times longer than sentences for comparable powder offenders. . . .

Second, the disparity between the treatment of crack cocaine and powder cocaine is matched by the disparity between the severity of the punishment imposed by federal law and that imposed by state law for the same conduct. . . . For example, if respondent Hampton is found guilty, his federal sentence might be as long as a mandatory life term. Had he been tried in state court, his sentence could have been as short as 12 years, less worktime credits of half that amount.

Finally, it is undisputed that the brunt of the elevated federal penalties falls heavily on blacks. While 65% of the persons who have used crack are white, in 1993 they represented only 4% of the federal offenders convicted of trafficking in crack. Eighty-eight percent of such defendants were black. . . . During the first 18 months of full guideline implementation, the sentencing disparity between black and white defendants grew from preguideline levels: blacks on average received sentences over 40% longer than whites. . . . Those figures represent a major threat to the integrity of federal sentencing reform, whose main purpose was the elimination of disparity (especially racial) in sentencing. . . .

The extraordinary severity of the imposed penalties and the troubling racial patterns of enforcement give rise to a special concern about the fairness of charging practices for crack offenses. . . .

The criticism that the affidavits were based on "anecdotal evidence" is also unpersuasive. I thought it was agreed that defendants do not need to prepare sophisticated statistical studies in order to receive mere discovery in cases like this one. Certainly evidence based on a drug counselor's personal observations or on an attorney's practice in two sets of courts, state and federal, can "ten[d] to show the existence" of selective prosecution. . . .

In sum, I agree with the Sentencing Commission that "[w]hile the exercise of discretion by prosecutors and investigators has an impact on sentences in almost all cases to some extent, because of the 100-to-1 quantity ratio and federal mandatory minimum penalties, discretionary decisions in cocaine cases often have dramatic effects. . . . The severity of the penalty heightens both the danger of arbitrary enforcement and the need for careful scrutiny of any colorable claim of discriminatory enforcement. Cf. *McCleskey v. Kemp,* 481 U.S. 279, 366 (1987) (Stevens, J., dissenting). In this case, the evidence was sufficiently disturbing to persuade the District Judge to order discovery that might help to explain the conspicuous racial pattern of cases before her Court. I cannot accept the majority's conclusion that the District Judge either exceeded her power or abused her discretion when she did so. I therefore respectfully dissent.

rights in the Constitution need not be applied if the individual who possesses the right waives the protection the right provides. Whenever a defendant gives up a right, the courts want to know that the waiver was voluntary. Supreme Court justices agree that waivers of rights must be voluntary, but they sometimes disagree about whether specific circumstances in fact demonstrate that a defendant willingly surrendered the right. Some justices, however, are also concerned that any waiver of rights be knowing as well as voluntary. Thus they have the additional concern that individuals completely understand the nature of the legal protections they are surrendering. Subsequent chapters will illustrate justices' debates about whether waivers of rights must be knowing and voluntary or merely voluntary. In the context of plea bargaining, judges typically inform defendants that they will forego their right to a trial if they plead guilty. Moreover, before accepting a guilty plea, judges usually ask defendants to acknowledge publicly that no one pressured them to plead guilty and surrender their rights. Defendants are often coached by their lawyers to reassure the judge about the voluntariness of the plea and the waiver of rights, even if the defendants, in fact, feel that they have been pressured by the defense attorney or prosecutor.

The U.S. Supreme Court has endorsed the legitimacy of plea bargaining. Although plea bargaining has existed for decades, until the 1960s many lawyers and judges denied that it occurred with any regularity. There seemed to be an effort to convince the public that defendants entered guilty pleas because that is what they wanted to do rather than in exchange for expectations about dropped charges or less-than-maximum sentences. The Supreme Court brought plea bargaining into public view and endorsed the legitimacy of the practice in *Santobello v. New York* (1971). As you read Chief Justice Warren Burger's majority opinion in the accompanying box, take note of the reasons that Burger provides for endorsing the existence of plea bargaining. In addition, what are the circumstances that must exist before a plea bargain can be accepted by a court?

The context of plea bargaining is shaped by several different factors and varies from courthouse to courthouse. Prosecutors use their discretion to set the stage for plea bargaining by determining how many charges to apply against the defendant. Prosecutors will often bring more charges than those that they know can be proven because they can use these extra charges as "bargaining chips" to be given away in the negotiation process. Thus the prosecutor may be able to compromise by dismissing charges in exchange for the defendant's agreement to plead guilty, yet ultimately arrive at the same charges and punishment that the defendant would likely have received after a trial.

Plea bargaining is also determined by the relationships between the prosecutor, defense attorney, and judge. Social scientists have identified the concept of the "courtroom workgroup," a set of actors that can reach agreements quickly and smoothly because of shared values and expectations. By reaching agreements on pleas and sentences in case after case within a particular courthouse, the courtroom workgroup members are able to predict how the other members will analyze particular cases. In many cases, the prosecutor and defense attorney do not need to "negotiate" in order to produce a plea agreement. Instead, their discussions focus on "settling the facts," which means reaching an agreement about what facts are provable by the available evidence. Once they agree on the provable facts, they know automatically what sentence will be applied by their courthouse's judge for the particular crime

| CASE | *Santobello v. New York,* 404 U.S. 257 (1971) |

[*Santobello was charged with two felonies for promoting gambling and possessing gambling records. He initially entered a plea of not guilty. After negotiations with the prosecutor, he agreed to plead guilty to one misdemeanor gambling charge in exchange for the prosecutor's promise to make no recommendations to the judge about the appropriate sentence. At sentencing, a new prosecutor recommended the maximum sentence of one year in jail and the judge imposed the sentence. Santobello sought to withdraw his guilty plea. The U.S. Supreme Court remanded the case to the state courts to determine whether Santobello should be resentenced by a different judge with no recommendation from the prosecutor or whether he would be permitted to withdraw his guilty plea. In examining Santobello's case, the Supreme Court discussed plea bargaining benefits and legitimacy*].

CHIEF JUSTICE BURGER delivered the opinion of the Court.

. . .

This record represents another example of an unfortunate lapse in orderly prosecutorial procedures, in part, no doubt, because of the enormous increase in the workload of the often understaffed prosecutor's offices. The heavy workload may well explain these episodes, but it does not excuse them. The disposition of criminal charges by agreement between the prosecutor and the accused, sometimes loosely called "plea bargaining," is an essential component of the administration of justice. Properly administered, it is to be encouraged. If every criminal charge were subjected to a full-scale trial, the states and the federal government would need to multiply by many times the number of judge and court facilities.

Disposition of charges after plea discussions is not only an essential part of the process but a highly desirable part for many reasons. It leads to prompt and largely final disposition of most criminal cases; it avoids much of the corrosive impact of enforced idleness during pretrial confinement for those who are denied release pending trial; it protects the public from those accused persons who are prone to continue criminal conduct even while on pretrial release; and, by shortening the time between the charge and the disposition, it enhances whatever may be the rehabilitative prospects of the guilty when they are ultimately imprisoned. . . .

However, all of these considerations presuppose fairness in securing agreement between an accused and a prosecutor. It is now clear, for example, that the accused pleading guilty must be counseled, absent a waiver. . . . Federal Rule of Criminal Procedure 11, governing pleas in federal courts, now makes clear that the sentencing judge must develop, on the record, the factual basis for the plea, as, for example, by having the accused describe the conduct that gave rise to the charge. The plea must, of course, be voluntary and knowing and if it was induced by promises, the essence of those promises must in some way be made known. There is of course, no absolute right to have a guilty plea accepted. . . . A court may reject a plea in exercise of sound judicial discretion.

This phase of the process of criminal justice, and the adjudicative element inherent in accepting a plea of guilty, must be attended by safeguards to insure the defendant what is reasonably due in the circumstances. Those circumstances will vary, but a constant factor is that when a plea rests in any significant degree on a promise or agreement of the prosecutor, so that it can be said to be part of the inducement or consideration, such promise must be fulfilled. . . .

that can be proven. Ultimately, the sentence will depend significantly on two elements, the seriousness of the charges and the defendant's prior criminal record. Obviously, the more serious the charge and the more extensive the defendant's prior record, the more severe the sentence will be.

Why does plea bargaining exist, and why is it so pervasive? As mentioned by Chief Justice Burger in *Santobello,* the practice exists because it provides benefits for criminal justice actors and the system itself. Prosecutors gain a sure conviction without expending the significant resources required for a trial. Defense attorneys can complete a case and move on to other cases quickly. Defendants gain greater certainty about their sentence and often avoid the risk of receiving the maximum possible sentence. Judges and the court system save time and resources as cases are completed quickly and without tying up courtrooms for lengthy trials.

Because the actors' self-interest provides the motivation for plea bargaining, there are risks that rights will not be respected in the process. Prosecutors may seek ways to pressure or deceive defendants into entering guilty pleas that are not entirely voluntary. Defense attorneys may fall short of fulfilling defendants' constitutional right to counsel if they focus on persuading defendants to plead guilty quickly without adequately considering defendants' best interests. Because defendants' rights and fates are at issue in the plea bargaining process, there is a need for lawyers and judges to make special efforts to fulfill proper procedures. However, because plea bargaining occurs during private conversations behind closed doors, it may be difficult for courts to supervise the process, especially when appellate courts are asked to consider alleged improprieties in plea bargaining that occurred many months earlier.

THE TRIAL

Defendants whose charges are not dismissed and who do not agree to plead guilty proceed to trial. They may have a jury trial in which a panel of citizens determines whether the prosecutor's evidence justifies a finding of guilt. Alternatively, they may choose to have a bench trial in which the judge serves as the decision maker. They may make this choice for several reasons. They may believe that jurors will be unable to remain detached and open-minded if there is a highly publicized or vicious crime at issue. They may also believe that the particular judge in whose courtroom the trial is to be held will be more receptive than jurors to the defense attorney's arguments and evidence. Defendants facing minor charges in lower courts may be required to have bench trials if their states' laws do not permit jury trials for lesser offenses.

Trial Process

As later chapters will discuss, the selection of jurors is a key element of jury trials. Courts face many challenges in attempting to summon a pool of citizens that reflects the demographic diversity of a community. Reliance on voter lists or driver's license records will exclude some people who are not voters or drivers. In addition, many people who are called will never show up. Potential jurors who arrive at court are questioned about their views and backgrounds in the "voir dire" process in order to determine if any jurors have biases that may prevent them from deciding the case fairly. Potential jurors may be excluded "for cause" if the judge agrees with claims by either attorney that a potential juror has demonstrated a bias in responding to questions. Such exclusions are based on **challenges for cause.** Both prosecutors and defense attorneys are authorized to exclude a few potential jurors without giving any reason for the exclusions. These jurors are excluded through **peremptory challenges.** Each side in the case is allotted a limited number of such challenges with the exact number determined by the state or federal law governing that jurisdiction.

In a trial, the defendant's fate hinges upon the actions and decisions of several actors within the courtroom. The attorneys must not only gather favorable evidence and witnesses; they must also make persuasive presentations to the judge and jury. Evidence about guilt or innocence alone may not win a case if it is not presented effectively. Thus a defendant's criminal conviction may be affected by the prosecutor's or defense attorney's style as well as by the substance of the evidence.

During the trial, the judge is responsible for ensuring that the defendant's Sixth Amendment rights are protected. The Sixth Amendment provides a variety of rights related to trials. Under the words of this amendment, defendants are entitled to

- a speedy trial,
- a public trial,
- an impartial jury,
- confrontation of witnesses,
- compulsory process to obtain favorable witnesses and evidence, and
- assistance of counsel.

In addition to these rights, the Supreme Court has interpreted the Sixth Amendment to require a fair trial and, in jury trials, a jury drawn in a nondiscriminatory manner from a fair cross-section of the community. This does not mean that a jury must be mixed by race, age, or other demographic factors. However, it does mean that the jury pool from which the jury was drawn must be created in a fair and impartial manner. The number and variety of rights mandated by the Sixth Amendment, in addition to general requirements that criminal cases provide defendants with the Fourteenth Amendment's rights of due process and equal protection, impose important responsibilities on judges for ensuring that trials are conducted properly.

Evidence must be presented in accordance with the rules of evidence applicable to that jurisdiction. The prosecution, which carries the burden of demonstrating the defendant's guilt, presents witness testimony and other evidence (e.g., murder weapon, fingerprints). The defense is permitted to question the prosecution's evidence by, for example, asking questions of witnesses on cross-examination. The defense can also present its own evidence and arguments. If evidence is presented that one side believes is not in accordance with the rules, that side will object to the presentation of evidence and ask that the judge exclude the evidence. The judge's ruling on evidentiary disputes and other matters can determine the outcome of the trial, especially if the judge decides to admit or exclude controversial evidence that is important to one side's case. The box on p. 56 gives examples of rules of evidence.

Trial Decision Making

The prosecution bears the burden of convincing the jury or judge that the evidence proves the defendant's guilt. In attempting to prove guilt, the prosecution must provide proof about each element of the crime. Every crime is comprised of elements that must be proven and that distinguish that crime from other crimes. For example, first-degree murder typically requires proof

Rules of Evidence

Rules of evidence are similar in federal and state courts. Differences exist from state to state in the definitions of admissible evidence, but generally similar principles apply. These principles guide judges' decisions about what evidence may be presented in court and considered by the jury in determining whether or not a defendant is guilty. In general, rules of evidence are concerned with ensuring that the information presented and considered is reliable and will advance an understanding of the truth. For each principle, can you see why this is important in determining the admissibility of evidence? What if each principle did not exist to guide the information presented at trial? The following list contains examples and does not provide any jurisdiction's complete rules of evidence.

1. Evidence of a person's character or trait is not admissible for the purpose of proving that the person committed a specific act.

2. Evidence of other crimes, wrongs, or acts is not admissible to prove the character of a person in order to show that he acted in conformity with his prior act.

3. The following are not admissible as evidence against a defendant: (a) a guilty plea that was later withdrawn; (b) a plea of nolo contendere (no contest); (c) any statement made in the course of plea discussions with an attorney for the prosecuting authority that do not result in a plea of guilty or which result in a plea of guilty later withdrawn.

4. Reputation or opinion evidence of the past sexual behavior of an alleged sex crime victim is not admissible.

5. A witness may not testify to a matter unless evidence is introduced sufficient to support a finding that the witness has personal knowledge of the matter.

6. The judge presiding at a trial may not testify in that trial as a witness.

7. The credibility of a witness may be attacked or supported by evidence in the form of opinion or reputation, but subject to limitations: (a) the evidence may refer only to character for truthfulness or untruthfulness, and (b) evidence of truthful character is admissible only after the character of the witness for truthfulness has been attacked by opinion or reputation evidence.

8. Cross-examination should be limited to the subject matter of the direct examination and matter affecting the credibility of the witness.

9. A witness qualified as an expert in scientific, technical, or other specialized knowledge may testify in the form of opinions. Other witnesses generally cannot provide opinions in their testimony.

10. Hearsay is generally not admissible except in specific circumstances. One example of hearsay is when a witness testifies about what someone else said. Examples of admissible hearsay are present sense impressions, excited utterances, and statements that a criminal defendant made contrary to his or her own self-interest, such as an admission of guilt to a third party.

11. Criminal defendants have a privilege to refuse to disclose or to prevent any other person from disclosing a confidential communication made by them to their lawyer, physician, psychotherapist, spouse, or cleric (e.g., minister, rabbi, priest).

of specific intent or premeditation on the part of the defendant. This is one of the elements that distinguishes murder from manslaughter, negligent homicide, and other criminal actions that lead to someone's death. Other crimes, such as burglary, may require proof of entry into a building without permission. In order to produce a conviction, the jury or judge must believe that the evidence demonstrated guilt "beyond a reasonable doubt." This is a high burden of proof to fulfill. By contrast, an attorney can prevail in a civil lawsuit by merely showing that one side should prevail by "a preponderance of evidence." Thus the civil case can be won by persuading the decision makers of a 51 percent likelihood that one side should prevail. In criminal cases, the bur-

Criminal Jury Instructions, U.S. District Court for the District of Maine

[excerpt]

Section 3.02

It is a cardinal principle of our system of justice that every person accused of a crime is presumed to be innocent unless and until his/her guilt is established beyond a reasonable doubt. The presumption is not a mere formality. It is a matter of the most important substance.

The presumption of innocence alone may be sufficient to raise a reasonable doubt and to require the acquittal of a defendant. The defendant before you, [NAME], has the benefit of that presumption throughout the trial, and you are not to convict him/her of a particular charge unless you are persuaded of his/her guilt of that charge beyond a reasonable doubt.

The presumption of innocence until proven guilty means that the burden of proof is always on the government to satisfy you that [the defendant] is guilty of the crime with which he/she is charged beyond a reasonable doubt. The law does not require that the government prove guilt beyond all possible doubt; proof beyond a reasonable doubt is sufficient to convict. This burden never shifts to [the defendant]. It is always the government's burden to prove each of the elements of the crime[s] charged beyond a reasonable doubt by the evidence and the reasonable inferences to be drawn from that evidence. [Defendant] has the right to rely upon the failure or inability of the government to establish beyond a reasonable doubt any essential element of a crime charged against him/her.

If, after fair and impartial consideration of all the evidence, you have a reasonable doubt as to [the defendant's] guilt of a particular crime, it is your duty to acquit him/her of that crime. On the other hand, if after fair and impartial consideration of all the evidence, you are satisfied beyond a reasonable doubt of [the defendant's] guilt of a particular crime, you should vote to convict him/her.

---

den is often described as showing that there is a 99 percent likelihood of guilt. In reality, jurors are not making such mathematical assessments. The judge instructs the jury that a finding of guilt requires a high level of confidence in the certainty of the defendant's culpability.

Read the example of federal court jury instructions in the box "Criminal Jury Instructions: U.S. District Court for the District of Maine." These are the exact words that a judge would say to a jury in a criminal case. The judge would also provide other information relevant to specific cases, such as details about the elements of the crime that must be proven and any particular questions about evidence that arose in the trial. If you were a juror, would these instructions give you sufficient guidance to determine whether a defendant should be convicted of a crime?

The standard for proof of guilt in criminal cases is an important component of the criminal justice process. Police and prosecutors must work toward finding and presenting evidence that will fulfill their burden of proof and persuade the judge or jury that guilt has been shown beyond a reasonable doubt. As you read the excerpt from *In re Winship* (1970) in the box on p. 58, ask yourself why the United States sets such a high standard of proof for criminal cases.

The biases and memory capabilities of witnesses and jurors also affect the defendant's fate. Human beings make decisions about defendants' fates through their perceptions of past events (witnesses) and their understanding and evaluation of conflicting stories (jurors) presented by professionals trained in the art of persuasion (attorneys). In addition, the judge must provide instructions to the jury based on the judge's interpretation of the law. Jurors

In re Winship, 397 U.S. 358 (1970)

[*The case arose out of a challenge to a New York statute that permitted juveniles to be convicted of crimes and committed to juvenile detention facilities if a preponderance of the evidence indicated that a child was guilty.*]

JUSTICE BRENNAN delivered the opinion of the Court.

. . .

The requirement that guilt of a criminal charge be established by proof beyond a reasonable doubt dates at least from our early years as a Nation. The "demand for a higher degree of persuasion in criminal cases was recurrently expressed from ancient times, [though] its crystallization into the formula 'beyond a reasonable doubt' seems to have occurred as late as 1798. It is now accepted in common law jurisdictions as the measure of persuasion by which the prosecution must convince the trier of all the essential elements of guilt" [quoting] C. McCormick, Evidence 321, pp. 681–682 (1954). . . . Although virtually unanimous adherence to the reasonable-doubt standard in common-law jurisdictions may not conclusively establish it as a requirement of due process, such adherence does "reflect a profound judgment about the way in which law should be enforced and justice administered." . . .

Expressions in many opinions of this Court indicate that it has long been assumed that proof of a criminal charge beyond a reasonable doubt is constitutionally required. . . .

The reasonable-doubt standard plays a vital role in the American scheme of criminal procedure. It is a prime instrument for reducing the risk of convictions resting on factual error. The standard provides concrete substance for the presumption of innocence—that bedrock "axiomatic and elementary" principle whose "enforcement lies at the foundation of the administration of our criminal law." . . . As the dissenters in the New York Court of Appeals observed, and we agree, "a person accused of a crime . . . would be at a severe disadvantage, a disadvantage amounting to a lack of fundamental fairness, if he could be adjudged guilty and imprisoned for years on the strength of the same evidence as would suffice in a civil case." . . .

The requirement of proof beyond a reasonable doubt has this vital role in our criminal procedure for cogent reasons. The accused during a criminal prosecution has at stake interests of immense importance, both because of the possibility that he may lose his liberty upon conviction and because of the certainty that he would be stigmatized by the conviction. Accordingly, a society that values the good name and freedom of every individual should not condemn a man for commission of a crime when there is a reasonable doubt about his guilt. As we said in *Speiser v. Randall* [1958] . . . [,] "There is always in litigation a margin of error, representing error in factfinding, which both parties must take into account. Where one party has at stake an interest of transcending value—as a criminal defendant [has an interest in] his liberty—this margin of error is reduced as to him by the process of placing on the other party the burden of . . . persuading the factfinder at the conclusion of the trial of his guilt beyond a reasonable doubt. Due process commands that no man shall lose his liberty unless the Government has borne the burden of . . . convincing the factfinder of his guilt." To this end, the reasonable-doubt standard is indispensable, for it "impresses on the trier of fact the necessity of reaching a subjective state of certitude of the facts in issue." . . .

Moreover, the use of the reasonable-doubt standard is indispensable to command the respect and confidence of the community in applications of the criminal law. It is critical that the moral force of the criminal law not be diluted by a standard of proof that leaves people in doubt whether innocent men are being condemned. It is also important in our free society that every individual going about his ordinary affairs have confidence that his government cannot adjudge him guilty of a criminal offense without convincing a proper factfinder of his guilt with utmost certainty.

Lest there remain any doubt about the constitutional stature of the reasonable-doubt standard, we explicitly hold that the Due Process Clause protects the accused against conviction except upon proof beyond a reasonable doubt of every fact necessary to constitute the crime with which he is charged. . . .

often have difficulty understanding these instructions, and they must do the best they can in reaching a decision based on their own perceptions of their duties and of the contradictory evidence presented in court. Thus, the outcomes of trials are determined by a complex combination of interactions by human beings with varying capacities for memory, impartial judgment, communication, and persuasion.

POST-TRIAL PROCEDURES AND APPEALS

After a defendant is convicted, the court's probation officer frequently plays a significant role in determining the punishment. The probation officer will usually prepare a presentence report for the judge that describes the defendant's characteristics, skills, and experiences. The probation officer will also frequently make a recommendation to the judge about a desirable sentence. The quality of the report and the credibility of the probation officer can have significant influence upon the sentence the judge imposes.

In a growing number of jurisdictions, sentencing decisions are guided by mandated guidelines that instruct judges on the punishments they must impose for specified crimes. If the judge has discretion in the sentencing process, however, the prosecutor and the defense attorney will attempt to persuade the judge about the merits of the ideal sentence they respectively envision. Ultimately, after listening to the recommendations from other actors, the judge will apply his or her own philosophy, attitudes, and biases to pronounce a sentence. Because judges' backgrounds and viewpoints can differ so dramatically, the sentences imposed upon similarly situated offenders can vary dramatically from courthouse to courthouse. Variations in sentencing practices may be influenced by resource scarcity (e.g., burdensome caseloads, overcrowded jails and prisons). Judges may not be able to punish offenders as they wish if their state's courts and corrections system cannot adequately absorb the number of cases presented.

Criminal offenders may be sentenced to a variety of punishments: restitution, fines, community service, home confinement, probation, incarceration, or execution. In carrying out these sentences, a variety of additional criminal justice actors, including probation officers and correctional officials, make judgments about the offenders' cooperative behavior and rehabilitative progress. These discretionary assessments subsequently affect how long the offenders are under correctional supervision. If correctional officials and prison counselors do not provide positive assessments of a prisoner's behavior, it reduces the likelihood that the offender will benefit from the parole board's discretionary decisions for early release. In the corrections stage, as in the other steps of the criminal justice process, there are a variety of opportunities for authoritative officials to affect the treatment received by people being processed through the system.

After defendants are convicted, they may file appeals. Appeals from a trial court of general jurisdiction generally go to an intermediate appellate court. If the appeal is unsuccessful, there may be an opportunity for a second appeal to a state supreme court. By contrast, appeals from misdemeanor convictions in lower trial courts may be filed first in higher-level trial courts instead of appellate courts, depending on the appeal process mandated by a state's laws. In some states, offenders who entered guilty pleas may need the permission of a court in order to file an appeal since they have already admitted their guilt and it seems contradictory for them to turn around immediately afterward to challenge the legitimacy of their convictions. However, even people who entered a guilty plea may have valid claims, such as ineffective assistance from a defense attorney who used untruthful statements to induce them to plead guilty.

Appeals are not an opportunity to have the case heard all over again before a new court. Appellate courts do not hold trials to make a new determination about the defendant's guilt. Instead, appeals present an opportunity for the defendant to assert that one or more specific mistakes in the case's investigation and trial processes justify having the conviction overturned. If the conviction is overturned on appeal, the defendant does not necessarily go free. Instead, a successful appeal simply gives the prosecutor an opportunity to decide whether to place the defendant on trial again. Presumably, the error that marred the first trial would be omitted from the second trial.

What kinds of errors do defendants raise on appeal? Often defendants claim that one of their rights was violated during the trial process and that rights violation biased the case against them. They may claim that police conducted an illegal search in order to obtain evidence and that the trial judge did not take adequate actions to remedy that error. They may claim that the trial judge permitted improper questioning to occur during jury selection that created prejudice against the defendant. They may claim that the trial judge misinterpreted or otherwise violated the rules of evidence and erroneously permitted the prosecution to present improper evidence. They may claim any number of other errors related to constitutional rights and proper court procedures. Relatively few criminal appeals are successful, but the appeals process is important because it presents an opportunity to correct errors that occurred in criminal cases. It must be remembered, however, that appellate judges, like their counterparts in the trial courts, are imperfect human beings with values and opinions who do not always agree with each other about the interpretation of the law. Thus two defendants presenting identical appeals could receive different results depending on which appellate court judges hear their cases.

After a defendant has exhausted his or her appeals, there is an opportunity to file a habeas corpus petition. **Habeas corpus** is a traditional legal action, enshrined in the words of the Constitution, that permits people being held by the government to claim that their detention is improper. Although the appeals process permits defendants to raise a variety of claims about errors made by judges during trial, such as improper rulings on evidence or jury instructions, the habeas corpus process is limited to consideration of rights violations. Prisoners may file habeas corpus petitions in state courts under the laws of their state. Alternatively, if prisoners in state or federal corrections institutions claim that their rights under the U.S. Constitution were violated, they may file their habeas corpus petition in federal court. In effect, habeas corpus may present an opportunity for convicted offenders to remove their cases from state courts in order to have federal judges review whether any federal constitutional rights violations occurred. As later chapters will discuss, the habeas corpus process has been a source of dissatisfaction for state judges who resent being second-guessed by federal judges and who view the process as permitting prisoners to delay confronting their own guilt because they can prolong the litigation process. U.S. Supreme Court decisions and congressional legislation in the 1980s and 90s placed new limitations on convicted offenders' opportunities to use the habeas corpus process.

CONCLUSION

The criminal justice process consists of a series of steps during which many different officials make discretionary decisions that will ultimately determine the fates of people drawn into the justice system. The process differs slightly from state to state because each state's laws determine the steps that will comprise its criminal process. States do not have complete freedom, however, to define their own processes because the rights described in the Bill of Rights and the Fourteenth Amendment place demands and limitations on all justice systems. During criminal investigations, police and prosecutors throughout the United States must take account of Fourth Amendment rights concerning search and seizure, the Fifth Amendment privilege against compelled self-incrimination, the Sixth Amendment right to counsel, and the right to due process in the Fourteenth Amendment. Judges must monitor whether the foregoing rights were respected in gathering evidence and must also ensure that various Sixth Amendment rights are protected during trial. Despite the importance of rights throughout the process, myriad opportunities exist for officials to make decisions that ultimately may lead similarly situated defendants to receive quite different treatment. The existence of rights and legal procedures does not automatically ensure that cases will result in fair and equal outcomes. Mistakes can and do occur. Some guilty defendants go free. Some innocent defendants are convicted. And constitutional rights are not always protected.

SUMMARY

- In the investigation stage of the criminal process, police officers use their discretionary authority to observe people's activities and gather evidence of crimes.

- Constitutional protections against unreasonable searches and seizures provide limitations on police officers' authority to conduct investigations, but the court decisions defining these protections are not always followed.

- Upon making an arrest, police officers draw individuals into the criminal justice process and thereby trigger additional constitutional protections because of the burden upon the individuals' interest in liberty.

- Cases are processed through various pretrial proceedings, which may include initial appearance, bail hearing, preliminary hearing, and grand jury proceedings.

- Most criminal cases that survive dismissal are terminated through plea bargaining, a process endorsed by the U.S. Supreme Court. Plea negotiations develop through discussions, agreements, and compromises between the prosecutor and the defense attorney.

- Cases pursued by a prosecutor that are not resolved through plea bargaining will proceed to trial, the adversarial setting in which the rules of evidence govern what may permissibly be presented to the judge and jury.

- After an individual has been convicted of a crime, the postconviction processes of appeals and habeas corpus petitions provide error-correction mechanisms that create an opportunity for appellate courts and federal courts to review state trial court proceedings in order to determine if any errors occurred that would justify ordering a new trial.

Key Terms

arraignment   Preliminary court proceeding in which charges are formally read to a defendant and the defendant enters an initial plea.

arrest   The exercise of a law enforcement officer's authority to take a person into custody and begin processing him or her through the criminal justice system because sufficient evidence exists to establish probable cause that the person may be guilty of a crime.

arrest warrant   A judicial order authorizing police officers to take a specific person into custody because of the existence of evidence showing that it is more likely than not that the person is guilty of a specific crime.

bail   A sum of money or property placed under court control in order for an arrested suspect to gain freedom pending trial that will be forfeited if the individual does not appear as required for court hearings.

balancing test   The Supreme Court's approach to deciding Fourth Amendment search and seizure cases in which justices decide whether the individual's constitutional rights outweigh society's need to combat crime, or whether crime control interests are more important in a specific situation.

booking   The initial processing of an arrestee at the police station, including taking fingerprints and photographs.

challenge for cause   The authority of prosecutors and defense attorneys to request the exclusion of any jurors whose responses to questions from the attorneys and judge indicate the existence of a bias that could interfere with the individual juror's capacity to be neutral decision makers in the trial at hand.

discretion   Authority possessed by police officers, prosecutors, and other justice system officials to make decisions according to their own judgments and values, despite the risk that such judgments will sometimes be incorrect or biased.

grand jury   A body of citizens that hears presentations of prosecutorial evidence in closed-door sessions to determine if the evidence provides a sufficient basis to issue indictments and thereby authorize the prosecution of specific defendants.

habeas corpus   A post-appeal legal petition used by convicted offenders to claim that their detention by the government is improper because one or more constitutional rights were violated during the investigation and prosecution of the case.

indictment   The formal order authorizing the prosecution of an individual that a grand jury issues after hearing a presentation of the prosecution's evidence against that individual.

initial appearance   A criminal suspect's first court hearing shortly after arrest to determine if there is sufficient evidence against the suspect to justify the arrest and to ensure that the suspect has been informed about her or his constitutional rights.

peremptory challenge   The authority of prosecutors and defense attorneys to exclude a limited number of potential jurors without giving any reason as long as the exclusion is not based on the juror's race or gender.

preliminary hearing   Pretrial court proceeding in which a judge determines whether sufficient evidence exists to proceed with a criminal prosecution.

probable cause   An amount of evidence establishing that it is more likely than not that evidence will be found in a specific location or that a specific person is guilty of a crime. The Constitution requires prosecutors and police officers to show a judge enough evidence to establish probable cause before an arrest warrant or search warrant may be issued.

search warrant   A judicial order authorizing police officers to search a certain location for evidence of a specific crime because of the existence of evidence showing that it is more likely than not that criminal evidence will be found at that location.

Additional Readings

Cole, George F., and Christopher E. Smith. 2002. *Criminal Justice in America*. 3rd ed. Belmont, Calif.: Wadsworth. A thorough overview of the criminal justice system, including each stage of the process from arrest through appeal.

Neubauer, David. 1998. *American Courts and the Criminal Justice System*. 6th ed. Belmont, Calif.: Wadsworth. A careful examination of criminal courts and the processes employed to determine guilt and punishment.

Walker, Samuel. 1993. *Taming the System: The Control of Discretion in Criminal Justice, 1950–1990.* New York: Oxford University Press. An analysis of policy initiatives intended to reform and reduce the use of discretion by police, prosecutors, and judges.

Notes

1. American Civil Liberties Union, *Driving While Black* (June 1999 Special Report).
2. Christopher E. Smith, *United States Magistrates in the Federal Courts: Subordinate Judges* (New York: Praeger, 1990).
3. American Civil Liberties Union, *Driving While Black;* Stuart Eskenazi, "Minorities Searched More Often By Patrol," *Seattle Times,* 17 January 2001 (www.seattletimes.com); "Blacks In Kentucky Said Pulled Over More," Associated Press Wire Service, 29 October 2000; John Cloud, "What's Race Got To Do With It," *Time,* 22 July 2001 (www.time.com); John P. McAlpin, "N.J. Police Stopped More Minorities, Documents Show," Associated Press Wire Service, 27 November 2000.
4. Jennifer Loven, "Black Women Searched More Often," Associated Press Wire Service, 10 April 2000; General Accounting Office, *U.S. Customs Service: Better Targeting of Airline Passengers for Personal Searches Could Produce Better Results* (Washington, D.C.: Government Printing Office, March 2000).
5. Charles H. Whitebread and Christopher Slobogin, *Criminal Procedure: An Analysis of Cases and Concepts,* 4th ed. (New York: Foundation Press, 2000), 90.
6. *United States v. Watson,* 423 U.S. 411 (1976).

CHAPTER THREE

Warrants, Seizures, and Arrests

You are leaving a shopping mall and walking toward your car while carrying two shopping bags. One bag contains your newly purchased sweatshirt and several pairs of socks. The other bag contains two criminal justice books that you purchased in order to work on a research paper. Just as you reach your car, you see a police car come around the corner of the mall and head into your area of the parking lot with its lights flashing. The police car slows as it passes each aisle within the parking lot as the officers peer intently along each row of cars. You do not want to stare, so you slowly begin to put your key into the door lock as your curiosity moves you to keep watching the police car out of the corner of your eye. When the police car reaches the row in which your car is parked, the patrol vehicle stops momentarily, then quickly turns down the aisle and speeds up before coming to an abrupt halt behind your car. Two officers jump out of the car. One stands behind the open driver's side door of the police vehicle while the other officer quickly moves to a position on the passenger side of your car. You stand up straight in surprise and feel your heart start to race.

The officer by the patrol car speaks to you in a very firm, loud voice. "Were you just in Johnson's Sporting Goods store?"

Your tongue feels thick and dry as you struggle to respond. "Uh, yeah."

"What's in the bag?" the officer says brusquely.

You cannot help noticing how distinctly *un*friendly the officer sounds. In addition, you can practically feel the other officer's eyes boring into the side of your face, but you are afraid to turn your head to look at her. "Just some stuff that I bought," you reply. "Just some socks, a sweatshirt, and books."

"Where's your receipt?"

"I think it's in my coat pocket." You start to reach into your coat's side pocket when you notice the officer by the patrol car has quickly put his hand on his gun and the other officer has started yelling at you.

"GET YOUR HAND AWAY FROM THE COAT. PUT BOTH HANDS UP IN THE AIR AND DON'T MOVE!"

You lift both hands, still holding the car keys and bags, as the officer moves swiftly around the front of your car and comes up to you from behind. She puts one hand on the back of your neck and presses you up against the car while she rifles through your coat's side pockets with her free hand. She has been joined by the other officer, who grabs the bags out your hands and begins to dig through them while also watching you carefully.

When she says, "There's nothing in either pocket," you are seized by a frightening thought: Did I accidentally throw out the receipts when I took those candy wrappers out of my pocket and put them in the trash can?

"You're coming with us," says the male officer as he takes the car keys from your hands, places your hands behind your back, and begins to secure handcuffs on your wrists.

"This must be some mistake. What did I do? I was just shopping. What is this about? I didn't do anything. I was just . . ."

The officers ignore your desperate, rambling comments and one officer says to the other, "I'll call the captain to see if we should take the suspect to the station to have the victim make an identification."

Could such a scenario actually happen? What if a crime victim gave the police a general description of an assailant that happened to match your appearance, clothing, and location near the scene of a crime? Did the police act properly in taking you into custody in the scene described above?

THE FOURTH AMENDMENT'S PROTECTION: AN OVERVIEW

People are drawn into the criminal justice process through the investigatory actions of police officers. Police officers serve many functions, including providing information to the public and providing services, such as medical assistance, roadside assistance, and searching for lost children. However, it is officers' crime control activities that lead people to be stopped, searched, arrested, and charged with crimes. Officers have significant discretionary authority to make stops and undertake the other activities that draw people into contact with the criminal justice system. This authority is not supposed to be unlimited. The officers' actions are supposed to be guided by the requirements of the Fourth Amendment, as interpreted by the U.S. Supreme Court and other courts, as well as policies and procedures developed by the law enforcement agencies that employ them. If officers exceed their authority, there are risks that judges will subsequently order the release of people who have been arrested or forbid certain evidence from being used against a criminal defendant who was searched or arrested improperly. When officers exceed their authority, there are also risks that they will be disciplined by their superiors or even sued by people whose rights were violated by improper searches and arrests. The possible sanctions that officers may face for exceeding their authority are mere *risks*. In many circumstances, officers exceed their authority and violate constitutional guidelines without any consequences because the harm to the citizen was so slight or the person subjected to the officer's actions cannot prove that the officer acted improperly.

Searches

The Fourth Amendment says that its purpose is to protect "the right of the people to be secure in their persons, houses, papers, and effects." In order to achieve that goal, the Fourth Amendment forbids "unreasonable searches and seizures." Thus the Supreme Court must interpret and define the meaning of "searches" and "seizures" before it can evaluate the reasonableness of specific actions by police officers. If a police action does not produce a "search" or a "seizure," then the Court need not be concerned whether the officer's action was reasonable. For example, if you are walking down the street and a police officer looks at you, is that a "search"? Most people would readily agree that such actions by a police officer do not constitute a search. The person walking down the street has chosen to appear in public. Whatever the officer can by looking at the person, such as clothing, height, and hairstyle, can be easily observed by anyone else, too.

As we will see when we examine searches in subsequent chapters, the Supreme Court defines **searches** as actions by law enforcement officials that intrude upon people's **reasonable expectations of privacy.** A person walking down the street does not possess a reasonable expectation that her publicly visible clothing cannot be viewed by police officers and others because of her constitutionally protected interest in her privacy. She has voluntarily placed herself in public view and must naturally expect that people can and will see her. By contrast, someone who places a personal diary in a locked drawer within her bedroom in her home obviously has demonstrated a significantly greater reasonable expectation that police officers cannot simply decide to enter her home and bedroom in order to open the drawer and read the diary. These two examples represent opposite ends of a spectrum. In between them, there are many situations that raise questions about people's reasonable expectations. Should people reasonably expect that police officers will not reach into their pockets in order to see if they have guns? Should people reasonably expect that police officers will not walk up to their houses and peer into the windows? These issues will be discussed in subsequent chapters concerning searches, but it is important to recognize that people's reasonable expectations about their privacy are important elements in the Supreme Court's determinations about when police officers' actions violate the Fourth Amendment. As you read the descriptions of limitations on the government's authority to undertake electronic surveillance in the accompanying box, ask yourself whether people's reasonable expectations might change as the federal government continues to expand its antiterrorism investigations.

Government Snooping and Reasonable Expectations of Privacy

In July 2000, Congress held hearings on the FBI's controversial "Carnivore" program, an Internet wiretap system that permits federal law enforcement officials to intercept email messages. Unlike traditional wiretaps, which are placed and maintained by the telephone company, "Carnivore" is maintained solely by the FBI and is capable of intercepting all messages in a particular Internet provider's system. Thus the FBI provides assurances that it will intercept only targeted messages, but once it is plugged into America Online, the agency could really intercept all AOL users' messages.[1] Does the FBI's program threaten Americans' Fourth Amendment rights? Do legislators or judges need to impose new safeguards to ensure that rights are protected?

The Supreme Court has established that people possess legally protected, reasonable expectations of privacy for their communications, even when there is no physical intrusion into their homes or persons. In *Katz v. United States* (1967), the Supreme Court recognized Fourth Amendment protections against governmental eavesdropping on a conversation from a public telephone booth. According to the majority opinion:

> [W]hat he sought to exclude when he entered the booth was not the intruding eye—it was the uninvited ear. He did not shed his right to do so simply because he made his calls from a place where he might be seen. No less than an individual in a business office, in a friend's apartment, or in a taxicab, a person in a telephone booth may rely upon the protection of the Fourth Amendment. One who occupies it, shuts the door behind him, and pays the toll that permits him to place a call is surely entitled to assume that the words he utters into the mouthpiece will not be broadcast to the world. To read the Constitution more narrowly is to ignore the vital role that the public telephone has come to play in private communication. *(389 U.S. 347, 352)*

Katz helped to establish the idea that the Fourth Amendment protects people, not places. In addition, the Court has expressed its expectation that legislation authorizing electronic surveillance will meet specific standards in order to comply with the Fourth Amendment (*Berger v. New York*, 1967).

Congress enacted a federal statute known as Title III of the Omnibus Crime Control and Safe Streets Act that incorporated the Court's requirements. This legislation has been refined by subsequent enactments. The federal statute prohibits the interception of "wire, oral, or electronic communications" unless that interception is authorized according to the procedures and requirements specified by the statute. In order to obtain a warrant under the statute, these requirements must be fulfilled:

1. The identity of the applicant, who must be a government attorney authorized by the U.S. attorney general to make such applications.

2. The details of the offenses to be investigated.

3. A description with particularity of the communications to be intercepted. It should be noted that officers are not required to ignore conversations about crimes that were not part of the original application for a warrant. They can intercept this information and must forward it to the court for examination to determine whether it was obtained within the rules of the law.

4. An indication that other, less intrusive investigative techniques could not successfully be used to gain the needed evidence.

5. A statement about the duration of the requested order, which cannot exceed thirty days.

Criminal enterprises make increasingly effective use of computers, cell phones, and other electronic communication devices. In response, the government has employed new technologies, such as devices attached to computer keyboards that can detect and record individual keystrokes in order to re-create what was typed even if no file was saved. Moreover, technological surveillance is not limited to communication devices. In 2001 the U.S. Supreme Court said that the police cannot point a thermal imaging device at a house without a warrant. The police had used the device in order to detect if there were "grow lights" inside the house that were used to cultivate marijuana (*Kyllo v. United States*). As new technologies develop, judges and legislators will continually face new challenges in seeking to find the correct balance between crime control interests and individual rights.

Seizures

Like "searches," "seizures" must also be defined by the Supreme Court in order to evaluate whether officers' actions were reasonable and therefore within the limits on police authority established by the Fourth Amendment. In defining seizures, the Supreme Court focuses on the nature and extent of officers' interference with people's liberty and freedom of movement. If an officer who is leaning against the wall of a building says to a passing pedestrian, "Where are you going?" and the person replies, "To the sandwich shop down the street," as she continues to walk without interference by the officer, there is virtually no interference with her liberty and freedom of movement. Thus officers are free to speak to people on the street. If people voluntarily stop in order to speak with the officer, they have not been "seized" because they are free to move along their way whenever they choose. However, if people are not free to leave when officers assert their authority to halt someone's movement, then a **seizure** has occurred and the Fourth Amendment requires that the seizure be reasonable.

In evaluating the reasonableness of a seizure, the Supreme Court examines the duration of the seizure and the extent of interference with a person's freedom of movement in determining whether there has been a sufficient justification for the interference to make the seizure reasonable under the Fourth Amendment. A **stop** is a brief interference with a person's freedom of movement for a duration that can be measured in minutes. When police require a driver to pull over in order to receive a traffic citation, that is a stop. Sometimes a person must spend an hour or more along the side of the road while officers fill out paperwork, check the driver's license and car registration, and see if any weapon or evidence of crime is visible on the seats of the vehicle. When officers require a pedestrian to stand still briefly while they pat down the person's clothing in search of weapons, that is a stop. In order to be reasonable under the Fourth Amendment, stops must be justified by reasonable suspicion. The Court has defined **reasonable suspicion** as a situation in which specific articulable facts lead officers to conclude that the person is engaging in criminal activity. In other words, if challenged later about whether the stop was proper, the officer must be able to describe specific aspects of the person's appearance, behavior, and circumstances that led him or her to conclude that the person should be stopped in order to investigate the occurrence of a crime. For example, the person's description may closely match that of someone wanted for a crime, especially if the person who matches the description is in the vicinity of the crime in its immediate aftermath and is behaving in a nervous or otherwise unusual manner. These facts must be such that they would justify the formulation of suspicion to an outside observer who encountered the same facts. Otherwise, officers would be stopping people based on mere "hunches" by saying, in effect, "These facts made *me* suspicious even though most other people would not have been suspicious upon encountering the same circumstances." Officers cannot make stops based on hunches. They must be able to describe specific facts that would justify the stop in the eyes of others. Bear in mind, however, that officers supply these descriptions in court after the stop has occurred and incriminating evidence has been discovered. Thus there is a risk that an unethical officer would have the opportunity to make up additional facts and justifications for the stop, even if the officer did not actually have those considerations in mind at the time the stop occurred.

Judges often defer to police officers' decisions about the circumstances that constitute reasonable suspicion and justify a stop because they know that officers must often make quick decisions and react swiftly to shifting situations on the streets in order to prevent crimes and apprehend offenders. Despite a general orientation toward deference, judges must still be willing to examine critically a police officer's explanation and justification for a stop in order to make the Fourth Amendment's protections meaningful. The Supreme Court has struck down ordinances, such as those defining vague crimes such as "loitering," that attempted to grant police officers the authority to stop or arrest people for merely appearing suspicious without requiring specific facts that justified the conclusion that criminal activity had occurred (*Papachristou v. City of Jacksonville*, 1972).

The Supreme Court has identified a number of special situations in which law enforcement officers may make stops without reasonable suspicion. The Court uses a balancing approach in interpreting the Fourth Amendment. If the justices determine that the interests of society outweigh the liberty or privacy interests of individuals in a specific situation, then the requirements of the Fourth Amendment are loosened. For example, the Court permits roadblocks at or near international borders in order to stop, question, and inspect the vehicles of people who have entered the country (*United States v. Martinez-Fuerte*, 1976). The justices have concluded that the nation's interest in preventing smuggling, illegal immigration, and other problems stemming from the flow of people and objects across national borders justifies stops that are not based on individualized suspicion. Similarly, the Supreme Court has approved sobriety checkpoints at which police officers can stop all vehicles to make a brief determination of whether each driver exhibits signs of alcohol consumption (*Michigan Department of State Police v. Sitz*, 1990). In 2000, however, the Supreme Court declined to extend police authority for suspicionless stops to roadblocks within cities intended to permit K-9 officers to have dogs sniff vehicles in order to detect illegal drugs (*City of Indianapolis v. Edmond*). The Court also permits suspicionless stops of boats (*United States v. Villamonte-Marquez*, 1983) and suspicionless stops of airline passengers who must pass through metal detectors and, potentially, have their persons and luggage searched to prevent hijacking, smuggling, and other harms to society. People can also be told not to leave certain premises while a search is being undertaken (*Michigan v. Summers*, 1981). The Court does not permit suspicionless stops of motor vehicles in order to check drivers' licenses (*Delaware v. Prouse*, 1979).

In a few cases, the Supreme Court has identified circumstances in which an investigatory stop is not a "seizure" and therefore need not be justified by reasonable suspicion. Police officers may ask to see a traveler's ticket and identification at an airport and, if their suspicions are aroused by the traveler's behavior or responses, ask the traveler to accompany them to a private room (*United States v. Mendenhall*, 1991). However, if the officers do not return the traveler's ticket and license and therefore effectively indicate that the traveler is not free to leave, then they have effected a "seizure" that must be based on reasonable suspicion (*Florida v. Royer*, 1983). Similarly, immigration officials may enter a workplace and momentarily ask individual employees a few questions without effecting a "seizure" that must be based on reasonable suspicion (*Immigration and Naturalization Service v. Delgado*, 1984). Seizures also do not occur when a passenger on a bus is blocked into a row of seats and asked questions by armed officers (*Florida v. Bostick,* 1991). The majority of justices believe that people know that they are free to terminate their contact with the officers in such situations.

Officers' actions that intrude more significantly on an individual's freedom of movement require a higher level of justification. An arrest is not a brief interference with movement. Instead, it is significant deprivation of liberty because a person is taken into police custody, transported to the police station or jail, and processed into the criminal justice system. A seizure need not be lengthy to be an arrest. Indeed, it is possible that some "stops" may be longer than "arrests" if, for example, a person transported to the police station is released on bail within an hour while a person stopped along a roadside must wait a longer period of time for the officer to write out a number of traffic citations. Typically, however, stops are much shorter in duration than arrests. More importantly, arrests involve a more significant interference with freedom of movement because arrestees are transported by the police to an official facility and may end up spending time in jail. Because arrests involve a more significant intrusion on liberty, they must be supported by a higher level of justification. Unlike stops, which require only reasonable suspicion, arrests must be supported by probable cause. As we will see in this chapter, probable cause is a vague concept that, in the context of arrests, essentially requires that sufficient evidence exists to support the reasonable conclusion that a person has committed a crime. All arrests must be supported by probable cause. Police officers must provide a judicial officer with sufficient evidence to support a finding of probable cause in order to obtain an arrest warrant. Alternatively, police officers' on-the-street determinations of probable cause that produce discretionary arrests are subsequently examined by a judge for the existence of probable cause in a hearing that must occur shortly after the arrest, typically within 48 hours (*County of Riverside v. McLaughlin,* 1991). Probable cause is also relevant for searches because sufficient evidence to support probable cause must be presented to a judicial officer in order to obtain a search warrant under the Fourth Amendment.

REASONABLE SUSPICION

How can a police officer or, after the fact, a judge determine which specific facts constitute reasonable suspicion and justify a stop? Individual officers and judges make discretionary judgments about these matters because the concept of "reasonable suspicion" cannot be defined with sufficient clarity to ensure that it is applied consistently in all cases. In order to test your sense of the facts that support a conclusion that "reasonable suspicion" exists to justify a stop, read the case of *People v. Oliver* (2001), which was decided by the Michigan Supreme Court, in the accompanying box. Notice that Michigan's state court of last resort is interpreting the Fourth Amendment of the U.S. Constitution and interpreting precedents established by the U.S. Supreme Court. In other cases, a state supreme court might limit its consideration to an interpretation of its own state constitution. Here, the court's interpretation establishes law within the state of Michigan. The court's decision does not control interpretations in other states, but courts elsewhere may look to the Michigan decision for guidance when confronted with similar kinds of cases.

Because the case involves the U.S. Constitution, it is possible for the U.S. Supreme Court to overturn the decision if the defendant moves the case to the nation's highest court and succeeds in convincing the justices to accept it for hearing.

As you read the lengthy excerpt, take note of the importance of the facts in determining whether a seizure is reasonable under the Fourth Amendment. There is no simple rule that determines whether reasonable suspicion exists. Instead, the judges must look closely at many facts and determine whether these facts, when added together and viewed as a totality of circumstances, support the conclusion that the police officer had reasonable suspicion which justified stopping the car. Examine the majority opinion's characterization of the U.S. Supreme Court's definition of reasonable suspicion. Does the state court succeed in following the U.S. Supreme Court's decision? Is the U.S. Supreme Court's definition understandable to judges and police officers?

Most state supreme courts have either five or seven members rather than nine members like the U.S. Supreme Court. Here, two of the seven justices dissented. Pay attention to the contrasting analyses by the majority and dissenting opinions. The state justices reach very different conclusions about the implications of specific facts. Which side presents the most convincing analysis?

| C A S E | *People v. Oliver,* **Michigan Supreme Court (June 12, 2001)** |

JUSTICE TAYLOR wrote the opinion for the Court [joined by JUSTICES CORRIGAN, WEAVER, YOUNG, and MARKMAN].

These consolidated cases arise from the same bank robbery and ensuing police stop of a car in the city of Jackson. In each case, the defendant argues that incriminating evidence resulting from the stop of the car should have been suppressed on the basis of the Fourth Amendment exclusionary rule. We conclude that the stop of the car was supported by reasonable suspicion and, thus, did not violate the Fourth Amendment. Accordingly, we agree with the refusal of the lower courts to suppress the evidence at issue.

I. FACTS AND PROCEDURAL HISTORY

Shortly before noon on December 1, 1994, an armed robbery was committed at a Republic Bank branch in Jackson. It was reported that two black males were the perpetrators and that they left the bank on foot. Pivotal to the issue at hand is the conduct of Jackson County Deputy Sheriff Roger Elder that led to his stopping of the motor vehicle containing both the defendants and two other passengers. Deputy Elder had

been a sheriff's deputy for over sixteen years at the time of the suppression hearing in *Oliver*. Notably, the great bulk of Deputy Elder's service with the sheriff's department was with the road patrol division. Before that, he was a township police officer for about $2\frac{1}{2}$ to three years. In the course of his career as a police officer, Deputy Elder was directly involved in investigating about twenty bank robberies.

Deputy Elder testified that while he was in his patrol car shortly before noon on the date of the robbery he (along with other police officers in the area) heard a general dispatch that an armed robbery had just occurred at the Republic Bank at the corner of North and Wisner Streets in Jackson. This dispatch advised that the suspects were two black males last seen heading northbound on foot from the bank. When he heard the dispatch, Deputy Elder, who was north of the bank, headed south to the general area of the bank to look for suspects. Deputy Elder explained at the suppression hearing in *Oliver* that he was not looking for just two suspects,

> [b]ecause it's my experience in the years I've been a police officer, that there is almost always

(continued)

a getaway car in a bank robbery, and if there's a getaway car, there's at least one more person with it.

In the course of driving toward the area of the armed robbery, Deputy Elder stopped at a New York Carpet World store where he encountered two store employees standing outside smoking cigarettes. This store was located north of the Republic Bank. Deputy Elder asked them if they had seen any black males running in the area, and they replied that they had been outside for about ten minutes and had not seen anyone except children across the street at a school.

He next went to the Westbay Apartments complex because he thought that the apartment complex would have been an excellent place for someone on foot to run and a good place to hide a getaway vehicle. The Westbay Apartments were located on the corner of North and Brown Streets, which was the first major intersection along North Street to the west of the Republic Bank, and this area was secluded. The Westbay Apartments complex was within a quarter mile of the Republic Bank.

When Deputy Elder was turning into an entrance to the Westbay Apartments complex, he saw a green Mercedes with four black male occupants heading out of the driveway. Deputy Elder testified at the suppression hearing in *Oliver* that "[a]s I was passing by them [the occupants of the Mercedes], I turned and looked over at them, and all four subjects looked directly ahead. They would not, any of them, look over at me." Deputy Elder said that he found this "very unusual" because, on the basis of his nineteen years of experience as a police officer, "[w]ell basically, because people always look at the cops. When you drive by, they always look over and see who's in the car or—they just always look at you." Deputy Elder testified that he saw the Mercedes within ten or fifteen minutes of the dispatch regarding the bank robbery and that he passed within six to eight feet of the Mercedes when they passed by each other at the entrance to the apartment complex.

After this, apparently concluding that these individuals were possibly implicated in the robbery, Deputy Elder requested backup over his police radio because he had spotted a "possible suspect vehicle." Deputy Elder, driving his patrol car, then followed the Mercedes as it proceeded west on North Street, then south on Brown Street, then east on Ganson Street, and finally south on Wisner Street. In driving this route, the Mercedes went through the intersec-

tion of Wisner and Ganson Streets. It would have been a more direct route to that intersection from the Westbay Apartments for the Mercedes to have simply gone east on North Street and then turned south on Wisner Street. Notably, this more direct route would have taken the Mercedes by the location of the Republic Bank that was robbed in this case. When backup patrol cars arrived, Deputy Elder stopped the Mercedes on Wisner Street.

Eventually, when another sheriff's deputy patted down Casual Banks, one of the passengers in the Mercedes, he found a large amount of money, including a bundle of money with a bank wrapper on it, and a Michigan identification for defendant Oliver. Later at the police station, a wad of money was found on defendant Oliver, who was a passenger in the Mercedes. Defendant Taylor was the driver and owner of the Mercedes. A search of the trunk of the Mercedes at the police station located a bag containing money and a .32 caliber automatic pistol. Also, defendant Taylor eventually made statements to the police that were later used against him.

Notably, at each suppression hearing, the trial court credited Deputy Elder's testimony about the basic facts surrounding the traffic stop. Defendants do not challenge that determination, but rather accept the basic facts related by Deputy Elder, while arguing that he nevertheless did not have legal justification consistent with the Fourth Amendment to effect the traffic stop. . . .

In [*People v LoCicero (After Remand),* 453 Mich 496, 501–502; 556 NW2d 498(1996)], this Court summarized the requirements for the police to make a valid investigatory stop based on reasonable suspicion consistently with constitutional protections:

The brief detention of a person following an investigatory stop is considered a reasonable seizure if the officer has a "reasonably articulable suspicion" that the person is engaging in criminal activity. The reasonableness of an officer's suspicion is determined case by case on the basis of the totality of all the facts and circumstances. "[I]n determining whether the officer acted reasonably in such circumstances, due weight must be given, not to his inchoate and unparticularized suspicion or 'hunch,' but to the specific reasonable inferences which he is entitled to draw from the facts in light of his experience."

Although this Court has indicated that fewer facts are needed to establish reasonable suspicion when a person is in a moving vehicle than in a house, some minimum threshold of reasonable suspicion must be established to justify an inves-

tigatory stop whether a person is in a vehicle or on the street. [Citations omitted.]

Further, in determining whether the totality of the circumstances provide reasonable suspicion to support an investigatory stop, those circumstances must be viewed "as understood and interpreted by law enforcement officers, not legal scholars. . . ." *People v Nelson,* 443 Mich 626, 632; 505 NW2d 266 (1993). Also, "[c]ommon sense and everyday life experiences predominate over uncompromising standards." *Id.* at 635–636.

In *Terry v Ohio,* 392 US 1, 30–31; 88 S Ct 1868; 20 L Ed 2d 889 (1968), the United States Supreme Court held that in certain circumstances a police officer may "stop" and briefly detain a person consistently with the Fourth Amendment on the basis of reasonable suspicion that criminal activity may be afoot. Notably, "[t]he type of intrusion authorized by [*Terry*] has been extended to permit investigative stops under various circumstances. . . ." *Nelson,* at 631. . . .

In itself, there is certainly nothing suspicious about four men occupying a car that is leaving an apartment complex. However, there were other factors in this case that provided Deputy Elder with reasonable suspicion to stop the car. First, as Deputy Elder explained in his testimony at both suppression hearings, he deduced that the two direct perpetrators of the bank robbery would most likely have the assistance of a getaway driver. Also, it was reported that the bank was robbed by two black males. Thus, the fact that the car had at least three occupants and at least two black males indicated that its occupants were consistent with the description of the suspected perpetrators. Of course, that in itself would not provide the particularized suspicion necessary for a valid investigatory stop.

However, there were other factors that provided a particularized basis for Deputy Elder to reasonably suspect that occupants of the Mercedes in which defendants were present had been involved in the bank robbery. The car was spotted by Deputy Elder in the Westbay Apartments complex within fifteen minutes of the report of the bank robbery. The complex was located to the west of the bank along North Street and within a quarter mile of the bank. Deputy Elder had first essentially eliminated the direction north of the bank on the basis of two men outside the carpet store (which was north of the bank) telling him that they had not seen anyone go by in that direction. He testified that he went to the Westbay Apartments complex because that would have been an excellent place to hide a get-

away vehicle as the apartment complex provided a secluded area to hide a car in contrast to the parking lots of businesses near the bank. In this regard, the fact that the car was *leaving* the apartment complex was consistent with it being a getaway vehicle that was attempting to leave the general vicinity of the crime. Thus, the suspicion of Deputy Elder reasonably focused on the Westbay Apartments. These deductions by Deputy Elder are particularly entitled to deference because

> [i]n analyzing the totality of the circumstances, the law enforcement officers are permitted, if not required, to consider "the modes or patterns of operation of certain kinds of lawbreakers. From [this] data, a trained officer draws inferences and makes deductions—inferences and deductions that might well elude an untrained person." [Nelson, supra at 636, quoting United States v Cortez, 449 US 411, 418; 101 S Ct 690; 66 L Ed 2d 621 (1981).]

On top of this, the occupants of the Mercedes drew further suspicion on themselves by their atypical conduct in each declining to look in the direction of Deputy Elder's passing marked patrol car. As the deputy explained, in his experience as a police officer, this was highly unusual. There is no basis to conclude that this observation was inaccurate, and, accordingly, we defer to his substantial experience as a law enforcement officer. *LoCicero, supra* at 501–502.

For conduct to support a finding of a reasonable suspicion, it need be, as we are instructed by the United States Supreme Court, merely evasive. Indeed, the United States Supreme Court has quite recently stated that "nervous, evasive behavior is a pertinent factor in determining reasonable suspicion." *Illinois v Wardlow,* 528 US 119, 124; 120 S Ct 673; 145 L Ed 2d 570 (2000). . . .

Further, in *United States v Orozco,* 191 F3d 578, 582 (CA 5, 1999), the Fifth Circuit United States Court of Appeals approved consideration of the "overall behavior of the vehicle driver," including "the avoidance of eye contact" as one factor that might be considered in determining whether there was reasonable suspicion to support a traffic stop. Likewise, we see no reason that the overall behavior of all occupants of a car in seeming to avoid looking in the direction of a marked police car cannot be considered as one factor in support of a finding of reasonable suspicion. Accordingly, we believe that Deputy Elder was entitled to rely on his perception that it was unusual that the occupants of the

(continued)

Mercedes seemed to avoid looking in his direction. As in *Wardlow,* we do not have, nor have we been offered, the benefit of any empirical studies rebutting Deputy Elder's experience-based conclusion regarding how people ordinarily react to marked police cars. Deputy Elder's observation that it was suspicious for all four occupants of a car not to look at his passing police car does not strike us as unreasonable. Indeed, it may well comport with "commonsense." Accordingly, we consider Deputy Elder's suspicion aroused by the occupants of the car not looking at his patrol car to be one factor that is properly considered, together with other factors such as the secluded nature of the apartment complex and that the apartments were located within a quarter mile of the bank, as supporting a finding of reasonable suspicion in this case. . . .

We conclude that, under the totality of the circumstances, Deputy Elder's investigatory stop of the car at issue was supported by reasonable suspicion that occupants of that car may have been involved in the robbery of the Republic Bank. The reasons for that conclusion include: (1) the deputy encountered the car near the crime scene, given that the apartment complex was within a quarter mile of the bank; (2) the time was short, with at most fifteen minutes elapsing from the time of the report of the robbery to the traffic stop; (3) the car was occupied by individuals who comported with the limited description that the officer had at his disposal; (4) Deputy Elder had tentatively eliminated the direction north of the bank as an escape route on the basis of the information he received from the carpet store employees; (5) on the basis of his familiarity with the area and experience with crimes of this nature, Deputy Elder formed the reasonable and well-articulated hypothesis that the robbers had fled to the secluded Westbay Apartments; (6) the deputy also reasonably hypothesized on the basis of his experience that the robbers would use a getaway car to try to escape from the area; (7) Deputy Elder also reasonably inferred on the basis of his experience that a driver would probably be at the getaway car waiting for the actual robbers; (8) the behavior of each of the car's four occupants in seeming to avoid looking in the direction of the deputy's marked police car was atypical; (9) the car was *leaving* the apartment complex, which is consistent with it being a getaway car whose occupants were attempting to leave the area; (10) the car followed a circuitous route that avoided driving by the site of the bank robbery.

The viewpoint of the dissent may best be summed up in its statement that "in this case, the sum of zero suspicion and zero suspicion is zero suspicion." Slip op, p 19. Whatever the obvious merits of this proposition, we respectfully disagree that it bears any relevance to this case. The factors that we have discussed above as supporting a finding of reasonable suspicion were not each of "zero suspicion" in themselves. Rather, as we have acknowledged, while the degree of suspicion from each of the factors in isolation may have fallen short of providing reasonable particularized suspicion to support the present traffic stop, that does not mean that these factors properly considered in the aggregate would not provide reasonable suspicion to support the stop under the totality of the circumstances. The validity of such a cumulative analysis, as we have discussed, is well established in our law. . . .

JUSTICE CAVANAGH, dissenting, joined by JUSTICE KELLY.

The primary issue in this case is whether reasonable suspicion existed to stop and search a vehicle and its four black occupants. I would hold that (1) the officer effectuating the stop failed to articulate a particularized and objective basis that would lead a reasonable person to suspect the occupants of the vehicle of criminal activity, and (2) evidence derived from the illegal stop is subject to analysis under the exclusionary rule.

I

The issue in this case implicates the Search and Seizure Clause of the Fourth Amendment of the United States Constitution, which protects individuals against unreasonable searches and seizures conducted by governmental actors. *Whren v United States,* 517 US 806, 809–810; 116 S Ct 1769; 135 L Ed 2d 89 (1996). When a police officer detains, even temporarily, the occupants of a vehicle, they have been "seized" within the meaning of the Fourth Amendment. *Delaware v Prouse,* 440 US 648, 683; 99 S Ct 1391; 59 L Ed 2d 660 (1979). Thus, the question becomes whether the seizure of the defendants was constitutionally reasonable.

Our United States Supreme Court has spoken on the requisite test to be applied in cases involving an investigatory stop of criminal defendants. The Court has held that "[a]n automobile stop is thus subject to the constitutional imperative that it not be 'unreasonable' under the circumstances." *Whren* at 810. In *United States v Cortez,* 449 US 411, 418; 101 S Ct

690; 66 L Ed 2d 621 (1981), the United States Supreme Court stated that the totality of the circumstances inquiry, in the event of a *Terry* stop, should take into account the whole picture. On the basis of that whole picture, the detaining officers must have a particularized and objective basis for suspecting criminal activity by the particular person stopped. In other words, to justify the seizure, the officer must act on more than an "inchoate and unparticularized suspicion or hunch." *Terry v Ohio,* 392 US 1, 27; 88 S Ct 1868; 20 L Ed 2d 889 (1968). Instead, the officer must have at least "a particularized suspicion, based on an objective observation, that the person stopped has been, is, or is about to be engaged in criminal wrongdoing." *People v Shabaz,* 424 Mich 42, 59; 378 NW2d 451 (1985). . . .

. . . The majority does a fair job of detailing the objective facts underlying this case and recapping Deputy Elder's testimony. However, the majority occasionally commingles the facts with Deputy Elder's deductions and with its own deductions, and omits a few facts that I find key to the case. This opinion offers a disentangled version of the underlying events in order to separate the circumstances giving rise to Deputy Elder's suspicions from the conclusions he drew on the basis of those factors. I find the distinction to be crucial, especially in light of the majority's conclusions that an officer's subjective deductions must be given special deference, and that factors not articulated by the officer may factor into a determination of whether a stop was objectively reasonable. Given the tests offered by the majority, I believe that the Court must distinguish which parts of Deputy Elder's testimony amount to facts and which parts compose the officer's articulated particularized reasonable suspicion. In addition, the Court should recognize which factors were extrinsic to the officer's articulated basis for effectuating the stop.

Deputy Elder's testimony in this case revealed the following facts . . . : (1) Deputy Elder overheard a dispatch that an armed robbery had just occurred at the Republic Bank and that two black male suspects had been last seen heading north on foot; (2) Deputy Elder spoke to two men outside a New York Carpet World, which was located north of the bank, who indicated that they had seen no one but some children across the street during the preceding ten minutes; (3) Deputy Elder then decided to go to the Westbay Apartments, which were located approximately one quarter mile west of the bank; (4) Deputy Elder came upon four black men in a car as they were exiting the Westbay Apartment complex, approximately ten to fifteen minutes after

hearing the dispatch; (5) Deputy Elder had previously observed that blacks lived at the Westbay Apartment complex; (6) according to Deputy Elder, the car's occupants did not look in the direction of his patrol car when he passed within six to eight feet of them; (7) Deputy Elder doubled back, began following the car, and radioed for back-up; (8) while being followed by Deputy Elder, the driver of the car drove cautiously and obeyed all traffic laws; (9) while being followed by Deputy Elder, the car drove west on one street, then turned south, then turned east, and then turned south again before being stopped.

From these objective facts, Deputy Elder testified that his experience as a police officer led him to deduce the following: (1) that the Westbay Apartment complex would be an excellent place for someone to run on foot or to hide a getaway vehicle because it was close and secluded, (2) that if there were a getaway vehicle, it would likely have at least three occupants because an additional person usually drives the getaway vehicle, (3) that it was very unusual for people not to look at an officer or patrol car driving by, and (4) that by driving the speed limit, using turn signals, and making complete stops, the driver of the car seemed to be overcautious. The majority adds one additional deduction—that the defendants were acting suspiciously by driving a "circuitous" route while being tailed by Deputy Elder.

According to the majority, reasonable suspicion is the sum total of all the circumstances presented by this case. I disagree. An analysis of the underlying facts and deductions reveals that Deputy Elder's suspicions were generalized, rather than particularized, articulable, and reasonable. Deputy Elder failed to demonstrate that these particular defendants were acting in a fashion that would support a suspicion that they had been or were about to be engaged in criminal wrongdoing. As such, the stop lacked reasonableness and was unjustified. . . .

This case boils down to a situation in which our defendants fell within the universe of possible suspects because they were of the race, gender, and minimal number described in the dispatch and because they were in the vicinity of the robbery shortly after the time that it had occurred. It is important to remember that the original description Deputy Elder heard was that two black men (not four), fled north (not west), on foot (not in a car). While Deputy Elder's testimony provided reasons to justify his belief that he should look for a broader class of suspects than the dispatch described, it is crucial to recognize that many of the factors cited by Deputy Elder and relied upon by the majority would justify a stop of any grouping of two or more black males

(continued)

who happened to be traveling within the vicinity of the robbery at the time of Deputy Elder's search. The law does not permit random stops of automobiles. Rather, officers may make a stop only when particularized facts lead them to reasonably believe that the occupants have transgressed or will transgress some law.

As a preliminary matter, it should also be recognized that the majority had to deduce that the Westbay Apartment complex was a reasonable place for Deputy Elder to look for suspects as a precursor to the conclusion that he had the requisite reasonable suspicion. Though Deputy Elder testified that he had headed to the Westbay Apartment complex after ruling out the area north of the bank, and also stated that a getaway car would probably be located in a secluded area, his search nonetheless began north of the bank and he made inquiries of individuals standing in a public parking lot. Thus, it is not entirely clear that the Westbay Apartment complex was an area any more suspicious than anywhere else near the robbery, or that Deputy Elder would have been any less suspicious of black males in a crowded parking lot. Further, Jackson is a mid-sized city with a population over 37,000; it seems reasonable to infer that there could be scores of places to hide a getaway vehicle. Additionally, ten to fifteen minutes had passed before Deputy Elder arrived at the Westbay Apartments. Given that the apartment complex was located only a block away from the bank, the amount of time that passed between when Deputy Elder received the dispatch and the time he encountered the defendants was well beyond the necessary time to escape. Thus, the passage of time made it less likely that there was a connection between the robbery and the presence of four black men.

Even assuming that it is appropriate to rely on the deduction that the Westbay Apartment complex was a reasonable place to hide a getaway car, almost all the factors noted in Deputy Elder's testimony reveal only that he believed that he was in a location where the suspects might reasonably be when he stopped the defendants: he had ruled out the area near the New York Carpet World, he was within a quarter mile of the bank, he thought a getaway car might be hidden there, he thought it was within walking distance of the bank, and he knew blacks lived there. None of these factors were tied to our defendants. Similarly, Deputy Elder also offered a few factors that tend to show that the defendants were not precluded from the list of suspects: they were black, they were male, and there were at least two of them. At most, these collective observations by Deputy Elder narrowed the list of possible suspects. None of these factors would tie our specific defendants to the crime. While Deputy Elder may have been justified in stopping *only* black males in the vicinity, nothing in his testimony indicates that he was justified in stopping *every* grouping of black males in the vicinity, or these black males in particular.

Even if special weight is given to the fact that Deputy Elder believed the apartment complex would be a good place to hide a getaway vehicle and that at least three people would have been involved in the crime, the prosecution was still required to show that Deputy Elder believed that these particular defendants had been or were about to be engaged in criminal activity. Instead, a review of the factors leading to Deputy Elder's suspicions of these particular defendants, as opposed to his suspicion of groups of black men in general, amount to nothing more than a hunch that they in fact may have been the robbers. For Fourth Amendment purposes, a hunch is an insufficient basis for initiating a stop. . . .

In *Oliver,* Deputy Elder testified that he was familiar with the Westbay Apartments, that he knew from personal experience that black individuals lived there, and that it would not be unusual for black individuals to be coming out of the Westbay Apartment complex. These factors undercut the reasonableness of Deputy Elder's suspicions that any particular black men or group of black men at the apartment complex were the bank robbers. This is especially true in light of the fact that the officer had absolutely no description of the suspects' size, age, or clothing.

Beyond the fact that the defendants were a group of black men traveling together in a car near the location of the robbery, Deputy Elder offered only two reasons for stopping these defendants: they overcautiously followed all traffic laws, and they did not look at him when he drove by them. The majority wisely has chosen not to place emphasis on the fact that the defendants were obeying all traffic laws while being followed by a police officer. On cross-examination, Deputy Elder conceded that it is not unusual for persons followed by a marked police car to drive cautiously. The trial judge also found that the way the car was driven was not unusual, as an average citizen would drive similarly.

The final factor, that the defendants did not look at the patrol car when leaving the apartment complex, is the only other factor enunciated by Deputy Elder that potentially tends to separate these particular defendants from the general populace of black men. With regard to this observation, the majority defers to Deputy Elder's experience as a law enforcement officer, and concludes that courts may consider "evasive" behavior as a factor in determining whether reasonable suspicion exists. I believe that the majority places too much weight on this solitary factor, and I disagree with the majority's analysis in several regards.

First, I disagree that the law somehow decisively supports the proposition that failure to look at a police officer constitutes a specific factor. The primary case relied upon by the majority is distinguishable. The majority cites *Illinois v Wardlow*, 528 US 119, 124; 120 S Ct 673; 145 L Ed 2d 570 (2000), for the proposition that "nervous, evasive behavior is a pertinent factor in determining reasonable suspicion." Slip op at 14. However, *Wardlow* involved a defendant who fled at the sight of police officers. Failure to react to police officers and reacting by fleeing are very different, even opposite, behaviors. *Wardlow* is in no way controlling. . . .

Even if Deputy Elder's conclusion that it is unusual for people to avoid looking at police is given a great deal of weight as the majority suggests, his observation is insufficient in and of itself to create reasonable suspicion in this case. The majority correctly points out that it does not suggest that "the mere fact that a car passes by a patrol car without any of its occupants looking at the patrol car would justify a traffic stop, but merely that such apparent avoidance of eye contact can be one factor that, together with others, may support a stop." Slip op at 17, n 8.

In sum, the factors cited by Deputy Elder in support of his decision to stop the defendants do not amount to reasonable suspicion. In this regard, I agree with the majority that the fact that four men are leaving an apartment complex is not suspicious. Similarly, the majority correctly concludes that the fact that the defendants fit within the description of possible suspects did not create particularized reasonable suspicion. Additionally, I find nothing particularly suspicious about the fact that the defendants were leaving Westbay Apartments at the time Deputy Elder was patrolling the area, especially in light of Deputy Elder's own testimony that it was not unusual for black men to be leaving the complex. Similarly, I find nothing suspicious about the fact that the defendants were obeying all traffic laws. Again, I would point out that even Deputy Elder's testimony indicated that it is not unusual for people to follow traffic laws when followed by a marked police car. Once these clearly nonsuspicious singular factors are subtracted from the list of factors offered by Deputy Elder, all we are left with is the fact that the defendants did not look at Deputy Elder's patrol car. I agree with the majority that taken alone, the failure to look at a passing patrol car would not justify a traffic stop. For these reasons, I would hold that Deputy Elder's decision to stop the defendants was not predicated upon reasonable, articulable, and particularized suspicion. . . .

An important question that emerges from such opinions is whether the court's decision provides any actual guidance and limitations on police officers' discretionary authority to make stops. What if the police officer had seen three African American men in a car pulling out of a home's driveway south of the crime scene? If the officer said that robbers often have an accomplice driving the getaway car, would the officer's analysis constitute reasonable suspicion? What if one African American man was driving west of the crime scene and he failed to look at the police officer? Would that situation constitute reasonable suspicion if the officer said that robbers often split up after the robbery? What if all four men in the car had looked at the police as they drove past him and the officer said that guilty people often look directly at passing police cars, would those facts justify a stop? If all of these circumstances would constitute reasonable suspicion, then does the Michigan case provide any limitation on police officers' stops as long as officers provide some explanation for the stop? Obviously, the majority and dissenting opinions disagree about whether the court was too deferential to the police officer in approving the stop. The dissenting opinion's examination of the facts of the case was much more critical than was the majority's analysis.

In its 2001–2002 term, the U.S. Supreme Court considered a comparable case to determine what elements constitute reasonable suspicion to justify stopping and searching a vehicle. In *United States v. Arvizu* the Supreme Court decided to reverse an appellate court that said a Border Patrol officer made an improper stop when his suspicions were aroused by a car driving thirty miles north of the Mexican border in which the driver slowed down, did not look at the officer, and apparently had children wave in a friendly manner at the officer without actually looking at the officer. Although the Court's decision clearly endorsed the permissibility of the officer's stop and search that led to the discovery of marijuana in the vehicle, the decision did not necessarily provide more clear guidance to law enforcement officers about the definition of reasonable suspicion.

PROBABLE CAUSE

Imagine that you are a judge. Two police officers come to your chambers to ask you to authorize a search warrant. They raise their right hands and swear that they observed frequent foot traffic of suspicious people going in and out of a house. Moreover, they swear that an informant, one whom they claim has supplied reliable information in the past, told them that he was inside the house two days earlier and that he saw crack cocaine being sold. Does this information rise to the level of "probable cause" that justifies issuance of a search warrant? Can you grant a warrant based purely on the word of police officers, or do you need more concrete evidence?

How are judicial officers supposed to conclude that "probable cause" exists to justify the issuance of a warrant? In order to understand the meaning of "probable cause," we must look at the guidance that the U.S. Supreme Court has provided about how the concept is to be defined.

Defining Probable Cause

Take note that the Fourth Amendment requires that "no Warrants shall issue, but upon probable cause, supported by Oath or affirmation, and particularly describing the place to be searched, and the persons or things to be seized." These particular elements of the amendment must be fulfilled in order to issue a warrant. If they are not fulfilled, then a defendant may later challenge the validity of the warrant. However, as we will see in the discussion of *United States v. Leon* (1984) in Chapter 4, the Court may find ways to admit evidence discovered through use of a faulty search warrant if the officers acted in good faith in seeking and relying on the warrant. The important elements are, first, the existence of probable cause, which we will discuss in greater detail. Second, presentation of evidence to the judicial officer supported by "oath or affirmation," which typically means that the officers must say "yes" when the judicial officer asks them if they swear or affirm that all information presented is true to the best of their knowledge. This requirement may be fulfilled by presenting an **affidavit** from the police officers, which is a written statement confirmed by oath or affirmation. Third, the warrant must describe the place to be searched. The authors of the Fourth Amendment did not want to give the government the authority to use a "general warrant," which could be used to search in many locations. And, fourth, the warrant must describe the person or items to be seized. Thus, if the warrant is authorized to search for a person suspected of robbery, the officers should not open small dresser drawers or other locations where they know that a person could not be hiding.

Probable cause determinations are supposed to be made and warrants issued by neutral officials who will not—in theory—automatically support law enforcement officials' desire to obtain the warrant. These officials are charged with protecting people's Fourth Amendment rights against improper intrusions by investigatory officers. Because of the neutrality requirement, it would be improper to permit executive branch officials responsible for law enforcement operations, such as governors, attorneys general, or prosecutors, to issue warrants. However, the neutrality requirement does not demand that the officials issuing warrants be full-time or regular judges in the courts. Many state court systems permit **magistrates** to issue warrants, and these officials are often lawyers who work part-time in a judicial capacity handling specific preliminary tasks or minor cases. In the federal district courts, warrants are often issued by **U.S. magistrate judges.** These are full-time judicial officers who are appointed to office by U.S. district judges and serve for renewable eight-year terms. U.S. magistrate judges are authorized by Congress to handle a full range of judicial responsibilities, except for presiding over felony trials. The specific duties they handle may vary from courthouse to courthouse depending on the assignments they receive from their supervising U.S. district judges. U.S. magistrate judges frequently handle preliminary processes in criminal cases, such as making recommendations and rulings on evidentiary motions, and these preliminary matters typically include issuing warrants.

Although probable cause determinations and warrants are often handled by magistrates in state courts and U.S. magistrate judges in federal courts, the Supreme Court does not require that all warrants be issued by people who are trained in law. The Court permitted municipal court clerks to issue arrest warrants for violations of city ordinances in *Shadwick v. Tampa* (1972). The key issue was the neutrality of the clerks. They were under the supervision of a judge and were not under the control of the police or prosecutor.

The U.S. Supreme Court has attempted to help judicial officers in defining "probable cause." Mere suspicion cannot constitute probable cause, yet the level of evidence to establish probable cause need not fulfill the high level of proof needed to justify a criminal conviction. In essence, **probable cause** is a level of evidence sufficient to provide a reasonable conclusion that the proposed objects of a search will be found in the location that law enforcement officers request to search. For an arrest warrant, the essential issue is whether sufficient evidence is presented to lead to the reasonable conclusion that a specific person should be prosecuted for an arrestable criminal offense. There is no hard-and-fast definition of "probable cause" that can be applied to every situation. It is a flexible concept that will be applied differently by different judicial officers.

Developing a Test

During the 1960s, the Supreme Court established a two-part test for probable cause in the cases of *Aguilar v. Texas* (1964) and *Spinelli v. United States* (1969). Under the so-called *Aguilar-Spinelli* test, the evidence presented to justify a warrant must, first, provide the basis for the law enforcement officer's knowledge about the alleged criminal activity and, second, provide substantiation for the truthfulness and reliability of the information source. In other words, law enforcement officers could not simply say that they had heard certain information about the existence of criminal activity or seizable objects at a certain location. They had to provide enough information to convince the judicial officer about the circumstances in which the source had gained the information. This is the "basis of knowledge" component of the test. If the officers' information came from their firsthand knowledge through observing the actions of a suspect, then the basis of knowledge would be strong because the officers are not relying on information from other people. Similarly, information that comes from upstanding citizens provides greater confidence than information from informants who are involved in criminal enterprises and are seeking rewards or bargains in exchange for their cooperation with the police. When informants of questionable character are used, then the judge may want to be presented with indications of the informant's reliability, such as accurate information that was verified by police on previous occasions.

The police also had to provide information to convince the judicial officer of the truthfulness and reliability of the information source. This is the "veracity" component of the test. If the officers could not fulfill both components of the *Aguilar-Spinelli* test in providing evidence to the judicial officer, then the warrant was not supposed to be issued. In the 1980s, however, the Supreme Court altered this test.

What is the test for probable cause as described in *Illinois v. Gates* (1983)? As you read the excerpt from the case in the accompanying box, ask yourself if you could always recognize how much evidence is required to establish probable cause based on the Supreme Court's opinion. The case was triggered by the issue of whether an anonymous letter can provide the basis for sufficiently trustworthy evidence to constitute probable cause and justify a warrant.

CASE   *Illinois v. Gates*, 462 U.S. 213 (1983)

JUSTICE REHNQUIST delivered the opinion of the Court.

. . .

. . . On May 3, 1978, the Bloomingdale (Ill.) Police Department received by mail an anonymous handwritten letter which read as follows:

This letter is to inform you that you have a couple in your town who strictly make their living on selling drugs. They are Sue and Lance Gates, they live on Greenway, off Bloomingdale Rd. in the condominiums. Most of their buys are done in Florida. Sue his wife drives their car to Florida where she leaves it to be loaded up with drugs, then Lance flies down and drives it back. Sue flies back after she drops the car off in Florida.

May 3 she is driving down there again and Lance will be flying down in a few days to drive it back. At the time Lance drives the car back he has the trunk loaded with over $100,000.00 in drugs. Presently they have over $100,000.00 worth of drugs in their basement.

They brag about the fact they never have to work, and make their entire living on pushers.

I guarantee if you watch them carefully you will make a big catch. They are friends with some big drugs dealers, who visit their house often.

[Police officers investigated and confirmed that a Gates family lived in the condominiums and that an "L. Gates" had plane reservations for Florida in a few days. Lance Gates was followed in Florida after he flew there, and police saw him enter a room registered to a "Susan Gates." They also saw Gates and a woman leave the room and drive north in a car with Illinois plates registered to Lance Gates. Back in Illinois, police officers presented the letter and other information to a judge and the judge, issued a search warrant for the Gateses' car and home.]

. . .

. . . At 5:15 A.M. on March 7th, only 36 hours after he had flown out of Chicago, Lance Gates, and his wife, returned to their home in Bloomingdale, driving the car in which they had left West Palm Beach some 22 hours earlier. The Bloomingdale police were awaiting them, searched the trunk of the [car], and uncovered approximately 350 pounds of marijuana. A search of the Gateses' home revealed marijuana, weapons, and other contraband. The Illinois Circuit Court ordered suppression of all these items, on the ground that the affidavit [i.e., information presented to a court under oath] submitted [by the police] to the Circuit Judge failed to support the necessary determination of probable cause to believe that the Gateses' automobile and home contained the contraband in question. This decision was affirmed in turn by the Illinois Appellate Court [and the Illinois Supreme Court]. . . .

The Illinois Supreme Court concluded—and we are inclined to agree—that, standing alone, the anonymous letter sent to the Bloomingdale Police Department would not provide the basis for a magistrate's determination that there was probable cause to believe contraband would be found in the Gateses' car and home. The letter provides virtually nothing from which one might conclude that its author is either honest or his information reliable; likewise, the letter gives absolutely no indication of the basis for the writer's predictions regarding the Gateses' criminal activities. . . .

. . . The Illinois Supreme Court, like some others, apparently understood [the test for probable cause from *Aguilar v. Texas* (1964) and *Spinelli v. United States* (1969)] as requiring that the anonymous letter satisfy each of two independent requirements before it could be relied on. . . . [T]he letter, as supplemented by [the police officer's affidavit], first had to adequately reveal the "basis of knowledge" of the letter writer—the particular means by which he came by the information given in his report. Second, it had to provide facts sufficiently establishing either the "veracity" of the . . . informant [i.e., letterwriter], or, alternatively, the "reliability" of the informant's report in this particular case. . . .

We agree with the Illinois Supreme Court that an informant's "veracity," "reliability," and "basis of knowledge" are all highly relevant in determining the value of his report. We do not agree, however, that these elements should be understood as entirely separate and independent requirements to be rigidly exacted in every case. . . . Rather, . . . they should be understood simply as closely intertwined issues that may usefully illuminate the commonsense, practical question whether there is "probable cause" to believe that contraband or evidence is located in a particular place.

This totality-of-circumstances approach is far more consistent with our prior treatment of probable cause than is any rigid demand that specific "tests" be satisfied by every informant's tip. Perhaps the central teaching of our decisions bearing on the probable cause standard is that it is a "practical, nontechnical conception." . . .

As these comments illustrate, probable cause is a fluid concept—turning on the assessment of probabilities in particular factual contexts—not readily, or even usefully, reduced to a neat set of legal rules. . . .

Moreover, the "two-pronged test" directs analysis into two largely independent channels—the informant's "veracity" or "reliability" and his "basis of knowledge." . . . [However,] [t]here are persuasive arguments against according these two elements such independent status. Instead, they are better understood as relevant considerations in the totality-of-circumstances analysis that traditionally has guided probable cause determinations: a deficiency in one may be compensated for, in determining the overall reliability of a tip, by a strong showing as to the other, or by some other indicia of reliability. . . .

Our decisions applying the totality-of-circumstances analysis outlined above have consistently recognized the value of corroboration of details of an informant's tip by independent police work. . . .

Finally, the anonymous letter contained a range of details relating not just to easily obtained facts and conditions existing at the time of the tip, but to future actions by third parties ordinarily not easily predicted. The letter writer's accurate information as to the travel plans of each of the Gateses was of a character likely obtained only from the Gateses themselves, or from someone familiar with their not entirely ordinary travel plans. If the informant had access to accurate information of this type, a magistrate could properly conclude that it was not unlikely that he also had access to reliable information of the Gateses' alleged illegal activities. . . . It is enough that there was a fair probability that the writer of the anonymous letter

(continued)

obtained his entire story either from the Gateses or from someone they trusted. And corroboration of major portions of the letter's predictions provides just this probability. It is apparent, therefore, that the judge issuing the warrant had a "substantial basis for . . . conclud[ing]" that probable cause to search the Gateses' home and car existed. The judgment of the Supreme Court of Illinois therefore must be reversed.

JUSTICE BRENNAN, with whom JUSTICE MARSHALL joins, dissenting.

Although I join Justice Stevens' dissenting opinion and agree with him that the warrant is invalid even under the Court's newly announced "totality of circumstances" test, . . . and I write separately to dissent from the Court's unjustified and ill-advised rejection of the two-prong test for evaluating the validity of a warrant based on hearsay announced in *Aguilar v. Texas* . . . (1964), and refined in *Spinelli v. United States* . . . (1969).

The Court's current Fourth Amendment jurisprudence, as reflected by today's unfortunate decision, patently disregards Justice Jackson's admonition in *Brinegar v. United States* . . . (1949):

> *[Fourth Amendment rights] are not mere second-class rights but belong in the catalog of indispensable freedoms. Among deprivations of rights, none is so effective in cowing a population, crushing the spirit of the individual and putting terror in every heart. Uncontrolled search and seizure is one of the first and most effective weapons in the arsenal of every arbitrary government. . . . But the right to be secure against searches and seizures is one of the most difficult to protect. Since the officers are themselves the chief invaders, there is no enforcement outside of the court. . . .*

While recognizing that a warrant may be based on hearsay, the Court established the following standard [in *Aguilar v. Texas*]:

. . .

> *The magistrate must be informed of some of the underlying circumstances from which the informant concluded that the narcotics were where he claimed they were, and some of the underlying circumstances from which the officer concluded that the informant, whose identity need not be disclosed . . . was "credible" or his information was "reliable." Otherwise, "the inferences from which lead to the complaint" will be drawn not "by a neutral and detached magistrate," as the*

Constitution requires, but instead, by a police officer "engaged in the often competitive enterprise of ferreting out crime" . . . or, as in this case, by an unidentified informant. . . .

The *Aguilar* standard was refined in *Spinelli v. United States* . . . (1969). In *Spinelli*, the Court reviewed a search warrant based on an affidavit that was "more ample," . . . than the one in *Aguilar*. The affidavit in *Spinelli* contained not only a tip from an informant, but also a report of an independent police investigation that allegedly corroborated the informant's tip. . . . Under these circumstances, the Court stated that it was "required to delineate the manner in which *Aguilar*'s two-pronged test should be applied. . . .

The Court held that the *Aguilar* test should be applied to the tip, and approved two additional ways of satisfying that test. First, the Court suggested that if the tip contained sufficient detail describing the accused's criminal activity it might satisfy *Aguilar*'s basis of knowledge prong. . . .

Second, the Court stated that police corroboration of the details of a tip could provide a basis for satisfying *Aguilar*. . . .

Although the rules drawn from the cases discussed above are cast in procedural terms, they advance an important underlying substantive value: Findings of probable cause, and attendant intrusions, should not be authorized unless there is some assurance that the information on which they are based has been obtained in a reliable way by an honest or credible person. . . .

. . . The *Aguilar* and *Spinelli* tests must be applied to anonymous informants' tips, however, if we are to continue to insure that findings of probable cause, and attendant intrusions, are based on information provided by an honest or credible person who has acquired the information in a reliable way. . . .

. . . [C]ontrary to the Court's implicit suggestion, *Aguilar* and *Spinelli* do not stand as an insuperable barrier to the use of even anonymous informants' tips to establish probable cause. . . . It is no justification for rejecting them outright that some courts may have employed an overly technical version of the *Aguilar-Spinelli* standards. . . .

The Court also insists that the *Aguilar-Spinelli* standards must be abandoned because they are inconsistent with the fact that nonlawyers frequently serve as magistrates. . . . To the contrary, the standards help to structure probable-cause inquiries and, properly interpreted, may actually help a nonlawyer magistrate in making a probable-cause determination. . . .

[Justice Stevens wrote a separate dissenting opinion.]

The Requirement of Probable Cause

Recall that the Fourth Amendment requires that "no Warrants shall issue, but upon probable cause, supported by Oath or affirmation, and particularly describing the place to be searched, and the persons or things to be seized." Clearly the warrant requirement is intended to prevent law enforcement officials from using their own discretion to determine whether or not to conduct searches. In theory, the judicial officer who issues warrants serves as a neutral protector of the individual citizen's rights. In reality, however, judicial officers in many courthouses are accustomed to working closely with law enforcement officers. Moreover, judges who are elected to office in states that hold judicial elections often campaign by portraying themselves as "tough on crime." Many of these judges are also former prosecutors who have worked in concert with law enforcement officers to try to stop crime. This may raise questions about the neutrality of many judicial officials who are empowered to approve warrants.

In addition, the judicial officers typically make quick decisions based solely on information the police provide. All of these factors combine to create a situation in which it is difficult for the warrant approval process to achieve its idealized role. In addition, we will learn from *United States v. Leon* (1984) in Chapter 4 that a warrant that is not supported by probable cause can still result in a permissible search and seizure of evidence as long as the police officers acted in "good faith." Do these practical factors mean that the protections purported to be provided by the Fourth Amendment's warrant requirement do not actually keep people from being subjected to searches based on weak justifications? Should any rules or procedures be changed to strengthen the power of the warrant requirement as a protection for (in the Fourth Amendment's words) "the right of the people to be secure in their persons, papers, and effects, against unreasonable searches and seizures"?

In *Gates* the Supreme Court turned away from the two-part test in order to embrace a more flexible **"totality of circumstances" test.** The Court's opinion indicated that "basis of knowledge" and "veracity" remain as important considerations, but "a deficiency in one may be compensated for, in determining the overall reliability of a tip, by a strong showing as to the other, or by some other indicia of reliability. . . ." In effect, the Court's decision gave judicial officers greater discretion to make a determination about the existence of "probable cause." Rather than requiring these officials to ensure that each of two required components was fulfilled, the judicial officers could make a more generalized determination about whether the evidence was both sufficient and reliable enough to justify a warrant. The problem of judicial officers' use of discretion in issuing warrants is further illuminated by the above box that examines the probable cause requirement.

EXECUTING A SEARCH WARRANT

After the search warrant has been issued, the officers must carry out the search. One of the key questions that arises in initiating a search is whether the officers must knock on the door of the premises or whether the warrant justifies a forced entry that will surprise the occupants. The issue is important because there are obviously risks if the occupants know that the police have arrived

Wilson v. Arkansas, 514 U.S. 927 (1995)

JUSTICE THOMAS delivered the opinion for the unanimous Court.

At the time of the framing, the common law of search and seizure recognized a law enforcement officer's authority to break open doors of a dwelling, but generally indicated that he first ought to announce his presence and authority. In this case, we hold that this common-law "knock and announce" principle forms a part of the reasonableness inquiry under the Fourth Amendment. . . .

. . . [P]olice officers applied for and obtained warrants to search [Wilson's] home and to arrest both [Wilson and her housemate]. Affidavits filed in support of the warrants set forth the details of the narcotics transactions [involving sales by Wilson to a police informant] and stated that [the housemate] had previously been convicted of arson and firebombing. The search was conducted later that afternoon.

Police officers found the main door to [Wilson's] home open. While opening an unlocked screen door and entering the residence, they identified themselves as police officers and stated that they had a warrant. Once inside the home, the officers seized marijuana, methamphetamine, valium, narcotics paraphernalia, a gun, and ammunition. They also found [Wilson] in the bathroom, flushing marijuana down the toilet. [Wilson and her housemate] were arrested and charged with delivery of marijuana, delivery of methamphetamine, possession of drug paraphernalia, and possession of marijuana.

Before trial, [Wilson] filed a motion to suppress the evidence seized during the search. [Wilson] asserted that the search was invalid on various grounds, including that the officers had failed to "knock and announce" before entering her home. The trial court summarily denied the suppression motion. After a jury trial, petitioner was convicted of all charges and sentenced to 32 years in prison. . . .

We granted certiorari to resolve the conflict among the lower courts as to whether the common-law knock-and-announce principle forms a part of the Fourth Amendment reasonableness inquiry. . . . We hold that it does. . . .

The common-law knock-and-announce principle was woven quickly into the fabric of early American law. Most of the States that ratified the Fourth Amendment had enacted constitutional provisions or statutes generally incorporating English common law. . . .

Our own cases have acknowledged that the common-law principle of announcement is "embedded in Anglo-American law," . . . but we have never

and are about to conduct a search. Some people involved in criminal activity may endanger the lives of police officers by picking up a weapon and attacking the officers as they come through the door. In addition, there is a risk that people on the premises will destroy the evidence the police are seeking. For example, news reports commonly describe drug traffickers attempting to flush drugs down the toilet as officers come through the door to make arrests and conduct a search. When officers have the element of surprise, they may be more likely to avoid defensive attacks that might otherwise await them. Moreover, they increase the likelihood that they will find the evidence they seek.

The "Knock and Announce" Principle

The Supreme Court addressed the issue of officers' entry under the authority of a warrant in *Wilson v. Arkansas* (1995). As you read Justice Clarence Thomas's opinion in the accompanying box, ask yourself whether the Court announces an appropriate rule in the case.

In *Wilson,* a unanimous Supreme Court recognized the common law **"knock and announce" principle** as a required component of judges' determi-

squarely held this principle is an element of the reasonableness inquiry under the Fourth Amendment. We now so hold. Given the longstanding common-law endorsement of the practice of announcement, we have little doubt that the Framers of the Fourth Amendment thought that the method of an officer's entry into a dwelling was among the factors to be considered in assessing the reasonableness of a search or seizure. Contrary to the decision below [by the Arkansas Supreme Court], we hold that in some circumstances an officer's unannounced entry into a home might be unreasonable under the Fourth Amendment.

This is not to say, of course, that every entry must be preceded by an announcement. The Fourth Amendment's flexible requirement of reasonableness should not be read to mandate a rigid rule of announcement that ignores countervailing law enforcement interests. As even [Wilson] concedes, the common-law principle of announcement was never stated as an inflexible rule requiring announcement under all circumstances. . . .

. . . The common-law principle gradually was applied to cases involving felonies, but at the same time the courts continued to recognize that under certain circumstances the presumption in favor of announcement necessarily would give way to contrary considerations.

. . . [C]ourts acknowledged that the presumption in favor of announcement would yield under circumstances presenting a threat of physical violence . . . . Similarly, courts held that an officer may dispense with announcement in cases where a prisoner escapes from him and retreats to his dwelling. . . . Proof of "demand and refusal" [i.e., demand by the police that the door be opened that is refused by those inside] was deemed unnecessary in such cases because it would be "senseless ceremony" to require an officer in pursuit of a recently escaped arrestee to make an announcement prior to breaking the door to retake him. Finally, courts have indicated that unannounced entry may be justified where police officers have reason to believe that evidence would likely be destroyed if advance notice were given. . . .

We need not attempt a comprehensive catalog of the relevant countervailing factors here. For now, we leave to the lower courts the task of determining the circumstances under which an unannounced entry is reasonable under the Fourth Amendment. We simply hold that although a search or seizure of a dwelling might be constitutionally defective if police officers enter without prior announcement, law enforcement interests may also establish the reasonableness of the unannounced entry. . . .

[The case was remanded to the Arkansas courts to determine whether the circumstances of the search justified the failure to knock and announce as a reasonable course of action.]

nations of whether a search was reasonable. This appears to create a presumption in favor of expecting police officers to knock on the door and announce their presence before coming through the door. However, the Court explicitly recognized that there may be circumstances in which other factors outweigh the presumption that officers should knock and announce before entering. The Court specifically mentioned several circumstances in which the officers may be able to justify an unannounced entry in executing a search warrant. First, situations posing the threat of physical violence can outweigh the knock-and-announce requirement. Similarly, situations in which officers are seeking to recapture an escaped prisoner may not require an announced entry. Finally, police may enter without knocking when evidence might be destroyed if advance notice is given. The Court specifically declined, however, to say that these were the only situations in which officers could make a direct entry. In effect, the Court permits lower-court judges to make discretionary decisions about whether the circumstances of each search justify the officers' failure to knock and announce.

Bear in mind that these disputes will arise after the search has occurred and the defendant is seeking to have evidence excluded for being improperly obtained. Thus officers have time to think about and present a clear set of reasons

Richards v. Wisconsin, 520 U.S. 385 (1997)

JUSTICE STEVENS delivered the opinion for the unanimous Court.

. . .

In this case, the Wisconsin Supreme Court concluded that police officers are never required to knock and announce their presence when executing a search warrant in a felony drug investigation. . . . We disagree with the court's conclusion that the Fourth Amendment permits a blanket exception to the knock and announce requirement for this entire category of criminal activity. But because the evidence presented to support the officers' actions in this case establishes that the decision not to knock and announce was a reasonable one under the circumstances, we affirm the judgment of the Wisconsin court.

On December 31, 1991, police officers in Madison, Wisconsin, obtained a warrant to search Steiney Richards' hotel room for drugs and related paraphernalia. The search warrant was the culmination of an investigation that had uncovered substantial evidence that Richards was one of several individuals dealing drugs out of hotel rooms in Madison. The police requested a warrant that would have given advance authorization for a "no knock" entry into the hotel room, but the magistrate explicitly deleted those portions of the warrant.

The officers arrived at the hotel room at 3:40 A.M. Officer Pharo, dressed as a maintenance man, led the team. With him were several plainclothes officers and at least one man in uniform. Officer Pharo knocked on Richards' door and, responding to the query from inside the room, stated that he was the maintenance man. With the chain still on the door, Richards cracked it open. Although there is some dispute as to what occurred next, Richards acknowledges that when he opened the door he saw a man in uniform standing behind Officer Pharo. . . . He quickly slammed the door closed and, after waiting two or three seconds, the officers began kicking and ramming the door to gain entry to the locked room. At trial, the officers testified that they identified themselves as police while they were kicking the door in. When they finally did break into the room, the officers caught Richards trying to escape through the window. They also found cash and cocaine hidden in plastic bags above the bathroom ceiling tiles.

Richards sought to have the evidence from his hotel room suppressed on the ground that the officers had failed to knock and announce their presence prior to forcing entry into the room. . . .

We recognize in *Wilson [v. Arkansas]* that the knock and announce requirement could give sway "under circumstances presenting a threat of physical violence," or "where police officers have reason to believe that evidence would likely be destroyed if advance notice were given." . . . It is indisputable

that they hope will persuade the judge that an unannounced search was justified. If officers are not professional and ethical, they may be tempted to manufacture reasons for their failure to knock and announce. For example, if they find a gun during the search, they may make an after-the-fact assertion that they had reason to fear that a firearm might be in the possession of the occupants of the premises. By contrast, they might have had no knowledge or reasonable suspicion about the presence of weapons at the time they initiated the search. In fact, they might have believed that no one was present on the premises at the time they entered. As with other aspects of the Bill of Rights, if justice system officials are not honest and ethical, they will diminish the intended protections provided for individuals by the Constitution.

The Court gave further attention to the importance of the "knock and announce" principle and to the circumstances in which an unannounced entry may be approved in *Richards v. Wisconsin* (1997). As you read the case excerpt in the accompanying box, ask yourself whether the Court has placed a limitation on police officers' authority to gain immediate entry in order to conduct a search.

that felony drug investigations may frequently involve both of these circumstances. The question we must resolve is whether this fact justifies dispensing with case by case evaluation of the manner in which a search was executed.

The Wisconsin [Supreme Court] explained its blanket exception [to the knock-and-announce principle] as necessitated by the special circumstances of today's drug culture, . . . and the State asserted at oral argument that the blanket exception was reasonable in "felony drug cases because of the convergence in a violent and dangerous form of commerce of weapons and the destruction of drugs." But creating exceptions to the knock and announce rule based on the "culture" surrounding a general category of criminal behavior presents at least two serious concerns.

First, the exception contains considerable overgeneralization. . . . For example, a search could be conducted at a time when the only individuals present in a residence have no connection with the drug activity and thus will be unlikely to threaten officers or destroy evidence. . . . In those situations, the asserted governmental interests in preserving evidence and maintaining safety may not outweigh the individual privacy interests intruded upon by a no knock entry. Wisconsin's blanket rule impermissibly insulates these cases from judicial review.

A second difficulty with permitting a criminal category exception to the knock and announce requirement is that the reasons for creating an exception in one category can, relatively easily, be applied to others. Armed bank robbers, for example, are, by definition, likely to have weapons, and the fruits of their crime may be destroyed without too much difficulty. If a per se exception were allowed for each category of criminal investigation that included a considerable—albeit hypothetical—risk of danger to officers or destruction of evidence, the knock and announce element of the Fourth Amendment's reasonableness requirement would be meaningless.

. . . [I]n each case, it is the duty of the court confronted with the question to determine whether the facts and circumstances of the particular entry justified dispensing with the knock and announce requirement.

In order to justify a "no knock" entry, the police must have a reasonable suspicion that knocking and announcing their presence, under the particular circumstances, would be dangerous or futile, or that it would inhibit the effective investigation of the crime by, for example, allowing the destruction of evidence. This standard—as opposed to a probable cause requirement—strikes the appropriate balance between the legitimate law enforcement concerns at issue in the execution of search warrants and the individual privacy interests affected by no knock entries. . . .

Although we reject the Wisconsin court's blanket exception to the knock and announce requirement, we conclude that the officers' no knock entry into Richards' hotel room did not violate the Fourth Amendment. We agree with the trial court . . . that the circumstances in this case show that the officers had a reasonable suspicion that Richards might destroy evidence if given further opportunity to do so. . . .

Notice that the law enforcement officers in this case had sought a so-called no-knock warrant through which they would be authorized by the judicial officer to make an unannounced entry to executing the warrant. What is the legality of a no-knock warrant after the *Richards* decision? The Court did not address the issue directly, but the decision's emphasis on situational factors makes it unclear if a judicial officer can give prior authorization for an unannounced entry. An unannounced entry must be based on officers' "reasonable suspicions" that there is a real threat of violence or loss of evidence from knocking. It is not clear what constitutes "reasonable suspicions." Obviously, officers must make a discretionary decision based on their prior knowledge of the criminal activity and the contextual factors they encounter. This is a significant discretionary judgment because it affects the privacy of people in their homes.

In addition, all searches can create their own risks to the people on the premises being searched. These risks may be heightened in cases where the entry is unannounced. On October 4, 2000 in Lebanon, Tennessee, police officers made a drug raid on a house. Unfortunately, they meant to search the house next door. Instead, they entered the home of an innocent couple where a 61-year-old man grabbed his shotgun when he saw men coming into his house. He fired at the police and they fired back. He was shot three times and died shortly thereafter at the hospital.[2] In this case, the officers say they knocked on the door as they entered. Even if that's true, because they entered immediately as they knocked, the residents had every reason to believe that robbers were invading their home. The situation illustrates the risks that can happen when there are mistakes. Sometimes the mistakes come from relying on faulty information from informants. In other situations, elderly people have suffered heart attacks when their homes were mistakenly entered by police executing an unannounced search. Citizens awakened by the sound of people breaking into their homes have good reason to be stricken with fear.

Is the knock-and-announce requirement meaningful? Because officers may knock and yell "Open up! Police!" as they break down a door, the actual impact may be no different than if the police made an unannounced entry. The occupants have no time to react. They may be confused about who is entering the premises by force. Much depends on how the police actually implement the requirement. Do they pause a few seconds to give the people inside the opportunity to open the door voluntarily? Or do they automatically crash through the door? The events that occur during each search depend on the attitudes of the officers and the officers' perceptions about the potential for danger or the need for surprise. Thus the discretionary elements that determine how a search is conducted may be more important for how people are treated than is any court decision defining or reinforcing a knock-and-announce requirement.

ARREST ISSUES

As discussed in Chapter 2, traditional common law rules permitted police to make arrests without warrants in two situations. First, they can use their discretion to make arrests when they have probable cause to believe that a person is committing or has committed a felony. Second, officers may make arrests without warrants for misdemeanors committed in their presence. The Supreme Court has also considered if warrantless arrests are permissible in other circumstances. As you read the case excerpt from *Warden v. Hayden* (1967) in the accompanying box, try to identify the justification for the officers' actions.

In *Warden v. Hayden*, the Supreme Court focused on the "exigencies" that required the police officers to take the actions they did. As we will see in other cases, the Supreme Court often points to **exigent circumstances** to justify quick police actions that arguably clash with the words of the Bill of Rights. Exigent circumstances exist in a situation in which urgent, immediate action is needed in order to protect an important public interest. In this case, the important public interest that justified the warrantless entry and arrest was the need to protect the lives of police officers and others who might be endangered by an armed robber. Thus the court has endorsed warrantless arrests and searches when officers are in "hot pursuit" of fleeing felony suspects. In other cases, we will see that the need to keep criminal suspects from destroying valuable evidence can also constitute exigent circumstances in some situations.

The concept of "exigent circumstances" is vague and subject to interpretation. Officers must make quick decisions about when to enter a house to ef-

C A S E	*Warden v. Hayden*, 387 U.S. 294 (1967)

JUSTICE BRENNAN delivered the opinion of the Court.

. . .

About 8 A.M. on March 17, 1962, an armed robber entered the business premises of the Diamond Cab Company in Baltimore, Maryland. He took some $363 and ran. Two cab drivers in the vicinity attracted by the shouts of "Holdup," followed the man to 2111 Cocoa Lane. . . . [The drivers radioed a description to their dispatcher.] The dispatcher relayed the information to police who were proceeding to the scene of the robbery. Within minutes, police arrived at the house in a number of patrol cars. An officer knocked and announced their presence, Mrs. Hayden answered, and the officers told her they believed that a robber had entered the house, and asked to search the house. She offered no objection.

The officers spread out through the first and second floors and the cellar in search of the robber. Hayden was found in an upstairs bedroom feigning sleep. He was arrested when the officers on the first floor and in the cellar reported that no other man was in the house. Meanwhile an officer was attracted to an adjoining bathroom by the noise of running water, and discovered a shotgun and a pistol in the flush tank; another officer who, according to the District Court, "was searching the cellar for a man and money" found in a washing machine a jacket and trousers of the type the fleeing man was said to have worn. A clip of ammunition for the pistol and a cap were found under the mattress of Hayden's bed, and ammunition for the shotgun was found in a bureau drawer in Hayden's room. All these items of evidence were introduced against respondent at his trial.

We agree with the Court of Appeals that neither the entry without a warrant to search for the robber, nor the search for him without a warrant, was invalid. Under the circumstances of this case, "the exigencies of the situation made that course imperative." . . . The police were informed that an armed robbery had taken place, and that the suspect had entered 2111 Cocoa Lane less than five minutes before they reached it. They acted reasonably when they entered the house and began to search for a man of the description they had been given and for weapons which he used in the robbery or might use against them. The Fourth Amendment does not require police officers to delay in the course of an investigation if to do so would gravely endanger their lives or the lives of others. Speed here was essential, and only a thorough search of the house for persons and weapons could have ensured that Hayden was the only man present and that police had control of all weapons which could be used against them or to effect an escape. . . .

fect an arrest or conduct a warrantless search. It is possible for them to perceive the existence of dangers that do not actually exist. For example, what if the cab drivers mistakenly reported that the suspected robber was armed with a shotgun when, in fact, he carried only an umbrella but no weapons? Would the officers' warrantless entry into the home still be justified? Do exigent circumstances exist when officers mistakenly believe that a danger exists, or must an actual danger to the public be posed by the situation? These are difficult questions that end up being decided by judges. Many judges are reluctant to second-guess police officers who must make immediate decisions in moments of perceived danger. Other judges place greater emphasis on protecting individuals' rights against intrusions based on police errors. There are also risks that unethical police officers may not be entirely truthful in later explaining why they neglected to obtain a warrant. An officer may, for example, claim that she thought the suspect had a gun in his pocket to justify an arrest that really occurred because the officer had a strong hunch that the person was involved in a crime. How can a judge who hears testimony about the incident weeks later in court possibly know what really happened when an arrest or search occurred? Thus the Supreme Court's decision to permit the police to act quickly in exigent circumstances necessarily rests on a need to trust officers to act professionally and ethically. Officers are given significant discretionary authority. If they misuse that authority, it is not always possible for judges to recognize those misdeeds later.

Minor Offenses

The Supreme Court has expanded the discretionary authority of police officers to make arrests. In 2001 a narrow majority of justices decided that police officers can make a warrantless arrest for a fine-only traffic offense (*Atwater v. City of Lago Vista*). Such an arrest is not an unreasonable seizure. A Texas mother driving home from her children's soccer practice was stopped by a police officer because she and her children were not wearing seat belts. Failing to wear a seat belt is a violation of Texas law that has a maximum punishment of a $50 fine. The officer handcuffed the driver and took her to jail where she was placed in a cell for an hour before she appeared before a judge and entered a no-contest plea to the seat-belt charge. Presumably the children, ages 3 and 5, would have been forced to accompany their mother to the jail if a friend of the mother's had not appeared on the scene and taken the children away to care for them. Thus such an arrest can have significant consequences for the arrestee and for people accompanying the arrestee. The woman later filed a lawsuit against the officer and the city government alleging a violation of her Fourth Amendment right against unreasonable seizures. A federal appellate court found that such police actions constituted a violation of her rights, but that decision was later overturned by full appellate court when it heard the case again while sitting *en banc* (*Atwater v. City of Lago Vista*, 1999, 5th Circuit, U.S. Court of Appeals). The U.S. Supreme Court supported the second appellate court decision and, in the eyes of most observers, effectively expanded police officers' discretionary authority to make arrests. This expansion may not have broad practical consequences because many police officers may not wish to fill out the necessary paperwork and conduct the other processing steps involved in effectuating an arrest when they are merely issuing a traffic citation. However, for some individuals, such a decision will have a major impact if they are among the relatively few people selected by police officers for arrest in such circumstances. As you read the brief case excerpt in the box "*Atwater v. City of Lago Vista* (2001)," ask yourself: What is the justification for the majority's decision?

Use of Force

Another issue affecting arrests concerns the level of force that officers are permitted to use in order to effectuate an arrest. Officers can use force in self-defense, and they use necessary nonlethal force to control individuals who are threatening the safety of officers and others. Thus uncooperative suspects often find themselves pinned to the ground while handcuffs are affixed, or they may be subject to painful (but not injurious) wrist and hand holds that officers use to incapacitate people resisting arrest. Because of the risk of successful lawsuits for significant sums of money against officers who injure or kill people unnecessarily, police departments have gradually eliminated the

| CASE | *Atwater v. City of Lago Vista*, 532 U.S. 318 (2001) |

[*Officer Bart Turek saw Gail Atwater driving her pickup truck with her 3-year-old son and 5-year-old daughter unbelted in the front seat. According to Atwater, he approached her vehicle and yelled that she was going to go to jail. She asked to take her frightened children to a friend's nearby house, but the officer refused. A friend came by and took the children before the officer handcuffed Atwater, drove her to the police station, took her mug shot, and placed her alone in a cell for one hour before she appeared in court and was released on $310 bond. Atwater pleaded no contest to the seat-belt offense and was fined $50. She subsequently sued the officer and the City of Lago Vista for allegedly violating her civil rights by subjecting her to an unreasonable seizure under the Fourth Amendment.*]

JUSTICE SOUTER delivered the opinion of the Court.

The question is whether the Fourth Amendment forbids a warrantless arrest for a minor criminal offense, such as a misdemeanor seatbelt violation punishable only by a fine. We hold that it does not.

. . . Violation of [the Texas law requiring seat belts for front-seat occupants of motor vehicles and for any small child riding in front] is a misdemeanor punishable by a fine not less than $25 or more than $50. . . . Texas law expressly authorizes "[a]ny peace officer [to] arrest a person" found committing a violation of these seat belt laws, . . . although it permits police to issue citations in lieu of arrest. . . .

. . . Atwater's specific contention is that founding-era common-law rules forbade peace officers to make warrantless misdemeanor arrests except in cases of breach of the peace, a category she claims was then understood narrowly as covering only those nonfelony offenses involving or tending toward violence. . . . Although her historical argument is by no means insubstantial, it ultimately fails.

. . . [T]he founding-era common-law rules were not nearly as clear as Atwater claims; on the contrary, the common-law commentators (as well as sparsely reported cases) reached divergent conclusions with respect to officers' warrantless misdemeanor arrest power. Moreover, in the years leading up to American independence, Parliament repeatedly extended express warrantless arrest authority to cover misdemeanor-level offenses not amounting to or involving any violent breach of the peace. . . .

[After reviewing in detail the writings of English judges and legal scholars from the colonial era,] [w]e thus find disagreement, not unanimity, among both the common-law jurists and the text-writers who sought to pull the cases together and summarize accepted practice. Having reviewed the relevant English decisions, as well as English and colonial American legal treatises, legal dictionaries, and procedure manuals, we simply are not convinced that Atwater's is the correct, or even necessarily the better, reading of the common-law history. . . .

. . . Atwater has cited no particular evidence that those who framed and ratified the Fourth Amendment sought to limit peace officers' warrantless misdemeanor arrest authority to instances of actual breach of the peace, and our own review of the recent and respected compilations of framing-era documentary history has likewise failed to reveal any such design. . . .

At first glance, Atwater's argument may seem to respect the values of clarity and simplicity, so far as she claims that the Fourth Amendment generally forbids warrantless arrests for minor crimes not accompanied by violence or some demonstrable threat of it (whether minor crime be defined as a fine-only traffic offense, a fine-only offense more generally, or a misdemeanor). But the claim is not ultimately so simple, nor could it be, for complications arise the moment we begin to think about the possible applications of the several criteria Atwater proposes for drawing a line between minor crimes with limited arrest authority and others not so restricted.

One line, she suggests, might be between jailable and fine-only offenses, between those for which conviction could result in commitment and those for which it could not. The trouble with this distinction, of course, is that an officer on the street might not be able to tell. It is not merely that we cannot expect every police officer to know the details of frequently complex penalty schemes . . . , but that penalties for ostensibly identical conduct can vary on account of facts difficult (if not impossible) to know at the scene of an arrest. Is this the first offense or is the suspect a repeat offender? Is the weight of the marijuana a gram above or a gram below the fine-only line? . . .

. . . Atwater's rule therefore would not only place police in an almost impossible spot but would guarantee increased litigation over many of the arrests that would occur. For all these reasons, Atwater's

(continued)

various distinctions between permissible and impermissible arrests for minor crimes strike us as "very unsatisfactory line[s] to require police officers to draw on a moment's notice." . . .

Accordingly, we confirm today what our prior cases have intimated: the standard of probable cause applies to all arrests, without the need to balance the interests and circumstances involved in particular situations. . . . If an officer has probable cause to believe that an individual has committed even a very minor criminal offense in his presence, he may, without violating the Fourth Amendment, arrest the offender. . . .

JUSTICE O'CONNOR, with whom JUSTICES STEVENS, GINSBURG, and BREYER join, dissenting.

The Fourth Amendment guarantees the right to be free from unreasonable searches and seizures. The Court recognizes that the arrest of Gail Atwater was a pointless indignity that served no discernible state interest, . . . and yet holds that her arrest was constitutionally permissible. Because the Court's position is inconsistent with the explicit guarantee of the Fourth Amendment, I dissent. . . .

We have often looked to the common law in evaluating the reasonableness, for Fourth Amendment purposes, of police activity. . . . But history is just one of the tools we use in conducting the reasonableness inquiry. . . . And when history is inconclusive, as the majority amply demonstrates it is in this case, . . . we will evaluate the search or seizure under traditional standards of reasonableness by assessing, on the one hand, the degree to which it intrudes upon an individual's privacy and, on the other, the degree to which it is needed for the promotion of legitimate governmental interests. . . . In other words, in determining reasonableness, "[e]ach case is to be decided on its own facts and circumstances." . . .

The majority gives a brief nod to this bedrock principle of our Fourth Amendment jurisprudence, and even acknowledges that Atwater's claim to live free of pointless indignity and confinement clearly outweighs anything the City can raise against it specific to her case. . . . But instead of remedying this imbalance, the majority allows itself to be swayed by the worry that every discretionary judgment in the field [will] be converted into an occasion for constitutional review. . . . It therefore mints a new rule that "[i]f an officer has probable cause to believe that an individual has committed even a very minor criminal offense in his presence, he may,

without violating the Fourth Amendment, arrest the offender." . . . This rule is not only unsupported by our precedent, but runs contrary to the principles that lie at the core of the Fourth Amendment. . . .

. . . Justifying a full arrest by the quantum of evidence that justifies a traffic stop even though the offender cannot ultimately be imprisoned for her conduct defies any sense of proportionality and is in serious tension with the Fourth Amendment's proscription of unreasonable seizures.

A custodial arrest exacts an obvious toll on an individual's liberty and privacy, even when the period of custody is relatively brief. The arrestee is subject to a full search of her person and confiscation of her possessions. . . . If the arrestee is the occupant of a car, the entire passenger compartment of the car, including packages therein, is subject to search as well. See *New York v. Belton* . . . (1981). The arrestee may be detained for up to 48 hours without having a magistrate determine whether there in fact was probable cause for the arrest. See *County of Riverside v. McLaughlin* . . . (1991). Because people arrested for all types of violent and nonviolent offenses may be housed together awaiting such review, this detention period is potentially dangerous. . . . And once the period of custody is over, the fact of the arrest is a permanent part of the public record. . . .

. . . If the State has decided that a fine, and not imprisonment, is the appropriate punishment for an offense, the State's interest in taking a person suspected of committing that [fine-only] offense into custody is surely limited, at best. . . .

Because a full custodial arrest is such a severe intrusion on an individual's liberty, its reasonableness hinges on the degree to which it is needed for the promotion of legitimate governmental interests. . . . In light of the availability of citations to promote a State's interests when a fine-only offense has been committed, I cannot concur in a rule which deems a full custodial arrest to be reasonable in every circumstance. Giving police officers constitutional carte blanche to effect an arrest whenever there is probable cause to believe a fine-only misdemeanor has been committed is irreconcilable with the Fourth Amendment's command that seizures be reasonable. Instead, I would require that when there is probable cause to believe that a fine-only offense has been committed, the police officer should issue a citation unless the officer is able to point to specific and articulable facts which, taken together with rational inferences from those facts, reasonably warrant [the additional] intrusion of a full custodial arrest.

The majority insists that a bright-line rule [a rule of such clarity that everyone can easily know when and how to apply it] focused on probable cause is necessary to vindicate the State's interest in easily administratable law enforcement rules. . . . Probable cause itself, however, is not a model of precision. The quantum of information which constitutes probable cause evidence which would "warrant a man of reasonable caution in the belief that a [crime] has been committed" must be measured by the facts of the particular case. . . . The rule I propose which merely requires a legitimate reason for the decision to escalate the seizure into a full custodial arrest thus does not undermine an otherwise clear and simple rule. . . .

While clarity is certainly a value worthy of consideration in our Fourth Amendment jurisprudence, it by no means trumps the values of liberty and privacy at the heart of the Amendment's protections. . . .

At bottom, the majority offers two related reasons why a bright-line rule is necessary: the fear that officers who arrest for fine-only offenses will be subject to personal [section] 1983 liability for the misapplication of a constitutional standard, . . . and the resulting systematic disincentive to arrest where arresting would serve an important societal interest. . . . These concerns are certainly valid, but they are more than adequately resolved by the doctrine of qualified immunity. . . .

In *Anderson v. Creighton* . . . (1987), we made clear that the standard of reasonableness for a search or seizure under the Fourth Amendment is distinct from the standard for reasonableness for qualified immunity purposes. . . . If a law enforcement officer "reasonably but mistakenly conclude[s] that the constitutional predicate for a search or seizure is present, he should not be held personally liable." . . .

The record in this case makes it abundantly clear that Ms. Atwater's arrest was constitutionally unreasonable. . . . [N]either law nor reason supports [the officer's] decision to arrest her instead of simply giving her a citation. The officer's actions cannot sensibly be viewed as a permissible means of balancing Atwater's Fourth Amendment interests with the State's own legitimate interests. . . .

The Court's error, however, does not merely affect the disposition of this case. The *per se* rule that the Court creates has potentially serious consequences for the everyday lives of Americans. A broad range of conduct falls into the category of fine-only misdemeanors. . . .

Such unbounded discretion [for police officers] carries with it grave potential for abuse. The majority takes comfort in the lack of evidence of an epidemic of unnecessary minor-offense arrests. . . . But the relatively small number of published cases dealing with such arrests proves little and should provide little solace. Indeed, as the recent debate over racial profiling demonstrates all too clearly, a relatively minor traffic infraction may often serve as an excuse for stopping and harassing an individual. After today, the arsenal available to any officer extends to a full arrest and the searches permissible concomitant to that arrest. An officer's subjective motivations for making a traffic stop are not relevant considerations in determining the reasonableness of the stop. . . . But it is precisely because these motivations are beyond our purview that we must vigilantly ensure that officers' post-stop actions which are properly within our reach comport with the Fourth Amendment's guarantee of reasonableness.

The Court neglects the Fourth Amendment's express command in the name of administrative ease. In so doing, it cloaks the pointless indignity that Gail Atwater suffered with the mantle of reasonableness. I respectfully dissent.

---

use of many choke holds, which posed excessively great risks of injury and death. Because laws in many jurisdictions permitted police officers to use deadly force to stop fleeing felons, the Supreme Court was forced to consider if there were constitutional limits on the police use of force against felony suspects. As you read *Tennessee v. Garner* (1985) in the box on pp. 94–95, consider whether you agree with the rule created by the Supreme Court.

Note that the Court did not rule out the use of deadly force in *Garner*. It prohibited the traditional permission to use deadly force simply because the police were attempting to stop a fleeing felony suspect. Instead, deadly force can be used only to stop the threat of serious physical harm to the police or the public. Such circumstances are not likely to apply when the officers know

Tennessee v. Garner, 471 U.S. 1 (1985)

JUSTICE WHITE delivered the opinion of the Court.

This case requires us to determine the constitutionality of the use of deadly force to prevent the escape of an apparently unarmed suspected felon. We conclude that such force may not be used unless it is necessary to prevent the escape and the officer has probable cause to believe that the suspect poses a significant threat of death or serious injury to the officer or others.

At about 10:45 P.M. on October 3, 1974, Memphis Police Officers Elton Hymon and Leslie Wright were dispatched to answer a "prowler inside call." Upon arriving at the scene they saw a woman standing on her porch and gesturing toward the adjacent house. She told them she had heard glass breaking and that "they" or "someone" was breaking in next door. While Wright radioed the dispatcher to say that they were on the scene, Hymon went behind the house. He heard a door slam and saw someone run across the backyard. The fleeing suspect, who was appellee-respondent's decedent, Edward Garner, stopped at a 6-foot-high chain link fence at the edge of the yard. With the aid of a flashlight, Hymon was able to see Garner's face and hands. He saw no sign of weapon, and, though not certain, was "reasonably sure" and "figured" that Garner was unarmed. He thought Garner was 17 or 18 years old and about 5'5" or 5'7" tall. While Garner was crouched at the base of the fence, Hymon called out "police, halt" and took a few steps toward him. Garner then began to climb over the fence. Convinced that if Garner made it over the fence he would elude capture, Hymon shot him. The bullet hit Garner in the back of the head. Garner was taken by ambulance to a hospital, where he died on the operating table.

Ten dollars and a purse taken from the house were found on his body.

In using deadly force to prevent the escape, Hymon was acting under the authority of a Tennessee statute and pursuant to a Police Department policy [that permitted the use of deadly force in cases of burglary]. . . . The incident was reviewed by the Memphis Police Firearm's Review Board and presented to a grand jury. Neither took any action. . . .

Whenever an officer restrains the freedom of a person to walk away, he has seized that person. . . . While it is not always clear just when minimal police interference becomes a seizure, . . . there can be no question that apprehension by the use of deadly force is a seizure subject to the reasonableness requirement of the Fourth Amendment.

A police officer may arrest a person if he has probable cause to believe that person committed a crime. . . . Petitioners and appellant argue that if this requirement is satisfied the Fourth Amendment has nothing to say about how that seizure is made. This submission ignores the many cases in which this Court, by balancing the extent of the intrusion against the need for it, has examined the reasonableness of the manner in which a search or seizure is conducted. To determine the constitutionality of a seizure, "[w]e must balance the nature and quality of the intrusion on the individual's Fourth Amendment interests against the importance of the governmental interests alleged to justify intrusion." . . . We have described "the balancing of competing interests" as "the key principle of the Fourth Amendment." . . . Because one of the factors is the extent of the intrusion, it is plain that reasonableness depends on not only when a seizure is made, but also how it is carried out. . . .

that the suspect is unarmed as in the *Garner* case. The decision adds complications to police officers' decision making because they must be very aware of the possibility of being sued if they make an improper decision about the level of force to apply in making an arrest.

Entrapment

Another issue affecting arrests and prosecutions concerns whether law enforcement officers improperly induced someone to commit a crime. If officers' actions led someone, who would otherwise not have committed a crime, to

Applying these principles to particular facts, the Court has held that governmental interests did not support a lengthy detention of luggage [*United States v. Place*, 1983], . . . an airport seizure not "carefully tailored to its underlying justification," [*Florida v. Royer*, 1983], . . . surgery under general anesthesia to obtain evidence [*Winston v. Lee*, 1985], . . . or detention for fingerprinting without probable cause [*Davis v. Mississippi*, 1969]. . . . On the other hand, under the same approach it has upheld the taking of fingernail scrapings from a suspect [*Cupp v. Murphy*, 1973], . . . an unannounced entry into a home to prevent the destruction of evidence [*Ker v. California*, 1963], . . . administrative housing inspections without probable cause to believe that a code violation will be found [*Camara v. Municipal Court*, 1967], . . . and a blood test of a drunken-driving suspect [*Schmerber v. California*, 1966]. . . . In each of these cases, the question was whether the totality of circumstances justified a particular sort of search or seizure.

The same balancing process applied in the cases cited above demonstrates that, notwithstanding probable cause to seize a suspect, an officer may not always do so by killing him. The intrusiveness of a seizure by means of deadly force is unmatched. The suspect's fundamental interest in his own life need not be elaborated upon. The use of deadly force also frustrates the interest of the individual, and of society, in judicial determination of guilt and punishment. Against these interests are ranged governmental interests in effective law enforcement. It is argued that overall violence will be reduced by encouraging the peaceful submission of suspects who know that they may be shot if they flee. Effectiveness in making arrests requires the resort to deadly force, or at least the meaningful threat thereof. . . .

Without in any way disparaging the importance of these goals, we are not convinced that the use of deadly force is a sufficiently productive means of accomplishing them to justify the killing of nonviolent suspects. . . . The use of deadly force is a self-defeating way of apprehending a suspect and so setting the criminal justice mechanism in motion. . . . Petitioners and appellants have not persuaded us that shooting nondangerous fleeing suspects is so vital as to outweigh the suspect's interest in his own life.

The use of deadly force to prevent the escape of all felony suspects, whatever the circumstances, is constitutionally unreasonable. It is not better that all felony suspects die than that they escape. Where the suspect poses no immediate threat to the officer and no threat to others, the harm resulting from failing to apprehend him does not justify the use of deadly force to do so. It is no doubt unfortunate when a suspect who is in sight escapes, but the fact that the police arrive a little late or are a little slower afoot does not always justify killing the suspect. A police officer may not seize an unarmed, nondangerous suspect by shooting him dead. The Tennessee statute is unconstitutional insofar as it authorizes the use of deadly force against such fleeing suspects.

It is not, however, unconstitutional on its face. Where the officer has probable cause to believe that the suspect poses a threat of serious physical harm, either to the officer or to others, it is not constitutionally unreasonable to prevent escape by using deadly force. Thus, if the suspect threatens the officer with a weapon or there is probable cause to believe that he has committed a crime involving the infliction or threatened infliction of serious physical harm, deadly force may be used if necessary to prevent escape, and if, where feasible, some warning has been given. As applied in such circumstances, the Tennessee statute would pass constitutional muster. . . .

break the law, then the defendant can use the defense of **entrapment** to claim that he or she should not be held responsible for the crime. Criminal law is intended to punish people who violated the law through their own motives and actions. There are some circumstances in which courts have determined that the police led people to commit crimes and that the arrest resulted from officers' improper actions.

The entrapment defense is widely available as a matter of statutory law. Congress and state legislatures provide for the defense in the statutes they enact concerning criminal law. There is no constitutional right to be free from entrapment. States are not obligated to provide the defense to suspects and defense. However, because the Due Process Clause has been interpreted historically in a flexible manner, it is possible for attorneys to argue that outrageous police conduct that entraps otherwise innocent citizens and induces them to commit crimes should be considered as a violation of the right to due process. Thus the majority view is that entrapment is a statutory protection.

Because entrapment has a statutory rather than constitutional basis, states can have different tests for determining when entrapment has occurred. Some states have used a subjective test, sometimes referred to as the "predisposition test." This test focuses on the thoughts of the person who committed the crime. In order to determine if entrapment occurred, the test attempts to examine whether the person was predisposed to commit the crime. Such subjective tests can be difficult to apply because they require courts to make an assessment of the thoughts in a specific person's mind at a particular moment in the past. The alternative approach is an objective test that looks at the conduct of the police authorities. In other words, instead of trying to determine whether the individual was predisposed to commit the crime, the court merely examines whether the police officers' conduct was improper or excessive. The objective test asks whether the average reasonable person would have been able to resist the government's inducements to commit a crime.

Entrapment claims are sometimes raised when undercover law enforcement officers pretend to be drug abusers seeking to buy drugs or businesspeople offering bribes to government officials. Although the offer to make a drug sale or a bribe creates the opportunity for a crime to occur, this is generally not entrapment. Officers may create opportunities for crimes to occur, but there is no entrapment when the individual's intentions and voluntary actions lead to the completion of the crime. The situation may be different if the police officers badger the person into dealing drugs or taking a bribe when they do not really want to. Obviously, it is difficult for judges to provide clear definitions of entrapment. And it is even more difficult for officers to always recognize the line between properly creating opportunities to catch criminal actions and improperly inducing someone to commit a crime. As you read *Jacobson v. United States* (1992) in the accompanying box, consider whether you agree with the Court's decision.

CONCLUSION

The decisions and actions of justice system officials in securing and executing warrants and in making investigatory stops and arrests significantly impact people's Fourth Amendment rights against unreasonable searches and seizures. The Supreme Court has emphasized the need for probable cause to support warrants and arrests and the need for reasonable suspicion to underlie most seizures. However, consistent with the balancing approach characteristic of judicial decision making affecting the Fourth Amendment, the Supreme Court has also attempted to give law enforcement officers sufficient flexibility to deal adequately with situations they may face. Thus the Court has, for example, permitted warrantless arrests and searches when police are in "hot pursuit" of

| **C A S E** | *Jacobson v. United States*, 503 U.S. 540 (1992) |

JUSTICE WHITE delivered the opinion of the Court.

. . .

In February 1984, a 56-year-old veteran-turned-farmer who supported his elderly father in Nebraska, ordered two magazines and a brochure from a California adult bookstore. . . .

The young men depicted in the magazines were not engaged in sexual activity, and petitioner's receipt of the magazines was legal under both federal and Nebraska law. Within three months, the law with respect to child pornography changed. . . . In the very month that the new provision became law, postal inspectors found petitioner's name on the mailing list of the California bookstore that had mailed him [the magazines]. There followed over the next 2$\frac{1}{2}$ years repeated efforts of two Government agencies, through five fictitious organizations and a bogus pen pal, to explore petitioner's willingness to break the new law by ordering sexually explicit photographs of children through the mail.

[The Postal Service sent Jacobson repeated mailings from fictitious consumer research companies and lobbying organizations seeking to repeal laws on sexual materials. There were also letters from a postal employee posing as a pen pal interested in sexually explicit materials. After 26 months, Jacobson responded to another fictitious solicitation from the Postal Service by ordering a pornographic magazine depicting young boys. He was indicted and convicted for violating the child pornography statute.]

. . .

There can be no dispute about the evils of child pornography or the difficulties that laws and law enforcement have encountered in eliminating it. . . . Likewise, there can be no dispute that the Government may use undercover agents to enforce the law. . . .

In their zeal to enforce the law, however, Government agents may not originate a criminal design, implant in an innocent person's mind the disposition to commit a criminal act, and then induce commission of the crime so that the Government may prosecute. . . . Where the Government has induced an individual to break the law and the defense of entrapment is at issue, as it was in this case, the prosecution must prove beyond reasonable doubt that the defendant was disposed to commit the criminal act prior to first being approached by Government agents. . . .

. . . Had the agents in this case simply offered the petitioner the opportunity to order child pornography through the mails, and petitioner—who must be presumed to know the law—had promptly availed himself of this criminal opportunity, it is unlikely that his entrapment defense would have warranted a jury instruction. . . .

But that is not what happened here. By the time petitioner finally placed his order, he had already been the target of 26 months of repeated mailings and communications from Government agents and fictitious organizations. Therefore, although he had become predisposed to break the law by May 1987, it is our view that the Government did not prove that this predisposition was independent, and not the product of the attention that the Government had directed at petitioner since January 1985. . . .

Law enforcement officials go too far when they "implant in the mind of an innocent person the disposition to commit the alleged offense and induce its commission in order that they may prosecute." . . . [W]e are "unable to conclude that it was the intention of the Congress in enacting this statute that its processes of detection and enforcement should be abused by the instigation of government officials of an act on the part of persons otherwise innocent in order to lure them to its commission and to punish them." . . . When the Government's quest for convictions leads to the apprehension of an otherwise law-abiding citizen who, if left to his own devices, likely would have never run afoul of the law, the courts should intervene. . . .

[The Court reversed Jacobson's conviction.]

felony suspects. Because new kinds of situations can develop that call into question the justification for a warrant or an arrest in a particular context, courts must regularly address Fourth Amendment issues each year without any realistic hope that a final, clear set of rules will handle all future circumstances that may arise.

SUMMARY

- Arrests are seizures that must be supported by probable cause. Investigatory stops that are seizures must be supported by reasonable suspicion or a strong governmental interest. Other interactions between the police and the public, such as asking questions of passersby, do not constitute seizures because people are free to terminate the encounter and leave.

- The Fourth Amendment presents specific requirements for warrants. Warrants must be supported by probable cause and describe with particularity the places to be searched and the things to be seized.

- Probable cause is defined by a totality-of-circumstances test that includes consideration of sources and reliability of evidence indicating that there is a strong likelihood that evidence of a crime will be discovered in a search or that a person committed a criminal offense.

- Warrants should normally be issued by a neutral official, which can be a regular judge, a U.S. magistrate judge, or a state magistrate. The Supreme Court has also recognized circumstances in which court clerks can issue warrants.

- Officers executing a warrant must normally knock and announce their presence before entering, although there may be circumstances in which they can make unannounced entries if there is a reasonable basis to believe that physical danger or the destruction of evidence will result from knocking and announcing.

- Government monitoring of telephone conversations and other electronic communications, even those that take place in public places such as phone booths, is covered by the Fourth Amendment because people have a reasonable expectation of privacy in such communications.

- Officers may make warrantless arrests when justified by exigent circumstances such as the "hot pursuit" of a fleeing felony suspect.

- Officers may make arrests whenever there is probable cause to believe that a person has committed a crime, even if it is a fine-only offense.

- Officers may use reasonable force in making arrests, but they may not use deadly force against unarmed, nondangerous suspects, even if those suspects are fleeing from the scene of a felony. Deadly force can be used only when suspects pose serious physical threats to officers or the public.

- Arrests and prosecutions can be invalidated if the officers entrapped someone by inducing the person to commit a crime that he or she otherwise would not have committed.

Key Terms

affidavit   Written statement of fact, supported by oath or affirmation, that police officers may submit to judicial officers to fulfill the requirements of "probable cause" for obtaining a warrant.

entrapment   A defense to a criminal charge when police officers improperly induce someone to commit a crime.

exigent circumstances   A situation in which a threat to public safety or the risk that evidence will be destroyed justifies officers' quick actions in searching, arresting, or questioning suspects without obtaining a warrant or following other usual rules of criminal procedure.

"knock and announce" principle   Principle drawn from English common law and regarded by the Supreme Court as a component of the Fourth Amendment that requires police officers to knock and announce their presence before entering a premises to conduct a search, unless there is reasonable suspicion that the announcement will create a risk of physical harm or destruction of evidence.

magistrate   A judicial officer, often an attorney working on a part-time basis, with limited responsibilities for processing minor criminal and civil cases and for handling preliminary matters in serious criminal cases, including the issuance of warrants.

probable cause   An amount of evidence establishing that it is more likely than not that evidence will be found in a specific location or that a specific person is guilty of a crime. The Constitution requires prosecutors and police officers to show a judge enough evidence to establish probable cause before an arrest warrant or a search warrant may be issued.

reasonable expectations of privacy   The objective standard developed by the court for determining whether a governmental intrusion into an individual's person or property constitutes a search because it interferes with the individual's interests that are normally protected from governmental examination.

search   Government officials' examination of and hunt for evidence in or on a person or place in a manner that intrudes on reasonable expectations of privacy.

seizures   Situations in which police officers use their authority to deprive people of their liberty and which must not be "unreasonable" according to the Fourth Amendment.

stop   Government officials' brief interference with an individual's freedom of movement for a duration that can be measured in minutes.

totality-of-circumstances test   Flexible test established by the Supreme Court for identifying whether "probable cause" exists to justify a judicial officer in issuing a search or arrest warrant.

U.S. magistrate judges   Federal judicial officers who assist U.S. district judges and who are empowered to handle nearly any matter handled by district judges except presiding over trials of felony defendants. These officials are frequently responsible for issuing federal warrants and setting bail for federal defendants.

Additional Readings

Amar, Akhil Reed. 1997. *The Constitution and Criminal Procedure: First Principles*. New Haven, Conn.: Yale University Press.

Klein, Irving J. 1994. *The Law of Arrest, Search, Seizure, and Liability Issues*. South Miami, Fla.: Coral Gables Publishing.

Miller, Marc L., and Ronald F. Wright. 1999. *Criminal Procedures: The Police*. Gaithersburg, Md.: Aspen Law and Business.

Notes

1. John Schwartz, "Lawmakers Skeptical of FBI's 'Carnivore' System," *Seattle Times*, 25 July 2000; D. Ian Hopper, "FBI's E-mail Snooping Device Under Fierce Attack," *Seattle Times*, 12 July 2000.

2. Vicki Brown, "Man Killed By Police After Raid Targets Wrong House," *Seattle Times*, 7 October 2000.

CHAPTER FOUR

The Exclusionary Rule

Imagine that you are an enthusiastic fan of college basketball. During the NCAA tournament in March, you are planted on the sofa in your apartment watching every televised game. You left your front door open because you know that your roommate forgot his keys. Suddenly, the front door opens and two uniformed police officers enter the room. You stand up with a puzzled look on your face. "What's the problem, officers? Is there something wrong?" you ask earnestly.

"Step aside!" one officer says as they both push past you and move freely about the apartment.

"What's going on?" you ask.

The officers ignore your question and begin looking around the room, spilling note cards and papers on the floor as they sift through books and papers on your table.

You confusion begins to turn into anger. "Hey, that's my research for my term paper on the Supreme Court. I need those note cards kept in order."

"Shut up and sit down," one officer says with annoyance.

Suddenly you remember something from one of your criminal justice courses. "Do you guys have a warrant? You can't be in here searching my apartment without a warrant, you know."

"Shut up, kid. We don't need a warrant."

"Yes you do. The Fourth Amendment says so."

"Look over here," one officer says to the other. He picks up several sheets of paper from the sofa and hands them to his partner.

"Just as I suspected," remarks the other officer. "Gambling materials. I know how much you college students like to gamble, so I had a hunch we might find something like this in an apartment with a loud television blasting the basketball games all the way down to the parking lot."

You realize instantly that the officers are holding the tournament brackets submitted to you by your friends who participate in an annual betting pool. Twelve people each put in ten dollars, and the person who comes closest to predicting the winners in the most NCAA tournament games wins all of the money. "That's not gambling material. That's just our NCAA tournament pool. It's just for fun. It's only ten bucks apiece."

"It's gambling under the laws of this state, buddy. And you're under arrest."

Hopefully such a scene would never occur. Citizens should obey the criminal laws, even those concerning seemingly small matters such as office betting pools on sporting events. Police officers should obtain search warrants before entering people's homes. In the real world, however, we know that many people violate criminal laws, including "good" people who do not think of their sports betting activities as crimes. In addition, police officers sometimes violate the Constitution, including the Fourth Amendment prohibition against unreasonable searches and seizures. What happens under such circumstances? Can police officers initiate a prosecution even though they violated your Fourth Amendment rights? Because you were actually in possession of gambling materials, should you be able to avoid punishment for your crime just because the police did not follow proper procedures? These are important questions that can arise in many contexts. In this chapter, we will explore how the criminal justice system deals with situations in which criminal evidence is discovered through improper means.

It should be noted that the issue of improperly obtained evidence does not arise solely with respect to the Fourth Amendment. Go back to the original scenario. What if the police officers entered the apartment, grabbed you by the shirt, jammed you up against the wall in a threatening manner, and said, "Tell us where your gambling stuff is right now or you're going to get hurt!" Such behavior by police could violate such rights as the Fifth Amendment privilege against compelled self-incrimination and the Fourteenth Amendment right to due process of law.

CRIMINAL INVESTIGATION AND CONSTITUTIONAL RIGHTS

Police officers are trained to be suspicious. They are constantly on the lookout for criminal activity. Many officers enter careers in law enforcement because they envision themselves catching criminals and keeping their fellow citizens safe from harm. The crime control function of police is central to officers' image of themselves and to the image the general public holds of police officers. Even though officers typically spend more of their time undertaking service and order maintenance functions, the public's preoccupation with crime as a social problem helps to reinforce police officers' image as crime fighters. When there is a crime, officers are expected to act quickly. If crimes are not solved, police officers are sometimes blamed for being ineffective. Thus public pressure as well as the officers' self-image motivate them to place extra emphasis on investigating crimes and apprehending offenders.

The police have strong motives to combat crime. But what motivates them to be careful about respecting the rights of individuals? Will police officers forego opportunities to catch criminals when a rights violation may occur if the police take action? The answers to these questions are going to vary from officer to officer. Officers who are well trained, concerned about ethics, and professional have alternative goals, including their own obedience to law, that may lead them to pass up opportunities to conduct questionable searches or to employ improper interrogation techniques. Other officers, however, may place the protection of suspects' rights above other goals only when they fear being punished if they are caught violating constitutional rights. For these officers, the most significant considerations might be the likelihood of being caught and the nature of the potential punishment. When there is a low likelihood of being caught, such as when an officer is alone with a suspect in an alley, then there may be little reason to observe rules about searches and interrogations. If their primary goal is to control crime, some officers may be tempted to use improper techniques, such as physical force, to make suspects answer questions. Similarly, if the punishment or other adverse consequence faced by the officer is minimal, there may be little incentive for some officers to respect individuals' constitutional rights. Because officers use their discretion in conducting investigations and so many of their interactions with suspects are in low-visibility situations (e.g., behind closed doors), there are always risks that rights violations will occur.

ADDRESSING RIGHTS VIOLATIONS: A FIRST LOOK AT ALTERNATIVES

In light of the motives, discretionary decisions, and low-visibility situations that are central to investigations, judges who are presented with legal disputes about constitutional rights violations face major challenges in attempting to develop workable and enforceable rules to protect rights. Return to the scenario at the beginning of the chapter. Now imagine that you are a judge rather than a suspect. What are your options for addressing the defendant's claim that the prosecution should be dismissed because the officers' warrantless search violated the Fourth Amendment?

One option is for the judge to declare that the search did not violate the Fourth Amendment. The Fourth Amendment deals with government searches and seizures:

> *The right of the people to be secure in their persons, houses, papers, and effects, against unreasonable searches and seizures, shall not be violated, and no Warrants shall issue, but upon probable cause, supported by Oath or affirmation, and particularly describing the place to be searched, and the persons or things to be seized.*

The basic purpose of the Fourth Amendment is to guarantee citizens the right to be free from arbitrary actions by law enforcement officials. Clearly, the officers did not have a warrant. This does not necessarily make the search improper. Judicial decisions have identified a variety of circumstances in which a warrantless search does not violate the prohibition on "unreasonable searches and seizures." We will learn about these decisions in subsequent chapters. In this case, the judge could simply declare that the search was "reasonable" and then explain reasons for the decision. However, as you will discover in later chapters, the circumstances of this search do not appear to fit any of the U.S. Supreme Court's approved exceptions to the Fourth Amendment's warrant requirement. Thus there is a significant likelihood that a decision declaring that the Fourth Amendment was not violated in this case would be overturned by a higher court on appeal. In some other circumstances, however, the trial judge might have a stronger basis for ending the legal dispute by simply declaring that the search was proper.

A second option might be to focus on the fact that it is a lawbreaker who is complaining about the police allegedly violating constitutional rights. Many Americans believe that people who violate criminal laws should not be entitled to the protections provided by the Constitution. Some commentators refer to this as a "social contract" approach to constitutional rights. The central premise is that individuals are bound to society in a contract which obligates them to obey rules in exchange for the benefits and protections of law. If individuals violate society's rules, they have broken the contract and forfeited any benefits provided by society. Applying this philosophy to the case, a judge might say that any alleged rights violation is irrelevant because evidence of criminal activity was found and therefore the defendant forfeited any constitutional rights that would have protected good, law-abiding citizens.

A major problem with this approach is that it ignores the wording of the U.S. Constitution. The Constitution is not written in social contract terms. Nothing in the document speaks of contingencies that either explicitly or implicitly indicate that rights are contingent on good behavior. Instead, the Bill of Rights is written in "natural law" terms that indicate all people, just by virtue of being human, are entitled to the rights listed. The Fourth Amendment speaks of the right of the "people." There is no qualifying adjective such as "good" or "law-abiding" or "obedient" to limit the protections against unreasonable searches. The protections apply to all people. Other amendments are written the same way. The Eighth Amendment, for example, forbids the government from imposing cruel and unusual punishments without limiting in any way the number or nature of people protected.

Some people look at Fourth Amendment legal cases and say, "If people are not engaged in illegal activities, then they should not mind if the police conduct searches. They should welcome the police and applaud efforts to conduct investigations that will stop crime." These sentiments reflect a view of the police as helpful professionals who are devoted to serving society. This view, however, is not universally shared. Many Americans have unpleasant encounters with police officers in which they believe they were treated harshly, unfairly, or in a discriminatory manner. Moreover, the men who wrote the Fourth Amendment did not share a trusting view of the police. They had vivid memories of British soldiers searching houses without any justification. The authors of the Fourth Amendment were distrustful of government authority. Thus they wrote the Amendment to protect the privacy of all people. They did not believe that anyone, innocent or guilty, should be forced to endure the hassle and invasion of privacy attendant to an unreasonable warrantless search.

Weeks v. United States, 232 U.S. 383 (1914)

[*The defendant was arrested by police, acting without a warrant, at the train station in Kansas City, Missouri, where he was employed by a freight company. He was charged and eventually convicted of using the mails to transport lottery tickets. At the time of his arrest, police officers and a U.S. marshal went to his home, learned the location of the key from a neighbor, entered the house, and conducted a thorough search. The U.S. marshal seized letters and papers found in a drawer. Both before and after his trial, the defendant challenged the warrantless search of his home and the seizure of his personal papers.*]

JUSTICE DAY delivered the opinion of the Court.

. . .

The history of [the Fourth] Amendment is given with particularity in the opinion of Mr. Justice Bradley, speaking for the court in *Boyd v. United States* [1886]. As was there shown, it took its origin in the determination of the framers of the Amendments to the Federal Constitution to provide for that instrument a Bill of Rights, securing to the American people, among other things, those safeguards which had grown up in England to protect the people from unreasonable searches and seizures, such as were permitted under the general warrants issued under authority of the government, by which there had been invasions of the home and privacy of the citizens, and seizure of their private papers in support of charges, real or imaginary, made against them. Such practices had also received sanction under warrants and seizures under the so-called writs of assistance, issued in the American colonies. . . . Resistance to these practices had established the principle which was enacted into the fundamental law in the [Fourth] Amendment, that a man's

house was his castle, and not to be invaded by a general authority to search and seize his goods and papers. . . . In *Ex parte Jackson* [1878], this court recognized the principle of protection as applicable to letters and sealed packages in the mail, and held that, consistent with this guaranty of the right of the people to be secure in their papers against unreasonable searches and seizures, such matter could only be opened and examined upon warrants issued on oath or affirmation, particularly describing the thing to be seized, "as is required when papers are subjected to search in one's own household." . . .

The effect of the [Fourth] Amendment is to put the courts of the United States and Federal officials, in the exercise of their power and authority, under limitations and restraints as to the exercise of such power and authority, and to forever secure the people, their persons, houses, papers, and effects, against all unreasonable searches and seizures under the guise of law. This protection reaches all alike, whether accused of crime or not, and the duty of giving to it force and effect is obligatory upon all [e]ntrusted under our Federal system with the enforcement of the laws. The tendency of those who execute the criminal laws of the country to obtain conviction by means of unlawful seizures and enforced confessions, the latter often obtained after subjecting accused persons to unwarranted practices destructive of rights secured by the Federal Constitution, should find no sanction in the judgments of the courts, which are charged at all times with the support of the Constitution, and to which people of all conditions have a right to appeal for the maintenance of such fundamental rights. . . .

The case in the aspect of which we are dealing with it involves the right of the court in a criminal

THE SUPREME COURT'S APPROACH

Does a recognition that the Fourth Amendment's protections cover people who are guilty of crimes automatically mean that a defendant will have his or her charges dismissed if a right is violated? No. In some Supreme Court cases, including those in subsequent chapters, the judicial decision acknowledges that a rights violation occurred but that acknowledgment is not used to interfere with the prosecution. In other decisions, judges permit the case to move forward but attempt to address the rights violation by considering how evi-

prosecution to retain for the purposes of evidence the letters and correspondence of the accused, seized in his house in his absence and without his authority, by a United States marshal holding no warrant for his arrest and none for the search of his premises. The accused, without awaiting his trial, made timely application to the court for an order for the return of these letters, as well [as for] other property. This application was denied, the letters retained and put in evidence, after a further application at the beginning of the trial, both applications asserting the rights of the accused under the 4th and 5th Amendments to the Constitution. If letters and private documents can thus be seized and held and used in evidence against a citizen accused of an offense, the protection of the [Fourth] Amendment, declaring his right to be secure against such searches and seizures, is of no value, and, so far as those thus placed are concerned, might as well be stricken from the Constitution. The efforts of the courts and their officials to bring the guilty to punishment, praiseworthy as they are, are not to be aided by the sacrifice of those great principles established by years of endeavor and suffering which have resulted in their embodiment in the fundamental law of the land. The United States marshal could only have invaded the house of the accused when armed with a warrant issued as required by the Constitution, upon sworn information, and describing with reasonable particularity the thing for which the search was to be made. Instead, he acted without sanction of law, doubtless prompted by the desire to bring further proof to the aid of the government, and under color of his office undertook to make a seizure of private papers in direct violation of the constitutional prohibition against such action. Under such circumstances, without sworn information and particular description, not even an order of the court would

have justified such procedure; much less was it within the authority of the United States marshal to thus invade the house and privacy of the accused. . . . To sanction such proceedings would be to affirm by judicial decision a manifest neglect, if not an open defiance, of the prohibitions of the Constitution, intended for the protection of the people against such unauthorized action. . . .

We therefore reach the conclusion that the letters in question were taken from the house of the accused by an official of the United States, acting under color of his office, in direct violation of the constitutional rights of the defendant; that having made a reasonable application for their return, which was heard and passed upon by the court, there was involved in the order refusing the application a denial of the constitutional rights of the accused, and that the court should have restored these letters to the accused. In holding them and permitting their use upon the trial, we think prejudicial error was committed. As to the papers and property seized by the [local] policemen [who accompanied the U.S. marshal], it does not appear that they acted under any claim of Federal authority such as would make the amendment applicable to such unauthorized seizures. The record shows that what they did by way of arrest and search and seizure was done before the finding of the indictment in the Federal court, under what supposed right or authority does not appear. What remedies the defendant may have against them, we need not inquire, as the [Fourth] Amendment is not directed to individual misconduct of such officials. Its limitations reach the Federal government and its agencies. . . .

It results that the judgment of the court below must be reversed, and the case remanded for further proceedings in accordance with this opinion. Reversed.

dence from the improper search or interrogation will be used. They may also consider ways that police officers can be punished for violating someone's rights. The case of *Weeks v. United States* (1914) was the U.S. Supreme Court's important early effort to address this problem. As you read the case excerpt in the accompanying box, think carefully about how the Supreme Court characterizes the nature and importance of Fourth Amendment rights.

The Supreme Court clearly declared that if prosecutors were permitted to use improperly obtained evidence, then the Fourth Amendment would lose all meaning and people's constitutional rights under the amendment would disappear. According to Justice William Day's opinion,

If letters and private documents can thus be seized and held and used in evidence against a citizen accused of an offense, the protection of the 4th Amendment, declaring his right to be secure against such searches and seizures, is of no value, and, so far as those thus placed are concerned, might as well be stricken from the Constitution. (232 U.S. at 393)

By deciding that improperly obtained evidence cannot be used by the prosecution, the Court endorsed the **exclusionary rule** as the means to address rights violations during police investigations. Under the exclusionary rule, evidence that is obtained in violation of a person's constitutional rights cannot be used against that person in a criminal prosecution. The exclusionary rule embodies the principle that the government should not benefit from its misconduct. The rule also gives greater protection to constitutional rights than to society's interest in crime control. Although the Supreme Court made a strong statement in favor of the exclusionary rule in *Weeks,* the rule was not applied automatically to criminal cases in state courts. The *Weeks* precedent applied only to federal criminal cases because the decision occurred before the Fourth Amendment and other criminal justice–related provisions of the Bill of Rights had been incorporated into the Fourteenth Amendment for application against the states. Because there were relatively few federal prosecutions in the early twentieth century, the *Weeks* decision did not apply to the vast majority of criminal investigations and prosecutions.

The exclusionary rule does not require that cases against defendants be dismissed when constitutional rights have been violated. The prosecution can continue, but it may not make use of the improperly obtained evidence. In some cases, the lost evidence will not prevent a person from being found guilty. In other cases, there may not be enough evidence for the prosecution to continue, so the prosecutor will drop charges or the defense attorney may persuade a judge to dismiss the charges at a preliminary hearing. The rule clearly accepts the possibility that a guilty person may go free despite the fact that evidence exists to demonstrate his or her guilt. This is one of the primary reasons that many people do not like the exclusionary rule.

"Fruit of the Poisonous Tree" Doctrine

The Supreme Court expanded the impact of the exclusionary rule in *Silverthorne Lumber Co. v. United States* (1920) by declaring that the government could not use information gained from an illegal search in order to secure a subpoena for the documents it had illegally viewed. This decision provided the basis for the **"fruit of the poisonous tree" doctrine** in which the Court excluded evidence indirectly discovered through illegal methods rather than through some independent, legal source. Thus, for example, in later cases, statements obtained during legal interrogation of a suspect could be excluded from evidence if the interrogation was preceded by an improper warrantless arrest (see *Wong Sun v. United States,* 1963). The suspect's statements could be excluded as the "fruit" of the original warrantless search. This is an especially important doctrine because it seeks to discourage the police from engaging in improper investigatory activities that violate the Fourth Amendment with the hope that such actions might later produce useful evidence. Under the doctrine, judges trace the sources of evidence back through the chain of events and activities undertaken by the police to see if a violation of constitutional rights occurred at some point in the process. If so, and if the subsequently obtained evidence was the "fruit" of that process, then that evidence should be excluded.

Imagine the consequences of an alternative approach. What if police officers knew that information obtained during an improper search, improper arrest, or improper interrogation could be used as a means to obtain evidence legally? For example, what if officers used physical force to coerce a confession out of a suspect in violation of the Fifth Amendment's privilege against compelled self-incrimination? Should they be able to use statements from that coerced confession as the basis for probable cause to obtain a search warrant for conducting a legal search? Officers would have less reason to respect Fourth and Fifth Amendment rights if they knew that the use of improper procedures would create opportunities to obtain usable evidence through later investigatory actions.

As the Supreme Court reached the middle years of the twentieth century, two developments affected the Court's consideration of the exclusionary rule doctrine. First, attorneys continued to argue that the Court should incorporate the Fourth Amendment, Fifth Amendment, and other amendments affecting criminal justice. Second, the Court's composition changed. The justices appointed by President Franklin Roosevelt (1932–1944) over the course of his terms in office were more inclined than their predecessors to expand the applicability of the Bill of Rights to the states. In considering which rights apply in state criminal cases, the Court also had to consider whether the exclusionary rule should apply to state court cases. As you read the excerpt of *Wolf v. Colorado* (1949) in the accompanying box, look closely at Justice Frankfurter's reasons for reaching his conclusions about the applicability of the exclusionary rule to the states.

| CASE | *Wolf v. Colorado*, 338 U.S. 25 (1949) |

JUSTICE FRANKFURTER delivered the opinion of the Court.

The precise question for consideration is this: Does a conviction by a State court for a State offense deny the "due process of law" required by the Fourteenth Amendment, solely because evidence that was admitted at trial was obtained under circumstances which would have rendered it admissible in a prosecution for violation of a federal law in a court of the United States because there deemed to be an infraction of the Fourth Amendment as applied in *Weeks v. United States* [1914] . . .

Unlike the specific requirements and restrictions placed by the Bill of Rights, Amendments I to VIII, upon the administration of justice by federal authority, the Fourteenth Amendment did not subject criminal justice in the States to specific limitations. The notion that "due process of law" guaranteed by the Fourteenth Amendment is shorthand for the first eight amendments of the Constitution and thereby incorporates them has been rejected by the Court again and again, after impressive consideration. . . . Only the other day the Court reaffirmed this rejection after thorough examination of the scope and function of the Due Process Clause of the Fourteenth Amendment. *Adamson v. California*, 332 U.S. 46 [1947]. . . . The issue is closed.

For purposes of ascertaining the restrictions which the Due Process Clause imposed upon the States in the enforcement of their criminal law, we adhere to the views expressed in *Palko v. Connecticut* [1937]. . . . [The Court] affirmed [a] deeper and

(continued)

more pervasive conception of the Due Process Clause. This Clause exacts from the States for the lowliest and the most outcast all that is "implicit in the concept of ordered liberty.". . .

Due process of law thus conveys neither formal nor fixed nor narrow requirements. It is the compendious expression for all those rights which the courts must enforce because they are basic to our free society as of any one time; even though, as a matter of human experience, some may not too rhetorically be called eternal verities. It is of the very nature of a free society to advance in its standards of what is deemed reasonable and right. Representing as it does a living principle, due process is not confined within a permanent catalogue of what may at a given time be deemed the limits or the essentials of fundamental rights. . . .

The security of one's privacy against arbitrary intrusion by the police—which is at the core of the Fourth Amendment—is basic to a free society. It is therefore implicit in "the concept of ordered liberty" and as such enforceable against the States through the Due Process Clause. The knock at the door, whether by day or by night, as a prelude to a search, without authority of law but solely on the authority of the police, did not need the commentary of recent history to be condemned as inconsistent with the conception of human rights enshrined in the history and the basic constitutional documents of English-speaking peoples.

Accordingly, we have no hesitation in saying that were a State affirmatively to sanction such police incursion into privacy it would run counter to the guaranty of the Fourteenth Amendment. But the ways of enforcing such a basic right raise questions of a different order. How such arbitrary conduct should be checked, what remedies against it should be afforded, the means by which the right should be made effective, are all questions that are not to be so dogmatically answered as to preclude the varying solutions which spring from an allowable range of judgment on issues not susceptible of quantitative solution.

In *Weeks v. United States,* this Court held that in a federal prosecution the Fourth Amendment barred the use of evidence secured through an illegal search and seizure. This ruling was made for the first time in 1914. It was not derived from the explicit requirements of the Fourth Amendment; it was not based on legislation expressing Congressional policy in the enforcement of the Constitution. The decision was a matter of judicial implication. Since then it has been frequently applied and we stoutly adhere to it. But the immediate question is whether the basic right to

protection against arbitrary intrusion by the police demands the exclusion of logically relevant evidence obtained by an unreasonable search and seizure because, in a federal prosecution for a federal crime, it would be excluded. As a matter of inherent reason, one would suppose this to be an issue to which men with complete devotion to the protection of the right of privacy might give different answers. When we find that in fact most of the English-speaking world does not regard as vital to such protection the exclusion of evidence thus obtained, we must hesitate to treat this remedy as an essential ingredient of the right. The contrariety of views of the States is particularly impressive in view of the careful consideration which they have given the problem in light of the *Weeks* decision.

I. Before the *Weeks* decision 27 States had [considered] the admissibility of evidence obtained by unlawful search and seizure.

  (a) Of these, 26 States opposed the *Weeks* doctrine.

  (b) Of these, 1 State anticipated the *Weeks* doctrine [Iowa].

II. Since the *Weeks* decision 47 States all told have [considered] the *Weeks* doctrine.

  (a) Of these, 20 [considered] it for the first time.

    (1) Of the foregoing States, 6 followed the *Weeks* doctrine.

    (2) Of the foregoing States, 14 rejected the *Weeks* doctrine.

  (b) Of these, 26 States reviewed prior decisions contrary to the *Weeks* doctrine.

    (1) Of these, 10 have followed *Weeks,* overruling or distinguishing their prior decisions.

    (2) Of these, 16 States adhered to their prior decisions against *Weeks*.

  (c) Of these, 1 State adhered to its prior formulation of the *Weeks* doctrine [Iowa].

III. As of today 30 States reject the *Weeks* doctrine, 17 States are in agreement with it.

IV. Of 10 jurisdictions within the United Kingdom and the British Commonwealth of Nations which have [considered] the question, none has held evidence obtained by illegal search and seizure inadmissible.

The jurisdictions which have rejected the *Weeks* doctrine have not left the right to privacy without other means of protection. Indeed, the exclusion of evidence is a remedy which directly serves only to protect those upon whose person or premises something incriminating has been found. We cannot, therefore, regard it as a departure from basic standards to remand such persons, together with those who emerge [unscathed] from a search, to the remedies of private action and such protection as internal discipline of the police, under the eyes of an alert public opinion, may afford. Granting that in practice the exclusion of evidence may be an effective way of deterring unreasonable searches, it is not for this Court to condemn as falling below the minimal standards assured by the Due Process Clause a State's reliance upon other methods which, if consistently enforced, would be equally effective. Weighty testimony against such an insistence on our own view is the opinion of Mr. Justice (then Judge) Cardozo in *People v. Defore* [New York state court case]. . . .We cannot brush aside the experience of States which deem the incidence of such conduct by the police too slight to call for a deterrent remedy not by way of disciplinary measures but by overriding the relevant rules of evidence. There are, moreover, reasons for excluding evidence unreasonably obtained by the federal police which are less compelling in the case of police under State or local authority. The public opinion of a community can far more effectively be exerted against oppressive conduct on the part of police directly responsible to the community itself than can local opinion, sporadically aroused, be brought to bear upon remote authority pervasively exerted throughout the country.

We hold, therefore, that in a prosecution in a State court for a State crime the Fourteenth Amendment does not forbid the admission of evidence obtained by an unreasonable search and seizure. And though we have interpreted the Fourth Amendment to forbid the admission of such evidence, a different question would be presented if Congress under its legislative powers were to pass a statute purporting to negate the *Weeks* doctrine. We would then be faced with the problem of the respect to be accorded the legislative judgment on an issue as to which, in default of that judgment, we have been forced to depend upon our own. Problems of a converse character, also not before us, would be presented should Congress under [section] 5 of the Fourteenth Amendment undertake to enforce the rights there guaranteed by attempting to make the *Weeks* doctrine binding upon the States.
Affirmed.

[Appendices omitted]

JUSTICE BLACK, concurring.

. . . For the reasons stated in my dissenting opinion in *Adamson v. California,* . . . I agree with the conclusion of the Court that the Fourth Amendment's prohibition of "unreasonable searches and seizures" is enforceable against the states. Consequently, I should be for reversal of this case if I thought the Fourth Amendment not only prohibited "unreasonable searches and seizures," but also, of itself, barred the use of evidence so unlawfully obtained. But I agree with what appears to be a plain implication of the Court's opinion that the federal exclusionary rule is not a command of the Fourth Amendment but is a judicially created rule of evidence which Congress might negate.

It is not amiss to repeat my belief that the Fourteenth Amendment was intended to make the Fourth Amendment in its entirety applicable to the states. The Fourth Amendment was designed to protect people against unrestrained searches and seizures by sheriffs, policemen, and other law enforcement officers. Such protection is essential in a free society. I am unable to agree that protection of people from overzealous or ruthless state officers is any less essential in a country of "ordered liberty" than is the protection of people from overzealous or ruthless federal officers. . . .

JUSTICE DOUGLAS, dissenting.

I believe for the reasons stated by Mr. Justice Black in his dissent in *Adamson v. California,* . . . that the Fourth Amendment is applicable to the States. I agree with Mr. Justice Murphy that evidence obtained in violation of it must be excluded in state prosecutions as well as in federal prosecutions, since in absence of that rule of evidence the Amendment would have no effective sanction. I also agree with him that under that test this evidence was improperly admitted and that the judgments of conviction must be reversed.

JUSTICE MURPHY, with whom Justice Rutledge joins, dissenting.

It is disheartening to find so much that is right in an opinion which seems to me to be so fundamentally wrong. Of course I agree with the Court that the Fourteenth Amendment prohibits activities which are proscribed by the search and seizure clause of the Fourth Amendment. . . . Quite apart from the blanket application of the Bill of Rights to the States, a devotee of democracy would ill suit his name were he to suggest that his home's protection

(continued)

against unlicensed governmental invasion was not "of the very essence of a scheme of ordered liberty.". . . It is difficult for me to understand how the Court can go this far and yet be unwilling to make the step which can give some meaning to the pronouncements it utters.

Imagination and zeal may invent a dozen methods to give content to the commands of the Fourth Amendment. But this Court is limited to the remedies currently available. It cannot legislate the ideal system. If we attempt the enforcement of the search and seizure clause in the ordinary case today, we are limited to three devices: judicial exclusion of the illegally obtained evidence; criminal prosecution of violators; and civil action against violators in the action of trespass.

Alternatives are deceptive. Their very statement conveys the impression that one possibility is as effective as the next. In this case their statement is blinding. For there is but one alternative to the rule of exclusion. That is no sanction at all. This has been perfectly clear since 1914, when a unanimous Court decided *Weeks v. United States*. . . . "If letters and private documents can thus be seized and held and used in evidence against a citizen accused of an offense," we said "the protection of the 4th Amendment, declaring his right to be secure against such searches and seizures, is of no value, and, so far as those thus placed are concerned, might as well be stricken from the Constitution." [In the words of Justice Holmes,] "It would reduce the Fourth Amendment to a form of words.". . . *Silverthorne Lumber Co. v. United States* [1920]. . . .

Today the Court wipes those statements from the books with its bland citation of "other remedies." Little need be said concerning the possibilities of criminal prosecution. Self-scrutiny is a lofty ideal but its exaltation reaches new heights if we expect a District Attorney to prosecute himself or his associates for well-meaning violations of the search and seizure clause during a raid the District Attorney or his associates have ordered. But there is an appealing ring in another alternative. A trespass action for damages is a venerable means of securing reparation for unauthorized invasion of the home. Why not put the old writ to a new use? When the Court cites cases permitting the action, the remedy seems complete.

But what an illusory remedy this is, if by "remedy" we mean a positive deterrent to police and prosecutors tempted to violate the Fourth Amendment. The appealing ring softens when we recall that in a trespass action the measure of damages is simply the extent of the injury to physical property. If the officer searches with care, he can avoid all but nominal damages—a penny, or a dollar. Are punitive damages possible? Perhaps. But a few states permit none, whatever the circumstances. In those that do, the plaintiff must show the real ill will or malice of the defendant, and surely it is not unreasonable to assume that one in honest pursuit of crime bears no malice toward the search victim. If that burden is carried, recovery may yet be defeated by the rule that there must be physical damages before punitive damages may be awarded. In addition, some states limit punitive damages to the actual expenses of litigation. . . . And even if the plaintiff hurdles all of these obstacles, and gains a substantial verdict, the individual officer's finances may well make the judgment useless—for the municipality, of course, is not liable without its consent. Is it surprising that there is so little in the books concerning trespass actions for violation of the search and seizure clause?

The conclusion is inescapable that but one remedy exists to deter violations of the search and seizure clause. That is the rule which excludes illegally obtained evidence. Only by exclusion can we impress upon the zealous prosecutor that violation of the Constitution will do him no good. And only when that point is driven home can the prosecutor be expected to emphasize the importance of observing constitutional demands in his instructions to the police. . . .

I cannot believe that we should decide due process questions by simply taking a poll of the rules in various jurisdictions, even if we follow the *Palko* "test." Today's decision will do inestimable harm to the cause of fair police methods in our cities and states. Even more important, perhaps, it must have tragic effect upon public respect for our judiciary. For the Court now allows what is indeed shabby business: lawlessness by officers of the law. Since the evidence admitted was secured in violation of the Fourth Amendment, the judgment should be reversed.

[The dissenting opinion of Justice Rutledge is omitted.]

Alternatives to Exclusion

Justice Felix Frankfurter's majority opinion in *Wolf v. Colorado* made a powerful statement about the right against unreasonable search and seizure when he incorporated the Fourth Amendment and applied it against the states:

> *The security of one's privacy against arbitrary intrusion by the police—which is at the core of the Fourth Amendment—is basic to a free society. It is therefore implicit in the "concept of ordered liberty" and as such enforceable against the States through the Due Process Clause [of the Fourteenth Amendment]. The knock at the door, whether by day or by night, as a prelude to search, without authority of law but solely on the authority of the police, did not need the commentary of recent history to be condemned as inconsistent with the conception of human rights enshrined in the history and the basic constitutional documents of English-speaking peoples. (338 U.S. at 27–28)*

Despite Frankfurter's emphatic assertion that the Fourth Amendment was applicable to the states, he and the other justices in the majority declined to require the states to adhere to the *Weeks* exclusionary rule. Frankfurter was a strong supporter of states' authority to handle their own affairs as much as possible without interference of federal courts. He indicated that the states should be able to apply their own remedies to problems of police conduct, such as disciplining officers who violate rights and permitting lawsuits against officers, and he expressed confidence that local public opinion would serve as an important check against abusive police practices. In dissenting opinions, Justices Rutledge, Murphy, and Douglas agreed that the Fourth Amendment should be incorporated and applied to the states, but they asserted that the exclusionary rule must also be applied to the states in order to prevent lawlessness by the police. They also questioned whether remedies other than the exclusionary rule would be effective in addressing rights violations by the police.

Think about the alternatives to the exclusionary rule endorsed by Frankfurter. How well would they work? Frankfurter says that states can choose to use "internal discipline of the police" instead of the exclusionary rule. Under this approach, police officers who conduct an improper search or interrogation will be punished by the police department rather than have the evidence excluded from use against the defendant. Police officers could be suspended, demoted, or fired, but the guilty would not go free because of their improper investigations. There is a question, however, whether it is realistic to expect a police chief to punish officers who have caught lawbreakers. Would a police chief say, "You caught a drug dealer, but I'm going to have to punish you for the way in which you did it." Perhaps this would happen. But perhaps the punishment would always be a slap on the wrist that officers would not take seriously because presumably police chiefs, whose jobs depend on how effectively they combat crime, would not really want to deter officers from conducting investigations and making arrests.

Frankfurter also says that the "remedies of private action," meaning lawsuits under civil law, could be an effective alternative to applying the exclusionary rule. However, the dissenters noted that available civil remedies have limitations that reduce their potential effectiveness. For actions seeking recovery of monetary damages, such as civil rights lawsuits that are available today but were not generally available in 1949, there are questions about how juries would decide such cases. Would a jury actually find a police officer liable and force that officer to pay money to an imprisoned drug dealer as a result of a search that violated the Fourth Amendment? Many citizens would want to give the officer a reward for fighting crime effectively and would object to the possibility that a convicted criminal should receive money from a police officer. If the police cause physical injuries or deaths in the course of undertaking improper actions, then juries are more likely to impose liability. But if the injury is something as abstract as the violation of the right against unreasonable searches, it may be more difficult to rely on juries to provide a meaningful remedy for rights violations. Moreover, how much should be awarded to someone who was improperly searched? Would juries place a sufficient monetary value on such rights violations to deter the police from undertaking improper investigatory actions?

Whether or not one believes that these alternatives will be effective in deterring rights violations or remedying violations that have occurred, the *Wolf* decision leaves a major question: If *Weeks* says that the Fourth Amendment is rendered meaningless with respect to the federal courts if there is no exclusionary rule, then how can the Fourth Amendment be meaningful in state courts without the exclusionary rule? Frankfurter seems to justify this inconsistency through two arguments. First, he takes note of how many states have declined to adopt the exclusionary rule for themselves. Frankfurter seems to treat this as evidence that the states are able to develop their own remedies. However, he does not give much attention to the issue of whether these alternatives will really work.

Second, Frankfurter says the following:

> *There are, moreover, reasons for excluding evidence unreasonably obtained by the federal police which are less compelling in the case of police under State or local authority. The public opinion of a community can far more effectively be exerted against oppressive conduct on the part of police directly responsible to the community itself than can local opinion, sporadically aroused, be brought to bear upon remote authority pervasively exerted throughout the country. (338 U.S. at 32–33)*

In other words, Frankfurter implies that the local public will monitor police behavior and keep police departments from engaging in improper conduct. By contrast, the entire country is too large for public opinion to be sufficiently focused on and aware of misbehavior by federal law enforcement officers. For example, people in Detroit would never hear about an improper search conducted by FBI agents in San Diego, and therefore they would not express their dissatisfaction to the government. As in the case of citizen-jurors asked to find police officers liable for rights violations, there are questions about whether the public is really opposed to improper searches by police when those searches result in the discovery of criminal activity.

Only a few years after *Wolf,* the Supreme Court faced a different situation of improper investigatory actions by police. In *Rochin v. California* (1952), a defendant sought to have evidence excluded when police entered his home without a warrant and eventually took him to the hospital to have his stomach pumped in order to look for drugs that he may have ingested. As you read the accompanying case excerpt, ask yourself whether Justice Frankfurter's opinion is consistent with his prior opinion in *Wolf v. Colorado.*

| C A S E | *Rochin v. California*, 342 U.S. 165 (1952) |

JUSTICE FRANKFURTER delivered the opinion of the Court.

Having "some information that [the petitioner here] was selling narcotics," three deputy sheriffs of the County of Los Angeles, on the morning of July 1, 1949, made for the two-story dwelling house in which Rochin lived with his mother, common-law wife, brothers and sisters. Finding the outside door open, they entered and then forced open the door to Rochin's room on the second floor. Inside they found petitioner sitting partly dressed on the side of the bed, upon which his wife was lying. On a "night stand" beside the bed the deputies spied two capsules. When asked "Whose stuff is this?" Rochin seized the capsules and put them in his mouth. A struggle ensued, in the course of which the three officers "jumped upon him" and attempted to extract the capsules. The force they applied proved unavailing against Rochin's resistance. He was handcuffed and taken to a hospital. At the direction of one of the officers a doctor forced an emetic solution through a tube into Rochin's stomach against his will. This "stomach pumping" produced vomiting. In the vomited matter were found two capsules which proved to contain morphine.

Rochin was brought to trial before a California Superior Court, sitting without a jury, on the charge of possessing "a preparation of morphine" in violation of the California Health and Safety Code. . . . Rochin was convicted and sentenced to sixty days' imprisonment. The chief evidence against him was the two capsules. They were admitted over petitioner's objection, although the means of obtaining them was frankly set forth in the testimony by one of the deputies, substantially as here narrated.

On appeal, the District Court of Appeal affirmed the conviction, despite the finding that the officers "were guilty of unlawfully breaking into and entering defendant's room and were guilty of unlawfully assaulting and battering defendant while in the room," and "were guilty of unlawfully assaulting, battering, torturing and falsely imprisoning the defendant at the alleged hospital.". . .

. . . The faculties of the Due Process Clause may be indefinite and vague, but the mode of their ascertainment is not self-willed. In each case "due process of law" requires an evaluation based on a disinterested inquiry pursued in the spirit of science, on a balanced order of facts exactly and fairly stated, on the detached consideration of conflicting claims . . . on a judgment not ad hoc and episodic but duly mindful of reconciling the needs of both continuity and of change in a progressive society.

Applying these general considerations to the circumstances of the present case, we are compelled to conclude that the proceedings by which this conviction was obtained do more than offend some fastidious squeamishness or private sentimentalism about combatting crime too energetically. This is conduct that shocks the conscience. Illegally breaking into the privacy of the petitioner, the struggle to open his mouth and remove what was there, the forcible extraction of his stomach's contents—this course of proceeding by agents of government to obtain evidence is bound to offend even hardened sensibilities. They are methods too close to the rack and screw to permit of constitutional differentiation. . . .

To attempt in this case to distinguish what lawyers call "real evidence" from verbal evidence is to ignore the reasons for excluding coerced confessions. Use of involuntary verbal confessions in State criminal trials is constitutionally obnoxious not only because of their unreliability. They are inadmissible under the Due Process Clause even though statements contained in them may be independently established as true. Coerced confessions offend the community's sense of fair play and decency. So here, to sanction the brutal conduct which naturally enough was condemned by the court whose judgment is before us, would be to afford brutality the cloak of law. Nothing would be more calculated to discredit law and thereby brutalize the temper of a society. . . .

On the facts of this case the conviction of the petitioner has been obtained by methods that offend the Due Process Clause. The judgment below must be Reversed.

JUSTICE BLACK, concurring.

. . . I think a person is compelled to be a witness against himself not only when he is compelled to testify, but also when as here, incriminating evidence is forcibly taken from him by contrivance of modern science. . . . California convicted this petitioner by using against him evidence obtained in this manner, and I agree with Mr. Justice Douglas that the case should be reversed on this ground.

In the view of a majority of the Court, however, the Fifth Amendment imposes no restraint of any kind on the states. They nevertheless hold that California's use of this evidence violated the Due Process

(continued)

Clause of the Fourteenth Amendment. Since they hold as I do in this case, I regret my inability to accept their interpretation without protest. But I believe that faithful adherence to the specific guarantees in the Bill of Rights ensures a more permanent protection of individual liberty than that which can be afforded by the nebulous standards stated by the majority. . . .

JUSTICE DOUGLAS, concurring.

The evidence obtained from this accused's stomach would be admissible in the majority of states where the question has been raised. So far as the reported cases reveal, the only states which would probably exclude the evidence would be Arkansas, Iowa, Michigan, and Missouri. Yet the Court now says that the rule which the majority of the states have fashioned violates the "decencies of civilized conduct.". . .

. . . But I think that words taken from [Rochin's] lips, capsules taken from his stomach, blood taken from his veins are all inadmissible provided that they are taken from him without his consent. They are inadmissible because of the command of the Fifth Amendment.

That is an unequivocal, definite and workable rule of evidence for state and federal courts. But we cannot in fairness free the state courts from that command and yet excoriate them for flouting the "decencies of civilized conduct" when they admit the evidence. That is to make the rule turn not on the Constitution but on the idiosyncrasies of the judges who sit here.

The damage of the view sponsored by the Court in this case may not be conspicuous here. But it is part of the same philosophy that produced *Betts v. Brady* [1942] . . . denying counsel to an accused in a state trial against the command of the Sixth Amendment, and *Wolf v. Colorado* [1949] . . . allowing evidence obtained as a result of a search and seizure that is illegal under the Fourth Amendment to be introduced in a state trial. It is part of the process of erosion of civil rights of the citizen in recent years.

Unlike in *Wolf,* this time Frankfurter wrote a majority opinion which ordered that the evidence against Rochin be excluded from use at trial. Frankfurter continued to believe that the exclusionary rule should not be imposed on the states, but the *Rochin* case forced him to recognize that some actions by state law enforcement officials were so abusive that they required clear, strong remedies. According to Frankfurter,

> [W]e are compelled to conclude that the proceedings by which this conviction was obtained do more than offend some fastidious squeamishness or private sentimentalism about combatting crime too energetically. This is conduct that shocks the conscience. Illegally breaking into the privacy of the petitioner, the struggle to open his mouth and remove what was there, the forcible extraction of his stomach's contents—this course of proceeding by agents of government to obtain evidence is bound to offend even hardened sensibilities. They are methods too close to the rack and the screw to permit of constitutional differentiation. (342 U.S. at 172)

After the *Rochin* case, police officers knew that federal courts might order the exclusion of evidence in "conscience-shocking" circumstances, but the officers had no way of knowing which circumstances would produce exclusion. Frankfurter endorsed exclusion in the *Rochin* case because the officers' actions "shock[ed] the conscience." Such a test, however, leaves it up to individual judges to determine when police officers have gone too far in violating individuals' rights and thereby provides little guidance to police about the consequences of various actions they may choose to take in conducting searches and seizures.

Frankfurter's opinion also raised the question of why he insisted in *Wolf* that the exclusionary rule was not necessary in state courts, yet he ordered exclusion of the evidence in a state court case in *Rochin*. If Frankfurter believed that police internal discipline, civil law remedies, and public opinion can prevent and remedy rights violations, then why did Frankfurter not say that such remedies would work in *Rochin*? In effect, Frankfurter's decision to exclude evidence in *Rochin* called into question the strength of the belief in alternatives that he previously expressed in *Wolf*.

THE WARREN COURT AND THE EXCLUSIONARY RULE

The appointment of Earl Warren as Chief Justice in 1953 ushered in an era in which the Supreme Court expanded the definitions of constitutional rights affecting a variety of issues, including criminal justice. During the Warren era (1953–1969), the Court incorporated most of the criminal justice–related rights so that state law enforcement officials were required to adhere to the same rules as federal law enforcement officials. Because the Warren Court was asked to consider whether to incorporate various Fifth, Sixth, and Eighth Amendment rights, it was no surprise that they faced the issue of whether to subject state officials to the exclusionary rule. As you read the case excerpt from *Mapp v. Ohio* (1961) in the box on pp. 116–117, compare Justice Clark's conclusions about the applicability of the exclusionary rule with those of Justice Frankfurter in the earlier cases of *Wolf v. Colorado* (1949) and *Rochin v. California* (1952).

In *Mapp* the Supreme Court incorporated the exclusionary rule and made all state and local cases subject to the same rule that had been imposed on federal cases in *Weeks* in 1914. In some respects, it is possible to see *Wolf* and *Rochin* as intermediate steps taken by the Court as it gradually, over the course of forty-seven years, moved from applying the exclusionary rule only against federal officials (*Weeks*, 1914) to applying it against all criminal justice officials (*Mapp*, 1961). In *Wolf* the Court moved a step toward its ultimate decision in *Mapp* by incorporating the Fourth Amendment, although Frankfurter's opinion declined to incorporate the exclusionary rule because of a belief in the effectiveness of alternatives. In *Rochin*, Frankfurter implicitly conceded that alternatives will not always work and that exclusion is sometimes necessary in state cases. The *Mapp* decision then took the additional step of mandating the exclusionary rule in state and local cases.

Why did the Supreme Court see the exclusionary rule as necessary? Several reasons emerge in looking at the cases from *Weeks* to *Mapp*. First, *Weeks* declared that the exclusionary rule is essential to make the Fourth Amendment meaningful. In essence, the justices believed that constitutional rights are nullified if government officials are permitted to benefit by violating those rights.

Second, the *Mapp* decision indicates that the exclusionary rule is required by the Constitution. According to Justice Clark's majority opinion,

> *There are in the cases of this Court some passing references to the* Weeks *[exclusionary] rule as being one of evidence. But the plain and unequivocal language of* Weeks—*and its later paraphrase in* Wolf—*to the effect that the* Weeks *rule is of constitutional origin, remains entirely undisturbed. (367 U.S. at 649)*

Clark's point is clear. The justices are obligated to impose the exclusionary rule because the Constitution demands that they do. However, critics of the exclusionary rule disagree. Indeed, one can accuse Clark of mischaracterizing

Mapp v. Ohio, 367 U.S. 644 (1961)

[*Police officers came to Ms. Mapp's house looking for a bombing suspect. She would not let them enter. They forced open a door and entered. She demanded to see their search warrant. They waved a piece of paper in her face that she grabbed and stuffed down her shirt. The officers forcibly retrieved the paper from her and it was never seen again. The officers handcuffed Ms. Mapp and rummaged through her house, opening dresser drawers and suitcases. They found a trunk in the basement that contained books with such titles as* The Affairs of a Troubador, London Stage Affairs, *and* Memories of a Hotel Man. *Because of the books, Ms. Mapp was convicted of having obscene materials in her possession. The case was brought to the Supreme Court on a claim that the Ohio obscenity statute violated the First Amendment. However, the Court focused on the issue of whether the evidence should be excluded because the police conducted an unreasonable warrantless search.*]

JUSTICE CLARK delivered the opinion of the Court.

. . . The State says that even if the search were made without authority, or otherwise unreasonably, it is not prevented from using the unconstitutionally seized evidence at trial, citing *Wolf v. Colorado* [1949], in which this Court did indeed hold "that in a prosecution in a State court for a State crime the Fourteenth Amendment does not forbid the admission of evidence obtained by unreasonable search and seizure." On this appeal, of which we have noted probable jurisdiction, . . . it is urged once again that we review that holding. . . .

There are in the cases of this Court some passing references to the *Weeks* [exclusionary] rule as being one of evidence. But the plain and unequivocal language of *Weeks*—and its later paraphrase in *Wolf*—to the effect that the *Weeks* rule is of constitutional origin, remains entirely undisturbed. . . .

In 1949, 35 years after *Weeks* was announced, this Court, in *Wolf v. People of the State of Colorado,* . . . again for the first time, discussed the effect of the Fourth Amendment upon the States through the operation of the Due Process Clause of the Fourteenth Amendment. . . . [T]he Court decided that the *Weeks* exclusionary rule would not then be imposed upon the States as "an essential ingredient of the right [against unreasonable search and seizure]."

. . . The Court's reasons for not considering essential to the right to privacy, as a curb imposed upon the States by the Due Process Clause, that which decades before had been posited as part and parcel of the Fourth Amendment's limitation upon federal encroachment of individual privacy, were bottomed on several factual considerations.

While they are not basically relevant to a decision that the exclusionary rule is an essential ingredient of the Fourth Amendment as the right it embodies is vouchsafed against the States by the Due Process Clause, we will consider the current validity of the factual grounds upon which *Wolf* was based.

. . . While in 1949, prior to the *Wolf* case, almost two-thirds of the States were opposed to the use of the exclusionary rule, now, despite the *Wolf* case, more than half of those since passing upon it, by their own legislative or judicial decision, have wholly or partly adopted or adhered to the *Weeks* rule. . . . Significantly, among those now following the rule is California, which, according to its highest courts, was "compelled to reach that conclusion because other remedies have completely failed to secure compliance with the constitutional provisions.". . . In connection with this California case, we note that the second basis elaborated in *Wolf* in support of its failure to enforce the exclusionary doctrine against the States was that "other means of protection" have been afforded "the right to privacy.". . . The experience of California that such other remedies have been worthless and futile is buttressed by the experience of other States. The obvious futility of relegating the Fourth Amendment to the protection of other remedies has, moreover, been recognized by this Court since *Wolf.* See *Irvine v. People of State of California* [1954]. . . .

It, therefore, plainly appears that the factual considerations supporting the failure of the *Wolf* Court to include the *Weeks* exclusionary rule when it recognized the enforceability of the right to privacy against the States in 1949, while not basically relevant to the constitutional consideration, could not, in any analysis, now be deemed to be controlling. . . .

Since the Fourth Amendment's right of privacy has been declared enforceable against the States through the Due Process Clause of the Fourteenth, it is enforceable against them by the same sanction of exclusion as is used against the Federal Government.

Were it otherwise, then just as without the *Weeks* rule the assurance against unreasonable federal searches and seizures would be "a form of words," valueless and undeserving of mention in a perpetual charter of inestimable human liberties, so too, without that rule the freedom from state invasions of privacy would be so ephemeral and so neatly severed from its conceptual nexus with the freedom from all brutish means of coercing evidence as not to merit this Court's high regard as a freedom "implicit in 'the concept of ordered liberty.'" At the time that the Court held in *Wolf* that the Amendment was applicable to the States through the Due Process Clause, the cases of this Court, as we have seen, had steadfastly held that as to federal officers the Fourth Amendment included the exclusion of the evidence seized in violation of its provision. Even *Wolf* "stoutly adhered" to that proposition. The right to privacy, when conceded operatively enforceable against the States, was not susceptible of destruction by avulsion of the sanction upon which its protection and enjoyment had always been deemed dependent under the *Boyd, Weeks,* and *Silverthorne* [*Lumber Co. v. United States* (1920)] cases. Therefore, in extending the substantive protections of due process to all constitutionally unreasonable searches—state or federal—it was logically and constitutionally necessary that the exclusion doctrine—an essential part of the right to privacy—be also insisted upon as an essential ingredient of the right newly recognized by the *Wolf* case. In short, the admission of the new constitutional right by *Wolf* could not consistently tolerate denial of its most important constitutional privilege, namely, the exclusion of the evidence which an accused had been forced to give by reason of the unlawful seizure. To hold otherwise is to grant the right but in reality to withhold its privilege and enjoyment. Only last year the Court itself recognized that the purpose of the exclusionary rule "is to deter—to compel respect for the constitutional guaranty in the only effectively available way—by removing the incentive to disregard it." *Elkins v. United States,* 364 U.S. at 217. . . .

. . . This Court has not hesitated to enforce as strictly against the States as it does against the Federal Government the rights of free speech and of free press, the rights to notice and to a fair, public trial, including, as it does, the right not to be convicted by use of a coerced confession, however logically relevant it be, and without regard to its reliability. . . . And nothing could be more certain than that when a coerced confession is involved, "the relevant rules of evidence" are overridden without regard to "the incidence of such conduct by the police," slight or frequent. Why should not the same rule apply to what is tantamount to coerced testimony by way of unconstitutional seizure of goods, papers, effects, documents, etc.? We find that, as to the Federal Government, the Fourth and Fifth Amendments and, as to the State, the freedom from unconscionable invasions of privacy and the freedom from convictions based upon coerced confessions do enjoy an "intimate relation" in their perpetuation of "principles of humanity and civil liberty [secured] . . . only after years of struggle." . . . The philosophy of each Amendment and of each freedom is complementary to, although not dependent upon, that of the other in its sphere of influence—the very least that together they assure in either sphere is that no man is to be convicted on unconstitutional evidence. . . .

Moreover, our holding that the exclusionary rule is an essential part of both the Fourth and Fourteenth Amendments is not only the logical dictate of prior cases, but it also makes very good sense. There is no war between the Constitution and common sense. Presently, a federal prosecutor may make no use of evidence illegally seized, but a State's attorney across the street may, although he supposedly is operating under the enforceable prohibitions of the same Amendment. Thus the State, by admitting evidence unlawfully seized, serves to encourage disobedience to the Federal Constitution which it is bound to uphold. . . .

Federal-state cooperation in the solution of crime under constitutional standards will be promoted, if only by recognition of their now mutual obligation to respect the same fundamental criteria in their approaches. . . .

The ignoble shortcut to conviction left open to the States tends to destroy the entire system of constitutional restraints on which the liberties of the people rest. Having once recognized that the right to privacy embodied in the Fourth Amendment is enforceable against the States, and that the right to be secure against rude invasions of privacy by state officers is, therefore, constitutional in origin, we can no longer permit the right to remain an empty promise. Because it is enforceable in the same manner and to like effect as other basic rights secured by the Due Process Clause, we can no longer permit it to be revocable at the whim of any police officer who, in the name of law enforcement itself, chooses to suspend its enjoyment. Our decision, founded on reason and truth, gives to the individual no more than that which the Constitution guarantees him, to the police officer no less than that to which honest

(continued)

law enforcement is entitled, and, to the courts, that
judicial integrity so necessary in the true administration of justice.

The judgment of the Supreme Court of Ohio is
reversed and the cause remanded for further proceedings not inconsistent with this opinion.
Reversed and remanded.

[Concurring opinions by Justices Black and Douglas
are omitted.]

Memorandum of Justice Stewart.

. . . I express no view as to the merits of the constitutional issue which the Court today decides. I
would, however, reverse the judgment in this case,
because I am persuaded that the [Ohio obscenity
statute], upon which the petitioner's conviction was
based, is, in the words of Mr. Justice Harlan, not
"consistent with the rights of free thought and expression assured against state action by the Fourteenth Amendment."

**JUSTICE HARLAN, with whom JUSTICE
FRANKFURTER and JUSTICE WHITTAKER
join, dissenting.**

In overruling the *Wolf* case the Court, in my opinion, has forgotten the sense of judicial restraint
which, with due regard for *stare decisis,* is one element that should enter into deciding whether a past
decision of this Court should be overruled. Apart
from that I also believe that the *Wolf* rule represents
sounder Constitutional doctrine than the new rule
which now replaces it.

. . . [T]he new and pivotal issue brought to the
Court by this appeal is whether [the Ohio obscenity
statute] . . . under which appellant has been convicted, is consistent with the rights of free thought
and expression assured against state action by the
Fourteenth Amendment. That was the principal
issue which was decided by the Ohio Supreme
Court, which was tendered by appellant's Jurisdictional Statement, and which was briefed and argued
in this Court.

Given this posture of things, I think it fair to
say that five members of this Court have simply
"reached out" to overrule *Wolf.* With all respect for
the views of the majority, and recognizing that *stare
decisis* carries different weight in constitutional adjudication than it does in nonconstitutional decision, I can perceive no justification for regarding
this case as an appropriate occasion for reexamining
Wolf. . . .

It cannot be too much emphasized that what was
recognized in *Wolf* was not that the Fourth Amendment *as such* is enforceable against the States as a
facet of due process. . . . It would not be proper to
expect or impose any precise equivalence, either as
regards the scope of the right or the means of its
implementation, between the requirements of the
Fourth and Fourteenth Amendments. For the
Fourth, unlike what was said in *Wolf* of the Fourteenth, does not state a general principle only; it is
a particular command, having its setting in a pre-
existing legal context on which both interpreting
decisions and enabling statutes must build. . . .

I would not impose upon the States this federal
exclusionary remedy. The reasons given by the majority for now suddenly turning its back on *Wolf*
seem to me notably unconvincing. . . .

The preservation of the proper balance between
state and federal responsibility in the administration
of criminal justice demands patience on the part
of those who might like to see things move faster
among the States in this respect. Problems of criminal law enforcement vary widely from State to State.
One State, in considering the totality of its legal picture, may conclude that the need for embracing the
Weeks rule is pressing because other remedies are
unavailable or inadequate to secure compliance with
the substantive Constitutional principle involved.
Another, though equally solicitous of Constitutional
rights, may choose to pursue one purpose at a time,
allowing all evidence relevant to guilt to be brought
into a criminal trial, and dealing with Constitutional
infractions by other means. Still another may consider the exclusionary rule too rough-and-ready a
remedy, in that it reaches only unconstitutional intrusions which eventuate in criminal prosecution of
the victims. Further, a State after experimenting
with the *Weeks* rule for a time may, because of unsatisfactory experience with it, decide to revert to a
non-exclusionary rule. And so on. . . . In my view
this Court should forbear from fettering the States
with an adamant rule which may embarrass them in
coping with their own peculiar problems in criminal
law enforcement. . . .

I regret that I find so unwise in principle and so
inexpedient in policy a decision motivated by the
high purpose of increasing respect for Constitutional
rights. But in the last analysis I think this Court can
increase respect for the Constitution only if it rigidly
respects the limitations which the Constitution
places upon it, and respects as well the principles
inherent in its own processes. In the present case I
think we exceed both, and that our voice becomes
only a voice of power, not a voice of reason.

the *Wolf* decision because Frankfurter's majority opinion in that case had said that the exclusionary rule "was not derived from the explicit requirements of the Fourth Amendment. . . . The decision was a matter of judicial implication." The justices who support the imposition of the exclusionary rule tend to argue that it is required by the Constitution while those who oppose the rule argue that it was created by judges—and therefore it can be changed by judges.

Third, the majority opinion in *Mapp* concluded that alternatives to the exclusionary rule do not work. Clark's opinion noted that many states that had attempted to follow Frankfurter's ideas in *Wolf* had found that nothing short of exclusion of evidence would work to correct constitutional rights violations and limit the number of violations that occur.

Fourth, the *Mapp* opinion argued that the use of improperly obtained evidence by officials who are responsible for upholding the law serves only to diminish respect for the law. In Clark's words, "Thus the State, by admitting evidence unlawfully seized, serves to encourage disobedience to the Federal Constitution which it is bound to uphold."

Fifth, the *Mapp* decision indicates that the absence of an exclusionary rule diminishes the protection of all rights because it would permit all constitutional rights "to be revocable at the whim of any police officer who, in the name of law enforcement itself, chooses to suspend . . . [the] enjoyment [of rights]."

Sixth, the exclusionary rule is justified as an effective means of deterring police and prosecutors from violating constitutional rights. As described in Justice Murphy's dissenting opinion in *Wolf,*

> [O]ne remedy exists to deter violations of the search and seizure clause. Only by exclusion can we impress upon the zealous prosecutor that violation of the Constitution will do him no good. And only when that point is driven home can the prosecutor be expected to emphasize the importance of observing constitutional demands in his instructions to the police. (338 U.S. at 44)

Despite the justification underlying the exclusionary rule, the rule has many critics, including justices on the Supreme Court. In the immediate aftermath of the *Mapp* opinion, many law enforcement officials, commentators, and politicians harshly criticized the Court's decision. They complained that the Court's decision would hamper police investigations and allow guilty criminals to go free. When Richard Nixon ran for president of the United States in 1968, he made law and order a central campaign issue, in part, by accusing the Supreme Court and other federal judges of being too soft on crime. He vowed to appoint new judges who would alter the balance between protection of rights and crime control by giving greater emphasis to the empowerment of law enforcement officials. After winning the election, he had the opportunity to appoint four new Supreme Court justices, each of whom was less inclined to support the protection of constitutional rights than his predecessors.

CRITICISMS OF THE EXCLUSIONARY RULE

The first justice appointed by Nixon was Warren Burger, a federal court of appeals judge appointed to replace the retiring Earl Warren as chief justice. Burger had a reputation as a law and order justice, and he was appointed as a result of Nixon's vow to make the high court less supportive of rights for criminal defendants. Burger was known as a critic of the exclusionary rule, and he made a detailed presentation of his views in *Bivens v. Six Unknown Named Agents of the Federal Bureau of Narcotics* (1971). As you read the case excerpt in the accompanying box, compare Chief Justice Burger's analysis of the exclusionary role with that presented by Justice Frankfurter in *Wolf v. Colorado* (1949) and by Justice Clark in *Mapp v. Ohio* (1961).

Burger's dissent set forth many of the arguments against the application of the exclusionary rule. First, Burger complains that guilty offenders will be freed because of mistakes by police officers. He indicates that this result imposes a high cost on society, presumably by endangering the public and failing to enforce criminal laws. Burger refers to "the high price it exacts from society—the release of countless guilty criminals." As you read the accompanying box about the measurement of the exclusionary rule's cost to society, think about whether you agree with Chief Justice Burger's conclusions.

C A S E **Bivens v. Six Unknown Named Agents of the Federal Bureau of Narcotics, 403 U.S. 388 (1971)**

[The case concerned whether federal law enforcement officers could be subject to a lawsuit by someone whose home was subjected to an aggressive search and was later taken into custody and strip searched. The majority opinion, written by Justice William Brennan, concluded that federal officers could be subject to lawsuits based on alleged constitutional rights violations.]

[Justice Brennan's majority opinion is omitted.]

CHIEF JUSTICE BURGER, dissenting.

This case has significance far beyond its facts and its holding. For more than 55 years this Court has enforced a rule under which evidence of undoubted reliability and probative value has been suppressed and excluded from criminal cases whenever it was obtained in violation of the Fourth Amendment. . . . This rule was extended to the States in *Mapp v. Ohio*. . . . The rule has rested on a theory that suppression of evidence in these circumstances was imperative to deter law enforcement authorities from using improper methods to obtain evidence.

The deterrence theory underlying the suppression doctrine, or exclusionary rule, has a certain appeal in spite of the high price society pays for such a drastic remedy. Notwithstanding its plausibility, many judges and lawyers and some of our most distinguished legal scholars have never quite been able to escape the force of [Justice Benjamin] Cardozo's statement of the doctrine's anomalous result:

The criminal is to go free because the constable has blundered. . . . A room is searched against the law, and the body of a murdered man is found. . . . The privacy of the home has been infringed, and the murderer goes free. People v. Defore [1926]. . . .

The plurality opinion in *Irvine v. California* [1954] . . . catalogued the doctrine's defects:

Rejection of the evidence does nothing to punish the wrong-doing official, while it may, and likely will, release the wrong-doing defendant. It deprives society of its remedy against one lawbreaker because he has been pursued by another. It protects one against whom incriminating evidence is discovered, but does nothing to protect innocent persons who are the victims of illegal but fruitless searches.

From time to time members of the Court, recognizing the validity of these protests, have articulated varying alternative justifications for the suppression of important evidence in a criminal trial. Under one of these alternative theories the rule's foundation is shifted to the "sporting contest" thesis that the government must "play the game fairly" and cannot be allowed to profit from its own illegal acts . . . ; [b]ut the exclusionary rule does not ineluctably flow from a desire to ensure that government plays the "game" according to the rules. If an effective alternative remedy is available, concern for official observance of the law does not require adherence to the exclusionary rule. Nor is it easy to understand how a court can be thought to endorse a violation of the Fourth Amendment by allowing illegally seized evidence to be introduced against a defendant if an effective remedy is provided against the government. . . .

. . . Rather, the exclusionary rule has rested on the deterrent rationale—the hope that law enforcement officials would be deterred from unlawful searches and seizures if the illegally seized, albeit trustworthy, evidence was suppressed often enough and the courts persistently enough deprived them of any benefits they might have gained from their illegal conduct.

This evidentiary rule is unique to American jurisprudence. Although the English and Canadian legal systems are highly regarded, neither has adopted our rule.

I do not question the need for some remedy to give meaning and teeth to the constitutional guarantees against unlawful conduct by government officials. Without some effective sanction, these protections would constitute little more than rhetoric. Beyond doubt the conduct of some officials requires sanctions. . . . But the hope that this objective could be accomplished by the exclusion of reliable evidence from criminal trials was hardly more than a wistful dream. Although I would hesitate to abandon it until some meaningful substitute is developed, the history of the suppression doctrine demonstrates that it is both conceptually sterile and practically ineffective in accomplishing its stated objective. This is illustrated by the paradox that an unlawful act against a totally innocent person—such as petitioner claims to be—has been left without an effective remedy, and hence the Court finds it necessary now—55 years later—to construct a remedy of its own.

Some clear demonstration of the benefits and effectiveness of the exclusionary rule is required to justify it in view of the high price it extracts from society—the release of countless criminals. . . . But there is no empirical evidence to support the claim that the rule actually deters illegal conduct of law enforcement officials. . . .

There are several reasons for this failure. The rule does not apply any direct sanction to the individual official whose illegal conduct results in the exclusion of evidence in a criminal trial. With rare exceptions law enforcement agencies do not impose direct sanctions on the individual officer responsible for a particular judicial application of the suppression doctrine. . . . Thus there is virtually nothing done to bring about a change in his practices. The immediate sanction triggered by the application of

the rule is visited upon the prosecutor whose case against a criminal is either weakened or destroyed. The doctrine deprives the police in no real sense; except that apprehending wrongdoers is their business, police have no more stake in successful prosecutions than prosecutors or the public. . . .

But the prosecutor who loses his case because of police misconduct is not an official in the police department; he can rarely set in motion any corrective action or administrative penalties. Moreover, he does not have control or direction over police procedures or police actions that lead to the exclusion of evidence. It is the rare exception when a prosecutor takes part in arrests, searches, or seizures so that he can guide police action. . . .

The presumed educational effect of judicial opinions is also reduced by the long time lapse—often several years—between the original police action and its final judicial evaluation. Given a policeman's pressing responsibilities, it would be surprising if he ever bcomes aware of the final result after such a delay. Finally, the exclusionary rule's deterrent impact is diluted by the fact that there are large areas of police activity that do not result in criminal prosecutions—hence the rule has virtually no applicability and no effect in such situations. . . .

. . . Suppressing unchallenged truth has set guilty criminals free but demonstrably has neither deterred deliberate violations of the Fourth Amendment nor decreased those errors in judgment that will inevitably occur given the pressures inherent in police work having to do with serious crimes.

. . . Inadvertent errors of judgment that do not work any grave injustice will inevitably occur under the pressure of police work. These honest mistakes have been treated in the same way as deliberate and flagrant . . . violations of the Fourth Amendment. . . .

In characterizing the suppression doctrine as an anomalous and ineffective mechanism with which to regulate law enforcement, I intend no reflection on the motivation of those members of this Court who hoped it would be a means of enforcing the Fourth Amendment. Judges cannot be faulted for being offended by arrests, searches, and seizures that violate the Bill of Rights or statutes intended to regulate public officials. But we can and should be faulted for clinging to an unworkable and irrational concept of law. My criticism is that we have taken so long to find better ways to accomplish these desired objectives. And there are better ways. . . .

Reasonable and effective substitutes can be formulated if Congress would take the lead, as it did

(continued)

for example in 1946 in the Federal Tort Claims Act. I see no insuperable obstacle to the elimination of the suppression doctrine if Congress would provide some meaningful and effective remedy against unlawful conduct by government officials. . . .

[Concludes that lawsuits against police officers may not work because "[j]urors may well refuse to penalize a police officer at the behest of a person they believe to be a 'criminal' and probably will not punish an officer for honest errors of judgment.". . .]

I conclude, therefore, that an entirely different remedy is necessary but it is one that in my view is as much beyond judicial power as the step the Court takes today. Congress should develop an administrative or quasijudicial remedy against the government itself to afford compensation and restitution for persons whose Fourth Amendment rights have been violated. . . .

Second, Burger argues that there is no evidence that the exclusionary rule actually deters police from conducting illegal searches or otherwise violating constitutional rights during criminal investigations.

Third, the opinion says that prosecutors are punished by the exclusionary rule rather than the police officers who committed the rights violation. Thus Burger indicates that the rule's sanctioning mechanism is misdirected, especially because he says that prosecutors do not oversee and guide police investigations. Because the prosecutor is not part of the police department, he or she cannot initiate any internal disciplinary actions against officers who conduct illegal searches or interrogations.

Fourth, because of the time lag between the commission of the alleged rights violation and ultimate court decisions about excluding evidence, Burger says that police officers may not hear about the result in the case. Thus the rule does not have any educational value in teaching police officers about the consequences of improper investigatory procedures.

Fifth, Burger complains that it is wrong to apply the same sanction to intentional, flagrant rights violations by police and inadvertent violations that may occur because of officers' mistakes. Police officers may violate rights when, for example, they believe a warrantless search is permitted under law in circumstances when, in fact, it is not. Burger implies that a stronger remedy, such as exclusion, might be justified for intentional rights violations, but that such sanctions are not appropriate when police officers make an inadvertent error.

Sixth, Burger returns, in effect, to Frankfurter's arguments in *Wolf* by arguing that alternative remedies can be developed that will be adequate to solve the problem of rights violations. Specifically, he suggests that legislatures can enact statutes to provide compensation for people whose rights are violated by law enforcement officers.

The arguments put forth by Burger do not merely represent his unique, personal views on the exclusionary rule. Burger's views are representative of those of many legislators, judges, and law professors. There are, however, significant numbers of other legal professionals who believe that the arguments in *Mapp* present a compelling case in favor of the exclusionary rule. The disagreement often has to do with the observers' values and what they see as the appropriate balance between individuals' rights and society's crime control interests. Those who place great emphasis on crime control are likely to be sympathetic to Burger's arguments. People who are concerned about police misbehavior and the preservation of rights are likely to find the *Mapp* opinion to be persuasive.

| A CLOSER LOOK | The Exclusionary Rule's Cost to Society |

Justices and other legal experts have debated the costs to society of the exclusionary rule. Society pays a price for the preservation of rights when guilty people are set free. This is true both because they may cause additional crimes that otherwise would not have occurred if they had been incarcerated and because the effectiveness and image of law are diminished when people see the guilty go free. While some people may argue that the cost to society is too high if even one guilty person goes free, many other people see such thinking as imposing a more significant cost on society by permitting law enforcement officials to violate people's constitutional rights.

Studies of the impact of the exclusionary rule have produced two consistent findings. First, only a small minority of defendants file a "motion to suppress," which is used to ask a judge to exclude evidence that has allegedly been obtained in violation of the defendant's rights. Second, only a very small fraction of motions to suppress evidence are granted. As summarized by one scholar:

[One study] found that motions to suppress physical evidence were made in fewer than 5 percent of all cases and were successful in only 0.69 percent of the total. A General Accounting Office (GAO) study of the federal courts found that motions to suppress evidence were filed in only 11 percent of all cases and that between 80 and 90 percent were denied. Finally, a study of search warrants by the National Center for State Courts showed that only 5 percent of all motions to suppress were successful.[1]

Other studies have found only 0.8 percent of felony cases rejected for prosecution because of illegally obtained evidence[2] and a 0.9 percent success rate for motions to suppress when rights were allegedly violated despite the issuance of a search warrant.[3]

What if you were a policy analyst and you were asked to calculate the cost to society of the exclusionary rule? What factors would you consider in calculating the costs? How much of a cost would have to be shown before you would conclude that the costs to society are "too high?"

What is most relevant for the preservation or alteration of the exclusionary rule is not how analysts view the rule but, rather, how the justices on the Supreme Court view the rule. President Nixon, the law and order advocate, was able to appoint four new justices during the 1970s. The next six appointees through 1991 were all placed on the Court by Republican presidents who shared Nixon's desire to give greater authority to police officers. Although these justices did not all fulfill their appointing presidents' hopes that the exclusionary rule would be weakened or eliminated, the philosophical composition of the Court changed significantly from what it was when the exclusionary rule was incorporated during the 1960s. The Court's new orientation toward limiting rights for criminal defendants created the opportunity for Burger to see decisions adopting and advancing his arguments in *Bivens*.

EXCEPTIONS TO THE "FRUIT OF THE POISONOUS TREE" DOCTRINE

One development that reduced the impact of the exclusionary rule was the Court's creation of three exceptions to the "fruit of the poisonous tree" doctrine. Under the circumstances of the three exceptions, evidence may be admissible in court despite the fact that police officers violated constitutional rights during the course of criminal investigations. The three exceptions are (1) the attenuation doctrine, (2) the independent source rule, and (3) the inevitable discovery doctrine.

The Attenuation Doctrine

Under the **attenuation doctrine,** courts must consider whether evidence obtained after illegal actions by the police was gathered as a result of the illegality or whether the evidence was gained by means that were distinguishable from the improper action. This is sometimes called the "purged taint" exception because it asks whether the means through which the police obtained the evidence was sufficiently distant from the prior illegal action to "purge," or remove, the taint of the rights violation. For example, imagine that a suspect is identified through an improper arrest and interrogation of her partner in crime. However, the suspect comes to the police station voluntarily and confesses of her own free will. Thus the voluntariness of the confession can "purge the taint" of the illegal arrest and questioning that first led to the suspect's identification. Even though the police violated Fourth and Fifth Amendment rights in identifying the suspect, the confession may be admissible in court because it was obtained through the suspect's voluntary action and was distinguishable from the specific information obtained through the rights violation.

In *Brown v. Illinois* (1975), the Supreme Court spelled out the tests for determining whether confessions are admissible when they are obtained after a chain of events that included improper actions by law enforcement officers.

> *The question whether a confession is the product of a free will . . . must be answered on the facts of each case. No single fact is dispositive. . . .*
> *The* Miranda *warnings are an important factor, to be sure, in determining whether the confession is obtained by exploitation of an illegal arrest. But they are not the only factor to be considered. The temporal proximity of the arrest and the confession, the presence of intervening circumstances, and, particularly, the purpose and flagrancy of the official misconduct are all relevant. The voluntariness of the statement is a threshold requirement. And the burden of showing admissibility rests, of course, on the prosecution. (422 U.S. 590, 603–604)*

If we rephrase the Court's tests, we see that the prosecution must establish that the mix of factors favors admitting the voluntary confession. The prosecution's cause will be advanced if the person confessing was informed of his or her *Miranda* rights by the police. In addition, the longer the time period between the illegal search or arrest and the subsequent confession, the more likely it is that the court will accept the confession. The long time period can help to demonstrate that the suspect made a deliberate decision to confess that was not directly influenced by the police officers' improper actions which occurred at some earlier point in time. A confession that occurs immediately after an improper arrest, by contrast, is more likely to be considered tainted by the illegal action. The prosecution's interests can be helped by "intervening circumstances" that create greater separation between the illegal action and the voluntary confession. For example, if a suspect is improperly arrested but released on bail, and then comes to the police station voluntarily to confess several days later, the release and the passage of time will diminish the impact of the illegal arrest.

Lastly, if the police conduct was especially flagrant, such as physical abuse of the suspect, then it will be much more difficult for the prosecutor to persuade the court that the confession should be accepted, even if it is made later.

Most cases that raise the issue of the attenuation doctrine concern confessions obtained after an illegal search. Sometimes, however, the illegal search or improper questioning may precede another search or a police lineup, and the attenuation question will concern the admissibility of evidence from the second search or lineup. In these circumstances, the courts must still examine the circumstances of each case and evaluate the *Brown* factors of time between illegal action and acquisition of evidence ("temporal proximity"), any intervening circumstances, and the outrageousness of the police actions.[4]

The Independent Source Rule

The exclusion of evidence can also be avoided if law enforcement officials can establish that they obtained the evidence from a source that was separate from and independent of improper searches or questioning that occurred. For example, in *Murray v. United States* (1988), police suspected several people of involvement with illegal drugs. They kept these individuals under surveillance and observed them going in and out of a warehouse. The police stopped two vehicles that left the warehouse and discovered that the vehicles contained marijuana. After confirming their suspicions about the existence of drugs and arresting the drivers, officers entered the unoccupied warehouse and observed many wrapped bales that they suspected contained large quantities of marijuana. The officers left the warehouse and obtained a search warrant. Upon reentering the warehouse with the warrant, the officers confirmed that the bales contained marijuana.

The defendants sought to have the marijuana excluded as the fruit of an improper warrantless entry into the warehouse. However, the Supreme Court concluded that the marijuana could be used in evidence against the defendants. When the officers had provided information to a judge in order to obtain the search warrant, they made no mention of the fact that they had entered the warehouse and observed the bales. Instead, probable cause was established based on their observations prior to entering the warehouse and information obtained in the legal stop and seizure of the vehicles and drivers. Thus the officers obtained the search warrant and the bales of marijuana through legal sources of information that were independent of the improper warrantless entry into the warehouse. According to Justice Antonin Scalia's majority opinion,

> *Knowledge that the marijuana was in the warehouse was assuredly acquired at the time of the unlawful entry. But it was also acquired at the time of entry pursuant to a warrant, and if that later acquisition was not the result of the earlier entry there is no reason why the independent source doctrine should not apply. Invoking the exclusionary rule would put the police (and society) not in the same position they would have occupied if no violation occurred, but in a worse one. (487 U.S. 533, 541)*

In dissent, Justice Thurgood Marshall complained that the majority "fail[ed] to provide sufficient guarantees that the subsequent search was, in fact, independent of the illegal search." In a separate dissent, Justice John Paul Stevens labeled the independent source doctrine "unacceptable" because it "provide[s] government agents with an affirmative incentive to engage in unconstitutional violations of the privacy of the home." In effect, Stevens illuminated the point that there is no practical remedy for the rights violations that become ignored when the independent source rule permits officials to avoid the exclusion of evidence. The same problem arguably exists with the attenuation doctrine and the inevitable discovery rule.

The Inevitable Discovery Rule

The Supreme Court's endorsement of the **inevitable discovery rule** arose from a controversial case involving the tragic abduction and murder of a young girl in 1968. The victim disappeared from a YMCA on Christmas Eve. The police sought an escapee from a psychiatric hospital who was seen carrying a large bundle out of the YMCA. The man being sought by police contacted an attorney and arranged to surrender to police in a town 160 miles away from the scene of the abduction. The Supreme Court subsequently found that the police had improperly questioned the suspect outside of the presence of his attorney while driving him back to the city where the abduction occurred (*Brewer v. Williams,* 1977). The comments directed at the suspect by the police had led the suspect to admit his guilt and led the officers to the location of the girl's body. The Supreme Court declared that the body and the suspect's statements had to be excluded from evidence because they were obtained in violation of his rights. Thus his murder conviction was overturned and he was given a new trial. At the second trial, he was convicted again. However, at the second trial, the prosecution used the body in evidence against him based on the claim that search parties would have found the body eventually. There was a search team within 2½ miles of the body at the time it was found. Although the body was actually found as a result of improperly obtained statements, the prosecution asserted that it could use the evidence anyway. As you read the case excerpt from *Nix v. Williams* (1984) in the accompanying box, ask yourself whether you agree with the Court's endorsement of the inevitable discovery rule.

As indicated by the opinions in *Nix,* all of the justices endorsed the validity of the inevitable discovery doctrine. The dissenting justices disagreed with the standard of proof necessary to show that the evidence would have been discovered inevitably. The majority required only that the prosecution show by "a preponderance of evidence" that the discovery would have occurred. This means merely that available information tilts in favor of the prosecution's claim. It is as if the prosecution must show that the evidence was *likely* to be discovered. It is a relatively low standard of proof. By contrast, the dissenters would require the prosecutor to show by "clear and convincing evidence" that the evidence would have been inevitably discovered. This is a much more difficult standard to fulfill because the prosecution must establish that it was *virtually certain* that the evidence would have been discovered.

ALTERATION OF THE EXCLUSIONARY RULE

Collateral Use Exception

Early in the 1970s, the Supreme Court's decision in *Harris v. New York* (1971) provided an indication that the exclusionary rule would not be a strong barrier to using improperly obtained evidence in a prosecution. In *Harris,* a suspect

C A S E *Nix v. Williams,* **467 U.S. 431 (1984)**

CHIEF JUSTICE BURGER delivered the opinion of the Court.

. . .

The Iowa Supreme Court correctly stated that the "vast majority" of all courts, both state and federal, recognize an inevitable discovery exception to the exclusionary rule. We are now urged to adopt and apply the so-called ultimate or inevitable discovery exception to the exclusionary rule.

Williams contends that the evidence of the body's location and condition is "fruit of the poisonous tree," i.e., the "fruit" or product [of the comments from the police to the suspect which we previously found to constitute improper questioning outside of the presence of counsel]. He contends that admitting the challenged evidence violated the Sixth Amendment whether it would have been inevitably discovered or not. . . .

The core rationale consistently advanced by this Court for extending the exclusionary rule to evidence that is the fruit of unlawful police conduct has been that this admittedly drastic and socially costly course is needed to deter police from violations of constitutional and statutory protections. This Court has accepted the argument that the way to ensure such protections is to exclude evidence seized as a result of such violations notwithstanding the high social cost of letting persons obviously guilty go unpunished for their crimes. On this rationale, the prosecution is not to be put in a better position than it would have been if no illegality had transpired.

By contrast, derivative evidence analysis ensures that the prosecution is not put in a worse position simply because of some earlier police error or misconduct. The independent source doctrine allows the admission of evidence that has been discovered by means wholly independent of any constitutional violation. That doctrine, although closely related to the inevitable discovery doctrine, does not apply here; Williams' statements to [the detective in the car] led police to the child's body, but that is not the whole story. The independent source doctrine teaches us that the interest of society in deterring unlawful police conduct and the public interest in having juries receive all probative evidence of a crime are properly balanced by putting the police in the same, not a worse, position than they would have been in if no police error or misconduct had

occurred. . . . When challenged evidence has an independent source, exclusion of such evidence would put the police in a worse position than they would have been in if no police error or misconduct had occurred. There is a functional similarity between these two doctrines in that exclusion of evidence that would inevitably have been discovered would also put the government in a worse position, because the police would have obtained the evidence if no misconduct had taken place. Thus, while the independent source exception would not justify admission of evidence in this case, its rationale is wholly consistent with and justifies our adoption of the ultimate or inevitable discovery exception to the exclusionary rule.

It is clear that the cases implementing the exclusionary rule "begin with the premise that the challenged evidence is in some sense the product of illegal governmental activity.". . . Of course, this does not end the inquiry. If the prosecution can establish by a preponderance of the evidence that the information ultimately or inevitably would have been discovered by lawful means—here the volunteers' search—then the deterrence rationale has so little basis that the evidence should be received. Anything less would reject logic, experience, and common sense. . . .

More than a half century ago, Judge, later Justice, Cardozo made his seminal observation that under the exclusionary rule "[t]he criminal is to go free because the constable has blundered.". . . Prophetically, he went on to consider "how far-reaching in its effect upon society" the exclusionary rule would be when "[t]he pettiest peace officer would have it in his power through overzeal or indiscretion to confer immunity upon an offender for crimes the most flagitious.". . . Some day, Cardozo speculated, some court might press the exclusionary rule to the outer limits of its logic—or beyond—and suppress evidence relating to the "body of a murdered" victim because of the means by which it was found. . . . Cardozo's prophecy was fulfilled in *Killough v. United States,* . . . 315 F.2d 241, 245 (1962) (*en banc*). But when, as here, the evidence in question would inevitably have been discovered without reference to the police error or misconduct, there is no nexus sufficient to provide a taint and the evidence is admissible. . . .

On [the] record it is clear that the search parties were approaching the actual location of the body,

(continued)

and we are satisfied, along with three courts earlier, that the volunteer search teams would have resumed the search had Williams not earlier led the police to the body and the body inevitably would have been found. . . .

JUSTICE STEVENS, concurring in judgment.

. . .

. . . The uncertainty as to whether the body would have been discovered can be resolved in [the prosecution's] favor here only because, as the Court explains . . . , petitioner adduced evidence demonstrating that at the time of the constitutional violation an investigation was already under way which, in the natural and probable course of events, would have soon discovered the body. This is not a case in which the prosecution can escape responsibility for a constitutional violation through speculation; to the extent uncertainty was created by the constitutional violation the prosecution was required to resolve that uncertainty through proof. Even if [the detective] acted in bad faith in the sense that he deliberately violated the Constitution in order to avoid the possibility that the body would not be discovered, the prosecution ultimately does not avoid that risk; its burden of proof forces it to assume the risk. The need to adduce proof sufficient to discharge its burden, and the difficulty in predicting whether such proof will be available or sufficient, means that the inevitable discovery rule does not permit state officials to avoid the uncertainty they would have faced but for the constitutional violation.

The majority refers to the "societal cost" of excluding probative evidence. . . . In my view, the more relevant cost is that imposed on society by police officers who decide to take procedural shortcuts instead of complying with the law. What is the consequence of the shortcut [that the detective] took when he decided to question Williams in this case and not to wait an hour or so until he arrived in [the city in which the abduction took place]? The answer is years and years of unnecessary but costly litigation. Instead of having a 1969 conviction affirmed in routine fashion, the case is still alive 15 years later. Thanks to [the detective], the State of Iowa has expended vast sums of money and countless hours of professional labor in his defense. That expenditure surely provides adequate deterrent to similar violations; the responsibility for that expenditure lies not with the Constitution, but rather with the constable.

JUSTICE BRENNAN, with whom JUSTICE MARSHALL joins, dissenting.

. . .

To the extent that today's decision adopts this "inevitable discovery" exception to the exclusionary rule, it simply acknowledges a doctrine that is akin to the "independent source" exception first recognized by the Court in *Silverthorne Lumber Co. v. United States* . . . (1920). . . . In particular, the Court concludes that unconstitutionally obtained evidence may be admitted at trial if it inevitably would have been discovered in the same condition by an independent line of investigation that was already being pursued when the constitutional violation occurred. As has every Federal Court of Appeals previously addressing this issue, . . . I agree that in these circumstances the "inevitable discovery" exception to the exclusionary rule is consistent with the requirements of the Constitution.

In its zealous efforts to emasculate the exclusionary rule, however, the Court loses sight of the crucial difference between the "inevitable discovery" doctrine and the "independent source" exception from which it is derived. When properly applied, the "independent source" exception allows the prosecution to use evidence only if it was, in fact, obtained by fully lawful means. It therefore does no violence to the constitutional protections that the exclusionary rule is meant to enforce. The "inevitable discovery" exception is likewise compatible with the Constitution, though it differs in one key respect from its next of kin: specifically, the evidence sought to be introduced at trial has not actually been obtained from an independent source, but rather would have been discovered as a matter of course if independent investigations were allowed to proceed.

In my view, this distinction should require that the government satisfy a heightened burden of proof before it is allowed to use such evidence. The inevitable discovery exception necessarily implicates a hypothetical finding that differs in kind from the factual finding that precedes application of the independent source rule. To ensure that this hypothetical finding is narrowly confined to circumstances that are functionally equivalent to an independent source, and to protect fully the fundamental rights served by the exclusionary rule, I would require clear and convincing evidence before concluding that the government had met its burden of proof on this issue. . . .

A CLOSER LOOK | **Collateral Use Exception: Contexts in Which the Exclusionary Rule Does Not Apply**

Grand jury proceedings (*United States v. Calandra,* 1974): A witness summoned to appear before a grand jury cannot refuse to answer questions simply because the questions were based on evidence obtained from an improper search.

Parole revocation hearings (*Pennsylvania Board of Pardons and Parole v. Scott,* 1998): Improperly obtained evidence can be used at parole revocation proceedings.

Immigration deportation hearings (*Immigration and Naturalization Service v. Lopez-Mendoza,* 1984): Improperly obtained evidence can be used at deportation hearings.

Impeachment of defendant testimony (*Harris v. New York,* 1971): Improperly obtained statements can be used to impeach the credibility of defendants who take the witness stand and testify in their own trials.

---

was questioned improperly without being adequately informed of his rights. During that questioning, he made statements regarding his activities that led to his arrest for selling drugs. When he took the witness stand at his trial, however, he gave a different version of events. The prosecution introduced his prior statements into evidence to show that his trial testimony was inconsistent with his prior statements. He sought to have his prior statements excluded from the trial because they had been obtained in violation of his rights. The Supreme Court decided that the improperly obtained statements could be used against him. But they could not be used as evidence to show his guilt. They could be used only for the limited purpose of questioning his truthfulness by showing that he had given inconsistent statements.

This exception to the exclusionary rule's prohibition on the use of improperly obtained evidence had limited applicability because it would arise only when defendants decide to testify at trial—a choice that many defendants decline to make—and when prior inconsistent statements had been given to the police. However, this situation provided an example of the Court's development of the **collateral use exception**. The potential impact of the exclusionary rule is further reduced because the rule is not applicable to various kinds of legal proceedings. The rule applies only with respect to the prosecution's presentation of a case seeking to convict a defendant of a crime. It does not apply in other proceedings, such as grand jury hearings before trial and parole revocation hearings long after a conviction has been obtained. The box "Collateral Use Exception" describes contexts outside of the standard criminal prosecution in which evidence is *not* excluded even if officials commit rights violations in the course of gathering evidence.

"Good Faith" Exception

In the 1980s, the Court's composition had changed significantly from the 1960s and decisions emerged that further reduced the applicability and impact of the exclusionary rule. One of the major decisions was *United States v. Leon* (1984), an excerpt of which appears in the box on pp. 130–133.

United States v. Leon, 468 U.S. 897 (1984)

[*After receiving a tip from a confidential informant of unproven reliability about people selling and storing drugs at certain houses five months earlier, police initiated an investigation of people living at and visiting the named addresses. The police obtained a search warrant from a judge, and they discovered large quantities of illegal narcotics when they conducted their searches. On appeal, the defendants challenged the validity of the search warrant, and the U.S. Court of Appeals determined that the police lacked an adequate basis for obtaining a warrant. The information used to gain the warrant was not sufficiently current because it relied on events from five months earlier. Moreover, the police did not establish the credibility of their confidential informant. Thus the Court of Appeals reversed the conviction and ordered a new trial.*]

JUSTICE WHITE delivered the opinion of the Court.

This case presents the question whether the Fourth Amendment exclusionary rule should be modified so as not to bar the use in the prosecution's case in chief of evidence obtained by officers acting in reasonable reliance on a search warrant issued by a detached and neutral magistrate but ultimately found to be unsupported by probable cause. To resolve this question, we must consider once again the tension between the sometimes competing goals of, on the one hand, deterring official misconduct and removing inducements to unreasonable invasions of privacy and, on the other, establishing procedures under which criminal defendants are "acquitted or convicted on the basis of all the evidence which exposes the truth." . . .

Language in opinions of this Court and of individual Justices has sometimes implied that the exclusionary rule is a necessary corollary of the Fourth Amendment, *Mapp v. Ohio* (1961), *Olmstead v. United States* (1928); or that the rule is required by the conjunction of the Fourth and Fifth Amendments, *Mapp v. Ohio* (Black, J., concurring), *Agnello v. United States* (1925). These implications need not detain us long. The Fifth Amendment theory has not withstood critical analysis or the test of time, see *Andresen v. Maryland* (1976), and the Fourth Amendment "has never been interpreted to proscribe the introduction of illegally seized evidence in all proceedings or against all persons." *Stone v. Powell*, 428 U.S. at 486 (1976).

The Fourth Amendment contains no provision expressly precluding the use of evidence obtained in violation of its commands, and an examination of its origin and purposes makes clear that the use of fruits of a past unlawful search or seizure "work[s] no new Fourth Amendment wrong." *United States v. Calandra*, 414 U.S. at 354 (1974). The wrong condemned by the Amendment is "fully accomplished" by the unlawful search or seizure itself, and the exclusionary rule is neither intended nor able to "cure the invasion of the defendant's rights which he has already suffered.". . . The rule thus operates as "a judicially created remedy designed to safeguard Fourth Amendment rights generally through its deterrent effect, rather than a personal constitutional right of the party aggrieved." *United States v. Calandra,* 414 U.S. at 348. Whether exclusionary sanction is appropriately imposed in a particular case, our decisions make clear, is "an issue separate from the question whether the Fourth Amendment rights of the party seeking to invoke the rule were violated by police conduct." . . . Only the former question is currently before us, and it must be resolved by weighing the costs and benefits of preventing the use in the prosecution's case in chief of inherently trustworthy tangible evidence in reliance on a search warrant issued by a detached and neutral magistrate that ultimately is found to be defective.

The substantial social costs exacted by the exclusionary rule for the vindication of Fourth Amendment rights have long been a source of concern. . . . An objectionable collateral consequence of this interference with the criminal justice system's truth-finding function is that some guilty defendants may go free or receive reduced sentences as a result of favorable plea bargains. Particularly when law enforcement officers have acted in objective good faith or their transgressions have been minor, the magnitude of the benefit conferred on such guilty defendants offends basic concepts of the criminal justice system.

. . . Indiscriminate application of the exclusionary rule, therefore, may well "generat[e] disrespect for the law and administration of justice." . . . Accordingly, "[a]s with any remedial device, the application of the rule has been restricted to those areas where its remedial objectives are thought most efficaciously served." . . .

As yet, we have not recognized any form of good-faith exception to the Fourth Amendment exclusionary rule. But the balancing approach that has evolved during the years of experience with the rule provides strong support for the modification currently urged upon us. As we discuss below[,] our evaluation of the costs and benefits of suppressing reliable physical evidence seized by an officer reasonably relying on a warrant issued by a detached and neutral magistrate leads to the conclusion that such evidence should be admissible in the prosecution's case in chief. . . .

. . . [W]e discern no basis, and are offered none, for believing that exclusion of evidence seized pursuant to a warrant will have a significant deterrent effect on the issuing judge or magistrate. Many of the factors that indicate that the exclusionary rule cannot provide an effective "special" or "general" deterrent for individual offending law enforcement officers apply as well to judges or magistrates. And, to the extent that the rule is thought to operate as a "systemic" deterrent on a wider audience, it clearly can have no such effect on individuals empowered to issue search warrants. Judges and magistrates are not adjuncts to the law enforcement team; as neutral judicial officers, they have no stake in the outcome of particular criminal prosecutions. The threat of exclusion thus cannot be expected significantly to deter them. Imposition of the exclusionary sanction is not necessary meaningfully to inform judicial officers of their errors, and we cannot conclude that admitting evidence obtained pursuant to a warrant while at the same time declaring that the warrant was somehow defective will in any way reduce judicial officers' professional incentives to comply with the Fourth Amendment, encouraging them to repeat their mistakes, or lead to the granting of all colorable warrant requests. . . .

We have frequently questioned whether the exclusionary rule can have any deterrent effect when the offending officers acted in the objectively reasonable belief that their conduct did not violate the Fourth Amendment. "No empirical researcher, proponent or opponent of the rule, has yet been able to establish with any assurance whether the rule has a deterrent effect." . . . But even assuming that the rule effectively deters some police misconduct and provides incentives for the law enforcement profession as a whole to conduct itself in accord with the Fourth Amendment, it cannot be expected, and should not be applied, to deter objectively reasonable law enforcement activity. . . .

. . . [W]hen an officer acting with objective good faith has obtained a search warrant from a judge or magistrate and acted within its scope[,] . . . [i]n most such cases, there is no police illegality and thus nothing to deter. It is the magistrate's responsibility to determine whether the officer's allegations establish probable cause and, if so, to issue a warrant comporting in form with the requirements of the Fourth Amendment. In the ordinary case, an officer cannot be expected to question the magistrate's probable-cause determination or his judgment that the form of the warrant is technically sufficient. . . . Penalizing the officer for the magistrate's error, rather than his own, cannot logically contribute to the deterrence of Fourth Amendment violations.

We conclude that the marginal or nonexistent benefits produced by suppressing evidence obtained in objectively reasonable reliance on a subsequently invalidated search warrant cannot justify the substantial costs of exclusion. We do not suggest, however, that exclusion is always inappropriate in cases where an officer has obtained a warrant and abided by its terms. . . . [T]he officer's reliance on the magistrate's probable-cause determination and on the technical sufficiency of the warrant he issues must be objectively reasonable, . . . and it is clear that in some circumstances the officer will have no reasonable grounds for believing that the warrant was properly issued.

Suppression therefore remains an appropriate remedy if the magistrate or judge in issuing a warrant was misled by information in an affidavit that the affiant knew was false or would have known was false except for his reckless disregard of the truth. . . . The exception we recognize today will also not apply in cases where the issuing magistrate wholly abandoned his judicial role. . . . [I]n such circumstances, no reasonably well trained officer should rely on the warrant. Nor would an officer manifest objective good faith in relying on a warrant based on an affidavit "so lacking in indicia of probable cause as to render official belief in its existence entirely unreasonable." . . . Finally, depending on the circumstances of the particular case, a warrant may be so facially deficient,—*i.e.*, in failing to particularize the place to be searched or the things to be seized—that the executing officers cannot reasonably presume it to be valid. . . .

. . . The good-faith exception for searches conducted pursuant to warrants is not intended to signal our unwillingness strictly to enforce the requirements of the Fourth Amendment, and we do not believe that it will have this effect. As we have already suggested, the good-faith exception, turning as it does on objective reasonableness, should not be difficult to apply in practice. When officers have acted pursuant to a warrant, the prosecution should ordinarily be able to establish objective good faith without a substantial expenditure of judicial time. . . .

(continued)

In the absence of an allegation that the magistrate abandoned his detached and neutral role, suppression is appropriate only if the officers were dishonest or reckless in preparing their affidavit or could not have harbored an objectively reasonable belief in the existence of probable cause. . . .

Accordingly, the judgment of the Court of Appeals is
Reversed.

JUSTICE BLACKMUN, concurring.

. . . [B]ecause I believe that the rule announced today advances the legitimate interests of the criminal justice system without sacrificing the individual rights protected by the Fourth Amendment[,] I write separately . . . to underscore what I regard as the unavoidable provisional nature of today's decisions. . . .

. . . If it should emerge from experience that, contrary to our expectations, the good-faith exception to the exclusionary rule results in a material change in police compliance with the Fourth Amendment, we shall have to reconsider what we have undertaken here. The logic of a decision that rests on untested predictions about police conduct demands no less.

If a single principle may be drawn from this Court's exclusionary rule decisions from *Weeks* through *Mapp v. Ohio* . . . to the decisions handed down today, it is that the scope of the exclusionary rule is subject to change in light of changing judicial understanding about the effects of the rule outside the confines of the courtroom. It is incumbent on the Nation's law enforcement officers, who must continue to observe the Fourth Amendment in the wake of today's decisions, to recognize the double-edged nature of that principle.

JUSTICE BRENNAN, with whom JUSTICE MARSHALL joins, dissenting.

. . .

The Court seeks to justify this result on the ground that the "costs" of adhering to the exclusionary rule in cases like those before us exceed the "benefits." But the language of deterrence and cost/benefit analysis, if used indiscriminantly, can have a narcotic effect. It creates an illusion of technical precision and ineluctability. It suggests that not only constitutional principle but also empirical data support the majority's result. When the Court's analysis is examined carefully, however, it is clear that we have not been treated to an honest assessment of the merits of the exclusionary rule, but have instead been drawn into a curious world where the "costs" of excluding illegally obtained evidence loom to exaggerated heights and where the "benefits" of such exclusion are made to disappear with a mere wave of the hand. . . .

. . . [I]n this bit of judicial stagecraft, while the sets sometimes change, the actors always have the same lines. Given this well-rehearsed pattern, one might have predicted with some assurance how the present case would unfold. First there is the ritual incantation of the "substantial social costs" exacted by the exclusionary rule, followed by the virtually foreordained conclusion that, given the marginal benefits, application of the rule in the circumstances of these cases is not warranted. Upon analysis, however, such a result cannot be justified even on the Court's own terms.

At the outset, the Court suggests that society has been asked to pay a high price—in terms either of setting guilty persons free or of impeding the proper functioning of trials—as a result of excluding relevant physical evidence in cases where the police, in conducting searches and seizing evidence, have made only an "objectively reasonable" mistake concerning the constitutionality of their actions. . . . But what evidence is there to support such a claim? Significantly, the Court points to none, and indeed, as the Court acknowledges [in a footnote], recent studies have demonstrated that the "costs" of the exclusionary rule—calculated in terms of dropped prosecutions and lost convictions—are quite low. Contrary to the claims of the rule's critics that exclusion leads to "the release of countless guilty criminals," . . . these studies have demonstrated that federal and state prosecutors very rarely drop cases because of potential search and seizure problems. For example, a 1979 study prepared at the request of Congress by the General Accounting Office [GAO] reported that only 0.4% of all cases actually declined for prosecution by federal prosecutors were declined primarily because of illegal search problems. . . . If the GAO data are restated as a percentage of *all* arrests, the study shows only 0.2% of all felony arrests are declined for prosecution because of potential exclusionary rule problems. . . . Of course, these data describe only the costs attributable to the exclusion of evidence in all cases; the costs that are due to the exclusion of evidence in the narrower category of cases where police have made objectively reasonable mistakes must necessarily be even smaller. The Court, however, ignores this distinction and mistakenly weighs the aggregated costs of exclusion in *all* cases, irrespective of the circumstances that led to exclusion . . . against the potential benefits associated with only those cases in which evidence is excluded because police reasonably but mistakenly believe that their conduct does not violate the Fourth Amendment. . . . When such faulty scales are used, it is little wonder that the balance tips in favor of restricting the application of the rule. . . .

If the overall educational effect of the exclusionary rule is considered, application of the rule to even those situations in which individual police officers have acted on the basis of a reasonable but mistaken belief that their conduct was authorized can still be expected to have a considerable long-term deterrent effect. If evidence is consistently excluded in these circumstances, police departments will surely be prompted to instruct their officers to devote greater care and attention to providing sufficient information to establish probable cause when applying for a warrant, and to review with some attention the form of the warrant that they have been issued, rather than automatically assuming that whatever document the magistrate has signed will necessarily comport with Fourth Amendment requirements.

After today's decisions, however, that institutional incentive will be lost. Indeed, the Court's "reasonable mistake" exception to the exclusionary rule will tend to put a premium on police ignorance of the law. Armed with the assurance provided by today's decisions that evidence will always be admissible whenever an officer has reasonably relied upon a warrant, police departments will be encouraged to train officers that if a warrant has simply been signed, it is reasonable, without more, to rely on it. Since in close cases there will no longer be any incentive to err on the side of constitutional behavior, police would have every reason to adopt a "let's-wait-until-it's-decided" approach in situations in which there is a question about a warrant's validity or the basis of its issuance. . . .

Although the Court brushes these concerns aside, a host of grave consequences can be expected to result from its decision to carve this new exception out of the exclusionary rule. A chief consequence of today's decisions will be to convey a clear and unambiguous message to magistrates that their decisions to issue warrants are now insulated from subsequent judicial review. Creation of this new exception for good-faith reliance upon a warrant implicitly tells magistrates that they need not take much care in reviewing warrant applications, since their mistakes will from now on have virtually no consequence: If their decision to issue a warrant was

correct, the evidence will be admitted; if their decision to issue the warrant was incorrect but the police relied in good faith on the warrant, the evidence will also be admitted. Inevitably, the care and attention devoted to such an inconsequential chore will dwindle. . . .

When the public, as it quite properly has done in the past as well as in the present, demands that those in government increase their efforts to combat crime, it is all too easy for those in government to seek expedient solutions. In contrast to such costly and difficult measures as building more prisons, improving law enforcement methods, or hiring more prosecutors and judges to relieve the overburdened court systems in the country's metropolitan areas, the relaxation of Fourth Amendment standards seems a tempting, costless means of meeting the public's demand for better law enforcement. In the long run, however, we as a society pay a heavy price for such expediency, because as Justice Jackson observed, the rights guaranteed in the Fourth Amendment "are not mere second-class rights but belong in the catalog of indispensable freedoms." . . . Once lost, such rights are difficult to recover. There is hope, however, that in time this or some later Court will restore these precious freedoms to their rightful place as a primary protection for our citizens against overreaching officialdom. I dissent.

JUSTICE STEVENS, dissenting.

. . .

The notion that a police officer's reliance on a magistrate's warrant is automatically appropriate is one the Framers of the Fourth Amendment would have vehemently rejected. The precise problem that the Amendment was intended to address was *the unreasonable issuance of warrants.* As we have often observed, the Amendment was actually motivated by the practice of issuing general warrants—warrants which did not satisfy the particularity and probable-cause requirements. . . .

In short, the Framers of the Fourth Amendment were deeply suspicious of warrants; in their minds the paradigm of an abusive search was the execution of a warrant not based on probable cause. The fact that colonial officers had magisterial authorization for their conduct when they engaged in general searches surely did not make their conduct "reasonable." The Court's view that it is consistent with our Constitution to adopt a rule that it is presumptively reasonable to rely on a defective warrant is the product of constitutional amnesia. . . .

The *Leon* case created a **"good faith" exception** to the exclusionary rule when officers use search warrants. When officers acted in good-faith reliance on a warrant, the evidence will not be excluded even if the warrant is issued improperly. "Good faith" means that the officers acted with the honest belief that they were following the proper rules. In addition, the reliance and honest belief must be reasonable. If officers knew that a magistrate issued a warrant based on no evidence whatsoever, the officers could not claim that they reasonably and honestly relied on the warrant. Here, they presented evidence of probable cause to the magistrate and the magistrate made the error by issuing a warrant based on information that fell below the standard of "probable cause." The information was deficient because it was stale—it referred to something that had occurred five months earlier—and it came from an informant of unknown reliability.

In his majority opinion in *Leon,* Justice White explicitly acknowledged the Court's need to weigh the costs and benefits of the exclusionary rule: "[T]he . . . question . . . before us . . . must be resolved by weighing the costs and benefits of preventing the use in the prosecution's case in chief of inherently trustworthy tangible evidence obtained in reliance on a search warrant issued by a detached and neutral magistrate that ultimately is found to be defective." In answering the question he posed about the appropriate balance, White also used the language of costs and benefits. White's opinion declared that "the marginal or nonexistent benefits produced by suppressing evidence obtained in objectively reasonable reliance on a subsequently invalidated search warrant cannot justify the substantial costs of exclusion." Moreover, he asserted that "when law enforcement officers have acted in objective good faith or their transgressions have been minor, the magnitude of the benefit conferred on such guilty defendants offends basic concepts of the criminal justice system."

Justice Brennan's dissenting opinion, joined by Justice Marshall, took issue with White's use of the language of cost-benefit analysis to justify his subjective value judgments. Brennan noted that in previous exclusionary rule cases his conservative colleagues had claimed that the costs to society of the exclusionary rule outweigh the rule's benefits without giving any indication of how they are measuring costs and benefits. According to Brennan, "Given this well-rehearsed pattern, one might have predicted with some assurance how the present case would unfold. First there is the ritual incantation of the 'substantial social costs' exacted by the exclusionary rule, followed by the virtually foreordained conclusion that, given the marginal benefits, application of the rule in the circumstances of these cases is not warranted." Brennan then proceeded to discuss the social science studies of the exclusionary rule, which indicated that the rule is seldom raised by defendants, even less frequently successful, and often offset by other kinds of evidence that ensure the conviction of the offender. Brennan worried that the Court was sending the wrong message to police officers by permitting them to take insufficient care in preparing warrant applications. After *Leon,* any deficiencies in approved warrants would be blamed on errant judges and thus improperly obtained evidence could be used at trial.

The *Leon* decision, as well as its companion case, *Massachusetts v. Sheppard* (1984), concerning police officers' good faith use of an improper warrant form, represented the fulfillment of one of Chief Justice Burger's criticisms of the exclusionary rule from his *Bivens* dissent thirteen years earlier. Burger complained that honest mistakes were treated as harshly as intentional rights violations, and the Burger Court acted to differentiate those two categories of actions. From the

| **A CLOSER LOOK** | **"Good Faith" Exceptions to the Exclusionary Rule** |

1. Reasonable reliance on a warrant (*United States v. Leon,* 1984): Officers conducted a search based on a warrant erroneously issued by a magistrate who found probable cause based on stale information from a source of unproven reliability. The exception exists even when the warrant was issued based on erroneous evidence provided by the police as long as the police honestly believed that they were providing correct information. In *Maryland v. Garrison* (1987), police officers relied on a warrant to search the wrong apartment in a building. When the officers obtained the warrant, they had thought there was only one apartment, rather than two, on the third floor of the targeted building. They were able to use evidence found in the apartment, even though there had been no probable cause to search that apartment in the first place.

2. Reliance on statutes later declared unconstitutional (*Illinois v. Krull,* 1987): Officers conducted a search of a junkyard based on a state statute that authorized warrantless searches of such regulated locations. Although the statute was later declared unconstitutional, the evidence found during the improper search could be used against the defendant.

3. Reliance on records maintained by justice system employees (*Arizona v. Evans,* 1995): Officers stopped a man for a traffic violation. A computer check of his license revealed that there was an outstanding warrant for his arrest. They arrested him and found marijuana in the car which they had searched in conjunction with the arrest. Although it later turned out that there was no warrant and that some unknown court employee had failed to clear the warrant from the driver's record, the marijuana could be used against him even though the arrest which justified the search was invalid.

4. Reasonable reliance on a consent to search provided by someone who lacked the authority to grant such consent (*Illinois v. Rodriguez,* 1990): A suspect's girlfriend provided the police with a key and granted permission to search an apartment even though she did not live in the apartment and she was not supposed to have a key. Evidence was admissible against the defendant because the officers reasonably believed that the girlfriend lived in the apartment.

perspective of the individual whose Fourth Amendment rights were violated, it makes little difference whether the violation occurs intentionally or inadvertently. However, the *Leon* decision made clear that a majority on the Court viewed some rights violations from the perspective of law enforcement officers rather than from the perspective of individual claimants. In other words, the justices began with the question "Did the police officers do anything wrong?" rather than with the question "Were any constitutional rights violated?"

It is important to note that the Supreme Court never created a general good-faith exception to permit the admissibility of improperly obtained evidence whenever police officers make an honest mistake. In *Leon,* there was good-faith reliance on a warrant, meaning that the fundamental error was made by the magistrate who issued the warrant. Evidence can still be excluded if officers undertake a warrantless search based on their own discretionary decision, even if they honestly (but wrongly) believe that a warrantless search is permitted in such circumstances. The above box provides examples of other circumstances in which the Supreme Court has recognized a good-faith exception to the exclusionary rule. Some of these cases will be discussed in more detail in subsequent chapters. After reading these exceptions, think about their implications for the protection of individuals' rights as you consider the question posed in the box on p. 136, which addresses exclusionary rule exceptions and the Fourth Amendment.

Exclusionary Rule Exceptions and the Fourth Amendment

The *Weeks* decision declared that "the protection of the [Fourth] Amendment . . . is of no value, and, so far as those thus placed are concerned, might as well be stricken from the Constitution" if law enforcement officials are permitted to use evidence obtained through improper means. This decision has never been overturned. Yet the creation of exceptions to the exclusionary rule now permits the use of evidence obtained in violation of constitutional rights in certain circumstances. Does this mean that the Fourth and Fifth Amendments have been "stricken from the Constitution" for the individuals who are prosecuted through the use of such improperly obtained evidence?

THE EXCLUSIONARY RULE: AN ENDURING IMPACT OR A DOOMED CONCEPT?

After the *Mapp* decision in 1961, the exclusionary rule seemed very clear. It was a **bright-line rule,** meaning that all police officers could understand it and recognize when it would apply. If officers obtained evidence through improper means, it could not be used in court. In effect, the exclusionary rule was a definite, strong "wall" that stopped criminal justice officials from using evidence gained in violation of constitutional rights. Arguably, each exception recognized by the Supreme Court poked a "hole" through this "wall" by identifying a situation in which improperly obtained evidence can be used by the prosecution. Does the exclusionary rule still stand as a "wall" against constitutional violations, or is it more like a figurative slice of "swiss cheese" that provides enough holes to permit ample opportunities for officials to make use of improperly obtained evidence?

The "holes" in the wall are not necessarily small. They may provide significant opportunities for officials to use evidence obtained in violation of constitutional rights. Judges must make decisions about when improperly obtained evidence would have otherwise been inevitably discovered or when police acted in good faith. These judgments may be made in a manner to strictly limit when improperly obtained evidence can be used. Alternatively, these decisions may be made by giving great deference to police officers and thereby give police significant flexibility. Bear in mind that judges are making decisions about the admissibility of evidence based on after-the-fact testimony and arguments by police officers and prosecutors. Thus criminal justice officials have the opportunity to think about how to characterize their thoughts and actions as fitting within one of the exclusionary rule exceptions. Because judges are listening to calculated re-creations of events, there is a risk that they will not be able to make accurate assessments about the police officers' true motives and behavior. In a hearing about the admissibility of evidence, the opposing testimony and arguments are being presented by people who have been caught being involved in criminal activities, so they may have less credibility and persuasiveness to the judge even if their version of events is actually more accurate.

In addition, as the exclusionary rule changed from a bright-line rule to an exception-laden principle that varies by situation, the Court may have made it more difficult for police officers to understand the rule and apply it. There is a greater likelihood that if police officers are concerned about having evidence excluded, they may feel confused about which investigative actions are permissible. Bear in mind, of course, that sometimes police officers do not care about the exclusion of evidence. For example, if officers want to disrupt illegal narcotics sales on a particular street, they may search everyone on the street—without adequate justification—knowing perfectly well that any evidence they find will be excluded in court. However, they are not required to return illegal items to their owners, even if those items were seized improperly. Thus they can seize drugs and disrupt drug dealers' businesses without any concern about the exclusionary rule, because they do not intend to make any arrests. They merely want to disrupt an illegal enterprise.

In light of the number and nature of exceptions created to diminish the impact of the exclusionary rule, why has the Supreme Court never simply eliminated the rule as advocated by Chief Justice Burger in *Bivens*? The exclusionary rule was criticized vigorously from the 1960s onward by political conservatives who have long claimed that the Warren Court provided too many rights for criminal suspects and defendants. Politically conservative presidents, who agreed with these criticisms, appointed ten justices to the Supreme Court from 1969 through 1991. As a result, the Court became less receptive to claims of right by criminal defendants and, as we will see in subsequent chapters, diminished the scope of several rights. Yet the exclusionary rule continues to exist and is applied to prevent the use of evidence in some cases. Why?

Apparently, the justices believe that the exclusionary rule is sometimes necessary. This applies even to those justices who come from politically conservative backgrounds and who believe that rights for criminal defendants have been defined too broadly. The fact is, despite complaints about the exclusionary rule by critics of the courts, political conservatives are still wary of governmental power and therefore see a role for the rule. This point became crystal clear when conservatives in Congress proposed legislation to reform the rule in 1995. The proposed bill purported to permit the admissibility of any improperly obtained evidence if it might have been reasonable for law enforcement officers to believe (albeit erroneously) that their actions were legal at the time they undertook a search. While the proposed legislation was designed and publicized as a means to diminish the exclusionary rule, the authors of the legislation revealed their true receptivity to the rule in some circumstances by declaring that exclusion would still apply to searches undertaken by the Internal Revenue Service and the Bureau of Alcohol, Tobacco, and Firearms. Those happen to be the federal law enforcement agencies that are most disliked by many political conservatives who would like to limit government efforts to collect taxes and seize firearms. The bill, which was never passed by Congress, was largely a symbolic means of generating publicity. The Supreme Court has not permitted Congress to change by statute doctrines that were produced as the result of constitutional interpretation. Thus there was a great risk that the Court would have declared the statute unconstitutional if it had been enacted. In sum, despite the criticism directed at the exclusionary rule and the successful effort to diminish its applicability, it appears to enjoy support across the political spectrum as a means to deter or remedy improper police conduct in some circumstances.

The greatest source of disagreement concerns which circumstances require the application of the exclusionary rule. As indicated by the opposing opinions in cases such as *Leon*, there are significant disagreements among the justices about when and how the rule should apply.

CONCLUSION

The existence of constitutional rights inevitably raises questions about how to remedy the violation of those rights. With respect to rights violations arising during law enforcement officials' efforts to investigate crimes and gather evidence, the Supreme Court has developed and applied the exclusionary rule as a mechanism to deter police misconduct and remedy rights violations. When police officers undertake an improper search or gain incriminating statements from improper questioning, that evidence may be excluded from use in court. The Supreme Court discussed the rule with respect to Fourth Amendment violations by federal officers in *Weeks v. United States* (1914) and, after discussing the concept in the context of state cases over the course of several decades, applied the exclusionary rule to the states in *Mapp v. Ohio* (1961).

The exclusionary rule is controversial because it excludes from use in court evidence that may be important for holding lawbreakers responsible for their actions. The application of the rule creates risks that a criminal may go free if there is no other evidence available to support a criminal conviction. Critics of the exclusionary rule have suggested that a variety of alternative remedies could be used when rights are violated, including disciplining law enforcement officers and filing lawsuits against officials who violate constitutional rights. It has been argued that these alternatives will permit the use of valuable evidence, no matter how it was obtained, while also protecting citizens' rights.

After the Supreme Court's composition changed in the early 1970s through President Richard Nixon's efforts to place four "law and order" justices on the Court, judicial decisions concerning the exclusionary rule began to soften the rule's impact on law enforcement officials. The Supreme Court created "good faith" exceptions to the rule and recognized other situations (i.e., "inevitable discovery") in which improperly obtained evidence could be used in court despite the fact that rights were violated when the police gathered the evidence.

Because of the number and nature of exceptions to the exclusionary rule, there are debates about the extent to which the rule still provides a deterrent and remedy. The rule continues to exist, but there are many situations in which it does not apply.

SUMMARY

- The existence of rights raises issues about how violations of those rights will be remedied.

- The U.S. Supreme Court applied the exclusionary rule to federal law enforcement officers in 1914 as a means to deter and remedy violations of Fourth Amendment rights (*Weeks v. United States*). The exclusionary rule bars the use of evidence obtained in violation of a defendant's constitutional rights.

- After endorsing the use of alternatives (e.g., lawsuits, internal police discipline) to the exclusionary rule in state cases (*Wolf v. Colorado,* 1949), the Supreme Court eventually applied the exclusionary rule to state and local law enforcement officials (*Mapp v. Ohio,* 1961).

- Law enforcement officials and politicians reacted angrily to the Supreme Court's incorporation of the exclusionary rule because of a belief that the rule would permit many criminals to go free. Among the critics of the Supreme Court was Richard Nixon, who promised to appoint "law and order" opponents of the exclusionary rule to the Supreme Court if he became president.

- President Nixon's first Supreme Court appointee, Chief Justice Warren Burger, articulated several criticisms of the exclusionary rule. Among other arguments, he said that the rule punishes the prosecutor and society rather than the police and that the rule should not treat inadvertent rights violations with the same harshness as intentional rights violations.

- After President Nixon appointed four justices to the Supreme Court, the Court began to soften its application of the exclusionary rule by creating "good faith" and other exceptions to the rule, especially during the early 1980s.

- Although critics of the exclusionary rule claim that it imposes significant costs on society, social science studies have found that the rule applies to relatively few criminal justice cases.

- The nature and number of exceptions to the exclusionary rule have created debates about the extent to which the rule operates as a deterrent and remedy for rights violations.

Key Terms

attenuation doctrine   Exception to the exclusionary rule, also known as the "purged taint" exception, which permits the admission of improperly obtained evidence when a subsequent event, such as a confession by the defendant, removes the "taint" of the constitutional violation that led to the discovery of the evidence.

bright-line rule   A clear rule that is understood by police officers and applies to all situations so that officers do not need to make judgments about when and how the rule will apply.

collateral use exception   The legal use of improperly obtained evidence in proceedings other than criminal prosecutions. These proceedings include immigration hearings and grand jury proceedings.

exclusionary rule   Legal principle that evidence obtained in violation of a person's constitutional rights cannot be used against the person in a criminal prosecution.

"fruit of the poisonous tree" doctrine   When evidence is obtained by improper means, any further evidence discovered indirectly as a result of the improper search or interrogation is also excluded because it has been tainted by the initial rights violation.

"good faith" exception   Exception to the exclusionary rule that permits the use of improperly obtained evidence when police officers acted in honest reliance on a warrant improperly issued by a magistrate, a defective statute, or a consent to search by someone who lacked authority to give such permission.

independent source rule   Exception to the exclusionary rule that permits the use of improperly obtained evidence that was also discovered through separate, legal means.

inevitable discovery rule   Exception to the exclusionary rule that permits the use of improperly obtained evidence when it would have been discovered eventually anyway through legal investigatory processes that were already under way.

Additional Readings

Schlesinger, Steven R. 1977. *Exclusionary Injustice: The Problem of Illegally Obtained Evidence.* New York: Dekker. Critical analysis of the exclusionary rule and its effects.

Walker, Samuel. 1998. *Sense and Nonsense About Crime and Drugs: A Policy Guide.* 4th ed. Belmont, Calif.: Wadsworth. Discussion of policy issues, including a response to the critics of the exclusionary rule.

Wilson, Bradford P. 1986. *Enforcing the Fourth Amendment: A Jurisprudential History.* New York: Garland. Historical review of court decisions on the exclusionary rule.

Notes

1. Samuel Walker, *Sense and Nonsense About Crime and Drugs: A Policy Guide,* 4th ed. (Belmont, Calif.: Wadsworth, 1998), 88.

2. Thomas Y. Davies, "A Hard Look at What We Know (And Still Need to Learn) About the 'Costs' of the Exclusionary Rule: The NIJ Study and Other Studies of 'Lost' Arrests," *American Bar Foundation Research Journal* (1983): 611–690.

3. Craig Uchida and Timothy Bynum, "Search Warrants, Motions to Suppress and 'Lost Cases': The Effects of the Exclusionary Rule in Seven Jurisdictions," *Journal of Criminal Law and Criminology* 81 (1991): 1034–1066.

4. Charles H. Whitebread and Christopher Slobogin, *Criminal Procedure: An Analysis of Cases and Concepts,* 4th ed. (New York: Foundation Press, 2000), 41–42.

CHAPTER FIVE

Warrantless Searches: Persons

Imagine that you are hurrying quickly down the street. You overslept and are late for your final exam in college algebra. As you round the corner in front of the university bookstore, you pass a police officer standing on the sidewalk. You zoom past the officer, barely noticing her.

"Hey, you. What's the hurry?" she yells in your direction.

You do not even notice her words because you are preoccupied with the impending exam. You hear someone running behind you and you glance back over your shoulder. It is the police officer running down the street in your direction. You slow down in surprise and look ahead of you to try to see who she might be chasing. Suddenly, she grabs your arm and pushes you up against the building.

"I asked you a question," she says angrily. "Where are you going in such a hurry?"

You are surprised by her anger. "Look, officer. I'm late for my final exam. I didn't hear you say anything. I have to get going." You assume that she will release your arm and you start walking again. But she tightens her grip and pulls you back again.

"What's in your coat pocket?" she asks with great seriousness.

You let out an audible, impatient sigh. In an exasperated tone, you blurt out, "Gosh, what's the big deal!" and you reach for the calculator in your pocket. As your hand touches your pocket, you are suddenly spun around and pushed face first into the brick wall at the side of the building.

"Put your hands up against the wall," the officer orders sharply. "Nobody told you to reach into your pocket."

Her tone strikes fear in your heart and you instantly put both hands against the wall. The officer reaches swiftly into your pocket and, with some difficulty, pulls out the calculator that was jammed inside.

"I was trying to tell you that it was just a calculator," you say.

She seems not to hear. "You can take down your hands and step back from the wall," she says. She hands you the calculator and says coldly, "Somebody just stole money from the cash register at the convenience store down the street. Next time you're asked questions, it would be better for you if you co-operate. Now go on your way."

You resume hurrying toward class at an even faster pace. Your mind is racing from your encounter with the officer. You ask yourself several questions. Should an officer treat you so roughly when you're just hurrying down the street? Can the officer fish around in your pockets when you have not done anything wrong?

This hypothetical encounter between a police officer and a student raises questions about the meaning of the Fourth Amendment. By stopping the student, the officer may have effected a "seizure" under the Fourth Amendment. As we saw in Chapter 3, if a person stopped by police officers is not free to leave, courts will usually label such encounters as "seizures." Seizures may not be "unreasonable," so courts look to see if the officer's action was reasonable under the circumstances. In addition, there was clearly a search when the officer reached into the student's pocket. Again, the Fourth Amendment says that searches may not be "unreasonable." Thus the essential question about this encounter is whether the officer's actions were reasonable.

One could argue that the officer should have gotten a warrant supported by probable cause before seizing and searching the student. As we know, the Fourth Amendment emphasizes the importance of warrants supported by probable cause and issued by neutral judicial officers as a primary method of protecting people's reasonable expectations of privacy. However, the Supreme Court treats the Fourth Amendment's warrant requirement separately from the prohibition against unreasonable searches and seizures. When a warrant is necessary, it must fulfill the Fourth Amendment's required elements of probable cause, particularity, and issuance by a neutral official. But the Court has recognized that a warrant is not feasible in all situations. Thus the justices will permit warrantless searches and seizures provided they are reasonable. For example, remember that arrests—a form of seizure—can be made without warrants in several specific circumstances, including exigent circumstances such as hot pursuit of a fleeing felon.

In this chapter, we will consider the Supreme Court's guidelines for warrantless searches of people. The invasion of someone's clothing or body by a law enforcement officer is generally recognized as a serious intrusion on liberty and reasonable expectations of privacy. Thus the Supreme Court has been presented with many opportunities to define the proper limits of police officers' authority in physically touching and exploring people's bodies while seeking evidence or weapons. Some of the contexts in which people are searched without warrants also enable officers to search places, too. For example, in *Chimel v. California* (1969), the Supreme Court approved warrantless searches of people and nearby areas in conjunction with an arrest. Thus warrantless searches cannot be neatly categorized as exclusively about people or exclusively about places. The divisions used in this chapter and the following chapter were made for clarity and convenience. However, it should be remembered that some warrantless searches affect both people and places.

INTRUSIVENESS AND BODY SEARCHES

Sometimes students say, "If someone has nothing to hide, then he or she shouldn't mind being searched for the good of society's interests in catching criminals." When students make such statements, they are typically thinking of a brief search of a room, a backpack, or a car. If you replied by saying, "So you wouldn't mind if a police officer said to you, 'Take off your pants, I want to search your body,'" the response might very well change. When we talk about searches, we must remember that searches can encompass a variety of extremely intrusive examinations, including close examinations of people's bodies. While people might view themselves as willing to have their backpacks searched, they may be much more reluctant to have law enforcement officers closely examining their bodies.

Our different responses to different kinds of searches reveal that we are likely to have differing expectations of privacy with respect to containers we carry, such as a backpack, and our own bodies. Because the courts recognize these differences in reasonable expectations of privacy, the definition of a "reasonable" warrantless search will vary from situation to situation. Fourth Amendment decisions are generally based on the efforts of courts to strike a balance between the protection of citizens' rights and society's interests in crime control. The more intrusive the search that law enforcement officers want to conduct, the more courts demand increasingly compelling societal interests to be at stake. Would courts permit police officers to strip-search every customer in a store if the store manager reported that a stick of gum was missing? No. Such actions would be so extreme as to be unreasonable. The societal interest in finding that stick of gum would not outweigh the individuals' interests in privacy for their bodies.

How intrusive can searches potentially be? Searches occur every day in the United States that are as intrusive as they could be, including physical probes inside people's bodies. What can justify such intrusive searches?

The Corrections Context

As you read *Bell v. Wolfish* (1979) in the box on p. 144, examine the Supreme Court's justification for **strip searches** in a specific context. Are there other situations in which the Court's balancing of interests and justifications would apply?

Take note of the fact that *Bell v. Wolfish* concerns a federal *jail*, not a *prison*. Although prisons hold people who have been convicted of crimes, jails hold people awaiting trial as well as people serving short sentences and those awaiting transfer to prison. Thus the Court approved strip searches and **body-cavity searches** of people whom the law presumes to be innocent because they have never been convicted of a crime. The Supreme Court concluded that unconvicted pretrial detainees may be subjected to body-cavity searches after contact visits without any probable cause to believe that they are hiding contraband. Notice that the Court reached this conclusion even though it conceded that guards conduct some searches in an abusive manner. Did the Court do anything to protect against abusive searches in this humiliating context? Did the Court adequately weigh the inmates' interests against those of the institution? It appears that the majority of

Bell v. Wolfish, 441 U.S. 520 (1979): Majority Opinion

JUSTICE REHNQUIST delivered the opinion of the Court.

. . .

Inmates at all [federal] Bureau of Prisons facilities, including the MCC [Metropolitan Correctional Center], are required to expose their body cavities for visual inspection as part of a strip search conducted after every contact visit with a person from outside the institution. Corrections officials testified that visual cavity searches were necessary not only to discover but also to deter the smuggling of weapons, drugs, and other contraband into the institution. The District Court upheld the strip search procedure but prohibited the body-cavity searches absent probable cause to believe that the inmate is concealing contraband. . . . Because [jail officials] proved only one instance in the MCC's short history where contraband was found during a body-cavity search, the Court of Appeals affirmed [the District Court's ban on body cavity searches]. . . . In its view, the "gross violation of personal privacy inherent in such a search cannot be outweighed by the government's security interest in maintaining a practice of so little actual utility.". . .

Admittedly, this practice instinctively gives us the most pause. However, assuming for present purposes that inmates, both convicted prisoners and pretrial detainees, retain some Fourth Amendment rights upon commitment to a corrections facility, . . . we nonetheless conclude that these searches do not violate that Amendment. The Fourth Amendment prohibits only unreasonable searches . . . and under the circumstances, we do not believe that these searches are unreasonable.

The test of reasonableness under the Fourth Amendment is not capable of precise definition or mechanical application. In each case it requires a balancing of the need for the particular search against the invasion of personal rights that the search entails. Courts must consider the scope of the particular intrusion, the manner in which it is conducted, the justification for initiating it, and the place in which it is conducted. . . . A detention facility is a unique place fraught with serious security dangers. Smuggling of money, drugs, weapons, and other contraband is all too common an occurrence. And inmate attempts to secrete these items into the facility by concealing them in body cavities are documented in th[e records presented for this case]. . . . That there has been only one instance when an MCC inmate was discovered attempting to smuggle contraband into the institution on his person may be more a testament to the effectiveness of this search technique as a deterrent than to any lack of interest on the part of the inmates to secrete and import such items when the opportunity arises.

We do not underestimate the degree to which these searches may invade personal privacy. Nor do we doubt, as the District Court noted, that on occasion a security guard may conduct the search in an abusive fashion. . . . Such abuse cannot be condoned. The searches must be conducted in a reasonable manner. . . . But we deal here with the question whether visual body-cavity inspections as contemplated by the MCC rules can ever be conducted on less than probable cause. Balancing the significant and legitimate security interests of the institution against the privacy interests of the inmates, we conclude that they can [conduct the searches]. . . .

justices have strong concerns about maintaining institutional security and order. It also appears that unconvicted detainees enjoy no more rights than convicted offenders. The fact that they have not yet been convicted of a crime—and may eventually be released without conviction—does not seem to matter when contrasted with the courts' concerns about the authority of jails to protect security and order.

For comparison, read Justice Thurgood Marshall's dissenting opinion concerning body-cavity searches in the box on p. 145. In light of the facts presented by Marshall, do you agree with the majority's conclusion that body-cavity searches are necessary for institutional security? Did the majority of justices strike the proper balance between the individual's rights and societal interests in approving warrantless body-cavity searches of people in jail?

Bell v. Wolfish, 441 U.S. 520 (1979): Dissenting Opinion

JUSTICE MARSHALL, dissenting.

. . .

In my view, the body-cavity searches of MCC inmates represent one of the most grievous offenses against personal dignity and common decency. After every contact visit with someone from outside the facility, including defense attorneys, an inmate must remove all of his or her clothing, bend over, spread the buttocks, and display the anal cavity for inspection by a correctional officer. Women inmates must assume a suitable posture for vaginal inspection, while men must raise their genitals. And, as the [majority] neglects to note, because of time pressures [during the search process], this humiliating spectacle is frequently conducted in the presence of other inmates.

The District Court found that the stripping was "unpleasant, embarrassing, and humiliating.". . . A psychiatrist testified that the practice placed inmates in the most degrading position possible, . . . a conclusion amply corroborated by the testimony of the inmates themselves. . . . There was evidence, moreover, that these searches engendered among detainees fears of sexual assault, . . . were the occasion for actual threats of physical abuse by guards, and caused some inmates to forgo personal visits.

Not surprisingly, the Government asserts a security justification for such inspections. These searches are necessary, it argues, to prevent inmates from smuggling contraband into the facility. In crediting this justification despite the contrary findings of the two courts below, the Court overlooks the critical facts. As respondents point out, inmates are required to wear one-piece jumpsuits with zippers in the front. To insert an object into the vaginal or anal cavity, an inmate would have to remove the jumpsuit, at least from the upper torso. . . . Since contact visits occur in a glass-enclosed room and are continuously monitored by corrections officers, . . . such a feat would seem extraordinarily difficult. There was medical testimony, moreover, that inserting an object into the rectum is painful and "would require time and opportunity which is not available in the visiting areas, . . . and that visual inspection would probably not detect an object once inserted. . . . Additionally, before entering the visiting room, visitors and their packages are searched thoroughly by a metal detector, fluoroscope, and by hand. . . . Corrections officers may require that visitors leave packages or handbags with guards until the visit is over. . . . Only by blinding itself to the facts presented on this record can the Court accept the Government's security rationale. . . .

That the Court [majority] can uphold these indiscriminate searches highlights the bankruptcy of its basic analysis. Under the test adopted today, the rights of detainees apparently extend only so far as detention officials decide that cost and security will permit. Such unthinking deference to administrative convenience cannot be justified where the interests at stake are those of presumptively innocent individuals, many of whose only proven offense is the inability to afford bail.

I dissent.

Justice Marshall argued that the Court was not carefully striking a balance between the individual's rights and societal interests in security at correctional institutions. Instead, he viewed his colleagues as automatically granting to jail officials whatever authority they claimed to need, despite the risk there could be abuses in the exercise of that authority. Although it is understandable that jail officials would need to be certain detainees are not carrying any contraband when they enter the facility from the outside, it is not clear that the risks of contraband are as high during supervised interactions in the visitors' room while the detainees are wearing full-body jumpsuits. Corrections officials often tell stories about individual prisoners who developed amazingly ingenious methods for acquiring contraband from visitors, such as transferring a balloon full of drugs mouth-to-mouth during a brief kiss. Although these individual stories highlight the need for great vigilance in supervising prisoners, do such stories provide an adequate justification for the most intrusive possible searches of all pretrial detainees? Justice Marshall would require an individualized basis for suspicion to justify the search of a particular detainee. However, the Court's ruling gives broad discretionary authority to jail officials for conducting such searches of all detainees who meet with visitors.

It might be easy to dismiss the issue of jail searches as simply part of the price that one pays for being arrested and therefore completely different from other contexts in society. However, jails and prisons are not the only context in which Fourth Amendment issues arise concerning intrusive body searches. Such searches also affect regular people who have never been arrested if they arouse suspicion while entering the United States after traveling abroad.

The Customs Context

As mentioned in Chapter 3, border crossings provide a specific context in which the Supreme Court has approved suspicionless stops. Both citizens and non-citizens may be detained, questioned, and subjected to searches of their persons and property when entering the United States from another country. Typically, these stops involve only a few moments as customs officers check any required documents, such as passports and visas, inquire about where the person traveled, and ask what the person is bringing into the United States. The customs officers may have a trained dog sniff around people and their luggage checking for drugs or large amounts of cash. The use of such dogs is not considered a search because it is not intrusive and does not violate reasonable expectations of privacy. At the Mexican and Canadian borders and at airports, people may be chosen at random to have their cars and luggage searched. They may also be chosen for such searches because their behavior or their answers to questions arouse the suspicions of customs officers. The justification for these stops and searches is the need to prevent guns, drugs, and other regulated items from entering the country illegally.

The Supreme Court has never defined precise rules for searches by customs officers. Any searches that take place at the discretion of customs officials are clearly warrantless searches. Although there might be some unusual circumstances in which probable cause supports a search, such as if a gun falls out of a traveler's pocket, the vast majority of searches will be justified by some lesser level of suspicion. Other searches may not be based on suspicion at all, if a traveler is chosen at random for a search. The U.S. Customs Service's own handbook permits some suspicion-based searches to be based on a discretionary determination of suspicion by an officer rather than meeting the standard of "reasonable suspicion" that would require the support of some articulable reasons or facts.

The Customs Service instructs its personnel to consider six categories of factors in determining if suspicion exists to justify searching a traveler at a border crossing or an airport:

1. *Behavioral analysis:* signs of nervousness, such as flushed face, avoiding eye contact, excessive perspiration.
2. *Observational techniques:* unexplained bulges in clothing or awkwardness in walking.
3. *Inconsistencies:* discrepancies in answers to questions posed by customs officers.
4. *Intelligence:* information provided to customs officers by informants or other law enforcement officials.
5. *K-9:* signals from law enforcement trained dogs that can sniff around people and luggage.

| A CLOSER LOOK | U.S. Customs Service Policies for Personal Searches |

Search Type	Suspicion Level	Approval
1. Immediate patdown (frisk): a search necessary to ensure that a person is not carrying a weapon.	Suspicion that a weapon may be present	None required
2. Patdown for merchandise: a search for merchandise, including contraband, hidden on a person's body.	One articulable fact	On-duty supervisor
3. Partial body search: the removal of some clothing by a person to recover merchandise reasonably suspected to be concealed on the body.	Reasonable suspicion, based on specific, articulable facts	On-duty supervisor
4. X-ray: medical x-ray by medical personnel to determine the presence of merchandise within the body.	Reasonable suspicion, based on specific, articulable facts	Port director and court order, unless person consents
5. Body-cavity: any visual or physical intrusion into the rectal or vaginal cavity.	Reasonable suspicion, based on specific, articulable facts	Port director and court order, unless person consents
6. MBM (monitored bowel movement): detention of a person for the purpose of determining whether contraband or merchandise is concealed in the alimentary canal.	Reasonable suspicion, based on specific, articulable facts	Port director

6. *Incident to a seizure or an arrest:* the discovery of contraband in one suitcase can justify the search of the person and the rest of the person's property.

As the officers look for these indicators of suspicion that may justify a search, they must also decide what level of search is justified when their suspicions are aroused. In response to complaints and lawsuits about improper searches, the Customs Service has developed and refined guidelines for its personnel to follow. The above box contains the Custom Service's policies for personal searches, including the level of suspicion that is required for each type of search and whether supervisory approval is required. Do you believe these guidelines strike a proper balance between individuals' rights and societal interests in stopping the flow of contraband?

The most intrusive searches on the list interfere significantly with personal privacy and have tremendous potential to cause feelings of embarrassment and humiliation. Moreover, many people are concerned that x-rays pose a health hazard by exposing people to radiation. Furthermore, unlike in prisons, these searches are being conducted on people who have not been convicted of a crime. And, unlike the jail context, these searches are being conducted on people who have not even been arrested. Yet the searches themselves are as or more intrusive than those in corrections settings.

Notice how discretion plays an important role in determining who is subject to search. Customs officers can conduct a **patdown or frisk search** if they suspect someone may have a weapon. They may conduct such a search for merchandise with a supervisor's approval if they present one articulable fact as the basis for suspicion. The conclusion that an articulable fact exists, in itself, may involve discretion. If that fact is based on someone avoiding eye contact or not answering questions directly, the *perceptions* of the officer will guide that officer's decision making. More intrusive searches are also affected by perceptions and discretionary decisions as officers decide if articulable facts exist to seek a court order for an x-ray or body cavity search or to seek the port director's approval to hold someone in custody for a monitored bowel movement. Can you imagine being held in custody for a day or two at the discretion of an officer and the port director while officials wait to see if you swallowed any contraband? Obviously, this is a significant exercise of authority that affects the liberty and personal privacy of selected individuals. As in other contexts in which discretion affects people's lives, it is very important for customs officers to be ethical and professional.

The U.S. General Accounting Office (GAO), the federal government's research agency, studied searches conducted at airports and found they appeared to be guided by either ineffective or discriminatory decision making. Specifically, the GAO study found that African American women were selected for more intrusive searches—strip searches and x-rays—than any other demographic group. African American women were nine times as likely as white American women to be x-rayed after being frisked, yet the white women were twice as likely to be found carrying contraband.[1]

The GAO study raises questions about whether racial biases may affect some customs officers' decisions about whom to search. Officers may be misreading cues in observing behavior and listening to responses by African American women. Alternatively, officers may be making assumptions about the inclinations of people from certain demographic groups to participate in various criminal acts. Obviously, any racially biased behavior by government officials in conducting searches is both unethical and a violation of the Fourteenth Amendment's Equal Protection Clause. Thus the Customs Service and members of Congress made suggestions for improved training and reexamination of the factors regarded as providing a basis for the suspicion that justifies a search.

The study of the Customs Service's searches at airports could examine patterns in officers' decision making because the searches occurred in a limited, controlled context in which accurate records were maintained. Thus it was easy to detect if members of some demographic groups were searched more frequently than members of other groups. By contrast, it is much more difficult to determine if discriminatory patterns exist when police officers on the streets are undertaking searches, questioning, and other investigatory activities. Officers undertake these activities in many settings that are visible neither to their supervisors nor the public. It is difficult to imagine how accurate records could be kept. Several states and cities have required officers to keep track of the demographic characteristics of people whom they stop and search. These requirements emerged because of concerns that racial profiling was guiding officers' decisions. **Racial profiling** is the practice of using a person's race as a key factor in deciding whether he or she fits the general demographic description of a drug dealer or other targeted criminal offender. Although some officers are

The Pervasiveness of Personal Searches

Have you ever been searched? Nearly everyone has been. Whenever you enter the flight departure gates at an airport, you must go through a metal detector. The same is true at many courthouses. Many children go through metal detectors every day when they go to school. People who go to political rallies or speeches attended by the president or vice president of the United States must often go through metal detectors. Many retail stores have detector devices in their doorways that signal when customers are carrying away merchandise that has not yet been purchased. Moreover, most college libraries have detection devices at their exits in order to discover if people are taking away library materials that they have not checked out.

Do all of these situations count as "searches" for purposes of the Fourth Amendment? No. The Bill of Rights defines the relationships between government and individuals. Rights are protections that individuals possess against interference by government. Thus a retail store's detection device or the detection device at a private college's library cannot be regarded as "searches" for Fourth Amendment purposes. This does not mean that they are free to make intrusive examinations of people's bodies. They are still subject to criminal laws and civil lawsuits against "battery," which means an unlawful, unconsented touching of one person by another. However, a detection device that does not cause a physical invasion does not implicate such laws.

One can certainly argue that airport metal detectors and other detection technologies employed by governmental agencies conduct "searches" under the Bill of Rights. However, there is little risk that these searches will be regarded as violating the Fourth Amendment. Remember that courts make decisions about the Fourth Amendment by striking a balance between the individual's interests and society's interests. When the intrusion is regarded as minimal (e.g.,

a detection device that most people do not even notice), then courts are willing to let government agencies use such devices to protect society's interests, such as ensuring no weapons are carried onto airplanes or no books are stolen from public libraries.

New technologies are being developed that may be applied to people walking down the street. When metal detectors are used at airports, libraries, and schools, the people entering these buildings know that they will be examined by visible devices. If they do not want to be examined by these devices, they can stay away from these buildings. However, new devices may be applied to people who have no idea that they are being examined. For example, scientists and engineers are working on mobile scanners that can be pointed at people walking down the street to detect if there are metal masses beneath their clothing that might be guns. People will never know that they have been "searched," unless the device detects something that leads to further questioning and more intrusive searches.

Look back at the types of searches conducted by the U.S. Customs Service. Is an x-ray any more intrusive than a metal detector? If not, why does its use require more justification and supervisory approval? Also consider whether there is a risk that detection technologies have become so pervasive that we do not even notice that these devices are "searching" us every day. If so, could Americans become less attentive to governmental actions that examine their bodies and the possessions they carry? Does this matter at all, or is it of interest only to people who are exceptionally fearful of the government? What do you think? Would your answer change if you could envision a time in the future when cameras and sensors could continuously monitor what everyone is carrying as they walk down the street?

now asked to keep records of their own stops, many observers believe that officers who are inclined to use race as part their decision making will simply neglect to keep accurate records or will intentionally falsify reports.

The government's capacity to conduct searches will change as new technology is developed. As you read the above box on the pervasiveness of searches, ask yourself if you have a definite viewpoint on how far the government should be able to go in monitoring people within the United States.

STOP AND FRISK ON THE STREETS

In corrections, customs, and other special situations, there is a recognized need for specific personal searches in order to advance certain important governmental objectives. What about in other situations? Do police officers have general authority to decide that they must search someone? The Supreme Court's most important case on the issue was *Terry v. Ohio* (1968). As you read the opinion in *Terry* in the accompanying box, pay particular attention to the circumstances that must exist in order for an officer to initiate a search. Also take note of how extensive such a search may be.

C A S E   *Terry v. Ohio*, 392 U.S. 1 (1968)

[*A police officer with thirty years of experience observed several men repeatedly walking back and forth in front of a store and peering into the window. Their behavior aroused the police officer's suspicions because he believed that they could be preparing to commit a robbery. The officer approached the men, identified himself as a police officer, and patted down the exterior clothing of one man. When he found a gun in the man's coat pocket, he ordered the other two men to stand against a wall and he discovered a weapon in the coat pocket of one of the other men. The two men sought to have the guns excluded from their trial on the charge of carrying a concealed weapon. They asserted that the officer's patdown search of their outer clothing was not justified by probable cause because the officer had no evidence to indicate that they had committed any crime. Thus, they argued that his search was unreasonable under the terms of the Fourth Amendment.*]

CHIEF JUSTICE WARREN delivered the opinion of the Court.

. . .

The Fourth Amendment provides . . . [t]his inestimable right of personal security [that] belongs as much to the citizen on the streets of our cities as to the homeowner closeted in his study to dispose of his secret affairs. . . .

We would be less than candid if we did not acknowledge that this question thrusts to the fore difficult and troublesome issues regarding a sensitive area of police activity—issues which have never before been squarely presented to this Court. Reflec-

tive of the tensions involved are the practical and constitutional arguments pressed with great vigor on both sides of the public debate over the power of the police to "stop and frisk"—as it is sometimes euphemistically termed—suspicious persons.

On the one hand, it is frequently argued that in dealing with the rapidly unfolding and often dangerous situations on city streets the police are in need of an escalating set of flexible responses, graduated in relation to the amount of information they possess. For this purpose it is urged that distinctions should be made between a "stop" and an "arrest" (or a "seizure" of a person), and between a "frisk" and a "search." Thus, it is argued, the police should be allowed to "stop" a person and detain him briefly for questioning upon suspicion that he may be connected with criminal activity. Upon suspicion that the person may be armed, the police should have the power to "frisk" him for weapons. If the "stop" and the "frisk" give rise to probable cause to believe that the suspect has committed a crime, then the police should be empowered to make a formal "arrest," and a full incident "search" of the person. This scheme is justified in part upon the notion that a "stop" and a "frisk" amount to a mere "minor inconvenience" and petty indignity, which can properly be imposed upon the citizen in the interest of effective law enforcement on the basis of a police officer's suspicion.

On the other side the argument is made that the authority of the police must be strictly circumscribed by the law of arrest and search as it has developed to date in the traditional jurisprudence of the Fourth Amendment. It is contended with some force that there is not—and cannot be—a variety of police activity which does not depend solely upon the voluntary cooperation of the citizen and yet which stops short of an arrest based upon probable cause to make such an arrest. The heart of the Fourth Amendment, the argument runs, is a severe requirement of specific justification for any intrusion upon protected personal security, coupled with a highly developed system of judicial controls to enforce upon the agents of the State the commands of the Constitution. Acquiescence by the courts in the compulsion inherent in the field interrogation practices at issue here, it is urged, would constitute an abdication of judicial control over, and indeed an encouragement of, substantial interference with liberty and personal security by police officers whose judgment is necessarily colored by their primary involvement in "the often competitive enterprise of ferreting out crime." . . . This, it is argued, can only serve to exacerbate police-community tensions in the crowded centers of our Nation's cities.

In this context we approach the issues in this case mindful of the limitations of the judicial function in controlling the myriad daily situations in which policemen and citizens confront each other on the street. The State has characterized the issue here as "the right of a police officer . . . to make an on-the-street stop, interrogate, and pat down for weapons (known in street vernacular as 'stop and frisk')." But this is only partly accurate. For the issue is not the abstract propriety of the police conduct, but the admissibility against petitioner of the evidence uncovered by the search and seizure. Ever since its inception, the rule excluding evidence seized in violation of the Fourth Amendment has been recognized as a principal mode of discouraging lawless police conduct . . . , and experience has taught that it is the only effective deterrent to police misconduct in the criminal context, and that without it the constitutional guarantee against unreasonable searches and seizures would be a mere "form of words." . . . Courts which sit under our Constitution cannot and will not be made party to lawless invasions of the constitutional rights of citizens by permitting unhindered governmental use of the fruits of such invasions. Thus in our system evidentiary rulings provide the context in which the judicial process of inclusion and exclusion approves some conduct as comporting with constitutional guarantees and disapproves other actions by state agents. A ruling admitting evidence in a criminal trial, we recognize, has the necessary effect of legitimizing the conduct which produced the evidence, while an application of the exclusionary rule withholds the constitutional imprimatur.

. . . Street encounters between citizens and police officers are incredibly rich in diversity. They range from wholly friendly exchanges of pleasantries or mutually useful information to hostile confrontations of armed men involving arrests, or injuries, or loss of life. Moreover, hostile confrontations are not all of a piece. Some of them begin in a friendly enough manner, only to take a different turn upon the injection of some unexpected element into the conversation. Encounters are initiated by police for a wide variety of purposes, some of which are wholly unrelated to a desire to prosecute for crime. Doubtless some police "field interrogation" conduct violates the Fourth Amendment. But a stern refusal by this Court to condone such activity does not necessarily render it responsive to the exclusionary rule. Regardless of how effective the rule may be where obtaining convictions is an important objective of the police, it is powerless to deter invasions of constitutionally guaranteed rights where the police either have no interest in prosecuting or are willing to forgo successful prosecution in the interest of serving some other goal.

Proper adjudication of cases in which the exclusionary rule is invoked demands a constant awareness of these limitations. The wholesale harassment by certain elements of the police community, of which minority groups, particularly Negroes, frequently complain, will not be stopped by the exclusion of evidence from any criminal trial. Yet a rigid and unthinking application of the exclusionary rule, in futile protest against practices which it can never be used effectively to control, may exact a high toll in human injury and frustration of efforts to prevent crime. . . . And, of course, our approval of legitimate and restrained investigative conduct undertaken on the basis of ample factual justification should in no way discourage the employment of other remedies than the exclusionary rule to curtail abuses for which that sanction may prove inappropriate. . . .

. . . It is quite plain that the Fourth Amendment governs "seizures" of the person which do not eventuate in a trip to the station house and prosecution for crime—"arrests" in traditional terminology. It must be recognized that whenever a police officer accosts an individual and restrains his freedom to walk away, he has "seized" that person. And it is nothing less than sheer torture of the English language to suggest that a careful exploration of the outer surfaces of a person's clothing all over his or her body in an attempt to find weapons is not a "search." Moreover, it is simply fantastic to urge

(continued)

that such a procedure performed in public by a policeman while the citizen stands helpless, perhaps facing a wall with his hands raised, is a "petty indignity." It is a serious intrusion upon the sanctity of the person, which may inflict great indignity and arouse strong resentment, and it is not to be undertaken lightly. . . .

. . . We therefore reject the notion that the Fourth Amendment does not come into play at all as a limitation upon police conduct if the officers stop short of something called a "technical arrest" or a "full-blown search."

In this case there can be no question, then, that Officer McFadden "seized" petitioner and subjected him to a "search" when he took hold of him and patted down the outer surfaces of his clothing. We must decide whether at that point it was reasonable for Officer McFadden to have interfered with petitioner's personal security as he did. And in determining whether the seizure and search were "unreasonable" our inquiry is a dual one—whether the officer's action was justified at its inception, and whether it was reasonably related in scope to the circumstances which justified the interference in the first place. . . .

. . . [I]n justifying the particular intrusion the police officer must be able to point to specific and articulable facts which, taken together with rational inferences from those facts, reasonably warrant that intrusion. The scheme of the Fourth Amendment becomes meaningful only when it is assured that at some point the conduct of those charged with enforcing the laws can be subjected to the more detached, neutral scrutiny of a judge who must evaluate the reasonableness of a particular search or seizure in light of the particular circumstances. And in making that assessment it is imperative that the facts be judged against an objective standard: would the facts available to the officer at the moment of the seizure or the search "warrant a man of reasonable caution in the belief" that the action taken was appropriate? . . . Anything less would invite intrusions upon constitutionally guaranteed rights based on nothing more substantial than inarticulate hunches, a result this Court has consistently refused to sanction. . . . And simple "'good faith on the part of the arresting officer is not enough.' . . . If subjective good faith alone were the test, the protections of the Fourth Amendment would evaporate, and the people would be 'secure in their persons, houses, papers, and effects,' only in the discretion of the police." . . .

Applying these principles to this case, we consider first the nature and extent of the governmental interests involved. One general interest is of course that of effective crime prevention and detection; it is this interest which underlies the recognition that a police officer may in appropriate circumstances and in an appropriate manner approach a person for purposes of investigating possibly criminal behavior even though there is no probable cause to make an arrest. It was this legitimate investigative function Officer McFadden was discharging when he decided to approach petitioner and his companions. He had observed Terry, Chilton, and Katz go through a series of acts, each of them perhaps innocent in itself, but which taken together warranted further investigation. . . . It would have been poor police work indeed for an officer of 30 years' experience in the detection of thievery from stores in this same neighborhood to have failed to investigate this behavior further.

The crux of this case, however, is not the propriety of Officer McFadden's taking steps to investigate petitioner's suspicious behavior, but rather, whether there was justification for McFadden's invasion of Terry's personal security by searching him for weapons in the course of that investigation. We are now concerned with more than the governmental interest in fighting crime; in addition, there is the more immediate interest of the police officer in taking steps to assure himself that the person with whom he is dealing is not armed with a weapon that could unexpectedly and fatally be used against him. Certainly it would be unreasonable to require that police officers take unnecessary risks in the performance of their duties. American criminals have a long tradition of armed violence, and every year in this country many law enforcement officers are killed in the line of duty, and thousands more are wounded. Virtually all of these deaths and a substantial portion of the injuries are inflicted with guns and knives.

In view of these facts, we cannot blind ourselves to the need for law enforcement officers to protect themselves and other prospective victims of violence in situations where they may lack probable cause for an arrest. When an officer is justified in believing that the individual whose suspicious behavior he is investigating at close range is armed and presently dangerous to the officer or to others, it would appear to be clearly unreasonable to deny the officer the power to take necessary measures to determine whether the person is in fact carrying a weapon and to neutralize the threat of physical harm. . . .

Our evaluation of the proper balance that has to be struck in this type of case leads us to conclude that there must be a narrowly drawn authority to permit a reasonable search for weapons for the protection of the police officer, where he has reason to believe that he is dealing with an armed and dangerous individual, regardless of whether he has probable cause to arrest the individual for a crime. The officer need not be absolutely certain that the individual is armed; the issue is whether a reasonably prudent man in the circumstances would be warranted in the belief that his safety or that of others was in danger. . . . And in determining whether the officer acted reasonably in such circumstances, due weight must be given, not to his inchoate and unparticularized suspicion or "hunch," but to the specific reasonable inferences which he is entitled to draw from the facts in light of his experience. . . .

. . . [W]hen Officer McFadden approached the three men gathered before the display window at Zucker's store he had observed enough to make it quite reasonable to fear that they were armed; and nothing in their response to his hailing them, identifying himself as a police officer, and asking their names served to dispel that reasonable belief. We cannot say his decision at that point to seize Terry and pat his clothing for weapons was the product of a volatile or inventive imagination, or was undertaken simply as an act of harassment; the record evidences the tempered act of a policeman who in the course of an investigation had to make a quick decision as to how to protect himself and others from possible danger, and took limited steps to do so. . . .

The scope of the search in this case presents no serious problem in light of these standards. Officer McFadden patted down the outer clothing of petitioner and his two companions. He did not place his hands in their pockets or under the outer surface of their garments until he had felt weapons, and then he merely reached for and removed the guns. He never did invade Katz's person beyond the outer surfaces of his clothes, since he discovered nothing which might have been a weapon. Officer McFadden confined his search strictly to what was minimally necessary to learn whether the men were armed and to disarm them once he discovered the weapons. He did not conduct a general exploratory search for whatever evidence of criminal activity he might find.

We conclude that the revolver seized from Terry was properly admitted in evidence against him. At the time he seized petitioner and searched him for weapons, Officer McFadden had reasonable grounds to believe that petitioner was armed and dangerous, and it was necessary for the protection of himself and others to take swift measures to discover the true facts and neutralize the threat of harm if it materialized. The policeman carefully restricted his search to what was appropriate to the discovery of the particular items which he sought. Each case of this sort will, of course, have to be decided on its own facts. We merely hold today that where a police officer observes unusual conduct which leads him reasonably to conclude in light of his experience that criminal activity may be afoot and that the persons with whom he is dealing may be armed and presently dangerous, where in the course of investigating this behavior he identifies himself as a policeman and makes reasonable inquiries, and where nothing in the initial stages of the encounter serves to dispel his reasonable fear for his own or others' safety, he is entitled for the protection of himself and others in the area to conduct a carefully limited search of the outer clothing of such persons in an attempt to discover weapons which might be used to assault him.

Such a search is a reasonable search under the Fourth Amendment, and any weapons seized may properly be introduced in evidence against the person from whom they were taken.
Affirmed.

[The concurring opinions of Justices Black, Harlan, and White are omitted.]

JUSTICE DOUGLAS, dissenting.

I agree that petitioner was "seized" within the meaning of the Fourth Amendment. I also agree that frisking petitioner and his companions for guns was a "search." But it is a mystery how that "search" and that "seizure" can be constitutional by Fourth Amendment standards, unless there was probable cause to believe that (1) a crime had been committed or (2) a crime was in the process of being committed or (3) a crime was about to be committed.

The opinion of the Court disclaims the existence of "probable cause." If loitering were in issue and that was the offense charged, there would be "probable cause" shown. But the crime here is carrying concealed weapons; and there is no basis for concluding that the officer had "probable cause" for believing that that crime was being committed. Had a warrant been sought, a magistrate would, therefore, have been unauthorized to issue one, for he can act only if there is a showing of "probable cause." We hold today that the police have greater

(continued)

authority to make a "seizure" and conduct a "search" than a judge has to authorize such action. We have said precisely the opposite over and over again.

In other words, police officers up to today have been permitted to effect arrests and searches without warrants only when the facts within their knowledge would satisfy the constitutional standard of *probable cause*. At the time of their "seizure" without a warrant they must possess facts concerning the person arrested that would have satisfied a magistrate that "probable cause" was indeed present. . . .

The infringement on personal liberty of any "seizure" of a person can only be "reasonable" under the Fourth Amendment if we require the police to possess "probable cause" before they seize him. Only that line draws a meaningful distinction between an officer's mere inkling and the presence of facts within the officer's personal knowledge which would convince a reasonable man that the person seized has committed, is committing, or is about to commit a particular crime. . . .

To give the police greater power than a magistrate is to take a long step down the totalitarian path. Perhaps such a step is desirable to cope with modern forms of lawlessness. But if it is taken, it should be the deliberate choice of the people through a constitutional amendment.

Until the Fourth Amendment, which is closely allied with the Fifth, is rewritten, the person and the effects of the individual are beyond the reach of all government agencies until there are reasonable grounds to believe (probable cause) that a criminal venture has been launched or is about to be launched.

There have been powerful hydraulic pressures throughout our history that bear heavily on the Court to water down constitutional guarantees and give the police the upper hand. That hydraulic pressure has probably never been greater than it is today.

Yet if the individual is no longer to be sovereign, if the police can pick him up whenever they do not like the cut of his jib, if they can "seize" and "search" him in their discretion, we enter a new regime. The decision to enter it should be made after a full debate by the people of this country.

Justifications for a *Terry* Stop

The Warren Court justices were often accused of favoring the rights of criminal defendants at the expense of police officers' crime-fighting authority. Contrary to their reputation in the eyes of critics, in the *Terry* case, the Warren Court justices explicitly recognized the needs of law enforcement. The Court's decision recognized that seizures short of arrest could be "reasonable" under the Fourth Amendment.[2] Here, the suspects were not free to leave, yet the officer would presumably have released them if he had not found the weapons. Thus the stop and search occurred as part of the investigation process before any arrest occurred. The justices were clearly concerned about striking an appropriate balance between Fourth Amendment rights and necessary police authority to investigate and prevent crimes.

Although the justices supported law enforcement authority, they struck the balance by carefully specifying the circumstances in which such patdown searches—more commonly known as **stop-and-frisk search**—can occur. Look closely at the holding in the case. The Court appears to demand that a number of specific facts exist in each situation in which a permissible stop and frisk can occur. If we break apart the Court's own words, we can see that the justices explicitly say, "We merely hold today that[:]

[1] where a police officer observes unusual conduct

[2] which leads him reasonably to conclude in light of his experience

[3] that criminal activity may be afoot and

[4] that the persons with whom he is dealing may be armed and presently dangerous,

[5] where in the course of investigating this behavior

[6] he identifies himself as a policeman and makes reasonable inquiries,

[7] and where nothing in the initial stages of the encounter serves to dispel his reasonable fear for his own or others' safety,

[8] he is entitled for the protection of himself and others in the area to conduct a carefully limited search of the outer clothing of such persons in an attempt to discover weapons which might be used to assault him.

These specified factors imposed an affirmative obligation on police officers to make observations, draw reasonable conclusions, identify themselves, and make inquiries before conducting the stop-and-frisk search. In addition, the reasonableness of the search was justified by a reasonable conclusion that a person was armed and therefore the officer needed to act in order to protect him- or herself and the public.

What do you think about Justice Douglas's argument in the *Terry* case that such governmental interference with a person's liberty to walk down the street should be supported by probable cause rather than merely reasonable suspicion? It appears that Douglas linked the probable cause requirements for warrants and the reasonableness requirement for searches. This is a plausible interpretation of the Fourth Amendment's words, but one that other justices have refused to support. How would law enforcement officers' authority and effectiveness be different if Douglas's view had prevailed?

The *Terry* search was not justified by an officer's desire to search for evidence of criminal activity. Thus Chief Justice Warren's decision would not justify a patdown frisk intended solely to see if someone had drugs or other contraband, even if the officer saw the person talking to known drug addicts and reaching into his pocket (*Sibron v. New York,* 1968). However, if an officer possesses the necessary reasonable suspicion to justify a frisk for weapons, the officer does not need to ignore contraband or other criminal evidence that is readily identifiable by touch beneath a person's clothing (*Minnesota v. Dickerson,* 1993). The officer may not dig into the suspect's pocket in order to pull out and examine objects that arouse curiosity. If the officer feels something that he or she is reasonably certain is a weapon, that item may be retrieved. If the officer feels a "crack pipe" or other contraband item that is identifiable by a patdown of outer clothing, that item may also be seized. Most observers have characterized the *Dickerson* case as establishing a "plain feel" rule that permits officers to retrieve items that are clearly contraband or criminal evidence. It must be emphasized, however, that this rule does not justify "fishing expeditions" in which officers pull out and examine items in people's pockets that arouse their curiosity.

In *Adams v. Williams* (1972), an officer was told by an informant with whom he was acquainted that a person sitting in a car had a gun in his waistband. Based on this information, the officer approached the car, reached through the driver's window, and removed the gun from the person's body. Unlike in *Terry,* where the officer's own observations provided the basis for the reasonable suspicions, in *Adams* the information came from a known informant. When the Court approved the frisk in *Adams,* the justices effectively expanded *Terry*'s requirements and gave police officers increased flexibility for conducting such searches.

In *Alabama v. White* (1990), the police received an anonymous tip that described a specific person and said that the person would enter a brown Plymouth station wagon and then drive to a certain hotel while transporting cocaine. The officers went as directed by the tip to the designated apartment complex where they watched the events unfold exactly as described by the anonymous informant. They stopped the car and found the cocaine. Upon subsequent review in court, the U.S. Supreme Court said that reasonable suspicion was established because the tip's accuracy was verified by the officers' observations. The strength of the tip seemed to rest, in part, on its accuracy in predicting a variety of specific details. If the anonymous tip had provided sketchier, incomplete information, police may not be able to verify its accuracy.

By contrast, an unverified anonymous tip is not adequate as a basis for a stop-and-frisk search. In 2000 the Rehnquist Court, composed of justices much more inclined than the Warren Court justices to give police officers greater flexibility despite critics' concerns about a reduction in the scope of constitutional rights, examined stop-and-frisk searches in *Florida v. J.L.* Police officers received an anonymous tip that a young African American male standing at a specific bus stop and wearing a plaid shirt was carrying a gun. Police officers went to the bus stop and frisked a young man matching the description. They found a gun and the young man was charged with unlawfully carrying a concealed weapon. The justices unanimously ruled that the gun must be excluded from evidence because the officers did not have a proper basis for conducting the patdown search. Florida argued that the *Terry* rule should be modified to permit officers to rely on anonymous tips to search for firearms because of an exceptionally strong societal interest in stopping gun violence. The Supreme Court declined to accept the state's argument. The justices were very concerned that there must be additional indicators of reliability to justify a search because an anonymous tip alone could provide deceptive or untrustworthy information. The Court did not rule out the possibility that an anonymous tip alone might be sufficient in extraordinary circumstances in which a greater societal interest is at stake, such as a report that someone is carrying a bomb—a device with greater risk and likelihood of harm than a handgun.

New Developments

Another issue for *Terry* searches concerns the factual circumstances observed by officers which can lead them to reasonably conclude that a frisk is justified. As you read *Illinois v. Wardlow* (2000) in the accompanying box, ask yourself how much discretion police officers possess to conduct permissible patdown searches. How much more discretion, if any, do officers possess now than they possessed in the immediate aftermath of the *Terry* decision in 1968?

In *Wardlow,* Chief Justice Rehnquist's majority opinion permits police officers to stop and frisk people whom they see running if they interpret the running as flight under suspicious circumstances at the sight of a police officer. In this case, the fact that the man was running in a high crime neighborhood as police officers drove down the street provided the basis for the stop under the "totality-of-circumstances" test. The Court declined to adopt the bright-line rule suggested by Illinois that police officers be permitted to stop anyone

| CASE | *Illinois v. Wardlow*, 528 U.S. 119 (2000) |

CHIEF JUSTICE REHNQUIST delivered the opinion of the Court.

Respondent Wardlow fled upon seeing police officers patrolling an area known for heavy narcotics trafficking. Two of the officers caught up with him, stopped him, and conducted a protective patdown search for weapons. Discovering a .38-caliber handgun, the officers arrested Wardlow. We hold that the officers' stop did not violate the Fourth Amendment to the United States Constitution.

On September 9, 1995, Officers Nolan and Harvey were working as uniformed officers in the special operations section of the Chicago Police Department. The officers were driving the last car of a four-car caravan converging on an area known for heavy narcotics trafficking in order to investigate drug transactions. The officers were traveling together because they expected to find a crowd of people in the area, including lookouts and customers.

As the caravan passed 4035 West Van Buren, Officer Nolan observed respondent Wardlow standing next to the building holding an opaque bag. Respondent looked in the direction of the officers and fled. Nolan and Harvey turned their car southbound, watched him as he ran through the gangway and an alley, and eventually cornered him on the street. Nolan then exited his car and stopped respondent. He immediately conducted a protective pat-down search for weapons because in his experience it was common for there to be weapons in the near vicinity of narcotics transactions. During the frisk, Officer Nolan squeezed the bag respondent was carrying and felt a heavy, hard object similar to the shape of a gun. The officer then opened the bag and discovered a .38-caliber handgun with five live rounds of ammunition. The officers arrested Wardlow.

. . . [T]he Illinois Supreme Court determined that sudden flight in such an area does not create a reasonable suspicion justifying a *Terry* stop. . . . [It said that] flight may simply be an exercise of this right to "go on one's way," and, thus, could not constitute reasonable suspicion justifying a *Terry* stop. . . .

. . . Accordingly, we have previously noted the fact that the stop occurred in a "high crime area" among the relevant contextual considerations in a *Terry* analysis. . . .

. . . Our cases have also recognized that nervous, evasive behavior is a pertinent factor in determining reasonable suspicion. Headlong flight—wherever it occurs—is the consummate act of evasion: it is not necessarily indicative of wrongdoing, but it is certainly suggestive of such. . . . We conclude Officer Nolan was justified in suspecting that Wardlow was involved in criminal activity, and, therefore, in investigating further.

. . . [U]nprovoked flight is simply not a mere refusal to cooperate. Flight, by its very nature, is not "going about one's business"; in fact, it is just the opposite. Allowing officers confronted with such flight to stop the fugitive and investigate further is quite consistent with the individual's right to go about his business or to stay put and remain silent in the face of police questioning. . . .

In allowing such detentions, *Terry* accepts the risk that officers may stop innocent people. Indeed, the Fourth Amendment accepts that risk in connection with more drastic police action; persons arrested and detained on probable cause to believe they have committed a crime may turn out to be innocent. The *Terry* stop is a far more minimal intrusion, simply allowing the officer to briefly investigate further. If the officer does not learn facts rising to the level of probable cause, the individual must be allowed to go on his way. But in this case the officers found respondent in possession of a handgun, and arrested him for violation of an Illinois firearms statute. . . .

The judgment of the Supreme Court of Illinois is reversed. . . .

JUSTICE STEVENS, with whom JUSTICE SOUTER, JUSTICE GINSBURG, and JUSTICE BREYER join, concurring in part and dissenting in part.

The State of Illinois asks this Court to announce a "bright-line rule" authorizing the temporary detention of anyone who flees at the mere sight of a police officer. . . . Respondent counters by asking us to adopt the opposite *per se* rule—that the fact that a person flees upon seeing the police can never, by itself, be sufficient to justify a temporary investigative stop of the kind authorized by *Terry v. Ohio*. . . .

The Court today wisely endorses neither *per se* rule. Instead, . . . [reasonable suspicion] must be determined by looking to "the totality of the circumstances—the whole picture." . . . Abiding by this framework, the Court concludes that "Officer Nolan was justified in suspecting that Wardlow was involved in criminal activity." . . .

(continued)

Although I agree with the Court's rejection of the *per se* rules proffered by the parties, unlike the Court, I am persuaded that in this case the brief testimony of the officer who seized respondent does not justify the conclusion that he had reasonable suspicion to make the stop. . . .

The question in this case concerns "the degree of suspicion that attaches to" a person's flight—or, more precisely, what "commonsense conclusions" can be drawn respecting the motives behind that flight. A pedestrian may break into a run for a variety of reasons—to catch up with a friend a block or two away, to seek shelter from an impending storm, to arrive at a bus stop before the bus leaves, to get home in time for dinner, to resume jogging after a pause for rest, to avoid contact with a bore or a bully, or simply to answer the call of nature—any of which might coincide with the arrival of an officer in the vicinity. A pedestrian might also run because he or she has just sighted one or more police officers. . . .

. . . The inference we can reasonably draw about the motivation for a person's flight, rather, will depend on a number of different circumstances. Factors such as the time of day, the number of people in the area, the character of the neighborhood, whether the officer was in uniform, the way the runner was dressed, the direction and speed of the flight, and whether the person's behavior was otherwise unusual might be relevant in specific cases. . . .

. . . [A] reasonable person may conclude that an officer's sudden appearance indicates nearby criminal activity. And where there is criminal activity there is also a substantial element of danger—either from the criminal or from a confrontation between the criminal and the police. These considerations can lead to an innocent and understandable desire to quit the vicinity with all speed.

Among some citizens, particularly minorities and those residing in high crime areas, there is also the possibility that the fleeing person is entirely innocent, but, with or without justification, believes that contact with the police can itself be dangerous, apart from any criminal activity associated with the officer's sudden presence. For such a person, unprovoked flight is neither "aberrant" nor "abnormal." Moreover, these concerns and fears are known to the police officers themselves, and are validated by law enforcement investigations into their own practices. . . .

Guided by the totality-of-the-circumstances test, the Court concludes that Officer Nolan had reasonable suspicion to stop respondent. . . . In this respect, my view differs from the Court's. The entire justification for the stop is articulated in the brief testimony of Officer Nolan. Some facts are perfectly clear; others are not. This factual insufficiency leads me to conclude that the Court's judgment is mistaken.

. . . Officer Nolan testified that he was in uniform on that day, but he did not recall whether he was driving a marked or unmarked car.

. . . [Nolan] was not even asked whether any of the other three cars in the caravan were marked, or whether any of the other seven officers were in uniform. . . . Officer Nolan's testimony also does not reveal how fast the officers were driving. It does not indicate whether he saw respondent notice the other patrol cars. And it does not say whether the caravan [of police cars], or any part of it, had already passed Wardlow by before he began to run. . . .

The State, along with the majority of the Court, relies as well on the assumption that this flight occurred in a high crime area. Even if that assumption is accurate, it is insufficient because even in a high crime neighborhood unprovoked flight does not invariably lead to reasonable suspicion. On the contrary, because many factors providing innocent motivations for unprovoked flight are concentrated in high crime areas, the character of the neighborhood arguably makes an inference of guilt less appropriate, rather than more so. Like unprovoked flight itself, presence in a high crime neighborhood is a fact too generic and susceptible to innocent explanation to satisfy the reasonable suspicion inquiry. . . .

---

whom they see running. As you may recall from Chapter 4, a bright-line rule is a clear rule that applies in all circumstances and does not require contextual interpretation. Instead, the Court adopted a rule that will require officers to make judgments and justify their actions.

What has happened to the original justification for stop-and-frisk searches in the *Terry* case? In *Terry* such searches were justified by the important societal interest in protecting the safety of police officers and other citizens. Thus a *Terry* search could be conducted only if police had reasonable suspicions that someone was armed and involved in criminal activity. In *Wardlow* the suspect turned out to be armed. However, what behavior on the part of the suspect led officers to believe that he was armed and involved in criminal activity? Even if the Court majority is correct in claiming that running at the sight of the police in a high crime area raises reasonable suspicion about criminal activity, why does that imply a person is armed? One of the unaddressed questions lurking in *Wardlow* is whether police and courts can automatically assume that someone behaving suspiciously in a high crime area is armed. Alternatively, perhaps the *Wardlow* decision provides evidence that the Court is moving away from the original public safety justification for *Terry* and is more willing to permit patdown searches aimed solely at finding evidence of criminal activity.

Justice Stevens argues that there are many reasons a person may run as police officers approach and that many of those reasons are understandable. They do not mean the person is engaged in criminal activity, even if they occur in a high crime area. In fact, Stevens claims that people in high crime areas have very good reasons to run at the sight of police officers, since the presence of police may signal that danger is nearby. Although Stevens accepts the majority's totality-of-circumstances rule, he (and the other three justices who joined his opinion) would look more closely at officers' justifications for a search.

Once again, we see the important role of police officers' discretion and perceptions of events. Who decides if a neighborhood is a "high crime area"? The term is not defined, yet officers know after *Wardlow* that if they use that term to describe a neighborhood, it greatly increases the likelihood that a stop and frisk will be permissible. Who decides if someone was running "at the sight of a police officer" or was running for some other reason? It is a matter of police officers' perceptions, but it could also be a matter of officers' rationalizations if they decided to frisk someone on a hunch and later want to justify their actions. Although the Court's decision in *Florida v. J.L.* (2000) warned police officers that they do not have complete discretion to conduct stop-and-frisk searches, the *Wardlow* case confirms that the Court gives officers' significant discretionary authority to initiate patdown searches on the streets.

Another question is whether, as a practical matter, the *Wardlow* decision creates a discriminatory impact on society. Does the decision mean, in effect, that police officers could stop and frisk anyone seen running in a poor neighborhood based on the claim that the person took "flight" in a high crime neighborhood? Thus, for poor people, the decision might mean "joggers beware." By contrast, will anyone ever be stopped for running in an affluent neighborhood? Probably only if their clothes—or racial characteristics—make them look out of place. Imagine two identical young men dressed in Nike sweatsuits—one in a suburban neighborhood and one in an inner-city neighborhood. Both begin to jog as a police car comes down the street. What assumptions might police officers make? Might they assume that the man in the affluent neighborhood has, as Justice Stevens hypothesized, continued jogging after a brief rest? Would they make the same assumption about the young man in the inner-city neighborhood? Obviously, perceptions and assumptions will vary by individual police officer with each officer's training, experience, and biases affecting a decision about whether the situation has produced reasonable suspicion for a stop and frisk under the *Wardlow* rule. If both young men are stopped and searched and a weapon is found in each case, will they have an equal likelihood of winning exclusion of the evidence by claiming that there was insufficient factual support to fulfill the reasonable suspicion standard? See the box "Protection from Arbitrary Stops" on the next page.

CONSTITUTIONAL RIGHTS: SYMBOL OR SUBSTANCE?

Protection from Arbitrary Stops

The Supreme Court said in *Florida v. J.L.* (2000) that a stop-and-frisk cannot be based solely on a tip from an anonymous informant. The decision appears to reconfirm the Court's commitment to keep officers from having complete discretion to conduct stop-and-frisk searches. However, what if the officers in that case had stopped and observed the youth at the bus stop for a few minutes before conducting the patdown? Could they then claim that reasonable suspicion was based on their own observations rather than solely on the anonymous tip? Because of the totality-of-circumstances test and the Court's deference to police officers' judgments (as demonstrated in *Wardlow*), police officers have tremendous discretionary authority to conduct searches. Are there any practical limitations if officers are shrewd enough to understand that they must provide an after-the-fact justification for the search?

If we shift our focus from officers' *authority* to officers' *power*—namely, what a gun and a badge permit them to do whether or not the courts intended to enable them to take the action—what will stop a police officer from frisking anyone and everyone? Cases generally arise in the courts only when a weapon or contraband is found on someone and the person seeks to have the items excluded from evidence. If no weapon is found or no arrest is made (e.g., the officer just seizes and destroys the contraband), there is no court case. A person might file a civil lawsuit against the officer for violating Fourth Amendment rights. However, the expense of litigation would outweigh the potential recovery, so very few attorneys would be willing to take such cases. How much money would a jury award as damages for being stopped on the street for a minute while an officer briefly pats down pockets and outer clothing? Not much.

In light of these realities, do the *Terry* and *Florida v. J.L.* decisions really provide any protection to citizens even though they purport to require officers to have reasonable suspicion before undertaking a stop-and-frisk search?

SEARCH INCIDENT TO A LAWFUL ARREST

We have seen that police officers have the authority to conduct stop-and-frisk searches on the street based on reasonable suspicions developed through their own observations of people's behavior. In light of the Court's recognition that officers need the authority to frisk people on the streets, it is not surprising that the justices approve more extensive warrantless searches for people arrested on the streets who are headed for custody in a correctional institution. Moreover, a **search incident to a lawful arrest** permits a warrantless search that is more extensive than the searches authorized under the *Terry* doctrine. In the next chapter, we will give more extensive attention to these searches with respect to the officer's authority to search places, such as rooms in a home in which an arrest has taken place.

The justification for searches of arrestees at the scene of an arrest is twofold. First, the officers must make sure that the arrestee does not have a weapon which could endanger the officers or others in the vicinity. Second, the officers must look for evidence on the arrestee's body that the arrestee might destroy or damage before or during the process of being transported to jail. Thus the officers are authorized to make a more extensive search of the person than is authorized under a *Terry* frisk. Officers are permitted to reach into pockets and open containers found in those pockets. For example, a *Terry* frisk would not justify opening a cigarette case found in a suspect's pocket because the officers can tell that a small box is not a gun, knife, or other weapon. By contrast, a search undertaken incident to lawful arrest would permit officers to open the cigarette case because they are also permitted to search for evidence (*Gustafson v. Florida,* 1973).

The authority to undertake a warrantless search incident to a lawful arrest is not limited by the crime for which the arrestee has been taken into custody. Even someone arrested for a traffic offense can be searched. Although there is no reason to suspect the person has a weapon or to believe that evidence related to the offense will be found in the person's pockets (*United States v. Robinson,* 1973), the arrestee is subject to the same arrest-scene search as someone taken into custody for murder or any other violent crime.

In the beginning of the chapter, we discussed searches in the context of corrections. The Supreme Court has granted exceptionally broad authority to conduct warrantless searches of people in jails and prisons. Because of the paramount concerns for safety and security in corrections institutions, the Court approved the most intrusive possible searches (i.e., body-cavity searches) without any individualized suspicion. Even presumptively innocent pretrial detainees may be subject to searches automatically if they have contact visits with friends and relatives. Thus it is permissible to do a complete physical search of an arrestee who has been taken to jail. The arrestee has just arrived from outside the institution, so corrections officials are justified in making certain that no contraband is hidden anywhere on the person's body.

SPECIAL NEED BEYOND THE NORMAL PURPOSE OF LAW ENFORCEMENT

Stop-and-frisk searches on the streets are supposed to be justified by reasonable suspicions determined by officers after consideration of the totality of the circumstances. The application of the reasonable suspicion standard in such searches is consistent with an interpretation of the Fourth Amendment that focuses on the language in the amendment barring "unreasonable searches and seizures." Presumably, the existence of reasonable suspicion provides the "reasonableness" required by the amendment to justify such stops and frisks. We have seen, however, other warrantless searches that do not require reasonable suspicion, such as metal detectors at airports and frisks for weapons by customs officers at borders and airports. In the case of metal detectors, there is no articulable suspicion at all. Everyone is automatically subject to the same search no matter how well-behaved, law-abiding, and suspicionless they may be. Clearly, the Court accepts that a governmental interest, such as public safety or border security, outweighs the nature of the intrusion on the Fourth Amendment protection for people's reasonable expectations of privacy. In fact, the intrusion of metal detectors may be regarded by courts as so minimal as to not collide at all with any expectation of privacy. Thus we see that the Supreme Court has defined specific situations as justifying searches or potential searches of everyone who enters that context. Everyone entering the flight gate area at an airport must pass through a metal detector. Everyone entering the United States may be stopped and potentially subject to some level of

Vernonia School District v. Acton, 515 U.S. 646 (1995)

JUSTICE SCALIA delivered the opinion of the Court.

The Student Athlete Drug Policy adopted by [the Vernonia, Oregon, School District] . . . authorizes random urinalysis drug testing of students who participate in the District's school athletics programs. We granted certiorari to decide whether this violates the Fourth and Fourteenth Amendments to the United States Constitution. . . .

Drugs had not been a major problem in Vernonia schools. In the mid-to-late 1980's, teachers and administrators observed a sharp increase in drug use. . . .

Not only were student athletes included among the drug users but, as the District Court found, athletes were the leaders of the drug culture. . . . This caused the District's administrators particular concern, since drug use increases the risk of sports-related injury. . . .

The Policy applies to all students participating in interscholastic athletics. Students wishing to play sports must sign a form consenting to testing and must obtain the written consent of their parents. Athletes are tested at the beginning of the season for their sport. In addition, once each week of the season the names of the athletes are placed in a "pool" from which a student, with the supervision of two adults, blindly draws the names of 10% of the athletes for random testing. Those selected are notified and tested that same day, if possible. . . .

[If a sample tests positive, it is retested. If it is positive again, the school principal meets with the student and his or her parents.] . . . [T]he student is given the option of (1) participating for six weeks in an assistance program that includes weekly urinalysis, or (2) suffering suspension from athletics for the remainder of the current season and the next athletic season. . . .

[Acton signed up to play seventh-grade football, but he and his parents refused to sign the consent form. Instead, they filed a legal action challenging the drug testing policy.]

. . .

The Fourth Amendment . . . [applies] to searches and seizures by state officers, . . . including public school officials, *New Jersey v. T.L.O.* [1985]. . . . In *Skinner v. Railway Labor Executives' Association* [1989], . . . we held that state-compelled collecting and testing of urine, such as that required by the Student Athlete Drug Policy, constitutes a "search" subject to the demands of the Fourth Amendment. See also *Treasury Employees v. Von Raab* [1989]. . . .

. . . [A] warrant is not required to establish the reasonableness of all government searches; and when a warrant is not required (and the Warrant Clause therefore not applicable), probable cause is not invariably required either. A search unsupported by probable cause can be constitutional, we have said, "when special needs, beyond the normal need

search. These situations in which governmental objectives always outweigh Fourth Amendment interests in a defined context—without relying for justification on an officer's determination of reasonable suspicion or probable cause—produce permissible searches based on the **special need beyond the normal purpose of law enforcement.** As described by the Supreme Court in a case concerning the warrantless search of the home of a criminal offender on probation, searches may go forward "when special needs, beyond the normal need for law enforcement, make the warrant and probable-cause requirement impracticable" (*Griffin v. Wisconsin*, 1987).

Searches of persons at airports and borders are based on the special need beyond the normal purpose of law enforcement. In the next chapter, we will see how the same justification provides a basis for searches of specific places. For now, we must ask two questions: Are there other contexts in which the special need beyond the normal purpose of law enforcement justifies searches of persons? and How does the Supreme Court determine if sufficient justification exists to determine that a specific context requires that the special need for law enforcement, make the warrant and probable-cause requirement impracticable.". . .

We have found such "special needs" to exist in the public-school context [with respect to searches of school lockers in *T.L.O. v. New Jersey* (1985)]. . . . We have upheld suspicionless searches and seizures to conduct drug testing of railroad personnel involved in train accidents; . . . to conduct random drug testing of federal customs officers who carry arms or are involved in drug interdiction; . . . and to maintain automobile checkpoints looking for illegal immigrants and contraband, . . . and drunk drivers. . . .

The first factor to be considered is the nature of the privacy interest upon which the search here at issue intrudes. The Fourth Amendment does not protect all subjective expectations of privacy, but only those that society recognizes as "legitimate.". . . Central, in our view, to the present case is the fact that the subjects of the Policy are (1) children, who (2) have been committed to the temporary custody of the State as schoolmaster.

Traditionally at common law and still today, unemancipated minors lack some of the most fundamental rights of self-determination—including even the right to liberty in its narrow sense, i.e., the right to come and go at will. . . .

Legitimate privacy expectations are even less with regard to student athletes [who must undress and shower together in order to participate]. . . .

. . . By choosing to "go out for the team," they voluntarily subject themselves to a degree of regulation even higher than that imposed on students generally.

In Vernonia's public schools, they must submit to a preseason physical exam . . . , they must acquire adequate insurance coverage or sign an insurance waiver, maintain a minimum grade point average, and comply with any "rules of conduct, dress, training hours and related matters as may be established for each sport by the head coach and athletic director with the principal's approval.". . . [S]tudents who participate in school athletics have reason to expect intrusions upon normal rights and privileges, including privacy. . . .

[The Court concluded that the intrusion into the student-athletes' privacy was minimal.]
. . .

That the nature of the concern is important—indeed, perhaps compelling—can hardly be doubted. Deterring drug use by our Nation's schoolchildren is at least as important as enhancing efficient enforcement of the Nation's laws against the importation of drugs, which was the governmental concern in *Von Raab,* . . . or deterring drug use by engineers and trainmen, which was the governmental concern in *Skinner.* . . . [The Court also said that the interest was especially important with respect to student-athletes because of a risk of immediate harm to themselves or others with whom they play sports.]
. . .

Taking into account all the factors we have considered above—the decreased expectation of privacy, the relative unobtrusiveness of the search, and the severity of the need met by the search—we conclude Vernonia's Policy is reasonable and hence constitutional. . . .

beyond the normal purpose of law enforcement permit warrantless searches? As you read *Vernonia School District v. Acton* (1995) in the accompanying box, look closely at the Court's reasoning as it analyzes the request to recognize a special-needs-of-law-enforcement context.

Justice Scalia's analysis in *Vernonia* demonstrates the Court's general approach in determining whether a special-needs-of-law-enforcement justification supports dispensing with a requirement of individualized suspicion. The Court first examined the nature of the privacy interest involved and the intrusiveness of the search. If the case concerned a body-cavity search of a general member of the public (as opposed to someone confined to a corrections institution), the privacy interest would be more significant than a brief patdown frisk or a urine sample. Second, the Court examined the importance of the government's justification for the warrantless search. Here, the Court concluded that the government's interest in combatting drug use was "compelling" and that it outweighed the minimal nature of the privacy interest and intrusion. Although the *Vernonia* case itself is not central to an understanding of criminal procedure, the Court's analysis is important for understanding and anticipating how the Court is likely to approach later cases. In 2002, the Court used similar reasoning to approve drug testing students in all after-school activities (*Board of Education v. Earls*).

As indicated in the *Vernonia* opinion, the Supreme Court previously used the special need beyond the normal purpose of law enforcement justification in order to approve drug testing of two other specific groups. In *Skinner v. Railway Labor Executives' Association* (1989), the Court approved drug testing of train engineers. The U.S. Department of Transportation established the practice after two fatal train crashes in which the engineers were found to have been using illegal substances prior to the accidents. Similarly, the Court approved the Customs Service's policy of drug testing customs officers in *Treasury Employees v. Von Raab* (1989). The majority of justices found that the governmental interests at issue outweighed the costs to the individual from the intrusiveness of the search.

None of the foregoing decisions enjoyed unanimous support. In each case, one or more dissenters argued that the government's interests did not outweigh the individual's rights, and therefore the government should justify each search individually rather than freely search an entire class of citizens through drug testing. As you read *Chandler v. Miller* (1997) in the accompanying box, try to identify why the Court treats the targeted class of citizens differently from the people targeted for drug testing in the other cases.

The Court took a critical view of the government's justification for and execution of the drug testing program aimed at political candidates. Thus the justices do not automatically approve all governmental requests for recognition of

---

CASE   *Chandler v. Miller,* 520 U.S. 305 (1997)

[*Georgia enacted a statute requiring candidates for political office to prove that they have passed a urinalysis drug test.*]

JUSTICE GINSBURG delivered the opinion of the Court.

. . .

To be reasonable under the Fourth Amendment, a search ordinarily must be based on individualized suspicion of wrongdoing. . . . But particularized exceptions to the main rule are sometimes warranted based on "special needs, beyond the normal need for law enforcement.". . . When such "special needs"—concerns other than crime detection—are alleged in justification of a Fourth Amendment intrusion, courts must undertake a context specific inquiry, examining closely the competing private and public interests advanced by the parties. . . . As *Skinner* stated: "In limited circumstances, where the privacy interests implicated by the search are minimal, and where an important governmental interest

furthered by the intrusion would be placed in jeopardy by a requirement of individualized suspicion, a search may be reasonable despite the absence of such suspicion.". . .

Skinner concerned Federal Railroad Administration (FRA) regulations that required blood and urine tests of rail employees involved in train accidents; the regulations also authorized railroads to administer breath and urine tests to employees who violated certain safety rules. . . . Recognizing that the urinalysis tests, most conspicuously, raised evident privacy concerns, the Court noted two offsetting considerations: First, the regulations reduced the intrusiveness of the collection process, . . . and, more important, railway employees, "by reason of their participation in an industry that is regulated pervasively to ensure safety," had diminished expectations of privacy. . . .

In *Von Raab,* the Court sustained a United States Customs Service program that made drug tests a condition of promotion or transfer to positions directly involving drug interdiction or requiring the employee to carry a firearm. . . . While the Service's regime was not prompted by a demonstrated drug abuse problem, . . . it was developed for an agency with an "almost unique mission,". . . as the "first line of defense" against the smuggling of illicit drugs into the United States. . . . The Court held that the government had a "compelling" interest in assuring that employees placed in these positions would not include drug users. . . . Individualized suspicion would not work in this setting, the Court determined, because it was "not feasible to subject [these] employees and their work product to the kind of day to day scrutiny that is the norm in more traditional office environments.". . .

Finally, in *Vernonia,* the Court sustained a random drug testing program for high school students engaged in interscholastic athletic competitions. The program's context was critical, for local governments bear large "responsibilities, under a public school system, as guardian and tutor of children entrusted to its care.". . . An "immediate crisis". . . caused by "a sharp increase in drug use" in the school district . . . sparked installation of the program. . . . Our decision noted that "'students within the school environment have a lesser expectation of privacy than members of the population generally.'". . . We emphasized the importance of deterring drug use by schoolchildren and risk of injury a drug-using athlete cast on himself and those engaged with him on the playing field. . . .

. . . We are aware of no precedent suggesting that a State's power to establish qualifications for state offices—any more than its sovereign power to prosecute crime—diminishes the constraints on state action imposed by the Fourth Amendment. We therefore reject respondents' invitation to apply in this case a framework extraordinarily deferential to state measures setting conditions of candidacy for state office. Our guides remain *Skinner, Von Raab,* and *Vernonia.* . . .

Our precedents establish that the proffered special need for drug testing must be substantial—important enough to override the individual's acknowledged privacy interest, sufficiently vital to suppress the Fourth Amendment's normal requirement of individualized suspicion. . . . Georgia has failed to show, in justification of [its statute], a special need of that kind.

Respondents' defense of the statute rests primarily on the incompatibility of unlawful drug use with holding high state office. The statute is justified, respondents contend, because the use of illegal drugs draws into question an official's judgment and integrity; jeopardizes the discharge of public functions, including antidrug law enforcement efforts; and un-

dermines public confidence and trust in elected officials. . . . The statute, according to respondents, serves to deter unlawful drug users from becoming candidates and thus stops them from attaining high office. . . . Notably lacking in respondents' presentation is any indication of a concrete danger demanding departure from the Fourth Amendment's main rule.

Nothing in the record hints that the hazards respondents broadly describe are real and not simply hypothetical for Georgia's polity. The statute was not enacted, as counsel for respondents readily acknowledged at oral argument, in response to any fear or suspicion of drug use by state officials[.] . . .

In contrast to the effective testing regimes upheld in *Skinner, Von Raab* and *Vernonia,* Georgia's certification requirement is not well designed to identify candidates who violate antidrug laws. Nor is the scheme a credible means to deter illicit drug users from seeking election to state office. The test date—to be scheduled by the candidate anytime within 30 days prior to qualifying for a place on the ballot—is not secret. As counsel for respondents acknowledged at oral argument, users of illegal drugs, save for those prohibitively addicted, could abstain for a pretest period sufficient to avoid detection. . . .

What is left, after close review of Georgia's scheme, is the image the State seeks to project. By requiring candidates for public office to submit to drug testing, Georgia displays its commitment to the struggle against drug abuse. The suspicionless tests, according to respondents, signify that candidates, if elected, will be fit to serve their constituents free from the influence of illegal drugs. But Georgia asserts no evidence of a drug problem among the State's elected officials, those officials typically do not perform high risk, safety sensitive tasks, and required certification immediately aids no interdiction effort. The need revealed, in short, is symbolic, not "special," as that term draws meaning from our case law. . . .

However well meant, the candidate drug test Georgia has devised diminishes personal privacy for a symbol's sake. The Fourth Amendment shields society against that state action. . . .

We reiterate, too, that where the risk to public safety is substantial and real, blanket suspicionless searches calibrated to the risk may rank as "reasonable"—for example, searches now routine at airports and at entrances to courts and other official buildings. . . . But where, as in this case, public safety is not genuinely in jeopardy, the Fourth Amendment precludes the suspicionless search, no matter how conveniently arranged.

(continued)

For the reasons stated, the judgment of the Court of Appeals for the Eleventh Circuit is Reversed.

CHIEF JUSTICE REHNQUIST, dissenting.

I fear that the novelty of this Georgia law has led the Court to distort Fourth Amendment doctrine in order to strike it down. . . .

The privacy concerns ordinarily implicated by urinalysis drug testing are "negligible," . . . when the procedures used in collecting and analyzing the urine samples are set up "to reduce the intrusiveness" of the process. Under the Georgia law, the candidate may produce the test specimen at his own doctor's office, which must be one of the least intrusive types of urinalysis drug tests conceivable. But although the Court concedes this, it nonetheless manages to count this factor against the State, because with this kind of test the person tested will have advance notice of its being given, and will

therefore be able to abstain from drug use during the necessary period of time. But one may be sure that if the test were random—and therefore apt to ensnare more users—the Court would then fault it for its intrusiveness. . . .

Although petitioners might raise questions as to some of the other positions covered by the Georgia statute, there is no question that, at least for positions like Governor and Lieutenant Governor, identical concerns [about handling sensitive information that justify drug testing for other jobs] are implicated. In short, when measured through the correct lens of our precedents in this area, the Georgia urinalysis test is a "reasonable" search; it is only by distorting [our] precedents that the Court is able to reach the result it does. . . .

Nothing in the Fourth Amendment or in any other part of the Constitution prevents a State from enacting a statute whose principal vice is that it may seem misguided or even silly to the members of the Court. I would affirm the judgment of the Court of Appeals.

---

special-needs contexts. But was the statute at issue in *Chandler* really any less compelling than the policies examined in *Vernonia, Von Raab,* and *Skinner*? Why, for example, is it more important to make sure that student-athletes do not use drugs than it is to enforce the same issue against government officials who will become key policy makers? Moreover, if the government justification in *Vernonia* was so important, why did they drug test only student-athletes and not all students? There is a risk that in examining the issue, the justices do not treat all targeted groups in an equal manner. It appears that the majority of justices was less critical in analyzing the case concerning student-athletes. Skeptics might wonder whether the justices felt greater empathy and understanding of intrusion directed at the privacy of politicians rather than at the privacy of schoolchildren. However, the Court subsequently demonstrated that its decisions are not driven by its affinity for a certain class of claimants. Instead, the justices appear genuinely concerned about making a considered judgment about the sufficiency of the justification for a special-needs exception.

In 1999 the U.S. Court of Appeals (4th Circuit) ruled that the special-needs exception to the warrant requirement applied to justify the actions of the Medical University of South Carolina Hospital in drug testing pregnant women for cocaine and then turning positive results over to the county prosecutor (*Ferguson v. City of Charleston*). In the first few months of the policy, women were arrested at the hospital shortly after giving birth. Despite claims by the women that the drug tests violated their Fourth Amendment rights, the appeals court ruled that the government's interest in preventing the adverse effects of cocaine on newborn babies was more important. The women also made other claims, including violation of patient-doctor confidentiality privilege when the hospital gave the test results to prosecutors. As you read the case in the accompanying box, can you identify what factors affect the justices' determination of when special needs justify granting law enforcement officials additional authority?

C A S E   *Ferguson v. City of Charleston,* **532 U.S. 67 (2001)**

JUSTICE STEVENS delivered the opinion of the Court.

. . .

Petitioners are 10 women who received obstetrical care at MUSC [Medical University of South Carolina] and who were arrested after testing positive for cocaine. . . .

Petitioners' complaint challenged the validity of the policy under various theories, including the claim that warrantless and nonconsensual drug tests conducted for criminal investigatory purposes were unconstitutional searches. Respondents advanced two principal defenses to the constitutional claim: (1) that, as a matter of fact, petitioners had consented to the searches; and (2) that, as a matter of law, the searches were reasonable, even absent consent, because they were justified by special non-law-enforcement purposes. . . .

Because MUSC is a state hospital, the members of its staff are government actors, subject to the strictures of the Fourth Amendment. *New Jersey v. T.L.O.,* 469 U.S. 325, 335–337 (1985). Moreover, the urine tests conducted by those staff members were indisputably searches within the meaning of the Fourth Amendment. *Skinner v. Railway Labor Executives' Assn.,* 489 U.S. 602, 617 (1989). . . .

Because the hospital seeks to justify its authority to conduct drug tests and to turn the results over to law enforcement agents without the knowledge or consent of the patients, this case differs from the four previous cases in which we have considered whether comparable drug tests "fit within the closely guarded category of constitutionally permissible suspicionless searches." *Chandler v. Miller,* 520 U.S. 305, 309 (1997). In three of those cases, we sustained drug tests for railway employees involved in train accidents, *Skinner v. Railway Labor Executives' Assn.,* . . . (1989), for United States Customs Service employees seeking promotion to certain sensitive positions, *Treasury Employees v. Von Raab,* 489 U.S. 656 (1989), and for high school students participating in interscholastic sports, *Vernonia School Dist. v. Acton,* 515 U.S. 646 (1995). In the fourth case, we struck down such testing for candidates for designated state offices as unreasonable. *Chandler v. Miller,* 520 U.S. 305 (1997).

In each of those cases, we employed a balancing test that weighed the intrusion on the individual's interest in privacy against the "special needs" that supported the program. As an initial matter, we note that the invasion of privacy in this case is far more substantial than in those cases. In the previous four cases, there was no misunderstanding about the purpose of the test or the potential use of the test results, and there were protections against the dissemination of the results to third parties. The use of an adverse test result to disqualify one from eligibility for a particular benefit, such as a promotion or an opportunity to participate in an extracurricular activity, involves a less serious intrusion on privacy than the unauthorized dissemination of such results to third parties. The reasonable expectation of privacy enjoyed by the typical patient undergoing diagnostic tests in a hospital is that the results of those tests will not be shared with nonmedical personnel without her consent. . . . In none of our prior cases was there any intrusion upon that kind of expectation.

The critical difference between those four drug-testing cases and this one, however, lies in the nature of the "special need" asserted as justification for the warrantless searches. In each of those earlier cases, the "special need" that was advanced as a justification for the absence of a warrant or individualized suspicion was one divorced from the State's general interest in law enforcement. This point was emphasized both in the majority opinions sustaining the programs in the first three cases [*Skinner, Treasury Employees,* and *Vernonia*], as well as in the dissent in the *Chandler* case. In this case, however, the central and indispensable feature of the policy from its inception was the use of law enforcement to coerce the patients into substance abuse treatment. This fact distinguishes this case from circumstances in which physicians or psychologists, in the course of ordinary medical procedures aimed at helping the patient herself, come across information that under the rules of law or ethics is subject to reporting requirements, which no one has challenged here. . . .

Respondents argue in essence that their ultimate purpose, is a beneficent one. In *Chandler,* however, we did not simply accept the State's invocation of a "special need." Instead, we carried out a "close review" of the scheme at issue before concluding that the need in question was not "special," as that term has been defined in our cases. In this case, a review of the [hospital's drug-testing policy] plainly reveals that the purpose actually served by the MUSC searches "is ultimately indistinguishable from the general interest in crime control." *Indianapolis v. Edmond . . .* (2000).

(continued)

In looking to the programmatic purpose, we consider all the available evidence in order to determine the relevant primary purpose. . . . Tellingly, the document codifying the policy incorporates the police's operational guidelines. It devotes its attention to the chain of custody, the range of possible criminal charges, and logistics of police notification and arrests. Nowhere, however, does the document discuss different courses of medical treatment for either mother or infant, aside from treatment for the mother's addiction.

Moreover, throughout the development and application of the policy, the Charleston prosecutors and police were extensively involved in the day-to-day administration of the policy. Police and prosecutors decided who would receive the reports of positive drug screens and what information would be included with those reports. . . . Law enforcement officials also helped to determine the procedures to be followed when performing screens. . . .

While the ultimate goal of the program may well have been to get the women in question into substance abuse treatment and off of drugs, the immediate objective of the searches was to generate evidence *for law enforcement purposes* in order to reach that goal. The threat of law enforcement may ultimately have been intended as a means to an end, but the direct and primary purpose of MUSC's policy was to ensure the use of those means. In our opinion, this distinction was critical. Because law enforcement involvement always serves some broader social purpose or objective, under respondents' view, virtually any nonconsensual suspicionless search could be immunized under the special needs doctrine by defining the search solely in terms of its ultimate, rather than immediate, purpose. Such an approach is inconsistent with the Fourth Amendment. Given the primary purpose of the Charleston program, which was to use the threat of arrest and prosecution in order to force women into treatment and given the extensive involvement of law enforcement officials at every stage of the policy, this case simply does not fit within the closely guarded category of "special needs."

The fact that positive test results were turned over to the police does not merely provide a basis for distinguishing our prior cases applying the "special needs" balancing approach to the determination of drug use. It also provides an affirmative reason for enforcing the strictures of the Fourth Amendment. While state hospital employees, like other citizens, may have a duty to provide the police with evidence of criminal conduct that they inadvertently acquire in the course of routine treatment, when they undertake to obtain such evidence from their patients *for the specific purpose of incriminating those patients,* they have a special obligation to make sure that the patients are fully informed about their constitutional rights, as standards of knowing waiver require. . . .

As respondents have repeatedly insisted, their motive was benign rather than punitive. Such a motive, however, cannot justify a departure from Fourth Amendment protections, given the pervasive involvement of law enforcement with the development and application of the MUSC policy. The stark and unique fact that characterizes this case is that [the drug-testing policy] was designed to obtain evidence of criminal conduct by the tested patients that would be turned over to the police and that could be admissible in subsequent criminal prosecutions. While respondents are correct that drug abuse both was and is a serious problem, "the gravity of the threat alone cannot be dispositive of questions concerning what means law enforcement officers may employ to pursue a given purpose." *Indianapolis v. Edmond* . . . (2000). The Fourth Amendment's general prohibition against nonconsensual, warrantless, and suspicionless searches necessarily applies to such a policy. . . .

[Justice Kennedy's opinion concurring in judgment is omitted.]

JUSTICE SCALIA wrote a dissenting opinion, joined by CHIEF JUSTICE REHNQUIST and JUSTICE THOMAS.

. . .

The first step in Fourth Amendment analysis is to identify the search and seizure at issue. What petitioners, the Court, and to a lesser extent the concurrence really object to is not the urine testing, but the hospital's reporting of positive drug-test results to police. But the latter is obviously not a search. At most it may be a "derivative use of the product of a past unlawful search," which, of course, "work[s] no new Fourth Amendment wrong" and "presents a question, not of rights, but of remedies." *United States v. Calandra* . . . (1974). There is only one act that could conceivably be regarded as a search of petitioners in the present case: the *taking* of the urine sample. I suppose the *testing* of that urine for traces of unlawful drugs could be considered a search of sorts, but the Fourth Amendment protects only against searches of citizens' "persons, houses, papers, and effects"; and it is entirely unrealistic to regard urine as one of the "effects" (*i.e.,* part of the property) of the person who has passed and abandoned it. Cf. *California v. Greenwood,* 486 U.S. 35 (1988) (garbage left at curb is not property protected by the Fourth Amendment). Some would argue, I suppose, that testing of the urine is prohibited by some generalized privacy right "emanating" from the "penumbras" of the Constitution (a question that is not before us); but it is not even arguable that the testing of urine that has been lawfully obtained is a Fourth Amendment search. . . .

It is rudimentary Fourth Amendment law that a search which has been consented to is not unreasonable. There is no contention in the present case that the urine samples were extracted forcibly. . . .

Until today, we have *never* held—or even suggested—that material which a person voluntarily entrusts to someone else cannot be given by that person to the police, and used for whatever evidence it may contain. Without so much as discussing the point, the Court today opens a hole in our Fourth Amendment jurisprudence, the size and shape of which is entirely indeterminate. . . .

As indicated by the majority's reasoning in *Ferguson,* the Court looked closely at the nature of the intrusion into individuals' privacy interests in determining whether society's interests outweighed those of the individual and justified the intrusion. The Court found that the intrusion was especially severe because law enforcement goals, which threaten the individual's liberty, were being advanced. This differed from other drug testing cases which concerned other goals, such as public safety and preventing drug abuse in youths, that were not aimed directly at imposing criminal sanctions on the individuals being tested. The majority appears unwilling to grant officials additional authority for such warrantless searches merely because such authority would provide greater ability to apprehend criminal offenders. Instead, the Court is looking for a significant societal interest, other than law enforcement, to justify the intrusion on individuals' Fourth Amendment protections.

Searches of people entering the United States at border points are not justified merely by a desire to enhance the capacity of police officers to control crime. The Supreme Court has explicitly endorsed the use of routine searches of people and their property at borders without any requirement of reasonable suspicion (*United States v. Montoya de Hernandez,* 1985). Such searches are justified on two grounds. First, people are presumed to have a diminished expectation of privacy when they cross a national border. In other words, they should expect to be questioned and possibly have their persons and property checked for illegal contraband. Second, the government's interests in guarding against the entry of people and items (e.g., weapons, drugs, toxic chemicals) that are harmful to national interests outweigh the individuals' diminished expectations of privacy.[3]

The special-needs exception will receive further attention in the next chapter because it has also been put forward as a justification for searching places, especially automobiles.

EXIGENT CIRCUMSTANCES

In the discussion of arrests in Chapter 3, one of the bases for making an arrest without a warrant was when there are **exigent circumstances.** With respect to arrests, for example, when officers are in hot pursuit of a fleeing suspected

Cupp v. Murphy, 412 U.S. 291 (1973)

JUSTICE STEWART delivered the opinion of the Court.

The respondent, Daniel Murphy, was convicted by a jury in an Oregon court of the second-degree murder of his wife. The victim died by strangulation in her home in the city of Portland, and abrasions and lacerations were found on her throat. There was no sign of break-in or robbery. Word of the murder was sent to the respondent, who was not then living with his wife. Upon receiving the message, Murphy promptly telephoned the Portland police and voluntarily came into Portland for questioning. Shortly after the respondent's arrival at the station house, where he was met by retained counsel, the police noticed a dark spot on the respondent's finger. Suspecting that the spot might be dried blood and knowing that evidence of strangulation is often found under the assailant's fingernails, the police asked Murphy if they could take a sample of scrapings from his fingernails. He refused. Under protest and without a warrant, the police proceeded to take the samples, which turned out to contain traces of skin and blood cells, and fabric from the victim's nightgown. This incriminating evidence was admitted at trial. . . .

We believe this search was constitutionally permissible under the principles of *Chimel v. California* (1969) [a precedent validating warrantless searches incident to a lawful arrest]. . . .

Where there is no formal arrest, as in the case before us, a person might well be less hostile to the police and less likely to take conspicuous, immediate steps to destroy incriminating evidence on his person. Since he knows he is going to be released, he might be likely instead to be concerned with diverting attention away from himself. Accordingly, we do not hold that a full [search incident to a lawful arrest] . . . would have been justified in this case without a formal arrest and without a warrant. But the respondent was not subjected to such a search.

. . . The rationale of [searches incident to a lawful arrest] justified the police in subjecting him to the very limited search necessary to preserve the highly evanescent evidence they found under his fingernails. . . .

On the facts of this case, considering the existence of probable cause, the very limited intrusion undertaken incident to the station house detention, and the ready destructibility of the evidence, we cannot say that this search violated the Fourth and Fourteenth Amendments. . . .

felon they need not stop to seek a warrant and thereby risk permitting the suspect to get away. Similarly, exigent circumstances can justify warrantless searches. As you read *Cupp v. Murphy* (1973) in the accompanying box, see if you can determine when the justices will recognize the existence of exigent circumstances that will justify a search without taking the time to obtain a warrant.

Although Justice Stewart's opinion claims to rely on the search-incident-to-a-lawful-arrest precedents, the *Cupp* case is clearly different because there was no arrest. Instead, the Court was really concerned with the fact that the evidence could disappear if the officers were not permitted to search immediately under the suspect's fingernails. Thus, despite not explicitly labeling the justification for the warrantless search as based on exigent circumstances, the facts of the case make the actual underlying justification clear. The Court responded to a specific factual situation by permitting the officers to act quickly in order to avoid the undesirable result of losing available evidence.

How does the *Cupp* decision compare to *Rochin v. California* (1952)? Remember from Chapter 4 that the Supreme Court ruled in *Rochin* that police could not use evidence of drugs obtained by forcibly retrieving (via forced vomiting) pills from the stomach of a man whose bedroom police officers invaded without a warrant. In the *Rochin* case, Justice Frankfurter declared that the police officer's actions "shocked the conscience" through actions that the justice equated with medieval torture. By contrast, there was no home invasion by officers in *Cupp*. The suspect came voluntarily to the police station. Moreover, taking fingernail scrapings in *Cupp* did not compare to the intrusiveness of the "stomach pumping" in *Rochin*. This instructive comparison helps to show that the Court is likely to react on a case-by-case basis in examining—after the fact—whether police officers were justified in acting quickly by conducting a search without seeking a warrant.

In other cases, the Supreme Court approved warrantless blood tests because, for example, evidence of alcohol in the blood will dissipate and disappear if not retrieved immediately through a blood test. In *Breihaupt v. Abram* (1957), the Court permitted police to have blood drawn from an injured, unconscious individual suspected of causing a fatal car accident as a result of ingesting alcohol before driving. The case did not solve the Fourth Amendment issue for such searches and seizures from a person's body because the decision came before the Court had incorporated the exclusionary rule. In the later case of *Schmerber v. California* (1966), decided after incorporation, a police officer arrested a driver at the hospital after an automobile accident. The Court considered whether the officer needed to seek a warrant before having blood drawn. According to Justice Brennan's majority opinion:

> *The officer in the present case, however, might reasonably have believed that he was confronted with an emergency, in which the delay necessary to obtain a warrant, under the circumstances, threatened "the destruction of evidence.". . . We are told that the percentage of alcohol in the blood begins to diminish shortly after drinking stops, as the body functions to eliminate it from the system. Particularly in a case such as this, where time had to be taken to bring the accused to a hospital and to investigate the scene of the accident, there was no time to seek out a magistrate and secure a warrant. Given these special facts, we conclude that the attempt to secure evidence of blood-alcohol content in this case was an appropriate incident to petitioner's arrest. (384 U.S. 757, 770–771)*

In addition, the Court concluded the search was reasonable because it was conducted by medical personnel (rather than police) using minimally intrusive techniques that are highly likely to result in the discovery of evidence.

The Court's acceptance of such searches from suspects' bodies does not imply that the Court will endorse all searches. In other Fourth Amendment cases, the justices continue to seek a balance between societal interests and constitutional rights. In *Winston v. Lee* (1985), the Court rejected a request to order surgery for a suspect when the police wanted to see if the suspect's body contained a bullet that they thought struck an armed robber when fired by a storeowner during an attempted robbery. If they could remove and examine the bullet from the suspect's body, then the officers could determine if the bullet was the one fired from the storeowner's gun and thereby help to prove that the suspect was, in fact, the robber. In relying on the balance of factors considered in *Schmerber,* the justices decided that the proposed surgery was too intrusive and imposed too many health risks to the suspect.

Note that the exigent circumstances justification for warrantless searches can be applied merely for the purpose of seeking evidence. Public safety does not need to be threatened in order for such a search to be justified. As a practical matter, police officers make quick judgments about undertaking certain searches. If incriminating evidence is discovered, courts may be asked to make an after-the-fact determination of whether the urgency of the situation justified a warrantless search and whether the nature and purpose of the search were reasonable.

CONCLUSION

The Fourth Amendment explicitly seeks to protect "persons" against governmental invasions. Although the amendment implies a preference for warrants supported by probable cause, warrantless searches are permitted as long as they are not "unreasonable." The Supreme Court has identified several circumstances in which criminal justice officials may conduct warrantless searches of persons. The broadest authority for such searches exists with respect to people confined within correctional institutions. These searches are justified by the compelling need to maintain safety and security in such institutions. Warrantless searches are also permitted when required by the special need beyond the normal purpose of law enforcement. The Court has identified specific contexts in which the special-needs exception to the warrant requirement applies. These contexts include searches at borders and airports as well as specific searches aimed at targeted populations, including students, transportation workers, and certain categories of government employees, such as customs officers. Police officers may conduct stop-and-frisk searches on the streets when they have reasonable suspicion that someone is armed and involved in criminal activity. More intrusive searches may be conducted of arrestees at the scene of an arrest in order to protect public safety and prevent the destruction of evidence. In addition, warrantless searches may be justified by exigent circumstances, such as the risk that evidence will disappear if a person is not searched immediately. As with other Fourth Amendment issues, the Supreme Court is typically concerned with striking an appropriate balance between society's goals and individuals' interests in constitutional rights.

SUMMARY

- Corrections officials have broad authority to conduct warrantless searches of people held in custody. This authority includes the ability to conduct extremely intrusive body-cavity searches, and it extends over unconvicted pretrial detainees in jails as well as convicted offenders in prison.

- Customs officers may conduct warrantless searches at airports and borders. Supervisory approval or court orders may be needed in order to conduct the most intrusive kinds of searches on travelers.

- There is evidence that customs searches impact African American women more than other demographic groups. There are risks of discriminatory applications of warrantless searches because officers' perceptions and discretionary judgments play such an important role in determining when searches will be conducted.

- Under the doctrine of *Terry v. Ohio*, police officers may conduct stop-and-frisk searches on the street when their reasonable suspicions indicate that someone is armed and involved in criminal activity.

- The Supreme Court has given police officers flexibility to consider suspicious flight by pedestrians and tips from reliable informants in determining whether reasonable suspicion exists to justify a patdown search.
- Warrantless searches may be conducted at the scene of an arrest to ensure that arrestees do not have weapons or will not destroy evidence.
- Warrantless searches are justified in specific recognized contexts by the special need beyond the normal purpose of law enforcement. Such situations include airports, borders, and specific categories of targeted individuals.
- Warrantless searches may be justified by exigent circumstances in which a quick search must be undertaken in order to avoid the risk that evidence, such as a blood-alcohol reading, will dissipate or disappear while a warrant is being sought.

Key Terms

body-cavity search   The most intrusive form of physical search that normally requires reasonable suspicion and special supervision and procedures for application at international borders or any context other than an incarcerated detainee or prisoner.

exigent circumstances   Justification for warrantless searches in circumstances in which immediate search must be undertaken in order to protect public safety or prevent the destruction of evidence.

patdown or frisk search   Limited search of the exterior of a clothed person's body by feeling for the presence of weapons or other contraband.

racial profiling   The practice of using a person's race as a key factor in deciding whether he or she fits the general demographic description of a drug dealer or other targeted criminal offender.

search incident to a lawful arrest   A warrantless search undertaken at the scene of an arrest to ensure that the arrestee has no weapons which may endanger public safety and to see if any criminal evidence can be recovered from the arrestee or the immediate vicinity of the arrestee.

special need beyond the normal purpose of law enforcement   Search situations in which governmental objectives always outweigh Fourth Amendment interests in a defined context, without relying for justification on an officer's determination of reasonable suspicion or probable cause.

stop-and-frisk search   Limited search approved by the Supreme Court in *Terry v. Ohio* that permits police officers to pat down the clothing of people whose behavior leads to a reasonable suspicion that they may be armed and involved in criminal activity.

strip search   Physical search that requires the suspect to disrobe and must be justified by reasonable suspicion and special procedures in contexts outside of corrections.

Additional Readings

Hall, John Wesley, Jr. 2000. *Search and Seizure*. Charlottesville, Va.: LEXIS Law Publishing. A reference book on court cases concerning search and seizure.

LaFave, Wayne R. 1996. *Search and Seizure*. St. Paul, Minn.: West Publishing. Comprehensive examination of search and seizure issues and cases.

Notes

1. Jennifer Loven, "Black Women Searched More Often," Associated Press Wire Service, 10 April 2000; General Accounting Office, *U.S. Customs Service: Better Targeting of Airline Passengers for Personal Searches Could Produce Better Results* (Washington, D.C.: General Accounting Office, March 2000).

2. Charles Whitebread and Christopher Slobogin, *Criminal Procedure: An Analysis of Cases and Concepts*, 4th ed. (New York: Foundation Press, 2000), 237.

3. Ibid., 303.

CHAPTER SIX

Warrantless Searches: Places

Imagine that you live in a large house with a tall wooden fence around the backyard. Early one morning you are studying for an exam when the doorbell rings. Two police officers are standing on the doorstep.

You open the door and ask, "Can I help you?"

"We received a complaint that a suspicious person was prowling around the neighborhood. Can you open your gate to the backyard so that we can look around?"

You hesitate. Your friends will be picking you up to drive you to school at any moment. You need to pack up your books and get ready. "Really, officer. I don't think it's likely that someone could scale the fence and walk around the backyard without me noticing out the window."

"Will you open the gate or not?" The officers seemed annoyed.

"I'm sorry. But my ride is coming any minute. I have to go now. Maybe if you come back after four o'clock."

"How about if we come through the house and just look around the yard for a minute until you leave?"

You look at your watch. You do not want to be late for the exam. "I'm really sorry. I'd like to help. But I just don't have time." The officers stand motionless staring at you as you close the door. You force a smile across your uncertain face as you say, "Thanks for coming. I'm really sorry."

You spend several minutes gathering up your papers and putting your books into your backpack. Then the doorbell rings again. It is the police officers.

"Please step outside," one officer says sharply.

"Why?" you ask with a tone of confusion.

An officer grasps your arm and begins to place your hands behind your back.

"What are you doing? What's going on?" you ask nervously.

"We climbed your back wall and discovered a plant that looks like marijuana growing in the backyard."

"Climbed the wall? Marijuana? You must be joking."

"This is no joke. You're going to jail."

If this happened to you, hopefully the plant would turn out to be something other than marijuana. If it was marijuana, however, could you seek to have the plant excluded from evidence? That depends, of course, on whether the officers' search of the backyard violated your Fourth Amendment rights. Do you think the officers conducted a legal search? If you were a judge, how would you explain your decision about whether the evidence can be used in court?

The Fourth Amendment does not merely protect "[t]he right of the people to be secure in their persons," it also protects that same security for their "houses, papers, and effects." People have reasonable expectations of privacy with respect to their property. The extent of the expectation will vary—in the eyes of judges—according to the nature of the property. People's homes generally receive the greatest protection. But protection is also provided for automobiles, luggage, and other places where people keep their possessions. We know that officers may obtain warrants to search any location, including homes, if they demonstrate the existence of probable cause to the issuing judicial officer. Yet a warrant is not required in all situations. Just as in the searches of persons discussed in Chapter 5, there are specific circumstances that justify searches of places without warrants. In this chapter, we will examine the circumstances in which warrantless searches of property are permitted. Some of the circumstances justifying such searches are the same as those justifying warrantless searches of people.

PLAIN VIEW DOCTRINE

Much of the Supreme Court's discussion of Fourth Amendment issues includes consideration of individuals' reasonable expectation of privacy. If people take actions that effectively surrender their expectation of privacy, then the Court typically sees Fourth Amendment protections as simultaneously surrendered, too. For example, a homeowner who places trash at the curb for pickup has surrendered a privacy interest in the trash, and the trash may be freely searched by the police without a warrant (*California v. Greenwood*, 1988). The trash was placed in the open in a manner that conveyed the owner's intention to give up possession and control of the property. When the trash is in a public location, there is no impediment to anyone, including the police, looking through the trash to see what items are contained therein. Underlying such decisions concerning the surrender of reasonable expectations of privacy is the notion that items placed in the open are not being protected by their owners. Therefore the owners are not asserting the same expectation of privacy that might exist if they took measures to protect their property from observation and examination by passersby.

What if a police officer is walking down a street and he sees a marijuana plant growing in the front window of a home? Has the officer conducted a search by looking into the window? If so, is the search legal? Or is it illegal because it took place by chance and was not supported by reasonable suspicion or probable cause? The Supreme Court addressed such circumstances in *Coolidge v. New Hampshire* (1971). In *Coolidge* the Court discussed the **plain view doctrine,** which permits officers to notice and use as evidence items that are visible to them when they are in a location that they are permitted to be. Officers could not break into a home and then claim that the drugs found inside were in plain view on a table. However, if the table was in front of an open window so that the drugs were visible from a public sidewalk, the plain view doctrine could apply. According to the *Coolidge* opinion,

> *An example of the applicability of the "plain view" doctrine is the situation in which the police have a warrant to search a given area for specified objects, and in the course of the search come across some other article of incriminating character. . . . (403 U.S. 443, 465)*

In the example of the open window, the officer's act in viewing a plainly visible object would not constitute a search. Because the object was in plain view, the owner of the property had lost any reasonable expectation of privacy with respect to the item. For example, if officers are invited into a home to provide emergency medical assistance and they see cocaine lying on a table, they may seize the drugs because they have lawfully entered the home by consent of the occupants and the obvious visibility of the drugs provides probable cause for the seizure. By contrast, if the officer spies marijuana plants in a window, the officer's plain view of the items provides probable cause for obtaining a warrant to gain entry into the home in order to seize the items.

The Court explained the basis for searches and seizures under the plain view doctrine in *Arizona v. Hicks* (1987):

> *We now hold that probable cause is required [for searches and seizures under the plain view doctrine]. To say otherwise would be to cut the "plain view" doctrine loose from its theoretical and practical moorings. The theory of the doctrine consists of extending to nonpublic places such as the home, where searches and seizures without a warrant are presumptively unreasonable, the police's longstanding authority to make warrantless seizures in public places of such objects as weapons and contraband. And the practical justification for that extension is the desirability of sparing police, whose viewing of the object in the course of a lawful search is as legitimate as it would have been in a public place, the inconvenience and the risk—to themselves or to preservation of evidence—of going to obtain a warrant. Dispensing with the need for a warrant is worlds apart from permitting a lesser standard of cause for the seizure than a warrant would require. (480 U.S. 321, 326–327)*

As explained by the Court, the plain view doctrine represents the extension of a traditional doctrine permitting officers to seize evidence in public places when they have probable cause for such a seizure. The same standard applies when officers are lawfully standing in a private location. If they have probable cause to seize items, they may do so without obtaining a warrant in order to prevent the risk that the evidence will be moved or destroyed while they seek a warrant.

Open Fields Doctrine

Related to the plain view doctrine is the **open fields doctrine.** Under this doctrine, first announced by the Supreme Court in *Hester v. United States* (1924), property owners have no reasonable expectation of privacy in open fields on and around their property. Thus, if marijuana plants or other criminal evidence is visible, then probable cause has been established for its seizure. The Court has approved cases in which police officers, acting without a warrant, walked past "no trespassing" signs and found marijuana plants in fields on private property (*Oliver v. United States,* 1984). The Court limited this doctrine by refusing to apply it to the "curtilage" immediately surrounding the home, which is the yard or other land area adjacent and closely connected to the home. The curtilage is protected against physical intrusion by officers, but it is still subject to the plain view doctrine if evidence of criminal activity is clearly visible from the vantage point of a location where officers can lawfully stand. However, the Court permits law enforcement officials to use aerial surveillance to see marijuana plants and any other evidence that may be visible in the curtilage. Thus, when low-flying helicopters hovered a few hundred feet over private property, the Court determined that this surveillance did not constitute a "search" that was subject to the requirements of the Fourth Amendment (*Florida v. Riley,* 1989; *California v. Ciraolo,* 1986).

Plain Feel and Other Senses

The existence of doctrines permitting warrantless seizure of items visible to law enforcement officers naturally raises questions about whether the same doctrine applies to criminal evidence detected through other senses. For example, if officers smell the distinctive aroma of marijuana, they may be justified in investigating further. In *United States v. Villamonte-Marquez* (1983), a customs officer and state police trooper boarded a sailboat in a river channel. When they smelled marijuana, they looked through a porthole to see bundles of marijuana stacked in the hold. The Court focused on the authority of customs officers to board ships, but they gave no indication that they questioned the utility of following an officer's sense of smell. Bear in mind that the sense of smell may be employed by a trained police dog, too. Court decisions have established that police dogs that sniff luggage in public places are not conducting searches and therefore not subject to the requirements of the Fourth Amendment (*United States v. Place,* 1983).

In Chapter 5, we noted that the sense of feel may be used to identify and seize contraband during a stop-and-frisk search of a person if the illegal item is immediately identifiable upon a patdown search of outer clothing (*Minnesota v. Dickerson,* 1993). How does an officer's sense of feel apply to searches of property? The Supreme Court addressed the issue in *Bond v. United States* (2000). As you read *Bond* in the box on pp. 178–179, ask yourself which opinion is more persuasive, the majority or the dissent.

Bond v. United States, 529 U.S. 334 (2000)

CHIEF JUSTICE REHNQUIST delivered the opinion of the Court.

This case presents the question whether a law enforcement officer's physical manipulation of a bus passenger's carry-on luggage violated the Fourth Amendment's proscription against unreasonable searches. We hold that it did.

Petitioner Steven Dwayne Bond was a passenger on a Greyhound bus that left California bound for Little Rock, Arkansas. The bus stopped, as it was required to do, at the permanent Border Patrol checkpoint in Sierra Blanca, Texas. Border Patrol Agent Cesar Cantu boarded the bus to check the immigration status of its passengers. After reaching the back of the bus, having satisfied himself that the passengers were lawfully in the United States, Agent Cantu began walking toward the front. Along the way, he squeezed the soft luggage which passengers had placed in the overhead storage space above the seats.

Petitioner was seated four or five rows from the back of the bus. As Agent Cantu inspected luggage in the compartment above petitioner's seat, he squeezed a green canvas bag and noticed that it contained a "brick-like" object. Petitioner admitted that the bag was his and agreed to allow Agent Cantu to open it [although the Government did not argue that this consent was the basis for admitting the evidence]. Upon opening the bag, Agent Cantu discovered a "brick" of methamphetamine. . . .

The Fourth Amendment provides that "[t]he right of the people to be secure in their persons, houses, papers, and effects, against unreasonable searches and seizures, shall not be violated. . . ." A traveler's personal luggage is clearly an "effect" protected by the Amendment. . . . Indeed, it is undisputed here that petitioner possessed a privacy interest in his bag.

But the Government asserts that by exposing his bag to the public, petitioner lost a reasonable expectation that his bag would not be physically manipulated. The Government relies on [the cases of helicopters hovering over private property to view marijuana plants to determine that the property was observable to public]. . . .

But [the helicopter cases] are different from this case because they involved only visual, as opposed to tactile, observation. Physically invasive inspection is simply more intrusive than purely visual inspection. For example, in *Terry v. Ohio* [1968], . . . we stated that a "careful [tactile] exploration of the outer surfaces of a person's clothing all over his or her body" is a "serious intrusion upon the sanctity of the person, which may inflict great indignity and arouse strong resentment, and is not to be undertaken lightly." Although Agent Cantu did not "frisk" petitioner's person, he did conduct a probing tactile examination of petitioner's carry-on luggage. Obviously, petitioner's bag was not part of his person. But travelers are particularly concerned about their carry-on luggage; they generally use it to transport personal items that, for whatever reason, they prefer to keep close at hand.

Here, petitioner concedes that, by placing his bag in the overhead compartment, he could expect that

The majority opinion provides guidance about the meaning of the privacy expectation that the Court seeks to protect under the Fourth Amendment. The Court asks two questions about the privacy expectation being asserted. First, is there an actual subjective expectation of privacy? In other words, did the person actually expect to keep her possession private? The Court looks to see if the person behaved in a manner to indicate that she believed she had a right to privacy. It does not matter whether comparable people shared the same belief. This is an assessment of the expectation that the individual had within her own mind. The fact that other passengers may have opened their luggage so that others could see it or that they did not complain when people felt their luggage does not determine whether someone may actually possess a different expectation about privacy.

it would be exposed to certain kinds of touching and handling. But petitioner argues that Agent Cantu's physical manipulation of his luggage "far exceeded the casual contact [petitioner] could have expected from other passengers.". . . The Government counters that it did not.

Our Fourth Amendment analysis embraces two questions. First, we ask whether the individual, by his conduct, has exhibited an actual expectation of privacy; that is, whether he has shown that "he [sought] to preserve [something] as private.". . . Here, petitioner sought to preserve privacy by using an opaque bag and placing that bag directly above his seat. Second, we inquire whether the individual's expectation of privacy is "one that society is prepared to recognize as reasonable.". . . When a bus passenger places his bag in an overhead bin, he expects that other passengers or bus employees may move it for one reason or another. Thus, a bus passenger clearly expects that his bag may be handled. He does not expect that other passengers or bus employees will, as a matter of course, feel the bag in an exploratory manner. But this is exactly what the agent did here. We therefore hold that the agent's physical manipulation of petitioner's bag violated the Fourth Amendment. . . .

JUSTICE BREYER, with whom JUSTICE SCALIA joins, dissenting.

. . .

. . . The law is clear that the Fourth Amendment protects against government intrusion that upsets an "actual (subjective) expectation of privacy" that is objectively "reasonable.". . . Privacy itself implies the exclusion of uninvited strangers, not just strangers who work for the Government. Hence, an individual cannot reasonably expect privacy in respect to objects or activities that he "knowingly exposes to the public.". . .

Indeed, the Court has said that it is not *objectively* reasonable to expect privacy if "[a]ny member of the public . . . could have" used his senses to detect "everything that th[e] officers observed.". . .

Nor can I accept the majority's efforts to distinguish "tactile" from "visual" interventions, . . . even assuming that distinction matters here. Whether tactile manipulation (say, of the exterior of luggage) is more intrusive or less intrusive than visual observation (say, through a lighted window) necessarily depends on the particular circumstances.

If we are to depart from established legal principles, we should not begin here. At best, this decision will lead to a constitutional jurisprudence of "squeezes," thereby complicating further already complex Fourth Amendment law, increasing the difficulty of deciding ordinary criminal matters, and hindering the administrative guidance (with its potential for control of unreasonable police practices) that a less complicated jurisprudence might provide. . . . At worst, this case will deter law enforcement officers searching for drugs near borders from using even the most non-intrusive touch to help investigate publicly exposed bags. At the same time, the ubiquity of *non*-governmental pushes, prods, and squeezes (delivered by driver, attendant, passenger, or some other stranger) means that this decision cannot do much to protect true privacy. Rather, the traveler who wants to place a bag in a shared overhead bin and yet safeguard its contents from public touch should plan to pack those contents in a suitcase with hard sides, irrespective of the Court's decision today.

Second, the Court examined whether the person's subjective expectation of privacy (i.e., the expectation that was in the person's own mind) was objectively reasonable. In the Court's words, was it an expectation of privacy that others in society would find reasonable? Even if everyone in society may not agree that a bus traveler has an expectation of privacy concerning the exterior of soft-sided luggage, would most people in society find it within the range of reasonableness for someone else to have such an expectation? If the person's expectation of privacy is reasonable, then the Court seeks to protect it under the Fourth Amendment.

An extreme hypothetical example may help to reinforce the point. If a man walked down a public street with no clothes on, in his own mind he may actually believe that no one should look at him (subjective expectation of privacy), but that would not be considered a reasonable expectation (objective assessment of reasonableness) by most people in a society where public nudity is rare and strongly discouraged. Moreover, the Court would also find the man's expectation of privacy unreasonable because his behavior indicated that he had surrendered any such expectation with respect to the privacy of his body when he took off his clothes. Thus the Court looks at the person's definition and assertion of the privacy interest through words and actions and then determines if society would find the person's expectation of privacy to be reasonable.

Notice that the majority opinion seeks to protect people's reasonable expectations of privacy and the justices accepted the claim that people expect that their luggage, including a soft-sided duffel bag, will not be physically manipulated by others. The majority opinion also distinguished between visual and tactile (touching) examinations of property. The Court concluded that tactile examinations are more intrusive and analogized the situation to that in *Terry v. Ohio* where a patdown frisk was obviously more intrusive than just looking at a suspect. Do you agree with these conclusions? Is it reasonable for people to expect privacy for their luggage that is riding on an interstate bus or any other common carrier? Is touching the outside of a piece of luggage really intrusive in a way that violates reasonable expectations of privacy?

The dissenters did not simply disagree with the majority's conclusions. Justice Breyer predicted that this rule will make it more difficult for law enforcement officers to know exactly what they can do in seeking evidence of criminal behavior. The dissenting opinion expressed the fear that the *Bond* decision will deter officers from actively seeking to find drugs and other contraband.

Although the Court has clearly endorsed the plain view and open fields doctrines as avenues for warrantless searches, the *Bond* decision serves as a reminder that there are limits on law enforcement officers' authority to examine accessible property.

SPECIAL NEED BEYOND THE NORMAL PURPOSE OF LAW ENFORCEMENT

Imagine that the same duffel bag carried on the bus by Bond was subsequently taken to an airport so that he could take a flight to a distant city. Let us assume that the airport has a scanning device above a conveyor belt that scans luggage before it is placed on the aircraft. What if the scanner identified the bricklike objects in the duffel bag and this led airport security officers to open the bag and discover the drugs? Would the Supreme Court still exclude the evidence from use against Bond in a criminal case?

In the Fourth Amendment context, we must remember that the justices are usually attempting to strike an appropriate balance between society's interests and those of the individual who believes that constitutional rights are threatened by governmental action. Based on what we already learned in Chapter 5 about warrantless searches of persons, the airport situation would be treated differently than the case involving the bus. The government's interests are regarded as significantly more important at the airport. The government must try to make sure that no one brings guns or bombs on an airplane. Experiences around the world during the last decades of the twentieth century taught governments about the dangers posed by bombers and hijackers who can terrorize and kill hundreds of people with a single destructive act aboard a flying aircraft. Public fears about such dangers and governmental security measures to prevent hijackings increased dramatically after the events of September 11, 2001, when airline hijackers killed more than two thousand people in suicide attacks on New York's World Trade Center and the Pentagon in Washington, D.C. The government has a compelling interest in protecting the public from such attacks. Moreover, because it is well known that luggage is being searched, scanned, and x-rayed with increasing frequency, people do not have a reasonable expectation of privacy in this context. The airport situation and the *Bond* case represent two situations that are arguably alike. A passenger with soft-sided luggage is traveling on a common carrier. However, the Court treats these situations very differently. These examples demonstrate the extent to which decisions about the propriety of searches are contextual. There is no single rule to determine the extent of Fourth Amendment protection afforded to a traveler's luggage. Instead, the degree of protection depends on the context into which the luggage is placed. Individuals' reasonable expectations of privacy and governmental interests vary from context to context, and thus the balancing of interests will differ in each case.

Vehicle Checkpoints

We saw in Chapter 5 that international borders and entry points are recognized as contexts in which the special needs of law enforcement justify warrantless searches and seizures of persons. Not surprisingly, the same rationale holds true for searches of people's property. Cars crossing into the United States from Mexico and Canada are always stopped and frequently searched. Trained dogs are led around some vehicles to determine if there is any aroma of drugs that the dogs' sensitive noses can detect. A positive reaction from a trained dog can provide probable cause for a search of the vehicle and its contents. Such searches need not rely on the reaction of a trained dog. Customs officers can make discretionary decisions about which vehicles to search, and there are often policies about searching a certain number of vehicles at random even when there is no suspicion whatsoever.

The Supreme Court has expanded the checkpoint concept by approving systematic stops along highways within the nation's interior in order to look for drunk drivers. Michigan's state police implemented a sobriety checkpoint program in order to combat drunk driving. They set up a checkpoint at which they stopped every vehicle and briefly questioned each driver. If the driver's behavior aroused suspicions, then the driver was field tested for driving under the influence of alcohol. The Michigan policy was challenged in court, but the U.S. Supreme Court declared that the state's interests outweighed the brief and minimal intrusion on drivers (*Michigan Department of State Police v. Sitz,* 1990). Chief Justice Rehnquist's majority opinion indicated that such stops were similar to the well-established investigatory stops at the national borders in the sense that most drivers experience only a temporary delay and inconvenience in answering a few questions. Thus he concluded that "the balance of the State's interest in preventing drunken driving, the extent to which this system can reasonably be said to advance that interest, and the degree of intrusion upon individual motorists who are briefly stopped, weighs in favor of the state program."

The dissenters, Justices Stevens, Brennan, and Marshall, protested that the program improperly interferes with the liberty and privacy of numerous law-abiding drivers while catching hardly any drunk drivers. Thus the dissenters

Federalism and Constitutional Rights

Ironically, although the Michigan case established the legality of sobriety checkpoints for the entire nation, the Michigan Supreme Court later barred the use of such checkpoints within the state of Michigan. The Michigan Supreme Court examined the protection against unreasonable searches and seizures contained in Article I, Section 11 of the Michigan Constitution. According to the state court:

> Indeed, our precedent regarding automobiles implicitly incorporates a balancing test that is inherent in assessing the reasonableness of warrantless searches and seizures. We hold only that the protection afforded to the seizures of vehicles for criminal investigatory purposes has both an historical foundation and a contemporary justification that is not outweighed by the necessity advanced. Suspicionless criminal investigatory seizures, and extreme deference to the judgments of politically accountable officials is, in this context, contrary to Michigan constitutional precedent. (Sitz v. Department of State Police, 443 Mich. 744, 778–779, Michigan Supreme Court, 1993)

Michigan's high court used a balancing test, but simply struck a different balance than that applied by the U.S. Supreme Court majority. The words prohibiting "unreasonable searches and seizures" are identical in both constitutions, but each court possesses the authority to interpret its own constitution as it sees fit.

The *Sitz* case serves as a reminder that states can make authoritative decisions about many of their own affairs in the American governmental system of federalism. The U.S. Supreme Court is the final authority over decisions concerning the interpretation of the U.S. Constitution, but state supreme courts control the interpretation of their own constitutions. The U.S. Supreme Court's decisions interpreting the U.S. Constitution apply to the entire country, so they establish a baseline for available rights. State supreme courts cannot interpret their constitutions to provide fewer or weaker rights for people in their states, but they can interpret their own constitutions to provide stronger rights than those recognized by the U.S. Supreme Court. This is what happened in the Michigan sobriety checkpoint case. It happens in other cases, too, and thus constitutional rights vary to some degree from state to state.

But since all of the states in the United States are part of one country, shouldn't rights be the same in every state? If people in Michigan are protected against surprise sobriety checkpoints as an invasion of their right against unreasonable seizures, shouldn't other Americans enjoy the same constitutional protection?

labeled the program as "nothing more than symbolic state action" taken to give the appearance of solving the problem of drunken driving. The dissenters also disagreed with the comparison of sobriety checkpoints to border stops. In a border stop, everyone knows that they will be stopped at the border and that they effectively surrender their expectation of privacy when they voluntarily approach the border. If they do not want to be stopped and possibly searched, they can choose to never cross the border. By contrast, the sobriety checkpoints can be set up at surprise locations so that drivers have no advance notice and no choice about whether they will be subjected to the stop and possible search.

As you read the material in the above box about federalism, think about whether the events in Michigan change your expectations about the rights that you think you possess. If the U.S. Supreme Court is not the final authority about rights in every case, how drastically can people's rights vary depending on the state in which they reside? Do you know if any of your rights are different from those of people who reside in a neighboring state?

In 2000 the U.S. Supreme Court decided another case concerning whether the special needs of law enforcement justify warrantless searches and seizures with respect to other kinds of checkpoints. The case concerned the practice of Indianapolis police who set up checkpoints and stopped cars in an effort to combat illegal drug sales and use. Officers stopped each car for approximately five minutes. As officers asked each driver for a license and registration, a trained law enforcement dog was led around the car to sniff for evidence of drugs. A positive signal from a dog would lead to a search. The U.S. Court of Appeals ruled that the city did not provide a sufficient justification for the stops and searches. According to the appellate judge, "Indianapolis does not claim to be concerned with protecting highway safety against drivers high on drugs. . . . Its program of drug roadblocks belongs to the genre of general programs of surveillance which invade privacy wholesale in order to discover evidence of crime" (*City of Indianapolis v. Edmond,* U.S. Court of Appeals, 7th Circuit, 2000). As you read the Supreme Court's opinion in the box on pp. 184–185, ask yourself whether the decision is consistent with the Court's approach to the special needs of law enforcement justification for other kinds of searches.

The Supreme Court rejected the vehicle stops for drug control purposes as constituting an improper general crime control objective that did not out-weigh citizens' Fourth Amendment protections. Some people question the con-sistency of the Court's definitions of special needs of law enforcment. Can you explain why the Supreme Court permits vehicle stops to see if drivers have been drinking but does not permit such stops to look for evidence of drugs? Similarly, is it consistent (in Chapter 5) to permit mandatory drug testing of high school student-athletes (*Vernonia* case) but to not permit the same policy to be applied to adults seeking political office (*Chandler* case)? Although law should ideally be predictable and consistent, the Supreme Court is reacting to individual situations on a case-by-case basis. Thus it is not surprising if ques-tions arise concerning the consistency of the Court's decisions.

Schools

As indicated in *Vernonia School District v. Acton,* which was discussed in Chapter 5, the Supreme Court has identified schools' efforts to protect chil-dren as constituting a context in which the special needs of law enforcement can justify warrantless searches. In *Vernonia* the Court approved the searches of persons through the school system's policy on drug testing student-athletes. The Court has also approved warrantless searches of lockers and students' property in schools. In *New Jersey v. T.L.O.* (1985), a case arose in which an assistant principal searched the purse of a high school student to look for mar-ijuana. The Court determined that the Fourth Amendment applies to prohibit unreasonable searches and seizures by public school officials. However, the Court concluded that "the accommodation of the privacy interests of school-children with the substantial need of teachers and administrators for freedom to maintain order in the schools does not require strict adherence to the re-quirement that searches be based on probable cause to believe that the subject of the search has violated or is violating the law." In striking the balance, the Court merely requires that the warrantless search be supported by reasonable suspicion that the student was engaged in law-breaking behavior.

City of Indianapolis v. Edmond, 531 U.S. 32 (2000)

JUSTICE O'CONNOR delivered the opinion of the Court.

In *Michigan Department of State Police v. Sitz* . . . (1990), and *United States v. Martinez-Fuerte* . . . (1976), we held that brief, suspicionless seizures at highway checkpoints for the purposes of combating drunk driving and intercepting illegal immigrants were constitutional. We now consider the constitutionality of a highway checkpoint program whose primary purpose is the discovery and interdiction of illegal narcotics. . . .

The Fourth Amendment requires that searches and seizures be reasonable. A search or seizure is ordinarily unreasonable in the absence of individualized suspicion of wrongdoing. *Chandler v. Miller* . . . (1997). While such suspicion is not an "irreducible" component of reasonableness, . . . we have recognized only limited circumstances in which the usual rule does not apply [citing examples of drug testing of student-athletes, customs service officers, railway employees involved in accidents]. . . .

We have also upheld brief, suspicionless seizures of motorists at a fixed Border Patrol checkpoint designed to intercept illegal aliens, *Martinez-Fuerte,* . . . and at sobriety checkpoints aimed at removing drunk drivers from the road, *Michigan Department of State Police v. Sitz.* . . . In addition, *Delaware v. Prouse* . . . (1979), we suggested that a similar type of roadblock with the purpose of verifying drivers' licenses and vehicle registrations would be permissi-

ble. In none of these cases, however, did we indicate approval of a checkpoint program whose primary purpose was to detect evidence of ordinary criminal wrongdoing.

. . . In *Martinez-Fuerte,* we found that the balance tipped in favor of the Government's interests in policing the Nation's borders. . . . In so finding, we emphasized the difficulty of effectively containing illegal immigration at the border itself. . . . We also stressed the impracticality of the particularized study of a given car to discern whether it was transporting illegal aliens, as well as the relatively modest degree of intrusion entailed by the stops. . . .

In *Sitz,* . . . [t]he gravity of the drunk driving problem and the magnitude of the State's interest in getting drunk drivers off the road weighed heavily in our determination that the program was constitutional. . . .

. . . [W]hat principally distinguishes these [Indianapolis drug] checkpoints from those we have previously approved is their primary purpose.

As petitioners concede, the Indianapolis checkpoint program unquesionably has the primary purpose of interdicting illegal narcotics. . . .

We have never approved a checkpoint program whose primary purpose was to detect evidence of ordinary criminal wrongdoing. Rather, our checkpoint cases have recognized only limited exceptions to the general rule that a seizure must be accompanied by some measure of individualized suspicion. We suggested in *Prouse* that we would not credit the

---

Because the Supreme Court permits warrantless drug testing for student-athletes (*Vernonia Schools v. Acton*) but not for adult political candidates (*Chandler v. Miller*), critics claim that the Constitution has been interpreted unfairly to provide children with fewer rights than adults. Among critics, this perception is enhanced by the decision that special needs of law enforcement justify warrantless searches of schoolchildren's property. Adults attending college, for example, could not have their purses or backpacks so readily searched by school officials. Instead, law enforcement officers can conduct limited outer-clothing frisks of adults—which would not include looking for marijuana cigarettes in a purse—only if the context met the reasonable suspicion standards about the existence of a weapon and criminal activity. Thus it seems clear that the Court interprets the Fourth Amendment in a way that permits a diminution of schoolchildren's rights based on the justification that there is a great need to protect, guide, and control children in the school setting.

"general interest in crime control" as justification for a regime of suspicionless stops. . . . Consistent with this suggestion, each of the checkpoint programs that we have approved was designed primarily to serve purposes closely related to the problems of policing. . . .

The primary purpose of the Indianapolis narcotics checkpoints is in the end to advance "the general interest in crime control.". . . We decline to suspend the usual requirement of individualized suspicion where the police seek to employ a checkpoint primarily for the ordinary enterprise of investigating crimes. We cannot sanction stops justified only by the generalized and ever-present possibility that interrogation and inspection may reveal that any given motorist has committed some crime. . . .

It goes without saying that our holding today does nothing to alter the constitutional status of the sobriety and border checkpoints that we approved in *Sitz* and *Martinez-Fuerte,* or of the type of traffic checkpoint that we suggested would be lawful in *Prouse.* The constitutionality of such checkpoint programs still depends on a balancing of the competing interests at stake and the effectiveness of the program. . . . When law enforcement authorities pursue primarily general crime control purposes at checkpoints such as here, however, stops can only be justified by some quantum of individualized suspicion.

Our holding also does not affect the validity of border searches or searches at places like airports and government buildings, where the need for such measures to ensure public safety can be particularly acute. Nor does our opinion speak to other intru-sions aimed primarily at purposes beyond the general interest in crime control. Our holding also does not impair the ability of police officers to act appropriately upon information that they properly learn during a checkpoint stop justified by lawful purpose, even where such action may result in the arrest of a motorist for an offense unrelated to that purpose. Finally, we caution that the purpose of the inquiry in this context is to be conducted only at a programmatic level and is not an invitation to probe the minds of individual officers acting at the scene.

Because the primary purpose of the Indianapolis checkpoint program is ultimately indistinguishable from the general interest in crime control, the checkpoints violate the Fourth Amendment. The judgment of the Court of Appeals is accordingly affirmed.

CHIEF JUSTICE REHNQUIST (with JUSTICE SCALIA and JUSTICE THOMAS), dissenting.

The State's use of a drug-sniffing dog, according to the Court's holding, annuls what is otherwise plainly constitutional under our Fourth Amendment jurisprudence: brief, standardized, discretionless, roadblock seizures of automobiles, seizures which effectively serve a weighty state interest with only minimal intrusion on the privacy of their occupants. Because these seizures serve the State's accepted and significant interests of preventing drunken driving and checking for driver's licenses and vehicle registrations, and because there is nothing in the record to indicate that the addition of the dog sniff lengthens these otherwise legitimate seizures, I dissent. . . .

CONSENT

Criminal justice officials are supposed to respect the constitutional rights of citizens with whom they come into contact. As indicated by prior discussions, there are situations in which officials can make discretionary judgments about investigatory actions they wish to take which effectively diminish the scope of certain individuals' constitutional rights. For example, people are subject to types of searches at the nation's borders which could not be conducted if officers merely walked up to a house, knocked on the door, and announced that they wanted to investigate possible criminal activity. Although rights are supposed to provide protection by virtue of the words in the Constitution, the rights are, in effect, "owned" by the individuals who are entitled to protection. Thus, if the individuals do not desire the protection of specific constitutional rights, they may voluntarily surrender those rights. The word used in the law for someone who voluntarily surrenders legal protections is the **waiver of rights.** People can waive specific rights if they do not desire the protection of those rights.

In the context of searches, the primary role of the waiver of rights is to permit police officers to conduct warrantless searches that they otherwise would not be able to do, either at their own discretion or with a warrant supported by probable cause. Waiver of Fourth Amendment rights arises when individuals **consent** to have their possessions and property searched. If people consent to a search, there is no need for the law enforcement officers to have probable cause or even any level of suspicion to justify the search. The consent effectively absolves law enforcement officers of any risk that evidence will be excluded from use at trial or that they will be found liable in a civil lawsuit alleging a violation of Fourth Amendment rights.

Consent searches provide a valuable investigatory tool for officers who wish to conduct warrantless searches. Officers in many police departments are trained to ask people if they will consent to a search. Thus some officers ask every motorist during a traffic stop, "Can I search your car?" Or, if called to the scene of a domestic dispute or a citizen complaint about noise, the officers may ask, "Do you mind if I look around the downstairs area of your house?" Criminal evidence is often uncovered in such consent searches—a fact which may indicate that many citizens do not know that they have the option to say "no" when officers ask for permission to search. Moreover, some citizens may fear that they will look more suspicious to the officers if they say "no," so they agree to searches in order to act as if they have nothing to hide.

Two key issues must be addressed in order to decide if a permissible consent search has occurred. First, the consent must be *voluntary.* There can be no coercion or threats used by police officers in order to obtain consent. Obviously, if officers threaten someone with violence or arrest if he or she declines to consent to a search, the consent will be ruled invalid (*Jones v. Unknown Agents of the Federal Election Commission,* D.C. Circuit, U.S. Court of Appeals, 1979). Even more subtle tricks, such as dishonestly telling someone that there is a search warrant and thereby implying that the person has no choice but to consent, will result in the search being declared improper (*Bumper v. North Carolina,* 1968). Second, the consent must be given by someone who *possesses authority to give consent* and thereby holds the power to waive the right. Someone cannot, for example, consent to have his or her neighbor's house searched. We will first examine the issue of consent, and then we will look at the issue of proper authority.

Voluntariness

As in other tests applied by the U.S. Supreme Court to determine the permissibility of police actions, the Court mandated a totality-of-circumstances test to determine whether a consent was voluntary. There is no simple rule, such as looking to see that an individual said a specific word or phrase, to see if a consent was given voluntarily. If criminal evidence is found during a consent search and a defendant wishes to have the evidence excluded by claiming that the consent was not voluntary, the trial court must examine the details of the interactions between the defendant and the police officers. What did the police officers say and do prior to the search? What were the words and actions of the defendant which indicated that he or she consented to the search? Frequently the police officer and the defendant will provide contradictory accounts of what was said when they testify before the court about the circumstances of the search. Thus it can be very difficult for a trial judge to know for certain what transpired at the time of the search. According to the Supreme Court, "[T]he Fourth and Fourteenth Amendments require that a consent not be coerced, by explicit or implicit means, by implied threat or covert force" (*Schneckloth v. Bustamonte,* 1973). In light of this guidance from the high court, trial judges primarily look for indications that improper pressure was applied by the police or that the defendant did not provide a clear indication of consent at the time of the search.

Critics of actions by law enforcement officials to induce people to waive their rights claim that waivers should not merely be voluntary—they should also be knowing and intelligent. In other words, officers should be required to show that individuals *knew* that they had the option of saying "no" to a request to consent and that the individuals understood the implications of the consent. The one clear way to show that individuals knew that they had the option of saying "no" is to require that officers inform people about the nature and existence of the right before asking for a waiver, such as a consent to search. As we will see when we discuss the Fifth Amendment's protection against compelled self-incrimination, this is the approach taken in the familiar *Miranda* warnings in which officers seek a suspect's consent to be questioned without a defense attorney present. The **Miranda rule** requires that officers provide suspects with a specific informative warning before beginning custodial questioning. There is no such comparable rule requiring officers to inform individuals of their right to refuse officers' requests to search. In *Miranda* the Supreme Court under Chief Justice Earl Warren emphasized the need to guard against the risks of coercing people to surrender their Fifth and Sixth Amendment rights. The Court was especially concerned about less educated, unsophisticated suspects who might be vulnerable to manipulation by the police. The opinion elicited significant public outcry from law enforcement officers and politicians who assumed that the rule would prevent officers from gaining confessions. No such opinion came from the Supreme Court with respect to Fourth Amendment consents to searches, even though one can see that there are similar risks of people unknowingly placing their interests in jeopardy by agreeing to searches because they do not know that they can refuse. Is there a justification for treating Fourth Amendment rights differently than Fifth and Sixth Amendment rights with respect to voluntary waivers? This issue is subject to debate by observers. In any case, a few years after *Miranda,* the Court's composition changed in ways that precluded any possibility that the majority of justices would be receptive to arguments about expanding officers' obligations to inform citizens about their right to say "no" to requests for searches.

Without any obligation for officers to inform individuals about their right to decline, the issue of whether individuals understood the implications of consenting to a search will arise most often when officers are dealing with people whose mental capacities are less complete than those of the average adult. Such people would include children, mentally retarded adults, and adults with psychological problems. Even if such people were informed that they could say "no" to an officer's request to search, would they understand the consequences of saying "yes"?

In *Ohio v. Robinette* (1996), an officer stopped a car for speeding. After handing the driver back his license, the officer asked if there were any drugs or weapons in the car and then asked for consent to search. The driver agreed to the search, and illegal drugs were found during the search. The Ohio Supreme Court said that the consent was not valid because the individual was not free to go during the traffic stop and therefore the restraint on his liberty constituted a form of coercion that made the consent involuntary. The U.S. Supreme Court, however, reversed the state court's decision. According to the federal high court, it would be impractical to require officers to inform people about their rights before seeking consent. Thus, unlike the *Miranda* situation, the consent-search context does not impose any affirmative obligation on police officers to inform people about their right to decline a request to search.

As you read *Florida v. Bostick* in the accompanying box, ask yourself whether the totality of circumstances indicate that the consent was voluntary. Also ask yourself how the Court knows whether any consent was given at all.

The majority opinion makes clear that there is no rule that prevents police officers from approaching a citizen and asking questions, including a request

---

C A S E   *Florida v. Bostick,* **501 U.S. 429 (1991)**

[*At a stop in Fort Lauderdale, Florida, two police officers boarded a bus bound from Miami to Atlanta. Without an articulable basis for suspicion, they picked out the defendant and asked to see his ticket and his identification. The identification matched the name on the ticket. The officer persisted in questioning the defendant and requested permission to search his luggage. The officers claimed that they informed the defendant of his right to refuse, but the defendant claimed that they had not informed him of this right and that they searched one of his bags without his permission. The bag contained illegal narcotics. The trial court found that the officers had advised the defendant of his right to refuse and that the search had been conducted with his permission. After he was convicted, the defendant challenged the police officers' authority to question people randomly and seek to conduct searches without any grounds for suspicion.*]

JUSTICE O'CONNOR delivered the opinion of the Court.

We have held that the Fourth Amendment permits police officers to approach individuals at random in airport lobbies and other public places to ask them questions and request consent to search their luggage, so long as a reasonable person would understand that he or she could refuse to cooperate. This case requires us to determine whether the same rule applies to police encounters that take place on a bus.

Drug interdiction efforts have led to the use of police surveillance at airports, train stations, and bus depots. Law enforcement officers stationed at such locations routinely approach individuals, either randomly or because they suspect in some vague way that the individuals may be engaged in criminal activity, and ask them potentially incriminating questions. Broward County has adopted such a program. County Sheriff's Department officers routinely board buses at scheduled stops and ask passengers for permission to search their luggage.

In this case, two officers discovered cocaine when they searched a suitcase belonging to Terrance Bostick. The underlying facts of the search are in dispute, but the Florida Supreme Court, whose decision we review here, stated explicitly the factual premise for its decision:

Two officers, complete with badges, insignia and one of them holding a recognizable zipper pouch, containing a pistol, boarded a bus bound from Miami to Atlanta during a stopover in Fort Lauderdale. Eyeing the passengers, the officers admittedly without articulable suspicion, picked out the defendant passenger and asked to inspect his ticket and identification. The ticket, from Miami to Atlanta, matched the defendant's identification and both were immediately returned to him as unremarkable. However, the two police officers persisted and explained their presence as narcotics agents on the lookout for illegal drugs. In pursuit of that aim, they then requested the defendant's consent to search his luggage. Needless to say, there is a conflict in the evidence about whether the defendant consented to the search of the second bag in which the contraband was found and as to whether he was informed of his right to refuse consent. However, any conflict must be resolved in favor of the state, it being a question of fact decided by the trial judge. . . .

Two facts are particularly worth noting. First, the police specifically advised Bostick that he had the right to refuse consent. Bostick appears to have disputed the point, but, as the Florida Supreme Court noted explicitly, the trial court resolved this evidentiary conflict in the State's favor. Second, at no time did the officers threaten Bostick with a gun. The Florida Supreme Court indicated that one officer carried a zipper pouch containing a pistol—the equivalent of carrying a gun in a holster—but the court did not suggest that the gun was ever removed from its pouch, pointed at Bostick, or otherwise used in a threatening manner. The dissent's characterization of the officers as "gun-wielding inquisitor[s]". . . is colorful, but lacks any basis in fact. . . .

The sole issue presented for our review is whether a police encounter on a bus of the type described above necessarily constitutes a "seizure" within the meaning of the Fourth Amendment. The State concedes, and we accept for purposes of this decision, that the officers lacked the reasonable suspicion required to justify a seizure and that, if a seizure took place, the drugs found in Bostick's suitcase must be suppressed as tainted fruit.

Our cases make it clear that a seizure does not occur simply because a police officer approaches an individual and asks a few questions. So long as a reasonable person would feel free "to disregard the police and go about his business,". . . the encounter is consensual and no reasonable suspicion is required. The encounter will not trigger Fourth Amendment scrutiny unless it loses its consensual nature. The Court made precisely this point in *Terry v. Ohio* (1968). . . . "Only when the officer, by means of physical force or show of authority, has in some way restrained the liberty of a citizen may we conclude that a 'seizure' has occurred.". . .

There is no doubt that if this same encounter had taken place before Bostick had boarded the bus or in the lobby of the bus terminal, it would not rise to the level of a seizure. . . .

Bostick insists that this case is different because it took place in the cramped confines of a bus. A police encounter is much more intimidating in this setting, he argues, because the police tower over a seated passenger and there is little room to move around. Bostick claims to find support in language

from *Michigan v. Chesternut* (1988) . . . and other cases, indicating that a seizure occurs when a reasonable person would believe that he or she is not "free to leave." Bostick maintains that a reasonable bus passenger would not feel free to leave under the circumstances of this case because there is nowhere to go on a bus. Also, the bus was about to depart. Had Bostick disembarked, he would have risked being stranded and losing whatever baggage he had locked away in the luggage compartment.

The Florida Supreme Court found this argument persuasive, so much so that it adopted a *per se* rule prohibiting the police from randomly boarding buses as a means of drug interdiction. The state court erred, however, in focusing on whether Bostick was "free to leave" rather than on the principle that those words were intended to capture. When police attempt to question a person who is walking down the street or through an airport lobby, it makes sense to inquire whether a reasonable person would feel free to continue walking. But when the person is seated on a bus and has no desire to leave, the degree to which a reasonable person would feel that he or she could leave is not an accurate measure of the coercive effect of the encounter.

Here, for example, the mere fact that Bostick did not feel free to leave the bus does not mean that the police seized him. Bostick was a passenger on a bus that was scheduled to depart. He would not have felt free to leave the bus even if the police had not been present. Bostick's movements were "confined" in a sense, but this was the natural result of his decision to take the bus; it says nothing about whether or not the police conduct at issue was coercive. . . .

. . . Accordingly, the "free to leave" analysis on which Bostick relies is inapplicable. In such a situation, the appropriate inquiry is whether a reasonable person would feel free to decline the officers' requests or otherwise terminate the encounter. This formulation follows logically from prior cases and breaks no new ground. We have said before that the crucial test is whether, taking into account all of the circumstances surrounding the encounter, the police conduct would "have communicated to a reasonable person that he was not at liberty to ignore the police presence and go about his business.". . . Where the encounter takes place is one factor, but only one factor. And, as the Solicitor General correctly observes, an individual may decline an officer's request without fearing prosecution. . . . We have consistently held that a refusal to cooperate, without more, does not furnish the minimal level of objective justification needed for a detention or seizure. . . .

(continued)

The dissent characterizes our decision as holding that police may board buses and by an *"intimidating* show of authority,". . . demand of passengers their "voluntary" cooperation. That characterization is incorrect. Clearly, a bus passenger's decision to cooperate with law enforcement officers authorizes the police to conduct a search without first obtaining a warrant *only* if the cooperation is voluntary. "Consent" that is the product of official intimidation or harassment is not consent at all. Citizens do not forfeit their constitutional rights when they are coerced to comply with a request that they would prefer to refuse. The question to be decided by the Florida courts on remand is whether Bostick chose to permit the search of his luggage.

The dissent also attempts to characterize our decision as applying a lesser degree of constitutional protection to those individuals who travel by bus, rather than by other forms of transportation. This, too, is an erroneous characterization. Our Fourth Amendment inquiry in this case—whether a reasonable person would have felt free to decline the officers' request or otherwise terminate the encounter—applies equally to police encounters that take place on trains, planes, and city streets. It is the dissent that would single out this particular mode of travel for differential treatment by adopting a *per se* rule that random bus searches are unconstitutional.

The dissent reserves its strongest criticism for the proposition that police officers can approach individuals as to whom they have no reasonable suspicion and ask them potentially incriminating questions. But this proposition is by no means novel; it has been endorsed by the Court any number of times. *Terry* [*v. Ohio*, 1968], [*Florida v.*] *Royer* [1983], [*Florida v.*] *Rodriguez* [1984], and [*Immigration and Naturalization Service v.*] *Delgado* [1984] are just a few examples. As we have explained, today's decision follows logically from those decisions and breaks no new ground. Unless the dissent advocates overruling a long, unbroken line of decisions dating back more than 20 years, its criticism is not well taken. . . .

JUSTICE MARSHALL, with whom JUSTICE BLACKMUN and JUSTICE STEVENS join, dissenting.

Our Nation, we are told, is engaged in a "war on drugs." No one disputes that it is the job of law-enforcement officials to devise effective weapons for fighting this war. But the effectiveness of a law-enforcement technique is not proof of its constitutionality. The general warrant, for example, was certainly an effective means of law enforcement. Yet it is one of the primary aims of the Fourth Amendment to protect citizens from the tyranny of being singled out for search and seizure without particularized suspicion *notwithstanding* the effectiveness of this method. . . . In my view, the law-enforcement technique with which we are confronted in this case—the suspicionless police sweep of buses in intrastate or interstate travel—bears all of the indicia of coercion and unjustified intrusion associated with the general warrant. Because I believe that the bus sweep issue in this case violates the core values of the Fourth Amendment, I dissent. . . .

To put it mildly, these sweeps "are inconvenient, intrusive, and intimidating.". . . They occur within cramped confines, with officers typically placing themselves in between the passenger selected for an interview and the exit of the bus. . . . Because the bus is only temporarily stationed at a point short of its destination, the passengers are in no position to leave as a means of evading the officers' questioning. Undoubtedly, such a sweep holds up the progress of the bus. . . . Thus, this "new and increasingly common tactic,". . . burdens the experience of traveling by bus with a degree of governmental interference to which, until now, our society was proudly unaccustomed. . . .

This aspect of the suspicionless sweep has not been lost on many of the lower courts called upon to review the constitutionality of this practice. Remarkably, the courts located at the heart of the "drug war" have been the most adamant in condemning this technique. . . .

I have no objection to the manner in which the majority frames the test for determining whether a suspicionless bus sweep amounts to a Fourth Amendment "seizure." I agree that the appropriate question is whether a passenger who is approached during such a sweep "would feel free to decline the officers' requests or otherwise terminate the encounter.". . . What I cannot understand is how the majority can possibly suggest an affirmative answer to this question. . . .

As far as is revealed by facts on which the Florida Supreme Court premised its decision, the officers did not advise respondent that he was free to break off this "interview." Inexplicably, the majority repeatedly stresses the trial court's implicit finding that the police officers advised the respondent that he was free to refuse permission to search his travel bag. . . . This aspect of the exchange between respondent and the police is completely irrelevant to the issue before us. For as the State concedes, and as the majority purports to "accept,". . . *if* respondent was unlawfully seized when the officers approached him and initiated questioning, the resulting search was likewise unlawful no matter how well advised respondent was of his right to refuse it. . . . Consequently, the issue is not whether a passenger in respondent's position would have felt free to deny consent to the search of his bag, but whether such a passenger—without being apprised of his rights—would have felt free to terminate the antecedent encounter with the police.

Unlike the majority, I have no doubt that the answer to this question is no. Apart from trying to accommodate the officers, respondent had only two options. First, he could have remained seated while obstinately refusing to respond to the officers' questioning. But in light of the intimidating show of authority that the officers made upon boarding the bus, respondent reasonably could have believed that such behavior would only arouse the officers' suspicions and intensify their interrogation. Indeed, officers who carry out bus sweeps like the one at issue here frequently admit that this is the effect of a passenger's refusal to cooperate. . . . The majority's observation that a mere refusal to answer questions, "without more," does not give rise to a reasonable basis for seizing a passenger, . . . is utterly beside the point, because a passenger unadvised of his rights and otherwise unversed in constitutional law *has no reason to know* that the police cannot hold his refusal to cooperate against him.

Second, respondent could have tried to escape the officers' presence by leaving the bus altogether. But because doing so would have required respondent to squeeze past the gun-wielding inquisitor who was blocking the aisle of the bus, this hardly seems like a course that respondent reasonably would have viewed as available to him. The majority lamely protests that nothing in the stipulated facts shows that the questioning officer "*point[ed]* [his] gu[n] at [respondent] or otherwise *threatened* him" with the weapon . . . (emphasis added). Our decisions recognize the obvious point, however, that the choice of the police to "display" their weapons during an encounter exerts significant coercive pressure on the confronted citizen. . . . We have never suggested that the police must go so far as to put a citizen in immediate apprehension of *being shot* before a court can take account of the intimidating effect of being questioned by an officer with weapon in hand.

Even if respondent had perceived that the officers would *let* him leave the bus, moreover, he could not reasonably have been expected to resort to this

means of evading their intrusive questioning. For so far as respondent knew, the bus's departure from the terminal was imminent. Unlike a person approached by the police on the street . . . or at a bus or airport terminal after reaching his destination, . . . a passenger approached by the police at an intermediate point in a long bus journey cannot simply leave the scene and repair to a safe haven to avoid unwanted probing by law-enforcement officials. The vulnerability that an intrastate or interstate traveler experiences when confronted by police outside of "his own familiar territory" surely aggravates the coercive quality of such an encounter. . . .

Rather than requiring the police to justify the coercive tactics employed here, the majority blames respondent for his own sensation of constraint. The majority concedes that respondent "did not feel free to leave the bus" as a means of breaking off the interrogation by the Broward County officers. . . . But this experience of confinement, the majority explains, "was the natural result of *his* decision to take the bus" (emphasis added). . . . Thus, in the majority's view, because respondent's "freedom of movement was restricted by a factor independent of police conduct—*i.e.*, by his being a passenger on a bus,". . . respondent was not seized for purposes of the Fourth Amendment. This reasoning borders on sophism and trivializes the values that underlie the Fourth Amendment. Obviously, a person's "voluntary decision" to place himself in a room with only one exit does not authorize the police to force an encounter upon him by placing themselves in front of the exit. It is no more acceptable for the police to force an encounter on a person by exploiting his "voluntary decision" to expose himself to perfectly legitimate personal or social constraints. By consciously deciding to single out persons who have undertaken interstate or intrastate travel, officers who conduct suspicionless, dragnet-style sweeps put passengers to the choice of cooperating or of exiting their buses and their possibly being stranded in unfamiliar locations. It is exactly because this "choice" is no "choice" at all that police engage this technique.

In my view, the Fourth Amendment clearly condemns the suspicionless, dragnet-style sweep of intrastate and interstate buses. Withdrawing this particular weapon from the government's drug-war arsenal would hardly leave the police without any means of combatting the use of buses as instrumentalities of the drug trade. The police would remain free, for example, to approach passengers whom they have a reasonable, articulable basis to suspect of criminal wrongdoing. Alternatively, they could continue to confront passengers without suspicion

(continued)

so long as they took simple steps, like advising passengers confronted of their right to decline to be questioned, to dispel the aura of coercion and intimidation that pervades such encounters. There is no reason to expect that such requirements would render the Nation's buses law-enforcement-free zones.

The majority attempts to gloss over the violence that today's decision does to the Fourth Amendment with empty admonitions. "If th[e] [war on drugs] is to be fought," the majority intones, "those who fight it must respect the rights of individuals, whether or not those individuals are suspected of having committed a crime." . . . The majority's actions, however, speak louder than its words.

I dissent.

to conduct a search. Officers do not need any suspicions in order to request the opportunity to search. In this case, they had no reason to suspect that Bostick had done anything wrong. They simply boarded the bus and asked questions of randomly selected passengers. In examining whether any improper pressure contributed to the search, the Court is concerned about whether the person was free to leave the encounter with the officers. If police have "seized" someone (in the words of the Fourth Amendment) so that they are not free to leave, then the alleged voluntariness of any consent will be highly questionable. Justice O'Connor's opinion noted that it did not matter whether Bostick felt free to leave the bus when the officers stood in the aisle and spoke to him. Instead, O'Connor expressed concern whether the police officers' actions "would have communicated to a reasonable person that he was not at liberty to ignore the police presence and go about his business." Thus the test does not examine the individual's subjective thoughts about whether a seizure had occurred. Instead, the Court applies an objective test to determine whether a reasonable person would have felt free to leave. The application of such a test is somewhat problematic in the sense that people's consent will be based on their own understanding of whether they are free to leave—not on whether other people would believe that they can break off the encounter with the police. In effect, the Court relies on a kind of fiction by basing the totality-of-circumstances analysis on what a person *should have known and thought* rather than on what he or she *actually knew and thought*. Because judges are trained in law, there is a risk that they will overestimate how much the reasonable person should know. Judges' knowledge of law and relatively isolated position as elites in society may obscure their understanding of the limitations of the public's actual knowledge about law and constitutional rights.

The dissenters argue that people do not know that they can break off such encounters with police and that it is reasonable for them to feel "seized" even if the technical rules of law indicate that they ought to be able to leave. The dissenters also claim that the context of such an encounter in a bus is not treated realistically by the majority. Buses are confined spaces in which people are physically trapped when police officers block the aisle. Moreover, someone with a ticket to go from Miami to Atlanta is not going to feel free to leave the bus in Ft. Lauderdale and thereby lose the opportunity to complete the planned trip. The dissenters would prefer a rule that prevents officers from questioning bus passengers unless either they have an articulable basis for suspicion or they explicitly advise passengers of their right to decline to answer questions and consent to searches. In 2002 a divided Court followed *Bostick*

| A CLOSER LOOK | Police Officers' Ethics and the Waiver of Rights |

How did the Florida courts determine that any consent had been given in the *Bostick* case? The officers claimed that they informed Bostick of his rights and then he consented to the search. Bostick claims that he never received any warning and that he never consented to the search. Imagine the information that the trial judge had available to make the decision. There was testimony from two police officers versus the contradictory testimony of one criminal defendant who was transporting a bag full of illegal drugs. Whom would you believe? One can understand why the judge would find the police officers more credible than the defendant. However, that does not mean officers are always truthful. Unethical officers may know they can exploit the poor

image of defendants by claiming that there was consent even if there was no consent since many judges are likely to believe whatever the police say. Once again, the rights of citizens are affected most directly by the decisions and actions of police officers because courts have only a limited ability to determine precisely what happened in an encounter that occurred between police officers and a criminal suspect.

If you were a police administrator who was concerned about both ethics and protection of constitutional rights, what steps could you take to make sure that officers are honest in such situations? Is there any way to ensure that officers never cross the line of unethical behavior?

and clearly expected that officers need not inform bus passengers of their right to decline requests to search (*United States v. Dragton*). As you read the material in the above box on waiver of rights, think about how judges' assumptions about police officers' ethics may influence the creation of rules.

Appropriate Authority

Because a voluntary consent to search involves the waiver of a constitutional right, it is important that people waive only their own rights and not the rights of others. This issue is complicated in property searches because someone's property may be located on the property of another person. In *Stoner v. California* (1964), the Court would not permit a hotel clerk to consent to the search of a guest's room. By paying for the room, the guest gained a reasonable expectation of privacy and control over the room for consent-search purposes, just like a tenant who rents a house. By contrast, the owner of an automobile can consent to a search of the car which may ultimately lead to the discovery of drugs or weapons that a passenger has placed under a seat (*Schneckloth v. Bustamonte,* 1973). The passenger's fate in the criminal justice system is certainly affected by the search, but that does not mean the passenger's rights were necessarily at issue. The owner of the car controls the vehicle, and the courts would not agree that a passenger has an equal expectation of privacy to be protected by the Fourth Amendment on someone else's property.

Someone can also consent to a search that affects the fates of others when they both share common authority over property. In *United States v. Matlock* (1974), a woman consented to the search of a rented room that she shared with a criminal suspect. Her roommate was prosecuted based on evidence found during the search to which she consented. Although a rule requiring common authority in order to validate a consent search may sound as if it

[*A woman summoned police officers to her home and presented her daughter, who showed signs of a severe beating. The daughter told officers that she had been assaulted by a man at an apartment elsewhere in the city. The daughter stated that the man was presently asleep at the apartment. She agreed to travel with the police to the apartment and unlock the apartment door with her key so that officers could enter. During the conversation with the police, she referred to the premises as "our" apartment and indicated that she had personal belongings there. When she unlocked the door to the apartment, officers discovered white powder in "plain view" in the living room that later proved to be cocaine. The defendant was charged with possession of narcotics with intent to deliver. He sought to suppress all evidence obtained by the police during their entry into the apartment on the grounds that his girlfriend, who had opened the door, lacked the authority to give consent to have the apartment entered and searched. The girlfriend did not reside at the apartment, she did not contribute to paying rent at the apartment, and the trial court concluded that she was merely an "infrequent visitor."*]

JUSTICE SCALIA delivered the opinion of the Court.

. . .

The Fourth Amendment generally prohibits the warrantless entry of a person's home, whether to make an arrest or to search for specific objects. . . . The prohibition does not apply, however, to situations in which voluntary consent has been obtained, either from the individual whose property is searched, . . . or from a third party who possesses common authority over the premises. . . . The State of Illinois contends that that exception applies in the present case.

As we stated in *[United States v.] Matlock* [1974] . . . , "Common authority" rests "on mutual use of the property by persons generally having joint access or control for most purposes. . . ." The burden of establishing that common authority rests upon the State. On the basis of this record, it is clear that burden was not sustained [in the state's effort to show the girlfriend's authority to give consent for the search]. The evidence showed although [the girlfriend], with her two small children, had lived with Rodriguez beginning in December 1984, she had

moved out on July 1, 1985, almost a month before the search at issue here, and had gone to live with her mother. She took [most of her possessions] with her, though leaving behind some furniture and household effects. During the period after July 1 she sometimes spent the night at Rodriguez's apartment, but never invited her friends there, and never went there herself when he was not home. Her name was not on the lease nor did she contribute to the rent. She had a key to the apartment, which she said at trial she had taken without Rodriguez's knowledge (though she testified at the preliminary hearing that Rodriguez had given her the key). On these facts the State had not established that, with respect to the South California [Street] apartment, [the girlfriend] had "joint access or control for most purposes." To the contrary, the Appellate Court's determination of no common authority over the apartment was obviously correct. . . .

. . . It is apparent that in order to satisfy the "reasonableness" requirement of the Fourth Amendment, what is generally demanded of the many factual determinations that must regularly be made by agents of the government—whether the magistrate issuing a warrant, the police officer executing a warrant, or the police officer conducting a search or seizure under one of the exceptions to the warrant requirement—is not that they always be correct, but that they always be reasonable. . . .

We see no reason to depart from this general rule with respect to facts bearing on the authority to consent to a search. Whether the basis for such authority exists is the sort of recurring factual question to which law enforcement officials must be expected to apply their judgment; and all the Fourth Amendment requires is that they answer it reasonably. The Constitution is no more violated when officers enter without a warrant because they reasonably (though erroneously) believe that the person who has consented to their entry is a resident of the premises, than it is violated when they enter without a warrant because they reasonably (though erroneously) believe they are in pursuit of a violent felon who is about to escape. . . .

. . . [W]hat we hold today does not suggest that law enforcement officers may always accept a person's invitation to enter premises. Even when the invitation is accompanied by an explicit assertion that the person lives there, the surrounding circumstances could conceivably be such that a reasonable person would doubt its truth and not act upon it without further inquiry. As with other factual determinations bearing upon search and seizure, determination of consent to enter must "be judged against an objective standard: would the facts available to the officer at the moment . . . 'warrant a man of reasonable caution in the belief'" that the consenting party had authority over the premises? . . . If not, then warrantless entry without further inquiry is unlawful unless authority actually exists. But if so, the search is valid. . . .

JUSTICE MARSHALL, with whom JUSTICE BRENNAN and JUSTICE STEVENS join, dissenting.

. . .

The majority agrees with the Illinois appellate court's determination that [the girlfriend] did not have authority to consent to the officers' entry of Rodriguez's apartment. . . . The Court holds that the warrantless entry into Rodriguez's home was nonetheless valid if the officers reasonably believed that [the girlfriend] had authority to consent. . . . The majority's defense of this position rests on a misconception of the basis for third-party consent searches. That such searches do not give rise to claims of constitutional violations rests not on the premise that they are "reasonable" under the Fourth Amendment, . . . but on the premise that a person may voluntarily limit his expectation of privacy by allowing others to exercise authority over his possessions. . . . Thus, an individual's decision to permit another "joint access [to] or control [over the property] for most purposes," . . . limits that individual's reasonable expectation of privacy and to that extent limits his Fourth Amendment protections. . . . If an individual has not so limited his expectation of privacy, the police may not dispense with the safeguards established by the Fourth Amendment. The baseline for the reasonableness of a search or a seizure in the home is the presence of a warrant. . . . Indeed, "[S]earches and seizures inside a home without a warrant are presumptively unreasonable." . . . Exceptions to the warrant requirement must therefore serve "compelling" law enforcement goals. . . . Because the sole law enforcement purpose underlying the third-party consent searches is avoiding the inconvenience of securing a warrant, a departure from the warrant requirement is not justified simply because an officer reasonably believes a third party

has consented to a search of the defendant's home. In holding otherwise, the majority ignores our longstanding view that "the informed and deliberate determinations of magistrates . . . as to what searches and seizures are permissible under the Constitution are to be preferred over the hurried action of officers and others who may happen to make arrests." . . .

The Court has tolerated departures from the warrant requirement only when an exigency makes a warrantless search imperative to the safety of the police and of the community. . . . The Court has often heard, and steadfastly rejected, the invitation to carve out further exceptions to the warrant requirement for searches of the home because of the burdens on police investigation and prosecution of crime. Our rejection of such claims is not due to a lack of appreciation of the difficulty and importance of effective law enforcement, but rather to our firm commitment to "the view of those who wrote the Bill of Rights that the privacy of a person's home and property may not be totally sacrificed in the name of maximum simplicity in enforcement of the criminal law." . . .

In the absence of an exigency, then, warrantless home searches and seizures are unreasonable under the Fourth Amendment. The weighty constitutional interest in preventing unauthorized intrusions into the home overrides any law enforcement interest in relying on the reasonable but potentially mistaken belief that a third party has authority to consent to such a search or seizure. Indeed, as the present case illustrates, only the minimal interest in avoiding the inconvenience of obtaining a warrant weighs in on the law enforcement side. . . .

Unlike searches conducted pursuant to the recognized exceptions to the warrant requirement, . . . third-party consent searches are not based on an exigency and therefore serve no compelling social goal. Police officers, when faced with the choice of relying on consent by a third party or securing a warrant, should secure a warrant, and must therefore accept the risk of error should they instead choose to rely on consent. . . .

The majority's assertion . . . is premised on the erroneous assumption that third-party consent searches are generally reasonable. The cases the majority cites thus provide no support for its holding. . . . Because reasonable factual errors by law enforcement officers will not validate unreasonable searches, the reasonableness of the officer's mistaken belief that the third party had authority to consent is irrelevant. . . .

(continued)

Our cases demonstrate that third-party consent searches are free from constitutional challenge only to the extent that they rest on consent by a party empowered to do so. The majority's conclusion to the contrary ignores the legitimate expectations of privacy on which individuals are entitled to rely. That a person who allows another joint access over his property thereby limits his expectation of privacy does not justify trampling the rights of a person who has not similarly relinquished any of his privacy expectation.

. . . Where this free-floating creation of "reasonable" exceptions to the warrant requirement will end, now that the Court has departed from the balancing approach that has long been part of our Fourth Amendment jurisprudence, is unclear. But by allowing a person to be subjected to a warrantless search in his home without his consent and without exigency, the majority has taken away some of the liberty that the Fourth Amendment was designed to protect.

clarifies such situations for officers conducting investigations, in fact, there may be problems in determining when common authority exists. After reading *Illinois v. Rodriguez* (1990) in the box on the previous page, ask yourself whether you agree with the rule the Supreme Court applied.

The Supreme Court permits consent searches to take place, even when the person providing consent lacks the authority to do so, as long as the officers reasonably believed that the person possessed the authority to consent. Notice how the Court's approach in *Rodriguez* parallels the approach in *United States v. Leon* (1984), which was discussed in Chapter 4 about the exclusionary rule. The Court, in effect, focuses on whether the police officers did anything "wrong" rather than on whether an individual's reasonable expectation of privacy was violated. How will police officers know whether someone possesses actual authority to grant consent? Does the *Rodriguez* decision encourage police officers to find out as much information as possible about whether the person has the authority to consent, or does it reward them for remaining ignorant about whether proper authority exists? As in other situations, courts must evaluate these questions after the fact. Not only are judges limited to listening to competing accounts about the information available to officers at the time the consent allegedly occurred, there is also the opportunity for officers to think about how to re-create their thoughts and actions in a way that will fit most neatly within the legal rules. If officers are unethical or are not committed to the protection of constitutional rights, this after-the-fact context raises risks that officers will paint a picture of the search context that does not accurately reflect the full details of what really occurred.

In its 2001–2002 term, the high court examined whether a probation agreement authorizing any law enforcement officer to search the person or premises of a probationer without a warrant can constitute a valid consent for police officers to conduct an investigative search. In *United States v. Knights* the U.S. Supreme Court reversed a federal appellate court and ruled that such a consent is valid for searches conducted for probation purposes and not for searches used to investigate other crimes that the probationer may have committed. In the case, police burst through the door of the probationer's home in the middle of the night because they suspected he was involved with acts of vandalism at a power company's facilities. During the search they found ammunition, bomb-making equipment, and other evidence of his involvement in the acts of vandalism.

INCIDENT TO A LAWFUL ARREST

As indicated in Chapter 5, police officers may conduct warrantless searches in conjunction with a lawful arrest. People and places may be searched. An arrest does not justify an unlimited search. Instead, the scope of the search is limited by its rationale. As you read the excerpt from *Chimel v. California* (1969) on the next page, try to identify the reasons that justify such a warrantless search. How extensively can officers search in such situations? What is the relationship between the permitted extent of the search and justifications for the search?

There are two justifications underlying the search incident to a lawful arrest in *Chimel*. First, police are permitted to protect themselves by making sure that the arrestee does not have a weapon and there is no weapon within reach. Second, the police can make sure that there is no evidence on or within the reach of the arrestee which could be destroyed. The scope of the search is limited by these justifications. Officers could, in effect, search only the arrestee and the immediate area around the arrestee. Thus commentators sometimes refer to *Chimel* as creating an "armspan" rule: Officers can search within the armspan of the arrestee.

Subsequently, the Supreme Court expanded the scope of permissible warrantless searches incident to lawful arrests. In *Maryland v. Buie* (1990), the arrestee came up from the basement of a house with his hands raised at the command of an officer shouting from the top of the stairs. An officer went into the basement where the arrestee had been and looked around, but did not conduct a thorough search. Although the basement was not within an armspan of an arrestee who had come upstairs, the Court permitted a **protective sweep** of the area where the arrestee had been hiding in order to make sure that no one else was hiding down there. The Court held in *Buie* that

> [A]s an incident to the arrest the officers could, as a precautionary matter
> and without probable cause or reasonable suspicion, look in closets and
> other spaces immediately adjoining the place of arrest from which an at-
> tack could be immediately launched. Beyond that, however, we hold that
> there must be articulable facts which, taken together with the rational in-
> ferences from those facts, would warrant a reasonably prudent officer in
> believing that the area to be swept harbors an individual posing a danger
> to those on the arrest scene. . . . (494 U.S. 325, 334)

The protective sweep rule does not authorize a thorough search based on an arrest, but it permits a limited warrantless search that expands the original scope of the *Chimel* search.

Although a lawful arrest justifies a limited search and protective sweep, the Court has been unwilling to permit thorough warrantless searches at crime scenes. In *Flippo v. West Virginia* (1999), police officers spent sixteen hours thoroughly searching a state park cabin where a murder victim was found. In the course of the search, they opened the husband's briefcase and found incriminating evidence. The Supreme Court said, "[W]e rejec[t] the contention that there is a 'murder scene exception' to the Warrant Clause of the Fourth Amendment. . . . [P]olice may make warrantless entries onto premises if they reasonably believe a person is in need of immediate aid and may make prompt warrantless searches of a homicide scene for possible other victims or killers

Chimel v. California, 395 U.S. 752 (1969)

[*Three police officers arrived at Chimel's home with an arrest warrant. They asked Chimel's wife if they could come into the house. She ushered them in, and they waited for Chimel to return home from work. When he arrived at his house, the officers handed him the arrest warrant and asked if they could "look around." He objected, but the officers told him that they could conduct a search "on the basis of the lawful arrest." In the company of Chimel's wife, the officers searched the entire three-bedroom house looking for evidence from the burglary of a coin shop. They opened dresser drawers and moved items around within the drawers. Chimel sought to have excluded from evidence coins and other items seized during the search of his home.*]

JUSTICE STEWART delivered the opinion of the Court.

. . .

Without deciding the question, we proceed on the hypothesis that the California courts were correct in holding that the arrest of the petitioner was valid under the Constitution. This brings us directly to the question whether the warrantless search of the petitioner's entire house can be constitutionally justified as incident to that arrest. . . .

. . . When an arrest is made, it is reasonable for the arresting officer to search the person arrested in order to remove any weapons that the latter might seek to use in order to resist arrest or effect his escape. Otherwise, the officer's safety might well be endangered, and the arrest itself frustrated. In addition, it is entirely reasonable for the arresting officer to search for and seize any evidence on the arrestee's person in order to prevent its concealment or destruction. And the area into which an arrestee might reach in order to grab a weapon or evidentiary items must, of course, be governed by a like rule. A gun on a table or in a drawer in front of one who is arrested can be as dangerous to the arresting officer as one concealed in the clothing of the person arrested. There is ample justification, therefore, for a search of the arrestee's person and the area "within his immediate control"—construing that phrase to mean the area from within which he might gain possession of a weapon or destructible evidence.

There is no comparable justification, however, for routinely searching any room other than that in which an arrest occurs—or, for that matter, for searching through all the desk drawers or other closed or concealed areas in that room itself. Such searches, in the absence of well-recognized exceptions, may be made only under the authority of a search warrant. The "adherence to judicial processes" mandated by the Fourth Amendment requires no less. . . .

It is argued in the present case that it is "reasonable" to search a man's house when he is arrested in it. But the argument is founded on little more than a subjective view regarding the acceptability of certain sorts of police conduct, and not on considerations relevant to Fourth Amendment interests. Under such an unconfined analysis, Fourth Amendment protection in this area would approach the evaporation point. It is not easy to explain why, for instance, it is less subjectively "reasonable" to search a man's house when he is arrested on his front lawn—or just down the street—than it is when he happens to be in the house at the time of arrest. . . .

. . . [O]ne result of [prior precedents] . . . is to give law enforcement officials the opportunity to engage in searches not justified by probable cause, by the simple expedient of arranging to arrest suspects at home rather than elsewhere. . . . [These prior precedents that justified broad searches incident to arrests are overturned.]

. . .

Application of sound Fourth Amendment principles to the facts of this case produces a clear result. The search here went far beyond the petitioner's person and the area from within which he might have obtained either a weapon or something that could have been used as evidence against him. There was no constitutional justification, in the absence of a search warrant, for extending the search beyond that area. The scope of the search was, therefore, "unreasonable" under the Fourth and Fourteenth Amendments, and the petitioner's conviction cannot stand. . . .

on the premises, . . . but we rejec[t] any general 'murder scene exception' to the Fourth Amendment warrant requirement."

AUTOMOBILE SEARCHES

The U.S. Supreme Court first addressed searches of automobiles in *Carroll v. United States* (1925), a case in which federal agents searched a car looking for illegal alcohol. The *Carroll* case, in which the warrantless search was approved, provided one of the two underlying justifications for permitting such searches of automobiles. In essence, because cars are mobile, they are quite different from houses and offices. Automobiles can be driven away and disappear in the time it would take officers to ask a judicial officer for a search warrant. A second justification that emerged in later cases was a recognition that people have a diminished expectation of privacy in cars. Cars operate on public streets, and they have windows into which passersby may look. People cannot reasonably have the same expectation of privacy that they have in their homes because people can look so easily into a car's windows to see any activities or items contained within. The visibility of cars' interiors also creates opportunities for the plain view doctrine to enable police officers to observe and seize drugs, weapons, and other illegal items that are visible from the street or sidewalk.

The two key questions that arise in automobile searches are (1) when can an officer stop a car? and (2) how extensively can an officer search the vehicle? Many automobile searches arise as a result of traffic stops. Police officers are free to make a visible inspection around a car's interior as they question a driver and ask for identification and other papers when preparing a citation for speeding or other traffic violation. All sworn officers can make traffic stops, even if they are in unmarked vehicles and serving in special vice or detective bureaus that do not normally handle traffic offenses (*Whren v. United States*, 1996). Because motorists can seldom prove that they did not commit a traffic offense, critics fear that unscrupulous officers will make pretextual traffic stops. In short, they may falsely claim that a motorist failed to use a turn signal or was speeding simply in order to question the driver and examine the interior of the vehicle.

In *Knowles v. Iowa* (1998), the Supreme Court limited the scope of automobile searches conducted in conjunction with traffic stops, although they did nothing to address the risk of pretextual traffic stops. Iowa had enacted a statute that authorized police officers to conduct a full search of the car whenever they issue a citation during a traffic stop. The Court rejected Iowa's arguments that complete automobile searches under such circumstances are justified by concerns about the officers' safety and the prevention of the destruction of criminal evidence. If an arrest is made or if there is a reasonable suspicion of danger, then a search for weapons or evidence may be justified. However, a mere traffic citation does not provide such justifications.

As indicated by the description of *Knowles*, the search incident to a lawful arrest exception to the warrant requirement applies to automobiles as well as to rooms within buildings. The Supreme Court has said that such a search can extend to the entire passenger compartment of the automobile (*New York v. Belton*, 1981). Moreover, the arrest of a driver justifies the search of a passenger's property. In *Wyoming v. Houghton* (1999), a police officer found a hypodermic needle in the pocket of a driver stopped for a traffic violation. The driver admitted that the needle was used for illegal drug activities. Upon arresting the driver, the officer had probable cause to search the car, and the Court said that this probable cause extended to a passenger's purse because the officer was permitted to search anywhere that—in this case—drug-related evidence might be found.

In addition, the Court has expanded officers' authority to search automobiles even when no formal arrest has yet occurred. In *Michigan v. Long* (1983), the Court approved a search of the car's interior around the driver's seat after officers found the car in a ditch and the driver standing outside the car appearing intoxicated. The Supreme Court justified the search as an expansion of the *Terry* doctrine. In effect, the officers were permitted to "frisk" the car in order to protect themselves and others by making sure no weapon was available to the not-yet-arrested driver. Such a search requires that the officers have reasonable suspicion that the person stopped may be armed and poses a potential danger to the officers.

The preceding section discussed the Supreme Court's approval of specific-purpose roadblocks as one of the "special needs" justifications for warrantless searches. One approved justification for roadblocks is the need for the Immigration and Naturalization Service to check vehicles near borders for the presence of illegal immigrants attempting to enter the United States (*United States v. Martinez-Fuerte*, 1976). Border areas also heighten the government's need to check vehicles in order to stem the flow of illegal drugs and other contraband being smuggled into the country. Automobiles may be stopped and searched at the border itself. In addition, the courts are also cognizant of the government's interest in stopping and examining vehicles near the border that have already entered the country. The United States' lengthy land borders with Canada and Mexico provide opportunities for drug traffickers and other smugglers to use motor vehicles to sneak their goods into the country. In 2002 the Supreme Court issued a decision that attempted to clarify the circumstances in which an officer has sufficient grounds to stop a vehicle traveling in the United States near an international border (*United States v. Arvizu*, 2002). As you read the case excerpt in the following box, ask yourself whether the Court's decision gives clear guidance to law enforcement officers and provides motorists with adequate protection against governmental intrusions.

CASE   *United States v. Arvizu*, 122 S.Ct. 744 (2002)

CHIEF JUSTICE REHNQUIST delivered the opinion for the unanimous Court.

. . . [Border Patrol] Agent Clinton Stoddard was working at a border patrol checkpoint along U.S. Highway 191 approximately 30 miles north of Douglas, Arizona [a town situated on the U.S.-Mexican border]. . . .

. . . Agents use roving patrols to apprehend smugglers trying to circumvent the checkpoint by taking backroads, including those roads through the sparsely populated area between Douglas and the national forest. Magnetic sensors, or "intrusion devices," facilitate agents' efforts in patrolling these areas. Directionally sensitive, the sensors signal the passage of traffic that would be consistent with smuggling activities.

Sensors are located along the only other north-bound road from Douglas. . . . It is unpaved beyond the 10-mile stretch leading out of Douglas and is very rarely traveled except for use by local ranchers and forest service personnel. Smugglers commonly try to avoid the 191 checkpoint [by using the other northbound road]. . . .

Around 2:15 p.m., Stoddard received a report via Douglas radio that a . . . sensor had triggered. This was significant to Stoddard for two reasons. First, it suggested to him that a vehicle might be trying to circumvent the checkpoint. Second, the timing coincided with the point when agents begin heading back to the checkpoint for a shift change. Stoddard knew that alien smugglers did extensive scouting and seemed to be most active when agents were en route back to the checkpoint. Another border patrol agent told Stoddard that the same sensor had gone off several weeks before and that he had apprehended a minivan using the same route and witnessed the occupants throwing bundles of marijuana out the door.

Stoddard drove eastbound on Rucker Canyon Road to investigate. . . . He saw the dust trail of an approaching vehicle about a half mile away. . . . He pulled off to the side of the road at a slight slant so he could get a good look at the oncoming vehicle as it passed.

It was a minivan, a type of automobile that Stoddard knew smugglers used. As it approached, it slowed dramatically, from about 50–55 to 25–30 miles per hour. He saw five occupants inside. An adult man was driving, an adult woman sat in the front passenger seat, and three children were in the back. The driver appeared stiff and his posture very rigid. He did not look at Stoddard and seemed to be trying to pretend that Stoddard was not there. Stoddard thought this suspicious because in his experience on patrol most persons look over and see what is going on, and in that area most drivers give border patrol agents a friendly wave. Stoddard noticed that the knees of the two children sitting in the back seat were unusually high, as if their feet were propped up on some cargo on the floor.

At that point, Stoddard decided to get a closer look, so he began to follow the vehicle as it continued westbound. . . . Shortly thereafter, all of the children, though still facing forward, put their hands up at the same time and began to wave at Stoddard in an abnormal pattern. It looked to Stoddard as if the children were being instructed. Their odd waving continued on and off for about four or five minutes.

. . . Stoddard did not recognize the minivan as part of the local traffic agents encounter on patrol. . . . He was not aware of any picnic grounds [that could be reached by the minivan's route]. . . .

Stoddard radioed for a registration check and learned that the minivan was registered to an address in Douglas that was four blocks north of the border in an area notorious for alien and narcotics smuggling. After receiving the information, Stoddard decided to make a vehicle stop. He approached the driver and learned that his name was Ralph Arvizu. Stoddard asked if respondent would mind if he looked inside and searched the vehicle. Respondent agreed, and Stoddard discovered marijuana in a black duffel bag under the feet of the two children in the back seat. Another bag containing marijuana was behind the rear seat. In all, the van contained 128.85 pounds of marijuana, worth an estimated $99,080.

. . . [Arvizu] moved to suppress the marijuana, arguing among other things that Stoddard did not have reasonable suspicion to stop the vehicle as required by the Fourth Amendment [but the U.S. District Court supported Stoddard's actions]. . . .

The Court of Appeals for the Ninth Circuit reversed [the District Court's decision and decided in Arvizu's favor]. In its view, fact-specific weighing of circumstances or other multifactor tests introduced "a troubling degree of uncertainty and unpredictability" into the Fourth Amendment analysis. . . . [After examining the facts in the case, the Court of Appeals] held that 7 of the factors, including respondent's slowing down, his failure to acknowledge Stoddard, the raised position of the children's knees, and their odd waving carried little or no weight in the reasonable-suspicion calculus. The remaining factors—the road's use by smugglers, the temporal proximity between respondent's trip and the agents' shift change, and the use of minivans by smugglers—were not enough to make the stop permissible. . . .

The Fourth Amendment['s] . . . protections extend to brief investigatory stops of persons or vehicles that fall short of traditional arrest. . . . Because the "balance between the public interest and the individual's right to personal security," . . . tilts in favor of a standard less than probable cause in such cases, the Fourth Amendment is satisfied if the officer's action is supported by reasonable suspicion to believe that criminal activity "may be afoot." . . .

When discussing how reviewing courts should make reasonable-suspicion determinations, we have said repeatedly that they must look at the "totality of circumstances" of each case to see whether the

(continued)

detaining officer has a "particularized and objective basis" for suspecting legal wrongdoing. . . . This process allows officers to draw on their own experience and specialized training to make inferences from and deductions about the cumulative information available to them that "might well elude an untrained person.". . . Although an officer's reliance on a mere "hunch" is insufficient to justify a stop, . . . the likelihood of criminal activity need not rise to the level required for probable cause, and it falls considerably short of satisfying a preponderance of the evidence standard. . . .

Our cases have recognized that the concept of reasonable suspicion is somewhat abstract. . . . But we have deliberately avoided reducing it to "a neat set of legal rules.". . . In *Sokolow* [*United States v. Sokolow,* 1989], for example, we rejected a holding by the Court of Appeals that distinguished between evidence of ongoing criminal behavior and probabilistic evidence because it "create[d] unnecessary difficulty in dealing with one of the relatively simple concepts embodied in the Fourth Amendment.". . .

We think that the approach taken by the Court of Appeals here departs sharply from the teachings of these cases. The court's evaluation and rejection of seven of the listed factors in isolation from each other does not take into account the "totality of circumstances," as our cases have understood that phrase. The court appeared to believe that each observation by Stoddard that was by itself readily susceptible to an innocent explanation was entitled to "no weight.". . . *Terry* [*v. Ohio,* 1968], however, precludes this sort of divide-and-conquer analysis. The officer in *Terry* observed the petitioner and his companions repeatedly walk back and forth, look into the store window, and confer with one another. Although each of the series of acts was "perhaps

innocent in itself," we held that, taken together, they "warranted further investigation.". . .

Having considered the totality of the circumstances and given due weight to the factual inferences drawn by the law enforcement officer and the District Court Judge, we hold that Stoddard had reasonable suspicion to believe that respondent was engaged in illegal activity. It was reasonable for Stoddard to infer from his observations, his registration check, and his experience as a border patrol agent that respondent had set out from Douglas along a little-traveled route used by smugglers to avoid the 191 checkpoint. Stoddard's knowledge further supported a commonsense inference that respondent intended to pass through the area at a time when officers would be leaving their backroads patrol to change shifts. The likelihood that respondent and his family were on a picnic outing was diminished by the fact that the minivan had turned away from known recreational areas. . . . The children's elevated knees suggested the existence of concealed cargo in the passenger compartment. Finally, for the reasons we have given, Stoddard's assessment of respondent's reactions upon seeing him and the children's mechanical-like waving, which continued for a full four or five minutes, were entitled to some weight.

Repondent argues that we must rule in his favor because the facts suggested a family minivan on a holiday outing. A determination that reasonable suspicion exists, however, need not rule out the possibility of innocent conduct. . . . Undoubtedly, each of these factors alone is susceptible to innocent explanation, and some factors are more probative than others. Taken together, we believe they sufficed to form a particularized and objective basis for Stoddard's stopping the vehicle, making the stop reasonable within the meaning of the Fourth Amendment. . . .

In the *Arvizu* case, the Supreme Court focused on the existence of "reasonable suspicion" as the basis for justifying an investigatory stop of an automobile. Determinations of probable cause are determined by the "totality of circumstances," which requires the police officer to add together individual facts within a specific context in order to decide whether a stop is justified. As indicated by Chief Justice Rehnquist's discussion, the fact that a car is traveling into the country is a key fact that underlies the analysis in *Arvizu*. If the same facts had occurred when a law enforcement officer encountered a car traveling through the backroads of Kansas, there would not be the same basis for suspecting that the vehicle was smuggling illegal immigrants, drugs, or other contraband. As a result, cars in border areas are more susceptible to stops and searches because of the government's heightened basis for suspicion of illegal activities by motorists.

The Role of Probable Cause

The Supreme Court struggled over the years with defining the scope of searches that extend beyond the passenger compartment within the vehicle. When can officers search a glove compartment and trunk? Moreover, when can officers search closed containers found within a trunk? Initially the Court treated containers and closed areas in automobiles differently. Even when officers had probable cause to search a car's trunk, they were expected to obtain a warrant for any containers found within the trunk (*Robbins v. California,* 1981). As you read the case excerpt from *California v. Acevedo* (1991) in the box on pp. 204–205, think about how the Supreme Court clarified the basis for searching closed containers within vehicles.

The Court arrived at a rule permitting the search of any area within a car for which officers have probable cause to justify a search and any container in the vehicle for which officers have probable cause to justify a search (*California v. Acevedo,* 1991). In the Court's words,

> *Until today, this Court has drawn a curious line between the search of an automobile that coincidentally turns up a container and the search of a container that coincidentally turns up in an automobile. The protections of the Fourth Amendment must not turn on such coincidences. We therefore interpret* Carroll *as providing one rule to govern all automobile searches. The police may search an automobile and the containers within it where they have probable cause to believe contraband or evidence is contained.*

The Court appears to have attempted to clarify the rules so that officers are not confused about whether they can search a container or an area of the automobile. However, the effort to create a rule that officers can understand and apply has effectively diminished the protection for property that is placed in automobiles. Police officers have significant authority to search automobiles and to issue commands to people riding in vehicles (e.g., during a traffic stop, officers can order passengers as well as the driver to exit the vehicle, even if there is no basis for suspicion that the passengers engaged in any wrongdoing (*Maryland v. Wilson,* 1997). As you read the material in the box on p. 206 about the determination of probable cause in automobile searches, ask yourself whether the Supreme Court has given police officers too much authority.

There are specific circumstances in which searches may take place without regard to probable cause or to "frisking" the car for weapons in light of a driver's arrest or suspicious behavior. In *New York v. Class* (1986), the Supreme Court endorsed a limited search to view a car's Vehicle Identification Number (VIN). Even if officers lack probable cause to believe that the vehicle has been stolen, an officer may enter the vehicle to see the VIN when a car has been validly stopped pursuant to a traffic violation or other permissible justification. In addition, the Court permits thorough searches of vehicles, without regard to probable cause, when police officers inventory the content of impounded vehicles (*South Dakota v. Opperman,* 1976). In addition, containers found within the course of the inventory search may also be opened and searched when the examination of such containers is consistent with a police department's inventory policies (*Colorado v. Bertine,* 1987). Thus the Court has, in effect, encouraged police departments to develop inventory search procedures that grant broad authority to officers to examine thoroughly impounded vehicles and their contents. The Supreme Court has said that the inventory

California v. Acevedo, 500 U.S. 565 (1991)

[*Drug enforcement agents in Hawaii seized a package containing marijuana that was to have been taken to a Federal Express office for delivery to an address in California. The package was sent to police officers in California who took it to the Federal Express office and waited to arrest the person who would come to pick up the package. When Jamie Daza arrived to pick up the package, officers followed him to an apartment. One officer left the scene to obtain a search warrant as another continued to watch. Charles Acevedo arrived at the apartment, stayed for ten minutes, and then left carrying a paper bag that was approximately the same size as one of the wrapped marijuana packages sent from Hawaii. Acevedo placed the bag in the trunk of a car and drove away. Officers stopped the car, opened the trunk, and found the marijuana. A state court of appeals overturned Acevedo's drug conviction by concluding that the officers "had probable cause to believe that the paper bag contained drugs, but lacked probable cause to suspect that Acevedo's car, itself, otherwise contained contraband." Thus the officers should have obtained a search warrant in order to open the bag contained in the trunk of the car.*]

JUSTICE BLACKMUN delivered the opinion of the Court.

. . .

. . . In *Carroll,* this Court established an exception to the warrant requirement for moving vehicles. . . . It therefore held that a warrantless search of an automobile based upon probable cause to believe that the vehicle contained evidence of a crime in the light of an exigency arising out of the likely disappearance of the vehicle did not contravene the Warrant Clause of the Fourth Amendment. . . .

The Court refined the exigency requirement in *Chambers v. Maroney* . . . (1970), when it held that the existence of exigent circumstances was to be determined at the time the automobile is seized. [This permitted officers to conduct a warrantless search of the vehicle at the police station after the car was in possession of the police and the driver was in custody]. . . . Following *Chambers,* if the police have probable cause to justify a warrantless seizure of an automobile on a public roadway, they may conduct either an immediate or a delayed search of the vehicle.

In *United States v. Ross* . . . (1982), we held that a warrantless search of an automobile under the *Carroll* doctrine could include a search of a container or package found inside the car when such a search was supported by probable cause. . . . [This rule altered the doctrines developed in *United States v. Chadwick* (1977) and *Arkansas v. Sanders* (1979) requiring police to obtain a warrant for searching personal luggage contained within a vehicle, even when police have probable cause to believe that the luggage contained criminal evidence.]

. . .

This Court in *Ross* rejected *Chadwick*'s distinction between containers and cars. It concluded that the expectation of privacy in one's vehicle is equal to one's expectation of privacy in the container, and noted that "the privacy interests in a car's trunk or glove compartment may be no less than those in a movable container.". . . It also recognized that it was arguable that the same exigent circumstances that permit a warrantless search of an automobile would justify the warrantless search of a movable container. . . . In deference to the rule of *Chadwick* and *Sanders,* however, the Court put that question to one side. . . . It concluded that the time and expense of the warrant process would be misdirected if the police could search every cubic inch of an automobile until they discovered a paper sack, at which point the Fourth Amendment required them to take the sack to a magistrate for permission to look inside. We now must decide the question deferred in *Ross*: whether the Fourth Amendment requires the police to obtain a warrant to open the sack in a movable vehicle simply because they lack probable cause to search the entire car. We conclude that it does not.

. . . We now agree that a container found after a general search of the automobile and a container found in a car after a limited search for the container are equally easy for the police to store and for the suspect to hide or destroy. In fact, we see no principled distinction in terms of either the privacy expectation or the exigent circumstances between the paper bag found by the police in *Ross* and the paper bag found by the police [in *Acevedo*]. Furthermore, by attempting to distinguish between a container for which the police are specifically searching and a container which they come across in a car, we have provided only minimal protection for privacy, and have impeded effective law enforcement.

The line between probable cause to search a vehicle and probable cause to search a package in that vehicle is not always clear, and separate rules that govern the two objects to be searched may enable the police to broaden their power to make warrantless searches and disserve privacy interests. . . . At the moment when officers stop an automobile, it may be less than clear whether they suspect with a high degree of certainty that the vehicle contains drugs in a bag or simply contains drugs. If the police know that they may open a bag only if they are actually searching the entire car, they may search more extensively than they otherwise would in order to establish the general probable cause required by *Ross*. . . .

To the extent that the *Chadwick-Sanders* rule protects privacy, its protection is minimal. Law enforcement officers may seize a container and hold it until they obtain a search warrant. . . .

The discrepancy between the two rules [for searching cars and for searching containers within cars] has led to confusion for law enforcement officers. For example, when an officer, who has developed probable cause to believe that a vehicle contains drugs, begins to search the vehicle and immediately discovers a closed container, which rule applies? The defendant will argue that the fact that the officer first chose to search the container indicates that his probable cause extended only to the container and that *Chadwick* and *Sanders* therefore require a warrant. On the other hand, the fact that the officer first chose to search in the most obvious location should not restrict the propriety of the search. The *Chadwick* rule, as applied in *Sanders,* has devolved into an anomaly such that the more likely the police are to discover drugs in a container, the less authority they have to search it. We have noted the virtue of providing "clear and unequivocal" guidelines to the law enforcement profession. . . . The *Chadwick-Sanders* rule is the antithesis of a "clear and unequivocal" guideline. . . .

. . . We conclude that it is better to adopt one clear-cut rule to govern automobile searches and eliminate the warrant requirement for closed containers set forth in *Sanders.*

The interpretation of the *Carroll* doctrine set forth in *Ross* now applies to all searches of containers found in an automobile. In other words, the police may search without a warrant if their search is supported by probable cause. The Court in *Ross* put it this way:

> *The scope of the warrantless search of an automobile . . . is not defined by the nature of the container in which the contraband is secreted. Rather, it is defined by the object of the search and the places in which there is probable cause to believe that it may be found. . . .*

It went on to note: "Probable cause to believe that a container placed in the trunk of a taxi contains contraband or evidence does not justify a search of the entire cab.". . . We reaffirm that principle. In the case before us, the police had probable cause to believe that the paper bag in the automobile's trunk contained marijuana. That probable cause allows a warrantless search of the paper bag. The facts in the record reveal that the police did not have probable cause to believe that contraband was hidden in any other part of the automobile and a search of the entire vehicle would have been without probable cause and unreasonable under the Fourth Amendment. . . .

Until today, this Court has drawn a curious line between the search of an automobile that coincidentally turns up a container and the search of a container that coincidentally turns up in an automobile. The protections of the Fourth Amendment must not turn on such coincidences. We therefore interpret *Carroll* as providing one rule to govern all automobile searches. The police may search an automobile and the containers within it where they have probable cause to believe contraband or evidence is contained. . . .

JUSTICE SCALIA, concurring in the judgment.

I agree with the dissent that it is anomalous for a briefcase to be protected by the "general requirement" of a prior warrant when it is being carried along the street, but for that same briefcase to become unprotected as soon as it is carried into an automobile. On the other hand, I agree with the Court that it would be anomalous for a locked compartment in an automobile to be unprotected by the "general requirement" of a prior warrant, but for an unlocked briefcase within an automobile to be protected. I join in the judgment of the Court because I think its holding is more faithful to the text and tradition of the Fourth Amendment, and if these anomalies in our jurisprudence are ever to be eliminated, that is the direction in which we should travel. . . .

JUSTICE STEVENS (joined by JUSTICES WHITE and MARSHALL), dissenting.

. . .

Even if the warrant requirement does inconvenience the police to some extent, that fact does not distinguish this constitutional requirement from any other procedural protection secured by the Bill of Rights. It is merely a part of the price that our society must pay in order to preserve its freedom. . . .

The Determination of Probable Cause

The Court's decisions regarding automobile searches focus on the existence of probable cause, which is a protective standard requiring a strong justification under the Fourth Amendment. However, the Fourth Amendment envisions the application of a probable cause standard in which a neutral judicial officer determines the existence of probable cause for the purposes of issuing a warrant and thereby prevents officers from making their own subjective, discretionary evaluations of probable cause. In the automobile context, the requirement of probable cause gives the appearance that officers' discretionary authority is limited. In reality, however, officers are making judgments about probable cause for themselves. Challenges to their decisions will occur only after the fact when officers have had time to develop justifications for their actions.

Is the probable cause requirement a real limitation on officers' authority to search automobiles thoroughly? Or does the fact that officers determine probable cause for themselves make the Court's probable cause requirement merely a symbolic protection?

search must not be a pretext for fishing through an automobile looking for evidence. Thus the officers are not supposed to search places in the vehicle where the driver's valuables and personal property could not be found. While this limitation should keep officers from tearing apart the vehicle's seats or exploring the engine compartment, officers appear to have the authority to search anywhere in the passenger compartment, glove compartment, and trunk.

EXIGENT CIRCUMSTANCES

Chapter 3 presented the case of *Warden v. Hayden* (1967) concerning the "hot pursuit" doctrine and its applicability to justify officers entering and searching premises in order to effect the arrest of felony suspects in the immediate aftermath of a crime. As indicated by that case, the hot pursuit situation justifies a search. The search must be contemporaneous with the detection and arrest of the suspect, and the search must be focused on finding weapons that might endanger officers. Officers may observe and seize any evidence in plain view, but the hot pursuit doctrine does not justify an investigatory search for evidence.

Cupp v. Murphy (1973), in Chapter 5, demonstrated the Court's willingness to justify warrantless searches of people based on exigent circumstances outside of the context of hot pursuits. In *Cupp* the Court permitted officers to take scrapings from under the suspect's fingernails because the evidence would likely have been destroyed if the officers had taken the time to seek a warrant. The possibility exists for officers to undertake warrantless searches of property when the urgency of a context justifies immediate action in order to preserve evidence or to protect people from danger. When football Hall-of-Famer O. J. Simpson's ex-wife, Nicole Brown Simpson, was stabbed to death in front of her home, police officers went to Simpson's home and climbed the wall to gain entry to his backyard. They claimed that they found a bloody glove in the backyard, and that glove was admitted into evidence against Simpson because a judge was persuaded that the officers made the warrantless entry and search based on the urgency of their need to make sure that no one at the Simpson house was injured or in danger. Now return to the hypothetical situation presented at the outset of the chapter. Would an exigent circumstances justification permit the warrantless search undertaken by the officers in that situation? In order to analyze the permissibility of the search, you would need to determine whether the officers had reason to believe that an immediate search was necessary to protect public safety or evidence that would otherwise disappear while a warrant was being sought.

CONCLUSION

The Supreme Court has recognized a number of contexts in which warrantless searches of property are deemed reasonable and therefore permissible under the Fourth Amendment. The plain view and open fields doctrines permit officers to observe property for which there is no reasonable expectation of privacy because of its visibility. The special needs of law enforcement justify searches in specific defined contexts, such as vehicle checkpoints and schools, where significant governmental interests outweigh the need to protect individuals' expectations of privacy. In addition, individuals can waive their Fourth Amendment protection by consenting to searches, provided that the consents are voluntary and made by people with authority to make such consent decisions concerning the property to be searched. Just as in the case of searches of persons, a lawful arrest will justify a limited search and protective sweep of the nearby area in order to protect the officers' safety and prevent the destruction of evidence. Over time, the Court consistently restricted the degree of Fourth Amendment protection available for automobiles because of the mobility of vehicles and people's diminished expectations of privacy with respect to cars and other vehicles. Some warrantless searches of automobiles are triggered by the other categories of search justifications, including consents, special needs of law enforcement, plain view, and lawful arrests. In addition, the Court has given police officers additional flexibility for searching automobiles without warrants, including searches in which officers determine probable cause for themselves and inventory searches of impounded vehicles. The hot pursuit doctrine and other exigent circumstances can justify searches in urgent circumstances requiring the protection of people or the preservation of evidence when there would not be time to get a warrant.

The nature and number of situations in which warrantless searches of property are permitted demonstrate the complexity of Fourth Amendment law. Although the Supreme Court has given police officers significant flexibility to undertake searches without warrants in a variety of circumstances, officers must learn a complex array of rules. The protection of constitutional rights requires that officers be knowledgeable and ethical. Because officers are authorized to make judgments about matters such as probable cause for automobile searches and exigent circumstances, the treatment of the public rests significantly in the hands of the officers making these decisions. Courts typically become involved only if incriminating evidence is found and the defendant seeks to have the evidence excluded by claiming that a search was improper. When officers conduct warrantless searches and do not find evidence, it is unlikely that any resulting rights violation will be remedied unless the search involved an improper home invasion, the Fourth Amendment property context in which a jury of citizens is likely to hold the police accountable in a civil lawsuit.

SUMMARY

- The Supreme Court has identified specific circumstances in which warrantless searches of property are permissible. These are often referred to as the exceptions to the Fourth Amendment's warrant requirement.

- Objects in plain view are subject to observation and seizure by officers who are standing in a location where they are legally permitted to be. Similarly, officers may use the open fields doctrine to observe items in fields and woods near houses, even if the items are on private property.

- The special needs of law enforcement justify seizures and potential searches at sobriety checkpoints and in schools. The justification rests on the conclusion that the government's interests outweigh the privacy interests of people within those defined contexts.

- People can waive their Fourth Amendment rights by consenting to a search.

- The validity of consents depends on whether consent was given voluntarily by a person with authority over the property to be searched.

- Warrantless searches may be undertaken incident to lawful arrests. Such searches are limited to the area around the arrestee and protective sweeps of rooms in which a confederate may be hidden.

- Searches incident to lawful arrests are justified and defined by the objectives of protecting the safety of officers and preventing evidence from being destroyed.

- Automobiles receive greatly diminished Fourth Amendment protection because they are mobile and because of people's diminished reasonable expectations of privacy with respect to vehicles.

- With respect to vehicles and containers within those vehicles, officers may search any area or container for which they have probable cause to search. Officers make determinations of probable cause for themselves in such automobile searches.

- Warrantless searches may be justified by exigent circumstances, including hot pursuits, in which an urgent need to protect public safety or prevent the destruction of evidence may preclude the officers from seeking a warrant.

Key Terms

consent   A justification for warrantless searches when people who possess authority over property voluntarily agree to permit the police to conduct a search of the property.

Miranda **rule**   Rule announced by the U.S. Supreme Court in *Miranda v. Arizona* (1966) that requires police officers to inform people in police custody of their right to remain silent and their right to counsel before they are subjected to questioning.

open fields doctrine   Doctrine that permits warrantless exploration for visible criminal evidence on private property beyond the curtilage of a house.

plain view doctrine   Doctrine that permits officers to identify criminal evidence that is openly visible from the vantage point of a location where they are legally permitted to be and to seize such items on public property or on private property where they are lawfully located.

protective sweep   A search incident to a lawful arrest in which officers may make a warrantless examination of rooms, closets, and other locations where a confederate of the arrestee may be hiding and thereby endanger the officers if not found.

waiver of rights   People waive their rights when they voluntarily surrender the protection of those rights, such as when people consent to a search that police officers otherwise could not conduct at their discretion.

Additional Readings

LaFave, Wayne R., and Jerald H. Israel. 1992. *Hornbook on Criminal Procedure*. 2nd ed. St. Paul, Minn.: West Publishing.

McWhirter, Darien A. 1994. *Search, Seizure, and Privacy*. Phoenix: Oryx Press.

Moylan, Charles E., Jr. 1979. *Right of the People to Be Secure: An Examination of the 4th Amendment*. Washington, D.C.: National College of District Attorneys.

CHAPTER SEVEN

Interrogation and Confessions

Imagine that you are at a large, noisy bar with several friends watching a football game on the big screen television (and you are at least twenty-one years of age, of course). After the game, all of your friends have departed except for one who has obviously had too much to drink. He is talking too loudly and his speech is slurred. You insist on driving him home and you take his car keys from him. He insists that he needs to use the restroom before you depart. He stumbles toward the back hallway in the bar where the restrooms are located.

When he returns a few minutes later, he looks annoyed. "You wouldn't believe it," he says in a rambling style of speaking. "There were two guys fighting in the bathroom. In the bathroom! They were really going at it."

"You didn't get involved, did you?" you ask with great concern.

"Naw. I didn't get involved. One guy kind of bumped into me, so I turned around and shoved him away from me. But they kept going at it, so I don't think they really noticed me."

You help him get his coat on and then take him by the arm to lead him toward the door. When you reach the door, you can see a crowd of people near the back hallway and a police officer pushing through the crowd as if leaving the restroom area. Suddenly you see someone in the crowd point in your direction and say loudly, "That's the guy that came out of the bathroom." You freeze as the police officer hurries in your direction.

"Did this guy just come out of the men's room?" asks the stern officer who stares at you intently.

"Yes, I did," answers your friend, loudly. "Who wants to know?"

The officer eyes your drunk friend. "Did you hit anyone when you were in there?"

"Yeah. I hit a guy in there. And I'd hit him again if he bumped into me while I'm trying to take care of business in there."

You interrupt. "What's this all about, officer?"

"Unless you're going to tell me that you saw what happened, then just shut your mouth and stay out of it."

You are annoyed by the officer's attitude. Because you have studied criminal procedure, you believe that your friend is not obligated to stay and answer the officer's questions. You are worried that your friend will create big problems for himself by answering wildly while under the influence of alcohol. You grab your friend's arm. "C'mon. Let's get you home."

The officer grabs your friend's other arm. "You aren't going anywhere. You're under arrest." He spins your friend face first into the door, pulls back your friend's arms, and swiftly places handcuffs on both wrists. Immediately the officer begins to recite the *Miranda* warnings that you have heard so frequently on police shows on television. "You have the right to remain silent. If you give up that right, anything you say can be used against you in a court of law. You have a right to have an attorney present during questioning. If you cannot afford one, one will be appointed to represent you. Do you understand your rights?"

Your friend reacts angrily. "Yeah, I understand. You're making a big mistake. So what if I hit some guy? I've done more than that to other people."

You later learn that a man was found in the restroom unconscious and seriously injured with a skull fracture. People saw your friend leave the restroom, but they did not see anyone else leave the restroom around the time that the injured man was found. Your friend is facing serious assault charges. Do you think that your friend's statements made in response to the police officer's questions should be admissible in court? How does this situation fit within the Fifth Amendment's privilege against compelled self-incrimination?

In this chapter we will examine constitutional limitations on police officers' investigatory techniques involving the questioning of suspects in order to seek incriminating statements and confessions. As with other provisions of the Bill of Rights affecting criminal justice, the Supreme Court has interpreted the Fifth Amendment to establish guidelines for permissible actions by law enforcement officers. However, as we have seen with Fourth Amendment search and seizure issues, the fact that rules exist for officers does not guarantee that officers actually follow those rules. Thus we must consider how the rules affect officers' behavior and not simply assume that the rules determine how criminal investigations are conducted.

THE PRIVILEGE AGAINST COMPELLED SELF-INCRIMINATION

The Fifth Amendment contains various rights, including the one most relevant to police officers' actions in questioning suspects. The relevant words of the Amendment are "No person shall . . . be compelled in any criminal case to be a witness against himself." The right had its root in the practices of religious courts in England centuries earlier that pressured people into admitting that their religious or political beliefs were at odds with those required by the king. Over time, suspects resisted this procedure and asserted that they were not required to provide evidence against themselves. The English law that abolished the religious courts in 1641 indicated that the principle of avoiding compelled self-incrimination had gained acceptance and legitimacy because Parliament forbade church tribunals from compelling suspects to answer questions. Gradually, the principle was incorporated into English common law courts, too. Americans adopted the principle by placing it in several state constitutions in 1776 and then imposing it on the federal government through the Fifth Amendment of the Bill of Rights.[1]

The privilege against compelled self-incrimination should not be viewed as simply a legal protection that seeks to assist individuals who may be guilty of crimes. By protecting individuals in this way, the Fifth Amendment discourages police officers from using any means available to push suspects to confess. As indicated by *Brown v. Mississippi* (1936), a case presented in Chapter 2, prior to the incorporation of the Fifth Amendment and the development of guidelines from the interpretation of that amendment, police officers in some places used physical coercion to induce suspects to confess. In *Brown* the police obtained a confession by hanging the suspect by the neck from a tree with a rope and by whipping the suspect. The Supreme Court found such actions to be a violation of the Fourteenth Amendment right to due process in *Brown,* but most such cases never made it into the appellate courts. Thus the protection against compelled self-incrimination can help to discourage abusive police practices that may inflict physical pain and psychological harm in ways that are contrary to the expected standards of official behavior in American society.

In addition to discouraging physical abuse of suspects, the privilege against compelled self-incrimination can diminish the risk of erroneous convictions. When police officers use coercive pressure to seek confessions, there is a significant risk that innocent people will succumb to the pressure by confessing to crimes that they did not commit. The worst case scenario is illustrated by the Hollywood film *In the Name of the Father,* based on a true story in England in which police officers gain a confession from a bombing suspect (played by Academy Award winner Daniel Day Lewis) whom they know to be innocent by placing a gun in the suspect's mouth and threatening to pull the trigger. Erroneous convictions cause several significant harms. First, an individual is punished unjustly. In the aforementioned film, the innocent man served fifteen years in prison before a lawyer discovered information about the case that had been hidden in prosecution files. In addition to producing injustices, such erroneous convictions damage the reputation of the courts and cast doubt on the ability of legal processes to make accurate determinations of guilt. Moreover, the actual guilty people are still out on the streets where they may continue to threaten the public with additional crimes.

Voluntariness Test

In *Brown* and other cases prior to the 1960s, the Supreme Court did not focus on the privilege against compelled self-incrimination for state criminal justice cases because the Fifth Amendment right had not yet been incorporated. The Supreme Court incorporated the Fifth Amendment privilege against compelled self-incrimination and applied it against the states in *Malloy v. Hogan* (1964).

In *Malloy,* Connecticut officials had threatened the defendant with a contempt of court citation if he did not testify about gambling activities. The Supreme Court decided by a vote of 5 to 4 that he could decline to testify by asserting his right not to incriminate himself.

Until the incorporation decision in *Malloy,* the Court examined whether confessions were obtained improperly by assessing whether the methods used to obtain those confessions violated the Fourteenth Amendment right to due process. In order to determine whether the right to due process had been violated, the Court applied a voluntariness test. The justices' primary concern was whether the suspect confessed voluntarily. For each confession case that it considered, the Court looked at the totality of circumstances in order to determine whether police officers' actions had eliminated the suspect's ability to resist (*Fikes v. Alabama,* 1957). In assessing whether a confession was voluntary, the Court examined both the actions taken by the law enforcement officers and the vulnerability of the suspect. Some individuals may be much more susceptible to police pressure because they are young, mentally retarded, psychologically troubled, or otherwise less able to protect their own interests than the average citizen.

After the incorporation of the Fifth Amendment in *Malloy,* the Supreme Court remained concerned about the voluntariness of confessions. However, instead of considering voluntariness as an issue of the right to due process in state cases, the Court looked at voluntariness as central to the Fifth Amendment right. Decisions during the 1960s made additional constitutional rights relevant to confessions, particularly the *Miranda* right to be informed about Fifth and Sixth Amendment protections and the right to counsel during police questioning while in custody. Although these new rights provided additional grounds for defendants to challenge the admissibility of their self-incriminating statements, the issue of voluntariness continues to provide a basis for seeking the exclusion of confessions. If incriminating statements are not provided voluntarily, then they are obtained in violation of the Fifth Amendment. Improper coercion that violates suspects' rights by producing involuntary confessions may include either physical abuse or perceived threats. Such issues continue to arise in contemporary cases. For example, in *Arizona v. Fulminante* (1991), an officer posing as an organized crime figure in prison promised to protect another prisoner who was being threatened by the inmate population because of a rumor that he had murdered a child. The "organized crime figure" (i.e., undercover officer) said that he would provide protection only if the other prisoner told him the truth about the rumors. In response, the prisoner made incriminating statements to the undercover officer. In this case, a divided court narrowly ruled that the confession was inadmissible because the fear of physical violence that had motivated the statements constituted coercion.

The Court's efforts to assess the voluntariness of confessions pose significant difficulties. As described by prominent criminal law scholars,

> *The major problem with the voluntariness test is a practical one: it gives neither the police nor the courts much guidance. . . . [A] host of factors can be relevant in the "totality of the circumstances"; rarely does one factor predominate.*[2]

In some respects, the Court's development of *Miranda* rules can be seen as an effort to alleviate some of the problems inherent in relying solely on a voluntariness test. The Court intended to prevent some issues of voluntariness from arising by providing specific rules for police officers' interactions with suspects.

Miranda Rules

After *Malloy* the Supreme Court decided two right-to-counsel cases that helped to set the stage for *Miranda v. Arizona* (1966). As we will see in the *Miranda* case, the Supreme Court has talked about two different kinds of "right to counsel." In *Miranda* and related cases, the right to counsel during custodial questioning is simply a mechanism to help suspects protect their Fifth Amendment right against self-incrimination. Chapters 8 and 9 will discuss the Sixth Amendment right to counsel, which concerns an entitlement to representation after prosecution has begun.

Escobedo v. Illinois (1964) concerned a situation in which police officers would not permit an arrestee to see his attorney, even though he asked to see the attorney and the attorney was at the police station trying to see him. The police questioned the defendant for fourteen hours without an attorney and then gained a damaging admission from the defendant when they arranged a face-to-face confrontation between two co-defendants. The Court's holding specified that defendants have a right to counsel when "the investigation is no longer a general inquiry into an unsolved crime, but has begun to focus on a particular suspect, the suspect has been taken into police custody, [and] the police carry out a process of interrogations that lends itself to eliciting incriminating statements." The Court effectively expanded the right to counsel to apply at an early point in the criminal justice process as a means to guard against law enforcement officers' actions that might violate the Fifth Amendment privilege against compelled self-incrimination.

In *Massiah v. United States* (1964), a defendant who had been indicted and was already represented by counsel was lured into an automobile containing a radio transmitter by a co-defendant who was working for the police. Discussions in the car initiated by the co-defendant produced incriminating statements that were recorded by the police. The Supreme Court declared that the questioning of the defendant by a police agent outside of the presence of defense counsel violated both the Fifth Amendment privilege against compelled self-incrimination and the Sixth Amendment right to counsel. This case included consideration of the Sixth Amendment right to counsel because the defendant had already been formally charged with a crime through indictment. Thus prosecution processes had begun and he was not merely being questioned as a suspect in an investigation—the context in which the Fifth Amendment first becomes relevant.

Law enforcement officials regarded the Court's decisions in *Escobedo* and *Massiah* as extremely harmful to their efforts to investigate crimes. They were accustomed to relying on interrogations as the means to solve crimes. According to one legal historian, "To interrogate a suspect behind closed doors in order to secure a confession not only was a concept based on the custom and usage of centuries, but it had become a deeply entrenched police practice, strongly supported by both 'traditional' and 'reform' elements in the ranks of those charged with the administration of criminal justice."[3] As indicated by these examples, as well as cases in prior chapters such as *Mapp v. Ohio* (1961), the Supreme Court's decisions during the 1960s expanded the definitions of defendants' rights and created new limitations on police officers' investigatory strategies. As a result, many law enforcement officials and crime control–oriented politicians harshly criticized the Supreme Court's decisions. These criticisms became even more strident after the Supreme Court's decision in *Miranda,* which you can read in the following box.

Miranda v. Arizona, 384 U.S. 436 (1966)

CHIEF JUSTICE WARREN delivered the opinion of the Court.

. . .

Our holding will be spelled out with some specificity in the pages which follow but briefly stated it is this: the prosecution may not use statements, whether exculpatory or inculpatory, stemming from custodial interrogation of the defendant unless it demonstrates the use of procedural safeguards effective to secure the privilege against self-incrimination. By custodial interrogation, we mean questioning initiated by law enforcement officers after a person has been taken into custody or otherwise deprived of his freedom of action in any significant way. As for the procedural safeguards to be employed, unless other fully effective means are devised to inform accused persons of their right to silence and to assure a continuous opportunity to exercise it, the following measures are required. Prior to any questioning, the person must be warned that he has a right to remain silent, that any statement he does make may be used as evidence against him, and that he has the right to the presence of an attorney, either retained or appointed. The defendant may waive effectuation of these rights, provided the waiver is made voluntarily, knowingly, and intelligently. If, however, he indicates in any manner and at any stage of the process that he wishes to consult with an attorney before speaking there can be no questioning. Likewise, if the individual is alone and indicates in any manner that he does not wish to be interrogated, the police may not question him. The mere fact that he may have answered some questions or volunteered some statements on his own does not deprive him of the right to refrain from answering any further inquiries until he has consulted with an attorney and thereafter consents to be questioned.

The constitutional issue we decide in each of these cases is the admissibility of statements obtained from a defendant questioned while in custody or otherwise deprived of his freedom of action in any significant way. In each, the defendant was questioned by police officers, detectives, or a prosecuting attorney in a room in which he was cut off from the outside world. In none of these cases was the defendant given a full and effective warning of his rights at the outset of the interrogation process. In all the cases, the questioning elicited oral admissions, and in all three of them, signed statements as well which were admitted at their trials. They all thus share salient features—incommunicado interrogation of individuals in a police-dominated atmosphere, resulting in self-incriminating statements without full warnings of constitutional rights.

An understanding of the nature and setting of this in-custody interrogation is essential to our decisions today. The difficulty in depicting what transpires at such interrogations stems from the fact that in this country they have largely taken place incommunicado. From extensive factual studies undertaken in the early 1930's, including the famous Wickersham Report to Congress by a Presidential Commission, it is clear that police violence and the "third degree" flourished at that time.

In a series of cases decided by this Court long after these studies, the police resorted to physical brutality—beatings, hanging, whipping—and to sustained and protracted questioning incommunicado in order to extort confessions. The Commission on Civil Rights in 1961 found much evidence to indicate that "some policemen still resort to physical force to obtain confessions." . . . The use of physical brutality and violence is not, unfortunately, relegated to the past or to any part of the country. Only recently in Kings County, New York, the police brutally beat, kicked, and placed lighted cigarette butts on the back of a potential witness under interrogation for the purpose of securing a statement incriminating a third party. . . .

The examples given above are undoubtedly the exception now, but they are sufficiently widespread to be the object of concern. Unless a proper limitation upon custodial interrogation is achieved—such as these decisions will advance—there can be no assurance that practices of this nature will be eradicated in the foreseeable future. . . .

Again we stress that the modern practice of in-custody interrogation is psychologically oriented rather than physically oriented. . . . Interrogation still takes place in privacy. Privacy results in secrecy and this in turn results in a gap in our knowledge as to what in fact goes on in the interrogation rooms. A valuable source of information about present police practices, however, may be found in various police manuals and texts which document procedures employed with success in the past, and which recommend various other effective tactics. These texts are used by law enforcement agencies as guides. . . .

To highlight the isolation and unfamiliar surroundings, the manuals instruct the police to display an air of confidence in the suspect's guilt and from outward appearance to maintain an interest in confirming certain details. The guilt of the subject is to be posited as a fact. The interrogator should direct his comments toward the reasons why the subject committed the act, rather than court failure by asking the subject whether he did it. Like other men, perhaps the subject has had a bad family life, had an unhappy childhood, had too much to drink, had an unrequited desire for women. The officers are instructed to minimize the moral seriousness of the offense, to place blame on the victim or on society. These tactics are designed to put the subject in a psychological state where his story is but an elaboration of what the police purport to know already—that he is guilty. Explanations to the contrary are dismissed and discouraged. . . .

The interrogators sometimes are instructed to induce a confession out of trickery [by falsely telling the defendant that he was positively identified by a witness in a line-up]. . . .

Even without employing brutality, the "third degree" or the specific stratagems described above, the very fact of custodial interrogation exacts a heavy toll on individual liberty and trades on the weakness of individuals. . . .

In the cases before us today, given this background, we concern ourselves primarily with this interrogation atmosphere and the evils it can bring. . . . [I]n No. 584, *California v. Stewart,* the local police held the defendant for five days in the station and interrogated him on nine separate occasions before they secured his inculpatory statement.

In these cases, we might not find the defendants' statements to have been involuntary in traditional terms. Our concern for adequate safeguards to protect precious Fifth Amendment rights is, of course, not lessened in the slightest. In each of these cases, the defendant was thrust into an unfamiliar atmosphere and run through menacing police interrogation procedures. The potentiality for compulsion is forcefully apparent, for example, in *Miranda,* where the indigent Mexican defendant was a seriously disturbed individual with pronounced sexual fantasies, and in *Stewart,* in which the defendant was an indigent Los Angeles Negro who had dropped out of school in the sixth grade. To be sure, the records do not evince overt physical coercion or patent psychological ploys. The fact remains that in none of these cases did the officers undertake to afford appropriate safeguards at the outset of the interrogation to insure that the statements were truly the product of free choice.

It is obvious that such an interrogation environment is created for no purpose other than to subjugate the individual to the will of his examiner. This atmosphere carries its own badge of intimidation. To be sure, this is not physical intimidation, but it is equally destructive of human dignity. The current practice of incommunicado interrogation is at odds with one of our Nation's most cherished principles—that the individual may not be compelled to incriminate himself. Unless adequate protective devices are employed to dispel the compulsion inherent in custodial surroundings, no statement obtained from the defendant can truly be the product of his free choice. . . .

Today, then, there can be no doubt that the Fifth Amendment privilege is available outside of criminal court proceedings and serves to protect persons in all settings in which their freedom of action is curtailed in any significant way from being compelled to incriminate themselves. We have concluded that without proper safeguards the process of in-custody interrogation of persons suspected or accused of crime contains inherently compelling pressures which work to undermine the individual's will to resist and to compel him to speak where he would not otherwise do so freely. In order to combat these pressures and to permit a full opportunity to exercise the privilege against self-incrimination, the accused must be adequately and effectively apprised of his rights and exercise of those rights must be fully honored. . . .

If the interrogation continues without the presence of an attorney and a statement is taken, a heavy burden rests on the government to demonstrate that the defendant knowingly and intelligently waived his privileges against self-incrimination and his right to retained or appointed counsel. . . . This Court has always set high standards of proof for the waiver of constitutional rights, and we reassert these standards as applied to in-custody interrogation. Since the State is responsible for establishing the isolated circumstances under which the interrogation takes place and has the only means of making available corroborated evidence of warnings given during incommunicado interrogation, the burden is rightly on its shoulders.

An express statement that the individual is willing to make a statement and does not want an attorney followed closely by a statement could constitute a waiver. But a valid waiver will not be presumed simply from the silence of the accused after warnings are given or simply from the fact that a confession was in fact eventually obtained. . . .

(continued)

Our decision is not intended to hamper the traditional function of police officers investigating crime. . . . When an individual is in custody on probable cause, the police may, of course, seek out evidence in the field to be used at trial against him. Such investigation may include inquiry of persons not under restraint. General on-the-scene questioning as to the facts surrounding a crime or other general questioning of citizens in the fact-finding process is not affected by our holding. It is an act of good citizenship for individuals to give whatever information they may have to aid in law enforcement. In such situations the compelling atmosphere inherent in the process of in-custody interrogation is not necessarily present.

In dealing with statements obtained through interrogation, we do not purport to find all confessions inadmissible. Confessions remain a proper element in law enforcement. Any statement given freely and voluntarily without any compelling influences is, of course, admissible in evidence. . . . There is no requirement that police stop a person who enters a police station and states that he wishes to confess to a crime, or a person who calls the police to offer a confession or any other statement he desires to make. Volunteered statements of any kind are not barred by the Fifth Amendment and their admissibility is not affected by our holding today. . . .

A recurrent argument made in these cases is that society's need for interrogation outweighs the privilege [against self-incrimination]. This argument is not unfamiliar to this Court. . . . The whole thrust of our foregoing discussion demonstrates that the Constitution has prescribed the rights of the individual when confronted with the power of government when it provided in the Fifth Amendment that an individual cannot be compelled to be a witness against himself. That right cannot be abridged. . . .

In announcing these principles, we are not unmindful of the burdens which law enforcement officials must bear, often under trying circumstances. We also fully recognize the obligation of all citizens to aid in enforcing the criminal laws. This Court, while protecting individual rights, has always given ample latitude to law enforcement agencies in the legitimate exercise of their duties. The limits we have placed on the interrogation process should not constitute an undue interference with a proper system of law enforcement. . . .

Over the years the Federal Bureau of Investigation has compiled an exemplary record of effective law enforcement while advising any suspect or arrested person, at the outset of an interview, that he is not required to make a statement, that any statement may be used against him in court, that the individual may obtain the services of an attorney of his own choice, and, more recently, that he has a right to free counsel if he is unable to pay. . . .

The practice of the FBI can readily be emulated by state and local enforcement agencies. The argument that the FBI deals with different crimes than are dealt with by state authorities does not mitigate the significance of the FBI experience. . . .

It is also urged upon us that we withhold decision on this issue until state legislative bodies and advisory groups have had an opportunity to deal with these problems by rule making. . . . Congress and the states are free to develop their own safeguards for the privilege [against self-incrimination], so long as they are fully as effective as those described above in informing accused persons of their right of silence and in affording continuous opportunity to exercise it. In any event, however, the issues presented are of constitutional dimensions and must be determined by the courts. The admissibility of a statement in the face of a claim that it was obtained in violation of the defendant's constitutional rights is an issue the resolution of which has long since been undertaken by this Court. . . . Judicial solutions to problems of constitutional dimension have evolved decade by decade. As courts have been presented with the need to enforce constitutional rights, they have found means of doing so. That was our responsibility when *Escobedo* was before us and it is our responsibility today. Where rights secured by the Constitution are involved, there can be no rule making or legislation which would abrogate them. . . .

We reverse [Miranda's conviction]. From the testimony of the officers and by the admission of respondent, it is clear that Miranda was not in any way apprised of his right to consult with an attorney and to have one present during the interrogation, nor was his right not to be compelled to incriminate himself effectively protected in any other manner. Without these warnings the statements were inadmissible. The mere fact that he signed a statement which contained a typed-in clause stating that he had "full knowledge" of his "legal rights" does not approach the knowing and intelligent waiver required to relinquish constitutional rights. . . .

JUSTICE CLARK, dissenting.

It is with regret that I find it necessary to write in these cases. However, I am unable to join the majority because its opinion goes too far on too little, while my dissenting brethren do not go quite far enough. Nor can I join in the Court's criticism of the present practices of police and investigatory agencies as to custodial interrogation. The materials it refers to as "police manuals" are, as I read them, merely writings in this field by professors and some police officers. Not one is shown by the record here to be the official manual of any police department, much less in universal use in crime detection. Moreover the examples of police brutality mentioned by this Court are rare exceptions to the thousands of cases that appear every year in the law reports. The police agencies—all the way from municipal and state forces to the federal bureaus—are responsible for law enforcement and public safety in this country. I am proud of their efforts, which in my view are not fairly characterized by the Court's opinion. . . .

The rule prior to today . . . depended upon a "totality of circumstances evidencing an involuntary . . . admission of guilt." . . . I would continue to follow that rule. . . .

Rather than employing the arbitrary Fifth Amendment rule which the Court lays down I would follow the more pliable dictates of the Due Process Clauses of the Fifth and Fourteenth Amendments which we are accustomed to administering and which we know from our cases are effective instruments in protecting persons in police custody. In this way we would not be acting in the dark nor in one full sweep changing the traditional rules of custodial interrogation which this Court has for so long recognized as a justifiable and proper tool in balancing individual rights against the rights of society. . . .

JUSTICE HARLAN, with whom JUSTICE STEWART and JUSTICE WHITE join, dissenting.

. . .

Without at all subscribing to the generally black picture of police conduct painted by the Court, I think it must be frankly recognized at the outset that police questioning allowable under due process precedents may inherently entail some pressure on the suspect and may seek advantage in his ignorance or weakness. . . . Until today, the role of the Constitution has been only to sift out *undue* pressure, not to assure spontaneous confessions.

The Court's new rules aim to offset these minor pressures and disadvantages intrinsic to any kind of police interrogation. The rules do not serve due process interests in preventing blatant coercion since, as I noted earlier, they do nothing to contain the policeman who is prepared to lie from the start. . . .

What the Court largely ignores is that its rules impair, if they will not eventually serve to frustrate, an instrument of law enforcement that has long and quite reasonably been thought worth the price paid for it. There can be little doubt that the Court's new code would markedly decrease the number of confessions. . . .

How much harm this decision will inflict on law enforcement cannot fairly be predicted with accuracy. . . . We do know that some crimes cannot be solved without confessions, that ample expert testimony attests to their importance in crime control, and that the Court is taking a real risk with society's welfare in imposing its new regime on the country. The social costs of crime are too great to call the new rules anything but a hazardous experiment. . . .

JUSTICE WHITE, with whom JUSTICE HARLAN and JUSTICE STEWART join, dissenting.

The proposition that the privilege against self-incrimination forbids in-custody interrogation without the warnings specified in the majority opinion and without a clear waiver of counsel has no significant support in the history of the privilege or in the language of the Fifth Amendment. As for the English authorities and the common-law history, the privilege, firmly established in the second half of the seventeenth century, was never applied except to prohibit compelled judicial interrogations. . . .

Criticism of the Court's opinion, however, cannot stop with a demonstration that the factual and textual bases for the rule it propounds are, at best, less than compelling. Equally relevant is an assessment of the rule's consequences measured against community values. . . . More than the human dignity of the accused is involved; the human personality of others in society must also be preserved. Thus the values reflected by the privilege are not the sole desideratum; society's interest in the general security is of equal weight.

The obvious underpinning of the Court's decision is a deep-seated distrust of all confessions. . . . This is the not so subtle overtone of the opinion— that it is inherently wrong for the police to gather evidence from the accused himself. And this is precisely the nub of this dissent. I see nothing wrong or immoral, and certainly nothing unconstitutional, in the police's asking a suspect whom they have reasonable cause to arrest whether or not he killed his wife or in confronting him with the evidence on which the arrest was based, at least where he has been plainly advised that he may remain completely silent. . . .

(continued)

The rule announced today will measurably weaken the ability of the criminal law to perform [its] tasks. It is a deliberate calculus to prevent interrogations, to reduce the incidence of confessions and pleas of guilty and to increase the number of trials. Criminal trials, no matter how efficient the police are, are not sure bets for the prosecution, nor should they be if the evidence is not forthcoming. Under the present law, the prosecution fails to prove its case in about 30% of the criminal cases actually tried in the federal courts. . . . But it is something else again to remove from the ordinary criminal case all those confessions which heretofore have been held to be free and voluntary acts of the accused and to thus establish a new constitutional barrier to the ascertainment of truth by the judicial process.

There is, in my view, every reason to believe that a good many criminal defendants who otherwise would have been convicted on what this Court has previously thought to be the most satisfactory kind of evidence will now under this new version of the Fifth Amendment, either not be tried at all or will be acquitted if the State's evidence, minus the confession, is put to the test of litigation.

I have no desire whatsoever to share the responsibility for any such impact on the present criminal process.

In some unknown number of cases the Court's rule will return a killer, a rapist or other criminal to the streets and to the environment which produced him, to repeat his crime whenever it pleases him. As a consequence, there will not be a gain, but a loss, in human dignity. . . .

The *Miranda* warnings apply only to *custodial interrogations*. If police officers walk up to someone on the streets and begin asking questions, there is no need to inform the person of his or her rights. Just as we saw in the Court's opinion in *Florida v. Bostick* (Chapter 6), the justices say that people know they can walk away when an officer asks them questions in a public place. If the suspect is in custody, there is a different situation. When police have taken someone into custody, the Supreme Court sees an inherently coercive situation. The loss of liberty and isolation experienced by detained suspects can make them vulnerable to abusive interrogation techniques, especially when interrogations take place out of view of anyone other than police officers. When a suspect is alone in a room with police officers, will anyone believe it if the suspect claims to have been beaten, even if it is true? If the police say that the suspect confessed, will anyone believe it if the suspect says that no confession was ever given? The *Miranda* warnings and presence of counsel during questioning are supposed to prevent such risks from occurring.

Note how the premise of *Miranda* warnings differs so significantly from the premise of consent searches. The *Miranda* decision begins with the assumption that police may not be trustworthy. It also assumes that citizens are not knowledgeable about their rights. It requires that the officers inform suspects of their rights and make sure that the suspects state that they understand those rights. In effect, any waivers of the Fifth Amendment privilege against compelled self-incrimination, including the related right to counsel, must be made both *knowingly and voluntarily*. By contrast, the Court tends to emphasize that waivers of other rights must merely be voluntary; there is no comparable requirement that the individual indicate knowledge of the right before waiving it. In the Fourth Amendment context, remember that officers are not required to inform people about their right to refuse to permit a search when officers seek to do a warrantless search by gaining the consent of someone who has authority over the property to be searched. The officers must merely be sure that the consent was voluntary. They do not need to worry about whether the person knew that he or she could say "no," because the Court speaks as if citizens are knowledgeable about their constitutional rights. By contrast, the Warren Court presumed that people did not possess sufficient knowledge about their Fifth Amendment rights, and therefore the justices imposed upon police officers the obligation to educate arrestees before questioning them.

The *Miranda* decision explicitly expressed the justices' skepticism about police interrogation techniques. This opinion as much as any other Supreme Court opinion is premised on the recognition that law enforcement officials may use coercive or abusive techniques in order to gain criminal convictions. Here, Chief Justice Warren gave explicit examples of documented abuses over the years:

> From extensive factual studies undertaken in the 1930s, including the famous Wickersham Report to Congress by a Presidential Commission, it is clear that police violence and the "third degree" flourished at that time.
>
> In a series of cases decided by this Court long after these studies, the police resorted to physical brutality—beatings, hangings, whipping—and to sustained and protracted questioning incommunicado in order to exhort confessions. . . . The use of physical brutality and violence is not, unfortunately relegated to the past or to any part of the country. Only recently in Kings County, New York, the police brutally beat, kicked, and placed lighted cigarette butts on the back of a potential witness under interrogation. . . . (384 U.S. 436 at 445–446)

Should these occurrences be viewed as exceptional situations by a few "bad apples"? If so, should the law be based on relatively rare situations? Alternatively, should the Supreme Court look at the worst situations and try to create rules to prevent those situations from occurring? One of the challenges in answering these questions is the uncertainty about the frequency of abusive police actions. Clearly, the justices in the majority viewed such actions as sufficiently frequent to justify the need for a clear rule intended to prevent abuses from occurring.

It is just as clear, however, that the justices were deeply divided about the creation of the rule for police behavior. Justice White's dissent contained a famous—and ominous—warning that the decision would lead to the release of violent criminals who would victimize society again. In many respects, his warning echoed the views of the Court's critics who saw the Supreme Court as acting inappropriately to provide excessive protection for criminals while "handcuffing" the police by depriving them of a needed investigatory technique. Because the *Miranda* warnings were linked to the exclusionary rule, any statements obtained without providing the warnings properly would result in incriminating statements being excluded from use in court. If the statements were the only evidence in a case, the suspect could go free. There is a question, however, about the number of cases in which the *Miranda* warnings have led to the release of guilty suspects.

Prior to the *Miranda* decision, the due process and, later, Fifth Amendment rights involved in confessions cases could be challenged by making a claim that the incriminating statement was not made voluntarily. After *Miranda*, however, the defendants had two additional bases for constitutional rights claims related to confessions. Defendants could claim that they were not informed of their rights by the police prior to custodial questioning. They could also claim that they did not receive the right to counsel protections that the *Miranda*

Reading the Brain

The focus of the Fifth Amendment privilege against compelled self-incrimination and the *Miranda* warnings is testimonial evidence—in other words, statements that a person may be coerced to provide against himself. As we will see in Chapter 9, a person may be required to participate in generating evidence about himself by appearing in a lineup or providing a handwriting sample, but these circumstances do not raise Fifth Amendment and *Miranda* issues because they do not concern testimony.

Although the foregoing paragraph describes the current state of the law, it is possible that advances in technology may raise new questions about what kinds of evidence the Fifth Amendment covers. For example, Dr. Lawrence Farwell has developed a technique for examining people's brain-wave responses to words and pictures. An electronic headband worn by the person detects their brain-wave responses when specific words or pictures are flashed on a screen.[4] In theory, if the person shows brain-wave response to words and pictures that would be familiar only to a witness or perpetrator of a crime, then law enforcement officials could make a giant step toward solving the crime. Similarly, a person who was wrongly convicted may be exonerated if her brain waves indicate no response to words and phrases concerning the crime.

The technique is the basis for a 2000 appeal of an Iowa murder case in which an imprisoned offender who has maintained his innocence for twenty-three years "passed" Dr. Farwell's test by showing no response to information about the crime. His brain did, however, respond to words and pictures about his alibi. Thus Farwell concludes that his brain never had the information about the crime and therefore it was logical to conclude that he was not present at the killing.[5]

Because the person being tested sits silently and a researcher notes brain-wave responses that appear on a screen, there is no testimonial evidence being produced by the person. Does this mean that this technology does not have any connection to the Fifth Amendment? If Dr. Farwell's technology develops further and is accepted in court, judges will need to determine whether any rights are implicated by this investigation technique.

Do you think the Fifth Amendment should apply to exclude evidence drawn from brain-wave readings about people's thoughts? If there is no coercion or pressure involved in flashing the words and pictures across the screen, is there any collision with *Miranda*'s desire to protect people from incriminating themselves?

warnings promise. Thus courts face three different kinds of cases in which defendants challenge the admissibility of their incriminating statements. As you read the accompanying box about the detection of brain-wave responses during questioning, ask yourself whether you expect the development of new technology to create additional issues concerning *Miranda* warnings.

THE CONSEQUENCES OF *MIRANDA*

People often erroneously presume that rules announced by the Supreme Court are applied as intended by the justices. But, as we have discussed in prior chapters, the actual impact of Supreme Court decisions depends on the actions of officials who must interpret and implement those decisions. In the case of *Miranda* warnings, police officers have adapted their techniques in various ways in order to question suspects without any impediment from the warnings. In addition, *Miranda* warnings do not necessarily have the effect on suspects that the critics of the rule tend to assume. During oral arguments at the Supreme Court, the opponents of *Miranda* assumed that every subject would cease to talk upon being informed that there is a right to silence. However, in practice, this has not proven to be the case.

Miranda is a rule concerning *custodial* interrogations. Thus police officers can ask questions freely of suspects who are not in custody. In order to avoid the risk that *Miranda* warnings will impede an effort to gain incriminating statements from suspects, officers often ask questions *before* they make an arrest. For example, officers can ask someone questions on the street or go to the front door of the suspect's house in order to ask questions from the doorstep.

Miranda rights must be provided *before questions are asked* during custodial interrogations. Many departments train their officers to read the *Miranda* warnings to suspects as soon as an arrest is made. This is done in order to make sure the warnings are not omitted as the suspect is processed in the system. The warnings may be read off a standard "Miranda card" to make sure that the rights are provided consistently and correctly. However, the courts do not require that police inform suspects of their rights immediately after arrest. The warnings do not have to be provided until the police begin to ask questions. Thus, after taking a suspect into custody, some officers may use their discretion to delay providing *Miranda* warnings in order to see if the suspect will talk on his or her own. The suspect may be kept in the backseat of a car as officers drive around town, or the suspect may be left alone in a room at the police station. Some suspects will take the initiative to talk to officers because of feelings of guilt. Other suspects may start conversations with officers because they are so eager to convince the officers that they have an alibi. This may lead the suspect to provide contradictory statements that will help to build the case.

After suspects in custody have been informed of their *Miranda* rights, officers may attempt to defuse the potential impact of the rights by presenting the rights in a manner intended to dissuade the suspects from keeping silent. For example, officers may inform suspects of their rights but then add, "But if you don't have anything to hide, why would you ask for an attorney or stay silent?"

Officers are also trained in interrogation techniques that are intended to encourage suspects to talk despite *Miranda* warnings. Officers may pretend to be sympathetic to the suspect.[6] They may say, for example, "We understand how bad stuff can happen when you never intended for it to happen. We know that you had a good reason to get mad and go after that guy with your knife. We probably would have done the same thing if we were in your situation. We know that you never really planned to stab him." Such statements are not honest. But police officers are not required to be honest during questioning. They are allowed to use deception to induce suspects to talk. It is not uncommon for officers to say, untruthfully, "We have five witnesses who saw you do it. If you tell us everything right now, we may be able to get you a good deal. If you don't help us, we don't know what we can do for you." Do such statements constitute coercion that would be regarded as improper pressure in violation of *Miranda?* Probably not—as long as the officers do not threaten suspects in ways that make them fear for their physical safety or the safety of their loved ones.

Miranda rights have become very familiar to the American public through television shows and movies in which police officers inform arrested suspects of their rights. By the time television-watching Americans reach adulthood, they have probably heard the *Miranda* warnings delivered hundreds of times on these shows. Many Americans can easily recite the warnings along with the television detectives without thinking about the meaning of the warnings at all—and that reality may be an impediment to effective implementation of *Miranda* warnings. Suspects may hear the familiar warnings being spoken by the officers, yet the very familiarity of the warnings interferes with the suspects' ability to think about what the warnings actually mean. Some new police officers express surprise at how few arrested suspects actually remain silent or request an attorney after being told that they possess those rights. Suspects' ability to focus on and comprehend the rights may be further diminished by the shock of being arrested with its attendant feelings of uncertainty about what will happen next and potential feelings of fear about the prospect of being locked in jail.

Many suspects talk to the police despite being informed of their right to remain silent and their right to have an attorney present during questioning. Some suspects do not fully understand the rights. They may believe that they will look guilty by remaining silent or asking for an attorney, and therefore they feel that they must talk to officers in order to have any hope of claiming innocence. Other suspects may be overly confident about their ability to fool the police, and therefore they talk to officers, despite the warnings, in an effort to act as if they have nothing to hide. More importantly, many suspects believe (often accurately) that they will gain a more favorable charge or plea bargain if they cooperate with officers as fully as possible and as early as possible. Thus a trio of suspects arrested together after a robbery who are read their *Miranda* rights and who are placed in separate interrogation rooms may, in effect, race to be the first one to tell a version of events in order to pin greater responsibility on the other arrestees and to seek police assistance in gaining a favorable deal with the prosecutor. This incentive to cooperate can completely negate many of the fears about *Miranda*'s potentially detrimental effect on law enforcement's effectiveness. It can also create problems, however. There are many cases in which the most culpable arrestee—for example, the one who pulled the trigger and killed a storeowner during a robbery—is the most eager to cooperate with the police. If police are not sufficiently skeptical and careful, the most serious offender may get the most favorable deal by having his or her version of events accepted by authorities and the least culpable defendant, such as the driver of the getaway car, can sometimes end up with the most severe punishment if he or she loses the "race" to confess.

The actual meaning and implementation of *Miranda* warnings are affected by the behavior of police officers and suspects. In addition, the application of rules from *Miranda v. Arizona* is shaped by changes in the composition of the judiciary. As you read the box "Adjustment and Change in Constitutional Doctrine," think about whether the Warren Court justices who wrote *Miranda* would believe that the rules created in the case are still being applied correctly by judges and police officers today.

MIRANDA'S VARIATIONS

The Definition of Custody

The characterization of *Miranda* as applying to **custodial interrogation** might imply that warnings must be given whenever police ask questions of someone who is not free to leave the presence of the police. People who are arrested are,

| A CLOSER LOOK | **Adjustment and Change in Constitutional Doctrine** |

When we talk about "the U.S. Supreme Court," we often act as if we are talking about a single, enduring entity. The institution of the Court has existed for more than 200 years, but the nature of the Court changes as its composition changes. The Court that decided *Miranda v. Arizona* in 1966 was not the same Court that decided later cases applying the decision to specific situations. Of the Court's nine members who decided *Miranda* in 1966, only three still remained on the Court in 1981. Thus it was a different group of justices who decided how *Miranda* applied—or did not apply—in various cases decided during the 1980s and 90s. The definitions of constitutional rights and the rules for police conduct are not permanent and enduring. They change over time as the Supreme Court, and its new members, revisits issues. Thus it makes little sense to view law as merely a set of rules. Law concerns rules, but these rules are malleable. They bend and change through interpretation. They take new forms or even disappear in the hands of new decision makers who possess different values or different approaches to constitutional interpretation. An understanding of criminal procedure requires not only knowledge of the currently existing rights and rules, but also a recognition of the nature and possibility of change.

If you recognize that law, including the definition of constitutional rights, changes in the hands of new judges, does that give you more or less confidence in law as an important, reliable element in ensuring that legal protections and liberties are enjoyed by people in the United States?

obviously, not free to leave. However, there may be other situations where people are not free to leave, yet *Miranda* does not apply. When people are questioned by customs officers at a border stop, they are not entitled to be informed of their *Miranda* rights. They are not free to leave, but they are not considered to be in custody for *Miranda* purposes. Similarly, drivers whom officers pull over for a traffic stop are not free to leave, but they are also not entitled to be informed of their right to remain silent (*Berkemer v. McCarty,* 1984).

Suspects who come to the police station voluntarily are not entitled to *Miranda* warnings if they are not arrested (*California v. Beheler,* 1983). This includes probationers who are instructed to come to meetings with their probation officers. If they make incriminating statements during a meeting with their probation officers, those statements can be used against them, even if their presence at the meeting was not "voluntary" in the sense in which people normally use the word (*Minnesota v. Murphy,* 1984).

In the foregoing situations, the individuals may not actually feel free to leave. However, the Court has adopted a relatively specific definition of "custodial" questioning. It is not based on individuals' subjective understanding of whether or not they are free to leave. It is based on the Court's characterization of arrest as the primary defining step in determining whether someone is in custody for the purposes of *Miranda.*

One circumstance in which the Court has permitted police officers to forego *Miranda* warnings is when there would be a threat to "public safety" by taking the time to provide the warnings. This exception is similar to the exigent circumstance justification for warrantless searches discussed in Chapters 5 and 6. The underlying premise is that some urgent situation of significant social importance outweighs the necessity of respecting individuals' rights in the fashion in which they are normally protected. As you read *New York v. Quarles* (1984) in the following box, ask yourself whether it makes sense to have a "public safety" exception and whether this particular case justifies that exception.

[*A woman flagged down a patrol car and told officers that she had been assaulted. She said that her assailant had run into a store. Police officers entered the store, saw the man fitting the description of the alleged assailant, and arrested him. After placing handcuffs on a man, the officers asked him where he had put his gun. The suspect responded, "The gun is over there," and nodded toward some boxes. The officers retrieved the gun from under the boxes. The suspect sought to have his statement and the gun excluded from evidence because they were obtained through an incriminating statement in response to police questioning prior to him being given his* Miranda *warnings. The trial court excluded the statement and the gun because they were obtained in violation of* Miranda, *and the Appellate Division of the New York Supreme Court and the New York Court of Appeals affirmed the trial judge's ruling. The U.S. Supreme Court considered whether the statement and gun should be admissible as evidence despite the officers' failure to provide* Miranda *warnings prior to questioning the handcuffed suspect.*]

JUSTICE REHNQUIST delivered the opinion of the Court.

Respondent Benjamin Quarles was charged in the New York trial court with criminal possession of a weapon. The trial court suppressed the gun in question, and a statement made by respondent, because the statement was obtained by police before they read respondent his "*Miranda* rights." That ruling was affirmed on appeal through the New York Court of Appeals. We granted certiorari, . . . and we now reverse. We conclude that under the circumstances involved in this case, overriding considerations of public safety justify the officer's failure to provide *Miranda* warnings before he asked questions devoted to locating the abandoned weapon. . . .

[The New York Court of Appeals] concluded that respondent was in "custody" within the meaning of *Miranda* during all questioning and rejected the State's argument that the exigencies of the situation justified Officer Kraft's failure to read respondent his *Miranda* rights until after he had located the gun. The court declined to recognize an exigency exception to the usual requirements of *Miranda* because it found no indication from Officer Kraft's testimony at the suppression hearing that his subjective motivation in asking the question was to protect his own or the safety of the public. . . . For the reasons which follow, we believe that this case presents a situation where concern for public safety must be paramount to adherence to the literal language of the prophylactic rules enunciated in *Miranda*.

The Fifth Amendment guarantees that "[n]o person . . . shall be compelled in any criminal case to be a witness against himself." In *Miranda* this Court for the first time extended the Fifth Amendment privilege against compulsory self-incrimination to individuals subjected to custodial interrogation by the police. . . . The *Miranda* Court, however, presumed that interrogation in certain custodial circumstances is inherently coercive and held that statements made under those circumstances are inadmissible unless the suspect is specifically informed of his *Miranda* rights and freely decides to forgo those rights. The prophylactic *Miranda* warnings therefore are "not themselves rights protected by the Constitution but [are] instead measures to insure that the right against compulsory self-incrimination [is] protected." *Michigan v. Tucker*, 417 U.S. . . . 444 (1974). Requiring *Miranda* warnings before custodial interrogation provides "practical reinforcement" for the Fifth Amendment right. . . .

In this case we have before us no claim that respondent's statements were actually compelled by police conduct which overcame his will to resist. . . . Thus the only issue before us is whether Officer Kraft was justified in failing to make available to respondent the procedural safeguards associated with the privilege against compulsory self-incrimination since *Miranda*.

The New York Court of Appeals was undoubtedly correct in deciding that the facts of this case come within the ambit of the *Miranda* decision as we have subsequently interpreted it. We agree that respondent was in custody. . . . Here Quarles was surrounded by at least four police officers and was handcuffed when the questioning at issue took place. . . . The New York Court of Appeals' majority declined to express an opinion as to whether there might be an exception to the *Miranda* rule if the police had been acting to protect the public, because the lower courts in New York had made no factual determination that the police had acted with that motive.

We hold that on these facts there is a "public safety" exception to the requirement that *Miranda* warnings be given before a suspect's answers may be admitted into evidence, and that the availability of that exception does not depend upon the motivation of the individual officers involved. In a kaleidoscopic situation such as the one confronting these officers, where spontaneity rather than adherence to a police manual is necessarily the order of the day, the application of the exception which we recognize today should not be made to depend on *post hoc* findings at a suppression hearing concerning the subjective motivation of the arresting officer. Undoubtedly most police officers, if placed in Officer Kraft's position, would act out of a host of different, instinctive, and largely unverifiable motives—their own safety, the safety of others, and perhaps as well the desire to obtain incriminating evidence from the suspect.

Whatever the motivation of individual officers in such a situation, we do not believe that the doctrinal underpinnings of *Miranda* require that it be applied in all its rigor to a situation in which police officers ask questions reasonably prompted by a concern for the public safety. . . . The *Miranda* majority . . . apparently felt that whatever the cost to society in terms of fewer convictions of guilty suspects, that cost would simply have to be borne in the interest of enlarged protection for the Fifth Amendment privilege.

The police in this case, in the very act of apprehending a suspect, were confronted with the immediate necessity of ascertaining the whereabouts of a gun which they had every reason to believe the suspect had just removed from his empty holster and discarded in the supermarket. So long as the gun was concealed somewhere in the supermarket, with its actual whereabouts unknown, it obviously posed more than one danger to the public safety: an accomplice might make use of it, a customer or employee might later come upon it.

In such a situation, if the police are required to recite the familiar *Miranda* warnings before asking the whereabouts of the gun, suspects in Quarles' position might well be deterred from responding. Procedural safeguards which deter a suspect from responding were deemed acceptable in *Miranda* in order to protect the Fifth Amendment privilege; when the primary social cost of those added protections is the possibility of fewer convictions, the *Miranda* majority was willing to bear that cost. Here, had the *Miranda* warnings deterred Quarles from responding to Officer Kraft's question about the whereabouts of the gun, the cost would have been something more than merely the failure to obtain evidence useful in convicting Quarles. Officer Kraft needed an answer to his question not simply to make his case against Quarles but to insure that further danger to the public did not result from the concealment of the gun in a public area.

We conclude that the need for answers to questions in a situation posing a threat to the public safety outweighs the need for the prophylactic rule protecting the Fifth Amendment's privilege against self-incrimination. We decline to place officers such as Officer Kraft in the untenable position of having to consider, often in a matter of seconds, whether it best serves society for them to ask the necessary questions without the *Miranda* warnings and render whatever probative evidence they uncover inadmissible, or for them to give the warnings in order to preserve the admissibility of evidence they might uncover but possibly damage or destroy their ability to obtain that evidence and neutralize the volatile situation confronting them.

In recognizing a narrow exception to the *Miranda* rule in this case, we acknowledge that to some degree we lessen the desirable clarity of that rule. . . . We think police officers can and will distinguish almost instinctively between questions necessary to secure their own safety or the safety of the public and questions designed solely to elicit testimonial evidence from a suspect.

The facts of this case clearly demonstrate that distinction and an officer's ability to recognize it. Officer Kraft asked only the question necessary to locate the missing gun before advising respondent of his rights. It was only after securing the loaded revolver and giving the warnings that he continued with investigatory questions about ownership and place of purchase of the gun. The exception which we recognize today, far from complicating the thought processes and the on-the-scene judgments of police officers, will simply free them to follow their legitimate instincts when confronting situations presenting a danger to the public safety. . . .

JUSTICE O'CONNOR, concurring in the judgment in part and dissenting in part.

In *Miranda v. Arizona*, . . . the Court held unconstitutional, because inherently compelled, the admission of statements derived from in-custody questioning not preceded by an explanation of the privilege against self-incrimination and the consequences of forgoing it. Today, the Court concludes that overriding considerations of public safety justify the admission of evidence—oral statements and a gun—secured without the benefit of such warnings. . . . In so holding, the Court acknowledges that

(continued)

it is departing from prior precedent, . . . and that it is "lessen[ing] the desirable clarity of [the *Miranda*] rule." . . . Were the Court writing from a clean slate, I could agree with its holding. But *Miranda* is now the law and, in my view, the Court has not provided sufficient justification for departing from it or blurring its now clear strictures. Accordingly, I would require suppression of the initial statement taken from respondent in this case. On the other hand, nothing in *Miranda* or the privilege itself requires exclusion of nontestimonial evidence derived from informal custodial interrogation, and I therefore agree with the Court that admission of the gun in evidence is proper. . . .

Since the time *Miranda* was decided, the Court has repeatedly refused to bend the literal terms of that decision. To be sure, the Court has been sensitive to the substantial burden the *Miranda* rules place on local law enforcement efforts, and consequently has refused to extend the decision or to increase its strictures on law enforcement agencies in almost any way. . . . Similarly, where "statements taken in violation of the *Miranda* principles [have] not be[en] used to prove the prosecution's case at trial," the Court has allowed evidence derived from those statements to be admitted. . . . But wherever an accused has been taken into "custody" and subjected to "interrogation" without warnings, the Court has consistently prohibited the use of his responses for prosecutorial purposes at trial. . . . As a consequence, the "meaning of *Miranda* has become reasonably clear and law enforcement practices have adjusted to its strictures." . . .

In my view, a "public safety" exception unnecessarily blurs the edges of the clear line heretofore established and makes *Miranda*'s requirements more difficult to understand. In some cases, police will benefit because a reviewing court will find that an exigency excused their failure to administer required warnings. But in other cases, police will suffer because, though they thought an exigency excused their noncompliance, a reviewing court will view the "objective" circumstances differently and require exclusion of admissions thereby obtained. The end result will be a finespun new doctrine on public safety exigencies incident to custodial interrogation, complete with the hair-splitting distinctions that currently plague our Fourth Amendment jurisprudence. . . .

The justification the Court provides for upsetting the equilibrium that has finally been achieved—that police cannot and should not balance considerations of public safety against the individual's interest in avoiding compulsory testimonial self-incrimination—really misses the critical question to be decided. . . . *Miranda* has never been read to prohibit police from asking questions to secure the public safety. Rather, the critical question *Miranda* addresses is who shall bear the cost of securing the public safety when such questions are asked and answered: the defendant or the State. *Miranda,* for better or worse, found the resolution of that question implicit in the prohibition against compulsory self-incrimination and placed the burden on the State. When police ask custodial questions without administering required warnings, *Miranda* quite clearly requires that the answers received be presumed compelled and they be excluded from evidence at trial. . . .

The Court concedes, as it must, both that respondent was in "custody" and subject to "interrogation" and that his statement "the gun is over there" was compelled within the meaning of our precedent. . . . In my view, since there is nothing about an exigency that makes custodial interrogation any less compelling, a principled application of *Miranda* requires that respondent's statement be suppressed.

The Court below assumed, without discussion, that the privilege against self-incrimination required that the gun derived from respondent's statement also be suppressed, whether or not the State could independently link it to him. That conclusion was, in my view, incorrect. . . .

Only the introduction of a defendant's own *testimony* is proscribed by the Fifth Amendment's mandate that no person "shall be compelled in any criminal case to be a witness against himself." That mandate does not protect an accused from being compelled to surrender *nontestimonial* evidence against himself. . . .

[This] case is problematic because police compelled respondent not only to provide the gun but also to admit that he knew where it was and that it was his. . . .

The values underlying the privilege [against self-incrimination] may justify exclusion of an unwarned person's out-of-court statements, as perhaps they may justify exclusion of statements and derivative evidence compelled under the threat of contempt. But when the only evidence to be admitted is derivative evidence such as a gun—derived not from actual compulsion but from a statement taken in the absence of *Miranda* warnings—those values simply cannot require suppression, at least no more so than they would for other such nontestimonial evidence. . . .

[W]hen the *Miranda* violation consists of a deliberate and flagrant abuse of the accused's constitutional rights, amounting to a denial of due process, application of a broader exclusionary rule is warranted. Of course, "a defendant raising [such] a coerced-confession claim . . . must first prevail in a voluntariness hearing before his confession and evidence derived from it [will] become inadmissible." . . . By contrast, where the accused proves only that the police failed to administer the *Miranda* warnings, exclusion of the statement itself is all that will and should be required. Limitation of the *Miranda* prohibition to testimonial use of the statements themselves adequately serves the purposes of the privilege against self-incrimination. . . .

JUSTICE MARSHALL, with whom JUSTICE BRENNAN and JUSTICE STEVENS join, dissenting.

. . .

The majority's entire analysis rests on the factual assumption that the public was at risk during Quarles' interrogation. This assumption is completely in conflict with the facts as found by New York's highest court. Before the interrogation began, Quarles had been "reduced to a condition of physical powerlessness." . . . Contrary to the majority's speculations, . . . Quarles was not believed to have, nor did he in fact have, an accomplice to come to his rescue. When the questioning began, the arresting officers were sufficiently confident of their safety to put away their guns. As Officer Kraft acknowledged at the suppression hearing, "the situation was under control." . . . Based on Officer Kraft's own testimony, the New York Court of Appeals found: "Nothing suggests that any of the officers was by that time concerned for his own physical safety." . . . The Court of Appeals also determined that there was no evidence that the interrogation was prompted by the arresting officers' concern for the public safety. . . .

The majority attempts to slip away from these unambiguous findings of New York's highest court by proposing that danger be measured by objective facts rather than the subjective intentions of arresting officers. . . . Though clever, this ploy was anticipated by the New York Court of Appeals: "[T]here is no evidence in the record before us that there were exigent circumstances posing a risk to the public safety. . . ."

The New York court's conclusion that neither Quarles nor his missing gun posed a threat to the public's safety is amply supported by the evidence presented at the suppression hearing. Again, contrary to the majority's intimations, . . . no customers or employees were wandering about the store in danger of coming across Quarles' discarded weapon. Although the supermarket was open to the public, Quarles' arrest took place during the middle of the night when the store was apparently deserted except for the clerks at the check-out counter. The police could easily have cordoned off the store and searched for the missing gun. Had they done so, they would have found the gun forthwith. The police were well aware that Quarles had discarded his weapon somewhere near the scene of the arrest. As the State acknowledged before the New York Court of Appeals: "After Officer Kraft had handcuffed and frisked the defendant in the supermarket, *he knew with a high degree of certainty that the defendant's gun was within the immediate vicinity of the encounter.* He undoubtedly would have searched for it in the carton a few feet away without the defendant having looked in that direction and saying that it was there." Brief of the Appellant [State of New York] . . . (emphasis added).

Earlier this Term, four Members of the majority joined an opinion stating: "[Q]uestions of historical fact . . . must be determined, in the first instance, by state courts and deferred to, in the absence of 'convincing evidence' to the contrary, by the federal courts." . . . In this case, there was convincing evidence, indeed almost overwhelming, evidence to support the New York court's conclusion that Quarles' hidden weapon did not pose a risk either to the arresting officers or to the public. The majority ignores this evidence and sets aside the factual findings of the New York Court of Appeals. More cynical observers might well conclude that a state court's findings of fact "deserv[e] a 'high measure of deference,'" . . . only when deference works against the interests of a criminal defendant.

The majority's treatment of the legal issues presented in this case is no less troubling than its abuse of the facts. Before today's opinion, the Court had twice concluded that, under *Miranda v. Arizona* . . . police officers conducting custodial interrogations must advise suspects of their rights before any questions concerning the whereabouts of incriminating weapons can be asked. *Rhode Island v. Innis* . . . (1980) (dicta); *Orozco v. Texas* . . . (1969) (holding). Now the majority departs from these cases and rules that police may withhold *Miranda* warnings whenever custodial interrogations concern matters of public safety. . . .

In a chimerical quest for public safety, the majority has abandoned the rule that brought 18 years of tranquility to the field of custodial interrogations. As the majority candidly concedes, . . . a public-safety exception destroys forever the clarity of *Miranda* for both law enforcement officers and members of the

(continued)

judiciary. The Court's candor cannot mask what a serious loss the administration of justice has incurred.

This case is illustrative of the chaos the "public-safety" exception will unleash. The circumstances of Quarles' arrest have never been in dispute. After the benefit of briefing and oral argument, the New York Court of Appeals, as previously noted, concluded that there was "no evidence in the record before us that there were exigent circumstances posing a risk to the public safety." . . . Upon reviewing the same facts and hearing the same arguments, a majority of this Court has come to precisely the opposite conclusion. . . .

If after plenary review two appellate courts so fundamentally differ over the threat to public safety presented by the simple and uncontested facts of this case, one must seriously question how law enforcement officers will respond to the majority's new rule in the confusion and haste of the real world. . . . Disagreements of the scope of the "public-safety" exception and mistakes in its application are inevitable. . . .

In fashioning its "public-safety" exception to *Miranda*, the majority makes no attempt to deal with the constitutional presumption established by that case. The majority does not argue that police questioning about issues of public safety is any less coercive than custodial interrogations into other matters. The majority's only contention is that police officers could more easily protect the public if *Miranda* did not apply to custodial interrogations concerning the public's safety. But *Miranda* was not a decision about public safety; it was a decision about coerced confessions. Without establishing that interrogations concerning the public's safety are less likely to be coercive than other interrogations, the majority cannot endorse the "public-safety" exception and remain faithful to the logic of *Miranda v. Arizona*. . . .

The majority should not be permitted to elude the [Fifth] Amendment's absolute prohibition simply by calculating special costs that arise when the public's safety is at issue. Indeed, were constitutional adjudication always conducted in such an ad hoc manner, the Bill of Rights would be a most unreliable protector of individual liberties. . . .

The **"public safety" exception** announced in this case was controversial, as evidenced by the divergent opinions among the justices. The idea that there might be threats to public safety that would require immediate action is not controversial. Dissenters, such as Justice Brennan, did not object to the idea that police officers might sometimes feel compelled to ask questions prior to providing *Miranda* warnings. However, they believed that if officers chose to take that approach, they should not benefit at the expense of the individual's rights. In other words, the officers could use Quarles's statements to find the gun, but in choosing to do so in the absence of *Miranda* warnings, they should not be able to use the gun and statements against him on the basis of the improperly obtained statements. Does this mean that an obviously guilty lawbreaker would go free? Not necessarily. Remember in Chapter 4 that the Supreme Court created an "inevitable discovery exception" to the exclusionary rule in the same year as *Quarles*. Under that concept, improperly obtained evidence can be used if it would have been discovered by the police eventually anyway. This concept could arguably have been applied to the *Quarles* situation, too.

One of the issues of debate within the case concerned whether the facts of *Quarles* actually justified the creation of a public safety exception. As the dissenters noted, the police could have searched the entire empty store without any danger to the public—and without questioning the suspect prior to giving the *Miranda* warnings. Critics of Justice Rehnquist have argued that the public safety exception was created in *Quarles* because the majority was looking for ways to give police officers increased flexibility, not because the case presented a truly compelling case for the protection of public safety.[7]

The public safety exception was questioned by both the dissenters and Justice O'Connor in her concurrence for making Fifth Amendment principles more difficult to understand. *Miranda* was a "bright-line rule." Officers were required to inform suspects of rights before any custodial questioning. *Quarles* made the rule much less clear. How will an officer know when a situation falls under the "public safety exception"? The majority acknowledged this concern but expressed confidence that this was a workable exception: "[W]e acknowledge that to some degree we lessen the desirable clarity of that rule. . . . We think police officers can and will distinguish almost instinctively between questions necessary to secure their own safety or the safety of the public and questions designed solely to elicit testimonial evidence from a suspect." Will it really be so easy for officers to know when the exception applies? Or will officers simply decide for themselves with the knowledge that judges are unlikely to second-guess decisions that were made in the heat of the apprehension of a suspected felon?

Because of uncertainty about whether judges will be willing to second-guess officers' determinations about public safety issues, there are questions about whether this is a "narrow" exception, as characterized by the majority, or whether this exception gives significant discretion and flexibility to police officers who can choose to skip *Miranda* warnings by claiming that they perceived a threat to public safety. This issue is likely to be a problem only when decisions are being made by officers who seek to exploit opportunities to avoid respecting constitutional rights. Most officers will always provide *Miranda* warnings for several reasons. First, they are trained to read rights automatically in the course of the arrest process. Second, they do not want to take the risk that evidence might be excluded because of their errors. Third, officers learn through experience that *Miranda* warnings are not necessarily an impediment to obtaining confessions because of questioning techniques used by officers and because of the previously discussed factors that lead suspects to talk despite being informed of the right to remain silent.

Note that Justice O'Connor's opinion also talked about the difference between **testimonial evidence** and **nontestimonial evidence**. According to the Supreme Court's decisions, the Fifth Amendment protection applies only to testimonial evidence, which normally means incriminating statements made by suspects. The Fifth Amendment does protect against the admission into evidence of nontestimonial evidence, such as objects or descriptions of behaviors manifested by the suspect. Thus O'Connor would have excluded Quarles's statement from evidence, but she would have permitted the gun to be used as evidence against him in court.

In another example of the distinction between types of evidence subject to examination under the Fifth Amendment, police could use evidence of a drunken-driving suspect's slurred speech and inability to answer questions, because such evidence was nontestimonial. By contrast, the police could not use as evidence a statement made by the same arrested suspect in response to a question that was posed prior to the delivery of *Miranda* warnings (*Pennsylvania v. Muniz*, 1990).

Coercive Questioning

In order to determine—after the fact—if *Miranda* warnings should have been given, the courts do not merely examine whether the suspect was in custody. They must also determine if interrogation occurred and, if so, whether it occurred in a coercive fashion. In *Oregon v. Mathiason* (1977), a parolee was told that the police would like to speak with him. He agreed to come to the police station. Once inside a room within the office, the officer closed the door, told the parolee that he wanted to discuss a burglary, and asserted, falsely, that the parolee's fingerprints had been found at the scene of the crime. The parolee confessed immediately. The officer then gave the parolee his *Miranda* warnings, and the confession was repeated. The Oregon Supreme Court disallowed the confession because it found that the confession occurred in a "coercive environment." However, the U.S. Supreme Court found the questioning acceptable. The justices noted that suspects are not entitled to *Miranda* warnings simply because questioning occurs at a police station. Suspects who come to police stations voluntarily are considered free to leave unless some specific circumstances indicate that the officer prevented the suspect from departing. Thus this context did fall within *Miranda*'s coverage of "custodial" questioning.

In *Illinois v. Perkins* (1990), a police undercover agent was planted in a jail cell to pose as an arrestee. One of the other detainees in the cell had been arrested on a battery charge. In the course of jail conversation, the agent asked his cellmate about an unsolved murder. The cellmate made incriminating statements in response to these questions. Even though the cellmate was clearly in police custody, the questioning did not constitute interrogation for *Miranda* purposes because he did not know that he was being questioned by a police officer. Because he did not know the other "prisoner" was a police officer, he could not feel that he was under police pressure to confess. Thus there was no coercion involved in this form of questioning.

The existence of interrogation itself is not always self-evident. In *Rhode Island v. Innis* (1980), police arrested a suspect for armed robbery. They informed him of his *Miranda* rights. The suspect indicated that he understood his rights and he asked to speak to a lawyer. Thus the officers were not allowed to question the suspect without his lawyer present. The officers were concerned about what had happened to the shotgun that was used in the robbery since it was not on the suspect when he was arrested shortly after the crime. They believed he had discarded or hidden the gun after committing the crime. While driving to the police station, the officers addressed each other in expressing concern about the location of the gun as the suspect sat handcuffed in the backseat. One officer later testified that he had said, "There's a lot of handicapped children running around in this area, and God forbid one of them might find a weapon with shells and they might hurt themselves." The suspect interrupted the officers and directed them to the location of the gun. The suspect said that he "wanted to get the gun out of the way because of the kids in the area in the school" located near the place where the gun was discarded.

The Rhode Island Supreme Court decided that the officers had improperly interrogated the suspect by holding this conversation that was likely to elicit an emotional response. The U.S. Supreme Court, however, disagreed. According to Justice Rehnquist's majority opinion:

> *The case thus boils down to whether, in the context of a brief conversation, the officers should have known that the [suspect] would suddenly be moved to make a self-incriminating response. Given the fact that the entire conversation appears to have consisted of no more than a few offhand remarks, we cannot say that the officers should have known that it was reasonably likely that [the suspect] would so respond. This is not a case where the police carried on a lengthy harangue in the presence of the suspect.*

> *Nor does the record support the [suspect's] contention that, under the cir-*
> *cumstances, the officers' comments were particularly "evocative." It is our*
> *view, therefore, that the respondent was not subjected by the police to*
> *words or actions that the police should have known were reasonably likely*
> *to elicit an incriminating response from him. (446 U.S. 291 at 303)*

Is there a risk that the *Innis* decision simply instructs officers on how to seek information from suspects who have asserted their right to remain silent? We must consider how Supreme Court decisions that clarify the applicability of precedents to different situations also serve to guide criminal justice officials on their options for developing strategies to avoid the impact of the underlying precedent. This may be especially true when the Court's composition changes and later justices do not agree completely with the decisions their predecessors established. If justices wish to dilute the impact of a precedent with which they disagree, they may decide cases concerning specific situations in which they say that the precedent does not apply. As you read about the Court's decisions defining exactly what police must tell suspects in the course of providing *Miranda* warnings, consider whether these decisions have altered the impact of *Miranda*.

The Content of *Miranda* Warnings

The *Miranda* decision was very specific about the content of the warnings that must be given to suspects prior to custodial questioning. According to Chief Justice Warren's opinion, "Prior to any questioning, the person must be warned that he has a right to remain silent, that any statement he does make may be used as evidence against him, and that he has a right to the presence of an attorney, either retained or appointed." Stated in this fashion, the warnings appear clear and direct. What happens, however, if police officers add extra information, leave out information, or state the warnings in a manner that differs from the description provided by Chief Justice Warren? As you read *Duckworth v. Eagan* (1989) in the following box, consider whether the warnings given by the officers posed a risk of confusing the suspect about the nature of his rights.

Many people had believed that warnings must be given exactly as described by Chief Justice Warren's opinion in the *Miranda* case. Indeed, many law enforcement agencies train their officers either to give the warnings exactly as described in the *Miranda* case or to read such precise warnings from a prepared "Miranda warning card." However, the *Duckworth* decision made clear that the warnings do not need to be given by using a specific set of words. Rehnquist's opinion focused on whether the warnings, as given by the officers, presented the essential elements of the warnings. Although the dissenters expressed the view that the warnings in the case could confuse suspects about the nature of their rights, Rehnquist and the majority did not believe that the altered warnings would cause that effect. The decision gave police officers flexibility in presenting the warnings. *Duckworth* spares officers from the risk that a confession will be excluded merely because they present the warnings in a slightly altered fashion. On the other hand, the decision also creates the risk that officers may intentionally alter the warnings in the hope that suspects will be confused or otherwise dissuaded from asserting the right to remain silent. As with other rights, the full enjoyment of legal protections by the public depends significantly on the ethics and professionalism of police officers and other officials in the criminal justice system. As you examine the version of the *Miranda* warnings

Duckworth v. Eagan, 492 U.S. 195 (1989)

[*The defendant was identified by a woman as her attacker who had stabbed her nine times and left her for dead. Before being questioned by police, the defendant signed a waiver form that included the following statement among the usual elements of the* Miranda *warnings: "We have no way of giving you a lawyer, but one will be appointed for you, if you wish, if and when you go to court." The defendant maintained that he was innocent during initial questioning. The following day, however, after being read the traditional* Miranda *rights by officers, he confessed to the crime. At trial, the defendant challenged the first* Miranda *warnings as defective, but the judge permitted the confession to be used against him. He was convicted and state appellate courts upheld his conviction. When he challenged his conviction through a habeas corpus petition in the federal courts, the U.S. Court of Appeals reversed his conviction by deciding that the initial* Miranda *warnings did not clearly indicate to him that he was entitled to representation by an attorney during questioning. The U.S. Supreme Court considered whether the phrasing of the* Miranda *warnings fulfilled the requirements of the Constitution.*]

CHIEF JUSTICE REHNQUIST delivered the opinion of the Court.

Respondent confessed to stabbing a woman nine times after she refused to have sexual relations with him, and he was convicted of attempted murder. Before confessing, respondent was given warnings by the police, which included the advice that a lawyer would be appointed "if and when you go to court." The United States Court of Appeals for the Seventh Circuit held that such advice did not comply with the requirements of *Miranda v. Arizona* . . . (1966). We disagree and reverse. . . .

We have never insisted that *Miranda* warnings be given in the exact form described in that decision. In *Miranda* itself, the Court said that "[t]he warnings required and the waiver necessary in accordance with our opinion today are, *in the absence of a fully effective equivalent,* prerequisites to the admissibility of any statement made by a defendant?" (emphasis added) 384 U.S. at 476. . . .

We think the initial warnings given to respondent touched all of the bases required by *Miranda.* The police told respondent that he had the right to remain silent, that anything he said could be used against him in court, that he had the right to speak to an attorney before and during questioning, that he had "this right to the advice and presence of a lawyer even if [he could] not afford to hire one," and that he had the "right to stop answering at any time until [he] talked to a lawyer." . . . As noted, the police also added that they could not provide respondent with a lawyer, but that one would be appointed "if and when you go to court." The Court of Appeals thought this "if and when you go to court" language suggested that "only those accused who can afford an attorney have the right to have one present before answering any questions," and "implie[d] that if the accused does not 'go to court,' *i.e.*[,] the government does not file charges, the accused is not entitled to counsel at all." . . .

In our view, the Court of Appeals misapprehended the effect of the inclusion of "if and when you go to court" language in *Miranda* warnings. First, this instruction accurately described the procedure for the appointment of counsel in Indiana. Under Indiana law, counsel is appointed at the defendant's initial appearance in court, . . . and formal charges must be filed at or before that hearing. . . . We think it must be relatively commonplace for a suspect after receiving *Miranda* warnings, to ask *when* he will obtain counsel. The "if and when you go to court" advice simply anticipates that question. Second, *Miranda* does not require that attorneys be producible on call, but only that the suspect be informed, as here, that he has the right to an attorney before and during questioning, and that an attorney would be appointed for him if he could not afford one. The Court in *Miranda* emphasized that it was not suggesting that "each police station must have a 'station house lawyer' present at all times to advise prisoners." . . . If the police cannot provide appointed counsel, *Miranda* requires only that the police not question a suspect unless he waives his right to counsel. . . . Here, respondent did just that. . . .

[Justice O'Connor's concurring opinion, joined by Justice Scalia, is omitted.]

JUSTICE MARSHALL, with whom JUSTICE BRENNAN, JUSTICE BLACKMUN, and JUSTICE STEVENS join, dissenting.

The majority holds today that a police warning advising a suspect that he is entitled to an appointed lawyer only "if and when he goes to court" satisfies the requirements of *Miranda v. Arizona.* . . . The majority reaches this result by seriously mischaracterizing that decision. Under *Miranda,* a police warning must *"clearly infor[m]"* a suspect taken into custody "that if he cannot afford an attorney one will be appointed for him *prior to any questioning* if he so desires?" . . . (emphasis added). A warning qualified by an "if and when you go to court" caveat does nothing of the kind; instead, it leads the suspect to believe that a lawyer will not be provided until some indeterminate time in the future *after questioning.* I refuse to acquiesce in the continuing debasement of this historic precedent [citing *Oregon v. Elstad,* 1985 and *New York v. Quarles,* 1984], . . . and therefore I dissent. . . .

In concluding that the first warning given to respondent Eagan, . . . satisfies the dictates of *Miranda,* the majority makes a mockery of that decision. Eagan was initially advised that he had the right to the presence of counsel before and during questioning. But in the very next breath, the police informed Eagan that, if he could not afford a lawyer, one would be appointed to represent him only "if and when" he went to court. As the Court of Appeals found, Eagan could easily have concluded from the "if and when" caveat that only "those accused who can afford an attorney have the right to have one present before answering any questions; those who are not so fortunate must wait." . . . Eagan was, after all, never told that questioning would be *delayed* until a lawyer was appointed "if and when" Eagan did, in fact, go to court. Thus, the "if and when" caveat may well have had the effect of negating the initial promise that counsel could be present. At best, a suspect like Eagan "would not know . . . whether or not he had a right to the services of a lawyer." . . .

In lawyerlike fashion, the Chief Justice parses the initial warnings given Eagan and finds that the most plausible interpretation is that Eagan would not be questioned until a lawyer was appointed when he later appeared in court. What goes wholly overlooked in the Chief Justice's analysis is that the recipients of police warnings are often frightened suspects unlettered in law, not lawyers or judges or others schooled in interpreting legal or semantic nuance. Such suspects can hardly be expected to interpret, in as facile a manner as the Chief Justice, "the pretzel-like warnings here—intertwining, contradictory, and ambiguous as they are." . . . The majority thus refuses to recognize that "[t]he warning of a right to counsel would be hollow if not couched in terms that would convey to the indigent—the person most often subjected to interrogation—the knowledge that he too has the right to have counsel present." . . .

Even if the typical suspect could draw the inference the majority does—that questioning will not commence until a lawyer is provided at a later court appearance—a warning qualified by an "if and

when" caveat still fails to give a suspect any indication of *when* he will be taken to court. Upon hearing the warnings given in this case, a suspect would likely conclude that no lawyer would be provided until trial. In common parlance, "going to court" is synonymous with "going to trial." Furthermore, the negative implication of the caveat is that, if the suspect is never taken to court, he "is not entitled to an attorney at all." . . . An unwitting suspect harboring uncertainty on this score is precisely the sort of person who may feel compelled to talk "voluntarily" to the police, without the presence of counsel, in an effort to extricate himself from his predicament:

> "The suspect is effectively told that he can talk now or remain in custody—in an alien, friendless, harsh world—for an indeterminate length of time. To the average accused, still hoping at this stage to be home on time, the implication that his choice is to answer questions right away or remain in custody until that nebulous time 'if and when' he goes to court is a coerced choice of the most obvious kind." Dickerson v. State . . . (1972) [Indiana state court opinion].

. . .

But if a suspect does not understand that a lawyer will be made available within a reasonable period of time after he has been taken into custody and advised of his rights, the suspect may decide to talk to the police *for that reason alone.* The threat of an indefinite deferral of interrogation, in a system like Indiana's, thus constitutes an effective means by which the police can pressure a suspect to speak without the presence of counsel. Sanctioning such police practices simply because the warnings given do not misrepresent state law does nothing more than let the state-law tail wag the federal constitutional dog. . . .

It poses no great burden on law enforcement officers to eradicate the confusion stemming from the "if and when" caveat. Deleting the sentence containing the offending language is all that needs to be done. . . . Purged of this language, the warning tells the suspect in a straightforward fashion that he has the right to the presence of a lawyer before and during questioning, and that a lawyer will be appointed if he cannot afford one. The suspect is given no reason to believe that the appointment of an attorney may come after interrogation. To the extent one doubts that it is the "if and when" caveat that is the source of the confusion, compare the initial warning given Eagan, . . . and the crystal-clear warning currently used by the FBI. . . . The majority's claim that the two are indistinguishable in the message conveyed to a suspect defies belief. I dissent.

Police officers tell an arrestee upon arrest:

"You can stay quiet if you want. That's your right. If you do the smart thing, the right thing—and that means telling us just what happened—we can use that information, but we can also use it to help you with the prosecutor and the judge. You can ask for an attorney if you want. If you do, we're supposed to get you one eventually, but we don't know if we can get one right now. The bottom line is that you know and we know that you would be talking to us and helping us unless you really have something to hide."

If you were a defense attorney, what arguments would you make about this form of the *Miranda* warnings? What would you say as a prosecutor? Imagine that you are a judge. How would you decide a request by the defense to exclude any confession from evidence? Whether or not you believe these warnings are proper, do you think that they are consistent with the intentions of the justices who decided the *Miranda* case?

presented in the above box, ask yourself whether they are consistent with ethical performance by police officers.

THE CHALLENGE TO *MIRANDA*

Critics of the *Miranda* decision continually put forward arguments about the warnings being illegitimate and undesirable.[8] The 1990s saw a flurry of academic articles debating the consequences of *Miranda*. The author of many of these articles was Paul Cassell, a University of Utah law professor, who devoted himself to a crusade against *Miranda* warnings. Cassell claimed that the warnings caused hundreds of thousands of crimes to go unsolved.[9] Although many police officers claimed that *Miranda* was not a major impediment to law enforcement and that it helped to professionalize police practices, legal critics continued to develop arguments and strategies for challenging *Miranda*.

In 1999, *Miranda*'s critics achieved a major legal victory. The Fourth Circuit U.S. Court of Appeals heard a case concerning a suspected bank robber's confession that was excluded from evidence because of a *Miranda* violation. The court considered the applicability of Title 18, United States Code, section 3501, a statute passed by Congress in the aftermath of the original *Miranda* decision in the 1960s. The statute said that the requirements of *Miranda* do not apply to federal law enforcement officers and that the admissibility of confessions made by suspects in federal cases will be made by using the old voluntariness standard. The statute had remained on the books for thirty years, but it had never been used because the U.S. Justice Department had never sought to have courts recognize the statute. The appellate court surprised the legal community when it said that the statute was valid and that the *Miranda* warnings were not really required by the Constitution (*United States v. Dickerson*, 4th Cir. U.S. Court of Appeals, 1999). The case next moved to the U.S. Supreme Court. As you read *Dickerson v. United States* (2000) in the box at right, ask yourself whether you agree with the reasoning in the majority opinion. Does the opinion have a strong basis for reaching the conclusion that it does?

Dickerson v. United States, 530 U.S. 428 (2000)

CHIEF JUSTICE REHNQUIST delivered the opinion of the Court.

In *Miranda v. Arizona* . . . (1966), we held that certain warnings must be given before a suspect's statement made during custodial interrogation could be admitted in evidence. In the wake of that decision, Congress enacted 18 U.S.C. [section] 3501 which in essence laid down a rule that the admissibility of such statements should turn only on whether or not they were voluntarily made. We hold that *Miranda,* being a constitutional decision of this Court, may not be in effect overruled by an Act of Congress, and we decline to overrule *Miranda* ourselves. We therefore hold that *Miranda* and its progeny in this Court govern the admissibility of statements made during custodial interrogation in both state and federal courts.

Petitioner Dickerson was indicted for bank robbery, conspiracy to commit bank robbery, and using a firearm in the course of committing a crime of violence, all in violation of the applicable provisions of Title 18 of the United States Code. Before trial, Dickerson moved to suppress a statement he had made at a Federal Bureau of Investigation field office, on the grounds that he had not received "*Miranda* warnings" before being interrogated. . . . [The Fourth Circuit U.S. Court of Appeals] agreed with the District Court's conclusion that petitioner had not received *Miranda* warnings before making his statement. But it went on to hold that [section] 3501, which in effect makes the admissibility of statements such as Dickerson's turn solely on whether they were made voluntarily, was satisfied in this case. It then concluded that our decision in *Miranda* was not a constitutional holding, and that therefore Congress could by statute have the final say on the question of admissibility. . . .

We have never abandoned [our pre-*Miranda*] due process jurisprudence, and thus continue to exclude confessions that were obtained involuntarily. But our decisions in *Malloy v. Hogan* . . . (1964) and *Miranda* changed the focus of much of the inquiry in determining the admissibility of suspects' incriminating statements. In *Malloy,* we held that the Fifth Amendment's Self-Incrimination Clause is incorporated in the Due Process Clause of the Fourteenth Amendment and thus applies to the States. . . . We decided *Miranda* on the heels of *Malloy.*

In *Miranda,* we noted that the advent of modern custodial police interrogation brought with it an increased concern about confessions obtained by coercion. . . . Because custodial police interrogation, by its very nature, isolates and pressures the individual, we stated that "[e]ven without employing brutality, the 'third degree' or [other] specific stratagems, . . . custodial interrogation exacts a heavy toll on individual liberty and trades on the weakness of individuals. . . . We concluded that the coercion inherent in custodial interrogation blurs the line between voluntary and involuntary statements, and thus heightens the risk that an individual will not be "accorded his privilege under the Fifth Amendment . . . not to be compelled to incriminate himself." . . . Accordingly, we laid down "concrete constitutional guidelines for law enforcement agencies and courts to follow." . . .

The law in this area is clear. This Court has supervisory authority over the federal courts, and we may use that authority to prescribe rules of evidence and procedure that are binding in those tribunals. . . . Congress retains the ultimate authority to modify or set aside any judicially created rules of evidence and procedure that are not required by the Constitution. . . .

But Congress may not legislatively supersede our decisions interpreting and applying the Constitution. . . . This case therefore turns on whether the *Miranda* Court announced a constitutional rule or merely exercised its supervisory authority to regulate evidence in the absence of congressional direction. Recognizing this point, the Court of Appeals surveyed *Miranda* and its progeny to determine the constitutional status of the *Miranda* decision. . . . Relying on the fact that we have created several exceptions to *Miranda*'s warnings requirement and that we have repeatedly referred to the *Miranda* warnings as "prophylactic" [quoting *New York v. Quarles* (1984)] . . . and "not themselves rights protected by the Constitution" [quoting *Michigan v. Tucker* (1974)], the Court of Appeals concluded that the protections announced in *Miranda* are not constitutionally required. . . .

We disagree with the Court of Appeals' conclusion, although we concede that there is language in some of our opinions that supports the view taken by that court. But first and foremost of the factors on the other side—that *Miranda* is a constitutional decision—is that both *Miranda* and two of its companion cases applied the rule to proceedings in state courts. . . . Since that time, we have consistently applied *Miranda*'s rule to prosecutions arising in

(continued)

state court. . . . With respect to proceedings in state courts, our "authority is limited to enforcing the commands of the United States Constitution." . . .

The *Miranda* opinion itself begins by stating that the Court granted certiorari "to explore some facets of the problems . . . of applying the privilege against self-incrimination to in-custody interrogation, *and to give concrete constitutional guidelines for law enforcement agencies and courts to follow.* . . . In fact, the majority opinion is replete with statements indicating that the majority thought it was announcing a constitutional rule. Indeed, the Court's ultimate conclusion was that the unwarned confessions obtained in the four cases before the Court in *Miranda* "were obtained from the defendant under circumstances that did not meet constitutional standards for protection of the privilege." . . .

The Court of Appeals also relied on the fact that we have, after our *Miranda* decision, made exceptions from its rule in cases such as *New York v. Quarles* . . . (1984) and *Harris v. New York* . . . (1971). . . . But we have also broadened the application of the *Miranda* doctrine in cases such as *Doyle v. Ohio* . . . (1976) and *Arizona v. Roberson* . . . (1988). These decisions illustrate the principle—not that *Miranda* is not a constitutional rule—but that no constitutional rule is immutable. No court laying down a general rule can possibly foresee the various circumstances in which counsel will seek to apply it, and the sort of modifications represented by these cases are as much a normal part of constitutional law as the original decision. . . .

Whether or not we would agree with *Miranda*'s reasoning and its resulting rule, were we addressing the issue in the first instance, the principles of *stare decisis* weigh heavily against overruling it now. . . .

We do not think there is such justification for overruling *Miranda*. *Miranda* has become embedded in routine police practice to the point where the warnings have become part of our national culture. . . . Our subsequent cases have reduced the impact of the *Miranda* rule on legitimate law enforcement while reaffirming the decision's core ruling that unwarned statements may not be used as evidence in the prosecution's case in chief.

The disadvantage of the *Miranda* rule is that statements which may be by no means involuntary, made by a defendant who is aware of his "rights," may nonetheless be excluded and a guilty defendant go free as a result. But experience suggests that the totality-of-circumstances test which [section] 3501 seeks to revive is more difficult than *Miranda* for

law enforcement officers to conform to, and for courts to apply in a consistent manner. . . .

In sum, we conclude that *Miranda* announced a constitutional rule that Congress may not supersede legislatively. Following the rule of *stare decisis*, we decline to overrule *Miranda* ourselves. The judgment of the Court of Appeals is therefore *Reversed*.

JUSTICE SCALIA, with whom JUSTICE THOMAS joins, dissenting.

. . .

. . . [T]o justify today's agreed-upon result, the Court must adopt a significant *new*, if not entirely comprehensible, principle of constitutional law. As the Court chooses to describe that principle, statutes of Congress can be disregarded, not only when what they prescribe violates the Constitution, but when what they prescribe contradicts a decision of this Court that "announced a constitutional rule." . . . That is an immense and frightening antidemocratic power, and it does not exist. . . .

. . . Moreover, history and precedent aside, the decision in *Miranda*, if read as an explication of what the Constitution *requires*, is preposterous. There is, for example, simply no basis in reason for concluding that a response to the very first question asked, by a suspect who already *knows* all of the rights described in the *Miranda* warning, is anything other than a volitional act. . . . And even if one assumes that the elimination of compulsion absolutely requires informing even the most knowledgeable suspect of his right to remain silent, it cannot conceivably require the right to have *counsel* present. There is a world of difference, which the Court recognized under the traditional voluntariness test but ignored in *Miranda*, between compelling a suspect to incriminate himself and preventing him from foolishly doing so of his own accord. Only the latter (which is *not* required by the Constitution) could explain the Court's inclusion of a right to counsel and the requirement that it, too, be knowingly and intelligently waived. Counsel's presence is not required to tell the suspect that he *need* not speak; the interrogators can do that. The only good reason for having counsel there is that he can be counted on to advise the suspect that he *should* not speak. . . .

. . . Nonthreatening attempts to persuade the suspect to reconsider that initial decision [to remain silent] are not, without more, enough to render a change of heart the product of anything other than the suspect's free will. Thus, what is more remarkable about the *Miranda* decision—and what made it unacceptable as a matter of straightforward constitutional interpretation . . .—is its palpable hostility toward the act of confession *per se,* rather than toward what the Constitution abhors, *compelled* confession. . . . The Constitution is not, unlike the *Miranda* majority, offended by a criminal's commendable qualm of conscience or fortunate fit of stupidity. . . .

Today's judgment converts *Miranda* from a milestone of judicial overreaching into the very Cheops' Pyramid (or perhaps the Sphinx would be a better analogue) of judicial arrogance. In imposing its Court-made code upon the States, the original opinion at least *asserted* that it was demanded by the Constitution. Today's decision does not pretend that it is—and yet *still* asserts the right to impose it against the will of the people's representatives in Congress. Far from believing that *stare decisis* compels this result, I believe we cannot allow to remain on the books even a celebrated decision—*especially* a celebrated decision—that has come to stand for the proposition that the Supreme Court has power to impose extraconstitutional constraints upon Congress and the States. This is not the system that was established by the Framers, or that would be established by any sane supporter of government by the people. . . .

The Supreme Court declared that the *Miranda* decision was based on the Constitution and was not merely a rule created by the justices as a well-intentioned policy for police practice. Although Congress can undo Supreme Court decisions that interpret statutes by passing new statutes that clarify the intended meaning of legislation, Congress cannot pass legislation to alter court decisions interpreting the Constitution. Although most analysts considered the Supreme Court in 2000 to be dominated by a majority of justices who tend to favor law enforcement interests more than broad protection of individuals' rights, the Court firmly endorsed and preserved *Miranda* warnings. Moreover, the *Dickerson* decision was written by one of the Court's most conservative justices, Chief Justice Rehnquist. Among the justices, Rehnquist is always one of the most consistent supporters of decisions to grant broader authority and discretion to law enforcement officials.

Why did the Court preserve *Miranda*? The original *Miranda* decision had a debatable basis. Nothing in the words of the Fifth Amendment indicates that police officers must provide warnings to suspects. Moreover, there was no tradition in legal history for providing such warnings. The decision was obviously produced as a matter of interpretation by justices who were concerned about evidence throughout history of abusive behavior directed by police toward crime suspects. Clearly, there is some disagreement among the justices about whether that interpretation was based on the Constitution. In addition, the majority in *Dickerson* expressed the idea that *Miranda* warnings had become thoroughly integrated and accepted in American legal culture and police practice. Is this a strong argument for preserving a controversial precedent? As indicated by the questions raised in the box on the next page, lurking beneath the entire discussion is a growing recognition that police adaptations to *Miranda* have diminished the frequency with which *Miranda* impedes police officers' interests in gathering evidence. If there was clear proof that *Miranda* prevents crimes from being solved, do you think the justices would have argued that it should be preserved because it has become part of culture and tradition?

RIGHT TO COUNSEL UNDER *MIRANDA*

The *Miranda* decision gave suspects an entitlement to the assistance of an attorney during custodial questioning. This right to counsel is closely connected to the Fifth Amendment privilege against compelled self-incrimination. The

The Impact of *Miranda*

To what extent does *Miranda* provide the protections envisioned by Chief Justice Warren? Police officers have developed strategies and techniques for questioning suspects without *Miranda* warnings preventing those suspects from supplying incriminating statements. Police officers seek ways to question suspects before taking them into custody. For example, they ask suspects to voluntarily come to the police station to answer questions. They also present *Miranda* warnings in ways that may lead suspects to think that a request for a lawyer or an assertion of the right to remain silent will be regarded as an admission of guilt. Officers also employ questioning techniques through which they seek to gain the trust of suspects by pretending to be sympathetic or friendly. In addition, many guilty suspects have a strong self-interest in cooperating and providing information. Does *Miranda* actually protect against abusive police practices? Does it merely serve as a symbolic reminder to police and the public that law enforcement officials are supposed to respect the rights of criminal suspects?

---

precedent set by the Supreme Court in *Escobedo v. Illinois* (1964) says that police may not prevent arrestees from seeing their attorneys when they have requested assistance of counsel during questioning. *Massiah v. New York* (1966) prohibits the police from using undercover agents or informants to question suspects who are already represented by counsel. *Massiah*, in particular, provides a basis for constitutional claims because police often use jailhouse informants as witnesses against other jail inmates. Hypothetically, the police instruct their informants to simply listen to their cellmates and not ask questions. In reality, however, there are many problems with jailhouse informants. These problems concern both their compliance with proper procedures and their truthfulness, especially when they have been promised that their own charges will be dismissed if they testify about hearing incriminating statements made by others in the jail.

Waiver of Rights

The right to have an attorney present during custodial questioning may be waived by the suspect. Unlike other waivers of rights, such as consent searches, in which the courts assume that people know their rights, *Miranda* places an obligation on criminal justice officials to show that people knowingly and intelligently waived their privilege against compelled self-incrimination and right to counsel. This does not require, however, that the suspect explicitly state that he or she is waiving *Miranda* rights. If suspects are read their rights and temporarily remain silent, but then begin to talk, the courts may regard their behavior as indicating that they are knowingly and intelligently waiving their rights (*North Carolina v. Butler,* 1979).

The suspect's mental state and physical condition may be relevant to the assessment of whether a valid waiver has been made. In *Colorado v. Connelly* (1986), an individual approached a police officer on the street and said that he wanted to talk about a homicide that he had committed. After being given *Miranda* warnings, he showed the officers the location of the crime and continued to talk about the killing. It later turned out that he was mentally ill and that he thought he had been commanded by God to confess. The Supreme Court found the confession to be admissible, despite his condition, because the police had done nothing to coerce him. By contrast, the Court has excluded confessions by injured suspects who were questioned in their hospital beds while medicated and in severe pain (*Beecher v. Alabama*, 1972; *Mincey v. Arizona*, 1978).

If a suspect asserts the right to remain silent, police officers are supposed to cease all questioning. However, the Court has permitted police to resume questioning later if they repeat *Miranda* warnings and focus on crimes other than those that were the subject of the initial questioning (*Michigan v. Mosley*, 1975). The Court may permit questioning about the same crime if *Miranda* warnings are made clear, the suspect agrees to talk, and the police do not appear intent on wearing down or badgering the suspect over a long period of time.

Suspects are permitted to waive their right to have an attorney present during custodial questioning after they have been informed of their *Miranda* rights. During custodial questioning by police officers, if suspects do not clearly assert their right to counsel, then an indication of waiver can provide the basis for permitting incriminating statements and confessions to be placed into evidence. In *Edwards v. Arizona* (1981), the suspect being questioned said that he wanted to see an attorney before making any deal. He refused to talk to police officers until they told him that he "had to" talk to them. Then he was read his *Miranda* rights again, and he made incriminating statements. The Supreme Court excluded those statements from evidence by asserting the rule that suspects who express a desire to deal with the police only through an attorney cannot be questioned further until the attorney is made available or the suspect initiates further communications with the police. Moreover, once the right is asserted, police cannot attempt to ask the suspect about separate crimes until the lawyer has been provided (*Arizona v. Roberson*, 1988). The lawyer must actually be present during questioning. The fact that a suspect has consulted with a lawyer outside of police presence does not give police permission to begin questioning anew when the right has been asserted (*Minnick v. Mississippi*, 1990). The provision of counsel does preclude the possibility that the police may question a suspect concerning other offenses. In *Texas v. Cobb* (2001), a burglary suspect who was represented by counsel for that charge was questioned by police concerning the disappearance of family members from the burglarized house. The suspect was informed of his *Miranda* warnings and waived his right to counsel before confessing to murdering the missing people. When he later claimed that the police should not have questioned him outside the presence of the attorney representing him on the burglary charge, the Supreme Court emphasized that assertions of the right to counsel apply to specific offenses. The defendant should have asserted his right to counsel for the murder case under investigation if he wanted the police questioning to cease.

By contrast, when a juvenile in *Fare v. Michael C.* (1979) expressed the desire to talk to his probation officer prior to questioning, that was not considered a request for assistance of counsel even though it was clearly an expressed desire for assistance from an adult authority figure. Indeed, the Court has required suspects to make a very clear assertion of a desire to speak to a lawyer in order to have questioning cease. In *Davis v. United States* (1994), the suspect's statement "Maybe I should talk to a lawyer" was not considered as a request for an attorney.

Waiver and Knowledge of Representation

What happens if the suspect does not have complete information about the availability of a defense attorney? In *Moran v. Burbine* (1986), the police knew that a defense attorney was ready to come to the station to be present during questioning, but the suspect was not told that his sister had already obtained an attorney's services for him. As you read the Supreme Court's opinion in *Moran*, ask yourself whether a waiver of the right to counsel should be valid when the defendant was not fully informed of the facts concerning his current representation.

C A S E   *Moran v. Burbine*, 475 U.S. 412 (1986)

[*After Cranston, Rhode Island, police arrested Brian Burbine for burglary, they realized that information previously obtained from a confidential informant indicated that Burbine might be the person responsible for an unsolved murder in Providence, Rhode Island, the previous year. Providence police officers came to the Cranston station at about 7 p.m. to question Burbine. Meanwhile, Burbine's sister, who was unaware that her brother was a murder suspect, telephoned the public defender's office to secure representation for Burbine on the burglary charge. At 8:15 p.m. a public defender telephoned the Cranston detective bureau at the police station to inform the police that she would represent Burbine and to inquire whether the police intended to question him that evening. The attorney was told that Burbine would not be questioned until the following morning. The attorney was not informed that Burbine was a murder suspect or that the Providence police had arrived in Cranston to question him. Shortly thereafter, Burbine was taken to an interrogation room for the first of a series of questioning sessions. He was given his* Miranda *warnings prior to each session, and he signed statements waiving his rights prior to signing a murder confession. The police did not inform Burbine that his sister had secured an attorney to represent him or that the attorney had offered to come to the station to advise Burbine if the police wished to question him. After being convicted of first degree murder, Burbine unsuccessfully filed an appeal with the Rhode Island Supreme Court alleging that his Fifth Amendment rights were violated. After losing his state appeals, Burbine filed a habeas corpus petition in the federal courts. He*

lost *his claim in a U.S. district court, but a U.S. court of appeals ruled that the police had violated his privilege against compelled self-incrimination and his right to counsel by not informing him of the attorney's call on his behalf before he waived his Fifth Amendment rights. The U.S. Supreme Court faced the issue of whether Burbine's confession should be rendered inadmissible because of a violation of his Fifth Amendment rights.*]

JUSTICE O'CONNOR delivered the opinion of the Court.

. . .

We granted certiorari to decide whether a prearraignment confession preceded by an otherwise valid waiver must be suppressed either because the police misinformed an inquiring attorney about their plans concerning the suspect or because they failed to inform the suspect of the attorney's efforts to reach him. . . . We now reverse [the Court of Appeals decision upholding Burbine's claim]. . . .

[W]e have no doubt that the respondent validly waived his right to remain silent and to the presence of counsel. The voluntariness of the waiver is not at issue. . . . Nor is there any question about respondent's comprehension of the full panoply of rights set out in the *Miranda* warnings and of the potential consequences of a decision to relinquish them. Nonetheless, the Court of Appeals believed that the "[d]eliberate or reckless" conduct of the police, in particular their failure to inform respondent of the telephone call, fatally undermined the validity of an otherwise proper waiver. . . . We find this conclusion untenable as a matter of both logic and precedent.

Events occurring outside of the presence of the suspect and entirely unknown to him surely can have no bearing on the capacity to comprehend and knowingly relinquish a constitutional right. . . . No doubt the additional information would have been useful to respondent; perhaps even it might have affected his decision to confess. But we have never read the Constitution to require that the police supply a suspect with a flow of information to help him to calibrate his self-interest in deciding whether to speak or stand by his rights. . . . Once it is determined that a suspect's decision not to rely on his rights was uncoerced, that he at all times knew he could stand mute and request a lawyer, and that he was aware of the State's intention to use his statements to secure a conviction, the analysis is complete and the waiver is valid as a matter of law. The Court of Appeals' conclusion to the contrary was in error.

Nor do we believe that the level of the police's culpability in failing to inform respondent of the telephone call [from the attorney] has any bearing on the validity of the waivers. . . . [W]hether intentional or inadvertent, the state of mind of the police is irrelevant to the question of the intelligence and voluntariness of respondent's election to abandon his rights. Although highly inappropriate, even deliberate deception of an attorney could not possibly affect a suspect's decision to waive his *Miranda* rights unless he were at least aware of the incident. . . . Nor was the failure to inform respondent of the telephone call the kind of "trick[ery]" [discussed in the *Miranda* opinion] that can vitiate the validity of a waiver. . . . Granting that the "deliberate or reckless" withholding of information is objectionable as a matter of ethics, such conduct is only relevant to the constitutional validity of a waiver if it deprives a defendant of knowledge essential to his ability to understand the nature of his rights and the consequences of abandoning them. Because respondent's voluntary decision to speak was made with the full awareness and comprehension of all the information *Miranda* requires the police to convey, the waivers were valid. . . .

At the outset, while we share respondent's distaste for the deliberate misleading of an officer of the court, reading *Miranda* to forbid police deception of an *attorney* "would cut [the decision] completely loose from its own explicitly stated rationale." . . . As is now well established, "[t]he . . . *Miranda* warnings are 'not themselves rights protected by the Constitution but [are] instead measures to insure that the [suspect's] right against compulsory self-incrimination [is] protected.'" . . . Their

objective is not to mold police conduct for its own sake. Nothing in the Constitution vests in us the authority to mandate a code of behavior for state officials wholly unconnected to any federal right or privilege. The purpose of the *Miranda* warnings instead is to dissipate the compulsion inherent in custodial interrogation and, in so doing, guard against abridgement of the suspect's Fifth Amendment rights. Clearly, a rule that focused on how the police treat an attorney—conduct that has no relevance at all to the degree of compulsion experienced by the defendant during interrogation—would ignore both *Miranda*'s mission and its only source of legitimacy.

Nor are we prepared to adopt a rule requiring that the police inform a suspect of an attorney's efforts to reach him. While such a rule might add marginally to *Miranda*'s goal of dispelling the compulsion inherent in custodial interrogation, overriding practical considerations counsel against its adoption. As we have stressed on numerous occasions, "[o]ne of the principal advantages" of *Miranda* is the ease and clarity of its application. . . . We have little doubt that the approach urged by respondent and endorsed by the Court of Appeals would have the inevitable consequence of muddying *Miranda*'s otherwise relatively clear waters. The legal questions it would spawn are legion: To what extent should the police be held accountable for knowing that the accused has counsel? Is it enough that someone in the station house know of counsel's efforts to contact the suspect? Do counsel's efforts to talk to the suspect concerning one criminal investigation trigger the obligation to inform the defendant before interrogation may proceed on a wholly separate matter? We are unwilling to modify *Miranda* in a manner that would so clearly undermine the decision's central "virtue of informing police and prosecutors with specificity . . . what they may do in conducting [a] custodial interrogation, and of informing courts under what circumstances statements obtained during such interrogation are not admissible." . . .

Moreover, problems of clarity to one side, reading *Miranda* to require the police in each instance to inform a suspect of an attorney's efforts to reach him would work a substantial and, we think, inappropriate shift in the subtle balance struck in that decision. Custodial interrogations implicate two competing concerns. On the one hand, "the need for police questioning as a tool for effective enforcement of criminal laws" cannot be doubted. . . . Admissions of guilt are more than merely "desirable[;]" . . . they are essential to society's compelling interest in finding, convicting, and punishing those who violate

(continued)

the law. On the other hand, the Court has recognized that the interrogation process is "inherently coercive" and that, as a consequence, there exists a substantial risk that the police will inadvertently traverse the fine line between legitimate efforts to elicit admissions and constitutionally impermissible compulsion. . . . *Miranda* attempted to reconcile these opposing concerns by giving the *defendant* the power to exert some control over the course of the interrogation. . . .

The position urged by respondent would upset this carefully drawn approach in a manner that is both unnecessary for the protection of the Fifth Amendment privilege and injurious to legitimate law enforcement. Because, as *Miranda* holds, full comprehension of the rights to remain silent and request an attorney are sufficient to dispel whatever coercion is inherent in the interrogation process, a rule requiring the police to inform the suspect of an attorney's efforts to contact him would contribute to the protection of the Fifth Amendment privilege only incidentally, if at all. This minimal benefit, however, would come at a substantial cost to society's legitimate and substantial interest in securing admissions of guilt. . . .

We acknowledge that a number of state courts have reached a contrary conclusion. . . . We recognize also that our interpretation of the Federal Constitution . . . is at odds with the policy recommendations embodied in the American Bar Association Standards of Criminal Justice. . . . Nothing we say today disables the States from adopting different requirements for the conduct of its employees and officials as a matter of state law. We hold only that the Court of Appeals erred in construing the Fifth Amendment to the Federal Constitution to require the exclusion of respondent's three confessions.

[Justice O'Connor's discussion and rejection of Burbine's Sixth Amendment arguments are omitted.]

JUSTICE STEVENS, with whom JUSTICE BRENNAN and JUSTICE MARSHALL join, dissenting.

This case poses fundamental questions about our system of justice. As this Court has long recognized, and reaffirmed only weeks ago, "ours is an accusatorial and not an inquisitorial system." . . . The Court's opinion today represents a startling departure from that basic insight.

The Court concludes that the police may deceive an attorney by giving her false information about whether her client will be questioned, and that the police may deceive a suspect by failing to inform him of his attorney's communications and efforts to represent him. For the majority, this conclusion, though "distaste[ful]," . . . is not even debatable. The deception of the attorney is irrelevant because the attorney has no right to information, accuracy, honesty, or fairness in the police response to her questions about her client. The deception of the client is acceptable, because, although the information would affect the client's assertion of his rights, the client's actions in ignorance of the availability of his attorney are voluntary, knowing, and intelligent; additionally society's interest in apprehending, prosecuting, and punishing criminals outweighs the suspect's interest in information regarding his attorney's efforts to communicate with him. Finally, even mendacious police interference in the communications between a suspect and his lawyer does not violate any notion of fundamental fairness because it does not shock the conscience of the majority. . . .

The murder of Mary Jo Hickey was a vicious crime, fully meriting a sense of outrage and a desire to find and prosecute the perpetrator swiftly and effectively. . . .

The recognition that ours is an accusatorial, and not an inquisitorial[,] system nevertheless requires that the government's actions, even in responding to this brutal crime, respect those liberties and rights that distinguish this society from most others. As Justice Jackson observed shortly after his return from Nuremberg, cases of this kind present "a real dilemma in a free society . . . for the defendant is shielded by such safeguards as no system of law except the Anglo-American concedes to him." . . .

The Court's holding focuses on the period after a suspect has been taken into custody and before he has been charged with an offense. The core of the Court's holding is that police interference with an attorney's access to her client during that period is not unconstitutional. The Court reasons that a State has a compelling interest, not simply in custodial interrogation, but in lawyer-free, incommunicado custodial interrogation. Such incommunicado interrogation is so important that a lawyer may be given false information that prevents her presence and representation; it is so important that police may refuse to inform a suspect of his attorney's communications and immediate availability. This conclusion flies in the face of this Court's repeated expressions of deep concern about incommunicado questioning. Until today, incommunicado questioning has been viewed with the strictest scrutiny by this Court; today, incommunicado questioning is embraced as a societal goal of the highest order that justifies police deception of the shabbiest kind.

It is not only the Court's ultimate conclusion that is deeply disturbing; it is also its manner of reaching that conclusion. The Court completely rejects an entire body of law on the subject—the many carefully reasoned state decisions that have come to precisely the opposite conclusion. The Court similarly dismisses the fact that the police deception which it sanctions quite clearly violates the American Bar Association's Standards for Criminal Justice—Standards which the Chief Justice has described as "the single most comprehensive and probably the most monumental undertaking in the field of criminal justice ever attempted by the American legal profession in our national history," and which this Court frequently finds helpful. And, of course, the Court dismisses the fact that the American Bar Association has emphatically endorsed the prevailing state-court position and expressed its serious concern about the effect that a contrary view—a view, such as the Court's, that exalts incommunicado interrogation, sanctions police deception, and demeans the right to consult with an attorney—will have in police stations and courtrooms throughout this Nation. Of greatest importance, the Court misapprehends or rejects the central principles that have, for several decades, animated this Court's decisions concerning incommunicado interrogation.

Police interference with communications between an attorney and his client is a recurrent problem. The factual variations in the many state-court opinions condemning this interference as a violation of the Federal Constitution suggest the variety of contexts in which the problem emerges. In Oklahoma, police led a lawyer to several different locations while they interrogated the suspect; in Oregon, police moved a suspect to a new location when they learned that his lawyer was on his way; in Illinois, authorities failed to tell a suspect that his lawyer had arrived at the jail and asked to see him; in Massachusetts, police did not tell suspects that their lawyers were at or near the police station. In all these cases, the police not only failed to inform the suspect, but also misled the attorneys. The scenarios vary, but the core problem of police interference remains. . . .

The near-consensus of state courts and the legal profession's Standards about this recurrent problem lends powerful support to the conclusion that police may not interfere with communications between an attorney and the client whom they are questioning. Indeed, at least two opinions from this Court seemed to express precisely that view [citing *Miranda v. Arizona,* 1966, and *Escobedo v. Illinois,* 1964]. The Court today flatly rejects that widely held view and responds to this recurrent problem by adopting the most restrictive interpretation of the federal constitutional restraints on police deception, misinformation, and interference with attorney-client communications. . . .

Well-settled principles of law lead inexorably to the conclusion that the failure to inform Burbine of the call from his attorney makes the subsequent waiver of his constitutional rights invalid. Analysis should begin with an acknowledgement that the burden of proving the validity of a waiver of constitutional rights is always on the *government.* When such a waiver occurs in a custodial setting, that burden is an especially heavy one because custodial interrogation is inherently coercive, because disinterested witnesses are seldom available to describe what actually happened, and because history has taught us that the danger of overreaching during incommunicado interrogation is so real. . . .

[T]he Court's truncated analysis, which relies in part on a distinction between deception accomplished by means of an omission of a critically important fact and deception by means of a misleading statement, is simply untenable. If, as the Court asserts, "the analysis is at an end" as soon as the suspect is provided with enough information to have the *capacity* to understand and exercise his rights, I see no reason why the police should not be permitted to make the same kind of misstatements to the suspect that they are apparently allowed to make to his lawyer. *Miranda,* however, clearly establishes that both kinds of deception vitiate the suspect's waiver of his right to counsel. . . .

The Court's balancing approach is profoundly misguided. The cost of suppressing evidence of guilt will always make the value of a procedural safeguard appear "minimal," "marginal," or "incremental." Indeed, the value of any trial at all seems like a "procedural technicality" when balanced against the interest in administering prompt justice to a murderer or a rapist caught redhanded. The individual interest in procedural safeguards that minimize the risk of error is easily discounted when the fact of guilt appears certain beyond doubt.

What is the cost of requiring the police to inform a suspect of his attorney's call? It would decrease the likelihood that custodial interrogation will enable the police to obtain a confession. This is certainly a real cost, but it is the same cost that this Court has repeatedly found necessary to preserve the character of our free society and our rejection of an inquisitorial system. . . .

(continued)

If the court's cost-benefit analysis were sound, it would justify repudiation of a right to a warning about counsel itself. There is only a difference in degree between a presumption that advice about the immediate availability of a lawyer would not affect the voluntariness of a decision to confess, and a presumption that every citizen knows that he has a right to remain silent and therefore no warnings of any kind are needed. In either case, the withholding of information serves precisely the same law enforcement interests. And in both cases, the cost can be described as nothing more than an incremental increase in the risk that an individual will make an unintelligent waiver of his rights. . . .

The possible reach of the Court's opinion is stunning. For the majority seems to suggest that police may deny counsel all access to a client who is being held. At least since *Escobedo v. Illinois,* it has been widely accepted that police may not simply deny attorneys access to their clients who are in custody. This view has survived the recasting of *Escobedo* from a Sixth Amendment to a Fifth Amendment case that the majority finds so critically important. That this prevailing view is shared *by the police* can be seen in the state-court opinions detailing various forms of police deception of attorneys. For, if there were no obligation to give attorneys access, there would be no need to take elaborate steps to avoid access, such as shuttling the suspect to a different location, or taking the lawyer to different locations; police could simply refuse to allow the attorneys to see the suspect. But the law enforcement profession has apparently believed, quite rightly in my view, that denying lawyers access to their clients is impermissible. The Court today seems to assume that this view was error. . . .

This case turns on a proper appraisal of the role of the lawyer in our society. If a lawyer is seen as a nettlesome obstacle to the pursuit of wrongdoers—as in an inquisitorial society—then the Court's decision makes a good deal of sense. If a lawyer is seen as an aid to the understanding and protection of constitutional rights—as in an accusatorial society—then today's decision makes no sense at all.

Like the conduct of the police in the Cranston station on the evening of June 29, 1977, the Court's opinion today serves the goal of insuring that the perpetrator of a vile crime is punished. Like the police on that June night as well, however, the Court has trampled on well-established legal principles and flouted the spirit of our accusatorial system of justice.

I respectfully dissent.

The disagreement among the justices centers, in large part, around the issue of what constitutes a knowing and intelligent waiver. The majority says it is adequate if you have been informed of the right, but the dissent believes suspects are entitled to more complete information in order to make an intelligent decision. In addition, the justices disagree about whether they should endorse police dishonesty directed at defense attorneys. The majority expresses "distaste at the deliberate misleading of an officer of the court" (i.e., the defense attorney), yet the justices implicitly approve the police actions by failing to sanction the police in any way for being untruthful with the attorney. By contrast, the dissenters worry that the Court is endorsing police interference in communications between defense lawyers and their clients. They are concerned that the Court is, in effect, diminishing the supposed importance of the adversary system of justice by permitting the police to cut the defense attorney out of the process in an effort to gain incriminating information. The bottom line is that the police do not have to give the suspect—or the attorney—complete information in order to fulfill the obligations of the right to counsel imposed by *Miranda*. As you read the box "Police Ethics and Interrogation," ask yourself whether a police officer's obligations would change if a suspect began to inquire about whether an attorney had already been called.

| **A CLOSER LOOK** | **Police Ethics and Interrogation** |

Imagine that you are a police officer in an interrogation room preparing to question a burglary suspect. There have been dozens of unsolved burglaries in your community, and this suspect was caught in the vicinity of a just-burglarized home carrying a stocking cap and burglar's tools in a bag. You read the suspect his *Miranda* rights and the suspect replies by saying, "You seem like a nice officer. I think I might talk to you. Do you know if my sister called my attorney yet?"

Would this constitute a request for counsel that would prevent you from asking further questions?

If you knew that the attorney had called the station and that you had told the attorney that questioning "would probably not occur until tomorrow" because you honestly believed, at the time, that no questioning would occur on this night, how should you answer the suspect's question?

Is this situation different from the one in *Moran v. Burbine* in any important respects?

CONCLUSION

The Supreme Court made a strong statement against coercive police practices in questioning suspects by imposing the requirement of *Miranda* warnings in 1966. The warnings require police to inform suspects of the right to remain silent, the fact that their statements will be used against, and their right to counsel, including the right to appointed counsel for defendants who cannot afford to hire their own attorneys. The *Miranda* decision has been criticized for impeding criminal investigations and for not being genuinely required by the Fifth Amendment's privilege against compelled self-incrimination. The warnings apply only to questioning that occurs in custody, which generally means when someone is arrested. It does not apply to people questioned during traffic stops or when they voluntarily appear at the police station. The warnings need not be given before questioning in an exigent circumstance in which public safety is threatened. Questions remain about the actual impact of *Miranda* because police have adapted their strategies and techniques to gain information from suspects without violating the ruling.

SUMMARY

- In order to guard against abusive police practices, the Supreme Court moved away from a voluntariness test for the admissibility of confessions and incriminating statements and instead imposed an affirmative obligation to inform suspects about their rights.

- *Miranda v. Arizona* (1966) requires police officers to inform suspects of their right to remain silent, the fact that any statements they make will be used against them, the right to counsel, and the right to have counsel provided if they cannot afford to hire their own.

- *Miranda* warnings are intended to protect the Fifth Amendment privilege against compelled self-incrimination. The right to counsel presented in the warnings is not the Sixth Amendment right to counsel applicable to prosecutions but is instead a Fifth Amendment right to counsel because the Court determined that defense attorneys may be essential during custodial questioning in order to protect against compelled self-incrimination.

- The warnings must be given prior to custodial questioning, which includes arrests but does not include traffic stops and voluntary appearances at police stations.

- Warnings do not have to be given to arrested suspects in exigent circumstances in which public safety may be threatened (*New York v. Quarles,* 1984).

- Warnings do not have to be given exactly as described in the *Miranda* case. Officers have flexibility in presenting the warnings as long as they convey the essential components of the rights (*Duckworth v. Eagan,* 1979).

- Police officers have adapted their strategies and techniques for questioning suspects in order to gain information without violating *Miranda.*

- Suspects often do not assert their *Miranda* rights both because they do not think care-fully about the warnings they receive and because they may seek expected benefits of leniency if they cooperate with the police.

- Despite challenges to the legal basis for *Miranda,* the Supreme Court has declared that *Miranda* is a constitutional decision that cannot be altered by legislative action (*Dickerson v. United States,* 2001).

- Questioning must cease when a defendant requests an attorney during police interrogation unless the attorney arrives or the suspect initiates further discussions with the police.

- Issues arise about whether suspects have actually waived their rights and whether they are capable of waiving those rights.

Key Terms

custodial interrogation   Questioning by law enforcement officials of people who are in government custody and not free to leave, and therefore must be given their *Miranda* warnings before the start of questioning.

nontestimonial evidence   Evidence from a person, such as behaviors (e.g., slurred speech) or material extracted from their bodies (e.g., blood tests), that is not covered by the privilege against compelled self-incrimination because they do not constitute statements from the person about him- or herself.

"public safety" exception   Exception to *Miranda* requirements that permits police to immediately question a suspect in custody without providing any warnings when public safety would be jeopardized by taking the time to supply the warnings.

testimonial evidence   The type of evidence covered under the privilege against compelled self-incrimination because it consists of statements by the suspect that might otherwise be used against him or her in court.

Additional Readings

Grano, Joseph D. 1993. *Confessions, Truth, and the Law.* 1993. Ann Arbor: University of Michigan Press. A thorough, scholarly examination of the law concerning confessions by one of the most well-known critics of the *Miranda* decision.

Leo, Richard, and George C. Thomas III, eds. 1998. *The Miranda Debate: Law, Justice, and Policing.* Boston: Northeastern University Press. A selection of readings concerning the Supreme Court's decisions about self-incrimination and their impact on criminal justice.

Levy, Leonard. 1968. *Origins of the Fifth Amendment: The Right Against Self-Incrimination.* New York: Oxford University Press. A history of the American constitutional protection against self-incrimination.

Notes

1. Leonard Levy, *Origins of the Fifth Amendment: The Right Against Self-Incrimination* (New York: Oxford University Press, 1968), 405–432; Stephen Schulhofer, "Some Kind Words for the Privilege against Self-Incrimination," *Valparaiso University Law Review* 26 (1991): 311–336.

2. Charles Whitebread and Christopher Slobogin, *Criminal Procedure: An Analysis of Cases and Concepts,* 4th ed. (New York: Foundation Press, 2000), 406–407.

3. Henry Abraham, *Freedom and the Court,* 5th ed. (New York: Oxford University Press, 1988), 158.

4. Kathy Bergstrom, "Source of Evidence: The Suspects Brain," *Lansing State Journal,* 30 August 1999, Business Extra section, 4.

5. "Brain Fingerprinting," *Sixty Minutes* (CBS television news show), 10 December 2000.

6. Richard Leo, "*Miranda*'s Revenge: Police Interrogation as a Confidence Game," *Law and Society Review* 30 (1996): 259–288.

7. Christopher E. Smith, "Bright-Line Rules and the Supreme Court: The Tension Between Clarity in Legal Doctrine and Justices' Policy Preferences," *Ohio Northern University Law Review* 16 (1989): 119–137.

8. Joseph D. Grano, *Confessions, Truth, and the Law* (Ann Arbor: University of Michigan Press, 1993).

9. Paul G. Cassell and Richard Fowles, "Handcuffing the Cops? A Thirty-Year Perspective on *Miranda*'s Harmful Effects on Law Enforcement," *Stanford Law Review* 50 (1998): 1055–1145.

CHAPTER EIGHT

Right to Counsel

After a college football game in which your university won the national championship, you run out into the streets to celebrate with thousands of other students and townsfolk. As you jump around, yell, and dance with strangers, you notice that some people have started to light bonfires in the street and others are throwing rocks through windows. Suddenly, dozens of police cars with sirens screaming race up to the crowded block where you are standing with hundreds of other celebrants. Officers rush into the crowd yelling, "Clear the streets!" Within a few feet of you, someone sticks out a foot and trips an officer who was running past. The officer falls to the sidewalk and scrapes her hands while trying to break her fall. You rush toward her to provide assistance when suddenly you are tackled by two other officers who were following close behind. They place handcuffs tightly on your wrists and drag you to a patrol car.

Before you know it, you are at the police station going through the booking process. You ask everyone, "What's going on? What did I do wrong?" but no officers speak to you except to bark orders in your direction—and in the direction of two dozen other people arrested on the street and brought to the police station with you.

After spending a night in jail, you are taken to court early in the morning. A judge informs you that you have been charged with assaulting a police officer and sets your bail at $20,000. The judge asks if you can afford to hire your own attorney. You say "no" and the judge says that she will appoint an attorney for you if you qualify. You are led away to fill out forms about your income and assets—which pretty much amount to zero—and then you are taken back to jail. You make a collect call to your parents from the jail, but they do not have any money to help you make bail or hire an attorney.

You spend one more night in jail, and then you are taken to court for a probable cause hearing. As you sit and wait with other defendants in the courtroom, a young woman in a suit calls out your name. When you wave your hand in her direction, she has the bailiff lead you to an empty row of chairs so that she can talk to you.

"I'm your attorney for this case," she says. "My name is Ms. Taylor and the judge appointed me to represent you."

"Good. I need help. I shouldn't be in jail."

"Look, if we act right now, I can get you the best deal possible. Right now you're facing a major felony charge, but the prosecutor is willing to let you plead to misdemeanor assault with a recommendation of a fine and community service if you plead guilty today."

You look at her with a shocked expression on your face. "Don't you even want to know what happened?"

"You need to understand the situation. They are going to throw the book at people for causing a public disturbance and destroying property. I don't want them to pin the whole disturbance on you."

"But I didn't do anything."

"Sure, sure. But look, you could get prison time for this charge. You need to really think about that. Do you want to wait in jail for weeks and weeks while this case moves forward slowly and then possibly end up in prison. Or would you rather get out now? If you want out now, take the plea—now."

This scenario poses a number of issues. What would you do under the circumstances? Do you assert your innocence and thereby assume the risk that the police officers or other witnesses may mistakenly believe that you tripped the officer and that you were moving forward to further assault the officer rather than to assist her? As you ponder those questions, turn your attention to the subject of this chapter. What do you think of the representation the defense attorney provided? Was the attorney's conversation with you proper and ethical in the context in which it occurred? More importantly, was this attorney fulfilling your right to counsel, or did this conversation somehow violate the Sixth Amendment?

In this chapter, we will examine the Sixth Amendment right to counsel, its development, and the issues that the U.S. Supreme Court has decided concerning the right. Most of the historical development of the right to counsel described in this chapter concerns the Sixth Amendment right that applies for pretrial and trial processes. In Chapter 7, we examined issues related to the right to counsel in the Fifth Amendment context when attorneys are considered necessary to prevent compelled self-incrimination during custodial questioning. As described in the preceding chapter, this right to counsel stems from the *Miranda* decision about the desirability of enabling suspects to have an entitlement to legal assistance during custodial questioning by the police. Such early representation is intended to guard the privilege against compelled self-incrimination and prevent coercive tactics by police. The Sixth Amendment right to counsel described in this chapter emphasizes the entitlement to an attorney during pretrial, trial, and post-trial court processes rather than in the context of police investigations. As in previous chapters, bear in mind that the Supreme Court's description of the right might not fit neatly with the actual behavior of people in the criminal justice system. Keep asking yourself whether the attorney's statements and actions in the hypothetical scenario are consistent with the Supreme Court's decisions about the right to counsel.

HISTORICAL DEVELOPMENT

For most of American history, the right to counsel contained in the Sixth Amendment meant only that the government could not stop you from hiring a defense attorney if you had enough money to do so. The right was not interpreted to supply criminal defendants with any tangible assistance. In addition, as we know from the history of incorporation in Chapter 1, the Sixth Amendment, like the other amendments, applied only against the federal government until the mid-twentieth century. Thus the majority of criminal defendants, whose cases are processed in state courts, did not have any entitlement to legal assistance unless their state's constitution or statutes provided them with such assistance.

Attorneys in the American Adversary System

The legal process in the United States portrays itself as an **adversary system**. The underlying assumption of the system is that the best way to discover the truth is to have two opposing advocates battle each other in a courtroom. It is presumed that the truth will emerge through the process of presenting opposing arguments and evidence. The alternative system commonly used in European democracies, such as France and Germany, is the **inquisitorial system** in which the judge takes a very active role in questioning witnesses and vigorously pursuing the truth. If one attorney is not performing adequately under the inquisitorial system, the judge can intervene to ask the questions that should be asked. By contrast, in the adversary system, the judge is supposed to be a relatively passive observer. If one side has a relatively weak or ineffective attorney, the American system simply says, in effect, "too bad for that side." In criminal cases, ineffective performance by defense attorneys can have significant impacts on whether and how long an individual is incarcerated.

In light of the importance of attorneys in the adversary system, you can picture the nature of criminal cases for most of American history when the Sixth Amendment right to counsel had little effect on cases. Trials were very brief, one-sided processes in which the prosecutor and the police presented evidence and the defendant had little chance of understanding the proceedings, let alone mounting an effective defense. Under such circumstances, there are grave risks that an innocent person could be wrongly convicted.

The U.S. Supreme Court's first major case concerning the right to counsel arose in the 1930s. As you read the case, *Powell v. Alabama,* on pp. 252–253, determine what part of the Constitution the Court interpreted in this famous case.

The *Powell* case is known in history as the "Scottsboro" case because it occurred in Scottsboro, Alabama, and it captured the nation's attention at the time. The case was viewed by many northerners as an example of racial discrimination in the southern criminal justice system. In reality, racial discrimination also existed in northern cities, but it was often more open and obvious in the South. Northern attorneys provided assistance to the defendants that enabled them to carry their case to the U.S. Supreme Court.

Note that the *Powell* decision arose prior to incorporation and that the Court did not incorporate the Sixth Amendment. Instead, the Court concluded that it was a violation of the Fourteenth Amendment right to due process for Alabama to not provide attorneys for these "indigent defendants" who were facing the death penalty. **Indigent defendants** are those who cannot afford to hire their own attorneys. The case was understood as setting a precedent that applied only to death penalty cases. Indigent defendants in other cases were on their own unless the state's own laws provided them with legal assistance.

In 1938 the Supreme Court interpreted the Sixth Amendment as imposing an obligation on the federal government to provide attorneys for indigent defendants facing serious criminal charges in federal court (*Johnson v. Zerbst*, 1938). Because relatively few cases arose under federal criminal law at that time, the new rule did not initially provide assistance to very many defendants. Because federal criminal law expanded substantially in the final decades of the twentieth century, especially with respect to drug and white-collar offenses, the decision serves as the basis for providing federal public defenders and appointed counsel for many federal defendants today.

The Supreme Court did not immediately apply the same rule to state courts, and thus many criminal defendants were not represented by attorneys when they appeared in court. In *Betts v. Brady* (1942), a defendant was indicted for robbery and prosecuted in the Maryland state courts. Because he was unable to afford an attorney, he requested that the judge appoint an attorney to represent him. The judge declined and informed him that attorneys were provided only to indigent defendants facing rape or murder charges. When the Supreme Court examined the case, the justices decided that states are not obligated to provide defense attorneys for indigent defendants in all cases—only in cases with special circumstances. The Supreme Court, in effect, instructed state judges to examine the defendant and the charges to determine if there was a special reason for requiring counsel to be appointed. The trial judge would look to see if the defendant was illiterate, mentally retarded, or otherwise suffering from a special disability that would interfere with the ability to present a defense on his or her own. In *Betts v. Brady,* the Court felt that no such special circumstances existed. According to the majority opinion, "[T]he accused was not helpless, but was a man forty-three years old, of ordinary intelligence, and ability to take care of his own interests on the trial of that narrow issue. He had once before been in a criminal court, pleaded guilty to larceny, and served a sentence and was not wholly unfamiliar with criminal procedure."

According to the Court's criteria at that time, if a defendant was an adult of normal intelligence who had been exposed to legal processes in the past, he or she was sufficiently capable to present a defense in court. If the goal was to fulfill the adversary system's ideal of equal advocates battling in court, it is very clear that this standard would not achieve that goal. Defendants had significant disadvantages when facing off against professional prosecutors who

Powell v. Alabama, 287 U.S. 45 (1932)

[*During the Depression, many people jumped aboard freight trains to travel from town to town looking for work. A group of whites ended up in the same freight car with a group of African Americans on one train. A fight broke out between the two groups, and most of the whites were ejected from the train by the other group. When the train arrived at the next station, two white women in the freight car claimed that they had been raped by the African Americans. Later, one of the women recanted and admitted that they had lied about the rape. The African American men were charged with the capital offense of rape. Although Alabama state law required that the defendants be represented by counsel, no attorneys actually prepared a defense for the defendants. During a brief trial, the young African American men were quickly convicted of rape and sentenced to death. The trial was conducted in such a hostile environment that the sheriff requested military assistance in guarding the prisoners to keep them safe from angry mobs of whites. The Alabama Supreme Court affirmed the convictions over the dissent of its chief justice, who believed that the defendants had not received a fair trial. The U.S. Supreme Court considered whether the men were denied due process of law and a fair trial because they were not represented by counsel.*]

JUSTICE SUTHERLAND delivered the opinion of the Court.

. . .

The indictment was returned in a state court of first instance on March 31, 1931, and the record recites that on the same day the defendants were arraigned and entered pleas of not guilty. There is a further recital to the effect that upon the arraignment they were represented by counsel. But no counsel had been employed, and aside from a state-

ment made by the trial judge several days later during a colloquy immediately preceding the trial, the record does not disclose when, or under what circumstances, an appointment of counsel was made, or who was appointed. During the colloquy referred to, the trial judge, in response to a question, said that he had appointed all the members of the bar for the purpose of arraigning the defendants and then of course anticipated that the members of the bar would continue to help the defendants if no counsel appeared. Upon the argument here, both sides accepted that as a correct statement of the facts concerning the matter. . . .

The record shows that immediately upon the return of the indictment defendants were arraigned and pleaded not guilty. Apparently they were not asked whether they had, or were able to employ, counsel, or wished to have counsel appointed; or whether they had friends or relatives who might assist in that regard if communicated with. . . .

It is hardly necessary to say that, the right to counsel [under Alabama state law] being conceded, a defendant should be afforded a fair opportunity to secure counsel of his own choice. Not only was that not done here, but such designation of counsel as was attempted was either so indefinite or so close upon the trial as to amount to a denial of effective and substantial aid in that regard. . . .

[U]ntil the very morning of the trial no lawyer had been named or definitely designated to represent the defendants. Prior to that time, the trial judge had "appointed all the members of the bar" for the limited "purpose of arraigning the defendants." Whether they would represent the defendants thereafter if no counsel appeared in their behalf, was a matter of speculation only, or, as the judge indicated, of mere anticipation on the part of the court. Such a

had police departments at their disposal to investigate cases and generate evidence. By contrast, the defendant would be unaware of court rules and incapable of locating evidence, especially since these defendants would likely remain in jail because they would be too poor to make bail.

Incorporation of the Right to Counsel

During the 1960s, the Supreme Court actively incorporated many rights affecting criminal justice in the Bill of Rights so that they would protect people in state

designation, even if made for all purposes, would, in our opinion, have fallen far short of meeting, in any proper sense, a requirement of appointment of counsel. . . .

In any event, the circumstance lends emphasis to the conclusion that during perhaps the most critical period of the proceedings against these defendants, that is to say, from the time of their arraignment until the beginning of their trial, when consultation, thoroughgoing investigation and preparation were vitally important, the defendants did not have the aid of counsel in any real sense, although they were as much entitled to such aid during that period as at the trial itself. . . .

The question, however, which it is our duty, and within our power, to decide, is whether the denial of assistance of counsel contravenes the due process clause of the Fourteenth Amendment to the federal Constitution. . . .

It thus appears that in at least twelve of the thirteen colonies the rule of the English common law [against a right to counsel for criminal defendants], in the respect now under consideration, had been definitely rejected and the right to counsel fully recognized in all criminal prosecutions, save that in one or two instances the right was limited to capital offenses or to the more serious crimes. . . .

. . . The fact that the right involved is of such a character that it cannot be denied without violating those "fundamental principles of liberty and justice which lie at the base of all our civil and political institutions" (*Hebert v. Louisiana* [1926]) is obviously one of those compelling considerations which must prevail in determining whether it is embraced within the due process clause of the Fourteenth Amendment, although it be specifically dealt with in another part of the federal Constitution. . . . While this question has never been categorically determined by this court, a consideration of the nature of the right and a review of the expressions of this and other courts,

makes it clear that the right to the aid of counsel is of this fundamental character. . . .

In light of the facts outlined in the forepart of this opinion—the ignorance and illiteracy of the defendants, their youth, the circumstances of public hostility, the imprisonment and the close surveillance of the defendants by military forces, the fact that their friends and families were all in other states and communication with them [was] necessarily difficult, and above all that they stood in deadly peril of their lives—we think the failure of the trial court to give them reasonable time and opportunity to secure counsel was a clear denial of due process.

But passing that, and assuming their inability, even if the opportunity had been given, to employ counsel, as the trial court evidently did assume, we are of opinion that, under the circumstances just stated, the necessity of counsel was so vital and imperative that the failure of the trial court to make an effective appointment of counsel was likewise a denial of due process within the meaning of the Fourteenth Amendment. Whether this would be so in other criminal prosecutions, or under other circumstances, we need not determine. All that it is necessary now to decide, as we do decide, is that in a capital case, where the defendant is unable to employ counsel, and is incapable adequately of making his own defense because of ignorance, feeblemindedness, illiteracy, or the like, it is the duty of the court, whether requested or not, to assign counsel for him as a necessary requisite of due process of law; and that duty is not discharged by an assignment at such a time or under such circumstances as to preclude the giving of effective aid in the preparation and trial of the case. . . .

The judgments must be reversed and the causes remanded for further proceedings not inconsistent with this opinion. *Judgments reversed.*

[The dissenting opinion of Justice Butler is omitted.]

criminal processes in the same manner that they protected defendants in federal criminal cases. In Chapter 4, we saw how the Supreme Court incorporated the exclusionary rule in *Mapp v. Ohio* (1961). Not surprisingly, as the Supreme Court incorporated individual rights, new cases arose requesting that additional rights be incorporated as well. Shortly after its controversial decision in *Mapp*, the Court turned its attention to the Sixth Amendment right to counsel.

The case that the Court chose to use as the vehicle to examine the right to counsel, *Gideon v. Wainwright* (1963), concerned a poor, high school dropout named Clarence Earl Gideon with a long record of nonviolent offenses and

Gideon v. Wainwright, 372 U.S. 335 (1963)

JUSTICE BLACK delivered the opinion of the Court.

. . .

We think the Court in *Betts* [*v. Brady,* 1942] had ample precedent for acknowledging that those guarantees of the Bill of Rights which are fundamental safeguards of liberty immune from federal abridgment are equally protected against state invasion by the Due Process Clause of the Fourteenth Amendment. This same principle was recognized, explained, and applied in *Powell v. Alabama* [1932] . . . , a case upholding the right of counsel, where the Court held that despite sweeping language to the contrary in *Hurtado v. California* [1884], . . . the Fourteenth Amendment "embraced" those "fundamental principles of liberty and justice which lie at the base of all our civil and political institutions," even though they had been "specifically dealt with in another part of the federal Constitution." [*Powell,*] 287 U.S. at 67. In many cases other than *Powell* and *Betts,* this Court has looked to the fundamental nature of the original Bill of Rights guarantees to decide whether the Fourteenth Amendment makes them obligatory on the States. Explicitly recognized to be of this "fundamental nature" and therefore made immune from state invasion by the Fourteenth, or some part of it, are the First Amendment's freedoms of speech, press, religion, assembly, association, and petition for redress of grievances. For the same reason, though not always in precisely the same terminology, the Court has made obligatory on the States the Fifth Amendment's command that private property shall not be taken for public use without just compensation, the Fourth Amendment's prohibition of unreasonable searches and seizures, and the Eighth's ban on cruel and unusual punishment. On

the other hand, this Court in *Palko v. Connecticut* (1937) refused to hold that the Fourteenth Amendment made the double jeopardy provision of the Fifth Amendment obligatory on the States. In so refusing, however, the Court, speaking through Mr. Justice Cardozo, was careful to emphasize that "immunities that are valid as against the federal government by force of the specific pledges of particular amendments have been found to be implicit in the concept of ordered liberty, and thus, through the Fourteenth Amendment, have become valid as against the states" and that guarantees "in their origin . . . effective against the federal government alone" had by prior cases "been taken over from the earlier articles of the federal bill of rights and brought within the Fourteenth Amendment by a process of absorption." [*Palko,*] 302 U.S. at 324–325, 326. We accept *Betts v. Brady*'s assumption, based as it was on our prior cases, that a provision of the Bill of Rights which is "fundamental and essential to a fair trial" is made obligatory upon the States by the Fourteenth Amendment. We think the Court in *Betts* was wrong, however, in concluding that the Sixth Amendment's guarantee of counsel is not one of these fundamental rights. Ten years before *Betts v. Brady,* this Court, after full consideration of all the historical data examined in *Betts,* had unequivocally declared that "the right to the aid of counsel is of this fundamental character." *Powell v. Alabama,* 287 U.S. 45, 68 (1932). While the Court at the close of its *Powell* opinion did by its language, as this Court frequently does, limit its holding to the particular facts and circumstances of that case, its conclusions about the fundamental nature of the right to counsel are unmistakable. Several years later, in 1936, the Court reemphasized

alcohol problems who was convicted in Florida of breaking into a pool hall and stealing some beer and coins from a cigarette machine. He was convicted and sentenced to five years in prison. During the trial, he told the judge that he thought he was entitled to have an attorney provided to represent him. The judge informed him that Florida law did not entitle him to an attorney and that the Sixth Amendment did not apply to his case. The judge was not hostile to his request. Indeed, the judge tried to be helpful by telling him to pick out any potential jurors whom he would like to exclude from his jury. However, the judge could not assist him in presenting his defense, and he was overmatched by the professional prosecutor

what it had said about the fundamental nature of the right to counsel in this language:

> We concluded that certain fundamental rights, safeguarded by the first eight amendments against federal action, were also safeguarded against state action by the due process of law clause of the Fourteenth Amendment, and among them the fundamental right of the accused to the aid of counsel in a criminal prosecution. Grosjean v. American Press Co., 297 U.S. 233, 243–244 (1936).

And again in 1938 this Court said:

> [The assistance of counsel] is one of the safeguards of the Sixth Amendment deemed necessary to insure fundamental human rights of life and liberty. . . . The Sixth Amendment stands as a constant admonition that if the constitutional safeguards it provides be lost, justice will not "still be done." Johnson v. Zerbst, 304 U.S. 458, 462 (1938). To the same effect, see Avery v. Alabama (1940), Smith v. O'Grady (1941).

In light of these and many other prior decisions of this Court, it is not surprising that the *Betts* Court, when faced with the contention that "one charged with crime, who is unable to obtain counsel, must be furnished counsel by the State," conceded that "[e]xpressions in the opinions of this court lend color to the argument. . . ." 316 U.S. at 462–463. The fact is that in deciding as it did—that "appointment of counsel is not a fundamental right, essential to a fair trial"—the Court in *Betts v. Brady* made an abrupt break with its own well-considered precedents. In returning to these old precedents, sounder we believe than the new, we but restore constitutional principles established to achieve a fair system of justice. Not only these precedents but also reason and reflection require us to recognize that in our adversary system of criminal justice, any person haled into court who is too poor to hire a lawyer cannot be assured a fair trial unless counsel is provided to him. This seems to us to be an obvious truth. Governments, both state and federal, quite properly spend vast sums of money to establish machinery to try defendants accused of crime. Lawyers to prosecute are everywhere deemed essential to protect the public's interest in an orderly society. Similarly, there are few defendants charged with crime, few indeed, who fail to hire the best lawyers they can get to prepare and present their defenses. That government hires lawyers to prosecute and defendants who have the money hire lawyers to defend are the strongest indications of the widespread belief that lawyers in criminal courts are necessities, not luxuries. The right of one charged with crime to counsel may not be deemed fundamental and essential to fair trials in some countries, but it is in ours. From the very beginning, our state and national constitutions and laws have laid great emphasis on procedural and substantive safeguards designed to assure fair trials before impartial tribunals in which every defendant stands equal before the law. This noble ideal cannot be realized if the poor man charged with crime has to face his accusers without a lawyer to assist him. . . . The Court in *Betts v. Brady* departed from the sound wisdom upon which the Court's holding in *Powell v. Alabama* rested. Florida, supported by two other States, has asked that *Betts v. Brady* be left intact. Twenty-two States, as friends of the Court, argue that *Betts* was "an anachronism when handed down" and that it should now be overruled. We agree.

The judgment is reversed and the cause is remanded to the Supreme Court of Florida for further action not inconsistent with this opinion. *Reversed.*

[The concurring opinions of Justices Douglas, Clark, and Harlan are omitted.]

who had extensive training in law. From his prison cell, Gideon attempted to appeal to the Florida Supreme Court. His appeal was summarily rejected, so he sent his case to the U.S. Supreme Court. He wrote out his own arguments in his own words in longhand on lined paper. The clerk's office initially returned the papers to him and instructed him to file an additional form concerning his indigent status and his request to waive the usual court fees. Upon his second submission of the filing, the Court accepted his filing, decided to accept his case for hearing, and then appointed an attorney to represent him in the arguments before the U.S. Supreme Court. As you read the Court's opinion in *Gideon,* take note of how Justice Black treats the prior precedent established in *Betts v. Brady* (1942).

The Legend of *Gideon*

Gideon v. Wainwright (1963) subsequently achieved the status as one of the most popular and famous cases decided by the Supreme Court. A best-selling book, *Gideon's Trumpet,* was written about the case by *New York Times* columnist Anthony Lewis. Actor Henry Fonda performed a one-man play that later became a film in which he portrayed Gideon. Americans seem to take pride in the fact that even the poorest or most despicable criminal defendant is entitled to representation by an attorney in court. One of the reasons the case has achieved mythical status is that it is often regarded as demonstrating that the U.S. Supreme Court is so committed to its motto, "Equal Justice Under Law," it will actively intervene to protect the rights of poor, uneducated citizens like Gideon. In reality, this view of the *Gideon* decision reinforces an erroneous view of the Supreme Court. There is nothing inevitable about the Court's intervention on behalf of poor people or even in cases in which rights violations have clearly occurred. Many right-to-counsel cases had been presented to the Supreme Court in the years prior to 1963. Gideon was simply lucky that his case appeared at the moment when the justices were ready to tackle the issue. He was no more worthy of assistance than prisoners sitting in cells in various states who had not been represented by attorneys at their trials. Gideon had good timing and, moreover, he presented a "safe" case for the Court's intervention. The justices could avoid some potential public criticism by establishing the right to counsel in the case of an unlucky, nonthreatening loser in life rather than in other cases presented by convicted robbers and child molesters. In addition, the attorney appointed to represent Gideon was Abe Fortas, one of the nation's most famous and powerful lawyers who would himself become a Supreme Court justice just two years later. Fortas's team of lawyers at his wealthy Washington, D.C., law firm overmatched the inexperienced assistant attorney general who represented Florida in the case.

The foregoing factors help to explain why Gideon won, but there is an additional reason why this victory did not cause the backlash and controversy that followed the Court's other famous criminal justice decisions of the 1960s, especially *Mapp v. Ohio* (1961) concerning the exclusionary rule and *Miranda v. Arizona* (1966) concerning self-incrimination. Although the Court's interpretation of the Sixth and Fourteenth Amendments in *Gideon* created a new rule and a strengthened right for criminal defendants, it was not a groundbreaking rule. At the time the Supreme Court decided *Gideon,* three dozen states already provided attorneys for indigent defendants under their own states' laws. In addition, judges in another half-dozen states had informally adopted the practice of appointing defense attorneys even though such appointments were not required under law. Thus the *Gideon* rule forced fewer than 10 states to change their practices. Instead of leading the nation with a new vision of this constitutional right, the U.S. Supreme Court was effectively trailing behind where most of the nation had already gone and the Court merely used its powers to make the rest of the states catch up. This point became very clear when the Florida attorney general's office asked that other states join in support of the written brief being submitted in opposition to Gideon's interpretation of the right to counsel. Florida's effort to present a united front of state governments opposed to the rule backfired when the attorney general of Minnesota, future U.S. Vice President Walter Mondale, organized more than twenty states to endorse Gideon's argument while Florida could find only five states willing to support its view.[1]

In *Gideon* the Supreme Court unanimously incorporated the Sixth Amendment right to counsel and applied it against the states. The rule in *Gideon* required all states to provide defense attorneys for indigent defendants who faced serious charges, which is usually defined as a potential sentence of six months or more in prison or jail. For those states that were not already providing public defenders or appointed counsel, this imposed new costs as they had to rearrange their governmental budgets in order to pay for these attorneys. The *Gideon* decision was important, but its actual impact was less profound than many people believe. As you read the box "The Legend of *Gideon,*" think about the reasons that Supreme Court decisions may be less influential than one might expect.

JUSTICE DOUGLAS delivered the opinion of the Court.

. . .

We agree, however, with Justice Traynor of the California Supreme Court, who said that the "[d]enial of counsel on appeal [to an indigent] would seem to be a discrimination at least as invidious as that condemned in *Griffin v. Illinois*. . . ." In *Griffin v. Illinois* . . . [1956], we held that a State may not grant appellate review in such a way as to discriminate against some convicted defendants on account of their poverty. There, as in *Draper v. Washington* [1963], . . . the right to a free transcript on appeal was in issue. Here the issue is whether or not an indigent shall be denied the assistance of counsel on appeal. In either case the evil is the same: discrimination against the indigent. For there can be no equal justice where the kind of an appeal a man enjoys "depends on the amount of money he has." . . .

In spite of California's forward treatment of indigents, under its present practice the type of an appeal a person is afforded in the District Court of Appeal hinges upon whether or not he can pay for the assistance of counsel. . . .

We are not here concerned with problems that might arise from the denial of counsel for the preparation of a petition for discretionary or mandatory review beyond the stage in the appellate process at which the claims have once been presented by a lawyer and passed upon by an appellate court. We are dealing only with the *first appeal,* granted as a matter of right to rich and poor alike . . . from a criminal conviction. We need not now decide whether California would have to provide counsel for an indigent seeking a discretionary hearing from the California Supreme Court after the District Court of Appeal had sustained his conviction . . . or whether counsel must be appointed for an indigent seeking review of an appellate affirmance of his conviction in this Court by appeal as of right or by petition for writ of certiorari which lies within the Court's discretion. But it is appropriate to observe that a State can, consistently with the Fourteenth Amendment, provide for differences so long as the result does not amount to a denial of due process or an "invidious discrimination." . . . Absolute equality is not required; lines can be and are drawn and we often sustain them. . . . But where the merits of the *one and only* appeal an indigent has as of right are decided without benefit of counsel, we think an unconstitutional line has been drawn between rich and poor.

. . . There is lacking that equality demanded by the Fourteenth Amendment where the rich man, who appeals as of right, enjoys the benefit of counsel's examination into the record, research of the law, and marshalling of arguments on his behalf, while the indigent, already burdened by a preliminary determination that his case is without merit, is forced to shift for himself. The indigent, where the record is unclear or the errors are hidden, has only the right to a meaningless ritual, while the rich man has a meaningful appeal.

We vacate the judgment of the District Court of Appeal and remand the case to that court for further proceedings not inconsistent with this opinion.

[Dissenting opinions by Justices Clark and Harlan, joined by Justice Stewart, are omitted.]

On the same day the Court issued its *Gideon* decision, the Court also addressed the issue of legal representation in criminal appeals. In *Douglas v. California* (1963), the Court recognized a right to counsel in criminal appeals. As you read the brief excerpt in the above box, try to identify the source and nature of the right to counsel on appeal.

Notice that Justice Douglas never mentioned the Sixth Amendment specifically in his opinion. He mentioned the right to counsel, but the only Amendment he references is the Fourteenth Amendment. Thus it was not entirely clear where in the Constitution Justice Douglas found this right to counsel in appellate cases. Much of Douglas's discussion indicates that the denial of representation was based on improper wealth discrimination, which implies that he was relying on the Equal Protection Clause of the Fourteenth Amendment.

It is also possible that he simply regarded the denial of counsel as a violation of the Fourteenth Amendment right to due process.

It is also important to note that Douglas explicitly limited the Court's decision to the **first appeal of right,** which would typically be taken to a state's intermediate appellate court. He says that his opinion is not addressing whether this right to counsel would exist for cases in state supreme courts, which usually have discretionary jurisdiction to select or turn down individual cases, and for cases subject to similar discretionary acceptance in the U.S. Supreme Court. Justice Douglas did not say that the right to counsel could not exist for subsequent appeals under discretionary jurisdiction. He simply said that the Court has not yet decided those issues, and he acknowledged that the Court accepts different practices in those courts as long as the practices are not discriminatory.

THE RIGHT TO COUNSEL AFTER *GIDEON*

Representation and Incarcerative Punishments

As indicated in prior chapters, the Supreme Court's composition changed in the early 1970s as President Nixon made a concerted effort to appoint "law and order" justices. Although these justices typically were less inclined to expand the definitions of constitutional rights, the Court made another important decision that expanded the right to counsel just as the Court's composition began to change. In *Argersinger v. Hamlin* (1972), the Court expanded the Sixth Amendment protection by declaring that indigent defendants were entitled to representation for petty offenses if they faced the possibility of incarceration as punishment. After *Gideon,* the right had applied only when defendants faced serious charges with the potential of six months or more of incarceration. Justice Douglas wrote the majority opinion in *Argersinger.* According to Douglas's opinion, "Under the rule we announce today, every judge will know when the trial of a misdemeanor starts that no imprisonment may be imposed, even though local law permits it, unless the accused is represented by counsel." The Court's rule that the deprivation of liberty as a form of punishment was contingent on the defendant's opportunity to receive the benefit of professional representation expanded the scope of the right as well as the potential cost to local governments that had to pay for attorneys. It also enhanced the risk that resources allocated for criminal defense would be stretched thin by a requirement that coverage be granted to a large number of defendants. Whenever resources are stretched, there is an increased likelihood that the resources expended per case may shrink in some courthouses. Thus public defenders could (and, in some places, do) find themselves handling hundreds of cases simultaneously. Such caseloads make it very difficult to ensure that adequate attention is devoted to each case. Similarly, limited resources can place abnormally low caps on the amounts paid to appointed counsel with attendant risks that the attorneys' efforts will be constrained by their sense that their compensation adequately covers only a limited range of activities. Some critics fear that limited resources ultimately lead attorneys to encourage their clients to plead guilty quickly rather than thoroughly investigate cases in order to prepare the strongest possible adversarial defense. The existence of these risks need not lead to the conclusion that the Court erred in expanding the right to counsel because it may be a far greater threat to the protection of constitutional rights and individual liberty when defendants face jail sentences without any representation at all. Thus many observers argue that the real problem is inadequate funding for criminal defense rather than rights to representation that are too broad.

Note that *Argersinger* attempted to guarantee the right to counsel for defendants facing deprivations of liberty as punishment for conviction of a crime. The expanded right to counsel in *Argersinger* applies only when a jail or prison sentence is imposed. The right does not apply to other contexts in which people may lose their liberty without enjoying the benefits of legal representation. When people are arrested, if they are jailed prior to trial, they lose their liberty even though they are presumptively innocent. There is no right to counsel at bail hearings, so many people are jailed initially without enjoying the right to counsel. Because liberty is considered a central value to be protected under the Constitution, scholars have argued that the right to counsel should be extended to an earlier point in the process—the bail hearing. At a bail hearing, a defense attorney may be able to prepare and present effective arguments to justify ROR (release on own recognizance) or a low bail based on the defendant's community ties and character references. It is extremely difficult for defendants to prepare and present effective arguments, especially since they are sitting in jail as the prosecutors, police, and probation officers prepare recommendations for judges concerning an appropriate set of conditions for pretrial release.

Shortly after *Argersinger,* the Supreme Court examined whether probationers and parolees are entitled to representation by attorneys when they are accused of violating their conditions of release and face the prospect of incarceration. **Probationers** are people whose sentence for a crime is probation, which is supervised release under a set of restrictive conditions (e.g., check in with probation officer weekly, do not drink or use drugs). The threat held over the head of many probationers is that they can be sent to jail or prison if they violate their release conditions or if they are arrested for a new offense. **Parolees** are people who have already served time in prison and are released on parole—supervised release under a set of restrictive conditions—prior to the completion of the sentence. A parole violation can lead to a return trip to prison, and many parolees are sent back to finish their sentences behind bars. In *Gagnon v. Scarpelli* (1973), the Supreme Court decided that defense attorneys are required only in *some* probation and parole revocation hearings. According to Justice Powell's opinion in the case, "In some cases, these modifications in the nature of the revocation hearing must be endured and the costs borne [by the state] because [the] probationer's or parolee's version of a disputed issue can fairly be represented only by a trained advocate." Unlike the prior cases from *Gideon* through *Argersinger,* the Court declined to make a clear expansion of the right to counsel. *Gagnon* is arguably an expansion because it acknowledged the possibility of a right to counsel in some cases, but it also clearly indicated that many—and probably most—cases would not require the involvement of an attorney. In reading the brief excerpt of Justice Powell's opinion in the box on p. 260, ask yourself how you would determine if a probationer or parolee facing revocation was entitled to representation by an attorney.

Limits on the Right to Counsel

The decision in *Gagnon* came in the immediate aftermath of a significant shift in the Supreme Court's composition. By the end of 1972, Chief Justice Warren, Justice Black, and two other justices who had decided *Gideon* (1963)

Gagnon v. Scarpelli, 411 U.S. 778 (1973)

JUSTICE POWELL delivered the opinion of the Court.

. . .

We thus find no justification for a new inflexible constitutional rule with respect to the requirement of counsel. We think, rather, that the decision as to the need for counsel must be made on a case-by-case basis in the exercise of a sound discretion by the state authority charged with responsibility for administering the probation and parole system. Although the presence and participation of counsel will probably be both undesirable and constitutionally unnecessary in most revocation hearings, there will remain certain cases in which fundamental fairness—the touchstone of due process—will require that the State provide at its expense counsel for indigent probationers or parolees.

It is neither possible nor prudent to attempt to formulate a precise and detailed set of guidelines to be followed in determining when the providing of counsel is necessary to meet the applicable due process requirements. The facts and circumstances in preliminary and final hearings are susceptible of almost infinite variation, and a considerable discretion must be allowed the responsible agency in making the decision. Presumptively, it may be said that counsel should be provided in cases where, after being informed of his right to request counsel, the probationer or parolee makes such a request, based on a timely and colorable claim (i) that he has not committed the alleged violation of the conditions upon which he is at liberty; or (ii) that, even if the violation is a matter of public record or is uncontested, there are substantial reasons which justified or mitigated the violation and make revocation inappropriate, and that the reasons are complex or otherwise difficult to develop or present. In passing on a request for the appointment of counsel, the responsible agency also should consider, especially in doubtful cases, whether the probationer appears to be capable of speaking for himself. In every case in which a request for counsel at a preliminary or final hearing is refused, the grounds for refusal should be stated succinctly in the record. . . .

were gone from the high court. In their place were four justices appointed by President Nixon with the express intention of altering the Court's orientation toward the expansion of rights for criminal suspects and defendants. Nixon could not control the Court's decisions, but he could appoint justices whose prior statements and records indicated that they favored giving more authority and autonomy to criminal justice officials.

The Supreme Court expressly curtailed the expansion of the right to counsel in *Ross v. Moffitt* (1974). *Ross* rejected a claim asserting that the entitlement to appointed counsel should continue in the appellate system beyond the first appeal of right. Recall that the Supreme Court's decision in *Douglas v. California* (1963), establishing the entitlement to counsel for initial appeals, had been written in language implying that the Equal Protection Clause barred discrimination against appellants who were too poor to hire their own attorneys. By 1974 the Supreme Court had determined quite clearly that the Constitution does not forbid wealth discrimination by the government. In 1973 the Supreme Court decided *San Antonio Independent School District v. Rodriguez.* This noncriminal justice case concerned a challenge to Texas's method of financing public schools in which wealthy districts gained more money than poor districts even when the wealthy districts had lower tax rates. The Court explicitly rejected the argument that the Equal Protection Clause protects people against government discrimination by wealth. The Court clarified that the Equal Protection Clause was focused primarily on racial discrimination and, later, made

Ross v. Moffitt, 417 U.S. 600 (1974)

JUSTICE REHNQUIST delivered the opinion of the Court.

. . .

This is not to say, of course, that a skilled lawyer, particularly one trained in the somewhat arcane art of preparing petitions for discretionary review, would not prove helpful to any litigant able to employ him. An indigent defendant seeking review in the Supreme Court of North Carolina is therefore somewhat handicapped in comparison with a wealthy defendant who has counsel assisting him in every conceivable manner at every stage in the proceeding. But both the opportunity to have counsel prepare an initial brief in the Court of Appeals and the nature of discretionary review in the Supreme Court of North Carolina make this relative handicap far less than the handicap borne by the indigent defendant denied counsel on his initial appeal as of right in *Douglas.* And the fact that a particular service might be of benefit to an indigent defendant does not mean that the service is constitutionally required. The duty of the State under our cases is not to duplicate the legal arsenal that may be privately retained by a criminal defendant in a continuing effort to reverse his conviction, but only to assure the indigent defendant an adequate opportunity to present his claims fairly in the context of the State's appellate process. . . .

The suggestion that a State is responsible for providing counsel to one petitioning [the U.S. Supreme] Court simply because it initiated the prosecution which led to the judgment sought to be reviewed is unsupported by either reason or authority. It would be quite as logical under the rationale of *Douglas* and *Griffin,* and indeed perhaps more so, to require that the Federal Government or [the U.S. Supreme] Court furnish and compensate counsel for petitioners who seek certiorari here to review state judgments of conviction. Yet this Court has followed a consistent policy of denying applications for appointment of counsel by persons seeking to file jurisdictional statements or petitions for certiorari in this Court. . . . In light of these [case precedents], it would be odd, indeed, to read the Fourteenth Amendment to impose such a requirement on the States, and we decline to do so.

We do not mean by this opinion to in any way discourage those States which have, as a matter of legislative choice, made counsel available to convicted defendants at all stages of judicial review. Some States which might well choose to do so as a matter of legislative policy may conceivably find that other claims for public funds within or without the criminal justice system preclude the implementation of such a policy at the present time. . . .

clear that the clause sometimes protects against discrimination based on gender, national origin, and illegitimacy (i.e., was a person born within a marriage or out-of-wedlock for inheritance purposes). The Equal Protection Clause has not been interpreted by the Court to bar discrimination based on other categories of characteristics. Because wealth discrimination is not prohibited by the Constitution, *Douglas v. California* could not have been based on a prohibition against wealth discrimination—otherwise, the Court would have been forced to overturn *Douglas* and it did not take that step. Instead, the Court in *Ross* treated *Douglas* as resting on the Fourteenth Amendment right to due process. However, the majority of justices did not agree with the claimant's argument that due process requires that an indigent appellant be provided with an attorney after the first appeal of right. Thus indigent offenders have no constitutional right to an attorney if they lose their initial appeal and seek to carry their case forward to a state supreme court, which has discretionary jurisdiction over what cases it will choose to hear, or to the U.S. Supreme Court, which has similar discretionary authority over its docket. As you read the Court's opinion in *Ross,* think about how this decision can affect convicted offenders who want to appeal their cases through the entire court system.

Scott v. Illinois, 440 U.S. 367 (1979)

JUSTICE REHNQUIST delivered the opinion of the Court.

We granted certiorari in this case to resolve a conflict among state and lower federal courts regarding the proper application of our decision in *Argersinger v. Hamlin*. . . . Petitioner Scott was convicted of theft [i.e., shoplifting merchandise valued at less than $150] and fined $50 after a bench trial in the Circuit Court of Cook County, Ill. His conviction was affirmed by the state intermediate appellate court and then by the Supreme Court of Illinois, over Scott's contention that the Sixth and Fourteenth Amendments to the United States Constitution required that Illinois provide trial counsel to him at its expense. . . .

There is considerable doubt that the Sixth Amendment itself, as originally drafted by the Framers of the Bill of Rights, contemplated any guarantee other than the right of an accused in a criminal prosecution in a federal court to employ a lawyer to assist in his defense. . . .

The number of separate opinions in *Gideon, Duncan, Baldwin* [*v. New York*, 1970, regarding the right to trial by jury whenever someone faces six months or more of incarceration], and *Argersinger,* suggests that constitutional line drawing becomes more difficult as the reach of the Constitution is extended further, and as efforts are made to transpose lines from one area of Sixth Amendment jurisprudence to another. . . . As a matter of constitutional adjudication, we are, therefore, less willing to extrapolate an already extended line when, although the general nature of the principle sought to be applied is clear, its precise limits and their ramifications become less so. We have now in our decided cases departed from the literal meaning of the Sixth Amendment. And

The *Ross* case signaled a new direction in Supreme Court decision making regarding legal entitlement to representation by defense counsel in the criminal justice system. The justices did not roll back any of the decisions by their predecessors defining the right to counsel. Instead, they effectively drew a line and said that they would expand the right to counsel no further with respect to post-trial proceedings. This did not preclude future criminal defendants from seeking to persuade the Court to change its decision, especially as the Court's composition changed in subsequent years. Just as the *Ross* decision indicated a stopping point for the expansion of an entitlement to counsel on appeals, the Court's later decision in *Scott v. Illinois* (1979) had the same effect for trial-level criminal cases. As you read the accompanying opinion from *Scott,* ask yourself whether this decision fulfills the words and purpose of the Sixth Amendment or whether the Court's decision is motivated by other priorities.

The Supreme Court called a halt to further expansion of the right to counsel. Notice, however, that Justice Rehnquist implies that *Argersinger* itself had mandated no further expansion of the right to counsel (i.e., "*Argersinger* did indeed delimit the constitutional right to appointed counsel"). In reality, the Court was determining for itself in *Scott* how far the right to counsel would go, but asserting reliance on a previous case helps to lend legitimacy to new opinions. Rehnquist's central justifications for the decision, aside from the claimed reliance on the *Argersinger* precedent, are that

1. incarceration is a sufficiently significant punishment to require the assistance of a defense attorney, but a fine is not sufficiently significant; and

we cannot fall back on the common law as it existed prior to the enactment of that Amendment, since it perversely gave less in the way of right to counsel to accused felons than to those accused of misdemeanors. . . .

In *Argersinger* the Court rejected arguments that social cost or a lack of available lawyers militated against its holding, in some part because it thought these arguments were factually incorrect. . . . But they were rejected in much larger part because of the Court's conclusion that incarceration was so severe a sanction that it should not be imposed as a result of a criminal trial unless an indigent defendant had been offered appointed counsel to assist in his defense, regardless of the cost to the States implicit in such a rule. The Court in its opinion repeatedly referred to trials "where an accused is deprived of his liberty" . . . and to "a case that actually leads to imprisonment even for a brief period," . . . [Chief Justice Burger] in his opinion concurring in the result also observed that "any deprivation of liberty is a serious matter." . . .

Although the intentions of the *Argersinger* Court are not unmistakably clear from its opinion, we conclude today that *Argersinger* did indeed delimit the constitutional right to appointed counsel in state criminal proceedings. Even were the matter *res nova* [i.e., an issue being presented to us for the first time], we believe that the central premise of *Argersinger* that actual imprisonment is a penalty different in kind from fines or the mere threat of imprisonment as the line defining the constitutional right to appointment of counsel. *Argersinger* has proved reasonably workable, whereas any extension would create confusion and impose unpredictable, but necessarily substantial, costs on 50 quite diverse States. We therefore hold that the Sixth and Fourteenth Amendments to the United States Constitution require only that no indigent criminal defendant be sentenced to a term of imprisonment unless the State has afforded him the right to assistance of appointed counsel in his defense. The judgment of the Supreme Court of Illinois is accordingly *Affirmed*.

2. it would be too costly to require the states to supply defense attorneys for minor cases.

Both of these justifications have been questioned. Some critics wonder whether Rehnquist and the other justices in the majority undervalued the impact of a criminal conviction with a non-incarcerative sanction. Because any criminal conviction can carry with it significant social stigma as well as harm to a person's job prospects and other important opportunities in life, an attorney might be needed to reduce the risk of erroneous convictions. Arguably, it would be terrible for someone to suffer lifelong harm to her or his job opportunities and to be treated as a criminal by others in society if, in fact, the person was wrongly convicted for lack of professional representation. With respect to the second justification, some people would argue that financial considerations should never determine whether people enjoy constitutional rights. In the real world, of course, there are limits to the resources possessed by state and local governments. Whether the provision of defense counsel in all criminal cases would be beyond this limit is a matter of speculation, but certainly the costs could be substantial. As you think about the correctness and impact of this issue, remember that this case, like the decisions in *Gideon, Douglas, Argersinger,* and *Ross,* really only affects the fates of poor people. People with sufficient resources to hire an attorney are unaffected by any of these decisions because they can always enjoy their right to counsel. These cases help to illustrate the difficulties involved and, indeed, the failure to fulfill the slogan, "Equal Justice Under Law," that is chiseled in marble across the top of the U.S. Supreme Court building in Washington, D.C.

In 2002, the Court examined a case in which a suspended sentence was imposed on a misdemeanor defendant who represented himself at trial (*Alabama v. Shelton*). The defendant was convicted of third-degree assault and sentenced to thirty days in jail, but the sentence was suspended and he was placed on probation. He would be jailed only if he violated the terms of probation. On appeal, he claimed that he was never informed that he faced the possibility of a jail sentence and therefore his waiver of the right to counsel was not knowing and voluntary. The Court divided on the issue of whether this situation fell under the rule of *Argersinger* or whether this case was comparable to *Scott*. A five-member majority applied the *Argersinger* rule and declared that the defendant's right to counsel was violated by the sentence. According to the Court, no one can be imprisoned without having the right to counsel, even if their risk of incarceration is small in the context of a suspended sentence connected to probation.

As you read the accompanying box about eligibility for appointed counsel, ask yourself whether you could afford to hire an attorney if you were arrested. Most of the Supreme Court's right-to-counsel cases focus on indigent defendants. Yet, many people who cannot readily afford to hire an attorney cannot actually benefit from the Court's Sixth Amendment decisions.

To summarize, the right to counsel—meaning the right to have a criminal defense attorney appointed to represent you if you cannot afford to hire one—was incorporated into the Fourteenth Amendment and applied to the states in 1963 (*Gideon*). The entitlement to appointed counsel applies at the trial level in any case in which incarceration is sought as a possible punishment (*Argersinger*) and in a first appeal of right after conviction, typically in an intermediate appellate court (*Douglas*). Bear in mind that a dozen states have no intermediate appellate court, so the first appeal of right may provide counsel for appeals that go directly from a trial court to a state supreme court. There is no right to counsel for discretionary appeals to a state supreme court or discretionary petitions to the U.S. Supreme Court (*Ross*). A state may, however, decide to provide representation for indigent appellants at any level if mandated by its own state's laws. The U.S. Constitution does not, however, require appointment of counsel after the first appeal of right.

There are other contexts in which there is no right to counsel. First, there is no right to counsel in habeas corpus proceedings. Habeas corpus in the postconviction process in which, after unsuccessfully pursuing appeals, a convicted offender may initiate an action asserting that a constitutional right was violated in the course of the investigation and prosecution of the case. Habeas corpus provides the mechanism through which offenders in state prisons can ask *federal* judges to review a case to determine whether state and local criminal justice officials made errors that violated federal constitutional rights (e.g., Fifth Amendment *Miranda* rights, Sixth Amendment right to counsel). The Supreme Court has said that convicted offenders do not have a constitutional right to assistance from attorneys, even in death penalty cases where habeas corpus petitions usually provide the prisoner's final opportunity to have a court review the case for errors (*Murray v. Giarratano*, 1989).

Second, there is no right to counsel for civil lawsuits. No matter how poor you are or what sort of legal difficulty you face (e.g., divorce, child custody battle, serious personal injury), there is no constitutional entitlement to assistance from an attorney in order to protect your legal interests. Some kinds of

A CLOSER LOOK	**Who Can Afford to Hire a Defense Attorney?**

Most college students do not have enough money to hire a defense attorney. Quite frankly, most of them feel as if they can barely keep up with the rising costs of tuition and textbooks. Despite the fact that they do not have sufficient funds, this does not mean that they cannot afford to hire a defense attorney if they are arrested for a crime. Are these statements apparent contradictions? No. We must distinguish between having money and being able to afford to hire a lawyer.

Lawyers are very expensive. Many lawyers charge more than $100 per hour for their services, and quite a few have fees that exceed $200 per hour. In criminal cases, by contrast, lawyers often do not charge by the hour. They know that they cannot send a bill to people who are sent to prison because people in prison simply will not pay. If clients end up in prison, they are often unhappy with the outcome and they figure that there is no way that the lawyer can force them to pay. Thus criminal defense lawyers in private practice typically require that clients pay a ballpark figure at the very start of the case. These amounts can be quite daunting. Lawyers often demand $10,000 for a serious felony, and murder cases can easily result in a required payment of $100,000.

Let us return to the provocative premise at the beginning of our discussion. How can someone with no money afford to pay these fees for representation? The answer lies in two simple words: family resources. When a family's loved one is arrested for a serious crime, family members make a determination about whether they wish to see their brother, son, daughter, niece, uncle, or cousin end up in prison. Often parents and siblings, in particular, will want to help ensure that their loved one receives a strong defense and a fair proceeding so that even if the person is, in fact, guilty of the crime, the punishment is no more severe than necessary. How do most families come up with the substantial sums of money required by defense attorneys? They often pool their resources and tap assets that they normally would not touch. Thus they may take out a second mortgage on a home or cash in retirement savings in order to try to rescue a loved one. This is a major, life-altering sacrifice for most middle-class people. It may ultimately result in the selling of a family home or someone not being able to retire at all. Yet these mechanisms often permit even middle-class people to come up with large sums of money. Thus, even though college students and most other middle-class (and below) Americans do not have the money to hire a criminal defense attorneys, they can often afford to hire attorneys because of assistance from the sacrifices and pooled resources of their family members.

What happens if the defense attorney, after being paid thousands of dollars, does an outstanding job of representation and convinces the judge or jury that the defendant is not guilty? Moreover, what if the defendant was, in fact, never guilty of anything but was arrested as a result of mistaken identification? The money is still gone. The house is still sold. The parent or sibling loses out on a chance to retire as planned. The system has no mechanism for reimbursing people who were arrested by mistake or for whom there was insufficient evidence to prove guilt. The innocent person may have spent weeks in jail awaiting trial, too. These are very harsh results for defendants and their families. These results again reinforce the idea that police officers and prosecutors must be careful and ethical in their decisions so that their exercises of authority and power do not unduly harm innocent people—and their families.

civil lawsuits will attract assistance from lawyers without any initial payment by the litigant. If a personal injury is sufficiently severe and caused by an entity that is presumed to be wealthy or insured (e.g., corporation, physician, government agency), the lawyers will take the case on a **contingency fee** basis. The lawyers are not actually working for free. Instead, they will typically take 30 percent of the award plus expenses from any settlement or verdict. Because these cases can be lucrative for lawyers, it is easier for poor people to find representation in such cases.

Petition Under 28 U.S.C. [Section] 2254 for Writ of Habeas Corpus by a Person in State Custody

(If petitioner is attacking a judgment which imposed a sentence to be served in the future, petitioner must fill in the name of the state where the judgment was entered. If petitioner has a sentence to be served in the future under a federal judgment which he wishes to attack, he should file a motion under 28 U.S.C. [section] 2255, in the federal court which entered the judgment.)

PETITION FOR WRIT OF HABEAS CORPUS BY A PERSON IN STATE CUSTODY

Instructions—Read Carefully

(1) This petition must be legibly handwritten or typewritten, and signed by the petitioner under penalty of perjury. Any false statement of a material fact may serve as the basis for prosecution and conviction for perjury. All questions must be answered concisely in the proper space on the form.

(2) Additional pages are not permitted except with respect to the facts which you rely upon to support your grounds for relief. No citation of authorities need be furnished. If briefs or arguments are submitted, they should be submitted in the form of a separate memorandum.

(3) Upon receipt of a fee of $5 your petition will be filed if it is in proper order.

(4) If you do not have the necessary funds for transcripts, counsel, appeal, and other costs connected with a motion of this type, you may request permission to proceed *in forma pauperis,* in which event you must execute form AO 240 or any other form required by the court, setting forth information establishing your inability to pay the costs. If you wish to proceed *in forma pauperis,* you must have an authorized officer at the penal institution complete the certificate as to the amount of money and securities on deposit to your credit in any account in the institution. If your personal account exceeds [an amount determined by the court] you must pay the filing fee as required by the rules of the district court.

(5) Only judgments entered by one court may be challenged in a single motion. If you seek to challenge judgments entered by different courts either in the same state or in different states, you must file separate petitions as to each court.

(6) Your attention is directed to the fact that you must include all grounds for relief and all facts supporting such grounds for relief in the petition you file seeking relief from any judgment of conviction.

The lack of a right to representation in civil cases is relevant to criminal justice because many lawsuits are filed against law enforcement and corrections officials for violating citizens' rights. If the case concerns a death or serious injury caused by alleged excessive use of force or careless high-speed driving by officers, lawyers will take the case on a contingency fee basis. If the case concerns improper searches or other alleged rights violations that do not lend themselves to substantial financial awards and verdicts because there was no significant medical injury, then it can be very difficult for poor people to gain the assistance of attorneys. This is particularly true for prisoners who believe that their religious freedoms or free speech rights are violated by prison policies, yet the lack of any likely financial award will deter lawyers from voluntarily assuming such cases. Thus many prisoners file their own civil rights lawsuits in addition to filing their own habeas corpus petitions. When people must represent themselves in litigation, they are called **pro se litigants.** Take a close look in the boxes on pp. 266–268 at the excerpted forms that courts

(7) When the petition is fully completed, the original and at least two copies must be mailed to the Clerk of the United States District Court whose address is _____.

(8) Petitions which do not conform to these instructions will be returned with a notation as to the deficiency.

. . .

(12) State *concisely* every ground on which you claim that you are being held unlawfully. Summarize *briefly* the *facts* supporting each ground. If necessary, you may attach pages stating additional grounds and *facts* supporting same.

CAUTION: *In order to proceed in the federal court, you must ordinarily first exhaust your available state court remedies as to each ground on which you request action by the federal court. If you fail to set forth all grounds in this petition, you may be barred from presenting additional grounds at a later date.*

For your information, the following is a list of the most frequently raised grounds for relief in habeas corpus proceedings. Each statement preceded by a letter constitutes a separate ground for possible relief. You may raise any grounds which you may have other than those listed if you have exhausted your state court remedies with respect to them. However, *you should raise in this petition all available grounds* (relating to this conviction) on which you base your allegations that you are being held in custody unlawfully.

Do not check any of these listed grounds. If you select one or more of these grounds for relief, you must allege facts. The petition will be returned to you if you merely check (a) through (j) or any one of these grounds.

(a) Conviction obtained by plea of guilty which was unlawfully induced or not made voluntarily with understanding of the nature of the charge and the consequences of the plea.

(b) Conviction obtained by use of coerced confession.

(c) Conviction obtained by use of evidence gained pursuant to an unconstitutional search and seizure.

(d) Conviction obtained by use of evidence obtained pursuant to an unlawful arrest.

(e) Conviction obtained by a violation of the privilege against self-incrimination.

(f) Conviction obtained by the unconstitutional failure of the prosecution to disclose to the defendant evidence favorable to the defendant.

(g) Conviction obtained by a violation of the protection against double jeopardy.

(h) Conviction obtained by action of a grand or petit jury which was unconstitutionally selected and impaneled.

(i) Denial of effective assistance of counsel.

(j) Denial of right of appeal.

provide to prisoners for filing their own legal actions. Would you be able to present an effective case without the assistance of an attorney? As you consider that question, remember that many prisoners are school dropouts, people with psychological problems, and people with weak or nonexistent literacy skills in the English language.

In the legal system of the United States, the right to counsel applies to most criminal trial contexts, except for minor offenses punishable only by a fine as explained in *Scott v. Illinois* (1979). The American reliance on appointed counsel and public defenders to provide representation for indigent criminal defendants represents particular choices about how to fulfill the Sixth Amendment right. These are not the only possible choices. As you read about the provision of counsel in Ontario, Canada, in the box on p. 269, think about other possible ways that the Sixth Amendment right could be fulfilled if courts in the United States sought to explore additional alternatives.

Form to Be Used by a Prisoner Filing a Complaint Under the Civil Rights Act, 42 U.S.C. [Section] 1983

. . .

This packet contains four copies of a complaint form. To start an action you must file an original and one copy of your complaint for each defendant you name and one copy for the court. For example, if you name two defendants you must file the original and three copies of the complaint. You should keep an additional copy of the complaint for your own records. *All copies of the complaint must be identical to the original.*

The clerk will not file your complaint unless it conforms to these instructions and to these forms.

Your complaint must be legibly handwritten or typewritten. You, the plaintiff, must sign and declare under penalty of perjury that the facts are correct. If you need additional space to answer a question, you must use the reverse side of the form or an additional blank page.

Your complaint can be brought in this court only if one or more of the named defendants is located within this district. Further, you must file a separate complaint for each claim that you have unless they are all related to the same incident or issue.

You are required to furnish, so that the United States marshal can complete service, the *correct name and address of each person you have named*

as a defendant. A PLAINTIFF IS REQUIRED TO GIVE INFORMATION TO THE UNITED STATES MARSHAL TO ENABLE THE MARSHAL TO COMPLETE SERVICE OF THE COMPLAINT UPON ALL PERSONS NAMED AS DEFENDANTS.

In order for this complaint to be filed, it must be accompanied by a filing fee of $120.00. In addition, the United States marshal will require you to pay the cost of serving the complaint on each of the defendants.

If you are unable to pay the filing fee and service costs for this action, you may petition the court to proceed *in forma pauperis* by completing and signing the attached declarations (pages 4 and 5). If you wish to proceed *in forma pauperis,* you must have an authorized officer at the penal institution complete the certificate as to the amount of money and securities on deposit to your credit in any account in the institution. If your prison account exceeds [an amount determined by the court], you must pay the filing fee and service costs.

You will note that you are required to give facts. THIS COMPLAINT SHOULD NOT CONTAIN ANY LEGAL ARGUMENTS OR CITATIONS.

When these forms are completed, mail the original and the copies to the Clerk of the United States District Court whose address is _____ .

WAIVER OF RIGHT TO COUNSEL

Defendants who waive their right to an attorney have a right to represent themselves at trial if they wish (*Faretta v. California,* 1975). Thus the right to counsel really does also encompass a right to *not* have counsel if the defendant so chooses. It is possible for a trial judge to refuse to permit the defendant to represent him- or herself if there are questions about the defendant's mental competence, but even a defendant who attempted suicide and was using several types of medication for psychiatric disorders was allowed to waive his right to counsel when psychiatric reports said that he was competent to stand trial (*Godinez v. Moran,* 1993). How far does the right to self-representation extend? The Supreme Court's decision in *Martinez v. Court of Appeal of California* (2000) addressed the question of a defendant's right to represent himself in an appeal. As discussed previously, there is no right to counsel for discretionary appeals beyond the first appeal of right (*Ross v. Moffitt,* 1974). There is, however, a right to counsel for the initial appeal if state law provides

Legal Advice in Ontario, Canada

In Ontario, defense attorneys staff a 24-hour-per-day hotline to answer questions from and advise arrestees. When people are arrested and advised of their right to have an attorney provided to represent them, they are given a toll-free telephone number that permits them to consult with an attorney immediately.[2] By contrast, indigent defendants in the United States might wait for many days before an attorney is assigned to represent them. In the interim, they may make damaging statements in the course of being brought to court for an initial appearance and a bail hearing. In Ontario, presum-ably the attorney on the telephone advises defendants to remain silent until they have an attorney at the police station to consult with them and advise them. This use of technology to provide quick advice to defendants about the protection of their rights after arrest could be readily implemented in each state with the expenditure of relatively modest resources. What if this system were implemented in the United States? What impact would it have on police investigations? What impact would it have on the quality of legal representation and the protection of constitutional rights?

a right to that appeal, typically presented to an intermediate appellate court (*Douglas v. California*, 1963). Moreover, a state may have its own laws and procedures that provide for the appointment of counsel during subsequent appeals. As you read the Court's opinion in *Martinez* in the box on pp. 270–272, ask yourself how the Court is interpreting the Sixth Amendment. Should the government be able to force someone to be represented by an attorney?

After having read the Court's opinion, do you think its conclusion makes sense? If an individual can waive his or her right to counsel under the Sixth Amendment, is it consistent to forbid that individual from making the same decision during appeals? The Court notes that it is considering the efficient administration of justice in its calculations about what is permitted or required under the Constitution. When courts must try to read legal papers prepared by people who are not trained in law, it often poses problems for understanding whether any actual legal issues exist in a case.

INEFFECTIVE ASSISTANCE OF COUNSEL

The right to counsel would mean very little if attorneys did not perform in a competent manner. When attorneys' performance on behalf of their clients is sufficiently inadequate, it may constitute **ineffective assistance of counsel**, which violates the Sixth Amendment. The Court has struggled to provide a workable definition of ineffective assistance of counsel. Part of the difficulty arises because the justices do not want to second-guess strategies employed by lawyers in an effort to win a case. For example, a defense attorney may decline to object to all questionable evidence presented by a prosecutor out of a fear that the jury will become alienated and hostile at the sight of the defense attorney interrupting and objecting every few minutes. Thus the defense attorney

Martinez v. Court of Appeal of California, 528 U.S. 152 (2000)

JUSTICE STEVENS delivered the opinion of the Court.

The Sixth and Fourteenth Amendments of our Constitution guarantee that a person brought to trial in any state or federal court must be afforded the right to assistance of counsel before he can be validly convicted and punished by imprisonment. In *Faretta v. California*, 422 U.S. 806 (1975), we decided that the defendant also "has a constitutional right to proceed *without* counsel when he voluntarily and intelligently elects to do so." . . . Although that statement arguably embraces the entire judicial proceeding, we also phrased the question as whether a State may "constitutionally hale a person into its criminal courts and there force a lawyer upon him, even when he insists that he wants to conduct his own defense." . . . Our conclusion in *Faretta* extended only to a defendant's "constitutional right to conduct his own defense." . . . Accordingly, our specific holding was confined to the right to defend oneself at trial. We now address the different question whether the reasoning in support of that holding also applies when the defendant becomes an appellant and assumes the burden of persuading a reviewing court that the conviction should be reversed. We have concluded that it does not.

Martinez describes himself as a self-taught paralegal with 25 years' experience at 12 different law firms. . . . While employed as an office assistant at a firm in Santa Ana, California, Martinez was accused of converting $6,000 of a client's money to his own use. He was charged in a two-count information with grand theft and the fraudulent appropriation of the property of another. He chose to represent himself at trial before a jury, because he claimed, "there wasn't an attorney on earth who'd believe me once he saw my past [criminal record]." . . . The jury acquitted him on Count 1, grand theft but convicted him on Count 2, embezzlement. The jury also found that he had three prior convictions; accordingly, under California's "three strikes" law, the court imposed a mandatory sentence of 25-years-to-life in prison. . . . Martinez filed a timely notice of appeal as well as a motion to represent himself and a waiver of counsel. The California Court of Appeal denied his motion, and the California Supreme Court denied his application for a writ of mandamus [i.e., a request for an order directed at the Court of Appeal to permit him to represent himself]. While the California Supreme Court did not issue an opinion in this case, the Court of Appeal previously had explained:

> There is no constitutional right to self-representation on the initial appeal as of right. The right to counsel on appeal stems from the due process and equal protection clauses of the Fourteenth Amendment, not from the Sixth Amendment, which is the foundation on which *Faretta* is based. The denial of self-representation at this level does not violate due process or equal protection guarantees. . . .

We granted certiorari because Martinez has raised a question on which both state and federal courts have expressed conflicting views. . . . We now affirm.

The *Faretta* majority based its conclusion on three interrelated arguments. First, it examined historical evidence identifying a right of self-representation that had been protected by federal and state law since the beginning of our Nation. . . . Second, it interpreted the structure of the Sixth Amendment, in the light of its English and colonial background, . . . Third, it concluded that even though it "is undeniable that in most criminal prosecutions defendants could better defend with counsel's guidance than by their own unskilled efforts," a knowing and intelligent waiver "must be honored out of that respect for the individual which is the lifeblood of the law." . . . Some of the Court's reasoning is applicable to appellate proceedings as well as to trials. There are, however, significant distinctions.

The historical evidence relied upon by *Faretta* as identifying a right of self-representation is not always useful because it pertained to times when lawyers were scarce, often mistrusted, and not readily available to the average person accused of crime. For one who could not obtain a lawyer, self-representation was the only feasible alternative to asserting no defense at all. Thus, a government's recognition of an indigent defendant's right to represent himself was comparable to bestowing upon the homeless beggar a "right" to take shelter in the sewers of Paris. Not surprisingly, early precedent demonstrates that this "right" was not always used to the defendant's advantage as a shield, but rather was often employed by the prosecution as a sword. . . .

. . . [A]n individual's decision to represent himself is no longer compelled by the necessity of choosing self-representation over incompetent or nonexistent representation; rather, it more likely reflects a genuine desire to "conduct his own cause in his own words." . . . Therefore, *Faretta* is correct in concluding that there is abundant support for the proposition that a right of self-representation has been recognized for centuries, the original reasons for protecting that right do not have the same force when the availability of competent counsel for every indigent defendant has displaced the need—although not always the desire—for self-representation. . . .

We are not aware of any historical consensus establishing a right of self-representation on appeal. . . . Historical silence, however, has no probative force in the appellate context because there simply was no long-respected right of self-representation on appeal. In fact, the right of appeal itself is of relatively recent origin.

Appeals as of right in federal courts were nonexistent for the first century of our Nation, and appellate review of any sort was "rarely allowed." . . . The States, also, did not generally recognize an appeal as of right until Washington became the first to constitutionalize the right explicitly in 1889. . . . Thus, unlike the inquiry in *Faretta*, the historical evidence does not provide any support for the affirmative constitutional right to appellate self-representation.

The *Faretta* majority's reliance on the structure of the Sixth Amendment is also not relevant. The Sixth Amendment identifies the basic rights that the accused shall enjoy in "all criminal prosecutions." They are presented strictly as rights that are available in preparation for trial and at the trial itself. The Sixth Amendment does not include any right to appeal. As we have recognized, "The right of appeal, as we presently know it in criminal cases, is purely a creature of statute." . . . It necessarily follows that the Amendment itself does not provide any basis for finding a right to self-representation on appeal. . . .

Finally, the *Faretta* majority found that the right of self-representation at trial was grounded in part in a respect for individual autonomy. . . . This consideration is, of course, also applicable to an appellant seeking to manage his own case. As we explained in *Faretta*, at the trial level "[t]o force a lawyer on a defendant can only lead him to believe that the law contrives against him." . . . On appellate review, there is surely a similar risk that the appellant will be skeptical of whether a lawyer, who is employed by the same government that is prosecuting him, will serve his cause with undivided loyalty. Equally true on appeal is the related observation that it is the appellant personally who will bear the consequences of the appeal. . . .

In light of our conclusion that the Sixth Amendment does not apply to appellate proceedings, any individual right of self-representation on appeal based on autonomy principles must be grounded in the Due Process Clause. Under the practices that prevail in the Nation today, however, we are entirely unpersuaded that the risk of either disloyalty or suspicion of disloyalty is a sufficient concern to conclude that a constitutional right of self-representation is a necessary component of a fair appellate proceeding. We have no doubt that instances of disloyal representation are rare. In both trials and appeals there are, without question, cases in which counsel's performance is ineffective. Even in those cases, however, it is reasonable to assume that counsel's performance is more effective than what the unskilled appellant could have provided for himself.

No one, including Martinez and the *Faretta* majority, attempts to argue that as a rule *pro se* representation is wise, desirable or efficient. . . .

In the appellate context, the balance between the two competing interests [of individual autonomy and effective court proceedings] surely tips in favor of the State. The status of the accused defendant, who retains a presumption of innocence throughout the trial process, changes dramatically when a jury returns a guilty verdict. . . .

The requirement of representation by trained counsel implies no disrespect for the individual inasmuch as it tends to benefit the appellant as well as the court. Courts, of course, may still exercise their discretion to allow a lay person to proceed *pro se*. We already leave to the appellate courts' discretion, keeping "the best interests of both the prisoner and the government in mind," the decision whether to allow a *pro se* appellant to participate in, or even be present at, oral argument. . . . Considering the change in position from defendant to appellant, the autonomy interests that survive a felony conviction are less compelling than those motivating the decision

(continued)

in *Faretta*. Yet the overriding state interest in the fair and efficient administration of justice remains as strong as at the trial level. Thus, the States are clearly within their discretion to conclude that the government's interests outweigh an invasion of the appellant's interest in self-representation.

For the foregoing reasons, we conclude that neither the holding nor the reasoning in *Faretta* requires California to recognize a constitutional right to self-representation on direct appeal from a criminal conviction. Our holding is, of course, narrow. It does not preclude the States from recognizing such a right under their own constitutions....

may adopt the strategy of objecting only to major errors made by the prosecutor. If the case is lost, the defendant may claim that the attorney should have objected to all errors, large and small, but a judge would be reluctant to say that the attorney's strategy, which was developed for the benefit of the client, was impermissible.

Strickland-Cronic Standards

In *Strickland v. Washington* (1984), a murder defendant rejected his attorney's advice to demand a jury's recommendation about a possible death sentence and instead waived his right to the jury and chose to have the trial judge decide the punishment. The defense attorney's "sense of hopelessness" led him to argue that the defendant's acceptance of responsibility and remorse justified sparing him from the death penalty. The attorney did not do everything possible on behalf of the client. After a death sentence was imposed, the defendant claimed that the attorney had provided ineffective assistance of counsel in violation of the Sixth Amendment for several reasons, including allegedly failing to request additional time to prepare for the sentencing hearing, failing to request a psychiatric evaluation of the defendant, failing to thoroughly investigate and present character witnesses, and failing to present meaningful arguments at sentencing. In establishing standards for assessing ineffective assistance of counsel, the U.S. Supreme Court said:

> *A convicted defendant's claim that counsel's assistance was so defective as to require reversal of a conviction or death sentence has two components. First, the defendant must show that counsel's performance was deficient. This requires showing that counsel made errors so serious that counsel was not functioning as the "counsel" guaranteed the defendant by the Sixth Amendment. Second, the defendant must show that the deficient performance prejudiced the defense. This requires showing that counsel's errors were so serious as to deprive the defendant of a fair trial, a trial whose result is reliable. Unless a defendant makes both showings, it cannot be said that the conviction or death sentence resulted from a breakdown in the adversary process that renders the result unreliable. (466 U.S. 668 at 687)*

In *United States v. Cronic* (1984), which was decided at the same time as *Strickland*, the federal government spent over four years investigating and preparing a mail fraud case against a defendant. Shortly before trial, the defense attorney was forced to withdraw because of illness, so the court appointed an inexperienced attorney as a replacement. The new attorney, whose experience was in real estate law rather than criminal law and who had never done a jury trial before, was given just twenty-five days to prepare for trial. After the defendant was convicted, he raised a claim of ineffective assistance of counsel, which was rejected by the U.S. Supreme Court.

Taken together with *Strickland,* these cases make clear that defendants face a significant challenge in attempting to prevail on a claim of ineffective assistance of counsel. It is not enough to assert generally that the attorney was inexperienced or had too little time to prepare; the defendant must show that the attorney made specific errors and that these errors were serious enough to deprive the defendant of a fair trial. The latter element is very difficult to prove. The defendant needs to show that there was a reasonable probability that outcome of the case was affected by a specific error. Thus courts have found instances in which attorneys clearly made serious errors, but there is a reluctance to label those errors as sufficient to affect the outcome of the case, especially because these cases all involve circumstances in which evidence of guilt persuaded either a judge or a jury that the defendant was guilty.

This does not mean that the courts never find that ineffective assistance violated the right to counsel. For example, when an attorney failed to file a statement of appeal and that failure resulted in the dismissal of an appeal, the Court found that the attorney's performance was sufficiently deficient to be recognized as a violation of the constitutional right (*Evitts v. Lacey,* 1985).

Critics complain that the standard for establishing ineffective assistance of counsel is so difficult, it effectively insulates incompetent lawyers from scrutiny and it severely disadvantages defendants whose rights were violated and those who may have been innocent. The challenge of succeeding with ineffective assistance of counsel claims is even more difficult because they frequently must be presented *pro se* in habeas corpus proceedings in which claimants have no right to representation. Critics of the Court's standards argue that a lawyer might have to be drunk and pass out in the courtroom in order to be found constitutionally ineffective, yet they can also point to cases in which this very event nearly happened and no rights violation was found.[3] Ineffective assistance of counsel issues are the most frequently alleged rights violation in habeas corpus petitions filed in federal court, but they are also among the least likely claims to be successful.[4] As you read the box on p. 274, ask yourself whether the standards for identifying ineffective assistance of counsel detract from the fulfillment of the Sixth Amendment right to counsel.

An excellent illustration of the difficulties faced by courts in applying the Supreme Court's standards arose in the case of *Burdine v. Johnson* (2001). Burdine was convicted of murder and sentenced to death in Texas in 1984. His conviction and sentence were affirmed on appeal to the Texas Court of Criminal Appeals. Later, Burdine filed habeas corpus petitions in state court alleging that his right to counsel was violated because his court-appointed attorney fell asleep repeatedly during his trial. A hearing was held on the habeas corpus petition in which witnesses testified about the attorney's slumber. In ruling on the habeas corpus claim, the Texas Court of Criminal Appeals acknowledged that the factual record of the case supported a finding that the attorney had fallen asleep repeatedly, yet the state court declined to provide any relief because it said that Burdine had not fulfilled the requirements of *Strickland v. Washington* by demonstrating that his attorney's sleep had "prejudiced" or harmed the presentation of his defense. Burdine filed a federal habeas corpus petition, and a U.S. district judge ruled the attorney's

The Effectiveness of Defense Attorneys

Does the right to counsel, in practice, mean anything more than having a licensed attorney stand next to you while you plead guilty? The majority of cases that are not dismissed end with guilty pleas. Defense attorneys often encourage their clients to plead guilty. This encouragement may be in their objectively considered best interest. However, there is a risk that public defenders who have overwhelming caseloads and appointed defense counselors who are paid a small fee for each case have personal incentives to end each case as quickly as possible. In other words, the structure of the criminal defense system for indigent defendants does not necessarily encourage the ideal of combative adversarialness

that characterizes the idealized description of the criminal justice process. In addition, because it is so difficult to establish a recognizable claim for ineffective assistance of counsel, there is little chance for defendants to remedy mistakes, incompetence, and apathy by defense attorneys that may have detracted from effective representation and the protection of constitutional rights. Is the right to counsel "real" only when a defendant happens to get an ethical, committed, and competent defense attorney? If a defendant is assigned an inexperienced, disinterested, or distracted attorney, is the Sixth Amendment right meaningful at all?

unconsciousness during the murder trial amounted to a denial of representation for substantial periods during the trial. On the appeal, a panel of judges from the 5th Circuit U.S. Court of Appeals decided that the attorney's slumber did not require a presumption that Burdine's case was prejudiced. Instead, Burdine was required to prove that the attorney slept during specific moments in the trial that required the attorney to be alert and active. Because of disagreement among the appellate judges, the case was reargued in an *en banc* hearing before the 5th Circuit, which meant that all fourteen judges heard the case as a group. As you read the court's opinion in the accompanying box, ask yourself whether the Supreme Court has provided standards for evaluating ineffective assistance of counsel that are sufficiently clear and demanding.

The *Burdine* case illustrates the fact that there is significant disagreement among judges about how to apply the U.S. Supreme Court standards for evaluating ineffective assistance of counsel. There were disagreements among state and federal courts, including a division among all the judges on the federal court of appeals. Do you believe that a sleeping defense attorney should automatically be regarded as providing ineffective assistance of counsel? Note that the majority opinion did not adopt that principle. Because the majority opinion focused narrowly on the facts of this case, the judges left open the possibility that attorneys can sleep during trials yet still be regarded as fulfilling the defendant's Sixth Amendment right to counsel as long as they do not sleep too much or during important moments in the trial.

In 2002 the U.S. Supreme Court examined a case in which a defendant claimed that he was denied effective assistance of counsel when he was not informed that his court-appointed attorney had recently represented the man he was accused of murdering (*Mickens v. Taylor*). At the heart of the case before the Court was the issue of whether the attorney had a conflict of interest because of his prior attorney-client relationship with the victim of the defen-

**Burdine v. Johnson, 262 F.3d 366
(U.S. Court of Appeals, 5th Cir., 2001)**

JUDGE BENAVIDES delivered the opinion of the court.

. . .

As an en banc court, we AFFIRM the judgment of the district court. The Supreme Court has long recognized that "a trial is unfair if the accused is denied counsel at a critical stage of his trial." *United States v. Cronic* . . . (1984). When a state court finds on the basis of credible evidence that defense counsel repeatedly slept as evidence was being introduced against a defendant, that defendant has been denied counsel at a critical stage of his trial. In such circumstances, the Supreme Court's Sixth Amendment jurisprudence compels the presumption that counsel's unconsciousness prejudiced the defendant.

[Description of the trial, including subsequent testimony during the habeas corpus hearing about the defense attorney's tendency to fall asleep. The foreman of the jury testified that he saw the attorney doze off between two and five times during the trial. Two other jurors also testified that they saw the attorney fall asleep repeatedly. The deputy clerk of the court also confirmed "lots of incidents" of the defense attorney sleeping during the trial. The judge, the prosecutor, and a fourth juror testified that they never saw the defense attorney fall asleep. However, a court administrator testified that he had spoken with the prosecutor during the trial and that the prosecutor had questioned the defense attorney's competence to handle capital cases. He also reported that the trial judge never again appointed the defense attorney to handle any capital trials. In his testimony, the defense attorney acknowledged that he had a habit of closing his eyes and tilting his head forward when he was concentrating. However, another attorney testified that Burdine's attorney fell asleep during other trials.]

. . .

. . . After detailing the evidence presented during the evidentiary hearing, the court entered "a finding that defense counsel dozed and actually fell asleep during portions of [Burdine's] trial on the merits, in particular the guilt-innocence phase when the State's solo prosecutor was questioning witnesses and presenting evidence." . . .

. . . In his appeal, the State concedes that we are bound by the habeas court's findings of fact. Specifically, the State "does not dispute that [defense coun-sel] dozed and actually fell asleep intermittently during Burdine's capital murder trial." The State maintains that habeas relief [i.e., a new trial] is nevertheless inappropriate [because] . . . the facts of Burdine's case do not warrant a presumption of prejudice because Burdine's counsel slept during indeterminate periods of what otherwise amounted to an adversarial trial.

The State's arguments fail to address the funda-mental unfairness in Burdine's capital murder trial created by the consistent unconsciousness of his counsel. It is well established that a defendant "re-quires the guiding hand of counsel at every step in the proceedings against him." *Powell v. Alabama*, 287 U.S. 45, 69 . . . (1932). Moreover, both the Supreme Court and this Court have recognized that the absence of counsel at critical stages of a defen-dant's trial undermines the fairness of the proceed-ing and therefore requires a presumption that the defendant was prejudiced by such deficiency. . . . Applying this longstanding principle, we conclude that a defendant's Sixth Amendment right to coun-sel is violated when that defendant's counsel is re-peatedly unconscious through not insubstantial portions of the defendant's capital murder trial. Under such circumstances, *Cronic* requires that we presume that the Sixth Amendment violation preju-diced the defendant. . . .

The State purports to accept the state trial court's findings that defense counsel slept during substantial portions of Burdine's trial. Nonetheless, the State painstakingly conducts a page-by-page analysis of the trial record in an apparent attempt to demon-strate that counsel was awake during significant portions of the trial. Yet, once we have accepted as presumptively correct the state court's finding that counsel slept "during portions of [Burdine's] trial on the merits, in particular during the guilt-innocence phase when the State's solo prosecutor was question-ing witnesses and presenting evidence," there is no need to attempt to further scrutinize the record. . . . The factual findings made during Burdine's state habeas proceedings demonstrate that Burdine's counsel was repeatedly asleep, and hence uncon-scious, as witnesses adverse to Burdine were exam-ined and other evidence against Burdine was introduced. This unconsciousness extended through a not insubstantial portion of the 12 hour and 51 minute trial. Unconscious counsel equates to no

(continued)

counsel at all. Unconscious counsel does not analyze, object, listen or in any way exercise judgment on behalf of a client. As recognized by the Second Circuit [U.S. Court of Appeals], "the buried assumption in our *Strickland* cases is that counsel is present and conscious to exercise judgment, calculation and instinct, for better or worse. But that is an assumption we cannot make when counsel is unconscious at critical times." *Tippins v. Walker,* 77 F.3d 682, 687 (2d Cir. 1996). When we have no basis for assuming that counsel exercised judgment on behalf of his client during critical stages of trial, we have insufficient basis for trusting the fairness of that trial and consequently we must presume prejudice.

The State suggests that because [the defense attorney] was physically present in the courtroom, his dozing constituted a form of performance that should be subjected to prejudice analysis. The State maintains that it is impossible to distinguish between sleeping counsel and other impairments that nevertheless have been subjected to prejudice analysis. We disagree. An unconscious attorney does not, indeed cannot, perform at all. This fact distinguishes the sleeping lawyer from the drunk or drugged one. Even the intoxicated attorney exercises judgment, though perhaps impaired, on behalf of his client at all times during a trial. Yet, the attorney that is unconscious during critical stages of a trial is simply not capable of exercising judgment. The unconscious attorney is in fact no different from an attorney that is physically absent from trial since both are equally unable to exercise judgment on behalf of their clients. Such absence of counsel at a critical stage of a proceeding makes the adversary process unreliable, and thus a presumption of prejudice is warranted pursuant to *Cronic.*

As in [a prior decision of the appellate court], we decline to adopt a per se rule that any dozing by defense counsel during trial merits a presumption of prejudice. Our holding, that the repeated unconsciousness of Burdine's counsel through not insubstantial portions of the critical guilt-innocence phase of Burdine's capital murder trial warrants a presumption of prejudice, is limited to the egregious facts found by the state habeas court in this case.

Based on the state court's findings that have been accepted by all as presumptively correct, we affirm the district court's grant of federal habeas corpus relief and vacate Burdine's capital murder conviction. The State is free to retry Burdine for capital murder.

[Five judges dissented in two separate dissenting opinions, in large part because they claimed that Burdine should not benefit from a presumption of prejudice when he waited for a decade after his trial to raise the issue of ineffective assistance of counsel based on his defense attorney's slumber. The *dissenting* opinion by Judge Jolly is omitted.]

JUDGE BARKSDALE, dissenting; joined by JUDGES JONES, SMITH, and GARZA.

. . .

The majority is not alone in its abhorrence at the spectacle of Cannon sleeping during a capital murder trial; but, our decision must not be influenced, much less dictated, by this. In focusing so narrowly and intently on [the defense attorney's] sleeping, the majority has lost sight of the reasons for the Sixth Amendment's requiring effective assistance of counsel in a criminal proceeding: adversarial testing of the prosecution's case and reliability of the result. . . .

The majority only pays lip service to these factors . . . ; it avoids applying them to this case. For example, it does not even mention Burdine's confession and [the defense attorney's] repeated efforts to keep it from the jury. Nor does it mention Burdine's testimony in which he *admitted* both robbing the victim and being present at his murder. The prosecution's case was more than tested; the result, more than reliable. [The defense attorney's] sleeping does not change that. . . .

. . . But, of utmost importance, and contrary to the majority's rule (again, applied only to this case), there is no state-finding that [the defense attorney] was "repeatedly unconscious" during "substantial" portions of the trial. Likewise, there are no state-findings as to:

> When [defense attorney] "dozed" as opposed to "slept";
>
> How long he slept, individually and collectively;
>
> How many times he slept;
>
> How deeply he slept;
>
> What happened while he slept, including which witness(es) was (were) testifying or other evidence was being presented; and
>
> When the sleeping occurred—which day(s), or whether during the morning or afternoon.

Moreover, the state habeas trial court did not discredit testimony by the trial judge and prosecutor that they did not observe [the defense attorney] sleeping. Because Burdine waited 11 years to raise the claim, memories have, of course, faded, making it impossible to determine what evidence was being presented while [the defense attorney] slept. . . .

Likewise, the state habeas trial court made no finding that [the defense attorney's] dozing or sleeping reached the level of "unconsciousness." Moreover, the testimony of the witnesses at the state habeas evidentiary hearing—describing [the attorney] as "dozing," "nodding," "bobbing his head," and "asleep"—does not support the majority's assumption that [the attorney] was, as a result, "repeatedly unconscious." . . .

Even assuming *arguendo* [the attorney] was "unconscious" each time he slept, the majority does not define "not insubstantial." Does it intend for substantiality to be judged by the length of sleep, or is it to be based on the significance of the evidence being presented while counsel slept and its impact on the defense? . . .

Therefore, I must respectfully dissent. I would hold that, under the circumstances of this case, prej-

udice must be proved. Accordingly, I would remand on that and the myriad ineffective assistance and other issues Burdine raised in his federal habeas application, which the district court did not address . . . It may well be that, on remand, Burdine could, *inter alia,* satisfy the *Strickland* two-prong test for ineffective assistance and be accorded a new trial on that basis. . . .

Burdine had the burden of proving [the attorney] was absent, by sleeping, during "critical stages" of trial. Because Burdine cannot demonstrate when [the attorney] slept, . . . he has not shown it was a "critical stage." The majority does not even discuss the facts of Burdine's case, much less the crucial point that, because Burdine admitted robbing Wise, the State's evidence of the robbery was uncontested by Burdine. Instead, the majority concludes that Burdine has established presumed-prejudice merely by demonstrating [the attorney] slept (characterized as "repeatedly unconscious") during some unidentified, "not insubstantial" portions of the guilt-innocence phase. . . .

dant's alleged crime. A closely divided Court rejected the ineffective-assistance-of-counsel claim. On behalf of a five-member majority, Justice Scalia concluded that the defendant did not prove that the apparent conflict of interest adversely affected the attorney's performance. Three separate dissenting opinions, representing the views of four justices, strenuously argued that the trial judge and the defense attorney had failed in their professional duties by not revealing the conflict of interest.

CONCLUSION

The Sixth Amendment right to counsel initially meant only that defendants in federal cases had the right to hire attorneys without interference from the government. As part of the incorporation process, the twentieth-century Supreme Court expanded the coverage of the right to require governments to provide attorneys for indigent defendants in both state and federal courts. Attorneys must be provided whenever defendants face the prospect of incarceration, and representation must continue only through the first appeal of right. The Supreme Court curtailed further expansion of the right to counsel after its composition changed in the early 1970s.

Police officers are supposed to cease questioning suspects who have asserted their desire to be represented by an attorney during interrogation. Interrogation can resume only in the presence of the requested attorney or if the suspect initiates further discussions with police. Suspects need not be informed that an attorney is waiting to represent them. They are entitled only to the formal elements of the *Miranda* warnings rather than complete information about their own situation. Defendants can waive their right to counsel in the early stages of the process during questioning as well as in later stages if they wish to represent themselves in court. There is, however, no right to represent oneself on appeal because the right to representation on appeal comes from the Due Process Clause rather than from the Sixth Amendment.

The Supreme Court has established a difficult standard that convicted offenders must fulfill in order to prove that their counsel's performance was so ineffective as to constitute a rights violation. Defendants must prove that their attorney made specific errors that were so significant that they had a reasonable probability of affecting the outcome of the case. Many convicted offenders are dissatisfied with their attorneys' performance, but very few are successful in raising such a claim.

SUMMARY

- The Sixth Amendment right to counsel initially meant that only federal defendants could hire their own attorneys if they could afford to do so.

- The Supreme Court gradually expanded the right to counsel by requiring the appointment of counsel for poor defendants facing the death penalty (*Powell v. Alabama*) and those facing serious charges in federal court (*Johnson v. Zerbst*).

- In the 1960s and early 1970s, the Supreme Court incorporated the right to counsel (*Gideon v. Wainwright*) for all trial-level cases with the prospect of incarceration as a punishment (*Argersinger v. Hamlin*) and the first appeal of right (*Douglas v. California*).

- When the Court's composition changed in the 1970s, expansion of the right to counsel ceased when the Court decided that no right applies for discretionary appeals (*Ross v. Moffitt*) and no counsel is required for minor cases when the punishment is merely a fine (*Scott v. Illinois*).

- Defendants can waive their right to counsel and represent themselves at trial but not in appeals.

- The Supreme Court has established a difficult-to-prove standard for ineffective assistance of counsel, which requires the demonstration of specific errors by the defense attorney that had a reasonable probability of affecting the outcome of the case.

Key Terms

adversary system   The legal process model employed in the United States in which the truth is presumed to emerge from the clash of opposing advocates in the courtroom, and therefore the attorney's performance can be a central element in determining the fate of individuals drawn into the court system.

contingency fee   Compensation method for lawyers in some civil legal cases in which they take no money from the clients but, instead, take 30 percent of any settlement or award plus reimbursement of expenses.

first appeal of right   The initial appeal provided for under state law that typically is presented to an intermediate appellate court and for which indi-

gents are entitled to representation supplied by the state.

indigent defendants   Criminal defendants who are too poor to hire their own attorneys and therefore are entitled to have attorneys supplied for them by the state.

ineffective assistance of counsel   A difficult-to-prove rights violation claim asserted by convicted offenders who claim that their attorneys' performances were so inadequate that they failed to fulfill the requirements of the Sixth Amendment.

inquisitorial system   Alternative legal process model employed by many European countries in which the judge takes an active role in questioning witnesses and evaluating evidence so that the lawyer is less central in determining the outcome of the case.

parolees　Convicted offenders who have already served a portion of their sentences in prison before being released into the community to live at home under restrictive conditions, including daily or weekly meetings with a parole officer. Any violations of parole conditions can lead to a return to prison.

probationers　Convicted offenders serving sentences of probation in which they live within their home communities under restrictive conditions, such as curfews and prohibitions on alcohol, with the threat of incarceration for violating any of their probation conditions.

***pro se* litigants**　Litigants who represent themselves in court, typically in a civil lawsuit or habeas corpus action in which they have no constitutional right to assistance of counsel.

Additional Readings

Goodman, James. 1994. *Stories of Scottsboro*. New York: Random House. Detailed analysis of the events surrounding *Powell v. Alabama*.

Lewis, Anthony. 1964. *Gideon's Trumpet*. New York: Random House. Best-selling true story of the stage-by-stage details of the case of *Gideon v. Wainwright*.

Tucker, John C. 1997. *May God Have Mercy: A True Story of Crime and Punishment*. New York: W. W. Norton. True story of a capital punishment case that reached the Supreme Court in which there are significant questions about whether the appointed defense attorneys were sufficiently effective to prevent the ultimate execution of a man who was very possibly innocent of the crime.

Notes

1. Anthony Lewis, *Gideon's Trumpet* (New York: Random House, 1964).

2. Kent Roach and Martin Friedland, "Borderline Justice: Policing in the Two Niagaras," *American Journal of Criminal Law* 23 (1996): 241–252.

3. Stephen B. Bright, "Counsel for the Poor: The Death Sentence Not for the Worst Crime but for the Worst Lawyer," *Yale Law Journal* 103 (1994): 1835–1883.

4. Roger Hanson and W. K. Daley, *Federal Habeas Corpus Review: Challenging State Court Convictions* (Washington, D.C.: U.S. Department of Justice, Bureau of Justice Statistics, 1995), 14.

CHAPTER NINE

Pretrial Processes

Imagine that you are driving back to college after spending a weekend with relatives. The traffic on the highway is backed up for miles because of road construction. After sitting for an hour in a line of cars moving at a snail's pace, you lose patience and decide to find your own shortcut. You leave the highway at the next exit and begin working your way through backroads and small towns in the direction that you think will take you back to your college's town. When you stop for gas in one small town, you have the strange perception that the guy working at the gas station is staring at you. As you take extra time to check your oil and tire pressure, a police car drives into the station and parks next to your car.

"Where you going?" the officer asks, as he stands above you while you check the tire.

"I'm going back to school in Collegeville."

"You're a little bit out of your way, aren't you?"

"Yeah, I was trying to avoid some construction on the interstate highway."

The officer looks over the station employee standing in the doorway and calls out, "Hey, Billy, c'mere."

The station employee saunters over slowly, looking at you closely.

The officer speaks again. "Take a good look now, Billy. Is this the person?"

Billy nods his head. "Yup, I think it is."

You look at both of them in confusion as the officer says, "I'm going to have to take you in. Put your hands up against the car and stand with your feet apart."

The officer proceeds to conduct a patdown search, places handcuffs on you, and drives you to the county jail in a neighboring small town. Along the way, the officer informs you of your *Miranda* rights and informs you that you have been identified by a witness as the perpetrator of a robbery that occurred in the town four months earlier. When you ask how long you have to stay in jail before bail is set and you can gain release to straighten out this mistake, the officer replies, "Well, the judge is sick, so you might not get into court for a few days yet. Maybe sometime next week."

As you sit in the jail cell feeling increasing frustration and anxiety waiting to be permitted to make a phone call, you search your mind to remember what you learned about arrests and pretrial processes in your criminal procedure class. You ask yourself whether you have any rights that might help you or whether you foresee any potential rights violations on the horizon.

Could such a scenario happen to you? While such events may be unlikely for many people, they *could* happen. Anyone can be drawn into the criminal justice process. Anyone can be arrested and placed in jail. Even the most innocent person is at risk if there is a mistaken identification or an unethical police officer who wants to give you a hard time. In November 2000, popular musician and singer Lenny Kravitz was taken into custody while walking down the street in Miami because police thought that he fit the description of a suspected bank robber. Fortunately for Kravitz, when the bank teller was brought to identify the suspect, the bank teller said that Kravitz was not the robber.[1] What would have happened if the bank teller had mistakenly told the police that Kravitz looked like the robber? Human imperfections, whether vision, memory, or ethics, can have significant impacts on people brought into contact with the criminal justice system, potentially even people who are rich and famous.

In this chapter, we will examine processes prior to trial after a suspect has been arrested. As with other aspects of the criminal procedure, court decisions interpreting the Constitution have created certain rules that define rights for arrestees and permissible practices for police and prosecutors. Despite these rights and rules, people's fates are still determined through discretionary decisions made by authoritative actors in the criminal justice process.

IDENTIFICATION PROCEDURES

Lineups, Showups, and Photographic Displays

When someone is at the police station, either through arrest or through a voluntary appearance to talk to officers, efforts may be made to gather additional evidence to either incriminate (prove guilt) or exculpate (prove innocence) the suspect. There are many investigation techniques used at this stage. In a **lineup,** the suspect is placed in a row with other people so that a witness or a victim can attempt to identify if the perpetrator is among them. By contrast, a **showup** involves showing the victim or witness only one person to see if that person is

Investigation and Record-Keeping

Technological advances have enhanced the possibilities for law enforcement officials to gather, store, and use potentially useful evidence. For example, new computer programs permit more rapid sorting of fingerprint records in order to match crime scene evidence with fingerprints on file from people arrested in the past. Debates have emerged about the use of new techniques and record-keeping in criminal justice. For example, Howard Safir, a former New York City police commissioner, has argued that DNA samples should be taken from all arrestees in order to build a database that can be used for unsolved and future crimes.[2] This proposal has faced opposition as an invasion of privacy. Moreover, anyone can be arrested, even if they are never convicted of a crime. Thus such a database would contain records from innocent people about whom there is no basis for suspicion of wrongdoing. In addition, many people do not trust criminal justice officials to take proper care of such evidence. There are fears that some police officers may be tempted to "solve" a case by placing an innocent person's DNA sample at a crime scene and later matching it with the DNA in the database. Unfortunately, there have been isolated examples of the misuse of evidence, such as the case of police officers in New York who took fingerprint samples from innocent people by lifting them off glasses at a bar and then placing those fingerprints on objects at the scene of an unsolved crime. Physical evidence is not automatically trustworthy. Its trustworthiness depends on ethical and careful handling, storage, and record-keeping.

Should DNA be collected and stored from all arrestees? Do you foresee problems with such a policy?

identified as the perpetrator. Showups often happen on the street around crime scenes, but it is possible that officers may try this technique at the station house or courthouse. **Photographic displays** involve having the victim or witness look through a set of photographs in order to attempt to make an identification. In all of these techniques, there are risks that the victim or witness did not get a good look at the perpetrator, especially because many crimes, such as muggings, robberies, and burglaries, involve very brief exposure to a criminal in a stressful context that often does not have good lighting. For example, read the completely inconsistent descriptions of a killer provided by eyewitnesses to a murder in *Kyles v. Whitley* (1995) presented in a box on pp. 298–299. These risks create the possibility of errors that will lead an innocent person to be drawn into the criminal justice process.

Other kinds of evidence-gathering techniques are also used. Two kinds of techniques, photographing and fingerprinting suspects, are used automatically as a matter of course in order to create records of arrests that may be used to confirm evidence drawn from the scene or from witnesses' statements. Other techniques, such as providing handwriting samples, are used only in certain cases in which such evidence might be relevant. As you read the material on technology in the above box, think about how effective use of technology depends on the behavior of the people who employ the new innovations.

The use of pretrial investigation procedures raises questions about the existence of any constitutional rights that may limit the extent of police authority to gather evidence from suspects who are in custody or voluntarily at the station house. We already know from *Cupp v. Murphy* (1973) in Chapter 5 that the Court permitted police officers to take scrapings from under the fingernails of a homicide suspect who appeared voluntarily for questioning. The Court justified this search of the person's body for evidence under the "exigent circumstances" rationale because evidence might have been lost in the time it would take to obtain a warrant. The investigation procedures that we will examine here do not rest on the same rationale. In *United States v. Wade* (1967), the Supreme Court discussed several important issues concerning these investigation techniques in examining the lineup identification procedure. As you read the Court's opinion in the box on pp. 284–286, think about the risks that the justices are seeking to avoid by creating the new rule in this case.

The opinion in *United States v. Wade* highlighted many important issues concerning the pretrial investigation techniques. First, the Court made clear that there are no Fifth Amendment self-incrimination problems with these techniques. Self-incrimination issues arise only with respect to testimonial evidence, which would be communication from the suspect that constitutes speaking about his or her guilt. Looking at the suspect's physical characteristics, including the sound of his or her voice, constitutes **real or physical evidence** and can be gathered without any worries about the Fifth Amendment. Thus fingerprints, photographs, lineups, handwriting samples, and the other pretrial techniques involve having the suspect provide potentially incriminating evidence. However, because this evidence is not in the form of communicated statements, it does not implicate the privilege against compelled self-incrimination.

Second, the Court presented the concept of **critical stages** in the criminal justice process and used this concept as the test to determine when the presence of a defense attorney is necessary to protect the rights of defendants. The Court defined *critical stages* as "any stage of the prosecution, formal or informal, in court or out, where counsel's absence might derogate from the accused's right to a fair trial." Justices have also described "critical stages" as steps in the justice process in which a defendant's rights and ultimate fate would be significantly disadvantaged by the absence of defense counsel. In other cases, the Court took this concept and attempted to determine when it applies. For example, in *Gilbert v. California* (1967), the Court decided that the production of a handwriting sample is not a critical stage. This is a systematic procedure that is less susceptible to error, especially as compared to identifications being made by witnesses and victims. Ultimately, the defendant is entitled to representation at certain stages—the "critical" ones—such as during custodial police interrogation and certain lineup contexts represented by the *Wade* case, but not in other settings such as bail hearings and questioning during traffic stops. Prominent legal scholars have observed that "identification procedures mentioned in *Wade* are more easily explained on right to effective cross-examination grounds than assistance-of-counsel grounds."[3] An attorney can conduct cross-examination effectively regarding the taking of a handwriting sample without being present when it is produced, but the same may not be true of lineup identification procedures.

Third, the Court determined that the lineup situation in *Wade* constituted a "critical stage," and therefore Wade's rights were violated when his attorney was not present during the identification procedure.

United States v. Wade, 388 U.S. 218 (1967)

JUSTICE BRENNAN delivered the opinion of the Court.

The question here is whether courtroom identifications of an accused at trial are to be excluded from evidence because the accused was exhibited to the witnesses before trial at a post-indictment lineup conducted for identification purposes without notice to and in the absence of the accused's appointed counsel.

. . . [After a bank robbery,] [o]n March 23, 1965, an indictment was returned against respondent Wade and two others for conspiring to rob the bank and against Wade and the accomplice for the robbery itself. Wade was arrested on April 2, and counsel was appointed to represent him on April 26. Fifteen days later an FBI agent, without notice to Wade's lawyer, arranged to have the two bank employees observe a lineup made up of Wade and five or six other prisoners and conducted in a courtroom of the local county courthouse. Each person in the line wore strips of tape such as allegedly worn by the robber and upon direction each said something like "put the money in the bag," the words allegedly uttered by each robber. Both bank employees identified Wade in the lineup as the bank robber.

. . . At trial, . . . Wade's counsel moved for a judgment of acquittal or, alternatively, to strike the bank officials' courtroom identifications on the ground that the conduct of the lineup, without notice to and in the absence of his appointed counsel, violated his Fifth Amendment privilege against self-incrimination and his Sixth Amendment right to assistance of counsel. The motion was denied, and Wade was convicted. . . .

Neither the lineup itself nor anything shown by this record that Wade was required to do in the line-up violated his privilege against self-incrimination. We have only recently reaffirmed that the privilege "protects an accused only from being compelled to testify against himself, or otherwise provide the State with evidence of a testimonial or communicative nature. . . ." *Schmerber v. California* [1966]. . . . We there held that compelling a suspect to submit to a withdrawal of a sample of his blood for analysis for alcohol content and the admission in evidence of the analysis report were not compulsion to those ends. . . .

We have no doubt that compelling the accused merely to exhibit his person for observation by a prosecution witness prior to trial involves no compulsion of the accused to give evidence having testimonial significance. It is compulsion of the accused to exhibit his physical characteristics, not compulsion to disclose any knowledge he might have. It is no different from compelling Schmerber to provide a blood sample or [other suspects to try on an article of clothing to see if it fits], and as in those instances, is not within the cover of the privilege. Similarly, compelling Wade to speak within hearing distance of the witnesses, even to utter words purportedly uttered by the robber, was not compulsion to utter statements of a "testimonial" nature; he was required to use his voice as an identifying physical characteristic, not speak his guilt. We held in *Schmerber* . . . that the distinction to be drawn under the Fifth Amendment privilege against self-incrimination is one between an accused's "communications" in whatever form, vocal or physical, and "compulsion which makes a suspect or accused the source of 'real or physical evidence'" . . . None of these activities becomes testimonial within the scope of the privilege because required of the accused in pretrial lineup. . . .

. . . [O]ur cases have construed the Sixth Amendment guarantee to apply to "critical" stages of the proceedings. The guarantee reads: "In all criminal prosecutions, the accused shall enjoy the right . . . to have the Assistance of Counsel *for his defence*" (emphasis supplied). The plain wording of this guarantee thus encompasses counsel's assistance whenever necessary to assure a meaningful "defence." . . .

. . . [T]he accused is guaranteed that he need not stand alone against the State at any stage of the prosecution, formal or informal, in court or out, where counsel's absence might derogate from the accused's right to a fair trial. The security of that right is as much the aim of the right to counsel as it is of the other guarantees of the Sixth Amendment. . . . The presence of counsel at such critical confrontations, as at the trial itself, operates to assure that the accused's interests will be protected consistently with our adversary theory of criminal prosecution.

In sum, the principle of *Powell v. Alabama* and succeeding cases requires that we scrutinize *any* pretrial confrontation of the accused to determine whether the presence of his counsel is necessary to preserve the defendant's basic right to a fair trial as affected by his right meaningfully to cross-examine the witnesses against him and to have effective assistance of counsel at the trial itself. It calls upon us to analyze whether potential substantial prejudice to defendant's rights inheres in the particular confrontation and the ability of counsel to help avoid that prejudice.

The Government characterizes the lineup as a mere preparatory step in the gathering of the prosecution's evidence, not different for Sixth Amendment purposes from various other preparatory steps, such as systematized or scientific analyzing of the accused's fingerprints, blood sample, clothing, hair, and the like. We think there are differences which preclude such stages being characterized as critical stages at which the accused has the right to the presence of his counsel. Knowledge of the techniques of science and technology is sufficiently available, and the variables in techniques few enough, that the accused has the opportunity for a meaningful confrontation of the Government's case at trial through the ordinary processes of cross-examination of the Government's expert witnesses and the presentation of the evidence of his own experts. The denial of a right to have his counsel present at such analyses does not therefore violate the Sixth Amendment; they are not critical stages since there is minimal risk that his counsel's absence at such stages might derogate from his right to a fair trial.

But the confrontation compelled by the State between the accused and the victim or witnesses to a crime to elicit identification evidence is peculiarly riddled with innumerable dangers and variable factors which might seriously, even crucially, derogate from a fair trial. The vagaries of eyewitness identification are well-known; the annals of criminal law are rife with instances of mistaken identification. Mr. Justice Frankfurter once said: "What is the worth of identification testimony even when uncontradicted? The identification of strangers is proverbially untrustworthy. The hazards of such testimony are established by a formidable number of instances in the records of English and American trials. . . ." A major factor contributing to the high incidence of miscarriage of justice from mistaken identification has been the degree of suggestion inherent in the manner in which the prosecution presents the suspect to witnesses for pretrial identification. A commentator has observed that "[t]he influence of improper suggestion upon identifying witnesses

probably accounts for more miscarriages of justice than any other single factor. . . . Suggestion can be created intentionally or unintentionally in many subtle ways. And the dangers for the suspect are particularly grave when the witness' opportunity for observation was insubstantial, and thus his susceptibility to suggestion the greatest.

Moreover, "[i]t is a matter of common experience that, once a witness has picked out the accused at the lineup, he is not likely to go back on his word later on, so that in practice the issue of identity may (in the absence of other relevant evidence) for all practical purposes be determined there and then, before the trial." . . .

In any event, neither witnesses nor lineup participants are likely to be schooled in the detection of suggestive influences. Improper influences may go undetected by a suspect, guilty or not, who experiences the emotional tension which we might expect in one being confronted with potential accusers. Even when he does observe abuse, if he has a criminal record he may be reluctant to take the stand and open up the admission of prior convictions. Moreover, any protestations by the suspect of the fairness of the lineup made at trial are likely to be in vain; the jury's choice is between the accused's unsupported version and that of the police officers present. In short, accused's inability effectively to reconstruct at trial any unfairness that occurred at the lineup may deprive him of his only opportunity meaningfully to attack the credibility of the witness' courtroom identification.

What facts have been disclosed in specific cases about the conduct of pretrial confrontations for identification illustrate both the potential for substantial prejudice to the accused at that stage and the need for its revelation at trial. . . . Similarly state reports, in the course of describing prior identifications admitted as evidence of guilt, reveal numerous instances of suggestive procedures, for example, that all in the lineup but the suspect were known to the identifying witness, that the other participants in a lineup were grossly dissimilar in appearance to the suspect, that only the suspect was required to wear distinctive clothing which the culprit allegedly wore, that the witness is told by the police that they have caught the culprit after which the defendant is brought before the witness alone or is viewed in jail, that the suspect is pointed out before or during a lineup, and that the participants in the lineup are asked to try on an article of clothing which fits only the suspect. . . .

(continued)

Since it appears that there is grave potential for prejudice, intentional or not, in the pretrial lineup, which may not be capable of reconstruction at trial, and since presence of counsel itself can often avert prejudice and assure a meaningful confrontation at trial, there can be little doubt that for Wade the post-indictment lineup was a critical stage of the prosecution at which he was "as much entitled to such aid [of counsel] . . . as at the trial itself." . . . Thus both Wade and his counsel should have been notified of the impending lineup, and counsel's presence should have been requisite to conduct of the lineup, absent an "intelligent waiver." . . . No substantially countervailing policy considerations have been advanced against the requirement of the presence of counsel. Concern is expressed that the requirement will forestall prompt identifications and result in obstruction of the confrontations. As for the first, we note that in the two cases in which the right to counsel is today held to apply [i.e., *Wade* and a companion case], counsel had already been appointed and no argument is made in either case that notice to counsel would have prejudicially delayed the confrontations. . . . And to refuse to recognize the right to counsel for fear that counsel will obstruct the course of justice is contrary to the basic assumptions upon which this Court has operated in Sixth Amendment cases. We rejected similar logic in *Miranda v. Arizona.* . . . In our view counsel can hardly impede legitimate law enforcement; on the contrary, for the reasons expressed, law enforcement may be assisted by preventing the infiltration of taint in the prosecution's identification evidence. That result cannot help the guilty avoid conviction but can only help assure that the right man has been brought to justice. . . .

Suggestiveness of Identification Procedures

Another important issue also appeared in *Wade*. The Court discussed the risks to defendants if there is no counsel present during lineups. The justices state that eyewitness testimony can be notoriously unreliable. Moreover, there is a concern about **suggestiveness,** meaning that police officers may intentionally or unintentionally give the witness clues about which suspect to identify in a lineup. The Court describes several blatant examples of suggestiveness, such as having the suspect stand with a group of people who are totally dissimilar in appearance (e.g., having an African American suspect stand in a lineup with a group of whites) or otherwise making the suspect distinctive within the group (e.g., having the suspect as the only person in the lineup wearing an orange jail jumpsuit and handcuffs). Suggestiveness can also be subtle and subconscious. Officers may not even realize that they are saying such things as "Are you sure it isn't suspect Number 3? Take a good long look," when they do not make any such specific references to the other individuals in the lineup. In *Moore v. Illinois* (1977), the Court invalidated an identification when officers told the witness that she was going to view the suspect as she was taken to make the identification. Moreover, the witness heard the prosecutor recite evidence that was going to be used to implicate the suspect. Such information conveyed to the witness went too far in suggesting that the suspect in custody was the person whom the witness had seen for a few brief seconds during the crime.

There are also risks that victims and witnesses who are susceptible to suggestiveness at the lineup will confidently testify about their identification later in court—not because they were so confident at the actual lineup, but because they remember the suspect quite clearly *from the lineup* and not from the crime.

The Court noted that it is extraordinarily difficult for witnesses to guard against suggestive actions by the police. In addition, the suspect may have no way to know what suggestive actions may be occurring, especially if the lineup is in one room and the witness is standing with officers in a separate room with a one-way mirror window. Even if the suspect recognizes elements of unfair suggestiveness, the trial court may not accept the word of a criminal suspect over that of the police officers who conducted the lineup. An attorney would be a perceptive observer of lineups who would know to look for suggestiveness and who would have the ability to bring it to the attention of the trial court.

Despite the concerns embodied in the Court's *Wade* decision, other decisions indicate a degree of flexibility in examining the permissibility of identification procedures. In *Stovall v. Denno* (1967), an assailant stabbed to death a man within his home. The man's wife jumped at the assailant and was herself stabbed eleven times. She was seriously injured and there was uncertainty about whether she would survive. The police brought the handcuffed suspect to her hospital room where she identified him as the assailant. The Supreme Court approved the identification procedure. Although the procedure was suggestive, because only one suspect was brought before the witness, the Court also indicated a concern about the necessity of using certain procedures. In this case, the victim could not come to the police station, and there were concerns that the victim might die at any time before a less suggestive procedure could be arranged. In addition to weighing the necessity of a certain procedure against the procedure's suggestiveness, the Court also is concerned about the reliability of the identification. Presumably, an unreliable identification, such as one in which the victim had an obscured and fleeting view of the offender running away down a dark alley, would not be as readily acceptable in suggestive circumstances. In *Stovall*, by contrast, the surviving victim had close contact with the assailant within the close confines of her own home.

Similarly, in *Simmons v. United States* (1968), the Court approved the actions of FBI agents who showed photographs of suspected robbers, who were still at large, to bank employees who witnessed the robbery. In establishing the rule of the case, the Court declared, "[W]e hold that each case must be considered on its own facts, and that convictions based on eyewitness identification at trial following a pretrial identification by photograph will be set aside on that ground only if the photographic identification procedure was so impermissibly suggestive as to give rise to a very substantial likelihood of irreparable misidentification." Here, the Court saw the FBI taking necessary actions under the circumstances, despite the risk of suggestiveness. As stated by the majority opinion, "It was essential for the FBI agents swiftly to determine whether they were on the right track, so that they could properly deploy their forces in Chicago and, if necessary, alert officials in other cities."

The Court illustrated its flexibility and concern about reliability when it accepted a suggestive identification in *Neil v. Biggers* (1972). In the case, a woman had been taken from her home at knifepoint and raped after being made to walk two blocks away into the woods. She had close contact with the assailant for fifteen to thirty minutes, first in her home and then in the relative brightness of a full-moon night. As you read the Court's opinion in the box on p. 288, ask yourself whether the justices struck the proper balance between investigating crime and protecting against the risk of misidentification.

Recall that in *Wade,* the Court emphasized the important role for defense attorneys at identification lineups in order to reduce the risk of misidentification and enhance reliability by facilitating the possibility of effective cross-examination at trial. In light of the Court's discussion of issues in *Wade,* can

Neil v. Biggers, 409 U.S. 188 (1972)

JUSTICE POWELL delivered the opinion of the Court.

. . .

On several occasions over the course of the next seven months, she viewed suspects in her home or at the police station, some in lineups and others in showups, and was shown between 30 and 40 photographs. She told the police that a man pictured in one of the photographs had features similar to those of her assailant, but identified none of the suspects. On August 17, the police called her to the station to view [the suspect], who was being detained on another charge. In an effort to construct a suitable lineup, the police checked the city jail and the city juvenile home. Finding no one at either place fitting petitioner's unusual physical description, they conducted the showup instead.

The showup consisted of two detectives walking [the suspect] past the victim. At the victim's request, the police directed [the suspect] to say "shut up or I'll kill you." The testimony at trial was not altogether clear as to whether the victim first identified him and then asked that he repeat the words or made her identification after he had spoken. In any event, the victim testified that she had "no doubt" about her identification. . . .

. . . The victim spent a considerable period of time with her assailant, up to half an hour. She was with him under adequate artificial light in her house and under a full moon outdoors, and at least twice, once in the house and later in the woods, faced him directly and intimately. She was no casual observer, but rather the victim of one of the most personally humiliating of all crimes. Her description to the police, which included the assailant's approximate age, height, weight, complexion, skin texture, build, and voice, . . . was more than ordinarily thorough. She had "no doubt" that respondent was the person who raped her. In the nature of the crime, there are rarely witnesses to a rape other than the victim, who often has limited opportunity of observation. The victim here, a practical nurse by profession, had an unusual opportunity to observe and identify her assailant. She testified at the habeas corpus hearing that there was something about his face "I don't think I could ever forget." . . .

There was, to be sure, a lapse of seven months between the rape and the confrontation. This would be a seriously negative factor in most cases. Here, however, the testimony is undisputed that the victim made no previous identification at any of the showups, lineups, or photographic showings. Her record for reliability was thus a good one, as she had previously resisted whatever suggestiveness inheres in a showup. Weighing all the factors, we find no substantial likelihood of misidentification. The evidence was properly allowed to go to the jury.

you understand the justices' conclusions and reasoning in *Kirby v. Illinois* (1972)? After the *Kirby* decision, what is the rule concerning the right to counsel during pretrial lineups? As you read the accompanying Court's opinion in *Kirby,* ask yourself whether the decision is consistent with the prior precedent established in *Wade.*

The reasoning in *Kirby* emphasized the formal initiation of prosecution as the triggering mechanism for "critical stages" that require the application of the Sixth Amendment right to counsel. In *Wade* the suspect had been indicted and thereby formally charged by a grand jury. Thus the lineup was a critical stage requiring the presence of counsel. By contrast, Kirby was identified by the victim prior to being charged with a crime. Therefore, according to the Court's reasoning, there was no need for an attorney to be present.

Are the decisions in *Wade* and *Kirby* consistent? *Wade* emphasized the grave risks of suggestiveness and error if no attorney was available at the identification procedure in order to monitor what was said and to be prepared to challenge the identification in court. The risks are no less grave for the

Kirby v. Illinois, 406 U.S. 682 (1972)

JUSTICE STEWART announced the Court's judgment and delivered an opinion joined by CHIEF JUSTICE BURGER and JUSTICES BLACKMUN and REHNQUIST. [JUSTICE POWELL concurred in the result of the case to provide the fifth vote needed to determine the outcome.]

In *United States v. Wade* . . . [1967] and *Gilbert v. California* . . . [1967], this Court held "that a post-indictment pretrial lineup at which the accused is exhibited to identifying witnesses is a critical stage of the criminal prosecution; that police conduct of such a lineup without notice to and in the absence of his counsel denies the accused his Sixth [and Fourteenth] Amendment right to counsel and calls in question the admissibility at trial of the in-court identification of the accused by witnesses who attended the lineup.". . . In the present case we are asked to extend the *Wade-Gilbert per se* exclusionary rule to identification testimony based upon a police station showup that took place *before* the defendant had been indicted or otherwise formally charged with any criminal offense. . . .

[A man was robbed by two men of his wallet and traveler's checks. Police later stopped two men on the street and found them in possession of the wallet, which they claimed to have won in a crap game. They were arrested and brought to the station where officers linked them to the robbery of the wallet, which had been reported two days earlier.]

. . . [A police car picked up the crime victim and brought him to the police station.] . . . Immediately upon entering the room in the police station where the petitioner and [his companion] were seated at a table, [the victim] positively identified them as the men who had robbed him two days earlier. No lawyer was present in the room, and neither the petitioner nor [his companion] had asked for legal assistance, or been advised of any right to the presence of counsel.

More than six weeks later, the [two men] were indicted for the robbery. . . .

The initiation of judicial criminal proceedings is far more than a mere formalism. It is the starting point of our whole system of adversary criminal justice. For it is only then that the government has committed itself to prosecute, and only then that the adverse positions of government and defendant have solidified. It is then that a defendant finds himself faced with the prosecutorial forces of organized society, and immersed in the intricacies of substantive and procedural criminal law. It is this point, therefore, that marks the commencement of the "criminal prosecutions" to which alone the explicit guarantees of the Sixth Amendment are applicable. . . .

In this case we are asked to import into a routine police investigation an absolute constitutional guarantee historically and rationally applicable only after the onset of formal prosecutorial proceedings. We decline to do so. Less than a year after *Wade* and *Gilbert* were decided, the Court explained the rule of those decisions as follows: "The rationale of those cases was that an accused is entitled to counsel at any 'critical stage of the *prosecution*,' and that a post-indictment lineup is such a 'critical stage.'" *Simmons v. United States* . . . . We decline to depart from that rationale today by imposing a *per se* exclusionary rule upon testimony concerning an identification that took place long before the commencement of any prosecution whatsoever.

What has been said is not to suggest that there may not be occasions during the course of a criminal investigation when the police do abuse identification procedures. Such abuses are not beyond the reach of the Constitution. As the Court pointed out in *Wade* itself, it is always necessary to "scrutinize any pretrial confrontation. . . ." . . . The Due Process Clause of the Fifth and Fourteenth Amendments forbids a lineup that is unnecessarily suggestive and conducive to irreparable mistaken identification. . . . When a person has not been formally charged with a criminal offense, [a prior precedent] strikes the appropriate constitutional balance between the right of a suspect to be protected from prejudicial procedures and the interest of society in the prompt and purposeful investigation of an unsolved crime.

defendants in *Kirby*. After all, the identification served as the crucial piece of evidence for the prosecution that led to their criminal convictions. Yet the justices do not appear concerned at all about risk of error in this context. The evidence is just as devastating to the defendant in both cases. The risk of an

Defense Attorneys and Identification Procedures

What is the message sent to police officers from the two co-existing but seemingly contradictory decisions in *Wade* and *Kirby*? The Court probably did not intend to send a specific message. The *Kirby* decision may simply reflect the fact that Nixon's four law-and-order appointees joined the Supreme Court after the *Wade* decision and that they constituted four-fifths of the justices who supported the outcome in *Kirby*. The practical impact for police practice, however, was to encourage officers to use lineups, showups, and other identification procedures *before filing formal charges against the defendant*. If the techniques are used prior to formal charging, then there is no need for an attorney to be present. If formal charges have been applied, then

the right to counsel exists at this "critical stage." If the new justices had hoped to overturn *Wade* but simply did not have enough votes to do so at the time of *Kirby*, they still may have advanced their underlying objective by giving police officers new opportunities to use identification procedures without any scrutiny from defense attorneys.

Is the legal protection promised by *Wade*—namely, the presence of a defense attorney during a lineup in order to combat the risk of prejudicial error—a real protection or an illusory right? If police officers' discretionary decisions determine whether a right is activated (i.e., by deciding whether to do a lineup before or after charges are formally filed), is the right merely symbolic?

unreliable identification may actually be worse in *Kirby* since it was a showup in which the victim saw only the suspects and did not have to pick them out of a lineup of people with similar characteristics. The risks that justified the presence of counsel in *Wade* are equally, if not more, threatening in *Kirby*, yet the Court drew a line—the moment of initiation of prosecution—to serve as the determining factor for the right to counsel rather than focusing on the practical risks of error and harm to a defendant's interests. As you read the above box on the symbolic nature of rights, ask yourself whether police officers will adjust their behavior to undercut the protection provided by *Wade*.

Subsequent In-Court Identifications

An important question that emerges from the identification cases decided by the Supreme Court is whether witnesses can make a valid in-court identification after an out-of-court lineup or photo array identification has been invalidated for suggestiveness or, after indictment, the absence of counsel. In other words, does an improper pretrial identification preclude the witness from identifying the suspect, or can the witness make a valid in-court identification? Should a witness identification that is both certain and accurate be invalidated and be precluded from subsequent remedy because the police used improper procedures? The Supreme Court addressed this issue in *Wade* by emphasizing that in-court identifications are permissible if they are not tainted by the prior identification. In the words of the majority opinion:

> We think it follows that the proper test to be applied in these situations is that quoted in Wong Sun v. United States [1963]. . . ." [W]hether granting establishment of the primary illegality, the evidence to which instant

objection is made has been come at by exploitation of that illegality or instead by means sufficiently distinguishably to be purged of the primary taint.". . . Application of this test in the present context requires consideration of various factors; for example, the prior opportunity to observe the alleged criminal act, the existence of any discrepancy between any pre-lineup description and the defendant's actual description, any identification prior to lineup of another person, the identification by picture of the defendant prior to the lineup, failure to identify the defendant on a prior occasion, and the lapse of time between the alleged act and the lineup identification. (388 U.S. 218 at 241)

Hypothetically, a witness's subsequent in-court identification of a suspect could be separate from a prior improper identification. In reality, however, do courts really have the ability to know if the in-court identification is independent from the prior exposure to the suspect? This poses a significant challenge for courts that take this issue seriously. There are risks, however, that judges will permit subsequent in-court identifications that are tainted by prior pretrial exposure to the suspect in invalid identification procedures by simply generating a list of factors that appear to make the second identification independent and presumptively reliable.

PRETRIAL COURT PROCEEDINGS

When an arrest warrant is used to take a suspect into custody, a judge has already seen evidence establishing probable cause to justify taking the individual into custody. However, many arrests are made without warrants. Remember that officers may make arrests for crimes committed in their presence, based on evidence of crimes that they discover during the course of investigations (e.g., *Terry* stop and frisk), and based on witness reports of felonies. In each of these circumstances, the officer must make a relatively quick discretionary judgment that leads to the loss of liberty for a crime suspect. There is always the risk of error in quick discretionary judgments. Witnesses can be mistaken. Police officers may misperceive playful mock fighting behavior among adolescents as an assault. Thus there is a need for a judicial examination of the basis of a warrantless arrest. This examination is required by the Fourth Amendment to ensure that the "seizure" was not unreasonable (*Gerstein v. Pugh*, 1975).

A hearing to examine the basis for arrests is frequently called an **initial appearance** or a "probable cause hearing." At this brief proceeding, the police must supply the judge with sufficient information to constitute probable cause justifying the arrest or, in Fourth Amendment terms, documenting the reasonableness of the seizure. There is no requirement that the arrestee be represented by counsel at this stage. The Supreme Court does not regard the initial appearance as a "critical stage" that can adversely affect the rights and interests of an unrepresented defendant. The police are providing information, the suspect is learning about the nature of the accusations, and the judge is making a determination about the existence of probable cause. The Supreme Court does not interpret the Fourth Amendment as requiring opportunities for cross-examination of witnesses or arguments by attorneys at this hearing. The criminal justice process provides subsequent opportunities to challenge the accuracy of the evidence and any improper actions by the police, and these later steps are the "critical stages" at which there is a right to counsel.

Gerstein v. Pugh (1975), the case which clarified the Fourth Amendment requirement of a probable cause hearing, said that a thirty-day time period after arrest for holding such hearings is unconstitutional. Instead, the Court said that such hearings must be "prompt." The Court addressed the acceptable time period for probable cause hearings in *County of Riverside v. McLaughlin* (1991). The Supreme Court rejected a lower-court decision mandating that such hearings be held within 36 hours of arrest. Instead, the Court took a flexible approach. The Court endorsed Riverside County's usual practice of holding such hearings within 48 hours. The justices indicated that the time period is flexible as long as it is prompt and there is no unreasonable delay. Thus the Court did not preclude the possibility that it could approve a time period longer than 48 hours if there were acceptable circumstances which dictated that length of time and thereby made the longer time period reasonable. The dissenters, by contrast, favored mandating a specific, brief time period, such as 24 hours or 36 hours, so that arrestees are not unreasonably deprived of their liberty, especially in cases of mistaken arrests that are not supported by probable cause.

Preliminary Hearings

At some point after the initial appearance, states' laws concerning criminal procedure typically require a **preliminary hearing** at which the defendant will have the opportunity to hear and challenge the evidence that the prosecution has prepared to present at trial. For defendants taken into custody through arrest warrants, this hearing provides the first opportunity for a judge to determine whether a prosecution is justified. The hearing provides a judicial check against excessive and unjustified prosecutions. It also provides an opportunity for the defense to learn about the basis for the prosecution's evidence and to challenge that evidence in order to try to have the charges dismissed. Rules vary by state about the presentation of evidence and permissibility of cross-examining witnesses because the hearing is not supposed to be as complex and involved as a full criminal trial.

Although the Constitution does not require the states to provide preliminary hearings, if state laws mandate such hearings, then the right to counsel applies because the hearing is a "critical stage" (*Coleman v. Alabama,* 1970). In discussing the defense attorney's role, the Court's opinion in *Coleman* illustrates the purposes of the preliminary hearing. According to Justice Brennan's majority opinion,

> *Plainly the guiding hand of counsel at the preliminary hearing is essential to protect the indigent accused against erroneous or improper prosecution. First, the lawyer's skilled examination and cross-examination of witnesses may expose fatal weaknesses in the State's case that may lead the magistrate to refuse to bind the accused over. Second, in any event, the skilled interrogation of witnesses by an experienced lawyer can fashion a vital impeachment tool for use in cross-examination of the State's witnesses*

at the trial, or preserve testimony favorable to the accused of a witness who does not appear at the trial. Third, trained counsel can more effectively discover the case the State has against his client and make possible the preparation of a proper defense to meet that case at the trial. Fourth, counsel can also be influential at the preliminary hearing in making effective arguments for the accused on such matters as the necessity for an early psychiatric evaluation or bail. (399 U.S. 1 at 9)

In many jurisdictions, defense attorneys advise their clients to waive their opportunity for a preliminary hearing. The defense attorney may know or presume that there is sufficient evidence to carry the prosecution. Thus the defense attorney may prefer to spend time focusing on the plea agreement that is likely to resolve the case rather than go through the process of preparing for and conducting an examination of evidence at the preliminary hearing. If the defense attorney anticipates that the case may ultimately result in a trial, either because the defendant faces very serious charges or because the defendant is wealthy enough to pay for a complete, unrelenting defense, then it is unlikely that the defense attorney would want to lose the opportunity to reveal and test the prosecution's evidence.

It is also possible that defense attorneys may tell their clients to waive the preliminary hearing because they do not want to annoy the prosecutors or judges whose time must be spent in such hearings. They may believe that they will gain greater cooperation during plea bargaining if they can spare the prosecutor and judge from extra work on an individual case. One study even identified an instance in which judges in one jurisdiction eventually appointed new attorneys to handle indigent criminal defense because they felt that other attorneys were too aggressive in demanding preliminary hearings and vigorously testing the prosecution in each case. The study found the following, with respect to the new defense attorneys,

They felt they knew what to look for in police reports, knew when to waive preliminary hearings, knew how to avoid wasting time filing nitpicking motions, and knew how to maintain good relations with police and prosecutors. As a result, [the defense attorneys in this jurisdiction] waived more than 60 percent of preliminary hearings, far more frequently than attorneys in the other [eight counties] studied [in three states]. They believed their style not only helped the county, the docket, and the judges, but also provided their clients with better representation.[4]

Although such considerations may reflect the reality of criminal justice officials' desire to have cases processed quickly and efficiently, they also raise questions about the officials' motives and whether defendants all receive the full benefits of the right to counsel and other legal entitlements.

Grand Jury Proceedings

Many states initiate criminal proceedings through the **information** process in which the prosecutor simply determines and files charges against a defendant. The Fifth Amendment provides a right for criminal defendants to have any serious criminal charges considered by a grand jury so that the actual imposition of charges stems from an indictment issued by a body of citizens. The relevant portion of the Fifth Amendment says, "No person shall be held to answer for a capital, or otherwise infamous crime, unless on a presentment or indictment of a grand jury." The purpose of the grand jury is to prevent inappropriate or vindictive prosecutions by interposing a body of citizen decision-makers between the defendant and the prosecutor. The prosecutor presents evidence in secret to a jury of citizens, and the citizens decide whether or not the person should be charged with the crime. The Grand Jury Clause is one of the few provisions of the Bill of Rights that was never incorporated, so it applies only against the federal government and is not applicable in state criminal cases (*Hurtado v. California*, 1884). Thus the structure and rules for grand jury proceedings vary from state to state depending on their respective laws. The same rules do not apply for such proceedings as apply to criminal trials. For example, illegally obtained evidence that would be subject to the exclusionary rule in a criminal trial may serve as the basis for questioning witnesses in a grand jury proceeding (*United States v. Calandra*, 1974).

Grand juries sit for a specified period of time, usually some number of months, in which they hear evidence concerning a number of cases and decide whether to issue indictments. The size of the grand jury will vary by jurisdiction. Some states have fewer than twelve members, but others are more like the federal judicial system in having twenty-three members.

Grand juries frequently hear evidence from witnesses. However, unlike the defendant's right to testify at a criminal trial, criminal suspects have no right to testify before grand juries and, indeed, may never know that the grand jury heard evidence about them until they are arrested after an indictment has been issued. People have no right to be told that they are the subject of a grand jury investigation (*United States v. Washington*, 1977). Witnesses before a grand jury have the right to assert their Fifth Amendment privilege against compelled self-incrimination by refusing to answer questions that might incriminate them. The U.S. Supreme Court has never required that grand jury witnesses be given their *Miranda* rights, even though their testimony could be used against them. The rules of many states require such warnings about the right to remain silent.[5] However, if a prosecutor grants them immunity from prosecution, there is the possibility that they could be held in contempt of court for refusing to answer if there is no longer any risk to them from the threat of self-incrimination (*Kastigar v. United States*, 1972).

Although witnesses may be warned about their right to remain silent, there is no right to counsel for witnesses appearing before a grand jury. If a witness has an attorney, the attorney generally is not permitted into the courtroom (unless a state's law indicates otherwise), since the testimony is taken in secret, only in the presence of the judge, prosecutor, witness, and grand jurors. There are instances in which attorneys wait outside courtrooms and witnesses leave the courtroom between questions to seek their attorneys' advice about whether or not to answer particular questions.

As a practical matter, grand juries only rarely decline to indict a suspect whom the prosecutor wishes to see charged with a crime. Grand juries are often referred to as a "tool" of the prosecutor rather than as a protection against excessive prosecution. Because the grand jury proceeding is not an adversarial process, the citizens on the grand jury do not hear challenges to the prosecutor's evidence or arguments that present the defendant's version of events.

EXCULPATORY EVIDENCE

During the pretrial stage of a case, both sides attempt to gather information and evidence. The defense attorney has a privileged relationship with the defendant so that all information the defendant gives to the attorney must be kept secret. Under ethics rules for attorneys, an attorney must vigorously defend his or her client, without regard to the person's innocence or guilt. In addition, attorneys can violate their client's trust only if they gain knowledge about any future crimes planned by the individual or any plan to be untruthful in sworn court testimony. Thus the defense attorney's required role can be described as a strong advocate on behalf of the client's interests.

By contrast, the prosecutor has dual roles. The prosecutor is responsible for combatting crime and making sure that guilty people are punished. In addition, the prosecutor is an officer of the court who is sworn to uphold legal rules and ensure that rights are protected. Sometimes, prosecutors feel tension or even outright conflict between their two sets of responsibilities. Many cases have arisen in which a prosecutor's zeal to gain a conviction has led to intentional and inadvertent violations of the defendant's rights.

Because of their responsibilities as officers of the court, prosecutors cannot keep all of their information secret. Typically, they must reveal some of their evidence at the preliminary hearing. Court rules in many jurisdictions also require that both sides exchange lists of witnesses and evidentiary exhibits (i.e., objects and documents) prior to the trial. As Chapter 10 will discuss, failure to provide the required information can lead to the exclusion of evidence, such as barring any testimony from a witness who was intentionally omitted from the witness list by a defense attorney (*Taylor v. Illinois,* 1988). However, the lists of witnesses to be used do not necessarily include all of the potential witnesses who are known to each side. There may be reasons that one side would like some witness to never be called at the trial. Witness lists also do not reveal exactly what each side may know about particular witnesses' knowledge about the crime and the defendant.

Many prosecutors have "open file" systems in which they give defense attorneys access to all information that they have gathered. Although open prosecutor files help defense attorneys to prepare arguments and evidence in opposition, such files also encourage guilty pleas if they demonstrate to the defense attorneys that there is little chance of success at trial. Cooperative practices can develop most readily when a "courtroom workgroup" exists within a courthouse so that defense attorneys, prosecutors, and judges have developed shared expectations about procedures and outcomes as they facilitate efficient processing of cases.

Other prosecutors, however, do not give defense attorneys access to their files. The only information they provide to defense attorneys is that which they are required to supply by court rules, such as lists of witnesses and exhibits. Defendants have no constitutional right of access to everything in prosecutors' files. This point was illustrated by the case of *United States v. Armstrong* (1996), which was excerpted in Chapter 2, where the Supreme Court said that the defense attorneys had not presented enough evidence of racial discrimination in cocaine prosecutions to justify a court order permitting them to evaluate prosecutors' files for patterns of racial discrimination in charging decisions. When the files are not open, there is an increased risk that the prosecutor may know about exculpatory evidence but never reveal to the defense the existence of that evidence which tends to show that the defendant is innocent. The worst possible situation for a criminal case in the American justice system would occur when a prosecutor knows that a defendant is innocent but proceeds with the prosecution anyway by not revealing to the defense attorney, judge, or jury that evidence exists showing that the defendant is not guilty. Unfortunately, such situations have arisen on occasion in American courts, and some innocent people have been sent to prison intentionally by prosecutors and police officers who were more intent on calling a case "solved" than on actually identifying the person responsible for the crime. For example, prosecutors in Florida told a jury that an illiterate farmworker poisoned his own children to collect insurance money even though they knew there was no insurance policy and that evidence pointed to the children's baby-sitter as the culprit.[6] A man in Alabama was released from death row when prosecutors later admitted that the three witnesses who placed him at the scene of the murder had presented their testimony either to collect reward money or to deflect attention away from their own guilt.[7]

The U.S. Supreme Court has sought to combat the risk of such blatant miscarriages of justice by requiring prosecutors to share exculpatory evidence with defense attorneys. In *Brady v. Maryland* (1963), the Supreme Court declared that it was a violation of the right to due process for the prosecution to suppress evidence favorable to the defendant that has been requested by the defense. The rights violation exists whether the prosecution withheld the exculpatory information either knowingly or by mistake. The existence of a due process violation does not depend on the motives of the prosecutors. After *Brady,* the Court faced additional cases concerning what information is "material" to the issue of culpability so that it must be provided upon request and concerning whether the prosecution has any obligation to hand over unrequested exculpatory information. As you read *Kyles v. Whitley* (1995) in the box on pp. 298–299, see if you can determine what kinds of evidence must be turned over by the prosecutor and what circumstances trigger the sharing of exculpatory information.

As described by the opinion in *Kyles,* the prosecution bears responsibility for turning over material exculpatory information, whether or not the defense attorney made a request for such information. The prosecutor is also responsible for finding out if the police, assistant prosecutors, or anyone else working on the case for the prosecution, such as lab technicians, know about unrevealed exculpatory information. All exculpatory information does not have to be given to the defense attorney. Only "material" information must be provided—namely, information that would have created a "reasonable probability" that the result in the case might have been different.

As indicated by the *Kyles* case, litigation concerning so-called *Brady* claims can be very complex and lengthy. Defense attorneys or convicted offenders must use appellate and habeas corpus processes to discover if the prosecution withheld exculpatory information and, if so, the court must be persuaded that the information meets the *Kyles* definition of "materiality." This is not necessarily an easy task. Hopefully, prosecutors will voluntarily follow the ethical and legal rules that require disclosure of exculpatory information. The litigation process is a difficult and imperfect tool for convicted offenders to use in seeking to pursue *Brady* claims, including those claims that have validity. This is especially so because convicted offenders have no constitutional right to counsel for discretionary appeals and habeas corpus proceedings, and therefore they may be forced to pursue this complex, difficult litigation on their own. *Pro se* litigants generally have a low likelihood of success, so it is possible that valid *Brady* claims remain unrevealed and unremedied.

PLEA BARGAINING

If charges are not dismissed during pretrial processes, then cases generally proceed to a resolution through negotiated guilty pleas. Because only about 10 percent of criminal cases nationally go to trial, it is clear that the vast majority of criminal convictions result from plea bargaining. There are different types of plea negotiations. Sometimes, prosecutors agree to reduce the number or severity of charges in exchange for a quick guilty plea. In other cases, the prosecutor agrees to recommend a specific sentence in exchange for the plea. Depending on the practices in particular courthouses, defense attorneys may discuss the plea agreement proposals with trial judges prior to accepting the deal to make sure that the judge will actually impose a sentence in accordance with the prosecutor's recommendations. In other courthouses, judges attempt to remain outside of the plea negotiation process. Thus defense attorneys and prosecutors base their agreements on their experience with and predictions about how specific judges will develop sentences for particular crimes and offenders. Because of the growing use of sentencing guidelines that reduce judges' discretion in imposing punishments in various states, it may be easier for prosecutors and defense attorneys to reach agreements. In these states, the lawyers may have greater confidence in anticipating the sentence that will be imposed after the guilty plea is entered.

The Dynamics of Plea Bargaining

The existence of plea bargaining does not mean that defendants are being "let off the hook" for the crimes they committed. Prosecutors frequently file more charges than they could prove in court so the plea negotiation process permits them to use the excess charges as bargaining chips. They may appear to surrender charges during the negotiations, but the defendant may actually end up with the same crimes and punishments that would have been the basis for conviction if the case had gone to trial. In addition, the plea negotiation process may not involve any actual "bargaining." It is often a discussion process in which the attorneys for each side work cooperatively to arrive at the charges and sentence that are most appropriate based on the provable facts in the case. The ultimate outcome is most heavily affected by the seriousness of the charges and the defendant's prior record as well as the usual punishment, sometimes called the "going rate," for that particular offense in a specific courthouse. Additional pressure to enter guilty pleas is created by the existence of habitual offender statutes, especially in the form of "three strikes" laws that mandate life sentences upon conviction for a third felony. Such laws can place extreme pressure on defendants to plead guilty quickly to a lesser offense rather than take the chance of being convicted at trial of an offense that will bring a harsh, mandatory sentence.

Kyles v. Whitley, 514 U.S. 419 (1995)

[*A woman was brutally murdered in the parking lot of a grocery store and her car was stolen. Eyewitnesses gave wildly divergent descriptions of the killer. A man who had the stolen car in his possession called the police and reported that he had purchased the car from Kyles. The informant talked to the police on several occasions and told police that Kyles was the killer. The various versions of events described by the informant were inconsistent with each other. The defense attorney filed "a lengthy motion for disclosure by the State of any exculpatory or impeachment evidence." However, the police did not inform the defense attorney about the divergent witness descriptions, the inconsistencies in the informant's statements, and other information which may have tended to show that the defendant was not guilty.*]

JUSTICE SOUTER presented the opinion of the Court.

. . .

New Orleans police took statements from six eyewitnesses, who offered various descriptions of the gunman. They agreed that he was a black man, and four of them said that he had braided hair. The witnesses differed significantly, however, in their descriptions of height, age, weight, build, and hair length. Two reported seeing a man of 17 or 18, while another described the gunman as looking as old as 28. One witness described him as 5′4″ or 5′5″, medium build, 140–150 pounds; another described the man as slim and close to six feet. One witness said he had a mustache; none of the others spoke of any facial hair at all. One witness said the murderer had shoulder-length hair; another described the hair as "short.". . .

Kyles was indicted for first-degree murder. Before trial, his counsel filed a lengthy motion for disclosure by the State of any exculpatory or impeachment evidence. The prosecution responded that there was "no exculpatory evidence of any nature," despite the government's knowledge of the following evidentiary items: (1) the six contemporaneous eyewitness statements taken by police following the murder; (2) records of [the informant's] initial call to the police; (3) the tape recording of the Saturday conversation between [the informant] and officers

Eaton and Miller; (4) the typed and signed statement given by [the informant] on Sunday morning; (5) the computer print-out of license numbers of cars parked at [the grocery store] on the night of the murder, which did not list the number of Kyles's car; (6) the internal police memorandum calling for the seizure of [Kyles's] rubbish after [the informant] had suggested that the [victim's] purse might be found there; and (7) evidence linking [the informant] to other crimes at [the grocery store] and to the unrelated murder . . . , committed in January before [the murder in question].

At the first trial, in November [which ended in a hung jury], . . . Kyles maintained his innocence, offered supporting witnesses, and supplied an alibi that he had been picking up his children from school at the time of the murder. The theory of the defense was that Kyles had been framed by [the informant], who had planted the evidence in Kyles's apartment and his rubbish for the purposes of shifting suspicion away from himself, removing [Kyles] as an impediment to romance [with a specific woman], and obtaining reward money. [The informant] did not testify as a witness. . . .

. . . [The informant changed the details of his story again when interviewed between the first and second trial by the police, but the defense was not provided with notes from this interview.]

[At the second trial, the police claimed that Kyles had left his car at the grocery store at the time of the murder in order to steal the victim's car. However, they knew that Kyles's car was not among those at the grocery store when police arrived after the crime. Defense witnesses testified that the informant actually matched the descriptions given by several of the eyewitnesses and that he was seen driving the victim's car within an hour after the crime.]

. . .

On rebuttal, the prosecutor had [the informant] brought into the courtroom. All of the testifying witnesses [i.e., the four eyewitnesses who picked Kyles out of a lineup], after viewing [the informant] standing next to Kyles, reaffirmed their previous identifications of Kyles as the murderer. Kyles was convicted of first-degree murder and sentenced to death. [The informant] received a total of $1,600 in reward money. . . . [In the appeal process it was revealed that the prosecution had failed to provide requested exculpatory information to Kyles.]

The prosecution's affirmative duty to disclose evidence favorable to a defendant can trace its origins to early 20th-century strictures against misrepresentation and is of course most prominently associated with this Court's decision in *Brady v. Maryland* [1963]. . . . *Brady* held "that the suppression by the prosecution of evidence favorable to an accused upon request violates due process where the evidence is material either to guilt or to punishment, irrespective of the good faith or bad faith of the prosecution.". . . In *United States v. Agurs* . . . (1976), however, it became clear that a defendant's failure to request favorable evidence did not leave the Government free of all obligation. There, the Court distinguished three situations in which a *Brady* claim might arise: first, where previously undisclosed evidence revealed that the prosecution introduced trial testimony that it knew or should have known was perjured, . . . ; second, where the Government failed to accede to a defense request for disclosure of some specific kind of exculpatory evidence, . . . ; and third, where the Government failed to volunteer exculpatory evidence never requested, or requested only in a general way. The Court found a duty on the part of the Government even in this last situation, though only when suppression of the evidence would be "of sufficient significance to result in the denial of the defendant's right to a fair trial.". . .

In the third prominent case on the way to current *Brady* law, *United States v. Bagley* . . . (1985), the Court disavowed any difference between exculpatory and impeachment evidence for *Brady* purposes, and it abandoned the distinction between the second and third *Agurs* circumstances, i.e., the "specific request" and "general or no request" situations. *Bagley* held that regardless of request, favorable evidence is material, and constitutional error results from its suppression by the government, "if there is a reasonable probability that, had the evidence been disclosed to the defense, the result of the proceeding would have been different.". . .

. . . Although the constitutional duty is triggered by the potential impact of favorable but undisclosed evidence, a showing of materiality does not require demonstration by a preponderance that disclosure of the suppressed evidence would have resulted ultimately in the defendant's acquittal. . . . *Bagley's* touchstone of materiality is a "reasonable probability" of a different result, and the adjective is important. The question is not whether the defendant would more likely than not have received a different verdict with the evidence, but whether in its absence he received a fair trial, understood as a trial resulting in a verdict worthy of confidence. A "reasonable probability" of a different result is accordingly shown when the Government's evidentiary suppression "undermines confidence in the outcome of the trial.". . .

. . . A defendant need not demonstrate that after discounting the inculpatory evidence in light of the undisclosed evidence, there would not have been enough evidence left to convict. . . .

The fourth and final aspect of *Bagley* materiality to be stressed here is its definition in terms of suppressed evidence considered collectively, not item by item. As Justice Blackmun emphasized in the portion of his opinion written for the Court, the Constitution is not violated every time the government fails or chooses not to disclose evidence that might prove helpful to the defense. . . . We have never held that the Constitution demands an open file policy (however such a policy might work out in practice), and the rule in *Bagley* (and, hence in *Brady*) requires less of the prosecution than the [American Bar Association] Standards for Criminal Justice, which call generally for prosecutorial disclosures of any evidence tending to exculpate or mitigate. . . .

. . . On the one side, showing that the prosecution knew of an item of favorable evidence unknown to the defense does not amount to a *Brady* violation, without more. But the prosecution, which alone can know what is undisclosed, must be assigned the consequent responsibility to gauge the likely net effect of all such evidence and make disclosure when the point of "reasonable probability" is reached. This in turn means that the individual prosecutor has a duty to learn of any favorable evidence known to the others acting on the government's behalf in the case, including the police. But whether the prosecutor succeeds or fails in meeting this obligation (whether, that is, a failure to disclose is in good faith or bad faith . . .), the prosecution's responsibility for failing to disclose known, favorable evidence rising to a material level of importance is inescapable. . . .

[In applying the foregoing standards to the *Kyles* case, the Supreme Court found that the prosecution had improperly failed to disclose evidence in violation of the defendant's right to due process.]

Plea negotiation does not occur because criminal justice officials desire to be lenient in addressing crime and criminals. It occurs because it serves the self-interest of every actor involved in the process. Prosecutors gain certain convictions. Judges are spared the time required to supervise lengthy trials. Defendants gain greater certainty about the punishments that they will receive. And defense attorneys are able to complete cases efficiently in order to produce more income by moving on to additional cases. For public defenders who receive a set salary, plea bargaining spares them from the time-consuming process of preparing for and conducting trials.

The plea bargaining process can raise questions about several different rights. For example, as discussed in Chapter 8, there may be a question about whether defense attorneys are providing ineffective assistance of counsel if they encourage their clients to plead guilty without adequately investigating and evaluating their clients' interests. There are also issues concerning the obligations of each side in the negotiating process.

One issue that lurks in all plea negotiations is the permissible range of promises or threats that a prosecutor may use in order to encourage a defendant to plead guilty. Obviously, if a prosecutor threatened to beat or shoot a defendant who did not plead guilty, we would have to be very concerned that the guilty plea would not be entered voluntarily. Threats may constitute improper coercion if they are too strong or otherwise impermissible. As you read *Bordenkircher v. Hayes* (1978) in the box on pp. 302–303, ask yourself whether you would consider the prosecutor's statements to constitute improper coercive pressure on the defendant.

As indicated by *Bordenkircher*, prosecutors are permitted to pressure defendants by threatening to impose additional charges if there is no guilty plea. The threat of additional charges, especially a habitual offender charge that may significantly increase the sentence, obviously imposed pressure on the defendant. The defendant must either make a choice about entering a guilty plea or take the risk of a more severe sentence if the prosecutor prevails in a trial. The threatened charges must be legitimate charges. A prosecutor cannot threaten to frame the defendant for a crime or to pursue charges that are unsupported by evidence.

Although pressure is permissible, there are limits to the form of that pressure. The Court is concerned that pressure goes too far when it becomes "vindictive." The line between permissible pressure and impermissible "vindictiveness" is not clear. Obviously, threats of physical violence go too far. Among other kinds of pressure, the Court has said that prosecutors cannot punish people by threatening additional charges for asserting their constitutional rights (*North Carolina v. Pearce,* 1969). In *Blackledge v. Perry* (1974), a defendant was charged with and convicted of misdemeanor assault and received a sentence of six months. He appealed his conviction and gained a new trial. The prosecutor reindicted him for *felony* assault. At the second trial, he was convicted and received a sentence of five to seven years. The Supreme Court overturned the second conviction and concluded that there was improper prosecutorial vindictiveness in imposing a more severe charge to punish the defendant for exercising a legal right to appeal.

In *Santobello v. New York* (1971), the Court declared that prosecutors must abide by the promises they made during plea negotiations. A defendant had entered a plea in exchange for the prosecutor's promise to make no recommendations about sentencing. At the sentencing phase, however, a new prosecutor handled the case who did not know about the promise. The new prosecutor requested the maximum sentence. The Supreme Court said that when defendants rely to a significant degree on prosecutors' promises in deciding to plead guilty, the prosecutors are obligated to fulfill those promises if the defendant is to be expected to stand by the plea. If the prosecutor fails to fulfill the promise, the defendant is not necessarily entitled to have a court order the prosecutor to deliver on that promise. The Supreme Court has implied that the prosecutor may be ordered to fulfill the promise, but most courts simply permit the defendant to withdraw the plea if the prosecutor reneges on the deal. Thus the defendant's practical ability to force the prosecution to deliver on the promise is quite limited.

Defendants also must fulfill their promises. In *Ricketts v. Adamson* (1987), the plea agreement for second-degree murder included a promise by the defendant to testify against his co-defendants in exchange for a lesser sentence. The defendant testified as agreed. Later, however, the co-defendants won an opportunity for a new trial on appeal, but the defendant refused to testify again because he said he had fulfilled his obligation in the first trial. Because of the defendant's refusal to provide further cooperation, the prosecutor treated the defendant as having violated the plea agreement by filing new first-degree murder charges. The U.S. Supreme Court supported the prosecution. The case demonstrates that defendants are in a very difficult position if they attempt to assert their own interpretation of a plea agreement rather than follow the prosecutor's interpretation. It also shows that defendants are obligated to fulfill the promises that they made during plea negotiations.

A guilty plea, in effect, constitutes a waiver of the right to trial and the other rights contained in the Sixth Amendment (e.g., right to confrontation, right to trial by jury). Thus trial judges are obligated to make sure that a guilty plea is entered knowingly and intelligently (*Boykin v. Alabama*, 1969). When a defendant stands in court to enter the plea, the judge typically asks the defendant a series of questions to make sure that the defendant understands the consequences of the plea and that the plea was not produced as the result of improper coercion. The box "The Guilty Plea Ceremony" on pp. 304–306 is drawn from the transcript of an actual armed robbery case and shows how trial judges attempt to ensure that the plea is proper.

In the guilty plea ceremony, the judge was concerned about ensuring several things. There was a concern that the plea was made knowingly and voluntarily. The judge checked to make sure that all parties agreed about the nature and details of the plea agreement. Each participant stated that he or she knew of no improper promises or threats. The judge provided a detailed list of the rights that the defendant would be waiving by entering a plea. Note that the defendant actually entered a **no contest** plea, which is the equivalent of admitting that the defendant accepts the fact that the prosecution can probably prove the defendant's guilt, so the defendant is willing to accept punishment for the crime. As was illustrated in this case, defendants often use the plea as a way of avoiding automatic liability if the crime victim were to file a civil lawsuit for personal injuries or destruction of property. In the civil lawsuit, the victim would still need to prove that the defendant was responsible. If you were a judge, would you permit the entry of a no contest plea?

The judge also sought to make sure that the defendant was actually guilty of the crimes. Thus the judge asked the defense attorney to state the factual basis for the plea and asked each attorney to verify that the facts support a

Bordenkircher v. Hayes, 434 U.S. 357 (1978)

[*Hayes was charged with forging a check, an offense punishable by a sentence of two to ten years in prison. During plea negotiations between his attorney and the prosecutor, the prosecutor offered to recommend a sentence of five years if Hayes would agree to plead guilty. The prosecutor also said that if Hayes chose not to plead guilty, the prosecutor would seek a new indictment against him under the state's habitual offender statute, which could lead to a mandatory life sentence because Hayes had already been convicted twice before on other felony charges. Hayes chose not to plead guilty. The prosecutor obtained the habitual offender indictment, and Hayes was sentenced to life in prison as a habitual criminal after being convicted for forging the check. The Kentucky Court of Appeals rejected Hayes's appeal. When Hayes initiated a habeas corpus action in the federal courts, the district court found no constitutional violations in his case. However, the federal circuit court of appeals found that the prosecutor's actions during plea bargaining had violated the principle from* Blackledge v. Perry *(1974), which forbids "vindictive" actions by prosecutors. The Supreme Court accepted the case to consider whether a prosecutor violates the right to due process of law when his or her charging decisions are influenced by the expectation of gaining advantages in the course of plea negotiations.*]

JUSTICE STEWART delivered the opinion of the Court.

. . .

We have recently had occasion to observe: "[W]hatever might be the situation in an ideal world, the fact is that the guilty plea and the often concomitant plea bargain are important components of this country's criminal justice system. Properly administered, they can benefit all concerned." *Blackledge v. Allison,* 431 U.S. 63, 71 (1977). . . . The open acknowledgement of this previously clandestine practice has led this Court to recognize the importance of counsel during plea negotiations, . . . the need for a public record indi-cating that a plea was knowingly and voluntarily made, . . . and the requirement that a prosecutor's plea-bargaining promise be kept. . . . The decision of the Court of Appeals in the present case, however, did not deal with considerations such as these, but held that the substance of the plea offer itself violated the limitations imposed by the Due Process Clause of the Fourteenth Amendment. . . . For the reasons that follow, we have concluded that the Court of Appeals was mistaken in so ruling. . . .

In those cases [of improper prosecutorial vindictiveness,] the Court was dealing with the State's unilateral imposition of a penalty upon a defendant who had chosen to exercise a legal right to attack his original conviction—a situation "very different from the give-and-take negotiation common in plea bargaining between prosecution and defense, which arguably possess relatively equal bargaining power.". . . The Court emphasized that the due process violation in [prosecutorial vindictiveness] cases . . . lay not in the possibility that a defendant might be deterred from the exercise of a legal right, . . . but rather in the danger that the State might be retaliating against the accused for lawfully attacking his conviction. . . .

Plea bargaining flows from "the mutuality of advantage" to defendants and prosecutors, each with his own reasons for wanting to avoid trial. . . . Defendants advised by competent counsel and protected by other procedural safeguards are presumptively capable of intelligent choice in response to prosecutorial persuasion, and unlikely to be driven to false self-condemnation. . . . Indeed, acceptance of the basic legitimacy of plea bargaining necessarily implies rejection of any notion that a guilty plea is involuntary in a constitutional sense simply because it is the end result of the bargaining process. . . .

[B]y tolerating and encouraging the negotiation of pleas, this Court has necessarily accepted as constitutionally legitimate the simple reality that the prosecutor's interest at the bargaining table is to persuade the defendant to forego his right to plead not guilty. . . .

To hold that the prosecutor's desire to induce a guilty plea is an "unjustifiable standard," which, like race or religion, may play no part in his charging decision, would contradict the very premises that underlie the concept of plea bargaining itself. Moreover, a rigid constitutional rule that would prohibit a prosecutor from acting forthrightly in his dealings with the defense would only invite unhealthy subterfuge that would drive the practice of plea bargaining back into the shadows from which it has so recently emerged. . . .

There is no doubt that the breadth of discretion that our country's legal system vests in prosecuting attorneys carries with it the potential for both individual and institutional abuse. And broad though that discretion may be, there are undoubtedly constitutional limits upon its exercise. We hold only that the course of conduct engaged in by the prosecutor in this case, which no more than openly presented the defendant with the unpleasant alternatives of forgoing trial or facing charges on which he was plainly subject to prosecution, did not violate the Due Process Clause of the Fourteenth Amendment.

Accordingly, the judgment of the Court of Appeals is *Reversed.*

JUSTICE BLACKMUN, with whom JUSTICE BRENNAN and JUSTICE MARSHALL join, dissenting.

. . .

The Court now says, however, that this concern with [prosecutorial] vindictiveness is of no import in the present case, despite the difference [in the defendant's sentence] between five years in prison and a life sentence, because we are here concerned with plea bargaining where there is give-and-take negotiation, and where, it is said [by the majority opinion] "there is no such element of punishment or retaliation so long as the accused is free to accept or reject the prosecution's offer." Yet in this case vindictiveness is present to the same extent as it was thought to be [in prior cases]; the prosecutor here admitted . . . that the sole reason for the new indictment was to discourage the respondent from exercising his right to a trial. Even had such an admission not been made, when plea negotiations, conducted in the face of the less serious charge under the first indictment, fail, charging by a second indictment a more serious crime for the same conduct creates "a strong inference" of vindictiveness. As then Judge McCree aptly observed, in writing for a unanimous panel of the Sixth Circuit [U.S. Court of Appeals], the prosecutor initially "makes a discretionary determination that the interests of the state are served by not seeking more serious charges." . . . I therefore do not understand why, as in [prior cases], due process does not require that the prosecution justify its action on some basis other than discouraging respondent from the exercise of his right to trial.

Prosecutorial vindictiveness, it seems to me, in the present narrow context, is the fact against which the Due Process Clause ought to protect. I perceive little difference between vindictiveness after what the Court describes . . . as the exercise of a "legal right to attack his original conviction" [in previous cases that found impermissible vindictiveness] and [permissible] vindictiveness in the "give-and-take negotiation common in plea bargaining." Prosecutorial vindictiveness in any context is still prosecutorial vindictiveness. The Due Process Clause should protect an accused against it, however it asserts itself. The Court of Appeals rightly so held, and I would affirm the judgment.

It might be argued that it really makes little difference how this case, now that it is here, is decided. The Court's holding gives plea bargaining full sway despite vindictiveness. A contrary result, however, merely would prompt the aggressive prosecutor to bring the greater charge initially in every case, and only thereafter to bargain. The consequences to the accused would still be adverse, for then he would bargain against a greater charge, face the likelihood of increased bail, and run the risk that the court would be less inclined to accept a bargained plea. Nonetheless, it is far preferable to hold prosecution to the charge it was originally content to bring and to justify in the eyes of the public.

[Justice Powell's dissenting opinion is omitted.]

[The names are changed from the original, and the transcript is edited to remove sidebar conversations concerning debates about the accuracy of the pre-sentence report.]

Judge: Your name is David Smith?
Smith: Yes.
Judge: And you're here with your attorney, Ms. Johnson. Is that correct?
Smith: Yes.
Judge: Mr. Smith, let me explain to you that the rights that I will read to you cover each of these files [charges] but rather than go through them twice I'm only going to go through them once. I want you to understand they apply to each case. Do you understand that, sir?
Smith: [Defendant nods head affirmatively.]
Judge: Now, Ms. Johnson, would you waive reading of the Information in each of these cases?
Ms. Johnson: I would, your Honor.
Judge: Mr. Smith, turning to the first case, this Information charges you with four counts as follows: Count 1 charges you with the crime known as home invasion in the first degree, and by virtue of this being allegedly your third offense the maximum penalty for that count is 40 years and/or a $10,000 fine. Do you understand that, sir?
Smith: Yes.
Judge: Count 2 charges you with the crime known as assault with intent to murder, and the maximum possible penalty for that offense is life. Do you understand that?
Smith: Yes.
Judge: Count 3 charges you with the crime known as armed robbery, and the maximum possible penalty for that offense is life. Do you understand that, sir?
Smith: Yes.
Judge: And Count 4 charges you with the crime known as assault with intent to rob while armed, and the maximum possible penalty for that offense is life. Do you understand that, sir?
Smith: Yes.
Judge: Ms. Johnson, what is it your client intends to do as relates to each of those cases?
Ms. Johnson: Your Honor, my client will be pleading no contest to Count 2 and an amended Count 5 of assault with intent to do great bodily harm less than the offense of murder.

Judge: Excuse me, then—the Prosecutor is moving to amend by adding Count 5; is that correct?
Prosecutor: That's correct. The armed robbery as charged, amending assault with intent to murder to assault with intent to do great bodily harm.
Judge: As a first offender?
Prosecutor: That's correct.
Judge: Ms. Johnson, any objection to that count being added?
Ms. Johnson: No, your Honor.
Judge: Mr. Smith, technically then the Information now charges you with a fifth count charging you with the crime known as assault with intent to do great bodily harm less than murder as a first offender, and the maximum possible penalty for that offense is 10 years. Do you understand that, sir?
Smith: Yes.
Judge: Ms. Johnson, what does your client intend to do with respect to the other charges?
Ms. Johnson: Entering pleas of not guilty.
Prosecutor: Gonna be dismissed, that's the plea agreement here.
Judge: Okay. Now I guess I'm up to speed.
Prosecutor: Sorry.
Judge: Okay. Ms. Johnson, the reason for the no contest plea is what?
Ms. Johnson: Potential civil liability, your Honor.
Judge: Do the People consent to a no contest plea?
Prosecutor: At this point, your Honor, we will.
Judge: All right. Mr. Smith, since I only have one file now, I'm going to read the rights once. Do you understand that, sir?
Smith: Yes.
Judge: All right. Raise your right hand, please. Do you solemnly swear that the testimony that you are about to give will be the truth, the whole truth, and nothing but the truth, so help you God?
Smith: Yes.
Judge: Mr. Smith, do you understand that if you plead no contest to these charges and I accept your plea, you would not have a trial of any kind? Do you understand that?
Smith: Yes.
Judge: Do you further understand that by not having a trial as a result of your plea, you are waiving and giving up the rights you would have had at the trial including the following: You're giving up your right to be tried by a jury; your right to

be tried by the Court without a jury, if you so choose, and the Prosecutor and the Court consent; your right to be presumed innocent until proven guilty; your right to have the Prosecutor prove beyond a reasonable doubt that you are guilty; your right to have the witnesses against you appear at the trial; your right to question the witnesses against you; your right to have the Court order any witnesses you have for your defense to appear at the trial; your right to remain silent during your trial; your right to not have your silence used against you; your right to testify at the trial, if you want to testify; and if your plea is accepted you will be giving up any claim that the plea was the result of promises or threats that were not disclosed to the Court at this plea proceeding, or that it was not your own choice to enter the plea? Do you understand that you have all of these rights and claims?

Smith: Yes.

Judge: Do you understand that you will be giving up each and every one of these rights and claims if your plea of no contest is accepted by the Court?

Smith: Yes.

Judge: Now, Ms. Johnson, would you outline the nature and extent of the plea bargain, please.

Ms. Johnson: Thank you, your Honor. In exchange for pleas of no contest to Count 2 and Count—amended Count 5, at the time of sentencing the prosecution would be moving to dismiss the other remaining counts and also not seek a charge under the Habitual Offender statute.

Judge: Is that the prosecution's understanding?

Prosecutor: That's accurate.

Judge: Mr. Smith, could you hear the plea bargain outlined by your lawyer and the Prosecutor?

Smith: Yes.

Judge: Did you understand it?

Smith: Yes.

Judge: Is it acceptable to you?

Smith: Yes.

Judge: Do you give up your right to a trial by jury?

Smith: Yes.

Judge: Do you give up a trial by the Court without a jury?

Smith: Yes.

Judge: Do you believe you've had enough time to talk to your lawyer before entering a plea this morning?

Smith: Yes.

Judge: Ms. Johnson, are you aware of any promises, threats, or inducements made to your client that have resulted in this plea other than what's been placed on the record?

Ms. Johnson: No, your Honor.

Judge: Same question for the prosecution.

Prosecutor: No, your Honor.

Judge: All right. Mr. Smith, to this charge in Count 2 of armed robbery, having had the advice of an attorney, understanding that this could carry up to life, understanding you could have a jury trial or a trial before the Court without a jury, and understanding the other rights that I've explained to you, what do you plead?

Smith: No contest.

Judge: Turning to the charge in Count 5 of assault with intent to do great bodily harm, having had the advice of an attorney, understanding this carries up to ten years, understanding you could have a jury trial or a trial by the Court without a jury, and understanding the other rights I've explained to you, what do you plead?

Smith: No contest.

Judge: Mr. Smith, has anyone promised you anything other than the plea bargain to get you to enter this plea?

Smith: No.

Judge: Has anyone threatened you or forced you or compelled you to enter the plea?

Smith: No.

Judge: Are you entering your plea based only on the plea bargain placed earlier on the record?

Smith: Yes.

Judge: Are you doing so of your own free will?

Smith: Yes.

Judge: Ms. Johnson, on what basis would you suggest that the Court accept a factual determination for your client's plea?

Ms. Johnson: I would request the Court consider Police Department report #555-67 and the preliminary examination [hearing] transcript that was filed in this matter. [The attorney then described the facts as set out in the police report and the preliminary hearing.]

Judge: All right. I will accept those facts as true. And having done so, Ms. Johnson, do you believe the elements of the offenses charged have been fully covered by those facts?

Ms. Johnson: I believe so, your Honor. [The Prosecutor agrees.]

(continued)

Judge: Mr. Smith, let me tell you that there's been no final agreement by this Court with the prosecution, defense counsel, or anyone acting in their interest as to any particular plea or possible sentence. Ms. Johnson, has the Court in your opinion fully complied with state laws concerning the acceptance of pleas?

Ms. Johnson: It has, your Honor.

Judge: Same question for the prosecution.

Prosecutor: Yes, your Honor.

Judge: Mr. Smith, in the event there's anything that I have said or your lawyer or the Prosecutor has said this morning that has caused you to change your mind, I want you to tell me once again what you plead to these charges.

Smith: No contest.

Judge: That's to each count; is that correct, sir?

Smith: Yes.

Judge: Mr. Smith, the Court believes your plea is accurate, is made freely, understandingly, and voluntarily, that the offense was committed by you, and that the potential of civil liability justifies the entry of a plea of no contest, and I hereby accept your plea of no contest to armed robbery and assault with intent to do great bodily harm less than murder. You're remanded to the custody of the Sheriff to await sentencing, which is hereby scheduled for June 27th at 8 a.m.

---

finding of guilt. The judge may make a finding of a factual basis even when the defendant refuses to admit guilt. In *North Carolina v. Alford* (1970), the defendant entered a guilty plea but refused to admit guilt. The Supreme Court said that the judge may accept such a plea if there is a factual basis for believing that the defendant is guilty.

The judge is not obligated to accept the guilty plea. For example, some judges will not accept a guilty plea if defendants' expressions and body language indicate that their verbal answers to questions may not, in fact, reflect their true feelings. A judge may also reject a plea agreement as inappropriate or unfair. In many courts, however, judges are reluctant to disturb agreements negotiated by the two sides as long as the plea is voluntary and has a factual basis.

In asking many questions during the proceeding, the judge builds a record of the case that makes it very difficult for defendants to later change their minds or to claim that they did not understand the implications of their pleas. A wise judge does not want inadvertently to leave open avenues for appeal that claim the judge failed to fulfill the requirements of the law.

When the judge in the example listed all of the rights that would be waived through a plea, do you think the defendant actually understood the implications of each and every right? In many respects, it seems unlikely that the defendant has a thorough understanding of all trial rights. But by asking and soliciting answers for such questions on the record in the courtroom, the judge makes it difficult for later realizations to provide the basis for appeals.

Plea bargaining is obviously a process that is driven by the discretionary decisions and ethical orientations of the actors involved. Prosecutors need to be honest in their dealings with defense attorneys. They need to follow the *Brady* rule for making material exculpatory evidence available since knowledge of such evidence may influence the defense posture during plea negotiations. Defense attorneys are ethically obligated to resist any self-interest they may feel in getting the case completed quickly. Instead, they should carefully evaluate and pursue the client's best interests as well as the client's wishes. Sometimes, clients will reject attorneys' advice to plead guilty. Although some attorneys resent clients who do not follow advice, the defendant is entitled to be the ultimate decision maker over his or her own fate. Judges must fulfill their professional responsibility to ensure that pleas are knowing, voluntary, and grounded in the factual record of the case. If judges are not conscientious, there is no check against errors or ethical blind spots by the attorneys involved in the case.

OTHER PRETRIAL PROCEEDINGS

There are a variety of pretrial proceedings that may occur depending on the issues in a case and how far the case moves along toward trial. Early in the process, there can be evidentiary hearings in which the two sides may seek rulings from the judge about what evidence will be admissible. Such proceedings would include **suppression hearings** in which the defense would seek to have prosecution evidence excluded because it was obtained in violation of the Fourth Amendment, Fifth Amendment, or state constitutional provisions.

In some cases, there will be questions about whether the defendant is competent to stand trial (*Pate v. Robinson,* 1966). Under American law, if people lack mental competence at the time of the crime, the insanity defense may be presented to determine if they can be held responsible for the crime. Competence to stand trial is slightly different because the focus is on the mental capability of the defendant at the time of the trial. In order to be competent to stand trial, the defendant must have a reasonable degree of ability to consult with the defense attorney and understand the criminal proceedings (*Dusky v. United States,* 1960). The trial court must rely on psychiatrists' testimony and arguments from attorneys in determining whether the defendant is competent. If defendants are found not competent to stand trial, they usually will be subject to civil commitment proceedings and sent to a mental health facility. They should be held and treated until their conditions improve sufficiently to permit them to stand trial, if that day ever comes.

The decisions in pretrial hearings are important. They will affect what happens at any eventual trial by determining which evidence will be presented to the judge or jury. In addition, pretrial hearing decisions may influence the plea bargaining process. If a defense attorney is unsuccessful in seeking to have evidence excluded from use at trial, the defendant may choose to engage in plea negotiations rather than face the ultimate likelihood of conviction by the strong evidence of guilt that the judge will permit the prosecutor to introduce in court.

CONCLUSION

Pretrial processes encompass a variety of steps. Investigatory steps occur, such as lineups and other identification procedures, after a suspect is taken into custody. There are also hearings to determine whether sufficient evidence exists to justify the arrest and the continuation of prosecution. The Supreme Court has focused on identifying" critical stages" to determine when the defendant is entitled to representation by counsel during pretrial processes. Thus counsel should be made available for lineups that occur after formal charges are filed and preliminary hearings, but counsel is not required for pre-indictment line-ups and probable cause hearings immediately after warrantless arrests.

Prosecutors bear special responsibilities in the criminal justice process. In addition to overseeing the prosecution of suspected criminals, they must uphold their oaths of office and ethical responsibilities by ensuring that laws are followed and defendants' rights are protected. A component of this responsibility is the obligation to share with the defense any exculpatory evidence that is "material," meaning evidence favorable to the defendant that has a reasonable probability of affecting the outcome of the case.

Most criminal charges that are not dismissed or dropped during the initial pretrial processes are ultimately terminated through plea bargaining. Plea bargaining raises a number of issues concerning constitutional rights, including ineffective assistance of counsel by defense attorneys, the voluntariness of pleas, and the obligations of prosecutors and defendants to fulfill the promises that they make during plea negotiations. Prosecutors may pressure defendants to plead guilty by threatening to impose additional legitimate charges, but they may not display "vindictiveness" by, for example, imposing more severe charges as a punishment for defendants asserting their constitutional rights.

There may be a variety of other pretrial processes, including hearings about the admissibility of evidence and hearings about the competence of the defendant to stand trial. The outcomes of these hearings are important because they may affect decisions about guilty pleas as well as what happens at any ultimate trial.

SUMMARY

- Pretrial proceedings include investigatory processes such as lineups, showups, and photographic displays. Despite significant risks of errors by eyewitnesses in identification procedures, defendants have a right to counsel only at "critical stages," which usually mean proceedings that take place after formal charges have been filed.

- After a warrantless arrest, arrestees are entitled to a probable cause hearing (initial appearance) that is conducted promptly within a reasonable time period. The Supreme Court has said that 48 hours is a reasonable time period but has not mandated that this time limit be met in all circumstances.

- At preliminary hearings to determine if there is enough evidence to prosecute, the defense attorney may challenge the evidence. By contrast, if the formal charge is produced through a grand jury proceeding, the defense

attorney has no opportunity to challenge the prosecution's presentation of evidence in the secret proceeding.

- Prosecutors are required to share with the defense any evidence favorable to the defendant (exculpatory evidence) that has a reasonable probability of affecting the outcome of the case.

- Most convictions result from plea negotiations. Prosecutors may pressure the defendant to plead guilty by threatening additional legitimate charges, but the prosecutor may not manifest "vindictiveness" by increasing the severity of charges to punish the defendant for exercising a legal right.

- Judges are responsible for ensuring that guilty pleas are entered voluntarily without improper threats or coercion, that the defendant understands the plea involves waiver of trial rights, and that there is a factual basis for the plea.

- Other pretrial hearings can involve disputes over the admissibility of evidence or the de-

fendant's competence to stand trial. Decisions in these proceedings can shape the defendant's determination about whether to plead guilty or go to trial.

Key Terms

critical stages Stages in the criminal process in which the absence of a defense attorney would significantly harm the defendant's rights and prospects for an accurate, fair proceeding. Thus the right to counsel applies at such stages in the process.

information In jurisdictions that do not use grand juries to issue formal charges, the document filed by the prosecutor to initiate prosecution.

initial appearance A hearing required by the Fourth Amendment within days of a warrantless arrest to determine whether there is probable cause to support the reasonableness of the seizure of the suspect.

lineup Investigation technique in which a suspect is placed in a line with other individuals who have similar physical characteristics in order to ask a victim or a witness to identify a criminal by picking the perpetrator out of the line.

no contest A plea, also known as *nolo contendere,* in which the criminal defendant does not contest the charges but accepts punishment without admitting guilt, usually in order to reduce the risk of civil liability related to the crime.

preliminary hearing Pretrial proceeding under the laws of many states, but not mandated by the Constitution, in which the defendant is entitled to have an attorney listen to and question the prosecution's preliminary evidence in an effort to get a judge to dismiss charges.

photographic display Investigation technique in which a victim or a witness looks through photographs of people arrested for previous offenses in order to attempt to identify the perpetrator of a crime.

real or physical evidence Noncommunicative evidence, such as physical objects related to an alleged crime, but also including physical characteristics of a suspect, fingerprints, handwriting samples, and other such evidence gathered during pretrial processes.

showup An identification procedure in which a victim or a witness is shown one suspect in order to ask whether that suspect is the perpetrator of the crime. This is often done near crime scenes but may also be done at police stations and in court depending on the circumstances of the case.

suggestiveness Actions by police officers during a lineup or other identification procedures that intentionally or unintentionally signal the witness about which individual the police suspect of committing the crime.

suppression hearings Pretrial proceedings in which the defense seeks to have prosecution evidence excluded from use at trial for being obtained in violation of constitutional rights or other legal requirements.

Additional Readings

Eisenstein, James, Roy B. Flemming, and Peter F. Nardulli. 1984. *The Contours of Justice: Communities and Their Courts.* Boston: Little, Brown. A study of the individual court communities in nine counties, including the local processes such as plea bargaining that lead to the resolution of criminal cases.

Heumann, Milton. 1978. *Plea Bargaining.* Chicago: University of Chicago Press. An examination of how prosecutors, defense attorneys, and judges adapt to plea bargaining.

Loftus, Elizabeth, and James M. Doyle. 1997. *Eyewitness Testimony: Civil and Criminal.* Charlottesville, Va.: Lexis Law Publishing. Psychological research on the flaws in eyewitness identification that can be a particularly important reason for errors in trials.

McCoy, Candace. 1993. *Politics and Plea Bargaining.* Philadelphia: University of Pennsylvania Press. A study of an effort in California to limit the use of plea bargaining that includes a thorough examination of the scholarly literature on plea negotiations.

Notes

1. "Not Going His Way," *Newsweek,* 11 December 2000, 87.

2. Richard Willing, "With DNA Databases on Fast Track, Legal Questions Loom," *USA Today,* 1 March 1999, 5A.

3. Charles Whitebread and Christopher Slobogin, *Criminal Procedure: An Analysis of Cases and Concepts,* 4th ed. (New York: Foundation Press, 2000), 475.

4. James Eisenstein, Roy B. Flemming, and Peter F. Nardulli, *The Contours of Justice: Communities and Their Courts* (Boston: Little, Brown, 1984), 147.

5. Charles H. Whitebread and Christopher Slobogin, *Criminal Procedure: An Analysis of Cases and Concepts,* 4th ed. (New York: Foundation Press, 2000), 596.

6. James N. Baker, "From Tragedy to Travesty," *Newsweek*, 24 April 1989, 68.

7. Garry Mitchell, "Murder Convict Is Cleared, Released," *Akron Beacon Journal*, 3 March 1993, A10.

CHAPTER TEN

Trial Processes

As we saw in Chapter 9, there are risks that eyewitnesses may make errors identifying specific individuals as lawbreakers. Imagine that an eyewitness had erroneously identified you as a murderer. You were seen angrily yelling at your landlord and, later that same day, a car the same color as yours quickly sped away after striking and killing the landlord as he walked across the street. One person says that you were the person driving the car. You know that you are innocent, but the prosecutor convinces the judge that strong evidence shows you had a motive and that you actually committed the criminal act. You are ordered to be held without bail. As you sit in your jail cell, you wonder how long you must wait before your trial. You know that, according to the Constitution, you have a right to a "speedy trial," but you have no idea what that means. Would your right be violated if you had to wait six months for a trial? What about two years? In your opinion, what is the longest you would have to wait without having your right to a speedy trial violated?

In this chapter, we will examine several constitutional rights relevant to criminal trials. These rights are drawn from both the Fifth and Sixth Amendments. Rights specifically related to jury trial will be discussed in Chapter 11. The Sixth Amendment is generally regarded as the "trial rights amendment." In addition to the right to counsel, the Amendment contains rights to speedy and public trials by impartial juries as well as confrontation with adverse witnesses and compulsory process. The Fifth Amendment contains the right against double jeopardy. As with other protections contained in the Bill of Rights, these rights are defined by court decisions, but they depend on the decisions and actions of prosecutors, judges, and defense attorneys in order to have practical effects.

THE HISTORY AND CONTEXT OF TRIALS

The fair trial guarantees of the Sixth Amendment came from the English development of trials as the means to determine the guilt of people accused of crimes. In England before the thirteenth century, the Angles, Saxons, and their conquerors, the Normans, determined criminal guilt by seeking divine decisions through the processes of battle, ordeal, and compurgation. Trial by battle was based on the presumption that divine intervention would ensure that the innocent combatant would not be killed. The value and attractiveness of trial by battle diminished in the twelfth century when accused persons began to have the opportunity to hire professional champions to fight for them. Trial by ordeal presented accused persons with a very undesirable situation. For example, criminal defendants had their hands and feet tied, and they were then thrown into a pond. If they managed to swim, they were judged guilty and executed. They were presumed to be able to swim in such a situation because they possessed (or were possessed by) some evil power. If they sank and drowned, then they were regarded as innocent and they received a respectful burial. There were other forms of trial by ordeal, such as lifting and carrying red-hot iron weights or placing human limbs into kettles of boiling water. Compurgation involved determining guilt by having people swear oaths attesting to an accused's honesty and innocence. These forms of "trials" were replaced by legalistic trials when Pope Innocent III forbade clergy from performing religious ceremonies in conjunction with ordeals in 1215. This declaration removed the religious sanction that had provided the basis for believing that divine intervention produced correct outcomes.[1]

The legal processes that are employed in the American criminal justice system continue the "combat" orientation of trials by pitting opposing attorneys against each other. The criminal trial provides one moment when the adversary system assumes its ideal form. The opposing legal gladiators present evidence and arguments favorable to their side as the judge or jury attempts to sift through the presentations to determine what constitutes the truth about the defendant's involvement in and culpability for the crime. In a jury trial, the judge serves as a "referee" who ensures that attorneys' presentations and jurors' deliberations follow court rules and the rules of evidence. The judge is the decision maker if the defendant requests a bench trial.

As we examine trial rights, we must remember that cases are not selected randomly for trial. Cases reach the trial stage as the result of decisions by specific actors in the criminal justice process. Prosecutors have no incentive to seek trials if they can gain satisfactory convictions and punishments through plea negotiation processes. Trials are very time-consuming, frequently requiring days or weeks of preparation followed by days or weeks in the courtroom. Defense attorneys, especially if they are appointed counsel for indigents, may not feel that they are adequately compensated for the extra time spent preparing for trial. Thus they also have an incentive to seek a resolution of the case during pretrial processes. Because none of the court professionals have any incentive to seek to take cases to trial, trials occur for other reasons, such as when the charges faced by the defendant are so serious that even a guilty plea will produce a very serious sentence. Thus for murders, sex offenses, and third-strike life sentence offenses, the defendant might as well see if the trial might produce an acquittal since there is little to be gained from plea bargaining. Trials also occur when the prosecution and defense have very different assessments of the provable facts in lesser cases so that they cannot reach an understanding about an appropriate plea agreement and sentence. If neither side is willing to compromise, then a trial is necessary to produce a decision about guilt and punishment. Trials may also occur when the defendant is wealthy enough to pay the costs of carrying a case through all steps in the process. Being wealthy does not necessarily lead to a trial because affluent defendants often hire attorneys who are especially skilled and effective at gaining very favorable plea agreements in cases in which the prosecution has strong evidence. In sum, trial rights are available to all defendants but are actually utilized by only a small percentage of people who are prosecuted for crimes.

SPEEDY TRIAL

One time limit affecting prosecutors is the **statute of limitations** for each crime. The statute of limitations is each state legislature's definition of the time limit for charging someone after a crime has been committed. The legislature has the authority to say that the prosecution must charge someone with a crime within a set period of time after the crime has been discovered, such as five years or ten years. The statute of limitations prevents prosecutors from waiting for many years before prosecuting a crime. It also encourages law enforcement officers to work expeditiously to solve crimes. Some crimes, such as murder, may not be affected by a statute of limitations. Murder is considered the most serious crime, and legislatures do not want to close the door on prosecutions, even if it takes years to identify a perpetrator. There is a growing movement to change states' laws so that sex crimes, which are also considered extremely serious offenses, do not have a time limit for prosecutions.

The Sixth Amendment right to a speedy trial applies after a suspect has been arrested for a crime. It is intended to keep defendants from languishing in jail for an indefinite period of time and to prevent people released on bail from having their lives disrupted by an ever-present cloud of criminal charges hanging over their heads. If prosecutors could accuse people of crimes but never follow through with prosecution, then people who are presumptively innocent could suffer from continuing adverse consequences including loss of job opportunities, social ostracism, and other effects of being accused of a crime. Thus the Sixth Amendment right seeks to force prosecutors to move forward if they have evidence justifying prosecution. If the prosecutor does not move forward in a timely manner, then the person should be freed from the adverse consequences of having unsettled charges simply hanging over his or her head.

The Test for Identifying Violations

The Sixth Amendment does not provide any specific details about the time limits required for fulfillment of the right to a speedy trial. Thus courts must interpret the provision in order to provide definitions that they can apply to actual cases. The U.S. Supreme Court's most important case defining the speedy trial right was *Barker v. Wingo* (1972). In *Barker* the time between arrest and trial became quite lengthy because the prosecution sought many **continuances,** which are requests from one side to the judge to order a delay in the proceedings. As you read the opinion in the accompanying box, pay attention to the length of the delay in the case and ask yourself whether that time period is "too long."

The Supreme Court was asked to create a definite "bright-line" rule for the right to a speedy trial. The prosecution wanted a "demand-waiver" rule which would say that any defendant who did not demand a quick trial thereby waived the right to complain later about any delays. The defense wanted a definite time rule that would say, for example, that all trials must commence within one year. Instead, the Court opted for a flexible rule that gives trial judges great discretion in interpreting when the commencement of the trial has been delayed too long. The Court created a four-part balancing test. The trial judge must weigh the following factors: (1) length of delay, (2) reason for the delay, (3) whether the defendant demanded a speedy trial, and (4) whether the defendant's case was disadvantaged by the delay ("prejudice to the defendant"). However, the Court's opinion gives no specific guidance on the weight of each factor. Judges have tremendous discretion to interpret the context of each case in light of the factors in order to come up with a decision. As you read the box on p. 319 on the symbolic nature of rights, ask yourself whether judges' discretionary decisions affect the fulfillment of the right to a speedy trial.

The Reality of Speedy Trial Claims

Allegations that the right to speedy trial has been violated do not arise frequently. In part, this is because legislatures in many jurisdictions enacted statutes establishing guidelines and time limits for the steps in the criminal justice process. By adhering to laws concerning the timing of hearings and other pretrial processes, speedy trial issues are avoided. For example, the federal Speedy Trial Act pushes federal cases to move from arrest to trial within 100 days, although there are many reasons that permissible delays lengthen this schedule. In addition, most convictions occur through plea negotiations and such agreements normally occur relatively quickly in a matter of weeks or possibly months, not over the course of years. Moreover, defense attorneys frequently request continuances on behalf of the defendant because they want additional time to prepare for trial. When the defense requests continuances, concerns about speedy trial issues essentially evaporate because a judge is not likely to find a right violated when it was actions by the defense that caused the delay.

There may be some unusual circumstances in which the defendant may contribute to the delay yet end up having the speedy trial right violated. In *Doggett v. United States* (1992), an American suspect remained outside of the

| C A S E | *Barker v. Wingo*, 407 U.S. 514 (1972) |

JUSTICE POWELL delivered the opinion of the Court.

. . .

On July 20, 1958, in Christian County, Kentucky, an elderly couple was beaten to death by intruders wielding an iron tire tool. Two suspects, Silas Manning and Willie Barker, the petitioner, were arrested shortly thereafter. The grand jury indicted them on September 15. Counsel was appointed on September 17, and Barker's trial was set for October 21. The Commonwealth had a stronger case against Manning, and it believed that Barker could not be convicted unless Manning testified against him. Manning was naturally unwilling to incriminate himself. Accordingly, on October 23, the day Silas Manning was brought to trial, the Commonwealth sought and obtained the first of what was to be a series of 16 continuances of Barker's trial. Barker made no objection. By first convicting Manning, the Commonwealth would remove possible problems of self-incrimination and would be able to assure his testimony against Barker.

The Commonwealth encountered more than a few difficulties in its prosecution of Manning. The first trial ended in a hung jury. A second trial resulted in a conviction, but the Kentucky Court of Appeals reversed because of the admission of evidence obtained by an illegal search. . . . At his third trial, Manning was again convicted, and the Court of Appeals again reversed because the trial court had not granted a change of venue. . . . A fourth trial resulted in a hung jury. Finally, after five trials, Manning was convicted, in March 1962, of murdering one victim, and after a sixth trial, in December 1962, he was convicted of murdering the other.

The Christian County Circuit Court holds three terms each year in February, June, and September. Barker's initial trial was to take place in the September term of 1958. The first continuance postponed it until the February 1959 term. The second continuance was granted for one month only. Every term thereafter for as long as the Manning prosecutions were in process, the Commonwealth routinely moved to continue Barker's case to the next term. When the case was continued from the June 1959 term until the following September, Barker, having spent 10 months in jail, obtained his release by posting a $5,000 bond. He thereafter remained free in the community until his trial. Barker made no objection, through his counsel, to the first 11 continuances.

When on February 12, 1962, the Commonwealth moved for the twelfth time to continue the case until the following term, Barker's counsel filed a motion to dismiss the indictment. The motion to dismiss was denied two weeks later, and the Commonwealth's motion for a continuance granted. The Commonwealth was granted further continuances in June 1962 and September 1962, to which Barker did not object.

In February 1963, the first term of court following Manning's final conviction, the Commonwealth moved to set Barker's trial for March 19. But on the day scheduled for trial, it again moved for a continuance until the June term. It gave as its reason the illness of the ex-sheriff who was the chief investigating officer in the case. To this continuance, Barker objected unsuccessfully.

The witness was still unable to testify in June, and the trial, which had been set for June 19, was continued again until the September term over Barker's objection. This time the court announced that the case would be dismissed for lack of prosecution if it were not tried during the next term. The final trial date was set for October 9, 1963. On that date, Barker again moved to dismiss the indictment, and this time specified that his right to a speedy trial had been violated. The motion was denied; the trial commenced with Manning as the chief prosecution witness; Barker was convicted and given a life sentence. . . .

The right to a speedy trial is generically different from any of the other rights enshrined in the Constitution for the protection of the accused. In addition to the general concern that all accused persons be treated according to decent and fair procedures, there is a societal interest in providing a speedy trial which exists separate from, and at times in opposition to, the interests of the accused. The inability of courts to provide a prompt trial has contributed to a large backlog of cases in urban courts which, among other things, enables defendants to negotiate more effectively for pleas of guilty to lesser offenses and otherwise manipulate the system. In addition, persons released on bond for lengthy periods awaiting trial have an opportunity to commit other crimes. It must be of little comfort to the residents of Christian County, Kentucky, to know that Barker was at large

(continued)

on bail for over four years while accused of a vicious and brutal murder of which he was ultimately convicted. Moreover, the longer an accused is free awaiting trial, the more tempting becomes his opportunity to jump bail and escape. Finally, delay between arrest and punishment may have a detrimental effect on rehabilitation.

If an accused cannot make bail, he is generally confined, as was Barker for 10 months, in a local jail. This contributes to the overcrowding and generally deplorable state of those institutions. Lengthy exposure to these conditions "has a destructive effect on human character and makes the rehabilitation of the individual offender much more difficult." At times the result may even be violent rioting. Finally, lengthy pretrial detention is costly. The cost of maintaining a prisoner in jail varies from $3 to $9 per day, and this amounts to millions across the Nation. In addition, society loses wages which might have been earned, and it must often support families of incarcerated breadwinners.

A second difference between the right to speedy trial and the accused's other constitutional rights is that deprivation of the right may work to the accused's advantage. Delay is not an uncommon defense tactic. As the time between the commission of the crime and the trial lengthens, witnesses may become unavailable or their memories may fade. If the witnesses support the prosecution, its case will be weakened, sometimes seriously so. And it is the prosecution which carries the burden of proof. Thus, unlike the right to counsel or the right to be free from compelled self-incrimination, deprivation of the right to speedy trial does not *per se* prejudice the accused's ability to defend himself.

Finally, and perhaps most importantly, the right to speedy trial is a more vague concept than other procedural rights. It is, for example, impossible to determine with precision when the right has been denied. We cannot definitely say how long is too long in a system where justice is supposed to be swift but deliberate. As a consequence, there is no fixed point in the criminal process when the State can put the defendant to the choice of either exercising or waiving the right to speedy trial. If, for example, the State moves for a 60-day continuance, granting that continuance is not a violation of the right to speedy trial unless the circumstances of the case are such that further delay would endanger the values the right protects. It is impossible to do more than generalize about when those circumstances exist. There is nothing comparable to the point in the process when a defendant exercises or waives his right to counsel or his right to a jury trial. Thus . . . any inquiry into a speedy trial claim necessitates a functional analysis of the right in the particular context of the case. . . .

The amorphous quality of the right also leads to the unsatisfactorily severe remedy of dismissal of the indictment when the right has been deprived. This is indeed a serious consequence because it means that a defendant who may be guilty of a serious crime will go free, without having been tried. Such a remedy is more serious than an exclusionary rule or a reversal for a new trial, but it is the only possible remedy.

Perhaps because the speedy trial right is so slippery, two rigid approaches are urged upon us as ways of eliminating some of the uncertainty which courts experience in protecting the right. The first suggestion is that we hold that the Constitution requires a criminal defendant to be offered a trial within a specified time period. The result of such a ruling would have the virtue of clarifying when the right is infringed and of simplifying courts' application of it. Recognizing this, some legislatures have enacted laws, and some courts have adopted procedural rules which more narrowly define the right. . . . This type of rule is also recommended by the American Bar Association.

But such a result would require this Court to engage in legislative or rulemaking activity, rather than in the adjudicative process to which we should confine our efforts. We do not establish procedural rules for the States, except when mandated by the Constitution. We find no constitutional basis for holding that the speedy trial right can be quantified into a specified number of days or months. The States, of course, are free to prescribe a reasonable period consistent with constitutional standards, but our approach must be less precise.

The second suggested alternative would restrict consideration of the right to those cases in which the accused has demanded a speedy trial. Most states have recognized what is loosely referred to as the "demand rule," although eight States reject it. It is not clear, however, precisely what is meant by that term. . . .

Such an approach, by presuming waiver of a fundamental right from inaction, is inconsistent with this Court's pronouncements on waiver of constitutional rights. . . .

We reject, therefore, the rule that a defendant who fails to demand a speedy trial forever waives his right. This does not mean, however, that the defendant has no responsibility to assert his right. We think the better rule is that the defendant's assertion of or failure to assert his right to a speedy trial is one of the factors to be considered in an inquiry into the deprivation of the right. . . .

We, therefore, reject both of the inflexible approaches: the fixed-time period because it goes further than the Constitution requires; the demand-waiver rule because it is insensitive to a right which we have deemed fundamental. The approach we accept is a balancing test, in which the conduct of both the prosecution and the defendant are weighed.

A balancing test necessarily compels courts to approach speedy trial cases on an *ad hoc* basis. We can do little more than identify some of the factors which courts should assess in determining whether a particular defendant has been deprived of his right. Though some might express them in different ways, we identify four such factors: Length of delay, the reason for the delay, the defendant's assertion of his right, and prejudice to the defendant.

The length of the delay is to some extent a triggering mechanism. Until there is some delay which is presumptively prejudicial, there is no necessity for inquiry into the other factors that go into the balance. Nevertheless, because of the imprecision of the right to speedy trial, the length of delay that will provoke such an inquiry is necessarily dependent upon the peculiar circumstances of the case. To take but one example, the delay that can be tolerated for an ordinary street crime is considerably less than for a serious, complex conspiracy charge.

Closely related to length of delay is the reason the government assigns to justify the delay. Here, too, different weights should be assigned to different reasons. A deliberate attempt to delay the trial in order to hamper the defense should be weighted heavily against the government. A more neutral reason such as negligence or overcrowded courts should be weighted less heavily but nevertheless should be considered since the ultimate responsibility for such circumstances must rest with the government rather than with the defendant. Finally, a valid reason, such as a missing witness, should serve to justify appropriate delay.

We have already discussed the third factor, and the defendant's responsibility to assert his right. Whether and how a defendant asserts his right is closely related to the other factors we have mentioned. The strength of his efforts will be affected by the length of the delay, to some extent by the reason for the delay, and most particularly by personal prejudice, which is not always readily identifiable, that he experiences. The more serious the deprivation, the more likely a defendant is to complain. The defendant's assertion of his speedy trial right, then, is entitled to strong evidentiary weight in determining whether the defendant is being deprived of the right. We emphasize that the failure to assert the right will make it difficult for a defendant to prove that he was denied a speedy trial.

A fourth factor is prejudice to the defendant. Prejudice, of course, should be assessed in the light of the interests of defendants which the speedy trial right was designed to protect. This Court has identified three such interests: (i) to prevent oppressive pretrial incarceration; (ii) to minimize anxiety and concern of the accused; and (iii) to limit the possibility that the defense will be impaired. Of these, the most serious is the last, because the inability of a defendant adequately to prepare his case skews the fairness of the entire system. If witnesses die or disappear during a delay, the prejudice is obvious. There is also prejudice if defense witnesses are unable to recall accurately events of the distant past. Loss of memory, however, is not always reflected in the record because what has been forgotten can rarely be known.

We have discussed previously the societal disadvantages of lengthy pretrial incarceration, but obviously the disadvantages for the accused who cannot obtain his release are even more serious. The time spent in jail awaiting trial has a detrimental impact on the individual. It often means loss of a job; it disrupts family life; and it enforces idleness. Most jails offer little or no recreational or rehabilitative programs. The time spent in jail is simply dead time. Moreover, if a defendant is locked up, he is hindered in his ability to gather evidence, contact witnesses, or otherwise prepare his defense. Imposing those consequences on anyone who has not yet been convicted is serious. It is especially unfortunate to impose them on those persons who are ultimately found to be innocent. Finally, even if an accused is not incarcerated prior to trial, he is still disadvantaged by restraints on his liberty, and by living under a cloud of anxiety, suspicion, and often hostility. . . .

We regard none of these four factors identified above as either a necessary or sufficient condition to

---

(continued)

the finding of a deprivation of the right of speedy trial. Rather, they are related factors and must be considered together with such other circumstances as may be relevant. In sum, these factors have no talismanic qualities; courts must still engage in a difficult and sensitive balancing process. But, because we are dealing with a fundamental right of the accused, this process must be carried out with full recognition that the accused's interest

in a speedy trial is specifically affirmed in the Constitution. . . .

[The Supreme Court applied the four-part balancing test to Barker's case and determined that although the delay was lengthy and caused by the prosecution, those factors were outweighed by the fact that Barker did not demand a speedy trial and the delay did not disadvantage him in presenting his defense. Thus the speedy trial right was not violated.]

United States in Central America for two years after he was indicted for drug smuggling. He subsequently returned to the United States and lived openly and lawfully under his own name for six years before he was arrested. A narrow majority of the Supreme Court seemed to attribute the delay to the government's negligence. In effect, because the government made Doggett's arrest and prosecution such a low priority that it made no effort to find him for a number of years, it violated his right to a speedy trial. The unusual example provided by this case may arise only rarely, but it demonstrates that the activation of the speedy trial right does not rest entirely on determining which party caused the delay.

Criminal defendants are not the only people who may benefit from an entitlement to speedy trials. Victim advocates believe that crime victims also deserve to see judicial proceedings completed with delays. The completion of a prosecution, especially if it results in a conviction and sentence, may help give victims a sense of closure in the aftermath of a traumatic experience with a criminal incident. As you read the box on p. 320 about a proposed constitutional amendment to give crime victims a right to a speedy trial, think about the problems that may arise from the creation of such a legal entitlement for victims.

COMPULSORY PROCESS

The Sixth Amendment contains a right to compulsory process. This means that the defendant can use the authority of the judicial process to obtain evidence for presentation at trial. For example, the defendant is entitled to use subpoenas to obtain documents, witnesses, and other evidence. To be effective, the right necessarily extends beyond the acquisition of evidence to also include a right to present evidence. The right was incorporated by the Supreme Court in *Washington v. Texas* (1967). This does not mean that the defendant can present any evidence that he or she may desire for the judge or jury to hear. Rules of evidence still apply, and the court must be concerned about the reliability of evidence. Thus, for example, the defendant cannot automatically introduce hearsay evidence (e.g., testimony about statements heard from a nontestifying individual) if such statements violate the court's evidentiary rules.

CONSTITUTIONAL RIGHTS: SYMBOL OR SUBSTANCE?

Speedy Trials and Judicial Discretion

In Barker's case, the crime occurred on July 20, 1958, and he was arrested and charged shortly thereafter. His trial did not take place, however, until October 9, 1963, more than five years later. Despite the lengthy period of time, the Supreme Court said his right to a speedy trial was not violated. If Barker had disappeared for several years so that the delay was his fault rather than the prosecution's, then it would be understandable that the lengthy delay would not violate his rights. In this case, however, Barker was available for prosecution the entire time and it was the prosecution that requested delay after delay.

Judges have significant discretion in weighing the four *Barker* factors in determining the validity of speedy trial claims. If the judge says that the length of the delay is outweighed by the fact that the defendant suffered no serious harm from the delay, how could anyone contest that decision? It is very much a matter of individual judgment.

In light of the flexible standard for assessing the right, the discretion of judges to determine violations, and the Supreme Court's lax view of very lengthy delays as evidenced by the final result in *Barker,* how "real" is the right to a speedy trial? In light of the *Barker* decision, what would have to happen for a situation to really result in a violation of this constitutional right?

Compulsory Process and Court Rules

What happens if the trial judge rules that evidence the defense wishes to present must be excluded from court? The Supreme Court addressed this issue in *Taylor v. Illinois* (1988). As you read the Court's opinion in the box on pp. 321–324, ask yourself whether the trial judge's ruling on the admissibility of evidence is analogous to the use of the exclusionary rule that we saw in prior chapters.

The Limited Right

The Supreme Court's decision in *Taylor* shows that the right to compulsory process is not absolute. Indeed, the Court is quite willing to limit the right in the interest of maintaining an emphasis on orderly trial proceedings according to established rules of procedure. Although few would argue that the right to compulsory process should be absolute, thus implying that the right should supersede all rules of evidence and procedure, critics see the *Taylor* decision as potentially placing too much emphasis on judicial administration and not enough on constitutional rights. In *Taylor* the excluded witness was potentially very important for the defendant because the witness may have provided the basis for a self-defense claim. If the jury had believed that the victim carried a lethal weapon to the altercation, the defendant had the possibility of gaining acquittal because self-defense could be a basis for avoiding a homicide conviction. This potential testimony was excluded, however, because the defense attorney violated court rules by trying to have a surprise witness, rather than supplying a complete witness list as required by court rules. As a sanction for violating the court rules, the trial judge excluded the witness and the Supreme Court endorsed this exclusion. Yet despite the fact that the defense

In 1996 a proposed constitutional amendment was introduced in Congress that sought to create constitutional rights for crime victims. In order to become part of the Constitution, the proposed amendment would need to be approved by two-thirds of both chambers of Congress and then ratified by three-fourths of the states through action by their state legislatures or state constitutional conventions. The proposed amendment says, in part:

> To ensure that the victim is treated with fairness, dignity, and respect, from the occurrence of a crime of violence and other crimes as may be defined by law pursuant to section 2 of this article, and throughout the criminal, military, and juvenile justice processes, as a matter of fundamental rights to liberty, justice, and due process, the victim shall have the following rights: to be informed of and given the opportunity to be present at every proceeding in which those rights are extended to the accused or convicted offender; to be heard at any proceeding involving sentencing, including the right to object to a previously negotiated plea, or a release from custody; to be informed of any release or escape; and to a speedy trial, a final conclusion free from unreasonable delay, full restitution from the con-

victed offender, reasonable measures to protect the victim from violence or intimidation by the accused or convicted offender, and notice of the victim's rights.

The proposed amendment raises many questions. Would police officers and prosecutors be subject to civil rights lawsuits if they failed to notify victims' about their rights and fulfill other affirmative obligations in the amendment? Does the right to be present and object to pleas and sentences really constitute a significant entitlement since such rights do not prevent prosecutors and judges from doing what they would have done anyway? In addition, are there any clashes between the proposed rights of victims and existing rights for defendants?

With respect to this final question, the victim's right to a speedy trial stands out as a possible source of problems. What if the victim's desire for a quick trial clashes with the defendant's need for additional time to prepare for trial? Could a victim force a defendant to go to trial before the defendant's attorney is completely prepared? Alternatively, would judges merely define the victim's right to a speedy trial in such a vague manner that the right would be more symbolic than substantive?

attorney violated the court rules, it was the defendant who paid the price. For this defendant, that may have made the difference between a long sentence and freedom. The trial judge had options for punishing the attorney alone. The attorney could have been found in contempt of court or sanctioned by losing his law license through attorney discipline proceedings. Instead, the defendant goes to prison and the attorney suffers no sanction for his misdeed. Is the Supreme Court correct in equating the interests and responsibility of the defense attorney with those of the defendant, or are the results too harsh for the defendant?

Another basis for questioning *Taylor* is to ask whether a court rule should be regarded as more important than a constitutional right. Here the right is sacrificed in order to make a strong statement about a rule of criminal procedure. The result is ironic in the eyes of the dissenters who note that the very justices who create exceptions to the exclusionary rule such as *United States v. Leon*'s good faith exception (see Chapter 4) are also the ones who are quite willing to exclude evidence to protect the court rule. In other words, the dissenters subtly note that these justices are willing to admit evidence into court despite violations of Fourth Amendment rights, but that the justices will not

Taylor v. Illinois, 484 U.S. 400 (1988)

[*Prior to the start of a murder trial, the prosecutor filed a discovery motion requesting a list of defense witnesses. The list submitted by the defense attorney did not contain the name of Mr. Wormley. A later witness list submitted by the defense attorney on the first day of trial also did not contain Mr. Wormley's name. On the second day of the trial, the defense attorney asked for permission to amend his list in order to call Mr. Wormley as a witness. The attorney claimed that he did not previously list Mr. Wormley's name as a witness because he had been unable to locate Mr. Wormley. Prior to permitting Mr. Wormley to testify, the judge learned from the potential witness that he had actually met with the defense attorney two weeks prior to the trial. The judge refused to permit Mr. Wormley to testify. The exclusion of the witness was the judge's sanction against the attorney for a blatant and willful violation of discovery rules by not listing a known witness on the list submitted on the first day of trial and then subsequently being untruthful in stating that he had not been able to locate the witness until the second day of trial. Discovery rules govern the sharing of information between attorneys for each side in a case. The defendant was convicted of attempted murder at the conclusion of the trial. The Illinois Appellate Court affirmed the defendant's conviction. The Illinois Supreme Court declined to hear the defendant's appeal. The U.S. Supreme Court accepted the case to consider whether the judge's action in excluding the witness violated the defendant's Sixth Amendment right to compulsory process in producing and submitting relevant evidence.*]

JUSTICE STEVENS delivered the opinion of the Court.

. . .

In this Court petitioner makes two arguments. He first contends that the Sixth Amendment bars a court from ever ordering the preclusion of evidence as a sanction for violating a discovery rule. Alternatively, he contends that even if the right to present witnesses is not absolute, on the facts of this case the preclusion of Wormley's testimony was constitutional error. Before addressing these contentions, we consider the State's argument that the Compulsory Process Clause of the Sixth Amendment is merely a guarantee that the accused shall have the power to subpoena witnesses and simply does not apply to rulings on the admissibility of evidence.

In the State's view, no Compulsory Process concerns are even raised by authorizing preclusion as a discovery sanction. . . . We have, however, consistently given the Clause the broader reading reflected in contemporaneous state constitutional provisions. . . .

Few rights are more fundamental than that of an accused to present witnesses in his own defense. . . . Indeed, this right is an essential attribute of the adversary system itself. . . . The right to compel a witness' presence in the courtroom could not protect the integrity of the adversary process if it did not embrace the right to have the witness' testimony heard by the trier of fact. The right to offer testimony is thus grounded in the Sixth Amendment even though it is not expressly described in so many words. . . .

The right of the defendant to present evidence "stands on no lesser footing than the other Sixth Amendment rights that we have previously held applicable to the States." . . . We cannot accept the State's argument that this constitutional right may never be offended by the imposition of a discovery sanction that entirely excludes the testimony of a material defense witness.

Petitioner's claim that the Sixth Amendment creates an absolute bar to the preclusion of the testimony of a surprise witness is just as extreme and just as unacceptable as the State's position that the Amendment is simply irrelevant. The accused does not have an unfettered right to offer testimony that is incompetent, privileged, or otherwise inadmissible under standard rules of evidence. The Compulsory Process Clause provides him with an effective weapon, but it is a weapon that cannot be used irresponsibly. . . .

The principle that undergirds the defendant's right to present exculpatory evidence is also the source of essential limitations on the right. The adversary process could not function effectively without adherence to rules of procedure that govern the orderly presentation of facts and arguments to provide each party with a fair opportunity to assemble and submit evidence to contradict or explain the opponent's case. The trial process would be a shambles if either party had an absolute right to control the time and content of his witnesses' testimony.

(continued)

Neither may insist on the right to interrupt the opposing party's case, and obviously there is no absolute right to interrupt the deliberations of the jury to present newly discovered evidence. The State's interest in the orderly conduct of a criminal trial is sufficient to justify the imposition and enforcement of firm, though not always inflexible, rules relating to the identification and presentation of evidence. . . .

The "State's interest in protecting itself against an eleventh-hour defense" is merely one component of the broader public interest in a full and truthful disclosure of critical facts. . . .

It may well be true that alternative sanctions are adequate and appropriate in most cases, but it is equally clear that they would be less effective than the preclusion sanction and that there are instances in which they would perpetuate rather than limit the prejudice to the State and the harm to the adversary process. . . .

It would demean the high purpose of the Compulsory Process Clause to construe it as encompassing an absolute right to an automatic continuance or mistrial to allow presumptively perjured testimony to be presented to a jury. We reject petitioner's argument that a preclusion sanction is never appropriate no matter how serious the defendant's discovery violation may be.

Petitioner argues that the preclusion sanction was unnecessarily harsh in this case because the [questioning] of Wormley [by the judge prior to his opportunity to testify before the jury] adequately protected the prosecution from any possible prejudice resulting from surprise. Petitioner also contends that it is unfair to visit the sins of the lawyer upon his client. Neither argument has merit.

More is at stake than possible prejudice to the prosecution. We are also concerned with the impact of this kind of conduct on the integrity of the judicial process itself. The trial judge found that the discovery violation in this case was both willful and blatant. . . . Regardless of whether prejudice to the prosecution could have been avoided in this particular case, it is plain that the case fits into the category of willful misconduct in which the severest sanction is appropriate. . . .

The argument that the client should not be held responsible for his lawyer's misconduct strikes at the heart of the attorney-client relationship. Although there are basic rights that the attorney cannot waive without the fully informed and publicly acknowledged consent of the client, the lawyer has—and must have—full authority to manage the conduct of the trial. The adversary process could not function effectively if every tactical decision required client approval. Moreover, given the protections afforded by the attorney-client privilege and the fact that extreme cases may involve unscrupulous conduct by both the client and the lawyer, it would be highly impracticable to require an investigation into their relative responsibilities before applying the sanction of preclusion. . . . Whenever a lawyer makes use of the sword provided by the Compulsory Process Clause, there is some risk that he may wound his own client.

The judgment of the Illinois Appellate Court is Affirmed.

JUSTICE BRENNAN, with whom JUSTICE MARSHALL and JUSTICE STEVENS join, dissenting.

. . .

The question in this case . . . is not whether discovery rules should be enforced, but whether the need to correct and deter discovery violations requires a sanction that itself distorts the truthseeking process by excluding material evidence of innocence in a criminal case. . . . I would hold that, absent evidence of the defendant's personal involvement in a discovery violation, the Compulsory Process Clause *per se* bars discovery sanctions that exclude criminal defense evidence. . . .

The Compulsory Process Clause and the Due Process Clause . . . require courts to conduct a searching inquiry whenever the government seeks to exclude criminal defense evidence. After all, "[f]ew rights are more fundamental than that of an accused to present witnesses in his own defense.". . . The exclusion of criminal defense evidence undermines the central truthseeking aim of our criminal justice system, . . . because it deliberately distorts the record at the risk of misleading the jury into convicting an innocent person. Surely the paramount value our criminal justice system places on acquitting the innocent, see, *e.g., In re Winship* . . . (1970), demands close scrutiny of any law preventing the jury from hearing evidence favorable to the defendant. On the other hand, the Compulsory Process Clause does not invalidate every restriction on the presentation of evidence. The Clause does not, for example, require criminal courts to admit evidence that is irrelevant, . . . testimony by persons who are mentally infirm, . . . or evidence that represents half-truth. . . . That the inquiry required under the Compulsory Process Clause is sometimes difficult does not, of course, justify abandoning the task altogether. . . .

[P]recluding witness testimony is clearly arbitrary and disproportionate to the purpose discovery intended to serve—advancing the quest for truth. Alternative sanctions—namely, granting the prosecution a continuance and allowing the prosecutor to comment [to the jury] on the witness concealment—can correct for any adverse impact the discovery violation would have on the truthseeking process. Moreover, the alternative sanctions, unlike the preclusion sanction, do not distort the truth-seeking process by excluding material evidence of innocence. . . .

Witness preclusion . . . punishes discovery violations in a way that is both disproportionate—it might result in a defendant charged with a capital offense being convicted and receiving a death sentence he would not have received but for the discovery violation—and arbitrary—it might, in another case involving an identical discovery violation, result in a defendant suffering no change in verdict, or if charged with a lesser offense, being convicted and receiving a light or suspended sentence. In contrast, direct punitive measures (such as contempt sanctions or, if the attorney is responsible, disciplinary proceedings) can gradate the punishment to correspond to the severity of the discovery violation.

The arbitrary and disproportionate nature of the preclusion sanction is highlighted where the penalty falls on the defendant even though he bore no responsibility for the discovery violation. In this case, although there was ample evidence that the defense attorney willfully violated [the discovery rule concerning listing all known witnesses], there was no evidence that the defendant played any role in that violation. Nor did the trial court make any effort to determine whether the defendant bore any responsibility for the discovery violation. Indeed, reading the record leaves the distinct impression that the main reason the trial court excluded Wormley's testimony was a belief that the defense counsel had purposefully lied about when he had located Wormley.

Worse yet, the trial court made clear that it was excluding Wormley's testimony not only in response to the defense counsel's actions in this case but also in response to the actions of other defense attorneys in other cases. The trial court stated:

". . . All right, I am going to deny Wormley the opportunity to testify here. He is not going to testify. I find this a blatent [sic] violation of the discovery rules, willful violation of the rules. I also feel that defense attorneys have been violating discovery in this courtroom in the last three or four cases blatently [sic] and I am going to put a stop to it and this is one way to do so."

Although the [Supreme Court's majority opinion] recognizes this problem, it offers no response other than the cryptic statement that "[u]nrelated discovery violations . . . would not . . . normally provide a proper basis for curtailing the defendant's constitutional right to present a complete defense.". . . We are left to wonder either why this case is abnormal or why an exclusion founded on an improper basis should be upheld. . . .

The situation might be different if the defendant willfully caused the discovery violation. . . . But that is no explanation for allowing defense witness preclusion where there is no evidence that the defendant bore any responsibility for the discovery violation. At a minimum, we would be obligated to remand for further factfinding to establish the defendant's responsibility. Deities may be able to visit the sins of the father on the son, but I cannot agree that courts should be permitted to visit the sins of the lawyer on the innocent client. . . .

In this case there is no doubt that willfully concealing the identity of witnesses one intends to call at trial is attorney misconduct, that the government seeks to deter such behavior in all instances, and that the attorney knows such behavior is misconduct and not a legitimate tactical decision at the time it occurs. Direct punitive sanctions against the attorney are available [under state court rules]. . . .

It seems particularly ironic that the Court should approve the exclusion of evidence in this case at a time when several of its Members have expressed serious misgivings about the evidentiary costs of exclusionary rules in other contexts. Surely the deterrence of constitutional violations cannot be less important than the deterrence of discovery violations. Nor can it be said that the evidentiary costs are more significant when they are imposed on the prosecution. For that would turn on its head what Justice Harlan termed the "fundamental value determination of our society that it is far worse to convict an innocent man than to let a guilty man go free." *In re Winship*, 397 U.S. at 372 (concurring opinion).

Discovery rules are important, but only as a means for helping the criminal justice system convict the guilty and acquit the innocent. Precluding defense witnesses' testimony as a sanction for a defense counsel's willful discovery violation not only directly subverts criminal justice by basing convictions on a partial presentation of facts, . . . but is also arbitrary and disproportionate to any of the purposes served by discovery rules or discovery sanctions. The Court today thus sacrifices the

(continued)

paramount values of the criminal justice system in a misguided and unnecessary effort to preserve the sanctity of discovery. We may never know for certain whether the defendant or [the victim's] brother fired the shot for which the defendant was convicted. We do know, however, that the jury that convicted the defendant was not permitted to hear evidence that would have both placed a gun in [the victim's] brother's hands and contradicted the testimony of [the victim] and his brother that they possessed no weapons that evening—and that, because of the defense counsel's 5-day delay in identifying a witness, an innocent man may be serving 10 years in prison. I dissent.

[The dissenting opinion of Justice Blackmun is omitted.]

do the same when it is merely a court rule, rather than a constitutional right, that has been violated. The dissenters, in effect, raise the question whether their colleagues are biased in favor of prosecutors by working so hard to have prosecutorial evidence avoid exclusion when rights are violated, but not showing similar concern about seeking ways to avoid exclusion when court rules are violated and the sanction is imposed against the defendant. Whether or not this provides evidence of bias among the justices, it is clear that the Court does not treat the right to compulsory process as a constitutional protection with sufficient importance that other judicial interests will be sacrificed in order to ensure that the right is fulfilled.

CONFRONTATION

The Sixth Amendment contains a right to confront adverse witnesses. This includes a right to be present at one's own trial and reflects long-standing American opposition to systems that may permit defendants to be tried *in absentia*—in their absence. Under such systems, there would be a risk that someone could be convicted of a crime without ever knowing that she or he had been accused and without ever having an opportunity to challenge the prosecution's evidence. This does not mean a defendant's right to be present at trial is absolute. If a defendant disappears during a trial, the court can treat the defendant's behavior as a waiver of the right to confrontation (*Taylor v. United States*, 1973). Defendants may also be excluded from their own trials if they are disruptive in the courtroom. The Supreme Court regards exclusion as an option of last resort, but it recognizes that there may be some circumstances in which trial judges have few other options in attempting to proceed with a trial in an orderly manner. In addressing the situation of a defendant who continually threatened and swore at the judge during courtroom outbursts (*Illinois v. Allen*, 1970), the Court presented the trial judge's options and noted that all of them are undesirable and should be applied only if absolutely necessary:

> It is essential to the proper administration of criminal justice that dignity, order, and decorum be the hallmarks of all court proceedings in our country. The flagrant disregard in the courtroom of elementary standards of proper conduct should not and cannot be tolerated. We believe trial judges confronted with disruptive, contumacious, stubbornly defiant

| A CLOSER LOOK | A Trial *in Absentia* |

In 1977 Helen "Holly" Maddux, a 30-year-old woman from a wealthy Texas family, disappeared. She had been living in Philadelphia with her boyfriend, Ira Einhorn, a former hippie leader who had developed a network of friends among prominent people as he ran for mayor and organized artistic events and self-discovery courses. Eighteen months after Einhorn claimed that Maddux went out and never returned from a trip to the store, her decomposed remains were found in a trunk in his closet. Einhorn proclaimed his innocence and gained release on bail with the support of prominent Philadelphians who thought this leading advocate of peace and love could never commit a murder.

When Einhorn's trial date approached, he disappeared. Investigators later learned that he had fled the country. Sightings of Einhorn were reported in Ireland and Sweden, but authorities could not find him. When Philadelphia's district attorney became concerned that witnesses' memories might fade over time, Einhorn was tried *in absentia* in 1993. Einhorn was convicted of murder.

Philadelphia officials continued to investigate Einhorn's whereabouts. In 1997 they gained information that led them to a house in France where Einhorn's former Swedish girlfriend resided under an assumed name. The French police found a man who said his name was "Mallon," but his fingerprints matched those of Ira Einhorn.

Einhorn hired a French attorney to fight against his extradition—the process of returning a fugitive to face charges in another jurisdiction. His attorney argued that the United States has an unfair criminal trial process because it permitted defendants to be tried *in absentia*, it used the death penalty, and it did not obey the European Convention on Human Rights. According to an American writer who followed Einhorn's case closely, his attorneys were fundamentally raising questions about the fairness of American trials and the justice process:

> *However, the underlying argument, it would appear, was to urge the French judges to send a message to the "barbarians" in the United States. . . . [They wanted France to] send a message in human rights to the new masters of the world order across the ocean.*[2]

The French judges agreed with the attorneys' arguments. The judges refused to send Einhorn back to the United States to stand trial and he was released from custody. Government officials in the United States protested the decision and its implication that American trial processes are unfair. In an effort to satisfy French criticisms of the trial *in absentia,* the Pennsylvania legislature passed a special law to give Einhorn a new trial if he were ever returned to the United States. After two additional years of appeals, a French court ordered Einhorn returned to the United States in 1999. He was not transported from France immediately because he was entitled to further appeals in the French courts. He was returned to the United States to face trial in 2001.

Are trials *in absentia* fair? Can the defendant's case be adequately prepared and argued in such circumstances? Were the French judges correct in thinking that the existence of such trials indicates a flaw in the American system of justice?

> *defendants must be given sufficient discretion to meet the circumstances of each case. No one formula for maintaining the appropriate courtroom atmosphere will be best in all situations. We think there are at least three constitutionally permissible ways for a trial judge to handle an obstreperous defendant like Allen: (1) bind and gag him, thereby keeping him present; (2) cite him for contempt; (3) take him out of the courtroom until he promises to conduct himself properly. (397 U.S. 337 at 343–344)*

Exclusion from trial is possible, but it should happen only under unusual circumstances. As you read the material in the above box about a trial without confrontation, think about the circumstances that would justify such a **trial *in absentia*** when the defendant is unwilling to appear voluntarily or is otherwise unavailable.

Confrontation and Vulnerable Witnesses

In the minds of many analysts, the right to confrontation can clash with important societal interests in protecting certain crime victims and witnesses, especially children and sex crime victims. Because it may be frightening and
psychologically traumatic for child victims and sex crime victims to see their
alleged victimizers sitting at the defense table during a trial, several jurisdictions tried to develop a way to protect such witnesses. In *Coy v. Iowa* (1988),
the court followed a state law by placing a large screen between the witness
stand and the defense table. Two teenage girls who were allegedly sexually assaulted by a neighbor were permitted to sit behind the screen when they testified. The judge and jury could see the girls, the defense attorney could
cross-examine the girls, and everyone in the courtroom, including the defendant, could hear the girls speak. However, the girls could not see the defendant
and the defendant could not see the girls. When the defendant later challenged
the use of the screen, the Supreme Court ruled that the use of the device violated the Sixth Amendment right to confrontation. The case is one of relatively few situations in which Justice Scalia, who usually sides with the
prosecution in criminal justice cases, joined his most liberal colleagues in supporting the confrontation right. Scalia takes a literal view of the Confrontation Clause by interpreting it as requiring face-to-face confrontation between
the defendant and the accusers. Within the divided court, some justices believed that such devices reasonably accommodate the defendant's right and
the need to protect child witnesses. Other justices indicated that the Iowa practice might have been proper if it permitted the use of screens on a case-by-case
basis rather than permitting the use whenever child-victims testify.

Two years later, the Supreme Court addressed the confrontation issue. This
time, however, the court in Maryland used closed-circuit television rather than
a screen to shield the child witnesses from seeing the defendant. As you read
Maryland v. Craig (1990) in the accompanying box, ask yourself whether it is
consistent with *Coy v. Iowa*.

It is difficult to declare that the decision in *Maryland v. Craig* (1990)
established any particular principle concerning the right to confrontation. Obviously, the Court was divided about the issue. Whenever there is deep division, it may be difficult to articulate a clear rule to guide officials in the
criminal justice system. The Court effectively used an *ad hoc* balancing approach by simply making a decision about whether this particular technique
properly weighed and protected the respective interests of the defendant and
society.

The Court does not always weigh the balance by favoring the protection
of juveniles over the rights of defendants. In *Davis v. Alaska* (1974), the Court
rejected a trial court's attempt to protect a juvenile witness from the rigors of
cross-examination, but the justices concluded that the defendant's rights and
interests would be seriously harmed if the defense attorney was not permitted
to use cross-examination to fully reveal the juvenile witness's criminal record,
questionable reliability, and potential self-interest in pointing the prosecution
toward the defendant rather than himself. In that case, the juvenile was a witness with a criminal record rather than a young crime victim whose need for
protection might provide greater weight for the state's interests.

CASE	*Maryland v. Craig*, 497 U.S. 836 (1990)

[*Mrs. Craig, the operator of a preschool program, was accused of child abuse and sexual misconduct. Under Maryland state law, if the trial judge determined that face-to-face contact between a child-victim and alleged victimizer "will result in the child suffering serious emotional distress such that the child cannot reasonably communicate," then the judge can permit the child to testify via closed-circuit television. A judge permitted four children to testify against Mrs. Craig through the use of closed-circuit television, and she was convicted at trial. The Maryland Court of Special Appeals affirmed the conviction, but the Maryland Court of Appeals ordered a new trial. The Maryland Court of Appeals rejected Craig's claim that the Confrontation Clause always requires face-to-face encounters between defendants and witnesses. However, this state appellate court ordered a new trial because the trial judge had not adequately fulfilled the statutory requirements for demonstrating the need for the television testimony. According to the Maryland Court of Appeals, the Confrontation Clause always requires face-to-face encounters unless such encounters would prevent the child from testifying. The U.S. Supreme Court accepted the case to decide whether or not the Confrontation Clause always requires face-to-face contact in the courtroom.*]

JUSTICE O'CONNOR delivered the opinion of the Court.

This case requires us to decide whether the Confrontation Clause of the Sixth Amendment categorically prohibits a child witness in a child abuse case from testifying against a defendant at trial, outside the defendant's physical presence, by one-way closed circuit television. . . .

We observed in *Coy v. Iowa* [1988] that "the Confrontation Clause guarantees the defendant a face-to-face meeting with witnesses appearing before the trier of fact. . . ." [citing seven cases from 1895 to 1987]. This interpretation derives not only from the literal text of the Clause, but also from our understanding of its historical roots. . . .

We have never held, however, that the Confrontation Clause guarantees criminal defendants the *absolute* right to a face-to-face meeting with witnesses against them at trial. Indeed, in *Coy v. Iowa,* we expressly "le[ft] for another day . . . the question whether any exceptions exist" to the "irreducible

literal meaning of the Clause["]. . . . We concluded [in *Coy*] that "[s]ince there ha[d] been no individualized findings that these particular witnesses needed special protection, the judgment [in *Coy*] could not be sustained by any conceivable exception.". . . Because the trial court in [*Craig*] made individualized findings that each of the child witnesses needed special protection, this case requires us to decide the question reserved in *Coy*. . . .

The combined effect of these elements of confrontation—physical presence, oath, cross-examination, and observation of demeanor by the trier of fact—serves the purposes of the Confrontation Clause by ensuring that evidence admitted against an accused is reliable and subject to the rigorous adversarial testing that is the norm of Anglo-American criminal proceedings. . . .

Although face-to-face confrontation forms "the core of the values furthered by the Confrontation Clause,". . . we have nevertheless recognized that it is not the *sine qua non* of the confrontation right. . . . [S]ee also [*Kentucky v.*] *Stincer* [1987] . . . (confrontation right is not violated by exclusion of the defendant from competency hearing of child witnesses, where defendant had opportunity for full and effective cross-examination at trial). . . .

For this reason, we have never insisted on an actual face-to-face encounter at trial in *every* instance in which testimony is admitted against a defendant. Instead, we have repeatedly held that the Clause permits, where necessary, the admission of certain hearsay statements against a defendant despite the defendant's inability to confront the declarant at trial. . . . In *Mattox* [*v. United States,* 1895], for example, we held that the testimony of a government witness at a former trial against the defendant, where the witness was fully cross-examined but had died after the first trial, was admissible in evidence against the defendant at his second trial. . . . Thus, in certain narrow circumstances, "competing interests, if 'closely examined,' may warrant dispensing with confrontations at trial.". . . We have recently held, for example, that hearsay statements of non-testifying co-conspirators may be admitted against a defendant despite the lack of any face-to-face encounter with the accused. See *Bourjaily v. United States* [1987]. . . . Given our hearsay cases, the word "confront," as used in the Confrontation Clause, cannot simply mean face-to-face confrontation, for the Clause would then, contrary to our cases,

(continued)

prohibit the admission of any accusatory hearsay statement made by an absent declarant—a declarant who is undoubtedly as much a "witness against" a defendant as one who actually testifies at trial.

In sum, our precedents establish that "the Confrontation Clause reflects a *preference* for face-to-face confrontation at trial.". . .

The critical inquiry in this case, therefore, is whether use of the [closed-circuit television] procedure is necessary to further an important state interest. The State contends that it has a substantial interest in protecting children who are allegedly victims of child abuse from the trauma of testifying against the alleged perpetrator and that its statutory procedure for receiving testimony from such witnesses is necessary to further that interest.

We have of course recognized that a State's interest in "the protection of minor victims of sex crimes from further trauma and embarrassment" is a "compelling" one [citations to four cases]. . . . In *Globe Newspaper* [*Co. v Superior Court,* 1982], for example, we held that a State's interest in the physical and psychological well-being of a minor victim was sufficiently weighty to justify depriving the press and public of their constitutional right to attend criminal trials, where the trial court makes a case-specific finding that closure of the trial is necessary to protect the welfare of the minor. . . .

We likewise conclude today that a State's interest in the physical and psychological well-being of child abuse victims may be sufficiently important to outweigh, at least in some cases, a defendant's right to face his or her accusers in court. That a significant majority of States has enacted statutes to protect child witnesses from the trauma of giving testimony in child abuse cases attests to the widespread belief in the importance of such a public policy. . . . Thirty-seven States, for example, permit the use of videotaped testimony of sexually abused children; 24 States have authorized the use of one-way closed circuit television testimony in child abuse cases; and 8 States authorize the use of a two-way system in which the child-witness is permitted to see the courtroom and the defendant on a video monitor and in which the jury and judge are permitted to view the child during the testimony. . . .

Given the State's traditional and "transcendent interest in protecting the welfare of children,". . . and buttressed by the growing body of academic literature documenting the psychological trauma suffered by child abuse victims who must testify in court [citations to psychology research] . . . , we will not second-guess the considered judgment of the Maryland Legislature regarding the importance of its interest in protecting child abuse victims from the emotional trauma of testifying. Accordingly, we hold that, if the State makes an adequate showing of necessity, the state interest in protecting child witnesses from the trauma of testifying in a child abuse case is sufficiently important to justify the use of a special procedure that permits a child witness in such cases to testify at trial against a defendant in the absence of face-to-face confrontation with the defendant.

The requisite finding of necessity must of course be a case-specific one: the trial court must hear evidence and determine whether use of the one-way closed circuit television procedure is necessary to protect the welfare of the particular child witness who seeks to testify. . . .

Because there is no dispute that the child witnesses in this case testified under oath, were subject to full cross-examination, and were able to be observed by the judge, jury, and defendant as they testified, we conclude that, to the extent that a proper finding of necessity has been made, the admission of such testimony would be consonant with the Confrontation Clause. . . .

We therefore vacate the judgment of the Court of Appeals of Maryland and remand the case for further proceedings not inconsistent with this opinion.

It is so ordered.

JUSTICE SCALIA, with whom JUSTICES BRENNAN, MARSHALL, and STEVENS join, dissenting.

Technological developments may affect the right to confrontation by providing new methods for communication in hearings and trials. As you read the material in the box on p. 330 about technology, think about whether the vision of confrontation originally possessed by the Constitution's authors should guide contemporary interpretations of the Sixth Amendment right.

Cross-examination is a key component of the adversarial trial process because it permits questioning under oath and in court of the opposition's witnesses or witnesses with adverse interests through the use of leading questions

Seldom has this Court failed so conspicuously to sustain a categorical guarantee of the Constitution against the tide of prevailing current opinion. The Sixth Amendment provides, with unmistakable clarity, that "[i]n all criminal prosecutions, the accused shall enjoy the right . . . to be confronted with the witnesses against him." The purpose of enshrining this protection in the Constitution was to assure that none of the many policy interests from time to time pursued by statutory law could overcome a defendant's right to face his or her accusers in Court. . . .

Because of this subordination of explicit constitutional text to currently favored public policy, the following scene can be played out in an American courtroom for the first time in two centuries: A father whose young daughter has been given over to the exclusive custody of his estranged wife, or a mother whose young son has been taken into custody by the State's child welfare department, is sentenced to prison for sexual abuse on the basis of testimony by a child the parent has not seen or spoken to for many months; and the guilty verdict is rendered without giving the parent so much as the opportunity to sit in the presence of the child, and to ask, personally or through counsel, "[I]t is really not true, is it, that I—your father (or mother) whom you see before you—did these terrible things?" Perhaps that is a procedure today's society desires; perhaps (though I doubt it) it is even a fair procedure; but it is assuredly not a procedure permitted by the Constitution.

Because the text of the Sixth Amendment is clear, and because the Constitution is meant to protect against, rather than conform to, current "widespread belief," I respectfully dissent. . . .

The Court characterizes the State's interest which "outweigh[s]" the explicit text of the Constitution as an "interest in the physical and psychological well-being of child abuse victims.". . . and "interest in protecting" such victims "from the emotional trauma of testifying.". . . This is not so. A child who meets the Maryland statute's requirement of suffering such "serious emotional distress" from confrontation that he "cannot reasonably communicate" would seem entirely safe. Why would a prosecutor want to call a witness who cannot reasonably communicate? And if he did, it would be the State's own fault. Protection of the child's interest—as far as the Confrontation Clause is concerned—is entirely within Maryland's control [by simply not calling on such children to be witnesses]. The State's interest here is in fact no more and no less than what the State's interest always is when it seeks to get a class of evidence admitted in criminal proceedings: more convictions of guilty defendants. That is not an unworthy interest, but it should not be dressed up as a humanitarian one.

And the interest on the other side is also what it usually is when the State seeks to get a new class of evidence admitted: fewer convictions of innocent defendants—specifically, in the present context, innocent defendants accused of particularly heinous crimes. The "special" reasons that exist for suspending one of the usual guarantees of reliability in the case of children's testimony are perhaps matched by "special" reasons for being particularly insistent upon it in the case of children's testimony. Some studies show that children are substantially more vulnerable to suggestion than adults, and often unable to separate recollected fantasy (or suggestion) from reality [citations to academic studies]. . . .

The Court today has applied "interest balancing" analysis where the text of the Constitution simply does not permit it. We are not free to conduct a cost-benefit analysis of clear and explicit constitutional guarantees, and then to adjust their meaning to comport with our findings. The Court has convincingly proved that the Maryland procedure serves a valid interest, and gives the defendant virtually everything the Confrontation Clause guarantees (everything, that is, except confrontation). I am persuaded, therefore, that the Maryland procedure is virtually constitutional. Since it is not, however, actually constitutional I would affirm the judgment of the Maryland Court of Appeals reversing judgment of conviction.

that push for a specific answer (i.e., "You were at the scene of the crime when it happened, weren't you?") rather than the open questions required during direct examinations (i.e., "Were you at the crime scene?"). Questions during cross-examination are generally limited to topics raised during the witness's testimony during direct examination. Consistent with *Davis,* the right to confrontation is generally presumed to include a right to cross-examine adverse witnesses (*Pointer v. Texas,* 1965) even if the defense is forced to call the witness to testify, as in the case of someone who has confessed to the crime for

Trials on Television

The use of closed-circuit television that was approved by the Supreme Court in *Maryland v. Craig* reinforces the conclusion that face-to-face confrontation is not required in all trials. The advancement of technology permits people to see, hear, and participate in "live" meetings being conducted across the country or elsewhere in the world. What if a jurisdiction decided to conduct trials by keeping defendants at the jail but training a camera on the defendant so that he or she can be seen by those in the courtroom and permitting the defendant to watch and participate in the proceedings via closed-circuit television. The defendant could see the witnesses and the witnesses could see the defendant. However, the local criminal justice officials would be spared the expense of transporting the prisoner to the courtroom and guarding the prisoner during the trial. There also would be no risk that the defendant would escape or leap up from the defense table in order to assault someone during the trial.

Through the use of closed-circuit, two-location trials, the government's interests in security and reduced costs could be advanced while still permitting the defendant to participate and to confront the accusers.

To what extent would such closed-circuit contact fall short of the expectations of the Sixth Amendment? Is there something different about a defendant seeing an accuser face-to-face than seeing the accuser on television that might impact the outcome of the trial? If a witness was lying under oath, would the witness find it easier to lie while looking at the defendant in person? What about seeing the defendant on television? For lying witnesses, does it matter at all if and how they see the person about whom they are lying? If you were a Supreme Court justice, would you interpret the Sixth Amendment to permit such televised trials in which the defendant is kept at the jail and not brought to the courtroom?

which the defendant is charged (*Chambers v. Mississippi,* 1973). Such a witness is unlikely to be called by the prosecution to present testimony and may have a significant interest in seeking to avoid making any admissions helpful to the defendant.

If the foregoing situation concerns a co-defendant rather than someone not charged with the crime, then the prosecutor will want to use any incriminating statements, including statements made by the co-defendant that implicate another person. However, the co-defendant whose testimony is needed will not necessarily be willing to testify, either because of an assertion of Fifth Amendment rights (if not already tried and convicted) or because of a refusal to cooperate with the prosecution. In some circumstances, the Supreme Court has approved the admission of hearsay testimony. Thus, for example, a police officer or other official would testify about what a witness had said during a preliminary hearing or police station interrogation if the witness is either unavailable or unable to remember what was said earlier (*United States v. Owens,* 1988). The varying circumstances that arise have caused the Court to struggle with the application of the Confrontation Clause. For example, the Court rejected an effort in one case to avoid the confrontation problem by replacing the defendant's name with the word "deleted" in presenting a co-defendant's confession to a jury. For example, the confession might be read to say, "Me and 'deleted' went into the bank with guns because we planned to rob the place." Because the defendant's attorney would have no opportunity to cross-examine the co-defendant, the word "deleted" seemed to invite juries to fill in the blank with the defendant's name (*Gray v. Maryland*, 1998). Such cases remind us that new confrontation problems may arise with uncertain consequences for Supreme Court decisions when trials present situations that differ from the standard situation of adult witnesses being available in the courtroom to provide testimony *and* undergo cross-examination.

DOUBLE JEOPARDY

The constitutional protection against double jeopardy is a Fifth Amendment right relevant to trials. The relevant portion of the Fifth Amendment says, "nor shall any person be subject for the same offence to be twice put in jeopardy of life or limb." Recall the case of *Barker v. Wingo* presented earlier in this chapter. In *Barker* a defendant was tried six times before a final verdict was produced. Obviously, this case raises the question about how someone can be tried multiple times when the Fifth Amendment says that people cannot even be tried "twice." The example in *Barker* illustrates the fact that the Double Jeopardy Clause places a limitation on the *prosecution*. The prosecutor cannot initiate a second prosecution simply because the first verdict produced an acquittal. If there is a hung jury in which a deadlocked vote within the jury prevents a verdict, it is as if the trial never happened and the prosecutor can try the defendant again. If the defendant files an appeal and wins a reversal of the conviction, the defendant's action also operates as if the first trial did not occur. Thus the prosecutor can also initiate a new trial, although often the appellate decision requires exclusion of some of the evidence used in the first trial.

In Chapter 1, we saw that the Supreme Court initially declined to apply the right against double jeopardy to state criminal proceedings (*Palko v. Connecticut*, 1937). However, the Court later incorporated this Fifth Amendment right in *Benton v. Maryland* (1969). Although most people think of double jeopardy as barring a second prosecution after a final judgment is entered in a first proceeding, various rules have been used to activate double jeopardy claims in cases that never reached a verdict or judgment. As leading legal scholars have noted, "Under the rule traditionally applied in the federal courts, jeopardy attaches in jury trials when the jury is 'empaneled or sworn' and it attaches in bench trials [i.e., trial before a judge but not a jury] when the 'first witness is sworn.'"[3] Thus questions arise about whether there can be a renewed prosecution if a mistrial is declared during the course of the initial proceeding. During the 1970s, the Supreme Court demonstrated an inclination to narrowly interpret the scope of double jeopardy protection. In *United States v. Scott* (1978), the Court permitted a second prosecution after dismissal of initial charges during trial. This decision placed greater emphasis on double jeopardy as a right to protect against reprosecution of cases that had received final judgments rather than as a bar to reprosecution of uncompleted cases. Four dissenters, in an opinion by Justice White, disagreed and declared that "[t]he purpose of the [Double Jeopardy] Clause, which the Court today fails sufficiently to appreciate, is to protect the accused against the agony and risks attendant upon undergoing more than one criminal trial for any single offense." In other words, the justices were divided over whether it is unconstitutionally burdensome for defendants to face new trials, even when their first trial never came to completion.

Identifying Violations

The Supreme Court has also faced questions concerning whether defendants could be subjected to multiple prosecutions for a single action or set of actions. The basic rule was established in *Blockburger v. United States* (1932). The *Blockburger* rule precludes a second prosecution when both offenses require the prosecution to prove the same elements of the crime. Although this rule might appear to prevent a second prosecution in most instances in which multiple charges arise out of a single act, there are a variety of circumstances in which the right against double jeopardy provides no protection against a second trial. In *Heath v. Alabama* (1985), for example, the Supreme Court's concerns about federalism and the need to respect the authority of states to handle their own affairs appeared to take precedence over concerns about double jeopardy. Heath hired two men from Georgia to kill his girlfriend in Alabama. The men abducted the woman in Alabama and took her to Georgia where they killed her. Heath was indicted for murder in Georgia in November 1981 and entered a guilty plea in February 1982 in exchange for a life sentence with parole eligibility. In May 1982, Alabama indicted Heath for the offense of murder during kidnapping, and in January 1983 Heath was convicted by an Alabama jury and sentenced to death. Heath sought to invalidate his Alabama conviction on double jeopardy grounds because he had already been convicted for his actions in the Georgia court before he was even charged by Alabama. The Supreme Court, however, rejected Heath's double jeopardy claim. According to Justice O'Connor's majority opinion, "A State's interest in vindicating its sovereign authority through enforcement of its laws by definition can never be satisfied by another State's enforcement of its own laws." In dissent, Justices Marshall and Brennan argued that "[w]hether viewed as a violation of the Double Jeopardy Clause or simply as an affront to the due process guarantee of fundamental fairness, Alabama's prosecution of petitioner cannot survive constitutional scrutiny." In fact, the second prosecution did survive judicial scrutiny because a majority of justices approved the practice of having a second trial concerning the same criminal acts if the second set of charges and the second trial are processed in a second jurisdiction. Thus, under some circumstances, people acquitted of crimes in state court may later be tried and convicted of *federal* crimes based on the same acts, if those acts constitute federal offenses. Los Angeles police officers were acquitted of state criminal charges for the videotaped beating of motorist Rodney King. In 1992 those acquittals led to riots in Los Angeles in which dozens of people died and millions of dollars worth of property was damaged, stolen, or destroyed.[4] Afterward, two of the officers were convicted of federal criminal charges based on the same beating incident. The two prosecutions did not violate the Supreme Court's interpretation of the right against double jeopardy.

It should be noted that an acquittal in state court will seldom lead to a subsequent federal prosecution because federal criminal laws are limited in scope. Many people asked, for example, whether football Hall-of-Famer O. J. Simpson could be tried on federal charges after being acquitted of murdering his ex-wife and a man on the sidewalk of his ex-wife's home. However, murder, assault, burglary, and other offenses are strictly matters of state law unless special circumstances exist. Police officers acquitted of state charges may be more susceptible to federal prosecution because of federal criminal laws focused on state and local officials violating the civil rights of citizens.

Disagreement Within the Rehnquist Court

The most notable and controversial double jeopardy decision in the 1990s concerned the *Blockburger* issue of when a second criminal charge can be pursued based on a single criminal act or set of actions. In *Grady v. Corbin* (1990), a motorist crossed the centerline on a highway and smashed into an oncoming car, resulting in one person's death and another person's serious injury. The motorist was immediately charged with driving while intoxicated, and an assistant prosecutor began gathering evidence for a homicide prosecution. This assistant prosecutor did not inform the prosecutors in traffic court about his investigation. The defendant appeared in traffic court two weeks after the accident and, with no prosecutors present, entered a guilty plea to the traffic citations. At the sentencing hearing three weeks later, neither the judge nor the prosecutor in attendance knew that the traffic accident had produced a fatality because the traffic court prosecutor could not locate the file for the case. Thus the judge fined the defendant and temporarily revoked his license as punishment for the traffic citations. Two months later, a grand jury indicted the defendant for reckless manslaughter, and the defendant challenged the indictment as a violation of the Double Jeopardy Clause. A five-member majority of the Supreme Court supported the defendant's claim and extended the *Blockburger* rule by holding that "the Double Jeopardy Clause bars subsequent prosecution if, to establish an essential element of an offense charged in that prosecution, the government will prove conduct that constitutes an offense for which the defendant has already been prosecuted." The case attracted attention and criticism from interested members of the public and legal community because of the unpopular outcome of an apparently guilty offender escaping punishment for a homicide simply because the prosecutor's office did not coordinate its case-processing procedures effectively. Justice Scalia's dissenting opinion castigated the majority's opinion and declared that "[e]ven if we had no constitutional text and no prior case law to rely upon, rejection of today's opinion is adequately supported by the modest desire to protect our criminal justice system from ridicule." Although Scalia's sarcastic characterization of the Court's opinion is questionable, he was correct in his prediction about what would happen in subsequent cases: "A limitation that is so unsupported in reason and so absurd in application is unlikely to survive." The *Grady* precedent did not survive, but its demise is directly attributable to a change in the Court's composition rather than to any inherent deficiencies in the majority opinion's reasoning.

The Court revisited the double jeopardy issue in 1993 after two members of the *Grady* majority, Warren Court holdovers Brennan and Marshall, had been replaced by President Bush's appointees, Justices Souter and Thomas. In *United States v. Dixon* (1993), two defendants violated the conditions of their pretrial release for a pending criminal charge by being arrested, respectively, for assault and possession of narcotics. When they were convicted of criminal contempt for violating their bail conditions, they sought dismissal of their narcotics and assault indictments based on double jeopardy claims from the *Grady* decision. They argued that their criminal contempt convictions for violating release conditions precluded their prosecution for other charges arising out of the same incidents because the government would have to prove conduct that constituted an offense for which they had already been prosecuted. As you read *United States v. Dixon* in the accompanying box, ask yourself whether the rule produced by the Supreme Court is more sensible and consistent with the Fifth Amendment than the rule produced in the *Grady v. Corbin* decision.

In *Dixon,* the four *Grady* dissenters, Scalia, Rehnquist, Kennedy, and O'Connor, had gained the fifth vote that they needed through Justice Thomas's replacement of Justice Marshall. Thus a slim five-member majority reversed the liberal *Grady* decision and returned to using the "same-elements" test from *Blockburger.* Thus, although the Court barred the narcotics prosecution, the majority found that the assault charges were not barred by the *Blockburger* test because of the differing knowledge and intent requirements for criminal contempt and assault. As often happens when a precedent is overturned in a few short years due to a change in the Court's composition, the dissenters complained about the propriety of the majority's actions. As expressed by Justice Blackmun, "I also share both [Justice Souter's] and Justice White's dismay that the Court so cavalierly has overruled a precedent that is barely three years old and that has proved neither unworkable nor unsound."

In *Ricketts v. Adamson* (1987), a case discussed in Chapter 9 concerning a defendant's obligation to fulfill commitments made during plea bargaining, the Supreme Court permitted reprosecution of a defendant on first-degree murder charges after the prosecution invalidated his plea agreement for second-degree murder by claiming that he had failed to fulfill the agreement. The state claimed that the agreement included a waiver of any potential double jeopardy claims. The defendant had agreed to testify against co-defendants as part of his plea agreement, and he did so. However, he refused to testify in a second set of trials when his co-defendants' convictions were overturned because he believed that he had fulfilled his plea agreement by testifying at the initial trials. While Justice White's majority opinion approved the state's decision to retry the defendant on first-degree murder charges and sentence him to death, the four dissenters (Brennan, Marshall, Stevens, and Blackmun) questioned the prosecution's assertion that the defendant had indeed violated his plea agreement and asserted that the defendant needed to violate the agreement knowingly in order to waive his double jeopardy rights.

Many people may believe the right against double jeopardy embodies a straightforward ban on pursuing a second trial after acquittal in the first trial for one or more specific criminal acts. As the foregoing discussion indicates, the Supreme Court's interpretation of the Fifth Amendment is much more complicated than this simple conception of double jeopardy. It is possible to be prosecuted a second time, especially if the second prosecution is in a different jurisdiction or involves charges that require the prosecution to prove different elements (e.g., intent) than those associated with the initial set of charges. As you read the box "The Fundamental Meaning of Double Jeopardy" on p. 338, ask yourself whether the Supreme Court has interpreted the Fifth Amendment in an appropriate manner.

CASE	***United States v. Dixon,* 509 U.S. 688 (1993)**

[The Supreme Court considered jointly the cases of two separate defendants, Dixon and Foster. The title to the case reflected merely an alphabetical listing of defendants, although most of the opinion actually discussed Foster's case. Dixon was arrested for second-degree murder and was released on bail. His release conditions specified that he was not to commit any other crime. While awaiting trial, however, he was arrested for narcotics possession. Because he had violated his pretrial release conditions, he was quickly convicted of contempt of court and sentenced to jail for six months. He later claimed his right against double jeopardy meant that this contempt conviction precluded his further prosecution on the narcotics charge. Dixon won his double jeopardy claim in the trial court, and that ruling was upheld by the court of appeals. Foster's wife had obtained a court order to prevent him from coming near her because of his abusive behavior. In violation of the order, on several occasions he came to his wife's home and assaulted her. After he was convicted of violating the court order and sentenced to 600 days in prison, he claimed that his double jeopardy right barred his prosecution on the assault charge. Foster's claim was rejected by the trial court, but the court of appeals reversed in his favor. The U.S. Supreme Court accepted the cases to consider whether the convictions for contempt of court and for violating a court order precluded further prosecution of the underlying felonies because of the defendants' rights against double jeopardy.]

JUSTICE SCALIA announced the judgment of the Court and delivered the opinion of the Court with respect to Parts I, II, and IV and an opinion with respect to Parts III and V, in which JUSTICE KENNEDY joins.

. . .

II

. . .

The Double Jeopardy Clause, whose application to this new context we are called upon to consider, provides that no person shall "be subject for the same offence to be twice put in jeopardy of life or limb." U.S. Const., Amdt. 5. This protection applies both to successive punishments and to successive prosecutions for the same criminal offense. . . .

In both the multiple punishment and multiple prosecution contexts, this Court has concluded that where the two offenses for which the defendant is punished or tried cannot survive the "same-elements" test, the double jeopardy bar applies. . . . The same-elements test, sometimes referred to as the *"Blockburger"* test, inquires whether each offense contains an element not contained in the other; if not, they are the "same offence" and double jeopardy bars additional punishment and successive prosecution. . . .

We recently held in *Grady* [*v. Corbin,* 1990] that in addition to passing the *Blockburger* test, a subsequent prosecution must satisfy a "same-conduct" test to avoid the double jeopardy bar. The *Grady* test provides that, "if, to establish an essential element of an offense charged in that prosecution, the government will prove conduct that constitutes an offense for which the defendant has already been prosecuted," a second prosecution may not be had. . . .

III

[In Part III of the opinion, Scalia, joined by Kennedy, found that all of Dixon's prosecutions and some of Foster's charges met the *Blockburger* "same-elements" test and therefore were barred by the Double Jeopardy Clause. Justices Blackmun, Souter, Stevens, and White concurred in this aspect of the judgment.]

. . .

The remaining four counts in *Foster,* assault with intent to kill . . . and threats to injure or kidnap . . . , are not barred under *Blockburger.* . . . On the basis of the same episode, Foster was then indicted for violation of . . . assault with intent to kill. Under governing law, that offense requires proof of specific intent to kill, simple assault does not. . . . Similarly, the contempt offense [for violating the court order] required proof of knowledge of the [Civil Protective Order], which assault with intent to kill does not. Applying the *Blockburger* elements test, the result is clear: These crimes were different offenses and the subsequent prosecution did not violate the Double Jeopardy Clause. . . .

Counts II, III, and IV of Foster's indictment are likewise not barred. . . . Conviction of the contempt required willful violation of the [Civil Protective Order]—which conviction under [threatening to injure or kidnap] did not; and conviction under

(continued)

[threatening to injure or kidnap] required that the threat be a threat to kidnap, to inflict bodily injury, or to damage property—which conviction of the contempt [for violating the Civil Protective Order] did not. Each offense therefore contained a separate element, and the *Blockburger* test for double jeopardy was not met.

IV

Having found that at least some of the counts [against Foster] at issue here are not barred by the *Blockburger* test, we must consider whether they are barred by the new, additional double jeopardy test we announced three Terms ago in *Grady v. Corbin* [1990]. They undoubtedly are, since *Grady* prohibits "a subsequent prosecution if, to establish an essential element of an offense charged in that prosecution [here, assault as an element of assault with intent to kill, or threatening as an element of threatening bodily injury], the government will prove conduct that constitutes an offense for which the defendant has already been prosecuted [here, the assault and the threatening, which conduct constituted the offense of violating the [Civil Protective Order]."...

We have concluded, however, that *Grady* must be overruled. Unlike *Blockburger* analysis, whose definition of what prevents two crimes from being the "same offence," U.S. Const., Amdt. 5, has deep historical roots and has been accepted in numerous precedents of this Court, *Grady* lacks constitutional roots. The "same-conduct" rule it announced is wholly inconsistent with earlier Supreme Court precedent and with the clear common-law understanding of double jeopardy. ... We need not discuss the many proofs of these statements, which were set forth at length in the *Grady* dissent. See 495 U.S. at 526 ... (Scalia, J., dissenting). ...

But *Grady* was not only wrong in principle; it has already proved unstable in application. Less than two years after it came down, in *United States v. Felix* ... (1992), we were forced to recognize a large exception to it. There we concluded that a subsequent prosecution for conspiracy to manufacture, possess, and distribute methamphetamine was not barred by a previous conviction for attempt to manufacture the same substance. We offered as a

justification for avoiding a "literal" (*i.e.,* faithful) reading of *Grady* "longstanding authority" to the effect that prosecution for conspiracy is not precluded by prior prosecution for the substantive offense. ... Of course the very existence of such a large and longstanding "exception" to the *Grady* rule gave cause for concern that the rule was not an accurate expression of the law. This "past practice" excuse is not available to support the ignoring of *Grady* in the present case, since there is no Supreme Court precedent even discussing this fairly new breed of successive prosecution (criminal contempt for violation of a court order prohibiting a crime, followed by prosecution for the crime itself).

A hypothetical based on the facts in *Harris* [*v. Oklahoma,* 1977] reinforces the conclusion that *Grady* is a continuing source of confusion and must be overruled. Suppose the State first tries the defendant for felony-murder, based on robbery, and then indicts the defendant for robbery with a firearm in the same incident. Absent *Grady,* our cases provide a clear answer to the double-jeopardy claim in this situation. Under *Blockburger,* the second prosecution is not barred—as it clearly was not barred at common law, as a famous case establishes. In *King v. Vandercomb* ... [1796], the government abandoned, midtrial, prosecution of defendant for burglary by breaking and entering and stealing goods, because it turned out that no property had been removed on the date of the alleged burglary. The defendant was then prosecuted for burglary by breaking and entering with intent to steal. That second prosecution was allowed, because "these two offences are so distinct in their nature, that evidence of one of them will not support an indictment for the other."...

Having encountered today yet another situation in which the pre-*Grady* understanding of the Double Jeopardy Clause allows a second trial, though the "same-conduct" test would not, we think it time to acknowledge what is now, three years after *Grady,* compellingly clear: the case was a mistake. We do not lightly reconsider a precedent, but, because *Grady* contradicted an "unbroken line of decisions," contained "less than accurate" historical analysis, and has produced "confusion," we do so here. ... Although *stare decisis* is the "preferred course" in constitutional adjudication, "when governing decisions are unworkable or are badly reasoned, 'this Court has never felt constrained to follow precedent.'" [citing *Payne v. Tennessee,* 1991]. . . . We would mock *stare decisis* and only add chaos to our double jeopardy jurisprudence by pretending that *Grady* survives when it does not. We therefore accept the Government's invitation to overrule *Grady,* and Counts II, III, IV, and V of Foster's subsequent prosecution are not barred. . . .

[Chief Justice Rehnquist's opinion concurring in part and dissenting in part, joined by Justice O'Connor and Justice Thomas, is omitted. Rehnquist argued that none of the prosecutions against Dixon and Foster were barred by double jeopardy. He dissented against Scalia's conclusion that the *Blockburger* test barred the prosecutions against Dixon.]

[Justice White's opinion concurring in the judgment in part and dissenting in part, joined by Justice Stevens and joined as to Part I by Justice Souter, is omitted. White argued that all further prosecutions against Dixon and Foster are barred by double jeopardy, and that the Court should not have overruled *Grady.*]

[Justice Blackmun's opinion concurring in the judgment in part and dissenting in part is omitted. Blackmun agreed with White's conclusions but sought to emphasize additional reasons.]

JUSTICE SOUTER, with whom JUSTICE STEVENS joins, concurring in the judgment in part and dissenting in part.

While I agree with the Court as far as it goes in holding that a citation for criminal contempt and an indictment for violating a substantive criminal statute may amount to charges of the "same offence" for purposes of the Double Jeopardy Clause . . . , I cannot join the Court in restricting the Clause's reach and dismembering the protection against successive prosecution that the Constitution was meant to provide. The Court has read our precedents so narrowly as to leave them bereft of the principles animating that protection, and has chosen to overrule the most recent of the relevant cases, *Grady v. Corbin* . . . , decided three years ago. Because I think that *Grady* was correctly decided, amounting merely to an expression of just those animating principles, . . . I respectfully dissent. . . .

An example will show why [*Blockburger* provides insufficient protection against successive prosecutions]. . . . Assume three crimes: robbery with a firearm, robbery in a dwelling and simple robbery. The elements of the three crimes are the same, except that robbery with a firearm has the element that a firearm be used in the commission of the robbery while the other two crimes do not, and robbery in a dwelling has the element that the robbery occur in a dwelling while the other two crimes do not.

If a person committed a robbery in a dwelling with a firearm and was prosecuted for simple robbery, all agree that he could not be prosecuted subsequently for either of the greater offenses of robbery with a firearm or robbery in a dwelling. Under the lens of *Blockburger,* however, if that same person were prosecuted first for robbery with a firearm, he could be prosecuted subsequently for robbery in a dwelling, even though he could not be prosecuted on the basis of that same robbery for simple robbery. This is true simply because neither of the crimes, robbery with a firearm and robbery in a dwelling, is either identical to or a lesser-included offense of the other. But since the purpose of the Double Jeopardy Clause's protection against successive prosecutions is to prevent repeated trials in which a defendant will be forced to defend against the same charge again and again, and in which the government may perfect its presentation with dress rehearsal after dress rehearsal, it should be irrelevant that the second prosecution would require the defendant to defend himself not only from the charge that he committed the robbery, but also from the charge of some additional fact, in this case, that the scene of the crime was a dwelling. If, instead, protection against successive prosecution were as limited as it would be by *Blockburger* alone, the doctrine would be as striking for its anomalies as for the limited protection it would provide. Thus, in the relatively few successive prosecution cases we have had over the years, we have not held that the *Blockburger* test is the only hurdle the government must clear. . . .

Grady simply applied a rule with roots in our cases going back over 100 years. . . . Overruling *Grady* cannot remove this principle from our constitutional jurisprudence. . . .

The Fundamental Meaning of Double Jeopardy

The Fifth Amendment purports to protect people from being twice put into "jeopardy" for the "same offence." The authors of the provision were concerned that government officials might attempt to detain a defendant indefinitely while they mounted trial after trial in an effort to gain a conviction. Even a defendant who is released on bail can suffer severe consequences from facing multiple trials. As the trials proceed, the defendant must focus on assisting the preparation of the defense. Thus family responsibilities and employment opportunities would suffer as a result. In addition, it would be enormously expensive for a defendant to pay the legal fees required for multiple trials if he or she was middle-class and thereby ineligible for an appointed attorney. There are also risks that the prosecution may keep changing its theories, arguments, and evidence as multiple trials provide the opportunity to test various presentations in "dress rehearsal" proceedings. Presumably, the prosecution should have a clear theory of the case and sufficient evidence to prove the defendant's guilt before any trial moves forward. Despite the words and purposes of the Double Jeopardy Clause, people can be tried more than once for the same act, especially when that act produces additional charges in a different jurisdiction. This does not mean that defendants will face endless trials after an acquittal depending on the circumstances of the case. In light of the Supreme Court's decisions about double jeopardy, have the justices interpreted the phrase "same offence" in a technical way that defeats the underlying intentions of the Fifth Amendment? If the amendment was intended to prevent people from being tried again, has the Supreme Court effectively nullified that purpose by permitting subsequent prosecutions?

CONCLUSION

The Sixth Amendment provides the source of several trial rights, including the rights to a speedy trial, compulsory process, and confrontation of accusers and adverse witnesses. In addition, the Fifth Amendment provides the right against double jeopardy. Because relatively few criminal cases produce trials, these rights have direct application in a small minority of cases. The right to speedy trial is not defined by a specific time limit between the date of arrest and the date of the trial. In *Barker v. Wingo*, the Supreme Court developed a four-part balancing test that effectively gives trial judges significant discretion to determine if and when the right to a speedy trial has been violated. In addition to the flexible test for determining violations of this right, the issue arises in relatively few cases because so many defense attorneys request additional time to prepare for trial.

The right to compulsory process permits defendants to testify in their own behalf and to use subpoenas to obtain documents and witnesses to assist the defense. The right is not absolute, as demonstrated by the trial judge's action in *Taylor v. Illinois* in which a defense witness was precluded from testifying because the judge wished to punish the defense attorney for failing to follow court rules by submitting lists of all witnesses prior to trial.

The right to confrontation includes the opportunity to be present at one's own trial. However, the Supreme Court has identified circumstances in which a defendant may be excluded from the courtroom for being disruptive. Such exclusions should be ordered only as a last resort after the defendant has been warned about the consequences of continued misbehavior. There are also some circumstances in which a defendant who disappears may be tried *in absentia*.

Confrontation also includes the right to confront accusers and adverse witnesses in the courtroom. In order to protect child victims from the trauma of facing their alleged victimizers, the Supreme Court has permitted such victims to testify by closed-circuit television. However, the Court would not approve the use of a screen in the courtroom to prevent the witness and the defendant from seeing each other.

The Fifth Amendment right against double jeopardy appears to protect defendants from being tried again after acquittal. In reality, however, the complexities of the Supreme Court's interpretations of the Fifth Amendment create opportunities for subsequent prosecutions, especially when the second prosecution is in a different jurisdiction or concerns new charges for which the prosecutor must prove different elements than those involved in the original crimes that served as the basis for prosecution.

SUMMARY

- The Sixth Amendment contains trial-related rights, including rights to a speedy trial, compulsory process, and confrontation. The Fifth Amendment contains the right against double jeopardy.

- The Supreme Court has created a flexible, four-part test for the right to a speedy trial (*Barker v. Wingo*). The trial judge must weigh four factors: the length of delay, the reason for delay, whether the defendant demanded a trial, and any prejudice to the defendant's case as a result of the delay.

- The right to compulsory process includes the right of the defendant to testify as well as the right to use subpoenas to secure documents, objects, and witnesses to present as evidence for the defense.

- The right to compulsory process is not absolute. Permissible defense evidence is subject to the rules of evidence, and defense evidence may be excluded by a trial judge in order to punish a defense attorney for violating court rules (*Taylor v. Illinois*).

- The right to confrontation includes the opportunity for the defendant to be present in the courtroom during the trial. However, the defendant may be restrained or excluded as a last resort for disruptive misbehavior.

- Defendants who disappear may be tried *in absentia* in some situations.

- The right to confrontation does not always guarantee face-to-face confrontation between defendants and accusers. The Supreme Court has permitted the use of child-victim testimony via closed-circuit television to protect such victims from the trauma of seeing their alleged victimizer in person.

- The right against double jeopardy does not prevent a second trial after acquittal when the reprosecution occurs based on charges in a different jurisdiction or charges requiring different elements of proof than those for the original charges.

Key Terms

continuance   A delay in court proceedings requested by one side in the case and approved by the trial judge.

cross-examination   A portion of the trial process generally protected by the right to confrontation in which attorneys can ask leading questions to challenge the testimony of witnesses for the opposition or witnesses with interests adverse to those of the defendant.

statute of limitations   Time limit established by legislatures within which prosecutors must file charges in a case. Such limitations normally do not apply to murders.

trial *in absentia*   A criminal trial conducted without the defendant present in court.

Additional Readings

Levy, Steven. 1988. *The Unicorn's Secret: Murder in the Age of Aquarius.* New York: Prentice Hall. Investigative report on the case of Ira Einhorn, the American accused of murder in Philadelphia who hid in Europe for many years.

Thomas, George C., III. 1998. *Double Jeopardy: The History, The Law.* New York: New York University Press. A scholarly examination of double jeopardy that traces American doctrines back to their twelfth-century English roots.

Notes

1. Francis H. Heller, *The Sixth Amendment to the Constitution of the United States* (New York: Greenwood Press, 1951), 3–5.

2. Steven Levy, "A Guru Goes Free," *Newsweek,* 15 December 1997, 58

3. Yale Kamisar, Wayne LaFave, and Jerold Israel, *Modern Criminal Procedure,* 7th ed. (St. Paul, Minn.: West Publishing, 1992), 1418.

4. Seth Mydans, "11 Dead in Los Angeles Rioting; 4,000 Guard Troops Called Out as Fires and Looting Continue," *New York Times,* 1 May 1992, A1, A20.

CHAPTER ELEVEN

Jury Trials

Imagine that you have been called for jury duty. After all of the potential jurors are questioned by the attorneys and the judge, you are among the twelve jurors and alternates chosen to serve. You listen to two days of testimony about a robbery that occurred at night in front of a bank's outdoor ATM machine. A woman was withdrawing money from the machine when a man grabbed her from behind, pushed her roughly into the wall of the bank, and ran away with her purse and money. Two hours later, a homeless man was found holding the empty purse in an alley just a few blocks away. He was arrested and charged with the robbery. He had a prior record of numerous misdemeanors, including several petty theft offenses. The camera inside the ATM machine produced grainy pictures of the robbery, but the robber was standing behind the victim so it was difficult to see the perpetrator clearly. The defendant claimed that he found the empty purse in the alley, but the victim testified that he was the man who had robbed her. During the trial, you felt concerned that the attorney appointed to represent the defendant did not seem to spend much time challenging the prosecution's evidence.

When the jury retires to deliberate, you listen as other jurors express their views.

"He obviously did it. She saw him and they caught him with the purse."

"People like that are always committing crimes."

"This has been a waste of two days. Let's take a vote and get out of here. He's obviously guilty."

You feel increasingly uncomfortable because the other jurors have made up their minds without even discussing the evidence that was presented. As each juror speaks, it becomes clear that your turn will come last because of where you are sitting at the table. You feel as if you should point out that the defense attorney never challenged the certainty of the victim's identification. The victim's back was to the robber and he pushed her face first into the wall, so it seems unlikely that she would have seen the robber clearly. Moreover, the defense attorney never emphasized the question of what happened to the money. The defendant was caught with the purse, but there apparently was no money in the purse when he found it and no evidence that anything had been purchased with the money.

Is it appropriate for you to raise these questions as a juror when the defense attorney did not raise them? Should you bother raising these issues when it is clear that you are unlikely to change anyone else's mind? If you raise these issues, it might make the jury deliberations drag on for hours. Is it worthwhile to go through this when you believe that the defendant is someone who is going to keep getting arrested over and over again anyway? What would you do?

In this chapter, we will examine the rules and rights related to jury trials. The relevant words of the Sixth Amendment state that "[i]n all criminal prosecutions, the accused shall enjoy the right to a speedy and public trial, by an impartial jury. . . ." The jury process provides the lone opportunity for citizens to participate directly in decision making within the judicial branch. If the prosecution is initiating prosecutions unfairly or attempting to convict people by using insufficient evidence, the jury can speak for the community by stopping such actions by the prosecutor. This adds an element of democracy to the judicial process, but, in addition, it adds uncertainty and inconsistency as people without training and experience in law make decisions about the fates of their fellow citizens. Throughout the criminal justice process, there are risks that biases and self-interest will affect the discretionary decisions of police officers, lawyers, and judges. These risks may be compounded in the jury process because the decision makers may lack knowledge, understanding, and experience with the rules of law and the justice system's goal of protecting defendants' constitutional rights.

HISTORICAL BACKGROUND

The early English jury differed significantly from modern juries because the jurors acted as witnesses to the alleged crime rather than merely as judges of evidence: "[Jurors] were expected to be already familiar with the facts when the trial began and to announce the verdict based on their own personal knowledge of crime and defendant. It was the jurors' duty, upon being summoned for jury service, to make inquiry into the facts of the case to be tried, to sift the information and then, in court, to state their conclusion in terms of guilt or innocence."[1] The shift toward jurors as judges rather than witnesses was gradual. The English colonists who came to North America regarded the jury trial as a fundamental component of their judicial processes. The American colonies used juries, although they did not always use uniform practices with respect to the size of juries and the population from which jurors were drawn. Early colonial laws and state constitutions, as well as the later Bill of Rights, contained declarations about the right to trial by jury.[2]

One of the U.S. Supreme Court's first important cases about juries was *Strauder v. West Virginia* (1880). The Court decided that a West Virginia statute permitting only white males to serve as jurors violated the right to equal protection of the laws because it excluded African American men. The case did nothing to create opportunities for women to serve on juries. In subsequent decades, various states still applied various means to exclude both women and African Americans from juries. The Court simply forbade states from having statutes that openly barred jury participation based on race. As we saw in Chapter 1, the Supreme Court's seminal incorporation case, *Palko v. Connecticut* (1937), used the Sixth Amendment right to trial by jury as an example of a right that is not fundamental and therefore not applicable to the states. However, in 1948 the Court invalidated the Michigan practice of secret sentencing procedures and thereby effectively incorporated the "public trial" provision of the Sixth Amendment (*In re Oliver*, 1948). The actual incorporation of the right to trial by jury came in *Duncan v. Louisiana* (1968; see Chapter 1) during the 1960s era in which most of the criminal-justice-related rights from the Bill of Rights were applied to the states.

RIGHT TO A JURY TRIAL

Taken literally, the words of the Constitution imply that defendants have a right to trial by jury in all criminal cases. In Article III, section 2, clause 3, the Constitution says, "The Trial of *all* Crimes, except in Cases of Impeachment, shall be by Jury . . ." (emphasis added). Although this provision has never been incorporated, it seems to indicate that all federal criminal cases shall be tried by a jury. The Sixth Amendment says, "In *all criminal prosecutions*, the accused shall enjoy the right to a speedy and public trial, by an impartial jury . . ." (emphasis added). This provision of the Constitution was incorporated in *Duncan v. Louisiana* (1968) and therefore applies to state cases. Despite this explicit language authorizing jury trials in "all" criminal cases, the Supreme Court has not interpreted the Constitution to provide a right to a jury trial for less serious crimes. As you read *Lewis v. United States* (1996) in the box on pp. 344–347, ask yourself which defendants are entitled to jury trials. Also ask yourself whether the Court's interpretation is consistent with the words and intentions of the Constitution.

In *Lewis v. United States* (1996), a majority of justices concluded that the right to a trial by jury does not exist for petty offenses, which are traditionally defined as offenses punishable by a sentence of sixth months or less of incarceration. Although it was a 7-to-2 decision, the justices were more deeply divided than they appeared. Lewis faced two counts of obstructing the U.S. mail and could have been sentenced to six months for each count. Justices Kennedy and Breyer believed that any defendant facing a total sentence in excess of sixth months should be entitled to a jury trial. Thus they disagreed with the

Lewis v. United States, 518 U.S. 322 (1996)

JUSTICE O'CONNOR delivered the opinion of the Court.

This case presents the question whether a defendant who is prosecuted in a single proceeding for multiple petty offenses has a constitutional right to a jury trial where the aggregate prison term authorized for the offenses exceeded six months. We are also asked to decide whether a defendant who would otherwise have a constitutional right to a jury trial may be denied that right because the presiding judge has made a pretrial commitment that the aggregate sentence will not exceed six months.

We conclude that no jury-trial right exists where a defendant is prosecuted for multiple petty offenses. The Sixth Amendment's guarantee of the right to a jury trial does not extend to petty offenses, and its scope does not change where a defendant faces a potential aggregate prison term in excess of six months for petty offenses charged. Because we decide that no jury-trial right exists where a defendant is charged with multiple petty offenses, we do not reach the second question.

I

Petitioner Ray Lewis was a mail handler for the United States Postal Service [who was caught opening letters and stealing their contents]. . . . Petitioner was charged with two counts of obstructing the mail, in violation of 18 U.S.C. 1701. Each count carried a maximum authorized prison sentence of six months. Petitioner requested a jury, but the magistrate judge granted the Government's motion for a bench trial. She explained that because she would not, under any circumstances, sentence petitioner to more than six months' imprisonment, he was not entitled to a jury trial. . . .

We granted certiorari . . . to resolve a conflict in the Courts of Appeals over whether a defendant prosecuted in a single proceeding for multiple petty offenses has a constitutional right to a jury trial, where the aggregate sentence authorized for the offenses exceeds six months' imprisonment, and whether such jury-trial right can be eliminated by a judge's pretrial commitment that the aggregate sentence imposed will not exceed six months. . . .

II

The Sixth Amendment guarantees that "[i]n all criminal prosecutions, the accused shall enjoy the right to a speedy and public trial, by an impartial jury of the State and district wherein the crime shall have been committed. . . ." It is well-established that the Sixth Amendment, like the common law, reserves this jury-trial right for prosecutions of serious offenses, and that "there is a category of petty crimes or offenses which is not subject to the Sixth Amendment jury trial provision." *Duncan v. Louisiana* . . . (1968).

To determine whether an offense is properly characterized as "petty," courts at one time looked to the nature of the offense and whether it was triable by a jury at common law. Such determinations became difficult, because many statutory offenses lack common-law antecedents. . . . Therefore, more recently, we have instead sought "objective indications of the seriousness with which society regards the offense." . . . Now, to determine whether an offense is petty, we consider the maximum penalty attached to the offense. This criterion is considered the most relevant with which to assess the character of an offense, because it reveals the legislature's judgment about the offense's severity. "The judiciary should not substitute its judgment as to seriousness for that of a legislature, which is far better equipped to perform the task." . . . In evaluating the seriousness of the offense, we place primary emphasis on the maximum prison term authorized. While penalties such as probation or fine may infringe on a defendant's freedom, the deprivation of liberty imposed by imprisonment makes that penalty the best indicator of whether the legislature considered the offense to be "petty" or "serious." . . . An offense carrying a maximum prison term of six months or less is presumed petty, unless the legislature has authorized additional statutory penalties so severe as to indicate that the legislature considered the offense serious. . . .

Petitioner argues that, where a defendant is charged with multiple petty offenses in a single prosecution, the Sixth Amendment requires that the aggregate potential penalty be the basis for determining whether a jury trial is required. Although each offense charged here was petty, petitioner faced a potential penalty of more than six months' imprisonment; and, of course, if any offense charged had authorized more than six months' imprisonment, he would have been entitled to a jury trial. The Court must look to the aggregate potential prison term to determine the existence of the jury-trial right, petitioner contends, not to the "petty" character of the offenses charged.

We disagree. The Sixth Amendment reserves the jury-trial right to defendants accused of serious crimes. As set forth above, we determine whether an offense is serious by looking to the judgment of the legislature, primarily as expressed in the maximum term of imprisonment. Here, by setting the maximum authorized prison term at six months, the legislature categorized the offense of obstructing the mail as petty. The fact that the petitioner was charged with two counts of a petty offense does not revise the legislative judgment as to the gravity of that particular offense, nor does it transform the petty offense into a serious one, to which the jury-trial right would apply. We note that there is precedent at common law that a jury trial was not provided to a defendant charged with multiple petty offenses. . . .

. . . Where we have a judgment by the legislature that an offense is "petty," we do not look to the potential prison term faced by a particular defendant who is charged with more than one such petty offense. The maximum authorized penalty provides an "objective indicatio[n] of the seriousness with which society regards the offense," . . . and it is that indication that is used to determine whether a jury trial is required, not the particularities of an individual case. Here, the penalty authorized by Congress manifests its judgment that the offense is petty, and the term of imprisonment faced by the petitioner by virtue of the second count does not alter that fact. . . .

Certainly the aggregate potential penalty faced by petitioner is of serious importance to him. But to determine whether an offense is serious for Sixth Amendment purposes, we look to the legislature's judgment, as evidenced by the maximum penalty authorized. Where the offenses charged are petty, and the deprivation of liberty exceeds six months only as a result of the aggregation of charges, the jury-trial right does not apply. As petitioner acknowledges, even if he were to prevail, the Government could properly circumvent the jury-trial right by charging the counts in separate informations and trying them separately. . . .

Because petitioner is not entitled to a jury trial, we need not reach the question whether a judge's self-imposed limitation on sentencing may affect the jury-trial right.

The judgment of the Court of Appeals for the Second Circuit is affirmed.

JUSTICE KENNEDY, with whom JUSTICE BREYER joins, concurring in the judgment.

This petitioner has no constitutional right to a jury trial because from the outset it was settled that he could be sentenced to no more than six months' imprisonment for his combined petty offenses. The particular outcome, however, should not obscure the greater consequence of today's unfortunate decision. The Court holds that a criminal defendant may be convicted of innumerable offenses in one proceeding and sentenced to any number of years' imprisonment, all without benefit of a jury trial, so long as no one of the offenses considered alone is punishable by more than six months in prison. The holding both in its doctrinal formulation and in its practical effect is one of the most serious incursions on the right to jury trial in the Court's history, and it cannot be squared with our precedents. The Sixth Amendment guarantees a jury trial to a defendant charged with a serious crime. *Duncan v. Louisiana* . . . (1968). Serious crimes, for purposes of the Sixth Amendment, are defined to include any offense which carries a maximum penalty of more than six months in prison; the right to jury trial attaches to those crimes regardless of the sentence in fact imposed. . . . This doctrine is not questioned here, but it does not define the outer limits of the right to trial by jury. Our cases establish a further proposition: The right to jury trial extends as well to a defendant who is sentenced in one proceeding to more than six months' imprisonment. . . . To be more specific, a defendant is entitled to a jury if tried in a single proceeding for more than one petty offense when the combined sentences will exceed six months' imprisonment; taken together, the crimes are considered serious for constitutional purposes, even if each is petty by itself. . . .

. . . Crimes punishable by sentences of more than six months are deemed by the community's social and ethical judgments to be serious. . . . Opprobrium attaches to conviction of those crimes regardless of the length of the actual sentence imposed, and the stigma itself is enough to entitle the defendant to a jury. . . . This rationale does not entitle

(continued)

a defendant to trial by jury if he is charged only with petty offenses; even if they could result in a long sentence when taken together, convictions for petty offenses do not carry the same stigma as convictions for serious crimes.

The imposition of stigma, however, is not the only or even the primary consequence a jury trial serves to constrain. As [our precedents] recogniz[e], and as ought to be evident, the Sixth Amendment also serves the different and more practical purpose of preventing a court from effecting a most serious deprivation of liberty—ordering a defendant to prison for a substantial period of time—without the Government's persuading a jury he belongs there. A deprivation of liberty so significant may be exacted if a defendant faces punishment for a series of crimes, each of which can be punished by no more than six months' imprisonment. The stakes for a defendant may then amount in the aggregate to many years in prison, in which case he must be entitled to interpose a jury between himself and the Government. If the trial court rules at the outset that no more than six months' imprisonment will be imposed for the combined petty offenses, however, the liberty the jury serves to protect will not be endangered, and there is no corresponding right to jury trial. . . .

The Court does not aid its position when it notes, with seeming approval, the Government's troubling suggestion that a committed prosecutor could evade the rule here proposed by bringing a series of prosecutions in separate proceedings, each

for an offense punishable by no more than six months in prison. . . . Were a prosecutor to take so serious a view of a defendant's conduct as to justify the burden of separate prosecutions, I should think the case an urgent example of when a jury is most needed if the offenses are consolidated. And if a defendant is subject to repeated bench trials because of a prosecutor's scheme to confine him in jail for years without the benefit of a jury trial, at least he will be provided certain safeguards as a result. . . .

. . . Just as alarming is the threat the Court's holding poses to millions of persons in agriculture, manufacturing, and trade who must comply with minute administrative regulations, many of them carrying a jail term of six months or less. Violations of these sorts of rules often involved repeated, discrete acts which can result in potential liability of years of imprisonment. . . . Still, under the Court's holding it makes no difference whether a defendant is sentenced to a year in prison or for that matter to 20 years: As long as no single violation charged is punishable by more than six months, the defendant has no right to a jury. . . .

Petitioner's proposal [to deny judges the opportunity to preempt jury trials by promising to sentence to less than six months of imprisonment] would impose an enormous burden on an already beleaguered criminal justice system by increasing to a dramatic extent the number of required jury trials. There are thousands of instances where minor offenses are tried before a judge, and we would err on the other side of sensible interpretation were we to hold that combining petty offenses in a single pro-

majority's conclusion that the right to a jury trial depends solely on whether the crimes charged are classified as petty offenses, no matter how many counts the defendant faces. However, because the presiding judicial officer promised at the start of the trial that he would receive no more than six months as his total sentence, even if he was convicted on both counts, Kennedy and Breyer concurred in the judgment that Lewis was not entitled to a jury trial. By contrast, Justices Stevens and Ginsburg argued in dissent that a judge cannot preempt a defendant's right to a jury by promising before the trial to impose a sentence no greater than six months. They believed that any defendant facing the possibility of more than six months' imprisonment is entitled to a jury regardless of the classification of the offenses or promises about sentencing made by judges.

What is the longest possible sentence that a defendant could receive without having been given the opportunity for a jury trial under the doctrine presented in *Lewis v. United States*? If one looks superficially at the rule from the

ceeding mandates a jury trial even when all possibility for a sentence longer than six months has been foreclosed.

When a defendant's liberty is put at great risk in a trial, he is entitled to have the trial conducted to a jury. This principle lies at the heart of the Sixth Amendment. The Court does grave injury to the Amendment by allowing a defendant to suffer a prison term of any length after a single trial before a single judge and without the protection of a jury. I join only the Court's judgment.

JUSTICE STEVENS, with whom JUSTICE GINSBURG joins, dissenting.

The Sixth Amendment provides that the accused is entitled to trial by an impartial jury "in all criminal prosecutions." As Justice Kennedy persuasively explains[,] the "primary purpose of the jury in our legal system is to stand between the accused and the powers of the State." . . . The majority, relying exclusively on cases in which the defendant was tried for a single offense, extends a rule designed with those cases in mind to the wholly dissimilar circumstance in which the prosecution concerns multiple offenses. I agree with Justice Kennedy to the extent he would hold that a prosecution which exposes the accused to a sentence of imprisonment longer than six months, whether for a single offense or for a series of offenses, is sufficiently serious to confer on the defendant the right to demand a jury. . . .

Unlike Justice Kennedy, however, I believe that the right to a jury trial attaches when the prosecution begins. I do not quarrel with the established view that only defendants whose alleged misconduct is deemed serious by the legislature are entitled to be judged by a jury. But in my opinion, the legislature's determination of the severity of the charges against a defendant is properly measured by the maximum sentence authorized for the prosecution as a whole. The text of the Sixth Amendment supports this interpretation by referring expressly to "criminal prosecutions." . . .

All agree that a judge may not strip a defendant of the right to a jury trial for a serious crime by promising a sentence of six months or less. This is so because "[o]pprobrium attaches to conviction of those crimes regardless of the length of the actual sentence imposed." . . . In my view, the same rule must apply to prosecutions involving multiple offenses which are serious by virtue of their aggregate possible sentence. I see no basis for assuming that the dishonor associated with multiple convictions for petty offenses is less than the dishonor associated with conviction of a single serious crime. Because the right attaches at the moment of prosecution, a judge may not deprive a defendant of a jury trial by making a pretrial determination that the crimes charged will not warrant a sentence exceeding six months.

Petitioner is entitled to a jury trial because he was charged with offenses carrying a statutory maximum prison sentence of more than six months. I therefore would reverse the judgment of the Court of Appeals and, for that reason, I respectfully dissent.

---

case, it appears that anyone facing more than six months is entitled to a jury. In reality, however, there is no maximum sentence that can be given when the defendant does not have a jury. The potential sentence depends on how many charges the defendant faces. Thus, if Lewis had been caught opening 100 pieces of mail and charged with one count for each letter opened, then he could have faced a possible sentence of 50 years in prison even though no individual count was worth more than six months.

Is this possibility of a lengthy sentence without a jury trial consistent with the language of Article III ("The Trial of *all* Crimes, except in Cases of Impeachment, shall be by Jury . . ." [emphasis added]) and the Sixth Amendment ("In *all criminal prosecutions,* the accused shall enjoy the right to a speedy and public trial, by an impartial jury . . ."[emphasis added])? Clearly, the rule produced by the Supreme Court does not fit neatly with the literal words of the Constitution. However, the rule exists because the Supreme Court possesses the authority to interpret the Constitution and define its meaning.

JURIES AND FAIR TRIALS

Pretrial Publicity

As one aspect of the attainment of fair trials, judges must be concerned about the impact of pretrial publicity on the possibility of finding fair jurors. If there is too much publicity about the case or defendant, there are risks that the potential jurors who live in the area will develop conclusions about the case before they have heard the complete evidence from both sides. In *Rideau v. Louisiana* (1963), a film of a defendant confessing to a murder was broadcast on television. The public's exposure to the confession would presumably make it difficult to find jurors who would be open-minded when hearing evidence presented by the defense during a trial. Although some countries bar news agencies from reporting about certain aspects of crimes, such as the names or descriptions of arrestees, in order to reduce the risk of bias at trial, there is some publicity about every criminal case in the United States. The news media tells the public about the details of crimes and the names of defendants. However, this level of information is not presumed to affect the possibility of finding open-minded jurors. Potential difficulties arise when the public hears too much about a case, such as information about a confession, or the population in the town from which the jury will be drawn is so small and close-knit that literally everyone in the town presumably knows all the details of the prosecution's version of the case prior to trial.

The criminal justice process provides several options for attempting to reduce the risk of adverse consequences from pretrial publicity. One possibility is the use of **gag orders** on the media. Judges have sometimes ordered news reporters to *not* report information about specific cases. In *Nebraska Press Association v. Stuart* (1976), a judge in a small Nebraska town forbade the news media from informing the public about the details of a controversial murder case. The U.S. Supreme Court, however, has indicated that it will permit such restraints on the news media only in extraordinary circumstances. Such orders create a clash between the Sixth Amendment right to a fair trial and the First Amendment right to freedom of the press. The justices overturned the trial judge's decision in *Nebraska Press Association* as too restrictive. The Court did not rule out the possibility of such orders in special circumstances, but clearly such gag orders can be imposed only as an absolute last resort.

Another possibility for counteracting the prejudicial effects of pretrial publicity is a **change of venue,** which involves moving the trial from the location where the crime occurred to a different city where the citizens have heard less information about the case and therefore are less likely to be biased. Normally, the defense attorney will request a change of venue if there are fears that the court will not be able to find a sufficient number of unbiased jurors. These fears might be substantiated by potential jurors' responses to questions during the jury selection process. Such requests are not automatically granted. Indeed, most such requests are turned down. In 1995, when 168 people were killed in Oklahoma City by a bomb that destroyed the federal building, the two defendants, Timothy McVeigh and Terry Nichols, requested a change of venue. The judge moved the trial from Oklahoma City to Denver because of fears that so many people in Oklahoma City knew people who were killed and injured in the blast and because feelings against the defendants were so strong that the defense might not have a fair opportunity for its arguments and evidence to be heard.

A third option for addressing the risks of pretrial publicity is the ***voir dire*** process for questioning potential jurors about their knowledge and biases during the jury selection process. *Voir dire* may be very extensive in controversial and highly publicized cases. *Voir dire* does not focus exclusively on pretrial publicity. It is used as a matter of course to attempt to identify whether potential jurors have biases that will interfere with their ability to make decisions fairly in criminal cases. The attorneys for each side may ask many questions of each potential juror or, alternatively, submit extensive lists of suggested questions to the trial judge who examines the potential jurors prior to trial. In other cases, the judge merely asks the potential jurors whether they know the defendant, whether they know any of the attorneys, whether they or their relatives have ever been victims of a similar crime, and whether they know of any reason they will not be able to make a fair decision in the case. More extensive questioning may ask about people's occupations, attitudes toward certain kinds of evidence, such as circumstantial evidence or police officers' testimony, and willingness to make decisions that will send people to prison or lead to the death penalty. In December 2000, for example, Sister Helen Prejean, the nun who was the author of the best-selling book on the death penalty that later became the award-winning movie *Dead Man Walking,* was excluded from two juries in Louisiana through the *voir dire* process. In one case, she said that she did not believe in sentencing anyone to prison without possibility of parole, and in the other case she said she would not convict someone solely on the testimony of police officers.[3] As with other jurors excluded during *voir dire,* Sister Helen's views do not mean that she possesses "biases" that are illegitimate or improper. It merely means that the judge agreed with the prosecution that her specific opinions would prevent her from making an open-minded decision in cases in which the law permits sentences of life without parole or proof of guilt based solely on police testimony.

Concerns about the prejudicial effects of publicity continue after the trial has begun. Judges typically instruct jurors not to read or watch any news reports about the case and not to talk with anyone about the case. If individual jurors violate the judge's instructions, they may be excluded from the jury during trial provided there are alternate jurors available to replace them. If too many jurors are excluded or a juror biases the entire jury by, for example, bringing a newspaper into the jury room, then the judge may be forced to declare a **mistrial.** A judge may also **sequester the jury** in order to limit the jurors' exposure to potentially prejudicial information. This means that the judge keeps the jury in seclusion by having them stay overnight in a hotel and being escorted by bailiffs during the course of the trial. The bailiffs may control what is seen on television to make sure that the jurors do not see any news reports about the case.

None of these measures guarantee that the jurors are neutral and objective. People bring their own attitudes and experiences into their interpretations of evidence and the decisions that they make. Not all of these attitudes and biases that might influence jury decisions will be revealed in the *voir dire* process.

Jury Selection

The right to a fair trial depends, in part, on fair jury selection processes. Legal adults (i.e., age 18 and above) who reside within the jurisdiction are typically eligible to be jurors, although some jurisdictions make ex-felons ineligible to serve on juries. The Constitution does not require that a defendant have a jury of his or her "peers." There is no requirement that a jury contain any specific percentage of people from a particular gender or race. The Supreme Court emphasized that the Sixth Amendment contains a requirement that juries be selected from a fair cross-section of the community. African American defendants can legally end up with an all-white jury as long as the pool of potential jurors was drawn from a fair cross-section of the community and no improper discrimination occurred during the selection of individual jurors in the *voir dire* process. The same may be true for white defendants who have all-black juries in certain jurisdictions in which African Americans comprise a majority of the population.

Central to the fair cross-section issue is the design of the system for calling potential jurors. Initially the Supreme Court had to make sure that jurisdictions did not use exclusionary practices that keep segments of the community from participating in judicial decision making as jurors. For example, the Court used this requirement to invalidate Louisiana's statute which provided that women would not be selected for jury duty unless they filed a written declaration asking to be considered, thus barring mechanisms that systematically exclude women from jury service (*Taylor v. Louisiana,* 1975). In practice, other issues arise when jurisdictions rely on voter registration lists or drivers' licenses for calling potential jurors. Frequently, the reliance on such lists results in underrepresentation of poor people, racial minorities, and young people. The Supreme Court has not imposed a specific requirement about how the jury pool is to be called as long as the procedure appears to seek a fair cross-section of the community.

The composition of juries is also shaped in the *voir dire* process when attorneys for each side use challenges to exclude potential jurors from the jury that is ultimately selected. There are two types of challenges that attorneys use. **Challenges for cause** can be requested whenever an attorney believes that a potential juror has exhibited a bias or the risk of bias during the questioning process of *voir dire*. For example, if a potential juror said that she was previously the victim of an armed robbery, the defense attorney will undoubtedly ask the judge to exclude the potential juror because of the risk that the person's prior experience will prevent her from being objective in considering the case. By the same token, if a potential juror says, as Sister Helen did, that he distrusts police officers and therefore would not convict someone based on police testimony alone, the prosecutor is likely to request exclusion of the person for demonstrating a bias that might interfere with objective consideration of the prosecution's case. Obviously, potential jurors will face challenges when they are related to a party or an attorney in a case. There is no limit to the number of potential jurors who may be excluded through challenges for cause. The judge may exclude every potential juror that the prosecutor and defense attorney ask the judge to exclude. The decision about exclusion rests with the judge. Some judges seek to accommodate the attorneys' concerns. Other judges are much more selective and frequently reject attorneys' arguments about whether specific jurors' responses or characteristics provide a sufficient indication of potential bias to justify exclusion.

The second kind of challenge, the **peremptory challenge,** may be used to exclude a potential juror for nearly any reason. Attorneys frequently exclude potential jurors based on hunches about which potential jurors look friendly and receptive and which people in the jury pool look hostile to them during the *voir dire* process. Peremptory challenges are also based on demographic considerations. For example, some defense attorneys may believe that parents of young women will be prone to support the prosecution in sex offense cases because of their fears about their own daughters' safety in society. Each side in a criminal case is allotted a limited number of peremptory challenges. The peremptory challenge provides a key opportunity for the attorneys to use their discretion to shape the body of decision makers who will determine the outcome of the case. In using these challenges, the attorneys are not seeking to ensure that the most open-minded people are selected as jurors. Instead, their goal is to have as many jurors as possible whom they believe will be receptive to their arguments and to limit the number who will by receptive to the opposition. In other words, this is a process in which the attorneys can use their discretion with a desire to add favorable bias to the jury.

The number of peremptory challenges permitted for each side varies by state law, but frequently the defense will have only a half-dozen such challenges and the prosecution will have the same number or one or two fewer. In death penalty cases, state laws often give each side a larger number of peremptory challenges.

Traditionally, attorneys could use peremptory challenges to exclude potential jurors without giving any reason for eliminating specific individuals from the jury pool. Over time, these practices created concerns about the existence of discrimination in jury selection, especially when prosecutors appeared to use these challenges in order to make sure that African American defendants were tried before all-white juries. Studies have shown that prosecutors often use their challenges to exclude potential jurors who are poor, young, or members of minority groups.[4] In order to advance its desire to preclude discrimination in jury selection, the Supreme Court used the Equal Protection Clause in 1986 to bar prosecutors from using peremptory challenges in a systematic way to exclude potential jurors from particular racial groups (*Batson v. Kentucky,* 1986). If the defense believes that the prosecutor is using peremptory challenges to systematically exclude potential jurors on the basis of race, the defense must raise an objection to the judge. If the judge believes that the pattern of exclusions indicates the possibility of racial motives, the judge will call the prosecutor to the bench to ask for a reason for the apparently improper use of the peremptory challenges. The judge must be satisfied with the explanation in order to avoid invalidating any exclusions that appear to be racially motivated.

After initially rejecting a claim by a white defendant that the exclusion of African Americans from his jury constituted a violation of his Sixth Amendment right to a jury drawn from a fair cross-section of the community (*Holland v. Illinois,* 1990), the Court began to apply the Equal Protection Clause instead to bar the use of racial and gender motivations in peremptory challenges. In 1991 the Court decided the same issue—a white defendant contesting the exclusion of African American jurors—and concluded that the Equal

Protection Clause, unlike the Sixth Amendment, barred such racially motivated use of peremptory challenges (*Powers v. Ohio,* 1991). The Court also applied the Equal Protection Clause to place a similar limitation on the use of challenges in civil trials (*Edmonson v. Leesville Concrete Co.,* 1991). In *Georgia v. McCollum,* which you can read in the accompanying box, the Court declared that in the jury selection process, neither defense attorneys nor prosecutors can use race as the basis for excluding jurors through the use of peremptory challenges.

Much of the discussion in *Georgia v. McCollum* concerned whether the Equal Protection Clause should be applied to defense attorneys. The Fourteenth Amendment says "no *state* shall" deny equal protection of the laws. Defense attorneys work for the defendant, who is being prosecuted by the state, rather than for the interests of the state itself. However, as you saw in the case, because the justices had already applied the equal protection requirement to private attorneys in civil cases (*Edmonson v. Leesville Concrete Co.,* 1991), it was easier for the majority of justices to apply the rule to criminal defense attorneys as part of the state-sponsored judicial process. Later, in *J.E.B. v. Alabama ex rel T.B.* (1994), the Court expanded its rationale to bar the use of gender-based peremptory challenges.

In 1995 the Court decided *Purkett v. Elem* based on attorneys' written submissions without accepting the case for complete briefing and oral argument. *Purkett* provided a clarification of the Supreme Court's views on the use of attorneys' and judges' discretionary authority in exercising peremptory challenges. As you read the Court's opinion in the box on pp. 356–357, ask yourself how well the rule produced in this decision operates to prevent discrimination in jury selection.

Purkett was a *per curiam* opinion, meaning that it was an opinion on behalf of the Court without any individual justice credited as the author. Although the defendant's attorney claimed that the prosecutor's excuses were clearly a pretext for making improper race-based exclusions from the jury pool, the Supreme Court, in a 7-to-2 decision supporting the trial judge's ruling in the prosecutor's favor, said that reasons for exclusion can be silly, superstitious, implausible, or fantastic. In other words, the Supreme Court gave trial judges the discretionary authority to accept any reasons for excluding jurors, including the systematic exclusion of jurors by race or gender, as long as prosecutors and defense attorneys do not admit that they are making the exclusions based on race or gender. Some trial judges may be skeptical of attorneys' statements and reject any use of peremptory challenges that appear to rest on race or gender. Other judges, however, may willingly accept any excuse given by attorneys even when the effect is to produce systematic exclusion of potential jurors by race or gender.

The ultimate composition of a jury depends on additional factors beyond the nature of the original pool and the use of challenges by attorneys. The jury's composition is shaped by the individuals who actually appear when called for jury service and those who do not attempt to get themselves removed from participation. Retired people and affluent suburbanites are often overrepresented on juries because they are less likely to have employment, transportation, and child-care problems that keep them from reporting for jury duty. In addition, many people who report for jury duty seek to gain exclusion by claiming that service would constitute a hardship because of their family or employment situations. These factors help to determine which

C A S E	*Georgia v. McCollum*, 505 U.S. 42 (1992)

[*A white couple was charged with committing assault and battery against an African American couple. Before jury selection began, the prosecutor made a motion to preclude the defense from exercising peremptory challenges in a discriminatory manner. The prosecutor intended to show that the victims' race was a factor in the assault. Because the defense had twenty peremptory challenges at its disposal, the prosecutor was worried that these challenges could be used to exclude African American jurors and thereby create an all-white jury. The trial judge ruled that criminal defendants are not subject to case precedents barring the racially motivated use of peremptory challenges. The Supreme Court of Georgia affirmed the trial court's ruling. The U.S. Supreme Court accepted the case to determine whether or not the Equal Protection Clause bars the racially motivated use of peremptory challenges by criminal defendants.*]

JUSTICE BLACKMUN delivered the opinion of the Court.

For more than a century, this Court consistently and repeatedly has reaffirmed that racial discrimination by the State in jury selection offends the Equal Protection Clause. See, e.g., *Strauder v. West Virginia* [1880]. . . . Last Term, this Court held that racial discrimination in a civil litigant's exercise of peremptory challenges also violates the Equal Protection Clause. See *Edmonson v. Leesville Concrete Co.* [1991]. . . . Today, we are asked to decide whether the Constitution prohibits a criminal defendant from engaging in purposeful racial discrimination in the exercise of peremptory challenges. . . .

"The harm from discriminatory jury selection extends beyond that inflicted on the defendant and the excluded juror to touch the entire community." *Batson* [*v. Kentucky,* 1986], 476 U.S. at 87. . . . One of the goals of our jury system is "to impress upon the criminal defendant and the community as a whole that a verdict of conviction or acquittal is given in accordance with the law by persons who are fair." . . . Selection procedures that purposefully exclude African Americans from juries undermine that public confidence—as well they should. . . .

The need for public confidence is especially high in cases involving race-related crimes. In such cases, emotions in the affected community will inevitably be heated and volatile. Public confidence in the in-

tegrity of the criminal justice system is essential for preserving community peace in trials involving race-related crimes. . . .

Be it at the hands of the State or the defense, if a court allows jurors to be excluded because of group bias, it is a willing participant in a scheme that could only undermine the very foundation of our system of justice—our citizens' confidence in it. Just as public confidence in criminal justice is undermined by a conviction in a trial where racial discrimination has occurred in jury selection, so is public confidence undermined where a defendant, assisted by racially discriminatory peremptory strikes, obtains an acquittal. . . .

The second question that must be answered is whether a criminal defendant's exercise of a peremptory challenge constitutes state action for purposes of the Equal Protection Clause. . . .

As in *Edmonson,* a Georgia [criminal] defendant's right to exercise peremptory challenges and the scope of that right are established by a provision of state law. . . .

The Court in *Edmonson* found that peremptory challenges perform a traditional function of government. "Their sole purpose is to permit litigants to assist the government in the selection of an impartial trier of fact." . . . And, as the *Edmonson* Court recognized, the jury system in turn, "performs the critical governmental functions of guarding the rights of litigants and insur[ing] continued acceptance of the laws by all of the people." . . . These same conclusions apply with even greater force in the criminal context because the selection of a jury in a criminal case fulfills a unique and constitutionally compelled governmental function. . . .

Finally, the *Edmonson* Court indicated that the courtroom setting in which the peremptory challenge is exercised intensifies the harmful effects of the private litigant's discriminatory act and contributes to its characterization as state action. These concerns are equally present in the context of a criminal trial. Regardless of who precipitated the jurors' removal, the perception and reality in a criminal trial will be that the court has excused jurors based on race, an outcome that will be attributed to the State. . . .

Nor does a prohibition of the exercise of discriminatory peremptory challenges violate a defendant's Sixth Amendment right to the effective assistance of

(continued)

counsel. Counsel can ordinarily explain the reasons for peremptory challenges without revealing anything about trial strategy or any confidential client communications. In the rare case in which the explanation for a challenge would entail confidential communications or reveal trial strategy, an *in camera* discussion can be arranged. . . . In any event, neither the Sixth Amendment right nor the attorney-client privilege gives a criminal defendant the right to carry out through counsel an unlawful course of conduct. . . .

Lastly, a prohibition of the discriminatory exercise of peremptory challenges does not violate a defendant's Sixth Amendment right to a trial by an impartial jury. The goal of the Sixth Amendment is "jury impartiality with respect to both contestants." *Holland v. Illinois*, 493 U.S. 474, 483 . . . (1990). . . .

We hold that the Constitution prohibits a criminal defendant from engaging in purposeful discrimination on the ground of race in the exercise of peremptory challenges. Accordingly, if the State demonstrates a prima facie case of racial discrimination by the defendants, the defendants must articulate a racially neutral explanation for the peremptory challenges. The judgment of the Supreme Court of Georgia is reversed and the case is remanded for further proceedings not inconsistent with this opinion. It is so ordered.

CHIEF JUSTICE REHNQUIST, concurring.

I was in dissent in *Edmonson v. Leesville Concrete Co.*, . . . and continue to believe that case to have been wrongly decided. But so long as it remains the law, I believe that it controls the disposition of this case on the issue of "state action" under the Fourteenth Amendment. I therefore join the opinion of the Court.

JUSTICE THOMAS, concurring in judgment.

As a matter of first impression, I think I would have shared the view of the dissenting opinions. A criminal defendant's use of peremptory strikes cannot violate the Fourteenth Amendment because it does not involve state action. Yet, I agree with the Court and the Chief Justice that our decision last term in *Edmonson v. Leesville Concrete Co.*, . . . governs this case and requires the opposite conclusion. Because the respondents do not question *Edmonson*, I believe that we must accept its consequences. I therefore concur in the judgment reversing the Georgia Supreme Court.

I write separately to express my general dissatisfaction with our continuing attempts to use the Constitution to regulate peremptory challenges. . . . In my view, by restricting a criminal defendant's use of such challenges, this case takes us further from the reasoning and the result in *Strauder v. West Virginia* [1880]. . . . I doubt that this departure will produce favorable consequences. On the contrary, I am certain that black criminal defendants will rue the day that this court ventured down this road that inexorably will lead to the elimination of peremptory strikes.

Our departure from *Strauder* has two negative consequences. First, it produces a serious misordering of our priorities. In *Strauder*, we put the rights of defendants foremost. Today's decision, while protecting jurors, leaves defendants with less means of protecting themselves. Unless jurors actually admit prejudice during *voir dire*, defendants generally must allow them to sit and run the risk that racial animus will affect the verdict. . . . In effect, we have exalted the right of citizens to sit on juries over the rights of the criminal defendant, even though it is the defendant, not the jurors, who faces imprisonment or even death. At a minimum, I think that this inversion of priorities should give us pause.

individuals will decide defendants' fates, and they also contribute to the relative lack of representativeness in the composition of criminal juries in many jurisdictions.

The Supreme Court decisions concerning racial and gender discrimination in jury selection conveyed the message that biased applications of peremptory challenges are not acceptable in the American legal system. However, the Court's subsequent decision in *Purkett v. Elem* perpetuated opportunities for such discrimination to exist. As you read the material in the box "Discrimination in Jury Selection" on p. 358, ask yourself whether the Supreme Court could have made a greater effort to diminish the risk of discrimination.

Second, our departure from *Strauder* has taken us down a slope of inquiry that has no clear stopping point. . . . Next will come the question whether defendants can exercise peremptories on the basis of sex. . . . The consequences for defendants of our decision and of these future cases remain to be seen. But whatever the benefits were that this Court perceived in a criminal defendant's having members of his class on the jury, see *Strauder,* 100 U.S. at 309–10, they have evaporated.

JUSTICE O'CONNOR, dissenting.

The Court reaches the remarkable conclusion that criminal defendants being prosecuted by the State act on behalf of their adversary when they exercise peremptory challenges during jury selection. The Court purports merely to follow precedents, but our cases do not compel this perverse result. To the contrary, our decisions specifically establish that criminal defendants and their lawyers are not government actors when they perform traditional trial functions. . . .

Considered in purely pragmatic terms, moreover, the Court's holding may fail to advance nondiscriminatory criminal justice. It is by now clear that conscious and unconscious racism can affect the way white jurors perceive minority defendants and the facts presented at their trials, perhaps determining the verdict of guilt or innocence. . . . Using peremptory challenges to secure minority representation on the jury may help to overcome such racial bias, for there is substantial reason to believe that the distorting influence of race is minimized on a racially mixed jury. . . . In a world where the outcome of a minority defendant's trial may turn on the misconceptions or biases of white jurors, there is reason to question the implications of this Court's good intentions.

That the Constitution does not give federal judges the reach to wipe all marks of racism from every courtroom in the land is frustrating, to be sure. But such limitations are the necessary and intended consequence of the Fourteenth Amendment's state action requirement. Because I cannot accept the Court's conclusion that government is responsible for decisions criminal defendants make while fighting state prosecution, I respectfully dissent.

JUSTICE SCALIA, dissenting.

I agree with the Court that its judgment follows logically from *Edmonson v. Leesville Concrete Co.* . . . For the reasons given in the *Edmonson* dissents, however, I think that case was wrongly decided. Barely a year later, we witness its reduction to the terminally absurd: A criminal defendant, in the process of defending himself against the state, is held to be acting on behalf of the state. Justice O'Connor demonstrates the sheer inanity of this proposition (in case the mere statement of it does not suffice), and the contrived nature of the Court's justification. I see no need to add to her discussion, and differ from her views only in that I do not consider *Edmonson* distinguishable in principle—except in the principle that a bad decision should not be followed logically to its illogical conclusion.

Today's decision gives the lie, once again to the belief that an activist, "evolutionary" constitutional jurisprudence always evolves in the direction of greater individual rights. In the interest of promoting the supposedly greater good of race relations in the society as a whole (make no mistake that that is what underlies all of this), we use the Constitution to destroy the ages-old right of criminal defendants to exercise peremptory challenges as they wish, to secure a jury that they consider fair. I dissent.

JURY SIZE AND UNANIMITY REQUIREMENTS

The Supreme Court stated in 1898 that it adopted the traditional view of the need for twelve-member juries rendering unanimous verdicts: "The wise men who framed the Constitution . . . [believed that] in criminal prosecutions, [justice] would not be adequately secured except through the unanimous verdict of twelve jurors" (*Thompson v. Utah*). This view was based on the historical traditions in England, especially the Magna Carta's statement that juries would have twelve members, and understandings of the common law

Purkett v. Elem, 514 U.S. 765 (1995)

Per Curiam

Respondent was convicted of second-degree robbery in a Missouri court. During jury selection, he objected to the prosecutor's use of peremptory challenges to strike two black men from the jury panel, an objection arguably based on *Batson v. Kentucky* . . . (1986). The prosecutor explained his strikes:

> I struck [juror] number twenty-two because of his long hair. He had long curly hair. He had the longest hair of anybody on the panel by far. He appeared to not be a good juror for that fact, the fact that he had long hair hanging down shoulder length, curly, unkempt hair. Also, he had a mustache and a goatee type beard. And juror number twenty-four also has a mustache and a goatee type beard. Those are the only two people on the jury . . . with any facial hair . . . and I don't like the way they looked, with the way the hair is cut, both of them. And the mustaches and the beards look suspicious to me.

The prosecutor further explained that he feared that juror number 24, who had had a sawed-off shotgun pointed at him during a supermarket robbery, would believe that "to have a robbery you have to have a gun, and there is no gun in this case." . . .

The state trial court, without explanation, overruled respondent's objection and empaneled the jury. On direct appeal, respondent renewed his *Batson* claim. The Missouri Court of Appeals affirmed, finding that the "state's explanation constituted a legitimate 'hunch'" and that "[t]he circumstances fail[ed] to raise the necessary inference of racial discrimination." . . .

The Court of Appeals for the Eighth Circuit reversed and remanded with instructions to grant the writ of habeas corpus. It said:

> Where the prosecution strikes a prospective juror who is a member of the defendant's racial group, solely on the basis of factors which are facially irrelevant to the question of whether that person is qualified to serve as a juror in a particular case, the prosecution must at least articulate some plausible race-neutral reason for believing those factors will somehow affect the person's ability to perform his or her duties as a juror. In the present case, the prosecutor's comments, "I don't like the way [he] look[s], with the way the hair is cut. . . . And the mustach[e] and the bear[d] look suspicious to me," do not constitute such legitimate race-neutral reasons for striking juror 22." . . .

It concluded that the "prosecution's explanation for striking juror 22 . . . was pretextual," and that the state trial court had "clearly erred" in finding that striking juror number 22 had not been intentional discrimination. . . .

Under our *Batson* jurisprudence, once the opponent of a peremptory challenge has made out a *prima facie* case of racial discrimination (step one), the burden of production shifts to the proponent of the strike to come forward with a race-neutral explanation (step two). If a race-neutral explanation is tendered, the trial court must then decide (step three) whether the opponent of the strike has proved purposeful racial discrimination. . . .

The Court of Appeals erred by combining *Batson*'s second and third steps into one, requiring that the justification tendered at the second step be not just neutral but also at least minimally persuasive, i.e., a "plausible" basis for believing "that the person's ability to perform his or her duties as a juror will be affected." . . . It is not until the third step that the persuasiveness of the justification becomes relevant—the step in which the trial court determines whether the opponent of the strike has carried his burden of proving purposeful discrimination. . . . At that stage, implausible and fantastic justifications may (and probably will) be found to

practices used in American courts in 1789 when the Bill of Rights was drafted. Decades later, the Court's view obviously changed. In *Williams v. Florida* (1970), the Court endorsed Florida's use of six-member juries in criminal cases. Small juries are used with great frequency in civil cases, even in jurisdictions that use twelve-member juries in criminal cases. For example, federal courts use twelve-member juries for criminal trials and six-member juries for civil trials. Although it permitted the use of small juries, the Court refused to

be pretexts for purposeful discrimination. But to say that a trial judge may choose to disbelieve a silly or superstitious reason at step three is quite different from saying that a trial judge must terminate the inquiry at step two when the race-neutral reason is silly or superstitious. The latter violates the principle that the ultimate burden of persuasion regarding racial motivation rests with, and never shifts from, the opponent of the strike. . . .

The Court of Appeals appears to have seized on our admonition in *Batson* that to rebut a *prima facie* case, the proponent of the strike "must give a 'clear and reasonably specific' explanation of his 'legitimate reasons' for exercising the challenges," . . . and that the reason must be "related to the particular case to be tried." . . . This warning was meant to refute the notion that a prosecutor could satisfy his burden of production by merely denying that he had a discriminatory motive or by merely affirming his good faith. What it means by a "legitimate reason" is not a reason that makes sense, but a reason that does not deny equal protection. . . .

The prosecutor's proffered explanation in this case—that he struck juror number 22 because he had long, unkempt hair, a mustache, and a beard—is race-neutral and satisfies the prosecution's step two burden of articulating a nondiscriminatory reason for the strike. . . .

. . . The judgment of the Court of Appeals is reversed. . . .

JUSTICE STEVENS, with whom JUSTICE BREYER joins, dissenting.

In my opinion it is unwise for the Court to announce a law-changing decision without first ordering full briefing and argument on the merits of the case. . . .

Today, without argument, the Court replaces the *Batson* standard with the surprising announcement that any neutral explanation, no matter how "implausible or fantastic," . . . even if it is "silly or superstitious," . . . is sufficient to rebut a *prima facie* case of discrimination. A trial court must accept that neutral explanation unless a separate "step three" inquiry leads to the conclusion that the peremptory challenge was racially motivated. The Court does not attempt to explain why a statement that "the juror had a beard," or "the juror's last name began with the letter 'S'" should satisfy step two, though a statement that "I had a hunch" should not. . . . It is not too much to ask that a prosecutor's explanation for his strikes be race neutral, reasonably specific, and trial related. Nothing less will serve to rebut the inference of race-based discrimination that arises when the defendant has made out a *prima facie* case [of race-based exclusion of potential jurors through the use of peremptory challenges]. . . . That, in any event, is what we decided in *Batson*. . . .

In some cases, conceivably the length and unkempt character of a juror's hair and goatee-type beard might give rise to a concern that he is a nonconformist who might not be a good juror. In this case, however, the prosecutor did not identify any such concern. He merely said he did not "'like the way [the juror] looked,'" that the facial hair "'look[ed] suspicious.'" . . . I think this explanation may well be pretextual as a matter of law; it has nothing to do with the case at hand, and it is just as evasive as "I had a hunch." Unless a reviewing court may evaluate such explanations when a trial judge fails to find that a *prima facie* case has been established, appellate or collateral review of *Batson* claims will amount to nothing more than the meaningless charade that the Missouri Supreme Court correctly understood *Batson* to disfavor. . . .

. . . The Court's unnecessary tolerance of silly, fantastic, and implausible explanations, together with its assumption that there is a difference of constitutional magnitude between a statement that "I had a hunch about this juror based on his appearance," and "I challenged this juror because he had a mustache," demeans the importance of the values vindicated by our decision in *Batson*.

I respectfully dissent.

---

permit states to use five-person juries in criminal cases (*Ballew v. Georgia*, 1978). States are allowed to define jury size for themselves provided they do not violate the Supreme Court's interpretation that criminal juries cannot have fewer than six members. The Court's decision that the Sixth Amendment permits juries smaller than the traditional twelve-member decision-making body produced criticism. Psychology research indicates that decision-making groups of smaller size are less likely to include alternative viewpoints. A dominant

Discrimination in Jury Selection

In several decisions (*Batson v. Kentucky, Georgia v. McCullom,* etc.), the U.S. Supreme Court forbade the use of race and gender as the basis for peremptory challenges. However, *Purkett v. Elem* subsequently said, in effect, that all members of a particular race or gender may be excluded from a jury pool as long as the attorney using peremptory challenges to make the exclusions does not admit that the exclusions rest on race or gender. In light of *Purkett,* do the decisions forbidding racial and gender discrimination in the use of peremptory challenges actually provide any protection for defendants? Rather than prevent discrimination, *Purkett* arguably tells attorneys how to discriminate and get away with it. What is the message of *Purkett* for an attorney interested in engaging in racial or gender discrimination? When asked about the reason for race- or gender-based use of peremptory challenges, simply make up some other reason. Even if the alternate reason is a silly pretext for discrimination (e.g., "I don't like to have jurors with curly black hair"), the Supreme Court has said that the reason does not have to be sensible. Thus the protection against racial discrimination in jury selection rests in the discretionary judgments of trial judges who accept or reject peremptory challenges rather than on the words of the U.S. Supreme Court, which claims that it seeks to prevent such discrimination.

leader is more likely to be able to sway the other members. Fewer people are available to help the group remember the evidence and to understand the jury instructions. In effect, the Court's decision may have reduced the quality of jury decision making in those states that use fewer than twelve jurors.

After moving the Sixth Amendment's requirements about jury size away from the traditional English practice, the Court considered what the Constitution required concerning jury unanimity. As you read the Court's opinion in *Apodaca v. Oregon* (1972), ask yourself how the ruling affects the fates of criminal defendants.

The *Apodaca* case interpreted the Sixth Amendment to enable states to find defendants guilty based on a non-unanimous vote of jurors. The Court endorsed the use of super majority votes (i.e., 10 to 2 or 9 to 3). It did not address the question whether a simple majority vote (i.e., 7 to 5) can serve as the basis for a criminal conviction. States have not sought to have convictions by simple majorities, and many observers believe that the Supreme Court would be reluctant to permit convictions by closely divided juries. The Supreme Court's endorsement of non-unanimous verdicts as constitutionally permissible produced great disagreement among the justices. The dynamics of group decision making can change significantly when the jury is not required to reach a consensus. If the majority favors conviction immediately, they have no need to listen to the few jurors who see the case in a different light. This may impede careful consideration of all of the evidence. In the famous film *Twelve Angry Men,* Henry Fonda is the lone juror who holds out for the defendant's innocence in a twelve-member jury that was required to reach a unanimous verdict in order to declare the defendant guilty. Over the course of the movie, Fonda gradually convinces all of the other jurors that the defendant is not guilty. If the Supreme Court's *Apodaca* rule had applied in the film, the actually-innocent defendant would have been found guilty within minutes

Apodaca v. Oregon, 406 U.S. 404 (1972)

[*Robert Apodaca, Henry Cooper, and James Madden were tried on charges of assault with a deadly weapon, burglary, and larceny. Under Oregon law, juries can convict defendants on less-than-unanimous votes. Apodaca and Madden were convicted by 11-to-1 votes, and Cooper was convicted by a 10-to-2 vote, the minimum requisite vote under state law for sustaining a conviction. Their convictions were sustained by the Oregon Court of Appeals and the Oregon Supreme Court. They petitioned the U.S. Supreme Court to assert their claim that less-than-unanimous verdicts in criminal cases violate the Sixth Amendment right to trial by jury. The case was decided simultaneously with a companion case,* Johnson v. Louisiana *(1972), concerning Louisiana's comparable split-verdict rules that permitted 9-to-3 decisions as the minimum standard to convict defendants at trial.*]

JUSTICE WHITE announced the judgment of the Court in an opinion in which CHIEF JUSTICE BURGER, JUSTICE BLACKMUN, and JUSTICE REHNQUIST joined.

. . .

In *Williams v. Florida* [1970], . . . we had occasion to consider a related issue: whether the Sixth Amendment's right to trial by jury requires that all juries consist of 12 men. After considering the history of the 12-man requirement and the functions it performs in contemporary society, we concluded that it was not of constitutional stature. We reach the same conclusion today with regard to the requirement of unanimity. Like the requirement that juries consist of 12 men, the requirement of unanimity arose during the Middle Ages and had become an accepted feature of the common-law jury by the 18th century. But, as we observed in *Williams,* "the relevant constitutional history casts considerable doubt on the easy assumption . . . that if a given feature existed in a jury at common law in 1789, then it was necessarily preserved in the Constitution" [399 U.S. at 92–93]. . . .

As we observed in *Williams,* one can draw conflicting inferences from the legislative history. . . . Surely one fact that is absolutely clear from this history is that, after a proposal had been made to specify precisely which of the common-law requisites of the jury were to be preserved by the Constitution, the Framers explicitly rejected the proposal and instead left such specification for the future. As in

Williams, we must accordingly consider what is meant by the concept of "jury" and determine whether a feature commonly associated with it is constitutionally required. And, as in *Williams,* our inability to divine "the intent of the Framers" when they eliminated references to the "accustomed requisites" requires that in determining what is meant by a jury we must turn to other than purely historical considerations. Our inquiry must focus upon the function served by the jury in contemporary society. . . . "[T]he essential feature of a jury obviously lies in the interposition between the accused and his accuser of the commonsense judgment of a group of laymen. . . ." [*Williams,* 399 at 100]. . . . A requirement of unanimity, however, does not materially contribute to the exercise of this commonsense judgment. . . . Requiring unanimity would obviously produce hung juries in some situations where non-unanimous juries will convict or acquit. But in either case, the interest of the defendant in having the judgment of his peers interposed between himself and the officers of the State who prosecute and judge him is equally well served.

Petitioners nevertheless argue that unanimity serves other purposes constitutionally essential to the continued operation of the jury system. Their principal contention is that a Sixth Amendment "jury trial" made mandatory on the States by virtue of the Due Process Clause of the Fourteenth Amendment [in *Duncan v. Louisiana*] should be held to require a unanimous jury verdict in order to give substance to the reasonable-doubt standard otherwise mandated by the Due Process Clause. See [*In re Winship* (1970), which required the reasonable-doubt standard for convictions in juvenile proceedings]. We are quite sure, however, that the Sixth Amendment itself has never been held to require proof beyond a reasonable doubt in criminal cases. The reasonable-doubt standard developed separately from both the jury trial and the unanimous verdict. As the Court noted in the *Winship* case, the rule requiring proof of crime beyond a reasonable doubt did not crystallize in this country until after the Constitution was adopted. . . . And in [*Winship*], which held such a burden of proof to be constitutionally required, the Court purported to draw no support from the Sixth Amendment.

. . . Petitioners also cite quite accurately a long line of decisions of this Court upholding the principle that the Fourteenth Amendment requires jury

(continued)

panels to reflect a cross section of the community. . . . They then contend that unanimity is a necessary precondition for effective application of the cross-section requirement, because a rule permitting less than unanimous verdicts will make it possible for convictions to occur without the acquiescence of minority elements within the community.

There are two flaws in this argument. One is petitioners' assumption that every distinct voice in the community has a right to be represented on every jury and a right to prevent conviction of a defendant in any case. All that the Constitution forbids, however, is systematic exclusion of identifiable segments of the community from jury panels and from the juries ultimately drawn from those panels; a defendant may not, for example, challenge the makeup of a jury merely because no members of his race are on the jury, but must prove that his race has been systematically excluded. . . . No group, in short, has the right to block convictions; it has only the right to participate in the overall legal processes by which criminal guilt and innocence are determined.

We also cannot accept petitioners' second assumption—that minority groups, even when they are represented on a jury, will not adequately represent the viewpoint of those groups simply because they may be outvoted in the final result. They will be present during all deliberations, and their views will be heard. We cannot assume that the majority of the jury will refuse to weigh the evidence and reach a decision upon rational grounds, just as it must now do in order to obtain unanimous verdicts, or that a majority will deprive a man of his liberty on the basis of prejudice when a minority is presenting a reasonable argument in favor of acquittal. We simply find no proof for the notion that a majority will disregard its instructions and cast its votes for guilt or innocence based on prejudices rather than the evidence.

We accordingly affirm the judgment of the Court of Appeals of Oregon. It is so ordered. Judgment affirmed.

JUSTICE BLACKMUN, concurring.

I join the Court's opinion and judgment in each of these cases. I add only the comment, which should be obvious and should not need saying, that in so doing I do not imply that I regard a State's split-verdict system as a wise one. My vote means only that I cannot conclude that the system is constitu-tionally offensive. Were I a legislator, I would disfavor it as a matter of policy. Our task here, however, is not to pursue and strike down what happens to impress us as undesirable legislative policy.

I do not hesitate to say, either, that a system employing a 7–5 standard, rather than a 9–3 or 75% minimum, would afford me great difficulty. As Mr. Justice White points out, . . . "a substantial majority of the jury" are to be convinced. That is all that is before us in each of these cases.

JUSTICE POWELL, concurring.

I concur in the judgment of the Court that conviction based on less-than-unanimous jury verdicts in these cases did not deprive criminal defendants of due process of law under the Fourteenth Amendment. As my reasons for reaching this conclusion in the Oregon case differ from those expressed in the plurality opinion of Mr. Justice White, I will state my views separately. . . .

[The plurality opinion's] premise is that the concept of jury trial, as applicable to the States under the Fourteenth Amendment, must be identical in every detail to the concept required in federal courts by the Sixth Amendment. I do not think that all of the elements of jury trial within the meaning of the Sixth Amendment are necessarily embodied in or incorporated into the Due Process Clause of the Fourteenth Amendment. . . .

In an unbroken line of cases reaching back into the late 1800's, the Justices of this Court have recognized, virtually without dissent, that unanimity is one of the indispensable features of *federal* jury trial. . . . In these cases, the Court has presumed that unanimous verdicts are essential in federal jury trials, not because unanimity is necessarily fundamental to the function performed by the jury, but because that result is mandated by history. The reasoning that runs throughout this Court's Sixth Amendment precedents is that, in amending the Constitution to guarantee the right to jury trial, the framers desired to preserve the jury safeguard as it was known to them at common law. At the time the Bill of Rights was adopted, unanimity had long been established as one of the attributes of a jury conviction at common law. It therefore seems to me, in accord both with history and precedent, that the Sixth Amendment requires a unanimous jury verdict to convict in a federal criminal trial.

But it is the Fourteenth Amendment, rather than the Sixth, that imposes upon the States the requirement that they provide jury trials to those accused of serious crimes. This Court has said, in cases decided when the intendment of that Amendment was not as clouded by the passage of time, that due process does not require that the States apply the federal jury-trial right with all its gloss. . . .

Viewing the unanimity controversy as one requiring a fresh look at the question of what is fundamental in jury trial, I see no constitutional infirmity in the provision adopted by the people of Oregon. It is the product of a constitutional amendment, approved by a vote of the people in the State, and appears to be patterned on a provision of the American Law Institute's Code of Criminal Procedure. A similar decision has been echoed more recently in England where the unanimity requirement was abandoned by statutory enactment. Less-than-unanimous verdict provisions also have been viewed with approval by the American Bar Association's Criminal Justice Project. . . .

JUSTICE STEWART, with whom JUSTICE BRENNAN and JUSTICE MARSHALL join, dissenting.

In *Duncan v. Louisiana* [1968] . . . , the Court squarely held that the Sixth Amendment right to trial by jury in a federal criminal case is made wholly applicable to state criminal trials by the Fourteenth Amendment. Unless *Duncan* is to be overruled, therefore, the only relevant question here is whether the Sixth Amendment's guarantee of trial by jury embraces a guarantee that the verdict of the jury be unanimous. The answer to that question is clearly "yes," as my Brother Powell has cogently demonstrated in that part of his concurring opinion that reviews almost a century of Sixth Amendment adjudication.

Until today, it had been universally understood that a unanimous verdict is an essential element of a Sixth Amendment jury trial . . . [citations to five cases].

I would follow these settled Sixth Amendment precedents and reverse the judgment before us.

JUSTICE DOUGLAS, with whom JUSTICE BRENNAN and JUSTICE MARSHALL join, dissenting.

. . .

With due respect to the majority, I dissent from this radical departure from American tradition. . . .

Do today's decisions mean that States may apply a "watered down" version of the Just Compensation Clause [or other rights contained in the Bill of Rights]? Or are today's decisions limited to a paring down of civil rights protected by the Bill of Rights

and up until now as fully applicable to the States as to the Federal Government?

These civil rights—whether they concern speech, searches and seizures, self-incrimination, criminal prosecutions, bail, or cruel and unusual punishments—extend, of course, to everyone, but in cold reality touch mostly the lower castes in our society. I refer, of course, to the blacks, the Chicanos, the one-mule farmers, the agricultural workers, the off-beat students, the victims of the ghetto. Are we giving the States the power to experiment in diluting their civil rights? It has long been thought that "thou shall nots" in the Constitution and Bill of Rights protect everyone against governmental intrusion or over-reaching. The idea has been obnoxious that there are some who can be relegated to second-class citizenship. But if we construe the Bill of Rights and the Fourteenth Amendment to permit States to "experiment" with the basic rights of people, we open a veritable Pandora's box. For hate and prejudice are versatile forces that can degrade the constitutional scheme. . . .

I would construe the Sixth Amendment, when applicable to the States, precisely as I would when applied to the Federal Government. The plurality approves a procedure which diminishes the reliability of a jury. . . .

The diminution of verdict reliability flows from the fact that nonunanimous juries need not debate and deliberate as fully as must unanimous juries. As soon as the requisite majority is attained, further consideration is not required either by Oregon or by Louisiana even though the dissident jurors might, if given the chance, be able to convince the majority. Such persuasion does in fact occasionally occur in States where the unanimous requirement applies: "In roughly one case in ten, the minority eventually succeeds in reversing an initial majority, and these may be cases of special importance" [quoted from a study of juries conducted by psychologists]. One explanation for this phenomenon is that because jurors are often not permitted to take notes and because they have imperfect memories, the forensic process of forcing jurors to defend their conflicting recollections and conclusions flushes out many nuances which otherwise would go overlooked. This collective effort to piece together the puzzle of historical truth, however, is cut short as soon as the requisite majority is reached in Oregon and Louisiana. Indeed, if a necessary majority is immediately obtained, then no deliberation at all is required in these States. (There is a suggestion that this may have happened in the 10–2 verdict rendered in only

(continued)

41 minutes in Apodaca's case.) . . . The Court now extracts from the jury room this automatic check against hasty fact-finding by relieving jurors of the duty to hear out fully the dissenters. . . .

Proof beyond a reasonable doubt and unanimity of criminal verdicts and the presumption of innocence are basic features of the accusatorial system. What we do today is not in that tradition but more in the tradition of the inquisition. Until new [constitutional] amendments are adopted setting new standards, I would let no man be fined or imprisoned in derogation of what up to today was indisputably the law of the land.

JUSTICE BRENNAN, with whom JUSTICE MARSHALL joins, dissenting.

. . .

It is in this context that we must view the constitutional requirement that all juries be drawn from an accurate cross section of the community. When verdicts must be unanimous, no member of the jury may be ignored by the others. When less than unanimity is sufficient, consideration of minority views may become nothing more than a matter of majority grace. In my opinion, the right of all groups in this Nation to participate in the criminal process means the right to have their voices heard. A unanimous verdict vindicates that right. Majority verdicts could destroy it.

JUSTICE MARSHALL, with whom JUSTICE BRENNAN joins, dissenting.

Today the Court cuts the heart out of two of the most important and inseparable safeguards the Bill of Rights offers a criminal defendant: the right to submit his case to a jury, and the right to proof beyond a reasonable doubt. Together, these safeguards occupy a fundamental place in our constitutional scheme, protecting the individual defendant from the awesome power of the State. After today, the skeleton of these safeguards remains, but the Court strips them of life and of meaning. I cannot refrain from adding my protest to that of my Brothers Douglas, Brennan, and Stewart, whom I join. . . .

More distressing still than the Court's treatment of the right to jury trial is the cavalier treatment the Court gives to proof beyond a reasonable doubt. The Court asserts that when a jury votes nine to three for conviction [in Louisiana], the doubts of the three do not impeach the verdict of the nine. . . . But . . . we know what has happened: the prosecutor has tried and failed to persuade those [three] jurors of the defendant's guilt. In such circumstances, it does violence to language and logic to say that the government has proved the defendant's guilt beyond a reasonable doubt. . . .

Each time this Court has approved a change in the familiar characteristics of the jury, we have reaffirmed the principle that its fundamental characteristic is its capacity to render a commonsense, laymen's judgment, as a representative body drawn from the community. To fence out dissenting jurors fences out a voice from the community, and undermines the principle on which our whole notion of the jury now rests. . . . The doubts of a single juror are in my view evidence that the government has failed to carry its burden of proving guilt beyond a reasonable doubt. I dissent.

without any consideration of the complete evidence that was highlighted by the dissenting juror.

In a later case, the Supreme Court tied together the issues of jury size and unanimity requirements by declaring that juries containing only six members must render unanimous verdicts (*Burch v. Louisiana,* 1979). It is not clear from the words of the Sixth Amendment how the Supreme Court developed its specific requirements concerning jury size and non-unanimous verdicts. Language in several opinions indicated that the justices were sensitive to research and criticism concerning the potential reduction in the quality of deliberations as the number of jurors shrinks and the opportunities to ignore dissenting jurors increases. Thus the Court set minimum requirements for both jury size (i.e., six members) and voting (i.e., unanimity required for six-member juries) rather than giving states complete freedom to define their own requirements for juries' structures and processes. As you read the material in

| A CLOSER LOOK | Representativeness and the Jury |

Although many Americans speak as if they believe defendants are entitled to a "jury of their peers," the Supreme Court's interpretation of the Sixth Amendment actually requires only that the jury pool be drawn from a fair cross-section of the community. There is no requirement that the actual jurors seated in a case reflect the diversity of a community's composition. The poor, members of minority groups, and young adults are often underrepresented within jury pools that rely on voter registration lists for calling jurors. In addition, retired people and middle-aged suburbanites are often overrepresented among the jurors who actually show up at court because they are less likely to have problems with child care, employment, and transportation that interfere with their ability to serve as jurors. Thus many jury pools and juries do not accurately reflect the demographic composition of the court's home community.

A lack of diversity in jury composition can affect deliberations because all people do not have the same reference points in evaluating evidence. For example, if someone arrested for a crime left his home in the morning carrying a knife in his pocket, middle-class suburbanites may presume he intended to commit a crime that day and infer that there was criminal intent behind whatever confrontation or incident led to the person's arrest. By contrast, because of their different experiences and reference points, people from poor neighborhoods may view it as normal to carry a knife in order to have the capacity for self-defense in walking around a neighborhood with crime problems. Thus they may not assume that the defendant began the day intending to commit a crime.

One of the consequences of the Supreme Court's decisions on jury size and unanimity is that the benefits of diverse jury composition are further reduced.

In small juries (less than twelve), there are fewer spaces available for which a poor, minority, or young juror may be chosen. In states that use nonunanimous verdicts, the jury's voting scheme may permit the majority of jurors to simply ignore dissenting, minority viewpoints rather than genuinely listening and attempting to understand the evidence from a different perspective.

An additional issue related to diversity and representation concerns the jury's image and legitimacy in the eyes of the community. When the composition of juries does not reflect the composition of the community, there is a risk that defendants and their families and others in the community will view the criminal justice process as illegitimate and exclusionary if only affluent people and suburbanites are visible as decision makers determining the fates of defendants whose lives they do not understand. Although someone might understandably say, "Who cares what criminals think?," a perceived lack of legitimacy poses risks for the system. Foremost among these risks is the possibility that people in certain segments of the community will be reluctant to cooperate with authorities in a system that they view as unfair. Thus, for example, it may be more difficult for police and prosecutors to find witnesses who will cooperate and provide necessary information about criminal activities.

In making decisions about juries, should the Supreme Court include consideration of the practical consequences of judicial decisions, including any detrimental effects on the ideal of jury composition that is broadly representative of the demographic groups (i.e., ethnicity, race, social class, etc.) within a community?

the box "Representativeness and the Jury," think about how the Supreme Court's decisions affect the composition of juries and their decision-making processes.

TRIAL PROCESSES

During a jury trial, the judge acts like a referee at a sporting event. The judge makes sure that rules are followed and penalizes the "team" that violates rules by declaring that evidence may not be admitted. Sometimes, however, the jury has already heard a statement from a witness or attorney before the opposing side has the opportunity to object to the statement as improper under the rules of evidence or court procedure. When this circumstance arises, the judge will instruct the jury to disregard the statement. There is a significant question about whether jurors are capable of making a decision that does not take account of something they actually heard. If the rule violation is so significant that the judge believes the jury is incapable of reaching a fair decision after hearing improper statements or evidence, the judge may declare a mistrial and force the prosecutor to decide whether to begin an entirely new trial in front of a different jury. Judges strongly desire to avoid declaring mistrials because of the time involved in calling and selecting new jurors and conducting a trial over again. Thus there is a risk that judges will naively hope or believe that jurors are capable of ignoring statements that they have actually heard in order to avoid tying up the court (and the judge's time) with the preparation for and presentation of a new trial. Does this understandable reluctance to declare mistrials pose risks for fairness in jury deliberations and the protection of defendants' rights? In some cases, risks undoubtedly exist. Yet it is difficult to carry out perfect processes that ensure all rules are followed to the letter.

Trial Rules

Specific rules apply to each stage of the trial process. During attorneys' opening statements, jurors are warned that these introductory speeches do not constitute evidence and should not be considered in the eventual deliberations about the defendant's possible guilt. Again, it is easy to issue warnings and to believe, in the abstract, that jurors can separate evidence from attorneys' statements. In reality, however, there must be significant doubts about jurors' ability to compartmentalize information in this manner. Attorneys recognize that jurors will be influenced by their opening statements, and thus they take those statements quite seriously.

During the prosecution's presentation of evidence, including physical evidence and witness testimony, as well as the subsequent presentation of evidence by the defense, the judge will be asked to make rulings on whether particular statements or items of evidence are admissible and whether they have been presented in accordance with the rules of evidence. One of the flaws in the adversarial process of American trials is that the judge does not rule automatically on issues of questionable evidence. The opposing attorney must normally raise an objection to evidence in order for the judge to make a decision about its admissibility. If the attorney is unprepared, uncaring, lazy, or incompetent, the opposing side may be able to present improper evidence to the jury. Judges sometimes find themselves sitting silently as they observe evidentiary presentations that they know to be improper. However, unless the opposing side recognizes the problems with the evidence, the judge will not act to prevent its presentation to the jury. This potential problem looms as an especially important issue in the American system of justice in which different cities and counties use varying methods of selecting and paying defense attorneys who represent indigent criminal defendants. There are concerns that some jurisdictions pay defense attorneys so little money that there is little incentive for the attorneys to put adequate efforts into trial preparation. Alternatively, low levels of compensation make truly skilled attorneys unwilling to handle criminal cases for indigent defendants, and thus those defendants may find themselves represented by attorneys who are less skilled, less experienced, and less successful.

Traditionally, jurors have been barred from taking notes during trial. They are expected to sit, listen, and remember on their own. Several reasons supported the prohibition on juror notes. First, there is a fear that jurors who are taking notes will not be able to listen to important information that is presented during the moments that they are busy writing. Second, there is a risk that if jurors misunderstand evidence or mishear statements that are made, then they will write down erroneous information. Because the incorrect information is written on paper, it will become "real" to the jurors and it will be difficult to convince them during jury deliberations that they misunderstood what was presented in court. Related to the second reason is a third justification. Jurors who have notes will feel in a stronger position to correct jurors who did not take notes on a particular piece of evidence, and therefore the notes, even if erroneous, are likely to have a more powerful impact on jury deliberations. In theory, the collective memories of the twelve (or fewer) jurors will permit them to reconstruct the evidence through their discussions with each other in the jury room. If no one has taken notes, then they will be on equal footing in attempting to find the truth as they sort through the evidence.

In recent years, many judges and scholars have come to the conclusion that there are benefits from permitting jurors to take notes. There is so much for jurors to remember that they are better served by having the opportunity to write down important evidence and information as they go through the trial. In addition, if all jurors are taking notes, then there should be less risk that any one juror's erroneous notes will be unduly influential in the jury's deliberations. Thus some judges pass out notepads and pens at the start of trials in order to encourage jurors to take notes.

Jury Instructions and Deliberations

One of the greatest challenges for judges is the presentation of understandable jury instructions. At the end of the trial, the judge must instruct the jury on its responsibilities, the consideration of evidence (as opposed to attorneys' arguments), and the "reasonable doubt" standard to be applied in order to issue a guilty verdict. Attorneys for both sides make suggestions to the judge about what instructions to give to jurors. Obviously, the prosecutor and the defense attorney seek to phrase instructions in a way that will place their evidence or arguments in a favorable light and potentially discount the opponent's case. Sometimes it takes hours for the judge to make the oral presentation of jury instructions to the juror. Jurors are often confused and bored by the instructions. In addition, many lawyers and scholars debate whether jurors are truly capable of understanding complex jury instructions.

When the jurors retire to the jury room, they are free to engage in open, unguided discussions and decisions. No one observes the jurors at work. The privacy of the jury room is one of the strongest traditions in American law. If jurors improperly include erroneous evidence or arguments in their deliberations, there is no authority figure present to correct them. If jurors make biased statements, there is nothing to prevent such statements from influencing the outcome of the case. The jury trial process is designed to follow rules in presenting evidence and instructing jurors in the consideration of that evidence, but there is no mechanism to ensure that the rules are followed in the jury's deliberations. The jury trial is a very human process in which people who lack training in law attempt to use legal concepts (e.g., the "reasonable doubt" standard for guilt) and legal rules (e.g., rules about which evidence is eligible for consideration in deliberations), most of which they may not fully understand, in determining the fate of one of their fellow citizens. Many attorneys consider trials to be a "crapshoot"; it's like rolling dice, so you never know what will happen. Even if a defendant is clearly guilty or clearly innocent in the eyes of objective analysts of the evidence, there is no assurance that the jury will not reach a contrary conclusion.

Jury deliberations can be guided by improper considerations because there is no outside authority figure present to observe and control the discussions. This does not preclude the possibility of overturning a verdict if a judge later learns that the jury focused on improper evidence and issues. For example, in December 2000 a judge in Los Angeles overturned the convictions of three police officers charged with conspiracy for framing gang members. After the trial, jurors spoke publicly about the case and it was revealed that their decision was based, in part, on issues that were never presented at trial.[5] The judge's action in overturning the jury's verdict was unusual because in most cases jurors follow the judge's advice to avoid talking about the deliberations after the case is over. In most cases, outsiders never know how and why the jury reached its decision.

One of the most important and controversial powers of the jury is called **jury nullification.** Juries possess the power to nullify the law by reaching a conclusion contrary to the clear dictates of the law. When this occurs, the jury may be expressing the sentiments of the community that the law, if followed, would be too harsh in a particular factual situation. The jury may also be making a statement in opposition to the decisions and practices of the police and the prosecutor in investigating and pursuing a particular defendant. For example, if a storeowner is continuously victimized by burglaries and robberies and therefore puts an unlicensed gun under the cash register, a jury may be unwilling to convict the storeowner of a weapons violation if a police officer happens to observe the illegal weapon behind the counter. The owner is factually guilty of possessing an illegal weapon, but the jury may be unwilling to impose a finding of legal guilt that brings with it a criminal record and punishment. Although a jury can nullify the criminal law by acquitting a defendant whose guilt is supported by the evidence, the jury cannot impose a guilty verdict on a defendant whose guilt is not supported by the evidence. It would be a violation of the right to due process to impose criminal punishment on someone against whom the evidence cannot support a finding of guilt beyond a reasonable doubt.

In the twentieth century, technological developments affecting mass communications created new possibilities for informing the public about judicial proceedings. By the dawn of the twenty-first century, many states permitted live television broadcasts from inside courtrooms during trials. As you read

TECHNOLOGY AND CONSTITUTIONAL RIGHTS

Television Cameras in Court

What is the impact of television cameras in court? There are disagreements among lawyers and judges about the effects of broadcasting trials on television. Some critics believe that the presence of cameras makes attorneys engage in "grandstanding" behavior in which they attempt to be flamboyant and provocative in order to attract future clients from among the television audience. If television actually makes people more self-conscious, however, is it possible that the impact actually works to improve the trial process? If attorneys are attempting to im-

press the audience, perhaps that motive leads them to perform more effectively and conscientiously in presenting their side's case. Perhaps the television cameras reduce the likelihood that judges or jurors will become inattentive and distracted during trial. Would any of them want to appear bored or sleepy on television?

What do you think? Do televised trials have a beneficial or adverse impact on trial processes and the protection of defendants' rights to a fair trial?

the material in the accompanying box, consider whether you think the presence of cameras creates an adverse impact for the trial process and its ability to fulfill its purposes for society.

CONCLUSION

Criminal trials decided by a jury of citizens are an important and unique element of the legal tradition inherited by the United States from England. Today most jury trials are in Great Britain, the United States, and other countries that were formerly British colonies. The use of citizens as judicial decision makers evolved in England and provides an important mechanism for the community's voice to be heard in determining the fates of criminal defendants.

The words of the U.S. Constitution in both Article III (federal cases) and the Sixth Amendment (state cases) indicate that jury trials are required in all criminal prosecutions. However, the U.S. Supreme Court has not adopted a literal interpretation of the Constitution's words with respect to this right. In *Lewis v. United States* (1996), the U.S. Supreme Court made it clear that the right to a jury arises only when a person is charged with a crime that can bring a sentence in excess of six months in prison. If the charge or charges are merely petty offenses for which the potential punishment is six months or less, then there is no right to a jury, even if the defendant faces multiple petty charges that could total many years in prison if imposed as a consecutive sentence.

The fulfillment of the right to a jury trial rests on the fairness of jury selection procedures. The Constitution does not guarantee a defendant will have a jury of his or her "peers." Instead, the Supreme Court's interpretation requires that the jury be drawn from a fair cross-section of the community. A jury may turn out to be all-white or all-black. Such juries are permissible as long as the pool is drawn from the range of demographic groups in the community.

Jurisdictions frequently use voter registration lists to draw the names of potential jurors. Such lists often lead to the underrepresentation of poor people, people from minority groups, and young people, all of whom frequently register to vote at lower rates than other adults in American society. Some jurisdictions attempt to broaden their lists of potential jurors by using drivers' licenses, hunting licenses, and other government lists as a source of potential jurors.

Potential jurors summoned to court are actually selected to serve on juries through the *voir dire* process in which the judge (or attorneys) ask questions that attempt to reveal whether the potential jurors possess any biases that would interfere with fair decision making. Personal acquaintance with the defendant or attorneys, prior victimization from a similar crime, or statements revealing prejudices can all serve as a basis for exclusion from juries. Attorneys can use an unlimited number of challenges for cause (subject to the approval of the trial judge) to exclude potential jurors for demonstrated biases. Each side in the case is also permitted to use a fixed number of peremptory challenges that permit them to exclude jurors without giving a reason. The only limitation on the use of peremptory challenges is that the attorneys may not exclude potential jurors because of race or gender. However, the Supreme Court's decision in *Purkett v. Elem* (1995) revealed that attorneys can mask their use of race and gender as the basis for exclusion by simply creating another excuse, no matter how flimsy, as the reason for challenging the potential juror. If trial judges are not vigilant in examining the attorneys' reasons when there appears to be racial or gender discrimination occurring, then the protection against discrimination in jury selection will go unfulfilled.

The Supreme Court has interpreted the Constitution to permit criminal juries with fewer than twelve members. In addition, there is no constitutional requirement that jury verdicts be unanimous in order to find a defendant guilty. States are permitted to create their own rules as long as there are at least six members on criminal juries and guilty verdicts are based on a super majority vote (i.e., 11 to 1, 10 to 2, or 9 to 3) rather than a simple majority vote (i.e., 7 to 5). If small, six-member juries are used in criminal cases, then the vote must be unanimous. Critics have raised concerns about the risk that the quality of jury deliberations, including broad representation of varying viewpoints from the community, is diminished when criminal trials are conducted using small juries or non-unanimous verdicts.

In the American model of the adversarial justice system, the judge assumes a relatively passive role as a "referee" during jury trials. The judge must ensure that rules are followed, but frequently the judge is permitted to correct rule violations (e.g., improper evidence submissions) only when the attorneys for each side are sufficiently competent and attentive to raise objections to questionable presentations by the opposing side. If a defendant's lawyer does not perform well, the judge's role as "referee" may not be activated sufficiently to protect all of the defendant's rights.

The jury deliberates in secret without any authority figure present to ensure that the law is followed. Jurors may have difficulty in accurately remembering and understanding the important details of a trial and the detailed jury instructions provided by the judge. Thus a jury trial, like other aspects of criminal procedure, is a very human process that is presumed to be guided by law but may, in fact, be determined by human biases and discretionary decisions.

SUMMARY

- The United States inherited the use of citizen-jurors in criminal trials as part of the legal tradition carried over from England.

- In the Constitution, the words of both Article III and the Sixth Amendment indicate that jury trials will be used in all criminal cases. However, the Supreme Court has not applied these words in a literal fashion.

- The Supreme Court has interpreted the Sixth Amendment as providing a right to jury trials only when a defendant is charged with a serious crime carrying a potential punishment of six months or more in prison (*Lewis v. United States*, 1996).

- A defendant could potentially serve many years in prison without having been given an opportunity for a jury trial if the charges were all petty (i.e., worth six months or less) and there was a conviction on multiple charges that produced a consecutive sentence (i.e., multiple six-month sentences to be served one after another).

- The Constitution requires that the jury pool be drawn from a fair cross-section of the community. There is no requirement that the ultimate jury have any particular composition.

- Attorneys use challenges for cause and peremptory challenges in the *voir dire* process in order to exclude potential jurors from the jury that is ultimately selected.

- The Supreme Court has formally barred the use of racial and gender discrimination in attorneys' use of peremptory challenges, but the enforcement of this rule depends on trial judges giving close scrutiny to the excuses provided by attorneys when discrimination appears to occur in jury selection.

- According to the U.S. Supreme Court's interpretation, there is no requirement that criminal juries be comprised of twelve members. States may set the size of juries for themselves, but criminal juries may not have fewer than six members.

- There is no requirement that juries reach unanimous verdicts to find a defendant guilty unless the decision is being made by a small, six-person jury.

- Critics complain that the use of small juries and non-unanimous verdicts diminishes the quality of jurors' deliberations and decisions.

- In the American adversarial system, trial judges act as "referees" during jury trials. Judges' effectiveness as referees depends, in large part, on the competence of attorneys who must raise issues concerning alleged rules violations by the opposition in order to have many court rules actively enforced.

- Juries' decisions may be affected by the jurors' biases and prejudices because it is unclear whether jurors always understand the evidence and the legal rules for applying that evidence in determining whether a defendant's guilt has been proven beyond a reasonable doubt.

Key Terms

challenge for cause   A challenge exercised by attorneys for both sides during *voir dire* when attorneys ask the judge to excuse potential jurors for saying something that demonstrates a risk that they will be improperly biased.

change of venue   An order moving the location of a trial from the jurisdiction where the crime occurred to a different city where the citizens who will have to serve as jurors have heard less information about the case.

gag order   In an effort to prevent pretrial publicity that might bias potential jurors, a judge may, under extraordinary circumstances, order news agencies to *not* report on certain details of criminal cases.

jury nullification   The power of juries to nullify the law by acquitting a defendant whose factual guilt is clear because of the jurors' view that criminal punishment is not appropriate in the particular situation presented in the case.

mistrial   A judge's declaration that terminates and nullifies a trial because of improper evidence or information that may have prejudiced the jury or because the jury was deadlocked in its deliberations. The prosecution may begin the trial again in front of a new jury if a mistrial is declared.

peremptory challenge   A limited number of challenges used at the discretion of attorneys for each side so they can exclude potential jurors at their discretion. They are not supposed to use such challenges to exclude potential jurors on the basis of race or gender.

sequester the jury   The isolation of jury members from society during the course of a trial and jury deliberations by keeping them under around-the-clock supervision in the courthouse and a hotel in order to prevent them from hearing news reports, discussing the case with non–jury members, or otherwise infecting their deliberations with information from outside sources.

voir dire   Process of questioning potential jurors to determine who should be selected for or excluded from the jury based on any attitudes or biases that might interfere with their ability to give open-minded consideration to the evidence presented by the prosecution and the defense.

Additional Readings

Adler, Stephen J. 1994. *The Jury: Disorder in the Court*. New York: Doubleday. A news reporter's inside look at jury deliberations through interviews with jurors.

Giles, Robert, and Robert W. Snyder, eds. 1999. *Covering the Courts: Free Press, Fair Trials, and Journalistic Performance*. New Brunswick, N.J.: Transaction Publishers. A series of articles on various aspects of trials including the issue of televised trials and attention to two famous cases, the O. J. Simpson murder trial and the Oklahoma City bombing case.

Hastie, Reid, Steven Penrod, and Nancy Pennington. 1983. *Inside the Jury*. Cambridge, Mass.: Harvard University Press, 1983. Scholarly examination of juries and jury decision making.

Levine, James. 1992. *Juries and Politics*. Pacific Grove, Calif.: Brooks/Cole. An overview of the jury system in the United States.

Notes

1. Francis H. Heller, *The Sixth Amendment to the Constitution of the United States* (New York: Greenwood Press, 1951), 8.

2. Heller, *The Sixth Amendment,* 13–14.

3. "Best-Selling Author Excused from 2 Juries," *Lansing State Journal,* 17 December 2000, 2A.

4. Valerie Hans and Neil Vidmar, *Judging the Jury* (New York: Plenum Press, 1986), 75.

5. Linda Deutsch, "Judge Overturns 3 L.A. Convictions," Associated Press Wire Service, 23 December 2000.

CHAPTER TWELVE

Sentencing and Postconviction Processes

Imagine that your college's president announces a new policy that forbids students from parking cars on campus. The college plans to build a new alumni center where the large student parking lot currently sits. The college expects students to park in town, pay for parking in municipal and private lots, and then take city buses to the college campus for classes. Many students are furious both because their parking costs will increase in city lots and because it will take a long time to ride the bus from the city to the campus. The students also suspect that the college is attempting to force students to move back into empty dormitory rooms so that the college will have more "room and board" revenue. The students organize a nighttime, torch-lit protest march that will begin at the football stadium and end at the president's house. You join the other marchers and participate in shouting protest chants. More and more students pour out of their dorm rooms to join the march. As the crowd of marchers swells in size, some students begin throwing rocks at various college buildings. Soon many windows in classroom buildings have been broken. The college police are joined by city police in blocking the marchers' path to the president's house. The police yell instructions over a bullhorn, but the chanting crowd is so noisy that you cannot hear what the police are saying. The next thing you know, police officers are grabbing and arresting many students.

As marchers begin to run in every direction, a police officer grasps your arm, places you in handcuffs, and thrusts you into a patrol car. After spending a night in jail, you learn that you are being charged with disorderly conduct and obstructing a police officer in the exercise of official duties.

When you are released on $100 bail, you join dozens of students who gather at the office of the student government association. The association has hired an attorney to give preliminary advice to students who were arrested. The attorney tells you that she has had discussions with the local prosecutor. The prosecutor has agreed to permit students charged with disorderly conduct and obstruction to plead guilty to the disorderly conduct offense only. The obstruction charge will be dropped, the prosecutor will recommend a $100 fine with no probation, and the students' criminal charges will be expunged from their records if they do not commit any further offenses for two years. The attorney tells you that this is a favorable deal. If you do not take the deal, you will probably be forced to pay at least $10,000 to hire a private attorney to contest the charges in court. You do not have any money to hire an attorney and you do not want your parents to know about the arrest, so you agree to accept the plea agreement.

When you go to court to plead guilty, you are accompanied by the student government association attorney. You enter your guilty plea and the prosecutor recommends the $100 fine and eligibility to have the criminal record cleared after two years. However, the judge surprises everyone by refusing to accept the prosecutor's recommendation. The judge looks directly at you and says,

> "I think you students need to learn a lesson about respecting the laws that govern our society. Thus I am imposing a fine of $500 and requiring you to spend 30 days in jail. Afterward, you will be on probation for six months. You must meet with your probation officer three times each week and obey an 8 p.m. curfew. In addition, you and your parents must attend counseling sessions on proper parent-child relationships and behavior management. You must also repay this community by doing community service work in a soup kitchen for forty hours per week for three weeks as soon as you are released from jail. In addition, you must write a letter of apology to each and every police officer who lost an evening at home with their families because they were called to campus to deal with you spoiled, disrespectful college students.". . .

Your attorney requests that the jail sentence be suspended pending an appeal. The judge reluctantly agrees with the comment, "I don't know what you think you're going to appeal about. Your client voluntarily entered a guilty plea. I'm suspending the jail sentence only because the sheriff says there are too many other students already in jail now from the window-breaking incidents. Instead, you must start working full-time at the soup kitchen tomorrow, even as you file your appeal."

You are devastated and bewildered. "How could this happen? I thought it was just a fine. If I have to work at a soup kitchen, I'll miss all of my classes and probably fail some of them. Then my parents are going to find out. Plus, how am I going to go to jail? I'll have to drop out of school."

"I know. I know," said the attorney with a look of disgust. "I knew this judge was unreasonable, but I never thought it would turn out like this. Normally you cannot appeal a sentence just because you think it's too harsh. But we're going to appeal the sentence because the law does not give him the power to order your parents to go to counseling and all of those other details. I think the judge went beyond his authority in cooking up this sentence."

Is there any aspect of the judge's sentence that is unfair? Is any aspect of the sentence impermissible? Have any of your rights been violated by this sentence? These are questions you would want to answer if you actually found yourself facing such punishments in these circumstances.

In this chapter, we will examine sentencing and postconviction processes. The final stage of the criminal justice process involves the determination and implementation of punishment for people convicted of criminal offenses. There are also opportunities for convicted offenders to challenge the accuracy of their convictions, the proper application of court rules, and the alleged violation of constitutional rights during the investigation, prosecution, and trial processes. In examining relevant constitutional rights, our attention will be focused on the Eighth Amendment in particular. The Eighth Amendment provides the prohibitions on excessive fines and on cruel and unusual punishments. These vague rights provide the constitutional limitations on the government's ability to select and impose punishment for criminal offenders.

BACKGROUND ON THE EIGHTH AMENDMENT

The Purpose of the Limitations on Government

Many Americans often wonder why convicted criminals have any rights at all. The words of the Constitution do not differentiate between the convicted and the unconvicted in providing constitutional rights. The Eighth Amendment is written in "natural law" terms which indicate that everyone possesses certain rights against the government no matter what. The words of the Eighth Amendment do not focus on the behavior of the individual. The Amendment says, "Excessive bail shall not be required, nor excessive fines imposed, nor cruel and unusual punishments inflicted."

The Eighth Amendment focuses on the risk of the abusive application of government power against individuals. Thus, although the precise meaning of the amendment is unclear and must be interpreted by the Supreme Court, the Eighth Amendment clearly intends to place limits on what the government can do in punishing individuals, including those convicted of crimes. This approach to defining rights makes historical sense because the men who wrote the Constitution and the Bill of Rights were accustomed to being regarded as "criminals" by the British. They recognized that government authorities define who is regarded as a criminal. Because they feared that government officials may abuse this power, they created rights that would apply to protect all "criminals" and thereby prevent excessive applications of power against those who fell out of favor with the government.

When interpreting the Eighth Amendment, the Supreme Court's justices face the difficult task of giving meaning to the terms "cruel and unusual punishments" and "excessive fines." There is no definition for these words in the

Constitution. Because the language of the amendment is so ambiguous, some scholars have characterized the Eighth Amendment as constituting a grant of authority for judges to define relevant rights rather than a constitutional provision that itself tells us what rights are protected. Judges must inevitably give meaning to the Eighth Amendment.

The Meaning of Cruel and Unusual Punishment

The major case that helped to develop the definition of "cruel and unusual punishments" was *Trop v. Dulles* (1958). Trop was a native-born American citizen who served in the U.S. Army during World War II. In May 1944, he was confined to a military stockade in French Morocco for a breach of military disciplinary rules. He escaped from the stockade and was missing for less than a day when he willingly surrendered himself to the occupants of a passing Army vehicle while he was walking back toward the stockade. A general court-martial convicted Trop of desertion and sentenced him to three years' hard labor and a dishonorable discharge. After he served his sentence and the war ended, Trop applied for a passport in 1952. His application was denied because under the Nationality Act of 1940 he had lost his American citizenship by virtue of his conviction and dishonorable discharge for wartime desertion. Seven thousand other American servicemen lost their citizenship during World War II for committing the same offense. Trop challenged the forfeiture of citizenship as an unconstitutional cruel and unusual punishment.

In a 5-to-4 decision, the Supreme Court supported Trop's claim. In his plurality opinion that announced the judgment of the Court, Chief Justice Warren declared that the Eighth Amendment "must draw its meaning from the evolving standards of decency that mark the progress of a maturing society." This famous statement became the primary standard that the Supreme Court would subsequently quote and apply in Eighth Amendment cases. Except for occasional criticisms during the Rehnquist Court era by Justices Scalia and Thomas, the search for contemporary values as the means to define the Eighth Amendment has enjoyed support from both liberal and conservative justices.

The Warren Court justices formally incorporated the Eighth Amendment into the Due Process Clause of the Fourteenth Amendment in 1962. The case of *Robinson v. California* (1962) made the Eighth Amendment fully applicable against the states. As you read the Court's opinion in the accompanying box, ask yourself whether you agree with the justices' conclusion that Robinson's Eighth Amendment rights were violated.

The *Robinson* case did not merely incorporate the Eighth Amendment and apply it to the states. It also established an important principle of criminal law. People may not be subjected to criminal punishment for a status. Crime must be based on actions or failures to act when a legal duty exists. They cannot be punished for being a drug addict. They could be punished for an illegal action related to drugs, such as possession, selling, transporting, or carrying drugs. Similarly, they cannot be punished for being indigent, gay, left-handed, a member of a particular organization, or any number of other status-related categories into which people may fit. Other countries may make it a crime for someone to be a Communist or a Nazi. In the United States, by contrast, people have constitutional rights to freedom of speech and freedom of association.

| CASE | *Robinson v. California,* 370 U.S. 660 (1962) |

[California had a statute that made it a criminal offense to "be addicted to the use of narcotics." Lawrence Robinson was arrested for violating this statute after an officer examined his arm and observed scar tissue and "what appeared to be numerous needle marks and a scab which was approximately three inches below the crook of the elbow." The officer also testified that Robinson admitted that he used narcotics. After a jury convicted Robinson of the offense, he appealed unsuccessfully to the Appellate Department of the Los Angeles County Superior Court, the highest court available in California's system to hear his appeal. In the U.S. Supreme Court, Robinson's case raised the issue of whether the California statute criminalizing the status rather than the actions of narcotics addicts violated the Eighth and Fourteenth Amendments.]

JUSTICE STEWART delivered the opinion of the Court.

. . .

The broad power of a State to regulate the narcotic drugs traffic within its borders is not here in issue. . . . Such regulation, it can be assumed, could take a variety of valid forms. A State might impose criminal sanctions, for example, against the unauthorized manufacture, prescription, sale, purchase, or possession of narcotics within its borders. In the interest of discouraging the violation of such laws, or in the interest of the general health or welfare of its inhabitants, a State might establish a program of compulsory treatment for those addicted to narcotics. Such a program of treatment might require periods of involuntary confinement. And penal sanctions might be imposed for failure to comply with established compulsory procedures. . . . Or a state might choose to attack the evils of narcotics traffic on broader fronts also—through public health education, for example, or by efforts to ameliorate the economic and social conditions under which those evils might be thought to flourish. In short, the range of valid choices which a State might make in this area is undoubtedly a wide one, and the wisdom of any particular choice within the allowable spectrum is not for us to decide. Upon that premise we turn to the California law in issue here.

It would be possible to construe the statute under which the appellant was convicted as one which is operative only upon proof of the actual use of narcotics. But the California courts have not so construed this law. Although there was evidence in the present case that the appellant had used narcotics in Los Angeles, the jury were instructed that they could convict him even if they disbelieved that evidence. The appellant could be convicted, they were told, if they found simply that the appellant's "status" or "chronic condition" was that of being "addicted to the use of narcotics." And it is impossible to know from the jury's verdict that the defendant was not convicted upon precisely such a finding. . . .

The statute, therefore, is not one which punishes a person for the use of narcotics, for their purchase, sale or possession, or for antisocial or disorderly behavior resulting from their administration. It is not a law which even purports to provide or require medical treatment. Rather we deal with a statute which makes the "status" of narcotics addiction a criminal offense, for which the offender may be prosecuted "at any time before he reforms." California has said that a person can be continuously guilty of this offense, whether or not he has ever used or possessed any narcotics within the State, and whether or not he has been guilty of any antisocial behavior there.

It is unlikely that any State at this moment in history would attempt to make it a criminal offense for a person to be mentally ill, or a leper, or to be afflicted with a venereal disease. A State might determine that the general health and welfare require that the victims of these and other human afflictions be dealt with by compulsory treatment, involving quarantine, confinement, or sequestration. But, in the light of contemporary human knowledge, a law which made a criminal offense of such disease would doubtless be universally thought to be an infliction of cruel and unusual punishment in violation of the Eighth and Fourteenth Amendments. See *Louisiana ex rel. Francis v. Resweber* [1947]. . . .

We cannot but consider the statute before us as of the same category. In this Court counsel for the State recognized that narcotic addiction is an illness. Indeed, it is apparently an illness which may be contracted innocently or involuntarily. We hold that a state law which imprisons a person thus afflicted as a criminal, even though he had never touched any narcotic drug within the State or been guilty of any irregular behavior there, inflicts a cruel and unusual

(continued)

punishment in violation of the Fourteenth Amendment. To be sure, imprisonment for ninety days is not, in the abstract, a punishment which is either cruel or unusual. But the question cannot be considered in the abstract. Even one day in prison would be a cruel and unusual punishment for the "crime" of having a common cold.

We are not unmindful that the vicious evils of the narcotics traffic have occasioned the grave concern of government. There are, as we have said, countless fronts on which those evils may be legitimately attacked. We deal in this case only with an individual provision of a particularized local law as it has so far been interpreted by the California courts. Reversed.

JUSTICE DOUGLAS, concurring.

While I join the Court's opinion, I wish to make more explicit the reasons why I think it is "cruel and unusual" punishment in the sense of the Eighth Amendment to treat as a criminal a person who is a drug addict. . . .

The impact that an addict has on a community causes alarm and often leads to punitive measures. Those measures are justified when they relate to acts of transgression. But I do not see how under our system *being an addict* can be punished as a crime.

If addicts can be punished for their addiction, then the insane can also be punished for their insanity. Each has a disease and each must be treated as a sick person. . . .

The addict is a sick person. He may, of course, be confined for treatment or for the protection of society. Cruel and unusual punishment results not from confinement, but from convicting the addict of a crime. . . . A prosecution for addiction, with its resulting stigma and irreparable damage to the good name of the accused, cannot be justified as a means of protecting society, where civil commitment would do as well. . . . We would forget the teachings of the Eighth Amendment if we allowed sickness to be made a crime and permitted sick people to be punished for being sick. This age of enlightenment cannot tolerate such barbarous action.

JUSTICE HARLAN, concurring.

I am not prepared to hold that on the present state of medical knowledge it is completely irrational and hence unconstitutional for a State to conclude that narcotics addiction is something other than an illness, nor that it amounts to cruel and unusual punishment for the State to subject narcotics addicts to its criminal law. . . . But in this case the trial court's instructions permitted the jury to find the appellant guilty on no more proof than that he was present in California while he was addicted to narcotics. Since

They are permitted to express and believe in ideas, no matter how misguided or hurtful. If they act on ideas by attacking people or burning buildings, then they can be prosecuted and punished for their actions. American crimes must focus on illegal actions or conspiracies, not on categories of people.

THE SENTENCING PROCESS

After a defendant's guilty plea has been accepted or a guilty verdict has been produced at trial, the judge must determine the punishment to be imposed. The extent of judges' discretion in formulating sentences is going to be determined by the criminal statutes enacted by a state legislature or, for federal judges, Congress. Historically, some legislatures gave judges broad authority to determine sentences. A statute could, for example, declare that robberies are to be punished by sentences ranging from one year to fifty years of imprisonment. Within those broad limits, the trial judge in each case could determine what—in the judge's view—constituted an appropriate sentence for that offender. Some of these sentencing schemes rested, in part, on a belief that of-addiction alone cannot reasonably be thought to amount to more than a compelling propensity to use narcotics, the effect of this instruction was to authorize criminal punishment for a bare desire to commit a criminal act.

If the California statute reaches this type of conduct, and for present purposes we must accept the trial court's construction as binding, . . . it is an arbitrary imposition which exceeds the power that a State may exercise in enacting its criminal law. Accordingly, I agree that the application of the California statute was unconstitutional in this case and join the judgment of reversal.

JUSTICE CLARK, dissenting.

. . .

The majority strikes down the conviction primarily on the grounds that the petitioner was denied due process by the imposition of criminal penalties for nothing more than being in a status. This viewpoint is premised upon the theme that [the California statute] is a "criminal" provision authorizing a punishment, for the majority admits that "a State might establish a program of compulsory treatment for those addicted to narcotics" which "might require periods of involuntary confinement." I submit that California has done exactly that. The majority's error is in instructing the California Legislature that hospitalization is the *only treatment* for narcotics

addiction—that anything less is a punishment denying due process. California has found otherwise after a study which I suggest was more extensive than that conducted by the Court. . . . The test is the overall purpose and effect of a State's act, and I submit that California's program relative to narcotic addicts—including both the "criminal" and "civil" provisions—is inherently one of treatment and lies well within the power of a State. . . .

JUSTICE WHITE, dissenting.

. . .

Finally, I deem this application of "cruel and unusual punishment" so novel that I suspect the Court was hard put to find a way to ascribe to the Framers of the Constitution the result reached today rather than to its own notions of ordered liberty. If this case involved economic regulation, the present Court's allergy to substantive due process would surely save the statute and prevent the Court from imposing its own philosophical predilections upon state legislatures or Congress. I fail to see why the Court deems it more appropriate to write into the Constitution its own abstract notions of how best to handle the narcotics problem, for it obviously cannot match either the States or Congress in expert understanding.

I respectfully dissent.

fenders could be rehabilitated if given an appropriate sentence and monitored for improved behavior. The use of broad judicial discretion in sentencing created many concerns. Similarly-situated offenders who had committed identical offenses could receive significantly different sentences. In some jurisdictions, it appeared that defendants who were poor or members of minority groups received harsher sentences than defendants with other demographic characteristics. In addition, some critics believed that judges used their discretion to be too lenient on offenders who deserved longer prison terms.

Sentencing Reform

As a means to seek greater equality in sentencing and to demonstrate to voters that legislators are "tough on crime," many legislatures rewrote their sentencing statutes to reduce judges' discretion. In addition, public faith in rehabilitation waned and legislators placed greater emphasis on retribution and incapacitation as the goals of punishment. This reduction in judicial discretion took two forms. If the legislature was primarily concerned that judicial discretion led to leniency, then the legislators might enact sentencing statutes with tougher mandatory minimum sentences. Judges might retain discretion about how long a prison sentence would be, but they could not impose a sentence less than the significant minimum sentence determined by the legislature.

Another common approach to sentencing reform was the legislative creation of **sentencing guidelines.** Under such sentencing schemes, judges merely identify each offender's "score," a point system typically determined by the severity of the current offense, the offender's prior criminal record, and any prior probation or parole violations. After the point total is determined, the judge looks at a grid that provides the sentence range for offenders with a particular score. The grid may require a sentence ranging between eight and ten years of imprisonment for robbery, so the judge has relatively little flexibility in determining the sentence. Sentencing guidelines are intended to create greater equity in sentencing, but they can also advance punitive goals if the sentence ranges are set at higher levels than those previously applied by judges for similar offenses.

The creation of legislative sentencing reforms intended to equalize and increase sentences does not prevent actors in the justice system from affecting the punishments ultimately imposed. During plea negotiations, prosecutors and defense attorneys can determine sentences by **charge bargaining.** A prosecutor will agree to reduce the number or severity of charges in exchange for a guilty plea because both sides know exactly what sentence will be dictated by the sentencing-guidelines grid. A defendant may plead guilty to an offense that is slightly different from the act actually committed because the attorneys for both sides agree that the sentencing-guidelines sentence for the actual offense is too severe. Thus a prosecutor can, in effect, show leniency toward first offenders or young offenders in the same way that judges previously used sentencing discretion to produce such results.

The Presentence Report

In determining sentences, judges rely heavily on the **presentence report** that is typically prepared by a probation officer who works for the court. The probation officer is the official who actually gathers the information about prior offenses and adds the points to create the sentence score. The judge probably will check to see that the points have been added correctly, but most judges have no time to check on the accuracy of the numbers supplied by the probation officer that provide the basis for the score. It is not unusual for presentence reports to contain inaccuracies, especially for offenders who have been arrested many times. Charges are dismissed for a variety of reasons, including witnesses' unwillingness to cooperate or a prosecutor's determination that police actions were improper in making the arrest. However, in reading an offender's file, it may not always be clear which arrests were dismissed and which arrests led to convictions, especially if there are numerous minor charges for which small fines were imposed as the sentences. A probation officer may erroneously count an arrest as a conviction or mistakenly omit a conviction from an offender's sentence score. Depending on the current charge for which the defendant was convicted, the addition or omission of a point may change a sentence by several years.

In addition, the probation officer includes personal information about the defendant in the presentence report. The report often describes the offender's employment history, child support obligations, education, substance abuse record, and family history. The judge may use these factors to determine whether to set the sentence near the top or the bottom of the permitted range. A defendant with a good employment history and strong family support may be viewed as more deserving of a lesser sentence because of a presumed greater likelihood of successfully reforming his or her life.

Finally, the presentence report also typically contains a recommendation from the probation officer. The officer's values and conclusions about the offender are reflected in these recommendations. Because these recommendations reflect the probation officer's discretionary judgments, there are risks that any biases possessed by the officer will be reflected in the recommendation. Judges in some courts are strongly inclined to accept probation officers' recommendations, either because they have great faith in the probation officer or because they have such heavy caseloads that they have little time and opportunity to make their own considered judgments.

The defense attorney bears significant responsibilities in the sentencing process. She or he must attempt to ensure that the presentence report is accurate with respect to the offender's score. The attorney should also see whether the background information on the offender is accurate. A conscientious attorney will also evaluate the tone and basis for the probation officer's recommendations. At sentencing, the attorney's job is to make arguments on the defendant's behalf that might lead the judge to impose a sentence at the lower end of the mandated sentence range. Often, this advocacy requires gathering additional information about the defendant and the defendant's family situation. The attorney may, for example, have the defendant tested in order to let the court know about psychological or other problems that may have affected the defendant's behavior. Although the code of professional responsibility that governs attorneys' behavior requires them to be zealous advocates on behalf of their clients' interests, not all defense attorneys are competent, committed, or ethical. Appellate courts have been presented with many appeals based on defense attorneys' inaction during the sentencing process. Attorneys have failed to note errors in their clients' presentence reports or failed to make available arguments in favor of less severe sentences. One of the worst-case examples of such failures emerged in November 2000 when a defense attorney in North Carolina admitted that he had intentionally sabotaged his client's death penalty case by failing to file the proper legal papers in a timely manner because he disliked his client and thought the client deserved to die.[1] As in other stages of the criminal justice process, the officials who make discretionary decisions in each case shape the defendant's ultimate fate and determine whether the defendant receives the full protection of constitutional rights.

PERMISSIBLE PUNISHMENTS

It would be possible to have a criminal justice system in which the government has unlimited authority to punish criminal behavior. In such a system, a person who violates society's rules may forfeit any right to complain about how the government responds to the violation. Under the American constitutional democracy, however, people who commit crimes are entitled to legal protections because of the nation's historical skepticism about the risks of excessive governmental power. The Eighth Amendment is the primary provision that judges use to determine if specific punishments are permissible. The Eighth Amendment, however, does not provide the only limits on retributive actions by government. The Due Process Clauses of the Fifth and Fourteenth Amendments, for example, prevent government officials from imposing punishment on people who have not been convicted of crimes through the proper procedures of the criminal justice system. If a local sheriff tried to lock someone in jail indefinitely without following proper court procedures, the sheriff would be susceptible to a lawsuit for violating the person's right to due process of law as well as Fourth Amendment protection against unreasonable seizures.

Disproportionate Sentences

Prior to the twentieth century, the Supreme Court interpreted the Eighth Amendment prohibition on cruel and unusual punishments as preventing only torturous punishments. The Court permitted the states and Congress to have freedom in defining the severity of punishments for each criminal offense as long as the punishment did not amount to a form of torture. Thus, for example, only three dissenting justices expressed concern in 1892 about a defendant who faced fifty-four years in prison because he was unable to pay a $6,600 fine for selling liquor illegally (*O'Neil v. Vermont*). In *Weems v. United States* (1910), the Court's view of the Eighth Amendment shifted and the justices declared that the prohibition against cruel and unusual punishments barred disproportionate punishments as well as torturous punishments. In *Weems* a minor government official had been sentenced to twelve years at hard labor in ankle chains and a loss of citizenship rights for making two false entries in government payroll records. The Court found his punishment to be unconstitutionally disproportionate because the sentence was more severe than that applied to people convicted of robbery and other more serious crimes.

The words of the Eighth Amendment do not provide any guidance on how to determine whether a criminal sentence is disproportionate to the crime. It appears that proportionality is purely a matter of whether a majority of justices regard a sentence to be so excessive as to be "cruel and unusual." Recall that Chapter 1 presented the case of *Rummel v. Estelle* (1980) in which Texas was permitted to impose a sentence of life imprisonment on a man who was convicted of three theft offenses over a nine-year period in which he stole a total of $229.11. Although the dissenters regarded the punishment as disproportionate to the crimes, the Supreme Court majority indicated that it wanted to give states freedom to determine for themselves the most appropriate sentences for criminal offenders.

In 1983 the Supreme Court revisited the proportionality issue with respect to noncapital sentences (*Solem v. Helm,* 1983). Helm was sentenced to life imprisonment without possibility of parole when he was convicted of issuing a "no account" check for $100. His sentence was based on South Dakota's habitual offender statute because during the preceding fifteen years Helm had been convicted six times of burglary, grand larceny, and driving while intoxicated. Unlike the *Rummel* case three years earlier, *Solem* produced a 5-to-4 decision invalidating Helm's sentence. Justice Powell's majority opinion clearly stated that the Eighth Amendment's prohibition on cruel and unusual punishments "prohibits not only barbaric punishments, but also sentences that are disproportionate to the crime committed" (463 U.S. at 284) and that this disproportionality principle is applicable to noncapital cases. The majority did not overturn the previous decision in *Rummel,* but distinguished *Solem* by observing that Rummel was eligible for parole consideration after serving twelve years in prison in Texas. By contrast, under South Dakota's law, Helm was ineligible for parole. Although the possibility existed that Helm could have his sentence commuted by the governor, the majority viewed commutation as much more difficult to attain than parole.

The decisions in *Rummel v. Estelle* and *Solem v. Helm* do not provide clear guidance for legislatures and judges about how to determine if a sentence will be considered unconstitutionally disproportionate. The endorsement of life sentences for habitual offenders in *Rummel* provides endorsement for the policies in states that have "three-strikes laws" in which repeat offenders face the possibility of life sentences.

However, the Court's opposition to life-without-possibility-of-parole sentences for nonviolent repeat offenders in *Solem v. Helm* creates the possibility that judges may scrutinize habitual offender statutes that do not leave open the hypothetical possibility of eventual release. Because many states have made it increasingly difficult for offenders to gain release on parole, it appears that the Court is willing to accept the fact that some nonviolent habitual offenders may, in fact, live out their days in prison if their hypothetical opportunity for parole is never realized.

The Supreme Court's disagreements about the Eighth Amendment's proportionality issue were illustrated in a 1991 case examining Michigan's toughest-in-nation punishments for possessing quantities of cocaine. Under Michigan's law, which has since been softened through decisions by the Michigan Supreme Court and the state legislature, there was a mandatory sentence of life without possibility of parole for a first offender (or anyone else) convicted of possessing more than 650 grams of cocaine. The sentence was more severe than that imposed by Michigan on murderers and other offenders who commit acts of violence. Because Michigan does not have the death penalty, the mandatory life sentence was the stiffest possible sentence in Michigan's criminal justice system. As you read the Court's opinion in the box on pp. 382–384, ask yourself whether you agree with Justice Scalia's view on the Eighth Amendment's applicability to claims about disproportionate punishments.

Portions of Scalia's opinion advocated complete abandonment of any proportionality principle for noncapital cases, but only Chief Justice Rehnquist joined those sections of Scalia's opinion. According to Scalia, because punishments must be cruel and unusual in order to violate the Eighth Amendment, the justices should dispense with considering whether any noncapital punishment is cruel and focus their attention on whether or not these punishments are unusual. Thus Scalia concluded that "[s]evere, mandatory penalties may be cruel, but they are not unusual in the constitutional sense, having been employed in various forms throughout our Nation's history." Taken to its logical conclusion, Scalia's reasoning might render the Eighth Amendment meaningless as a limitation on government officials. In Scalia's eyes, if government officials choose to impose a punishment that has been used previously in Anglo-American history, it is apparently, therefore, not unusual and thus constitutionally acceptable. Scalia's reasoning contradicted his published speech

Harmelin v. Michigan, 501 U.S. 957 (1991)

[*Harmelin was convicted of possessing 672 grams of cocaine and was sentenced to a mandatory term of life imprisonment without possibility of parole pursuant to a Michigan statute requiring such sentences for persons convicted of possessing more than 650 grams of cocaine. The severe mandatory punishment applied even to first-time offenders. Harmelin claimed that his sentence was cruel and unusual because it was disproportionate to the crime and because the mandatory sentence did not permit the judge to take into account the particularized circumstances of the crime.*]

JUSTICE SCALIA announced the judgment of the Court and delivered the opinion of the Court with respect to Part V, and an opinion with respect to Parts I, II, III, and IV, in which CHIEF JUSTICE REHNQUIST joins.

I

. . .

. . . *Solem v. Helm*, 463 U.S. 277 . . . (1983), set aside under the Eighth Amendment, because it was disproportionate, a sentence of life imprisonment without possibility of parole, imposed under a South Dakota recidivist statute for successive offenses that included three convictions of third-degree burglary, one of obtaining money by false pretenses, one of grand larceny, one of third-offense driving while intoxicated, and one of writing a "no account" check with intent to defraud. . . .

. . . [O]ur 5–4 decision eight years ago in *Solem* was scarcely the expression of clear and well accepted constitutional law. We have long recognized, of course, that the doctrine of *stare decisis* is less rigid in its application to constitutional precedents . . . , and we think that to be especially true of a constitutional precedent that is both recent and in apparent tension with other decisions. Accordingly, we have addressed anew, and in greater detail, the question whether the Eighth Amendment contains a proportionality guarantee. . . . We conclude from this examination that *Solem* was wrong; the Eighth Amendment contains no proportionality guarantee. . . .

In sum, we think it most unlikely that the English Cruel and Unusual Punishments Clause [which served as the foundation for the Clause incorpor-ated into the American Bill of Rights] was meant to forbid "disproportionate" punishments. There is even less likelihood that proportionality of punishment was one of the traditional "rights and privileges of Englishmen" apart from the Declaration of Rights which happened to be included in the Eighth Amendment. Indeed, even those scholars who believe the [proportionality] principle to have been included within the Declaration of Rights do not contend that such a prohibition was reflected in English practice—nor could they. . . . [I]n 1791, England punished over 200 crimes with death. . . .

The Eighth Amendment received little attention during the proposal and adoption of the Federal Bill of Rights. However, what evidence exists from debates at the state ratifying conventions that prompted the Bill of Rights as well as the Floor debates in the First Congress which proposed it "confirm[s] the view that the cruel and unusual punishments clause was directed at prohibiting certain *methods* of punishment." . . .

We think it is enough that those who framed and approved the Federal Constitution chose, for whatever reason, not to include within it the guarantee against disproportionate sentences that some State Constitutions contained. It is worth noting, however, that there was good reason for that choice—a reason that reinforces the necessity of overruling *Solem*. While there are relatively clear historical guidelines and accepted practices that enable judges to determine which *modes* of punishment are "cruel and unusual," *proportionality* does not lend itself to such analysis. Neither Congress nor any state legislature has ever set out with the objective of crafting a penalty that is "disproportionate," yet as some of the examples . . . indicate, many enacted dispositions seem to be [disproportionate]—because they were made for other times or other places, with different social attitudes, different criminal epidemics, different public fears, and different prevailing theories of penology. This is not to say that there are no absolutes; one can imagine extreme examples that no rational person, in no time or place, could accept. But for the same reason these examples are easy to decide, they are certain never to occur. . . .

The first holding of this Court unqualifiedly applying a requirement of proportionality to criminal penalties was issued 185 years after the Eighth

Amendment was adopted. In *Coker v. Georgia* [1977], the Court held that, because of the disproportionality, it was a violation of the Cruel and Unusual Punishments Clause to impose capital punishment for rape of an adult woman. Four years later, in *Enmund v. Florida* . . . (1982), we held that it violates the Eighth Amendment, because of disproportionality, to impose the death penalty upon a participant in a felony that results in murder, without any inquiry into the participant's intent to kill. *Rummel* . . . treated this line of authority as an aspect of our death penalty jurisprudence, rather than a generalizable aspect of Eighth Amendment law. We think that is an accurate explanation, and we reassert it. Proportionality review is one of several respects on which we have held that "death is different," and have imposed protections that the Constitution nowhere else provides. . . . We would leave it there, but will not extend it further. . . .

V

. . . [Petitioner] apparently contends that the Eighth Amendment requires Michigan to create a sentencing scheme whereby life in prison without possibility of parole is simply the most severe of a range of available penalties that the sentencer may impose after hearing evidence in mitigation and aggravation.

As our earlier discussion should make clear, this claim has no support in the text and history of the Eighth Amendment. Severe, mandatory penalties may be cruel, but they are not unusual in the constitutional sense, having been employed in various forms throughout our Nation's history. As noted earlier, mandatory death sentences abounded in our first Penal Code. They were also common in the several States—both at the time of the founding and throughout the 19th century. . . . There can be no serious contention, then, that a sentence which is not otherwise cruel and unusual becomes so simply because it is "mandatory." . . .

Our cases creating and clarifying the "individualized capital sentencing doctrine" have repeatedly suggested that there is no comparable requirement outside the capital context, because of the qualitative difference between death and all other penalties. . . .

JUSTICE KENNEDY, with whom JUSTICE O'CONNOR and JUSTICE SOUTER join, concurring in part and concurring in the judgment.

. . . Regardless of whether Justice SCALIA or the dissent has the best of the historical argument . . . , *stare decisis* counsels our adherence to the narrow proportionality principle that has existed in our Eighth Amendment jurisprudence for 80 years. Although our proportionality decisions have not been clear or consistent in all respects, they can be reconciled, and they require us to uphold petitioner's sentence.

Our decisions recognize that the Cruel and Unusual Punishments Clause encompasses a narrow proportionality principle. We first interpreted the Eighth Amendment to prohibit "'greatly disproportioned'" sentences in *Weems v. United States* . . . (1910), quoting *O'Neil v. Vermont* . . . (1892), (Field, J., dissenting). Since *Weems,* we have applied the principle in different Eighth Amendment contexts. Its most extensive application has been in death penalty cases. . . .

The Eighth Amendment proportionality principle also applies to noncapital sentences. In *Rummel v. Estelle* . . . (1980), we acknowledged the existence of the proportionality rule for both capital and noncapital cases, . . . but we refused to strike down a sentence of life imprisonment, with possibility of parole, for recidivism based on three underlying felonies. . . .

All of [the relevant] principles—the primacy of the legislature, the variety of legitimate penological schemes, the nature of our federal system, and the requirement that proportionality review be guided by objective factors—inform the final one: the Eighth Amendment does not require strict proportionality between crime and sentence. Rather, it forbids only extreme sentences that are "grossly disproportionate" to the crime. . . .

A penalty as severe and unforgiving as the one imposed here would make this a most difficult and troubling case for any judicial officer. Reasonable minds may differ about the efficacy of Michigan's sentencing scheme, and it is far from certain that Michigan's bold experiment [in applying harsh sentences] will succeed [in reducing drug trafficking]. The accounts of pickpockets at Tyburn hangings [in England] are a reminder of the limits of the law's deterrent force, but we cannot say the law before us has no chance of success and is on that account so disproportionate as to be cruel and unusual punishment. The dangers flowing from drug offenses and the circumstances of the crime committed here

(continued)

demonstrate that the Michigan penalty does not surpass constitutional bounds. . . .

JUSTICE WHITE, with whom JUSTICE BLACK-MUN and JUSTICE STEVENS join, dissenting.

. . .

The language of the [Eighth] Amendment does not refer to proportionality in so many words, but it does forbid "excessive" fines, a restraint that suggests that a determination of excessiveness should be based at least in part on whether the fine imposed is disproportionate to the crime committed. Nor would it be unreasonable to conclude that it would be both cruel and unusual to punish overtime parking by life imprisonment . . . , or, more generally, to impose any punishment that is grossly disproportionate to the offense for which the defendant has been convicted. . . .

. . . Justice SCALIA argues that all of the available evidence of the day indicated that those who drafted and approved the Amendment "chose . . . not to include within it the guarantee against disproportionate sentences that some State Constitutions contained." . . . Even if one were to accept the argument that the First Congress did not have in mind the proportionality issue, the evidence would hardly be strong enough to come close to proving an affirmative decision against the proportionality component. Had there been an intention to exclude it from the reach of the words that otherwise could reasonably be construed to include it, perhaps as plain-speaking Americans, the Members of the First Congress would have said so. And who can say with confidence what the members of the state ratifying conventions had in mind when they voted in favor of the Amendment? . . .

. . . The Court's capital punishment cases requiring proportionality reject Justice SCALIA's notion that the Amendment bars only cruel and unusual modes or methods of punishment. Under that view, capital punishment—a mode of punishment—would either be completely barred or left to the discretion of the legislature. Yet neither is true. The death penalty is appropriate in some cases and not in others. The same should be true of punishment by imprisonment. . . .

[C]ontrary to Justice SCALIA's suggestion, . . . the fact that a punishment has been legislatively

mandated does not automatically render it "legal" or "usual" in the constitutional sense. Indeed, . . . if this were the case, then the prohibition against cruel and unusual punishments would be devoid of any meaning. . . .

The first *Solem* factor requires a reviewing court to assess the gravity of the penalty. . . .

Mere possession of drugs—even in such large quantity—is not so serious an offense that it will always warrant, much less mandate, life imprisonment without possibility of parole. . . .

The second prong of the *Solem* analysis is an examination of "the sentences imposed on other criminals in the same jurisdiction." . . . [T]here is no death penalty in Michigan; consequently, life without parole, the punishment mandated here, is the harshest punishment available. . . . Crimes directed against the persons and property of others—such as second-degree murder, . . . rape, . . . and armed robbery, . . . do not carry such a harsh mandatory sentence, although they do provide for the possibility of a life sentence in the exercise of judicial discretion. It is clear that petitioner "has been treated in the same manner as, or more severely than, criminals who have committed far more serious crimes." . . .

The third factor set forth in *Solem* examines "the sentences imposed for commission of the same crime in other jurisdictions." . . . No other jurisdiction imposes a punishment nearly as severe as Michigan's for possession of the amount of drugs at issue here. Of the remaining 49 States, only Alabama provides for a mandatory sentence of life imprisonment without possibility of parole for a first-time drug offender, and then only when a defendant possesses *ten kilograms* or more of cocaine. . . . Possession of the amount at issue here would subject an Alabama defendant to a mandatory minimum sentence of only five years in prison. . . .

Application of *Solem*'s proportionality analysis leaves no doubt that the Michigan statute at issue fails constitutional muster. The statutorily mandated penalty of life without possibility of parole for possession of narcotics is unconstitutionally disproportionate in that it violates the Eighth Amendment's prohibition against cruel and unusual punishment. . . .

[The separate dissenting opinions of Justice Marshall and Justice Stevens are omitted.]

expressing opposition to the reintroduction of public flogging as a constitutional means of criminal punishment.[2]

Justices Kennedy, O'Connor, and Souter supported Michigan's statute, and they joined only the final section of Scalia's opinion, which declined to invalidate the statute. However, they also advocated maintaining a proportionality principle within the Eighth Amendment for noncapital cases. In dissent, Justice White found Scalia's ideas sufficiently disturbing that he implicitly raised the possibility in his opinion that Scalia's reasoning could lead to the judicial endorsement of life imprisonment as a punishment for parking tickets. In sum, although the majority of justices regard the Eighth Amendment as prohibiting disproportionate punishments, it remains unclear how a legislature or judge would know when a sentence is constitutionally excessive.

Excessive Fines

The Eighth Amendment prohibits "excessive fines" as criminal punishments, but the Court never provided an example of a constitutionally excessive fine until the very end of the twentieth century. Notice that the Excessive Fines Clause of the Eighth Amendment is separate from the Cruel and Unusual Punishments Clause. Thus the excessiveness of a fine need not depend on whether the Court concludes that the fine is disproportionate, cruel, or unusual. The Court could simply establish standards for what constitutes excessiveness or, more accurately, determine on a case-by-case basis that specific fines violate some not-clearly-defined boundary between permissible and excessive fines.

During the 1980s and 90s, law enforcement officials began to expand the use of **forfeiture** as a means to combat drug trafficking and other criminal enterprises. Statutes permitted the government to seize property and cash used in or gained from criminal activities. Under some laws, the government did not even have to prove beyond a reasonable doubt that the person was guilty of a crime or that the particular property was related to criminal activities. There were highly publicized cases of grandmothers losing their homes because they did not realize that one of their grandchildren was using the home to sell marijuana. As a result of these cases and other instances in which critics believed law enforcement authorities had moved too aggressively to seize property, Congress and various courts acted to require law enforcement officials to fulfill higher standards of proof to initiate the forfeiture of property. Two Supreme Court decisions warned law enforcement officials that property forfeitures could be subject to the limitations imposed by the Excessive Fines Clause of the Eighth Amendment. In *Austin v. United States* (1993), the Court said it might be an unconstitutionally excessive fine when officials seized an offender's mobile home and auto body shop after he was convicted of possessing a small amount of cocaine. *Alexander v. United States* (1993) concerned the forfeiture of a bookstore and millions of dollars in assets after a conviction for racketeering and selling pornographic materials. In both cases, the Supreme Court instructed lower courts to consider whether the Eighth Amendment was violated by these property forfeitures. In 1998 the Supreme Court finally addressed an excessive fines issue for itself. As you read the Court's opinion in *United States v. Bajakajian* (1998), see if you can identify a test that enables you to know when a fine is unconstitutionally "excessive."

United States v. Bajakajian, 524 U.S. 321 (1998)

[*A law enforcement dog trained to sniff for cash in suitcases indicated to officers that the defendant's suitcase contained money as the defendant prepared to board an international flight at a Los Angeles airport. The defendant was informed that federal law requires travelers to make a report to the government if they are carrying more than $10,000 in cash out of the country. The defendant denied that he had more than $10,000 in the suitcase. The defendant's luggage was searched and officers found $357,144 in cash. When the defendant pleaded guilty to the failure-to-report offense, a judge followed the federal statute in ordering the defendant to forfeit all of the cash in the luggage.*]

JUSTICE THOMAS delivered the opinion of the Court.

. . .

III

Because the forfeiture of respondent's currency constitutes punishment and is thus a "fine" within the meaning of the Excessive Fines Clause, we now turn to the question of whether it is "excessive."

A

The touchstone of the constitutional inquiry under the Excessive Fines Clause is the principle of proportionality: The amount of the forfeiture must bear some relationship to the gravity of the offense that it is designed to punish. . . . Until today, however, we have not articulated a standard for determining whether a punitive forfeiture is unconstitutionally excessive. We now hold that a punitive forfeiture violates the Excessive Fines Clause if it is grossly disproportional to the gravity of the defendant's offense.

The text and history of the Excessive Fines Clause demonstrate the centrality of proportionality to the excessiveness inquiry; nonetheless, they provide little guidance as to how disproportional a punitive forfeiture must be to the gravity of an offense in order to be "excessive." Excessive means surpassing the usual, the proper, or a normal measure of proportion [citing dictionary entries]. . . . The constitutional question that we address, however, is just how proportional to a criminal offense a fine must be, and the text of the Excessive Fines Clause does not answer it.

Nor does history. The Clause was little discussed in the First Congress and the debates over the ratification of the Bill of Rights. As we have previously noted, the Clause was taken verbatim from the English Bill of Rights of 1689. . . . That document's prohibition on excessive fines was a reaction to the abuses of the King's judges during the reigns of the Stuarts, . . . but the fines that those judges imposed were described contemporaneously only in the most general terms. . . . Similarly, Magna Charta—which the Stuart judges were accused of subverting—required only that amercements (the medieval predecessor of fines) should be apportioned to the offense and that they should not deprive a wrongdoer of his livelihood. . . .

None of these sources suggest how disproportional to the gravity of the offense a fine must be in order to be deemed constitutionally excessive.

We must therefore rely on other considerations in deriving a constitutional excessiveness standard, and there are two that we find particularly relevant. The first, which we have emphasized in our cases interpreting the Cruel and Unusual Punishments Clause, is that judgments about the appropriate punishment for an offense belong in the first instance to the legislature. . . . The second is that any judicial determination regarding the gravity of a particular criminal offense will be inherently imprecise. Both of these principles counsel against requiring strict proportionality between the amount of a punitive forfeiture and the gravity of a criminal offense, and we therefore adopt the standard of gross disproportionality articulated in our Cruel and Unusual Punishments precedents. . . .

In applying this standard, the district courts in the first instance, and the courts of appeals, reviewing the proportionality determination *de novo,* must compare the amount of the forfeiture to the gravity of the defendant's offense. If the amount of the forfeiture is grossly disproportionate to the gravity of the defendant's offense, it is unconstitutional.

B

Under this standard, the forfeiture of respondent's entire $357,144 would violate the Excessive Fines Clause. Respondent's crime was solely a reporting offense. It was permissible to transport the currency out of the country so long as he reported it. Section

982 (a) (1) [of the relevant federal statute] orders currency to be forfeited for a "willful" violation of the reporting requirement. Thus, the essence of the respondent's crime is a willful failure to report the removal of currency from the United States. Furthermore, as the District Court found, respondent's violation was unrelated to any illegal activities. The money was proceeds of legal activity and was to be used to repay a lawful debt. Whatever his other vices, respondent does not fit the class of persons for whom the statute was principally designed: He is not a money launderer, a drug trafficker, or a tax evader. . . . And under the [federal] Sentencing Guidelines, the maximum sentence that could have been imposed on respondent was six months, while the maximum fine was $5,500. . . . Such penalties confirm a minimal level of culpability.

The harm that respondent caused was also minimal. Failure to report his currency affected one party, the Government, and in a relatively minor way. There was no fraud on the United States, and respondent caused no loss to the public fisc. Had his crime gone undetected, the Government would have been deprived of only information that $357,144 had left the country. The Government and the dissent contend that there is a correlation between the amount forfeited and the harm that the Government would have suffered had the crime gone undetected. . . . We disagree. There is no inherent proportionality in such a forfeiture. It is impossible to conclude, for example, that the harm respondent caused is anywhere near 30 times greater than that caused by a hypothetical drug dealer who willfully fails to report taking $12,000 out of the country in order to purchase drugs.

Comparing the gravity of respondent's crime with the $357,144 forfeiture the Government seeks, we conclude that such a forfeiture would be grossly disproportional to the gravity of the offense. It is larger than the $5,000 fine imposed by the District Court by many orders of magnitude, and it bears no articulable correlation to any injury suffered by the Government.

C

Finally, we must reject the contention that proportionality of full forfeiture is demonstrated by the fact that the First Congress enacted statutes requiring full forfeiture of goods involved in customs offenses or the payment of monetary penalties proportioned to the goods' value. It is argued that the enactment of these statutes at roughly the same time as the Eighth Amendment was ratified suggests that full forfeiture, in the customs context at least, is a proportional punishment. The early customs statutes, however, do not support such a conclusion because, unlike [section] 982(a)(1), the type of forfeiture that they imposed was not considered punishment for a criminal offense. . . .

JUSTICE KENNEDY, with whom The CHIEF JUSTICE [REHNQUIST], JUSTICE O'CONNOR, and JUSTICE SCALIA join, dissenting.

For the first time in history, the Court strikes down a fine as excessive under the Eighth Amendment. The decision is disturbing both for its specific holding and for the broader upheaval it foreshadows. At issue is a fine Congress fixed in the amount of the currency respondent sought to smuggle or to transport without reporting. If a fine calibrated with this accuracy fails the Court's test, its decision portends serious disruption of a vast range of statutory fines. The Court all but says the offense is not serious anyway. This disdain for the statute is wrong as an empirical matter and disrespectful of the separation of powers. The irony of the case is that, in the end, it may stand for narrowing of constitutional protection rather than enhancing it. To make its rationale work, the Court appears to remove important classes of fines from any excessiveness inquiry at all. This, too, is unsound; and with all respect, I dissent. . . .

II

. . .

Money launderers will rejoice to know they face forfeitures of less than 5% of the money transported, provided they hire accomplished liars [who will claim that the money was acquired legally] to carry their money for them. Five percent, of course, is not much of deterrent or punishment; it is comparable to the fee one might pay for a mortgage lender or broker. . . .

III

The Court's holding may in the long run undermine the purposes of the Excessive Fines Clause. One of the main purposes of the ban on excessive fines [in England] was to prevent the King from assessing unpayable fines to keep his enemies in debtor's prison. . . . Concern with imprisonment may explain why the Excessive Fines Clause is coupled with, and follows right after, the Excessive Bail Clause. While

(continued)

the concern is not implicated here—for of necessity the money is there to satisfy the forfeiture—the Court's restrictive approach could subvert this purpose. Under the Court's holding, legislators may rely on mandatory prison sentences in lieu of fines. Drug lords will be heartened by this, knowing the prison terms will fall upon their couriers while leaving their own wallets untouched.

At the very least, today's decision will encourage legislatures to take advantage of another avenue the majority leaves open. The majority subjects this for-feiture to scrutiny because it is *in personam*, but it then suggests most *in rem* forfeitures (and perhaps most civil forfeitures) may not be fines at all. . . . The suggestion, one might note, is inconsistent or at least in tension with *Austin v. United States*, 509 U.S. 602 (1993). In any event, these remarks may encourage a legislative shift from *in personam* to *in rem* forfeitures, avoiding *mens rea* as a predicate and giving owners fewer procedural protections. By invoking the Excessive Fines Clause with excessive zeal, the majority may in the long run encourage Congress to circumvent it. . . .

The Court's decision in *Bajakajian* established that there are actual limits to the government's ability to levy fines. Prior to the Court's decision, the limits were purely hypothetical because the Court had never actually declared that any fine was unconstitutionally excessive. The *Austin* and *Alexander* decisions in 1993 had merely said that forfeitures *could* violate the Excessive Fines Clause. The Court had not actually used the Eighth Amendment to overrule any financial punishments imposed as part of a criminal sentence. Although the *Bajakajian* decision demonstrated that the Court was willing to draw a line between permissible and excessive fines, the case did not define where the line sits. Moreover, the justices were so deeply divided that it is uncertain if the Court will find any fines to be excessive in the future, especially if any members of the majority retire from the Court. In essence, legislatures and trial judges have been warned that some financial sanctions may be unconstitutional, but they still retain significant freedom to impose fines as they see fit.

Double Jeopardy and *Ex Post Facto* Limitations

In addition to the Eighth Amendment, other constitutional provisions provide important potential limitations on governmental efforts to punish criminal offenders. One is the Double Jeopardy Clause of the Fifth Amendment. Punishing someone twice for the same offense is considered as much of a violation of double jeopardy as improperly placing the person on trial twice for the same offense in the same jurisdiction. Another is the **Ex Post Facto Clause,** which forbids the government from creating rules that impose punishments *after* the person already committed the acts for which the punishment is applied. Under American criminal law, crimes and punishments must be defined prospectively. The legislature cannot punish someone for a past act that was not illegal or otherwise covered by punitive laws at the time it occurred. Similarly, legislatures and judges cannot change someone's sentence by creating new rules that were not in existence at the time the sentence was determined and imposed.

In the earlier chapter on the Fifth Amendment, we examined the Supreme Court's complicated interpretation of the Double Jeopardy Clause of the Fifth Amendment. Contrary to popular understandings of the prohibition on multiple trials, the Court interpreted the clause narrowly to permit subsequent trials for the same criminal acts when the later trials occur in different jurisdictions or focus on criminal charges for which different elements of the crime must be proven. The right against double jeopardy is also relevant to sentencing because the Court has determined that people cannot be punished a second time for the same offense. Although this principle of the Double Jeopardy Clause may sound straightforward, in fact courts must evaluate individual situations to determine whether a second punishment has actually been imposed. Some kinds of burdens and deprivations imposed on criminal offenders are not regarded by the Supreme Court as "punishment," and therefore they do not trigger double jeopardy protections even when they are applied in addition to a criminal sentence of imprisonment. For example, in *United States v. Ursery* (1996), the Court found no double jeopardy violation when a man was sentenced to prison for growing marijuana after already having paid $13,000 to the government to settle a civil forfeiture action through which the government sought to seize his house. Ursery argued that the financial penalty constituted punishment for his crime and thereby precluded the government from later pursuing his imprisonment through a criminal prosecution. The Supreme Court disagreed and declared that such forfeiture actions do not constitute punishment that would trigger double jeopardy protection in criminal cases.

In 1997 the Supreme Court faced a more controversial double jeopardy claim because it involved continued deprivation of liberty after the completion of a criminal sentence for sex offenses. The case posing the double jeopardy claim also raised the issue of an *Ex Post Facto* Clause violation because the offender claimed that the state created and imposed new punishments after the criminal acts had already occurred. As you read the Court's opinion in *Kansas v. Hendricks* (1997) on pp. 390–393, consider whether you agree with the justices' reasoning and conclusions.

The *Hendricks* case is important because it represents an expansion of social control that raises questions about traditional principles within American criminal justice. To what extent is the government genuinely interested in providing meaningful treatment, or is the purpose really selective incapacitation—namely, the detention of people whom society fears because of their past behavior? Would the Supreme Court permit the government to expand indefinite detention to other repeat offenders whom we fear? For example, would the logic of *Hendricks* apply to people who repeatedly commit burglaries, robberies, or drug offenses and therefore arguably need treatment to keep them from endangering society?

As with the issues of excessive fines and disproportionate punishments, the Court was deeply divided. A slim majority of justices saw the state's actions as advancing the goal of treating mental illnesses. By contrast, other justices put greater emphasis on the deprivation of liberty and lack of evidence that Kansas genuinely regarded medical treatment as the primary purpose for the act. Because of the justices' disagreements about permissible punishments, there is a strong possibility that future cases concerning these issues may reach different conclusions as the Court's composition changes. In the 2001–2002 term, the Supreme Court endorsed the new argument that the Due Process Clause requires the state to prove that a sexually violent predator "cannot control" his criminal sexual behavior before he can be civilly committed for residential treatment (*Kansas v. Crane*, 2002).

Kansas v. Hendricks, 521 U.S. 346 (1997)

[Kansas enacted the Sexually Violent Predator Act, which mandated indefinite confinement in mental institutions for individuals who, due to "mental abnormality" or a "personality disorder," are likely to engage in "predatory acts of sexual violence." The civil commitment statute targeted several categories of sex offenders: those scheduled to be released from prison; those found incompetent to stand trial on criminal charges; those who have been found not guilty by reason of insanity; and those found not guilty because of a mental disease or defect. Kansas sought to commit Hendricks, a man with a forty-year record of sexually molesting children, immediately upon his completion of a prison term. Hendricks claimed that the state's action violated double jeopardy by punishing him again after he had served a complete prison sentence. He also claimed an ex post facto *violation because the new law was imposing punishment for acts that he committed before the new law was enacted.]*

JUSTICE THOMAS delivered the opinion of the Court.

. . .

We granted Hendricks' cross petition to determine whether the Act violates the Constitution's double jeopardy prohibition or its ban on *ex post facto* lawmaking. The thrust of Hendricks' argument is that the Act establishes criminal proceedings; hence confinement under it necessarily constitutes punishment. He contends that where, as here, newly enacted "punishment" is predicated upon past conduct for which he has already been convicted and forced to serve a prison sentence, the Constitution's Double Jeopardy and *Ex Post Facto* Clauses are violated. We are unpersuaded by Hendricks' argument that Kansas has established criminal proceedings.

The categorization of a particular proceeding as civil or criminal "is first of all a question of statutory construction." . . . We must initially ascertain whether the legislature meant the statute to establish "civil" proceedings. If so, we ordinarily defer to the legislature's stated intent. Here, Kansas' objective to create a civil proceeding is evidenced by its placement of the Sexually Violent Predator Act within the Kansas probate code, instead of the criminal code, as well as its description of the Act as creating

a *"civil commitment procedure."* . . . Nothing on the face of the statute suggests that the legislature sought to create anything other than a civil commitment scheme designed to protect the public from harm.

. . . [W]e will reject the legislature's manifest intent only where a party challenging the statute provides "the clearest proof" that "the statutory scheme [is] so punitive either in purpose or effect as to negate [the State's] intention" to deem it "civil." . . . In those limited circumstances, we will consider the statute to have established criminal proceedings for constitutional purposes. Hendricks, however, has failed to satisfy this heavy burden.

As a threshold matter, commitment under the Act does not implicate either of the two primary objectives of criminal punishment: retribution or deterrence. The Act's purpose is not retributive because it does not affix culpability for prior criminal conduct. Instead, such conduct is used solely for evidentiary purposes, either to demonstrate that a "mental abnormality" exists or to support a finding of future dangerousness. . . .

Hendricks focuses on his confinement's potentially indefinite duration as evidence of the State's punitive intent. That focus, however, is misplaced. Far from any punitive objective, the confinement's duration is instead linked to the stated purposes of the commitment, namely, to hold the person until his mental abnormality no longer causes him to be a threat to others. . . .

Finally, Hendricks argues that the Act is necessarily punitive because it fails to offer any legitimate "treatment." Without such treatment, Hendricks asserts, confinement under the Act amounts to little more than disguised punishment. Hendricks' argument assumes that treatment for his condition is available but that the State has failed (or refused) to provide it. . . .

. . . Even if we accept . . . that the provision of treatment was not the Kansas Legislature's "overriding" or "primary" purpose in passing the Act, this does not rule out the possibility that an ancillary purpose of the Act was to provide treatment, and it does not require us to conclude that the Act is punitive. Indeed, critical language in the Act itself demonstrates that the Secretary of Social and Rehabilitation Services, under whose custody sexually violent predators are committed, has an obligation to provide treatment to individuals like Hendricks. . . .

Although the treatment program initially offered to Hendricks may have seemed somewhat meager, it must be remembered that he was the first person committed under the Act. That the State did not have all of its treatment procedures in place is thus not surprising. . . . [B]efore this Court, Kansas declared "[a]bsolutely" that persons committed under the Act are now receiving in the neighborhood of "31.5 hours of treatment per week." . . .

Where the State has "disavowed any punitive intent"; limited confinement to a small segment of particularly dangerous individuals; provided strict procedural safeguards; directed that confined persons be segregated from the general prison population and afforded the same status as others who have been civilly committed; recommended treatment if such is possible; and permitted immediate release upon a showing that the individual is no longer dangerous or mentally impaired, we cannot say that it acted with punitive intent. We therefore hold that the Act does not establish criminal proceedings and that involuntary confinement pursuant to the Act is not punitive. Our conclusion that the Act is nonpunitive thus removes an essential prerequisite for both Hendricks' double jeopardy and *ex post facto* claims. . . .

We hold that the Kansas Sexually Violent Predator Act comports with due process requirements and neither runs afoul of double jeopardy principles nor constitutes an exercise in impermissible *ex post facto* lawmaking. Accordingly, the judgment of the Kansas Supreme Court is reversed.
It is so ordered.

JUSTICE KENNEDY, concurring.

. . .

Notwithstanding its civil attributes, the practical effect of the Kansas law may be to impose confinement for life. At this stage of medical knowledge, although future treatments cannot be predicted, psychiatrists or other professionals engaged in treating pedophilia may be reluctant to find measurable success in treatment even after a long period and may be unable to predict that no serious danger will come from release of the detainee.

A common response to this may be, "A life term is exactly what the sentence should have been anyway," or, in the words of a Kansas task force member, "So be it." . . . The point, however, is not how

long Hendricks and others like him should serve a criminal sentence. With his criminal record, after all, a life term may well have been the only sentence appropriate to protect society and vindicate the wrong. The concern instead is whether it is the criminal system or the civil system which should make the decision in the first place. If the civil system is used simply to impose punishment after the State makes an improvident plea bargain on the criminal side, then it is not performing its proper function. These concerns persist whether the civil confinement statute is put on the books before or after the offense. We should bear in mind that while incapacitation is a goal common to both the criminal and civil systems of confinement, retribution and general deterrence are reserved for the criminal system alone.

On the record before us, the Kansas civil statute conforms to our precedents. If, however, civil confinement were to become a mechanism for retribution or general deterrence, or if it were shown that mental abnormality is too imprecise a category to offer a solid basis for concluding that civil detention is justified, our precedents would not suffice to validate it.

JUSTICE BREYER, with whom JUSTICES STEVENS and SOUTER join, and with whom JUSTICE GINSBURG joins as to Parts II and III, dissenting.

. . .

Kansas' 1994 Act violates the Federal Constitution's prohibition of "any . . . *ex post facto* Law" if it "inflicts" upon Hendricks "a greater punishment" than did the law "annexed to" his "crime[s]" when he "committed" those crimes in 1984. . . . The majority agrees that the Clause "'forbids the application of any *new punitive measure* to a crime already consummated.'" . . . But it finds the Act is not "punitive." With respect to that basic question, I disagree with the majority.

Certain resemblances between the Act's "civil commitment" and traditional criminal punishments are obvious. Like criminal imprisonment, the Act's civil commitment amounts to "secure" confinement, . . . and "incarceration against one's will." . . .

Moreover, the Act, like criminal punishment, imposes its confinement (or sanction) only upon an individual who has previously committed a criminal offense. . . .

(continued)

In this circumstance, with important features of the Act pointing in opposite directions [in light of its stated "civil" intentions but characteristics that look like punishment], I would place particular importance upon those features that would likely distinguish between a basically punitive and a basically nonpunitive purpose. . . . [F]or reasons that I will point out, when a State believes that treatment does exist, and then couples that admission with a legislatively required delay of such treatment until a person is at the end of a jail term (so that further incapacitation is therefore necessary), such a legislative scheme begins to look punitive. . . .

Several important treatment related factors . . . in this case suggest [that there is a punitive rather than civil purpose]. First, the State Supreme Court here . . . has held that treatment is not a significant objective of the Act. The Kansas court wrote that the Act's purpose is "segregation of sexually violent offenders," with "treatment" a matter that was "incidental at best." . . .

We have generally given considerable weight to the findings of state and lower federal courts regarding the intent or purpose underlying state officials' actions. . . .

The record provides support for the Kansas court's conclusion. The court found that, as of the time of Hendricks' commitment, the State had not funded treatment, it had not entered into treatment contracts, and it had little, if any, qualified treatment staff. . . . Hendricks, according to the commitment program's own director, was receiving "essentially no treatment." . . .

It is not surprising that some of the Act's official supporters had seen in it an opportunity permanently to confine dangerous sex offenders. . . .

Second, the Kansas statute insofar as it applies to previously convicted offenders, such as Hendricks, commits, confines, and treats those offenders *after* they have served virtually their entire criminal sentence. That time related circumstance seems deliberate. . . . But why, one might ask, does the Act not commit and require treatment of sex offenders sooner, say soon after they begin to serve their sentences?

. . . [I]t is difficult to see why rational legislators who seek treatment would write the Act in this way—providing treatment years after the criminal act that indicated its necessity. . . . And it is particularly difficult to see why legislators who specifically wrote into the statute a finding that "prognosis for rehabilitating . . . in a prison setting is poor" would leave an offender in that setting for months or years before beginning treatment. This is to say, the timing provisions of the statute confirm the Kansas Supreme Court's view that treatment was not a particularly important legislative objective.

Third, the statute, at least as of the time Kansas applied it to Hendricks, did not require the commit-

---

CAPITAL PUNISHMENT

Reform of Procedures

The federal government and thirty-eight states provide for the possibility of capital punishment as sanction for the most serious offenses. Although capital punishment was used frequently in American history, it fell into disfavor among industrialized democracies around the world during the 1960s. Capital punishment was abolished in Canada and the countries of western Europe. Public opinion in the United States began to turn against capital punishment and the Supreme Court began to examine aspects of the issue. In *Furman v. Georgia* (1972), a slim majority of Supreme Court justices declared that capital punishment as applied in the United States violated the Constitution. Two justices, William Brennan and Thurgood Marshall, clearly believed that capital punishment was inconsistent with contemporary values and the Constitution's ideal of advancing the protection of human rights and dignity. They applied the Court's flexible approach to the Cruel and Unusual Punishments Clause established in *Trop v. Dulles* (1958) in order to conclude that capital punishment was out of step with contemporary values. By contrast, other justing authority to consider the possibility of using less restrictive alternatives, such as postrelease supervision, halfway houses, or other methods that *amici* supporting Kansas here have mentioned. . . .

This Court has said that a failure to consider, or to use, "alternative and less harsh methods" to achieve a nonpunitive objective can help to show that legislature's "purpose . . . was to punish." . . .

Fourth, . . . I have found 17 States with laws that seek to protect the public from mentally abnormal, sexually dangerous individuals through civil commitment or other mandatory treatment programs. Ten of those statutes, unlike the Kansas statute, begin treatment of an offender soon after he has been apprehended and charged with a serious sex offense. Only seven, like Kansas, delay "civil" commitment (and treatment) until the offender has served his criminal sentence (and this figure includes the Acts of Minnesota and New Jersey, both of which generally do not delay treatment). Of these seven, however, six (unlike Kansas) require consideration of less restrictive alternatives. . . . Only one State other than Kansas, namely Iowa, both delays civil commitment (and consequent treatment) and does not explicitly consider less restrictive alternatives. But the law of [Iowa] applies prospectively only [considering those committing offenses after July 1, 1997], thereby avoiding *ex post facto* problems. . . .

To find a violation of [the *Ex Post Facto*] Clause here, however, is not to hold that the Clause prevents Kansas, or other States, from enacting dangerous sexual offender statutes. A statute that operates prospectively, for example, does not offend the *Ex Post Facto* Clause. . . . Neither does it offend the *Ex Post Facto* Clause for a State to sentence offenders to the fully authorized sentence, to seek consecutive, rather than concurrent, sentences, or to invoke recidivism statutes to lengthen imprisonment. Moreover, a statute that operates retroactively, like Kansas' statute, nonetheless does not offend the Clause *if the confinement that it imposes is not punishment*—if, that is to say, the legislature does not simply add a later criminal punishment to an earlier one.

The statutory provisions before us do amount to punishment primarily because, as I have said, the legislature did not tailor the statute to fit the non-punitive civil aim of treatment, which it concedes exists in Hendricks' case. The Clause in these circumstances does not stand as an obstacle to achieving important protections for the public's safety; rather, it provides an assurance that, where so significant a restriction of an individual's basic freedoms is at issue, a State cannot cut corners. Rather, the legislature must hew to the Constitution's liberty protecting line. . . .

I therefore would affirm the judgment below.

tices saw capital punishment processes as violating the right to due process because the ultimate criminal sanction was applied so inconsistently that some murderers were sentenced to death, but others were not. These justices judged the death penalty to be excessively unfair because it was applied in such a random and capricious manner. The dissenting justices argued that capital punishment and the processes used to impose it were consistent with the Constitution and did not violate any rights.

Justice William O. Douglas did not explicitly oppose the death penalty as an inherent violation of the Eighth Amendment. His opinion focused on the unconstitutionally "cruel and unusual" nature of death sentences that are imposed in a discriminatory manner against the poor and minorities because decision makers have too much discretion. Many observers believe that he would have eventually endorsed the position held by Brennan and Marshall if he had remained on the Court past 1975 and thus participated in more post-*Furman* death penalty cases.

Furman ended the death penalty, but only temporarily. The remaining two justices in the majority (White and Stewart) believed that the death penalty violated the Constitution only in the way that it was being applied. They did not rule out the possibility that new sentencing procedures designed to reduce the capriciousness of capital punishment would correct the constitutional flaws in the application of the death penalty. State legislatures responded by enacting new laws that would provide guidelines to enable prosecutors, judges, and juries to make more consistent decisions about the death penalty. In the new procedures, states sought mechanisms to guide the discretion of judges and juries in deciding who would receive the death penalty. Many states created **bifurcated proceedings** in which a first trial was held to determine if the defendant was guilty and a second proceeding focused exclusively on the issue of punishment. The idea was to focus the judges' and juries' attention specifically on the issue of whether the defendant should live or die in order to avoid the risk that decisions on punishment were lumped together with the decisions about guilt. The laws sought to force judges and juries to make specific considered judgments about whether capital punishment should be imposed. In order to focus attention on the sentencing decisions, states also required judges and juries to identify aggravating factors that made the crime especially brutal or heinous and thus deserving of the death penalty. States also required consideration of mitigating factors, such as a perpetrator's youthful age or difficult family life, that made the offender less worthy of receiving a death sentence. Other states sought to make the death penalty mandatory for specific crimes in order to avoid capriciousness in the judges' and juries' discretionary sentencing decisions.

The Supreme Court examined these new death penalty statutes in a series of cases in 1976. The lead case, *Gregg v. Georgia* (1976), considered Georgia's new capital sentencing procedures. As you read the Court's opinion in *Gregg,* ask yourself whether the new procedures will solve the risks and problems identified by the Supreme Court in *Furman v. Georgia* (1972).

According to the Court's decision in *Gregg,* the new procedures cured the defects that led a majority of justices to halt executions in the *Furman* decision. The bifurcated proceedings served to provide a sufficient focus for the judges' and juries' decisions so that a majority of justices were reassured that the death penalty would no longer be imposed in an unfair and random manner. In 2002, the Supreme Court forced several states to reexamine their capital sentencing procedures by requiring that juries make findings about the existence of aggravating factors that trigger the imposition of the death penalty (*Ring v. Arizona,* 2002). Previously, some states permitted judges to identify the existence of aggravating factors.

At the same time that the Court reactivated the death penalty with the *Gregg* decision, slim majorities on the Court struck down laws that mandated the death penalty for specific crimes (*Roberts v. Louisiana,* 1976; *Woodson v. North Carolina,* 1976). A majority of justices believed that each capital case deserved individualized attention and a careful decision by the judge and jury. The justices saw mandatory sentences as preventing thorough consideration of each case on its own merits. Thus the Court approved bifurcated proceedings that focused the judges' and juries' attention on mitigating and aggravating factors. Mandatory sentences sought to avoid capriciousness by eliminating discretion, but the Court's decisions indicated that discretion should be guided and channeled rather than eliminated.

| C A S E | *Gregg v. Georgia*, 428 U.S. 153 (1976) |

[*In the aftermath of* Furman v. Georgia, *Georgia and other states enacted new capital punishment statutes. Georgia's statute mandated new procedures: a bifurcated trial with a separate sentencing hearing after a determination of guilt; the consideration of aggravating and mitigating factors during the sentencing phase; the requirement of finding beyond a reasonable doubt of the existence of at least one of ten specified aggravating factors before a death sentence may be imposed; and automatic appellate review by the state supreme court. Troy Gregg was convicted of armed robbery and murder after he and a companion killed the men who gave them a ride when they were hitchhiking. Gregg challenged the imposition of the death penalty as a violation of the Eighth Amendment's prohibition on cruel and unusual punishments.*]

JUSTICE STEWART announced the judgment of the Court and an opinion joined by JUSTICES POWELL and STEVENS.

The issue in this case is whether the imposition of the sentence of death for the crime of murder under the law of Georgia violates the Eighth and Fourteenth Amendments. . . .

. . . [Under the Georgia statute,] [t]he capital defendant's guilt or innocence is determined in the traditional manner, either by a trial judge or a jury, in the first stage of a bifurcated trial.

. . . After a verdict, finding, or plea of guilty to a capital crime, a presentence hearing is conducted before whoever made the determination of guilt. The sentencing procedures are essentially the same in both bench and jury trials. At the hearing:

"The judge [or jury] shall hear additional evidence in extenuation, mitigation, and aggravation of punishment, including the record of any prior criminal convictions and pleas of guilty or pleas of nolo contendere of the defendant, or the absence of any prior conviction and pleas: Provided, however, that only such evidence in aggravation as the State has made known to the defendant prior to his trial shall be admissible. The judge [or jury] shall also hear argument by the defendant or his counsel and the prosecuting attorney . . . regarding the punishment to be imposed."

The defendant is accorded substantial latitude as to the types of evidence that he may introduce. . . .

. . . Before a convicted defendant may be sentenced to death, however, except in cases of treason or aircraft hijacking, the jury, or the trial judge in cases tried without a jury, must find beyond a reasonable doubt one of the 10 aggravating circumstances specified in the statute. The sentence of death may be imposed only if the jury (or judge) finds one of the statutory aggravating circumstances and then elects to impose that sentence. . . .

. . . [In *Furman*,] [f]our Justices would have held that capital punishment is not unconstitutional *per se*; two Justices would have reached the opposite conclusion; and three Justices, while agreeing that the statutes then before the Court were invalid as applied, left open the question whether such punishment may ever be imposed. We now hold that the punishment of death does not invariably violate the Constitution. . . .

In assessing a punishment selected by a democratically elected legislature against the constitutional measure, we presume [the statute's] validity. We may not require the legislature to select the least severe penalty possible so long as the penalty selected is not cruelly inhumane or disproportionate to the crime involved. And a heavy burden rests on those who would attack the judgment of the representatives of the people. . . .

The imposition of the death penalty for the crime of murder has a long history of acceptance both in the United States and in England. . . . It is apparent from the text of the Constitution itself that the existence of capital punishment was accepted by the Framers. . . . For nearly two centuries, this Court, repeatedly and often expressly, has recognized that capital punishment is not invalid *per se*. . . .

The petitioners in the capital cases before the Court today renew the "standards of decency" argument, but developments during the four years since *Furman* have undercut substantially the assumptions upon which their argument rested. Despite the continuing debate, dating back to the 19th century, over the morality and utility of capital punishment, it is now evident that a large proportion of American society continues to regard it as an appropriate and necessary criminal sanction.

The most marked indication of society's endorsement of the death penalty for murder is the legislative response to *Furman*. The legislatures of 35 States have enacted new statutes that provide for the death

(continued)

penalty for at least some crimes that result in the death of another person. . . .

The concerns expressed in *Furman* that the penalty of death not be imposed in an arbitrary or capricious manner can be met by a carefully drafted statute that ensures that the sentencing authority is given adequate information and guidance. As a general proposition these concerns are best met by a system that provides for a bifurcated proceeding at which the sentencing authority is apprised of the information relevant to the imposition of sentence and provided with standards to guide its use of the information. . . .

In short, Georgia's new sentencing procedures require as a prerequisite to the imposition of the death penalty, specific jury findings as to the circumstances of the crime or the character of the defendant. Moreover, to guard further against a situation comparable to that presented in *Furman*, the Supreme Court of Georgia compares each death sentence with the sentences imposed on similarly situated defendants to ensure that the sentence of death in a particular case is not disproportionate. On their face these procedures seem to satisfy the concerns of *Furman*. . . .

The basic concern of *Furman* centered on those defendants who were being condemned to death capriciously and arbitrarily. Under the procedures before the Court in that case, sentencing authorities were not directed to give attention to the nature or circumstances of the crime committed or to the character or record of the defendant. Left unguided, juries imposed the death sentence in a way that could only be called freakish. The new Georgia sentencing procedures, by contrast, focus the jury's attention on the particularized nature of the crime and the particularized characteristics of the individual defendant. While the jury is permitted to consider any aggravating or mitigating circumstances, it must

find and identify at least one statutory aggravating factor before it may impose a penalty of death. In this way the jury's discretion is channeled. No longer can a jury wantonly and freakishly impose the death sentence; it is always circumscribed by the legislative guidelines. In addition, the review function of the Supreme Court of Georgia affords additional assurance that the concerns that prompted our decision in *Furman* are not present to any significant degree in the Georgia procedure applied here.

For the reasons expressed in this opinion, we hold that the statutory system under which Gregg was sentenced to death does not violate the Constitution. Accordingly, the judgment of the Georgia Supreme Court is affirmed.

JUSTICE WHITE, with whom CHIEF JUSTICE BURGER and JUSTICE REHNQUIST join, concurring in the judgment.

. . .

Petitioner's argument that prosecutors behave in a standardless fashion in deciding which cases to try as capital felonies is unsupported by any facts. Petitioner simply asserts that since prosecutors have the power not to charge capital felonies they will exercise that power in a standardless fashion. This is untenable. Absent facts to the contrary it cannot be assumed that prosecutors will be motivated in their charging decision by factors other than the strength of the case and the likelihood that a jury would impose the death penalty if it convicts. . . .

Petitioner's argument that there is an unconstitutional amount of discretion in the system which separates those suspects who receive the death penalty from those who receive life imprisonment, a lesser penalty or are acquitted or never charged seems to be in the final analysis an indictment of our entire system of justice. Petitioner has argued in effect that

Capital Punishment in Specific Circumstances

In a series of subsequent decisions, the Supreme Court imposed further limits on capital punishment. Historically, capital punishment for rape had been applied to African American defendants in southern states in a grossly disproportionate and discriminatory manner. It was relatively rare for a white defendant to receive the death penalty for rape, yet hundreds of African Americans were sentenced to death row and executed for this crime. In 1977 the Supreme Court decided by a 7-to-2 vote that capital punishment could not be imposed for the crime of rape (*Coker v. Georgia*, 1977). The Court later added

no matter how effective the death penalty may be as a punishment, government, created and run as it must be by humans, is inevitably incompetent to administer it. This cannot be accepted as a proposition of constitutional law. Imposition of the death penalty is surely an awesome responsibility for any system of justice and those who participate in it. Mistakes will be made and discriminations will occur which will be difficult to explain. However, one of society's most basic tasks is that of protecting the lives of its citizens and one of the most basic ways in which it achieves the tasks is through criminal laws against murder. I decline to interfere with the manner in which Georgia has chosen to enforce such laws on what is simply an assertion of lack of faith in the ability of the system of justice to operate in a fundamentally fair manner. . . .

[The statement of Chief Justice Burger and the concurring opinion of Justice Blackmun are omitted.]

JUSTICE BRENNAN, dissenting.

. . .

The fatal constitutional infirmity in the punishment of death is that it treats "members of the human race as nonhumans, as objects to be toyed with and discarded. [It is] thus inconsistent with the fundamental premise of the [Cruel and Unusual Punishments] Clause that even the vilest criminal remains a human being possessed of common human dignity" [quoting his own opinion in *Furman*]. . . . As such it is a penalty that "subjects the individual to a fate forbidden by the principle of civilized treatment guaranteed by the [Eighth Amendment]." I therefore would hold on that ground alone, that death is today a cruel and unusual punishment prohibited by the Clause. "Justice of this kind is obviously no less shocking than the crime itself, and the new 'official' murder, far from offering redress for the offense committed against society, adds instead a second defilement to the first." . . .

JUSTICE MARSHALL, dissenting.

. . .

Since the decision in *Furman,* the legislatures of 35 States have enacted new statutes authorizing the imposition of the death sentence for certain crimes, and Congress has enacted a law providing for the death penalty for air piracy resulting in death. . . . I would be less than candid if I did not acknowledge that these developments have a significant bearing on a realistic assessment of the moral acceptability of the death penalty to the American people. But if the constitutionality of the death penalty turns, as I have urged, on the opinion of an *informed* citizenry, then even the enactment of new death statutes cannot be viewed as conclusive. In *Furman,* I observed that the American people are largely unaware of the information critical to a judgment on the morality of the death penalty, and concluded that if they were better informed they would consider it shocking, unjust, and unacceptable. . . . A recent study, conducted after the enactment of the post-*Furman* statutes, has confirmed that the American people know little about the death penalty, and that the opinions of an informed public would differ significantly from those of a public unaware of the consequences and effects of the death penalty [citing Sarat and Vidmar, "Public Opinion, the Death Penalty, and the Eighth Amendment: Testing the Marshall Hypothesis," *Wisconsin Law Review* (1976): 171]. . . .

The death penalty, unnecessary to promote the goal of deterrence or to further any legitimate notion of retribution, is an excessive penalty forbidden by the Eighth and Fourteenth Amendments. I respectfully dissent from the Court's judgment upholding the sentences of death imposed upon the petitioners in these cases.

a further limitation to capital punishment by ruling 5-to-4 that insane prisoners could not be executed (*Ford v. Wainwright,* 1986). Defendants who are determined to be legally insane at the time of the crime can successfully be acquitted by reason of insanity, and those who are determined to be insane at the time of trial may be found not competent to stand trial. This decision applied to a prisoner who had become insane while awaiting execution on death row. In practice, however, many people with serious mental problems have been executed. The *Ford v. Wainwright* decision has not been applied rigorously to other cases by either the Supreme Court or lower courts.

In other cases defining the permissible circumstances of capital punishment, the Court decided that teenagers may receive the death penalty for any capital offenses committed at age sixteen and above (*Stanford v. Kentucky,* 1989). The death penalty may no longer be applied to mentally retarded defendants. In 2002 the Court reversed its prior precedents and declared that the execution of mentally retarded defendants violates the Eighth Amendment prohibition on cruel and unusual punishments (*Atkins v. Virginia,* 2002). In a 6-to-3 decision, the Court found that such executions violate the Eighth Amendment standards established in *Trop v. Dulles* (1958) because they are inconsistent with society's evolving values. As evidence of contemporary societal values, the Court noted that legislatures in many death penalty states had enacted statutes prohibiting the application of capital punishment to mentally retarded defendants.

In 1982 the Court applied the proportionality principle to a capital case by finding that a felony-murder accomplice who did not participate in the killing and did not intend for a life to be taken could not be sentenced to death (*Enmund v. Florida,* 1982). Enmund was convicted of driving the getaway car after two of his associates shot and killed an elderly couple during a robbery. In a 5-to-4 decision, Justice White's majority opinion concluded that the offender's punishment must be tailored to fit his personal responsibility and moral guilt. Thus, Enmund could be punished for his participation in the fatal robbery that came under the felony-murder law but could not be executed for a killing that he did not commit and did not intend to commit.

Although the *Enmund* decision appeared to stand for the principle that the death penalty was an excessively disproportionate punishment for accomplices who do not participate in the actual murder, the Supreme Court later refined its decision to permit the execution of some accomplices. In *Tison v. Arizona* (1987), the Supreme Court examined the case of two teenage boys who helped their family smuggle guns into an Arizona prison in order to free their father, a convicted murderer. The boys joined their father, an older brother, and their father's convicted-murderer cellmate in fleeing from the prison. The father and his cellmate eventually executed four Good Samaritans who had stopped to help with the escapees' broken down car. In a 5-to-4 decision, the Court declared that accomplices who do not plan or participate in a killing may receive the death penalty if they demonstrate "reckless indifference to human life" as participants in a felony-murder. Although the decision purported to make only a modest clarification of *Enmund*'s meaning, the opinion virtually nullified *Enmund* without formally overruling it. The *Enmund* decision had established a bright-line rule for the death penalty by stating that only those who plan or participate in a killing can receive the death penalty as felony-murder accomplices. In the aftermath of *Tison,* however, capital punishment decisions concerning accomplices became determined by the discretion of prosecutors and jurors. Prosecutors use their discretion to seek a death sentence for some felony-murder accomplices, but not to seek it for others. Jurors use their discretion to find some murders so despicable that they place the label of "reckless indifference" on accomplices who did not participate directly in the killings and thereby make those accomplices eligible for execution. By increasing the role of discretion in death penalty cases, the *Tison* decision increased the risk that prosecutors' and jurors' biases will determine capital cases and thereby reduce the consistency and fairness that the Supreme Court sought to advance in *Gregg v. Georgia.*

Although *Gregg* endorsed the constitutionality of the death penalty, new legal challenges arose regarding specific aspects of capital punishment. One of the most important cases concerned evidence that the imposition of the death penalty may be infused with racial discrimination in violation of the Equal Protection Clause of the Fourteenth Amendment. In *McCleskey v. Kemp* (1987), the Supreme Court examined statistical evidence showing that the race of the murder victim and the race of the defendant influenced the determination of which killers would be sentenced to death in Georgia. As you read the Court's opinion in the box on pp. 400–404, ask yourself whether the decision adequately fulfills the purposes of the Fourteenth Amendment's Equal Protection Clause.

By a narrow vote, the Court rejected the use of statistical evidence to show systemic racial discrimination in capital sentencing. In order to raise an equal protection claim, the majority required that defendants show evidence of discrimination in their own cases. What sort of evidence could this be? Unless the prosecutor or judge made an openly prejudicial statement, it is difficult to see how a defendant could demonstrate the existence of discrimination. If no such statement was made, does that mean that the decision was not affected by racial discrimination? No. We must remember that the ultimate decision to impose a death sentence is the product of cumulative decisions. The prosecutor must identify the individual cases in which the death penalty will be pursued. This is a discretionary decision that may be influenced by various factors. When former football star O. J. Simpson faced double murder charges, the prosecutor declined to seek the death penalty, despite the grisly nature of the stabbings, because he feared that some jurors might be reluctant to convict the handsome, popular athlete and actor if they thought he might be executed. In that case, Simpson's status as a celebrity helped him avoid the possibility of a death sentence. By contrast, most murder defendants have no status or fame to help them. Moreover, there is a risk that prosecutors may subconsciously weigh the "value" of the victim in determining when to seek the death penalty. A prosecutor may view a murder as more horrible if the victim is prominent, popular, or even white without even realizing that these factors are affecting the decision about what punishment to seek.

The defense attorney makes discretionary decisions in the course of preparing and presenting the defense. If the attorney is unprepared, inexperienced, or uncaring, these decisions might not be strategically sound and thus the defense attorney's performance may increase the likelihood of a death sentence. This risk is greatest when the defendant is indigent and must rely on whatever attorney the state provides. Unfortunately, investigations have revealed a number of instances in which inadequate defense representation contributed to the imposition of the death penalty.[3] Could an attorney's biases affect his or her effort in mounting a defense? It is possible that the attorney's view of the client could be affected by prejudicial attitudes.

Similarly, the judge and the jury must make judgments, and those judgments may be affected by biases that influence which defendants they view as most threatening or which victims they view as most deserving of sympathy. Thus racial attitudes can affect these cumulative discretionary decisions without any overt expression at trial. The impact of these biases may be detectable throughout a state's criminal justice system through the use of sophisticated statistical analysis, but the Supreme Court majority was unwilling to accept such evidence.

McCleskey v. Kemp, 481 U.S. 279 (1987)

[*McCleskey, an African American defendant, was convicted of shooting and killing a white police officer in the course of robbing a furniture store along with several accomplices. McCleskey challenged his death sentence by using a sophisticated social science study that indicated that defendants, especially African American defendants, convicted of killing white victims were much more likely to be sentenced to death than defendants convicted of killing black victims. He sought to invalidate his death sentence by claiming that racial discrimination was pervasive in Georgia's system for determining which defendants would receive capital punishment.*]

JUSTICE POWELL delivered the opinion of the Court.

This case presents the question whether a complex statistical study that indicates a risk that racial considerations enter into capital sentencing determinations proves that petitioner McCleskey's capital sentence is unconstitutional under the Eighth or Fourteenth Amendment.

McCleskey, a black man, was convicted of two counts of armed robbery and one count of murder in the Superior Court of Fulton County, Georgia, on October 12, 1978. . . . During the course of [a furniture store] robbery, a police officer, answering a silent alarm, entered the store through the front door. As he was walking down the center aisle of the store, two shots were fired. Both struck the officer. One hit him in the face and killed him.

Several weeks later, McCleskey was arrested in connection with an unrelated offense. He confessed that he participated in the furniture store robbery, but denied that he had shot the police officer. At trial, the State introduced evidence that at least one of the bullets that struck the officer was fired from a .38 caliber Rossi revolver. This description matched the description of the gun that McCleskey had carried during the robbery. The State also introduced the testimony of two witnesses who had heard McCleskey admit to the shooting.

The jury convicted McCleskey of murder. . . . The jury recommended that he be sentenced to death on the murder charge and to consecutive life sentences on the armed robbery charges. The court followed the jury's recommendation and sentenced McCleskey to death. . . .

McCleskey . . . filed a petition for a writ of habeas corpus in [federal court]. . . . His petition raised 18 claims, one of which was that the Georgia capital sentencing process is administered in a racially discriminatory manner in violation of the Eighth and Fourteenth Amendments to the United States Constitution. In support of his claim, McCleskey proffered a statistical study performed by Professors David C. Baldus, George Woodworth, and Charles Pulaski (the Baldus study) that purports to show disparity in the imposition of the death sentence in Georgia based on the race of the murder victim and, to a lesser extent, the race of the defendant. The Baldus study is actually two sophisticated statistical studies that examine over 2,000 murder cases that occurred in Georgia during the 1970s. The raw numbers collected by Professor Baldus indicate that defendants charged with killing white persons received the death penalty in 11% of cases, but defendants charged with killing blacks received the death penalty in only 1% of cases. The raw numbers also indicate a reverse racial disparity according to the race of the defendant: 4% of the black defendants received the death penalty, as opposed to 7% of the white defendants.

Baldus also divided the cases according to the combination of the race of the defendant and the race of the victim. He found that the death penalty was assessed in 22% of the cases involving black defendants and white victims; 8% of the cases involving white defendants and white victims; 1% of the cases involving black defendants and black victims; and 3% of the cases involving white defendants and black victims. Similarly, Baldus found that prosecutors sought the death penalty in 70% of the cases involving black defendants and white victims; 32% of the cases involving white defendants and white victims; 15% of the cases involving black defendants and black victims; and 19% of the cases involving white defendants and black victims.

Baldus subjected his data to an extensive analysis, taking account of 230 variables that could have explained the disparities on nonracial grounds. One of his models concludes that, even after taking account of 39 nonracial variables, defendants charged with killing white victims were 4.3 times as likely to receive a death sentence as defendants charged with killing blacks. According to this model, black defendants were 1.1 times as likely to receive a death sentence as other defendants. Thus, the Baldus study indicates that black defendants, such as McCleskey, who kill white victims have the greatest likelihood of receiving the death penalty.

The District Court . . . concluded that McCleskey's "statistics do not demonstrate a prima facie case in support of the contention that the death penalty was imposed upon him because of his race, because of the race of the victim, or because of any Eighth Amendment concern." . . . As to McCleskey's Fourteenth Amendment claim, the court found that the methodology of the Baldus study was flawed in several respects. . . .

. . . As a black defendant who killed a white victim, McCleskey claims that the Baldus study demonstrates that he was discriminated against because of the race of his victim. In its broadest form, McCleskey's claim of discrimination extends to every actor in the Georgia capital sentencing process, from the prosecutor who sought the death penalty and the jury that imposed the sentence, to the State itself that enacted the capital punishment statute and allows it to remain in effect despite its allegedly discriminatory application. We agree with the [lower courts] . . . that this claim must fail.

. . . [T]o prevail under the Equal Protection Clause, McCleskey must prove that the decision-makers in *his* case acted with discriminatory purpose. He offers no evidence specific to his own case that would support an inference that racial considerations played a part in his sentence. Instead, he relies solely on the Baldus study. McCleskey argues that the Baldus study compels an inference that his sentence rests on purposeful discrimination. . . .

The Court has accepted statistics as proof of intent to discriminate in certain limited contexts. First, this Court has accepted statistical disparities as proof of an equal protection violation in the selection of the jury venire in a particular district. . . . Second, this Court has accepted statistics in the form of multiple regression analysis to prove statutory violations under Title VII [regarding employment discrimination]. . . .

But the nature of the capital sentencing decision, and the relationship of the statistics to that decision, are fundamentally different from the corresponding elements in the venire-selection or Title VII cases. Most importantly, each particular decision to impose the death penalty is made by a petit jury selected from a properly constituted venire. Each jury is unique in its composition and the Constitution requires that its decision rest on consideration of innumerable factors that vary according to the characteristics of the individual defendant and the facts of the particular capital offense. . . . Thus, the application of an inference drawn from the general statistics to a specific decision in a trial and sentencing simply is not comparable to the application of an inference drawn from general statistics to a specific venire-selection or Title VII case. In those cases, the statistics relate to fewer entities, and fewer variables are relevant to the challenged decisions.

Another important difference between the cases in which we have accepted statistics as proof of discriminatory intent and this case is that, in the venire-selection and Title VII contexts, the decision-maker has an opportunity to explain the statistical disparity. . . .

Finally, McCleskey's statistical proffer must be viewed in the context of his challenge . . . at the heart of the State's criminal justice system. . . . Implementation of [criminal justice] laws necessarily requires discretionary judgments. Because discretion is essential to the criminal justice process, we would demand exceptionally clear proof before we would infer that the discretion has been abused. . . . [W]e hold that the Baldus study is clearly insufficient to support an inference that any of the decision-makers in McCleskey's case acted with discriminatory purpose. . . .

. . . As legislatures necessarily have wide discretion in the choice of criminal laws and penalties, and as there were legitimate reasons for the Georgia Legislature to adopt and maintain capital punishment, . . . we will not infer a discriminatory purpose on the part of the State of Georgia. . . .

. . . McCleskey argues that the sentence in his case is disproportionate to the sentences in other murder cases. . . .

. . . [A]bsent a showing that the Georgia capital punishment system operates in an arbitrary and capricious manner, McCleskey cannot prove a constitutional violation by demonstrating that other defendants who may be similarly situated did *not* receive the death penalty. . . .

Because McCleskey's sentence was imposed under Georgia sentencing procedures that focus discretion "on the particularized nature of the crime and the particularized characteristics of the individual defendant," . . . we lawfully may presume that McCleskey's death sentence was not "wantonly and freakishly" imposed, . . . and thus that the sentence is not disproportionate within any recognized meaning under the Eighth Amendment.

(continued)

. . . McCleskey further contends that the Georgia capital punishment system is arbitrary and capricious in *application,* and therefore his sentence is excessive, because racial considerations may influence capital sentencing decisions in Georgia. . . .

. . . Even Professor Baldus does not contend that his statistics *prove* that race enters into any capital sentencing decisions or that race was a factor in McCleskey's particular case. Statistics at most show only a likelihood that a particular factor entered into some decisions. There is, of course, some risk of racial prejudice influencing a jury's decision in a criminal case. There are similar risks that other kinds of prejudice will influence other criminal trials. . . . The question "is at what point that risk becomes constitutionally unacceptable. . . ." McCleskey asks us to accept the likelihood allegedly shown by the Baldus study as the constitutional measure of unacceptable risk of racial prejudice influencing capital sentencing decisions. This we decline to do. . . .

McCleskey's argument that the Constitution condemns the discretion allowed decisionmakers in the Georgia capital sentencing system is antithetical to the fundamental role of discretion in our criminal justice system. Discretion in the criminal justice system offers substantial benefits to the criminal defendant. Not only can a jury decline to impose the death sentence, it can decline to convict. . . .

At most, the Baldus study indicates a discrepancy that appears to correlate with race. Apparent disparities in sentencing are an inevitable part of our criminal justice system. . . .

. . . McCleskey's claim, taken to its logical conclusion, throws into serious question the principles that underlie our entire criminal justice system. The Eighth Amendment is not limited in application to capital punishment, but applies to all penalties. . . . Thus, if we accepted McCleskey's claim that racial bias has impermissibly tainted the capital sentencing decision, we could soon be faced with similar claims as to other types of penalty. . . .

. . . McCleskey's arguments are best presented to legislative bodies. . . . Legislatures . . . are better qualified to weigh and "evaluate the results of statistical studies in terms of their own local conditions." . . .

JUSTICE BRENNAN, with whom JUSTICE MARSHALL joins, and with whom JUSTICE

BLACKMUN and JUSTICE STEVENS join in all but Part I, dissenting.

I

. . . [M]urder defendants in Georgia with white victims are more than four times as likely to receive the death sentence as are defendants with black victims. . . . Nothing could convey more powerfully the intractable reality of the death penalty: "that the effort to eliminate arbitrariness in the infliction of that ultimate sanction is so plainly doomed to failure that it—and the death penalty—must be abandoned altogether." . . .

II

At some point in this case, Warren McCleskey doubtless asked his lawyer whether a jury was likely to sentence him to die. A candid reply to this question would have been disturbing. First, counsel would have to tell McCleskey that few of the details of the crime or of McCleskey's past criminal conduct were more important than the fact that his victim was white. . . . Furthermore, counsel would feel bound to tell McCleskey that defendants charged with killing white victims in Georgia are 4.3 times as likely to be sentenced to death as defendants charged with killing blacks. . . . In addition, frankness would compel the disclosure that it was more likely than not that the race of McCleskey's victim would determine whether he received a death sentence: 6 of every 11 defendants convicted of killing a white person would not have received the death penalty if their victims had been black. . . .

The Court today . . . finds no fault in a system in which lawyers must tell their clients that race casts a large shadow on the capital sentencing process. The Court arrives at this conclusion by stating that the Baldus Study cannot "*prove* that race enters into any capital sentencing decisions." . . . [W]e can identify only "a likelihood that a particular factor entered into some decisions," . . . and "a discrepancy that appears to correlate to race." . . . This "likelihood" and "discrepancy," holds the Court, is insufficient to establish a constitutional violation. The Court reaches this conclusion by placing four factors on the scales opposite McCleskey's evidence: the desire to encourage sentencing discretion, the existence of "statutory safeguards" in the Georgia scheme, the fear of encouraging widespread challenges to other sentencing decisions, and the limits of the judicial role. The Court's evaluation of the significance of petitioner's evidence is fundamentally at odds with our consistent concern for rationality in capital sentencing, and the considerations that the majority invokes to discount that evidence cannot justify its force.

It is important to emphasize at the outset that the Court's observation that McCleskey cannot prove the influence of race on any particular sentencing decision is irrelevant in evaluating his Eighth Amendment claim. Since *Furman v. Georgia* [1972], . . . the Court has been concerned with the *risk* of the imposition of an arbitrary sentence, rather than the proven fact of one. *Furman* held that the death penalty "may not be imposed under sentencing procedures that create a substantial risk that the punishment will be inflicted in an arbitrary and capricious manner." . . .

Defendants challenging their death sentences thus never have had to prove that impermissible considerations have actually infected sentencing decisions. We have required instead that they establish that the system under which they were sentenced posed a significant risk of such an occurrence. McCleskey's claim does differ, however, in one respect from these earlier cases: it is the first to base a challenge not on speculation about how a system *might* operate, but empirical documentation of how it *does* operate.

The Court assumes the statistical validity of the Baldus study, . . . and acknowledges that McCleskey has demonstrated a risk that racial prejudice plays a role in capital sentencing in Georgia. . . . Nevertheless, it finds the probability of prejudice insufficient to create constitutional concern. . . . Close analysis of the Baldus study, however, in light of both statistical principles and human experience, reveals that the risk that race influenced McCleskey's sentence is intolerable by an imaginable standard. . . .

. . . [B]lacks who kill whites are sentenced to death at nearly *22 times* the rate of blacks who kill blacks, and more than *7 times* the rate of whites who kill blacks. . . . Since our decision upholding the Georgia capital-sentencing system in *Gregg,* the State has executed 7 persons. All of the 7 were executed for killing whites, and 6 of the 7 executed were black. Such execution figures are especially striking in light of the fact that, during the period encompassed by the Baldus study, only 9.2% of Georgia homicides involved black defendants and white victims, while 60.7% involved black victims.

McCleskey's statistics have particular force because most of them are the product of sophisticated multiple-regression analysis. Such analysis is designed precisely to identify patterns in the aggregate, even though we may not be able to reconstitute with certainty any individual decision that goes to make up that pattern. Multiple-regression analysis is particularly well-suited to identify the influence of impermissible considerations in sentencing, since it is able to control for permissible factors that may explain an apparent arbitrary pattern. . . . In this case, Professor Baldus in fact conducted additional regression analyses in response to criticisms and suggestions by the District Court, all of which confirmed, and some of which even strengthened, the study's original conclusions.

The statistical evidence in this case thus relentlessly documents the risk that McCleskey's sentence was influenced by racial considerations. . . .

. . . We must also ask whether the conclusion suggested by those numbers [in the Baldus study] is consonant with our understanding of history and human experience. Georgia's legacy of a race-conscious criminal justice system, as well as this Court's own recognition of the persistent danger that racial attitudes may affect criminal proceedings, indicate that McCleskey's claim is not a fanciful product of mere statistical artifice. . . .

The Court maintains that petitioner's claim "is antithetical to the fundamental role of discretion in our criminal justice system." . . .

Reliance on race in imposing capital punishment, however, is antithetical to the very rationale for granting sentencing discretion. Discretion is a means, not an end. It is bestowed in order to permit the sentencer to "trea[t] each defendant in a capital case with that degree of respect due the uniqueness of the individual." . . .

Considering the race of the defendant or victim in deciding if the death penalty should be imposed is completely at odds with this concern that an individual be evaluated as a unique human being. . . . Enhanced willingness to impose the death sentence on black defendants, or diminished willingness to render such a sentence when blacks are victims, reflects a devaluation of the lives of black persons. . . .

The Court . . . states that its unwillingness to regard the petitioner's evidence as sufficient is based in part on the fear that recognition of McCleskey's claim would open the door to widespread challenges to all aspects of criminal sentencing. . . . Taken on its face, such a statement seems to suggest a fear of too much justice. Yet surely the majority would acknowledge that if striking evidence indicated that other minority groups, or women, or even persons with blond hair, were disproportionately sentenced

(continued)

to death, such a state of affairs would be repugnant to deeply rooted conceptions of fairness. . . .

JUSTICE BLACKMUN, with whom JUSTICE MARSHALL and JUSTICE STEVENS join, and with whom JUSTICE BRENNAN joins in all but Part IV-B, dissenting.

. . .

IV

A

One of the final concerns discussed by the Court may be the most disturbing aspect of its opinion. Granting relief to McCleskey in this case, it is said, could lead to further constitutional challenges. . . . That, of course, is no reason to deny McCleskey his rights under the Equal Protection Clause. If a grant of relief to him were to lead to a closer examination of the effects of racial considerations throughout the criminal-justice system, the system, and hence society, might benefit. Where no such factors come into play, the integrity of the system is enhanced. Where such considerations are shown to be significant, efforts can be made to eradicate their impermissible

influence and to ensure an evenhanded application of criminal sanctions. . . .

JUSTICE STEVENS, with whom JUSTICE BLACKMUN joins, dissenting.

. . .

The Court's decision appears to be based on a fear that the acceptance of McCleskey's claim would sound the death knell for capital punishment in Georgia. If society were indeed forced to choose between a racially discriminatory death penalty (one that provides heightened protection against murder "for whites only") and no death penalty at all, the choice mandated by the Constitution would be plain. . . . But the Court's fear is unfounded. One of the lessons of the Baldus study is that there exist certain categories of extremely serious crimes for which prosecutors consistently seek, and juries consistently impose, the death penalty without regard to the race of the victim or the race of the offender. If Georgia were to narrow the class of death-eligible defendants to those categories, the danger of arbitrary and discriminatory imposition of the death penalty would be significantly decreased, if not eradicated. As Justice BRENNAN has demonstrated in his dissenting opinion, such a restructuring of the sentencing scheme is surely not too high a price to pay.

Victim Impact Statements

In the late 1980s, a majority of justices demonstrated a recognition of the risk that jurors' biases and sympathies for particular victims may affect death penalty sentencing without regard to the nature of the crime or the record of the defendant. In *Booth v. Maryland* (1987), a 5-to-4 majority decided that "victim impact statements" were impermissible during the sentencing phase of capital cases. Prosecutors attempted to use victim impact statements to inform jurors about how a particular homicide had devastated surviving family members or had eliminated a valued and admired member of society. According to Justice Lewis Powell's majority opinion, victim impact statements are irrelevant to a capital sentencing decision, and their introduction creates the risk of capricious application of capital punishment. Such testimony was regarded as creating a risk that capital punishment would be imposed based on how much society values a particular victim's life rather than based on the viciousness of the defendant's actions or the defendant's prior criminal record. Thus the murderer of a town's doctor might be more likely to receive the death penalty than the murderer of a janitor, or the murderer of a white person might receive the penalty more freely than the murderer of an African American person, if the jurors valued whites' lives more highly. The Court reaffirmed this principle in *South Carolina v. Gathers* (1989) despite a dissenting opinion by Justice Scalia that warned that the dissenters were merely waiting for the Court's composition to change so that they could rewrite constitutional law to permit victim impact statements. Scalia foretold a future change by reassuring the other justices that a rapid change in the law would not adversely affect the Court's image as a legal institution. According to Scalia, "I doubt that overruling *Booth* will so shake the citizenry's faith in the Court. Overrulings of precedent rarely occur without a change in the Court's personnel. The only distinctive feature here is that the overruling would follow not long after the original decision. But that is hardly unprecedented."

As Scalia predicted, the Court overturned *Booth* and *Gathers* in *Payne v. Tennessee* (1991) after the Court's composition changed. Despite the two precedents within the previous four years barring the use of victim impact statements during the sentencing phase of capital cases, *Payne* permitted prosecutors to present testimony from family members about the impact of the victim's death on their lives. The *Payne* decision may increase the risk of discrimination illuminated by the *McCleskey* statistical study indicating that death penalty decisions are affected by jurors' differential valuation of murder victims' lives. The decision also illustrates how quickly criminal procedure rules can change. The meaning of the Constitution is not enduring. The retirement of one justice can potentially lead to the quick creation or elimination of rights and rules that had previously been in existence for a long time or had only recently been reaffirmed by the Supreme Court.

The public's awareness of capital punishment increased dramatically at the dawn of the twenty-first century as people convicted of murder were regularly released from death row in various states after new evidence emerged that demonstrated their innocence. For example, by the time a man was released from Idaho's death row in August 2001 after spending 18 years in prison for a rape and murder that DNA evidence now showed he did not commit, at least 96 people had been released from their death sentences in the preceding two decades.[4] The highly publicized releases from death row highlighted questions about the adequacy of procedures in capital cases and the fairness of the death penalty. As a result, public opinion polls showed that support for the death penalty dropped. For example, only 58 percent of Californians supported capital punishment in 2000 as compared to 78 percent supporting the death penalty in the state in 1990. Politicians also responded. The governor of Illinois declared a moratorium on the death penalty after 13 men on that state's death row were found to be innocent after serving for as long as 18 years in prison. In addition, newspaper investigations showed that in Illinois, a large number of people sentenced to death were represented by attorneys who had been disbarred or suspended and were convicted based on the self-serving testimony of jailhouse informants.[5] In 2001 alone, five states enacted legislation to prohibit the application of the death penalty to mentally retarded defendants. Thus 18 of the 38 states with capital punishment did not permit it to be imposed on mentally retarded people.[6] Even Justice Sandra Day O'Connor, a conservative jurist who generally supported the Supreme Court's decisions permitting capital punishment, publicly questioned the death penalty for the first time. In a July 2001 speech to the Minnesota Women Lawyers organization, O'Connor said that "the system may well be allowing some innocent defendants to be executed."[7] All of these developments indicate that social and political forces are turning against capital punishment, but it remains to be seen whether these developments will gain enough support and momentum to lead to more significant changes in states' laws. It also remains to be seen whether, as reflected in O'Connor's comment, any Supreme Court justices will begin to alter their own views in ways that affect their decisions in cases.

APPEALS

The appeals process enables convicted offenders to ask appellate courts to review trial court proceedings to determine whether any errors justify overturning the conviction. An appeal does not involve the reexamination of evidence by the appellate court. There is no jury, no presentation of witnesses and evidence, and no determination of guilt. Instead, the defendant must identify specific errors in law and procedure, such as a trial judge's improper ruling on evidence or improper jury instruction, that justify ordering a new trial. Intermediate appellate courts, the courts that hear the bulk of criminal appeals, are typically comprised of a three-judge panel that reads written submissions from attorneys and sometimes orders oral arguments. Subsequent appeals may go to state supreme courts, which typically have five or seven members. Appellate courts are deliberative bodies in which the judges must interact with each other in order to reach a decision. Usually, appellate judges receive substantial assistance from law clerks and staff attorneys. In states with high appellate caseloads, staff attorneys may serve a substantial screening function by reading attorneys' submissions and drafting recommended decisions for the judges before the judges have even looked at the cases. To some critics, the reliance on staff attorneys and law clerks raises risks of bureaucratic decision making in which unknown people within an organization make the actual decisions while the public continues to believe erroneously that the official decision makers (i.e., the judges) are the only ones who determine the outcomes of cases.[8]

There is no constitutional right to appeal. All state legislatures and Congress have created opportunities for appeals by statute. These statutes typically provide a statutory right to an initial appeal to an intermediate appellate court. There are not always opportunities for all convicted offenders to appeal. In Michigan, for example, there is no statutory right to appeal for offenders who enter guilty pleas. There is a presumption that offenders who voluntarily plead guilty have freely admitted their guilt and accepted their punishment, so they should not be able to turn around immediately and seek to have their convictions thrown out. There are, however, some circumstances in which defendants convicted by plea may have legitimate grounds to appeal. For example, what if they claim defense attorneys or trial judges misled them about the consequences of their plea? In order to handle such situations, even offenders who plead guilty are allowed to ask the court of appeals for permission to file an appeal.

Although the U.S. Constitution does not provide a right to appeal, there are constitutional rights that shape the appellate process. For example, indigent defendants have a right to receive free copies of their trial transcripts (*Griffin v. Illinois,* 1956). These transcripts are essential for appeals because the offender must be able to identify and document any alleged errors that occurred in the trial court. People who are not indigent are required to pay for copies of trial transcripts. These costs may be substantial. If the court has already paid to have the record transcribed from the court reporter's notes into text, then the costs may involve only photocopying. In some circumstances, however, the person requesting a court record may actually have to pay to have the record transcribed as well as copied. As we saw in the earlier examination of the Sixth Amendment, the Supreme Court has said that an indigent person's right to counsel continues from the trial stage through the first appeal of right (*Douglas v. California*, 1963). However, the right to counsel does not continue during any subsequent discretionary appeals to the state supreme courts (*Ross v. Moffitt*, 1974). States provide counsel for indigent defendants in various ways, such as by compensating their trial counsel to carry the case through the first appeal (and possibly beyond). Alternatively, states may provide legal counsel throughout the appellate process through systems of state appellate defenders and appointed appellate counsel that represent offenders in state supreme courts as well as in the intermediate courts of appeals.

One of the crucial issues in appellate procedure is the state-mandated time limit for filing a notice of appeal. If state law requires the offender to file notice within the first weeks after conviction, there are risks that legal grounds for appeal may be lost. An offender may fail to file in a timely manner, either because of attorney error or because some potential grounds for appeal were not known immediately after trial (i.e., discovery of new evidence months or years after the trial). Depending on how the state law is written and interpreted by state courts, failure to file a timely notice may result in a forfeiture of claims. In addition, forfeiture of constitutional claims for failing to meet the requirements of state appellate procedure can also provide grounds for forfeiting any opportunity to pursue those claims in federal courts through the habeas corpus process (*Coleman v. Thompson*, 1991). In theory, appellate procedures provide a mechanism for correcting errors that occur at the trial court level. However, the design of such procedures may prevent the appellate process from actually correcting all errors.

The Harmless Error Doctrine

Criminal defendants are not entitled to perfect processes. Appellate courts are willing to accept the existence of some errors as long as they did not produce an unfair process or an unfair result. **Harmless error** is one legal concept that limits the completeness of appellate processes as an error-correction mechanism. Underlying the concept is the sensible idea that some kinds of errors that occur in trial courts are so minor and harmless, they do not provide sufficient justification to overturn convictions on appeal and order new trials. Controversy arises, however, when analysts debate which errors courts should be willing to label as "harmless." The Supreme Court has instructed appellate courts to ask whether it can be established beyond reasonable doubt that the error did not contribute to the guilty verdict (*Chapman v. California*, 1967). However, it is not always clear how this standard should be applied, especially since it may require making guesses about how a judge or jury may have responded to the admission of improper evidence or some other error.

The Supreme Court has applied the harmless-error concept in controversial ways. For example, in *Arizona v. Fulminante* (1991), a majority of justices ruled that a coerced confession could be regarded as a "harmless error" that would not require reversal of a conviction. The ruling did not mean that all coerced confessions would be viewed as "harmless errors." Courts must look at each case and each rights violation individually to determine if an error was "harmless." However, the decision shocked many commentators who had previously believed that all coerced confessions justified reversal of convictions because of the seriousness of the rights violation and the significant impact of confessions on the likelihood of conviction. The Court's decision opened the question of whether there are any rights that are not subject to harmless-error analysis. This is a particularly important question because some commentators fear that courts use the harmless-error doctrine to ensure that there is no risk that certain offenders will gain a release after a new trial despite the occurrence of rights violations in the investigation and prosecution of their criminal offenses. Because the standards for determining whether errors are "harmless" are not clear-cut, there are risks that judges will make subjective, discretionary, and inconsistent decisions about whether convictions should be overturned. If, for example, someone is convicted of murder, would a judge be tempted to find that constitutional errors are "harmless" in order to avoid the possibility that the offender might gain an acquittal in a second trial in which a confession or other improperly obtained evidence might be excluded from presentation in court?

New technological developments affecting the discovery and testing of evidence have created controversies about the adequacy of postconviction legal procedures. Should people have a right to present newly discovered evidence in court? Should appeals courts be cautious about ordering new trials? These and other questions are matters of debate among scholars, judges, and lawyers who consider ways to reform the appeals process. As you read the accompanying material about the impact of new DNA testing methods, think about whether you would recommend that convicted offenders gain greater access to appeals courts.

HABEAS CORPUS

As you'll recall from Chapter 2, habeas corpus provides the traditional mechanism from Anglo-American law through which people can go to court to claim that they are being detained improperly. Habeas corpus procedures are governed by state and federal statutes, although the importance of the mechanism is apparent by its enshrinement in the Constitution. Article I of the Constitution forbids the government from suspending access to habeas corpus unless such a suspension may be required during a rebellion or an invasion.

Hypothetically, anyone being deprived of their liberty by the government can file a habeas corpus petition to challenge the basis for their detention. Thus someone confined in a mental hospital could file such a petition. In practice, the vast majority of habeas corpus petitions are filed by convicted offenders. After offenders have gone unsuccessfully through the appeals process, they may file a habeas corpus petition. Unlike the appeals process in which the offenders may seek to have convictions overturned for various trial court errors in law or procedure, habeas corpus petitions focus on the alleged violations of constitutional rights. In order for someone to have a federal court consider a habeas corpus petition, the offender must allege that a federal constitutional right was violated in the course of the investigation and prosecution of the case. All constitutional rights are not equally eligible for review in

TECHNOLOGY AND CONSTITUTIONAL RIGHTS

DNA Testing and Appeals

The development of DNA testing has enhanced the capacity of law enforcement officials to rule out suspects and to identify perpetrators through scientific testing on blood, hair, and other materials containing traces of human genes. DNA testing has also created new opportunities for convicted offenders to attempt to persuade courts of their innocence. By the end of 2000, nearly eighty convicted offenders had been released from prison after DNA testing was applied to evidence that had been saved from their cases. Some of these offenders served in prison for many years before the development of new scientific techniques made it possible to rule out their participation in the rapes and murders for which they had been convicted.

There is no constitutional right to have new evidence heard in court. Defendants have a right to a fair trial but no legal guarantee that the trial will produce a correct result. As Justice Scalia once wrote, "[T]here is no basis in text, tradition, or even in contemporary practice (if that were enough), for finding in the Constitution a right to demand judicial consideration of newly discovered evidence of innocence brought forward after conviction"

(*Herrera v. Collins*, 1993). Thus evidence may be available which could prove that a convicted offender is actually innocent, yet the offender has no right to have the evidence tested and, even if the tests exonerate him or her, no right to have a court hear the evidence and order a release from prison.

Under current practice, offenders must attempt to convince a judge to order testing and then to accept the results in court. However, there are many examples of prosecutors arguing that old evidence samples should not be tested, even when new scientific techniques might shed light on the offender's actual guilt or possible innocence. How should appellate courts deal with the issue of new evidence? Should there be specific rules that describe how claims of new evidence should be handled? Should courts interpret the Due Process Clause or the prohibition on cruel and unusual punishments as guaranteeing a release from prison if DNA testing leads to the conclusion that the prosecutor's original theory about the offender's involvement in a rape or murder is incorrect? Should the meaning of the Constitution adapt in response to the development of new technology?

---

the habeas corpus process. If a state appellate court has considered and rejected an offender's claims about Fourth Amendment search and seizure rights violations, a federal court will not examine this claim again because it has had a "full and fair hearing" already (*Stone v. Powell*, 1976). The most frequent claims raised in habeas corpus petitions concern Sixth Amendment rights, especially allegations of ineffective assistance of counsel, and Fourteenth Amendment due process rights.[9]

There is no right to counsel for habeas corpus proceedings. Offenders must submit their own petitions using forms supplied by the courts and legal resources contained in prison law libraries. Chapter 8, on the right to counsel, provided an example of a form used by prisoners to prepare a habeas corpus petition (see page 266). Because these are typically *pro se* actions, prisoners are often ineffective in identifying rights violations and describing the basis for their claims. Many petitions are rejected because prisoners do not understand what kinds of claims concern constitutional rights violations, and they mistakenly use the habeas corpus process to file every kind of complaint they can think of concerning their conviction and their treatment in prison. Habeas corpus petitions present a special challenge for court personnel, especially law clerks who first read the petitions, because they must try to cut through an unskilled litigator's frequently-less-than-clear legal writing in order to determine if any valid claim may lurk beneath the often rambling allegations. Only about 1 percent of habeas corpus petitions are approved by the federal courts as presenting a valid constitutional claim.[10]

Criticism and Reform

Many criticisms have been directed at the habeas corpus process. State judges object to the process being used to have federal judges second-guess their decisions. From the perspective of many state judges, the offenders have already had their cases reviewed by state appellate courts, so there is no need for additional judicial review in federal courts. Prosecutors and state attorneys general are frustrated that they must devote time and money to the preparation of responses to petitions that are ultimately judged as without merit in 99 percent of cases. Law enforcement officials are frustrated that the habeas corpus process permits offenders to drag out litigation processes and thereby delay confronting their guilt and the punishment they deserve for violating criminal laws. Federal judicial officials have expressed frustration that they must use their time to review petitions that seldom present valid claims.

During the 1980s and 90s, the Supreme Court made it more difficult for offenders to file successful habeas corpus petitions. For example, in 1991, the Court rejected a second case from Warren McCleskey, the defendant who lost his claim in 1987 concerning systemic racial discrimination in Georgia. McCleskey claimed that the police and prosecutors violated his rights when they planted an informant in his cell and then hid from McCleskey, his attorney, and the jury the fact that the informant-witness was working for the police and testifying against McCleskey in exchange for favors. Rather than consider whether the informant's activities violated McCleskey's Sixth Amendment right to be represented by counsel when questioned by police agents, a 6-to-3 majority on the Court emphasized a procedural rule to block McCleskey's claim. The Court ruled that a prisoner must normally use a single habeas corpus petition to present all claims (*McCleskey v. Zant*, 1991). Thus, McCleskey exhausted his opportunity to bring claims to the federal court when he brought his action using statistics to show the existence of racial discrimination. McCleskey's claim about the unconstitutional use of a police informant was barred despite the fact that the prosecutors allegedly hid relevant information from McCleskey's attorney until long after he had filed McCleskey's first challenge.

In *Teague v. Lane* (1989), the Court said that a habeas petitioner cannot benefit from "new rules" about constitutional rights that courts announce after their conviction has been finalized. In effect, a court may recognize that an offender's rights were violated, but decline to vindicate those rights because those rights were not clearly recognized in judicial precedents that existed at the time of conviction and appeal. In one case, a mentally retarded defendant was sentenced to death based on incriminating statements he made while being questioned without his attorney present. The Supreme Court acknowledged that the questioning was improper but said that the rule declaring such questioning to be improper had not been sufficiently clear for all judges to recognize it at the time the defendant's appeal was completed (*Butler v. McKellar,* 1990). Thus a defendant of limited mental capability remained on death row, despite significant questions about whether he had any connec-

tion to the physical evidence at the crime scene (e.g., hair evidence), even though the Supreme Court acknowledged that the police acted improperly in obtaining incriminating statements from him. Critics' discomfort with the outcome of this case was compounded because the prosecutor later said that he never would have sought the death penalty if the inexperienced defense attorney had brought forward information about the defendant's childlike mental capacity.[11] In deciding habeas cases, justices on the Supreme Court often disagree about whether a particular rule concerning constitutional rights was recognized by judges at the time a particular case occurred. In *Butler v. McKellar,* the justices were deeply divided on this question.

In *Coleman v. Thompson* (1991), the Supreme Court decided that violations of state court procedures preclude federal habeas review of alleged constitutional rights violations. Thus, if a defendant's attorney forfeits an opportunity to appeal an issue to the state intermediate appellate court by missing the deadline for filing a notice of appeal, the attorney also forfeits the opportunity to have a federal court review the claim in the habeas corpus process. In *Coleman* there were significant questions about whether the defendant was actually guilty as well as questions about the adequacy of his defense attorneys' performance. Despite these questions, Coleman could not gain review of his claims through habeas corpus, and ultimately he was executed in 1992 because his appeal was filed a few days too late.[12] In 2001 attorneys sought to have the evidence in Coleman's case tested using DNA techniques that were unavailable at the time of his trial. Because a thorough reexamination of the case by a lawyer-turned-writer had raised serious doubts about Coleman's guilt, many observers suspected that DNA tests would clear Coleman and implicate the victim's neighbor. According to the writer's interviews with witnesses, the neighbor should have been a strong suspect in the case, but he was never thoroughly investigated by the police.[13] Virginia's attorney general vigorously resisted permitting the evidence to be subjected to DNA testing. While the attorney general said that there was no reason to retest the evidence since Coleman had already been executed, several attorneys, interest groups, and newspapers believed that the testing was important in order to see whether the legal process in the case was so flawed that it had made the most tragic kind of error. After lower courts in Virginia refused to permit the DNA test, attorneys planned to appeal the decision to the Virginia Supreme Court.[14]

In another case, the development of DNA tests after the conviction might have demonstrated that the convicted offender's blood did not match the murderer's blood at the crime scene, but there was no opportunity for federal court review because the defendant's attorney had made a procedural error by filing the wrong document with the court.[15] In many respects, the law governing habeas corpus processes may place a greater emphasis on technical compliance with procedural rules than on careful examination of alleged violations of constitutional rights.

In 1996 Congress reinforced the strictness of habeas corpus procedures and made it even more difficult for offenders to file successful habeas corpus petitions. The legislature enacted and President Bill Clinton signed into law a new statute titled the "Antiterrorism and Effective Death Penalty Act." Included in the new law were provisions setting stricter time limits for filing habeas corpus petitions and requiring greater deference to state court decisions by federal judges receiving habeas petitions.[16]

Access to Postconviction Legal Process

Do constitutional rights have substance if there are no accessible and effective mechanisms for correcting violations of those rights? The habeas corpus process is difficult for convicted offenders to utilize because of the many technical procedural requirements and the lack of a right to representation by counsel. Supreme Court decisions concerning habeas corpus have said, in effect, that courts may recognize that a defendant's constitutional rights were violated, yet no actions may be taken to correct those violations. If the offender files more than one habeas petition, makes a claim concerning a right about which there is a dispute whether it was clearly established at the time of the case, or violates a procedural rule in the appellate process, the court will not act to correct recognizable rights violations.

Does the habeas corpus process provide an illusory promise when it purports to provide a mechanism for the protection of rights? Does the habeas corpus process ultimately convey the message that the court system would rather have efficient procedures than devote resources to the examination of individual offenders' claims to see if any rights violations occurred during the investigation and prosecution of criminal cases?

The habeas corpus process provides the traditional mechanism to seek release from unjustified detention. In practice, convicted criminals file such petitions but they are seldom successful in gaining new trials or release. The challenges of meeting the specific deadlines and procedures of the habeas process are too difficult for most prisoners to overcome, especially since there is no right to counsel during the habeas process. Thus, even if an offender had a valid constitutional claim, it is unlikely that the habeas process would provide vindication for any rights violation. As you read the material in the accompanying box, ask yourself whether the contemporary habeas corpus process can effectively fulfill its traditional purpose.

CONCLUSION

The sentencing process is influenced by the decisions of several different actors. Prosecutors have an especially powerful influence over sentences in the plea bargaining process because they determine what charges and sentence recommendations will be part of the final agreements that lead to guilty pleas. After trials, prosecutors make sentence recommendations and defense attorneys make counterarguments about appropriate punishments. Probation officers prepare presentence reports that make recommendations and provide information that will guide judges' decisions. Judges possess discretion to determine sentences in some jurisdictions, but in others the legislature has acted to limit judges' discretion. Under sentencing reforms that produced sentencing guidelines and mandatory minimum sentences, legislators have used their judgment to determine punishments for various crimes. Many judges and lawyers object to these sentencing reforms because they prevent decision makers

in the courthouse from individualizing sentences to fit the circumstances of each case.

The Constitution imposes several limitations on the sentencing process and criminal punishments. Punishments cannot violate the Eighth Amendment prohibitions on excessive fines and on cruel and unusual punishments. Punishments may be impermissibly cruel and unusual either because they are disproportionate to the crime or because they are torturous. The Cruel and Unusual Punishments Clause is to be interpreted flexibly in light of changing social values (*Trop v. Dulles,* 1958). In addition to the limitations imposed by the Eighth Amendment, punishments may not violate the Double Jeopardy Clause or the *Ex Post Facto* Clause. The Supreme Court's justices have been divided in their assessments of when punishments are disproportionate, violate the Excessive Fines Clause, or constitute double jeopardy and *ex post facto* violations. Changes in the Court's composition may produce changes in the rules affecting these issues.

After the Supreme Court briefly halted capital punishment in 1972 because it was applied too randomly and capriciously to meet the requirements of due process (*Furman v. Georgia,* 1972), states that employ the death penalty reformed their capital sentencing procedures. The Court approved bifurcated capital sentencing procedures in *Gregg v. Georgia* (1976). Although the Supreme Court has limited the use of capital punishment by barring its application for rape and as a mandatory sentence, the Court was unwilling to accept statistical evidence as a basis for finding systemic racial discrimination as a violation of the Equal Protection Clause (*McCleskey v. Kemp,* 1987).

The appeals process provides an opportunity for convicted offenders to seek new trials by having appellate courts review allegations of trial court errors in applying the relevant law and following procedural rules. The habeas corpus process provides a final opportunity to seek vindication of alleged rights violations after the appeals process has been completed. Offenders rarely succeed in the habeas corpus process, in part because there is no right to counsel and they must fulfill specific procedural requirements to have their petitions considered by the court.

SUMMARY

- Criminal sentences are shaped by the decisions of prosecutors, defense attorneys, judges, probation officers, and state legislators.

- The sentencing discretion of judges in many jurisdictions has been reduced by reforms including sentencing guidelines and mandatory minimum sentences.

- The probation officer's production of the presentence report is a key element in sentencing, and conscientious defense attorneys must examine the report carefully to ensure its accuracy and objectivity.

- Constitutional limitations on the government's authority to impose criminal punishments are contained in the Eighth Amendment's Excessive Fines Clause and Cruel and Unusual Punishments Clause as well as the *Ex Post Facto* Clause and the Fifth Amendment's Double Jeopardy Clause.

- The Cruel and Unusual Punishments Clause covers both disproportionate and torturous punishments. The Supreme Court has declared that the clause must be interpreted flexibly in light of changing societal values (*Trop v. Dulles,* 1958).

- The Supreme Court's justices have been divided in their assessment of cases concerning the proportionality of punishment, excessive fines, and double jeopardy and *ex post facto* issues. The rules affecting these issues may change as the Court's composition changes in the future.

- The Supreme Court temporarily halted the death penalty in 1972 (*Furman v. Georgia*), but reactivated capital punishment after states created bifurcated procedures that satisfied the Court's expectations for the right to due process (*Gregg v. Georgia,* 1976).

- The Supreme Court rejected the use of statistics to demonstrate the existence of systemic racial discrimination in capital punishment (*McCleskey v. Kemp,* 1987).

- The Supreme Court has decided that capital punishment may be applied to teenagers who are at least sixteen, but the death penalty may not be applied as a mandatory sentence, imposed on insane or mentally retarded people, or used as a punishment for the crime of rape.

- The appeals process provides an opportunity for convicted offenders to seek review of errors that allegedly occurred in the trial court's application of law and adherence to legal procedures.

- The habeas corpus process provides an opportunity to seek vindication of alleged constitutional rights violations after the appeals process has been exhausted, but very few prisoners are successful in filing habeas corpus petitions, in part because there is no right to counsel for habeas proceedings.

Key Terms

bifurcated proceedings   Proceedings that are split into two parts, especially in death penalty cases in which the trial to determine guilt is separate from the later proceeding to determine whether the offender should be sentenced to death.

charge bargaining   Negotiations between the prosecutor and the defense attorney about what charges will be reduced or dropped in order to determine what sentence will be imposed when the defendant pleads guilty.

Ex Post Facto **Clause**   Constitutional provision forbidding after-the-fact criminal laws that define crimes and punishments for application to people who committed acts before the new laws were in existence.

forfeiture   Government seizure of property under statutory authority, especially when that property may have been used in or acquired from criminal enterprises.

harmless error   Legal concept applied by appellate courts to trial court errors that are not believed to have affected the verdict and therefore do not justify overturning a conviction.

presentence report   Report prepared by a probation officer describing a convicted offender's prior criminal record and personal history which, along with the probation officer's recommendation about an appropriate punishment, is used by the judge in determining the sentence for a criminal offense.

sentencing guidelines   Sentencing reform enacted by legislatures to reduce judicial discretion in sentencing and equalize sentences imposed on similar offenders. The offender's current charge and prior record determine a narrow sentencing range in which the judge establishes the actual sentence.

Additional Readings

Costanzo, Mark. 1997. *Just Revenge: Costs and Consequences of the Death Penalty.* New York: St. Martin's Press. Review of capital punishment as an issue of public policy.

Tigar, Michael E., and Jane B. Tigar. 1999. *Federal Appeals: Jurisdiction and Practice.* St. Paul, Minn.: West Publishing. Detailed overview of appellate process and relevant law governing appellate procedures.

White, Welsh. 1991. *The Death Penalty in the Nineties.* Ann Arbor: University of Michigan Press. Detailed analysis of legal decisions shaping procedures in capital punishment cases.

Notes

1. Paul Nowell, "Lawyer Says He Sabotaged Inmate," Associated Press Wire Service, 2 November 2000.

2. Antonin Scalia, "Originalism: The Lesser Evil," *Cincinnati Law Review* 57: 849–865.

3. Stephen B. Bright, "Counsel for the Poor: The Death Sentence Not for the Worst Crime but for the Worst Lawyer," *Yale Law Journal* 103 (1994): 1835–1883; John C. Tucker, *May God Have Mercy* (New York: W. W. Norton, 1997); Nowell, "Lawyer Says He Sabotaged Inmate."

4. Raymond Bonner, "Death Row Inmate Is Freed After DNA Test Clears Him," *New York Times,* 24 August 2001 (www.nytimes.com).

5. William Claiborne, "Illinois Governor to Block Executions During Death Penalty Probe," *Seattle Times,* 21 January 2000 (www.seattletimes.com).

6. Raymond Bonner, "North Carolina to Prohibit Execution of the Retarded," *New York Times,* 4 August 2001 (www.nytimes.com).

7. "Death-Penalty Foes Split on O'Connor," *Seattle Times,* 4 July 2001 (www.seattletimes.com).

8. Mary Lou Stow and Harold Spaeth, "Centralized Research Staff: Is There a Monster in the Judicial Closet?" *Judicature* 76 (1992): 216–221.

9. Roger Hanson and Henry W. K. Daley, *Federal Habeas Corpus Review: Challenging State Court Convictions* (Washington, D.C.: Bureau of Justice Statistics, 1995), 14.

10. Ibid.

11. Ruth Marcus, "Waiting Forever on Death Row," *Washington Post National Weekly Edition,* 18 June 1990, 12.

12. Tucker, *May God Have Mercy.*

13. Ibid.

14. David G. Savage, "'92 Execution Haunts Death Penalty Foes," *Los Angeles Times,* 22 July 2001 (www.latimes.com).

15. Linda Greenhouse, "In Shift, O'Connor Urges Appeal in Murder Case," *New York Times,* 3 December 1991, B10.

16. Christopher E. Smith, *Law and Contemporary Corrections* (Belmont, Calif.: Wadsworth, 2000), 37–39.

Selected Provisions of the U.S. Constitution

Article I

Section 9.

. . .

The Privilege of the Writ of Habeas Corpus shall not be suspended, unless when in Cases of Rebellion or Invasion the public safety may require it.

No Bill of Attainder or ex post facto Law shall be passed.

. . .

Article II

Section 2.

. . .

. . . [The President] shall nominate, and by and with the Advice and Consent of the Senate, shall appoint Ambassadors, other public Ministers and Consuls, Judges of the supreme Court, and all other Officers of the United States, whose Appointments are not herein otherwise provided for, and which shall be established by Law: but the Congress may by Law vest the Appointment of such inferior Officers, as they think proper, in the President alone, in the Courts of Law, or in the Heads of Departments.

. . .

Article III

Section 1.   The judicial Power of the United States, shall be vested in one supreme Court, and in such inferior Courts as the Congress may from time to time ordain and establish. The Judges, both of the supreme and inferior Courts, shall hold their Offices during good Behavior, and shall, at stated Times, receive for their Services, a Compensation, which shall not be diminished during their Continuance in Office.

Section 2.   The judicial Power shall extend to all Cases, in Law and Equity, arising under this Constitution, the Laws of the United States, and Treaties made, or which shall be made, under their Authority. . . .

In all Cases affecting Ambassadors, other public Ministers and Consuls, and those in which a State shall be a Party, the supreme Court shall have original Jurisdiction. In all the other Cases before mentioned, the supreme Court shall have appellate Jurisdiction, both as to Law and Fact, with such Exceptions, and under such Regulations as the Congress shall make.

The Trial of all Crimes, except in cases of Impeachment, shall be by Jury; and such Trial shall be held in the State where said Crimes shall have been committed; but when not committed within any State, the Trial shall be at such Place or Places as the Congress may by law have directed.

AMENDMENT 1

Congress shall make no law respecting an establishment of religion, or prohibiting the free exercise thereof; or abridging the freedom of speech, or of the press; or the right of the people peaceably to assemble, and to petition the Government for redress of grievances.

AMENDMENT 2

A well regulated Militia, being necessary for the security of a free State, the right of the people to keep and bear Arms, shall not be infringed.

AMENDMENT 3

No Soldier shall, in time of peace be quartered in any house, without the consent of the Owner, nor in time of war, but in a manner to be prescribed by law.

AMENDMENT 4

The right of the people to be secure in their persons, houses, papers, and effects, against unreasonable searches and seizures, shall not be violated, and no Warrants shall issue, but upon probable cause, supported by Oath or affirmation, and particularly describing the place to be searched, and the persons or things to be seized.

AMENDMENT 5

No person shall be held to answer for a capital or otherwise infamous crime, unless on a presentment or indictment of a Grand Jury, except in cases arising in the land or naval forces, or in the Militia, when in actual service in time of War or public danger; nor shall any person be subject for the same offence to be twice put in jeopardy of life or limb; nor shall be compelled in any criminal case to be a witness against himself, nor be deprived of life, liberty, or property, without due process of law; nor shall private property be taken for public use, without just compensation.

AMENDMENT 6
In all criminal prosecutions, the accused shall enjoy the right to a speedy and public trial, by an impartial jury of the State and district wherein the crime shall have been committed, which district shall have been previously ascertained by law, and to be informed of the nature and cause of the accusation; to be confronted with the witnesses against him; to have compulsory process for obtaining witnesses in his favor, and to have the Assistance of Counsel for his defence.

AMENDMENT 7
In Suits at common law, where the value in controversy shall exceed twenty dollars, the right of trial by jury shall be preserved, and no fact tried by a jury, shall be otherwise re-examined in any Court of the United States, than according to the rules of the common law.

AMENDMENT 8
Excessive bail shall not be required, nor excessive fines imposed, nor cruel and unusual punishments inflicted.

AMENDMENT 9
The enumeration in the Constitution, of certain rights, shall not be construed to deny or disparage others retained by the people.

AMENDMENT 10
The powers not delegated to the United States by the Constitution, nor prohibited by it to the States, are reserved to the States respectively, or to the people.

. . .

AMENDMENT 14
Section 1.   All persons born or naturalized in the United States, and subject to the jurisdiction thereof, are citizens of the United States and of the State wherein they reside. No State shall make or enforce any law which shall abridge the privileges or immunities of citizens of the United States; nor shall any State deprive any person of life, liberty, or property, without due process of law; nor deny to any person within its jurisdiction the equal protection of the laws.

Section 5.   The Congress shall have the power to enforce, by appropriate legislation, the provisions of this article.

GLOSSARY

adversary system   The legal process model employed in the United States in which the truth is presumed to emerge from the clash of opposing advocates in the courtroom, and therefore the attorney's performance is a key factor in determining the fate of individuals drawn into the court system.

affidavit   Written statement of fact, supported by oath or affirmation, that police officers may submit to judicial officers to fulfill the requirements of "probable cause" for obtaining a warrant.

arraignment   Preliminary court proceeding in which charges are formally read to a defendant and the defendant enters an initial plea.

arrest   The exercise of a law enforcement officer's authority to take a person into custody and begin processing him or her through the criminal justice system because sufficient evidence exists to establish probable cause that the person may be guilty of a crime.

arrest warrant   A judicial order authorizing police officers to take a specific person into custody because of the existence of evidence showing that it is more likely than not that the person is guilty of a specific crime.

attenuation doctrine   Exception to the exclusionary rule, also known as the "purged taint" exception, which permits the admission of improperly obtained evidence when a subsequent event, such as a confession by the defendant, removes the "taint" of the constitutional violation that led to the discovery of the evidence.

bail   A sum of money or property placed under court control in order for an arrested suspect to gain freedom pending trial that will be forfeited if the individual does not appear as required for court hearings.

balancing test   The Supreme Court's approach to deciding Fourth Amendment search and seizure cases in which justices decide whether the individual's constitutional rights outweigh society's need to combat crime, or whether crime control interests are more important in a specific situation.

bifurcated proceedings   Proceedings that are split into two parts, especially in death penalty cases in which the trial to determine guilt is separate from the later proceeding to determine whether the offender should be sentenced to death.

body-cavity search   The most intrusive form of physical search that normally requires reasonable suspicion and special supervision and procedures for application at international borders or any context other than an incarcerated detainee or prisoner.

booking   The initial processing of an arrestee at the police station, including taking fingerprints and photographs.

bright-line rule   A clear rule that is understood by police officers and applies to all situations so that officers do not need to make judgments about when and how the rule will apply.

case law   Legal rules produced by judges' decisions.

case precedent   Legal rules created in judges' decisions that serve to guide the decisions of other judges in subsequent similar cases.

challenge for cause   The authority of prosecutors and defense attorneys to request the exclusion of any jurors whose responses to questions from the attorneys and judge indicate the existence of a bias that could interfere with the individual jurors' capacity to be neutral decision makers in the trial at hand.

change in venue   An order moving the location of a trial from the jurisdiction where the crime occurred to a different city where the citizens who will have to serve as jurors have heard less information about the case.

charge bargaining   Negotiations between the prosecutor and the defense attorney about what charges will be reduced or dropped in order to determine what sentence will be imposed when the defendant pleads guilty.

citation   Formal abbreviated notation that identifies the case reporter, volume, and page where a complete printed version of a judicial opinion can be found.

civil law   Rules governing the relationships among individuals, corporations, and government agencies, including disputes about contracts, property, and personal injuries.

collateral use exception   The legal use of improperly obtained evidence in proceedings other than criminal prosecutions. These proceedings include immigration hearings and grand jury proceedings.

common law   Legal system that the United States inherited from England in which judges create law by deciding cases while relying on judges' opinions in prior similar cases.

concurring opinion   Opinion by an appellate judge who agrees with the outcome of a case but disagrees with some aspect of the reasoning in the majority opinion.

consent   A justification for warrantless searches when people who possess authority over property voluntarily agree to permit the police to conduct a search of the property.

constitution   Fundamental law contained in a state or federal document that provides the design of government and basic rights for individuals.

constitutional rights Legal guarantees, which are specified in the fundamental legal document of a state or nation, to protect individuals against improper actions by government.

contingency fee Compensation method for lawyers in some civil legal cases in which they take no money from the clients but, instead, take 30 percent of any settlement or award plus reimbursement of expenses.

continuance A delay in court proceedings requested by one side in the case and approved by the trial judge.

court of last resort Highest court in a judicial system, either a state supreme court or the U.S. Supreme Court.

critical stages Stages in the criminal process in which the absence of a defense attorney would significantly harm the defendant's rights and prospects for an accurate, fair proceeding. Thus the right to counsel applies at such stages in the process.

cross-examination A portion of the trial process generally protected by the right to confrontation in which attorneys can ask leading questions to challenge the testimony of witnesses for the opposition or witnesses with interests adverse to those of the defendant.

custodial interrogation Questioning by law enforcement officials of people who are in government custody and not free to leave, and therefore must be given their *Miranda* warnings before the start of questioning.

discretion Authority possessed by police officers, prosecutors, and other justice system officials to make decisions according to their own judgments and values, despite the risk that such judgments will sometimes be incorrect or biased.

discretionary jurisdiction Power of court of last resort to pick and choose which cases will be heard and thereby decline to hear other cases brought forward from lower courts.

dissenting opinion Judicial opinion by an appellate judge who disagrees with the court majority's decision on the outcome of a case.

***en banc* hearing** Hearing in which all the judges of an appellate court hear and decide a case together as a group rather than in three-member panels.

entrapment A defense to a criminal charge when police officers improperly induce someone to commit a crime.

exclusionary rule Legal principle that evidence obtained in violation of a person's constitutional rights cannot be used against the person in a criminal prosecution.

exigent circumstances A situation in which a threat to public safety or the risk that evidence will be destroyed justifies officers' quick actions in searching, arresting, or questioning suspects without obtaining a warrant or following other usual rules of criminal procedure.

***Ex Post Facto* Clause** Constitutional provision forbidding after-the-fact criminal laws that define crimes and punishments for application to people who committed acts before the new laws were in existence.

facts The events and circumstances that produced a legal case. In a court case, the decision is based on legal facts developed through the presentation of admissible evidence.

first appeal of right The initial appeal provided for under state law that typically is presented to an intermediate appellate court and for which indigents are entitled to representation supplied by the state.

forfeiture Government seizure of property under statutory authority, especially when that property may have been used in or acquired from criminal enterprises.

"fruit of the poisonous tree" doctrine When evidence is obtained by improper means, any further evidence discovered indirectly as a result of the improper search or interrogation is also excluded because it has been tainted by the initial rights violation.

gag order In an effort to prevent pretrial publicity that might bias potential jurors, a judge may, under extraordinary circumstances, order news agencies to *not* report on certain details of criminal cases.

"good faith" exception Exception to the exclusionary rule that permits the use of improperly obtained evidence when police officers acted in honest reliance on a warrant improperly issued by a magistrate, a defective statute, or a consent to search by someone who lacked authority to give such permission.

grand jury A body of citizens that hears presentations of prosecutorial evidence in closed-door sessions to determine if the evidence provides a sufficient basis to issue indictments and thereby authorize the prosecution of specific defendants.

habeas corpus A post-appeal legal petition used by convicted offenders to claim that their detention by the government is improper because one or more constitutional rights were violated during the investigation and prosecution of the case.

harmless error Legal concept applied by appellate courts to trial court errors that are not believed to have affected the verdict and therefore do not justify overturning a conviction.

holding The statement of the legal rule in a judicial opinion that will serve a precedent for later cases.

incorporation Process through which the U.S. Supreme Court applied provisions of the Bill of Rights against state and local governments by including them in the Due Process Clause of the Fourteenth Amendment.

independent source rule Exception to the exclusionary rule that permits the use of improperly obtained evidence that was also discovered through separate, legal means.

indictment The formal order authorizing the prosecution of an individual that a grand jury issues after hearing a presentation of the prosecution's evidence against that individual.

indigent defendants Criminal defendants who are too poor to hire their own attorneys and therefore are entitled to have attorneys supplied for them by the state.

ineffective assistance to counsel   A difficult-to-prove rights violation claim asserted by convicted offenders who claim that their attorneys' performances were so inadequate that they failed to fulfill the requirements of the Sixth Amendment.

inevitable discovery rule   Exception to the exclusionary rule that permits the use of improperly obtained evidence when it would have been discovered eventually anyway through legal investigatory processes that were already under way.

information   In jurisdictions that do not use grand juries to issue formal charges, the document filed by the prosecutor to initiate prosecution.

initial appearance   A criminal suspect's first court hearing shortly after arrest to determine if there is sufficient evidence against the suspect to justify the arrest and to ensure that the suspect has been informed about her or his constitutional rights.

inquisitorial system   Alternative legal process model employed by many European countries in which the judge takes an active role in questioning witnesses and evaluating evidence so that the lawyer is less central in determining the outcome of the case.

issue   The question of law or procedure being addressed by an appellate court in a legal case.

judicial opinion   A written document issued by a judge that announces and explains a legal decision.

judicial review   The power of American judges to review actions by other branches of government to determine if those actions should be invalidated for violating constitutional law.

jurisdiction   The legal issues and territory under the authority of a court.

jury nullification   The power of juries to nullify the law by acquitting a defendant whose factual guilt is clear because of the jurors' view that criminal punishment is not appropriate in the particular situation presented in the case.

"knock and announce" principle   Principle drawn from English common law and regarded by the Supreme Court as a component of the Fourth Amendment that requires police officers to knock and announce their presence before entering a premises to conduct a search, unless there is reasonable suspicion that the announcement will create a risk of physical harm or destruction of evidence.

law   Rules and policies produced by government officials, especially legislators and judges, that define and limit the authority of government, including protections for individuals and rules for settling disputes.

lineup   Investigation technique in which a suspect is placed in a line with other individuals who have similar physical characteristics in order to ask a victim or a witness to identify a criminal by picking the perpetrator out of the line.

magistrate   A judicial officer, often an attorney working on a part-time basis, with limited responsibilities for processing minor criminal and civil cases and for handling preliminary matters in serious criminal cases, including the issuance of warrants.

***Miranda* rule**   Rule announced by the U.S. Supreme Court in *Miranda v. Arizona* (1966) that requires police officers to inform people in police custody of their right to remain silent and their right to counsel before they are subjected to questioning.

mistrial   A judge's declaration that terminates and nullifies a trial because of improper evidence or information that may have prejudiced the jury or because the jury was deadlocked in its deliberations. The prosecution may begin the trial again in front of a new jury if a mistrial is declared.

no contest   A plea, also known as *nolo contendere,* in which the criminal defendant does not contest the charges but accepts punishment without admitting guilt, usually in order to reduce the risk of civil liability related to the crime.

nontestimonial evidence   Evidence from a person, such as behaviors (e.g., slurred speech) or material extracted from their bodies (e.g., blood tests), that is not covered by the privilege against compelled self-incrimination because they do not constitute statements from the person about him- or herself.

open fields doctrine   Doctrine that permits warrantless exploration for visible criminal evidence on private property beyond the curtilage of a house.

parolees   Convicted offenders who have already served a portion of their sentences in prison before being released into the community to live at home under restrictive conditions, including daily or weekly meetings with a parole officer. Any violations of parole conditions can lead to a return to prison.

patdown or frisk search   Limited search of the exterior of a clothed person's body by feeling for the presence of weapons or other contraband.

peremptory challenge   The authority of prosecutors and defense attorneys to exclude a limited number of potential jurors without giving any reason as long as the exclusion is not based on the juror's race or gender.

photographic display   Investigation technique in which a victim or a witness looks through photographs of people arrested for previous offenses in order to attempt to identify the perpetrator of a crime.

plain view doctrine   Doctrine that permits officers to identify criminal evidence that is openly visible from the vantage point of a location where they are legally permitted to be and to seize such items on public property or on private property where they are lawfully located.

preliminary hearing   Pretrial proceeding under the laws of many states, but not mandated by the Constitution, in which the defendant is entitled to have an attorney listen to and question the prosecution's preliminary evidence in an effort to get a judge to dismiss charges.

presentence report   Report prepared by a probation officer describing a convicted offender's prior criminal record and personal history which, along with the probation officer's recommendation about an appropriate punishment, is used by the judge in determining the sentence for a criminal offense.

probable cause   An amount of evidence establishing that it is more likely than not that evidence will be found in a specific location or that a specific person is guilty of a crime. The Constitution requires prosecutors and police officers to show a judge enough evidence to establish probable cause before an arrest warrant or a search warrant may be issued.

probationers   Convicted offenders serving sentences of probation in which they live within their home communities under restrictive conditions, such as curfews and prohibitions on alcohol, with the threat of incarceration for violating any of their probation conditions.

procedural criminal law   Statutes and judicial decisions that mandate the steps in the criminal justice process and provide legal protections for criminal suspects, defendants, and convicted offenders.

pro se **litigants**   Litigants who represent themselves in court, typically in a civil lawsuit or habeas corpus action in which they have no constitutional right to assistance of counsel.

protective sweep   A search incident to a lawful arrest in which officers may make a warrantless examination of rooms, closets, and other locations where a confederate of the arrestee may be hiding and thereby endanger the officers if not found.

"public safety" exception   Exception to *Miranda* requirements that permits police to immediately question a suspect in custody without providing any warnings when public safety would be jeopardized by taking the time to supply the warnings.

racial profiling   The practice of using a person's race as a key factor in deciding whether he or she fits the general demographic description of a drug dealer or other targeted criminal offender.

real or physical evidence   Noncommunicative evidence, such as physical objects related to an alleged crime, but also including physical characteristics of a suspect, fingerprints, handwriting samples, and other such evidence gathered during pretrial processes.

reasonable expectations of privacy   The objective standard developed by the court for determining whether a governmental intrusion into an individual's person or property constitutes a search because it interferes with the individual's interests that are normally protected from governmental examination.

reasoning   The portion of a judicial opinion that provides justifications for a judge's decision.

search   Government officials' examination of and hunt for evidence in or on a person or place in a manner that intrudes on reasonable expectations of privacy.

search incident to a lawful arrest   A warrantless search undertaken at the scene of an arrest to ensure that the arrestee has no weapons which may endanger public safety and to see if any criminal evidence can be recovered from the arrestee or the immediate vicinity of the arrestee.

search warrant   A judicial order authorizing police officers to search a certain location for evidence of a specific crime because of the existence of evidence showing that it is more likely than not that criminal evidence will be found at that location.

seizures   Situations in which police officers use their authority to deprive people of their liberty and which must not be "unreasonable" according to the Fourth Amendment.

sentencing guidelines   Sentencing reform enacted by legislatures to reduce judicial discretion in sentencing and equalize sentences imposed on similar offenders. The offender's current charge and prior record determine a narrow sentencing range in which the judge establishes the actual sentence.

sequester the jury   The isolation of jury members from society during the course of a trial and jury deliberations by keeping them under around-the-clock supervision in the courthouse and a hotel in order to prevent them from hearing news reports, discussing the case with non–jury members, or otherwise infecting their deliberations with information from outside sources.

showup   An identification procedure in which a victim or a witness is shown one suspect in order to ask whether that suspect is the perpetrator of the crime. This is often done near crime scenes but may also be done at police stations and in court depending on the circumstances of the case.

special need beyond the normal purpose of law enforcement   Search situations in which governmental objectives always outweigh Fourth Amendment interests in a defined context, without relying for justification on an officer's determination of reasonable suspicion or probable cause.

statute of limitations   Time limit established by legislatures within which prosecutors must file charges in a case. Such limitations normally do not apply to murders.

statutes   Law created by the people's elected representatives in legislatures.

stop   Government officials' brief interference with an individual's freedom of movement for a duration that can be measured in minutes.

stop-and-frisk search   Limited search approved by the Supreme Court in *Terry v. Ohio* that permits police officers to pat down the clothing of people whose behavior leads to a reasonable suspicion that they may be armed and involved in criminal activity.

strip search   Physical search that requires the suspect to disrobe and must be justified by reasonable suspicion and special procedures in contexts outside of corrections.

substantive criminal law   Laws that define which behaviors will be subject to punishment by government.

suggestiveness   Actions by police officers during a lineup or other identification procedures that intentionally or unintentionally signal the witness about which individual the police suspect of committing the crime.

suppression hearings   Pretrial proceedings in which the defense seeks to have prosecution evidence excluded from use at trial for being obtained in violation of constitutional rights or other legal requirements.

testimonial evidence   The type of evidence covered under the privilege against compelled self-incrimination because it consists of statements by the suspect that might otherwise be used against him or her in court.

totality-of-circumstances test   Flexible test established by the Supreme Court for identifying whether "probable cause" exists to justify a judicial officer in issuing a search or arrest warrant.

trial *in absentia*   A criminal trial conducted without the defendant present in court.

U.S. circuit courts of appeals   The intermediate appellate courts in the federal court system that each handle initial appeals from cases within a specific geographic region.

U.S. district court   The trial courts in the federal court system.

U.S. magistrate judges   Federal judicial officers who assist U.S. district judges and who are empowered to handle nearly any matter handled by district judges except presiding over trials of felony defendants. These officials are frequently responsible for issuing federal warrants and setting bail for federal defendants.

voir dire   Process of questioning potential jurors to determine who should be selected for or excluded from the jury based on any attitudes or biases that might interfere with their ability to give open-minded consideration to the evidence presented by the prosecution and the defense.

waiver of rights   People waive their rights when they voluntarily surrender the protection of those rights, such as when people consent to a search that police officers otherwise could not conduct at their discretion.

Warren Court era   Time period from 1953 to 1969 in which the U.S. Supreme Court, under the leadership of Chief Justice Earl Warren, incorporated the Bill of Rights and expanded interpretations of constitutional protections for individuals.

writ of certiorari   Legal petition used to ask the U.S. Supreme Court to accept a case for hearing by calling up the case from a lower court.

TABLE OF CASES

Index